The Parisian Summit, 1377–78

Emperor Charles IV
and King Charles V of France

František Šmahel

THE PARISIAN SUMMIT, 1377–78

EMPEROR CHARLES IV AND KING CHARLES V OF FRANCE

FRANTIŠEK ŠMAHEL

Charles University in Prague
Karolinum Press 2014

CATALOGUING-IN-PUBLICATION – NATIONAL LIBRARY OF THE CZECH REPUBLIC

Šmahel, František
The Parisian Summit, 1377–78 : Emperor Charles IV and King Charles V of France / František Šmahel. – 1st English ed. – Prague : Karolinum, 2014
Published by: Charles University in Prague
ISBN 978-80-246-2522-5

929.731 * 910.4 * 316.72/.75 * 94(437.3) * 94(44) * (430)
– Charles IV, Holy Roman Emperor, 1316–1378
– kings and rulers – Czechia – 14th century
– kings and rulers – Holy Roman Empire – 14th century
– voyages and travels – France – 14th century
– culture and society – Czechia – 14th century
– culture and society – France – 14th century
– Czechia – history – 14th century
– France – history – 14th century
– monographs

940 – General history of Europe, Western Europe [8]

ISBN 978-80-246-2522-5

To my wife, Hana Šmahelová, for her extraordinary patience and understanding.

Contents

This book was born from the feeling of relief after weathering a severe illness. I put my other projects aside, revived a subject from the time of my youth and began to deal with the last great journey of Emperor Charles IV – to *la belle France*. That journey and the summit with Charles IV, king of France, aroused interest not only in Paris, but also throughout Europe. I had at my disposal an uncommonly valuable set of written as well as artistic testimonies, which I could assemble into multiple mosaics. I have selected the ones that preserved the authenticity of one of the main sources, namely the official Account of the *Great Chronicles of France* on the visit to Paris by Charles IV and his son Wenceslas at Christmas 1377/78. In this report the words and the illuminations complement each other in such a compelling and comprehensible way that they deserve to take centre stage in this book. The *Account* did not restrict itself merely to the surface of the colourful ceremonies and sumptuous banquets. In places, it plunges deeply into the interpersonal relationships of the main actors, while also providing an entirely singular look behind the scenes of European high politics. In the *Prologue*, it was more or less sufficient to hint briefly at what preceded the departure of the two Luxemburgs. The *Epilogue* merely finished by telling what followed it. In the second part of the book, the platform is already given to the historian, because the *Account* has not recorded everything that was related to this summit of the most influential statesmen of Europe. Finally, the third and the final part offers information on the illustrations, a bibliography of primary sources and secondary literature, as well as the indispensable glossaries in for all who are those seriously interested in expert commentaries. The study of medieval history is no longer a place of quiet contemplation of past events. The information explosion in this research field continues to bring new monographs that enriched and affected the work on this book, even during the translation stage. Those titles are included only in the list of publications.

No preface would be complete without words of thanks. Without the support of Prof. Maurice Aymard, the Director of the *Maison des Sciences de l'Homme*, in Paris, it would not have been possible to undertake the necessary study visits to French museums and libraries. I am also grateful to the *British*

Academy, which has repeatedly made it possible for me to study the *British Library* manuscripts. The specialist libraries of the Warburg and Courtauld Institutes, University of London as well as the *Monumenta Germaniae Historica* Institute in Munich always did their best to accommodate my needs. At the *Centre for Mediaeval Studies* in Prague, I was willingly helped by Robert Novotný, I am deeply obliged to František Kavka for his encouraging words after reading the manuscript and to my good friend Petr Sommer for his encouraging help. My heartfelt thanks belong to Martin Nejedlý with whom I shared exciting discussions in Paris as well as in Prague, and to Martyn Rady from UCL School of Slavonic and East European Studies for his consultations and advices. For the translation I am deeply indebted to Sean Mark Miller and Kateřina Miller, for graphic design to Zdeněk Ziegler. Last but not least, I am grateful to The Carolinum Press, and namely to Director Petr Valo and Kamila Veselá for launching the book into the wider world.

In Prague, Spring 2014

PROLOGUE
THE LUXEMBURGS AND FRANCE
1322–1377

The Childhood Years of the Two Charleses

The dates that frame this Prologue may cause confusion or curiosity. Even experts in the history of the Late Middle Ages would be hard pressed to remember what momentous events happened in either year. Indeed, the two dates are important more or less only in relation to an extensive description of the visit by Emperor Charles IV and his son, then already King of the Romans and of Bohemia, Wenceslas IV, to the court of Charles V the Wise in Paris in the first days of 1378. This separate chapter of the *Great Chronicles of France*, which forms the backbone of our entire story, will hereinafter be referred to simply as the Account. History is already such that historians select from it only that which is interesting, whatever they regard as important for history itself, for their readers and ultimately also for themselves. If history is according to one catchphrase merely an 'extract' or selection, it does not necessarily have to mean that likewise everything in this description will be haphazard and distorted by a subjective approach. It simply is not necessary, nor would it be bearable for the reader, to detail every known circumstance merely because we know it. All three of the main participants at the summit of January 1378 were among the most influential men of the contemporary European world; therefore any attempt at completeness would be to the detriment of the cause. We will depict only those events and circumstances that preceded this memorable meeting and attempt to explain why it happened at all.

Naturally, the focus of attention will be those events linked to the year 1377. Also the year 1322, which might at first glance seem distant, has its justification, because that was the year in which the decision was made regarding the first journey to France of the future Charles IV for education as well as for a bride. Never before, or again, were events in Bohemia so tied to France as in the second quarter of the fourteenth century. It was precisely at this time that, thanks to the efforts of Charles' father John of Luxembourg, a knight on the Bohemian throne, most of the personal and other bonds were forged that would surface much later, namely in connection with the celebrations in Paris at the beginning of 1378. If this explanation is satisfactory, we may start from the very beginning of the actual story.

1. The wedding of John the Blind of Luxembourg to Elisabeth of Bohemia in Speyer in 1310 (Codex Balduini Trevoriensis. Koblenz Landeshauptstadtarchiv, Bestand 1C, Nr. 1, fol. 3b)

A BLEAK CHILDHOOD

The future Emperor Charles IV set out on his first journey to France at the age of seven. At the time, he still bore the name Wenceslas, after the patron saint of Bohemia and in memory of his grandfather, Wenceslas II, King of Bohemia and Poland (1283–1305). Despite having been born the son of John of Luxembourg and his wife Elizabeth I of Bohemia (in Czech: Eliška Přemyslovna), his early childhood was not exactly enviable. There was nothing to suggest this on the day that he was born, Friday, 14 May 1316. Quite the reverse, the *Chronicon Aulae Regiae* (Zbraslav Chronicle) states that the day 'brought joy and jubilation to all who wished the king and kingdom well'.[1] His baptism on Whitsunday, 30 May, was among the most memorable to be performed in St Vitus' Cathedral. The ceremony was conducted by Archbishop of Mainz Peter of Aspelt, an uncommonly successful diplomat and man of influence, who up until his death in 1320 pulled strings not only in Prague but also at other European courts. Other than by Bishop of Prague John (Jan) of Dražice and Suffragan Bishop of Prizren Hermann, he was assisted also by another of the imperial electors, Archbishop of Trier Baldwin (1285–1354). This uncle of King of Bohemia John (1296–1346) and at this time already the patriarch of the Luxembourg family, was to intervene in the baby's life in an entirely exceptional fashion.[2]

However, this transient family cosiness soon began to fade. When, shortly after the middle of August 1316, the twenty-year-old king went to Germany

1/ The citations have been truncated, the full titles can be found in the bibliography. *Chronicon Aulae Regiae*, p. 230.

2/ See the anthology *Balduin von Luxemburg*; there, especially Hlaváček, 'Johann der Blinde', pp. 151–173.

on a military campaign, his wife (his elder by four years), who played her own political games on the domestic scene and consequently had her own enemies, put her four-month-old infant into the care of one of her supporters, William (Vilém) Zajíc of Valdek, residing at Křivoklát Castle.

The situation in the country was at times threatened by malicious acts with allies changing sides – and William Zajíc was no exception. As soon as the queen lost her confidence in him in 1317, she had Wenceslas moved to her stronghold of Loket Castle. Not quite two years later, the situation had changed, and this time it was Elizabeth who had to confront her husband's accusations that she had re-allied with William of Valdek. Elizabeth did not know what to do. In January 1319, she and her children took refuge anew at Loket Castle, where they were however besieged by her husband and his retinue in the middle of February and compelled to capitulate the following day.

2. Elizabeth of Bohemia (1292–1330), Queen of Bohemia. A bust in the inner triforium of the Cathedral of St Vitus at Prague Castle

3. Castle Křivoklát, the place of the residence of Charles IV during his childhood

The main victim in this marital dispute was the three-year-old Wenceslas, over whom both of the contending power parties of nobles struggled, as he was the next heir to the throne. Wenceslas was taken from his mother by force and imprisoned for two months in a cellar room lit only by a window slit. According to the chronicler Beneš Krabice of Weitmile,[3] Wenceslas felt like a prisoner here even later and was left entirely at the mercy of juvenile 'vanities'. What this pious Canon of Prague meant by this can only be speculated on;[4] he might have merely been teasing the castle servants to pass the time. Wences-

3/ In Latin: Benessius de Weitmil, in German: Benesch von Weitmühl (translators' note).
4/ *Chronicon Benessii de Weitmil*, p. 475.

4. John of Luxembourg (1296–1346), King of Bohemia. A bust in the inner triforium of the Cathedral of St Vitus at Prague Castle

las experienced nothing pleasant at Loket, and it would be no wonder if this incident had not left its mark on his relationship with his father, but this is a question more for a psychoanalyst than for an historian.

Wenceslas was left at Loket Castle for more than a year and then taken back to Křivoklát, which after the death of William Zajíc of Valdek in October 1319 had lapsed to King John. He remained at this castle residence until April 1323, without being able to see his mother for the entire time. During that time, however, he seems not to have met either his father or his aunt Marie (1304–1324), who in June 1318 had come along with her younger sister Beatrix from Luxembourg to Prague, where for three years she was a companion to Queen Elizabeth. Her fate is typical of girls of royal or other noble families, who were already engaged in childhood, taken into a strange environment from which they would sometimes be returned to their parents in disgrace, only to be engaged again before finally being married.

Marie, whose story interests and moves us, because it would soon intertwine with that of Wenceslas', experienced various trials of this type. Her royal brother John had her brought to Prague as bait for the widowed King Charles I of Hungary (Charles Robert of Anjou) despite her already being a novice in the Dominican convent at Marienthal. The Hungarian delegation, however, chose Beatrix for their King, and that under circumstances that were more than degrading. 'I was there and saw,' testifies Abbot of Zbraslav Peter of Zittau, 'the Hungarians standing before the two girls, fixating their open eyes on them with repose, carefully examining the lovely faces of these maidens, studying their proportions, assessing their gait and carefully investigating which they should choose'.[5] Beatrix was given preference, but it did not bring her good fortune – in the autumn of the following year she died giving premature birth.

Marie was to linger on the shelf in Prague. The next groom that they wanted to force her to marry was the fifty-six-year-old Duke Henry of Carinthia, who had worn the royal crown of Bohemia in 1307–1310 until it was taken from him by force by John of Luxembourg. Marie apparently opposed her brother and, although the years were passing quickly for her, she awaited her opportunity, which came in the first half of 1322, namely under peculiar circumstances illustrating this time the situation in the ruling dynasty of France. When, at the beginning of January 1322, King Philip V the Tall died without a male heir, the only legitimate successor was his brother Charles, known as the Fair, the taciturn and somewhat neglected youngest son of Philip IV the Fair (1285–1314). Few had previously believed in his lucky star, and not even he himself had anticipated his succession. When he was crowned as Charles IV

5/ *Chronicon Aulae Regiae*, p. 249.

of France in Rheims on 21 February 1322, one of his royal duties was to secure an heir for his own branch of the family, which is where a certain complication arose. He was actually married, namely to Blanche of Burgundy, who was courted by other men while her female relatives could not stand her. In 1314, the attractive Blanche fell victim to intrigues, which culminated in her humiliating condemnation and imprisonment at Château-Gaillard. Under the circumstances, the only solution was to achieve an annulment of the marriage through legal manoeuvring. Blanche readily agreed to a divorce when offered release from the prison and adequate provisions for her to reside in a selected convent. The rest was arranged by the lawyers, who presented evidence to Pope John XXII in the form of testimony by Blanche's mother, who as the baptismal godmother became a relation of Charles' in contravention of the demands of Canon Law. It all proceeded with unbelievable speed, because already on 19 May 1322 the pope pronounced the first marriage of the King of France annulled. This course of events had already been expected, so the bidding for a possible bride had begun.[6]

Luxemburg diplomacy was quick to act, and because both of the representatives of the family – King John and Elector Baldwin – guaranteed the royal matchmakers an advantageous political dowry, fortune finally smiled upon the waiting Marie. Her husband must have been a handsome man; otherwise, he would not have been given his appellation 'the Fair' in historical consciousness. Not even this time was it devoid of obstacles, because she had to face the slanders of Count Charles of Valois, the father of several unmarried daughters at once. This elderly count was jealous of the successful Luxemburgs, with whom he appears to have had scores to settle as well, and therefore spread gossip about Marie of the coarsest kind. She had allegedly grown up in Bohemia, a land of questionable morals; she had a squint; she was too old for the king, supposedly being over 20 years of age… The king saw everything in a different light when he saw the mature and elegant 18-year-old Marie for the first time, which happened in the late summer at a banquet held by Archbishop of Trier Baldwin on the occasion of a hunt on the French-Luxembourg border. Whether the wedding arrangements were speeded up by some secret promises as to the King of France's potential prospects for the imperial crown or not, the couple were soon hand in glove. As soon as the court had received the dispensation by which, on 30 August 1322, the pope declared the fourth degree of consanguinity between the betrothed pair to be unobjectionable, nothing stood in the way of the wedding, which took place with all the usual festivities in

6/ The essential information on the mentioned kings who quickly succeeded one another on the French throne can be found in the anthology of biographies *Die französischen Könige des Mittelalters*.

5. The wedding of Charles IV the Fair and Marie Luxembourg on 21 September 1322. Les Grandes Chroniques de France, illumination by Jean Fouquet (BnF, ms. fr. 6465, fol. 332r)

the town of Provins in Champagne on 21 September 1322. This was followed by a quick removal to Paris, where on 30 September a banquet followed after homage was paid by the French nobility, clergy and towns.[7] Marie was to wait a few more months for her coronation.

Archbishop Baldwin could be content, for the wedding of his niece was primarily the result of his own diplomatic skills and political dexterity. The self-centred King John did not even know that his uncle had had Marie and her retinue escorted to France already in April. He did not even appear at the wedding, as he could not miss the Battle of Mühldorf, where on 28 September 1322 the decisive clash took place between King of the Romans Louis IV, called the Bavarian (1328–1347), and his rival, also elected King of the Romans (Anti-King), Frederick the Fair (Habsburg, Frederick I of Austria, III of the HRE). The victorious Louis repaid his Bohemian ally with a num-

7/ On the reception of Marie in France and her welcome in Paris, see de Puymaigre, 'Jean l'Aveugle en France', p. 401.

ber of privileges and material advantages. John of Luxembourg continued to squeeze money out of the Kingdom of Bohemia, but on the other hand he was expanding it with some considerable territorial gains. This time, he achieved the definitive annexation of Cheb (Eger) with its entire surrounding area to Bohemia and moreover acquired some hereditary holdings in the Meissen region and Thuringia. His reception in Prague was his triumph. He did not, however, remain in Bohemia for long and headed back to Luxembourg, where at the turn of 1323 he was attempting to establish contacts with the French royal court, which had moved to Toulouse for the winter.

6. Blanche of Valois (1316–1348), Queen of Bohemia, the first wife of Charles IV. A bust in the inner triforium of the Cathedral of St Vitus at Prague Castle

King John had hitherto appeared to be a monarch indifferent to religion, but when it was politically expedient, he had nothing against a lengthy pilgrimage to the Shrine of Our Lady at Rocamadour, near Cahors. After all, this was a pilgrimage site for knights of John's type, as it was from there that the fabulous hero Roland was supposed to have departed to fight against the Moors. According to one of the tales, Roland bequeathed his famous sword Durandal to the sanctuary. Since the original was stolen by King Henry II of England, John could only see its replica. Whether a religious motive played a certain role or was merely a pretext, it moved John closer to the French royal family, who had also not foregone the pilgrimage to the church with its 278 stone steps. In Toulouse, John must have colourfully described the Battle of Mühldorf, and also various political and kinship affairs are likely to have been discussed, during which it turned out that it would do no harm to relieve Charles of Valois of the burden of at least one of his daughters, thereby reducing some of the pressure left on both sides after the wedding of the ruling Charles IV to the Luxembourg princess Marie. Whether she herself had the greatest share in these familial negotiations cannot be said for certain. Either way, the engagement was agreed between John's son Wenceslas and Charles of Valois' youngest daughter, who came from his third marriage to Mahaut, daughter of Count Guy III de Châtillon.[8] Margaret, which was the bride's original name before they with the typical local arbitrariness began to call her Blanche, had forebears who were more than august. It is most unlikely that the young bride would have been asked for her agreement to the selected groom, who was after all still far away. As soon as the agreement had been reached, King John sent word to Bohemia that his eldest son be taken to the French court without delay. The date of Wenceslas' departure from Křivoklát Castle is known precisely to the day: it was on Sunday, 4 April 1323. The journey must

8/ Cf. Margue, *Un itineraire européen*, pp. 61–86. Šusta, *Král cizinec*, p. 355, Note 1 and after him also Spěváček, *Karel IV.*, p. 671 confused her with Mahaut, daughter of Count Robert II of Artois, about whom we will hear later in connection with John of Luxembourg. The correct identification can be found in Bobková, *Velké dějiny zemí Koruny české*, IVa, p. 91.

have been rapid, for by the middle of the following month Wenceslas was already in Paris, where ceremonial clothing was hastily prepared, on which his father spared no expense this time.

Sunday, 15 May 1323 entered the historical memory through several ceremonial acts. First of all, it was the day of the coronation of Marie of Luxembourg – sister of King John of Luxembourg and aunt of his son Wenceslas – as Queen of France. The seven-year-old Wenceslas was not to retain his Christian name for good. By coincidence, that same May Sunday was Whitsunday, when adolescents traditionally received the Sacrament of Confirmation. The Czech name Václav (Wenceslas) sounded strange and foreign to French ears, which was the reason that on this occasion the boy was given the name Charles by his royal godfather, which moreover evoked one of the greatest figures of domestic as well as European history. The prince of Bohemia appreciated this later as we know from his *Autobiography*, and since his new name quickly came into use, he had no problem adopting it as his own. In Bohemia, not surprisingly, it aroused at the very least wonder.[9]

This, however, was not the end of the festive events on this memorable Sunday. In compliance with prior papal approval, the first-born son of the king of Bohemia, to whom we shall henceforth refer only as Charles, was joined in the church Sacrament of Matrimony with his coeval princess Blanche of Valois. On the basis of period reports, both of the Luxemburgs – King John and Archbishop Baldwin – were resplendent in marvellous vestments during the ceremony. Princess Blanche was in no way inferior to the Czech wedding party, whose bridal gown and jewellery, including her crown, had conversely been paid for by the Royal Treasury of France.[10] Particular attention is aroused by a gold belt with precious stones, whose elements may have been used later for the arch of the Crown of St Wenceslas.[11]

To have numerous offspring and marry them to advantage could sometimes be more profitable than military campaigns. We need to admit that King John did not neglect either. Having negotiated two marriages at the French court, why not add another and extend his network of alliances in another direction as well? Shortly beforehand, John had learnt that the marriage of his second daughter Jutta alias Guta to the son of the Landgrave of Thuringia

9/ *Karoli IV Vita*, p. 23. For more on that, see Schneider, 'Karolus, qui et Wenceslaus', pp. 365–387, and Thomas, 'Vater und Sohn', pp. 446–447.

10/ The accounting documents were published by Viard, *Les Journaux du Trésor*; they were broadly used by Mezník, 'Berichte der französischen königlichen Rechnungen', pp. 291–295, from whom information was taken by Spěváček, *Jan Lucemburský*, pp. 341–342. On that exhaustively, Otavsky, *Die Sankt Wenzelskrone*, whose knowledge was summarised by Gaborit-Chopin, 'Les arts précieux à Paris', pp. 58–59.

11/ This opinion, expressed by Otavský, *Die Sankt Wenzelskrone*, p. 60, was later supported by an X-ray investigation of the Crown of St Wenceslas.

and Margrave of Meissen Frederick I the Bitten had been cancelled. To no little dishonour to her entire family, Guta was returned from Wartburg Castle to Prague, and it was thus necessary to have her wed without delay. Do not think ill of the author for constantly introducing one character after another on the scene. Like in other cases, it will be shown also that Guta is an actor in this play. Why not kill two birds with one stone when such an opportunity arises? King John had had a long-running dispute with Edward, Count of Bar and a neighbour of his Luxemburg holdings, over the castles of Mirvault and Monçy, and since also the King of France laid sovereign claims to several, likewise controversial, rights in the town of Verdun, the idea suggested itself of achieving through him reconciliation, and therewith also the arrangement of Guta's engagement to Count of Bar's eldest son. Everything seemed to be coming to a promising conclusion when it was agreed at Le Mans on 28 May 1323 that the wedding would take place within a year.

King John did not stay long in Paris either and already on 25 June was back in Prague. His son Charles lingered in France – which may seem surprising to us today – because it was usually the juvenile bride who travelled to the foreign court. Elizabeth, and doubtless her political confidants as well, would have preferred to have the heir to the throne in Bohemia, as close to them as possible, so that they could have influence on him and jointly inculcate in him the local customs. It was precisely this that John sought to avoid, as he wished to raise him as a Western European knight of his own mould. Charles could actually already speak Czech, but the question remains as to whether in isolation at Loket and Křivoklát he had also learnt something of colloquial German. With the agreement of Queen Marie and the family of his wife Blanche, Charles at his father's behest continued to be brought up in France.

'MONSEIGNEUR CHARLES DE BOHÊME'

No later than 8 November 1323, the Royal Treasury of France began to contribute to the costs of Charles' household and other needs. The commissioned middleman for this and at the same time for Charles' education was the cleric Jean de Viviers, of whom little is otherwise known. The sum of items paid by 6 April 1324 was 880 pounds, after which the accounts of the Royal Chamber do not mention the prince of Bohemia for several months.[12] It is possible that this was related to the unexpected demise of his aunt Marie. The young queen had tried to be at her husband's side even in difficult times and thus accom-

12/ The expenditures are recorded synoptically by Mezník, 'Berichte der französischen königlichen Rechnungen', pp. 291–293. Jean de Viviers once appears in the accounts also as *clericus et doctor*; despite all my efforts, I have not been able to verify his university degree. More on the Office of 'Almoner' below.

panied him on a military campaign to Languedoc against the rebellious city of Toulouse. The conflict was successfully averted with the aid of a mounted division of John of Luxembourg, who met his sister in the pacified city for the last time.[13] After a bad fall from her carriage at the village of Issoudun near Bourges on the return journey, Marie gave premature birth to a boy, who was barely baptised before dying. Marie herself died on 26 March 1324 and was buried with her infant son in the church of the Dominican convent at Montargis.[14] Her body was later transported to the royal necropolis in the Abbey of Saint-Denis near Paris, where her nephew Emperor Charles IV would stop at her tomb in January 1378. His wife Blanche seems to have received a precious royal crown worth 840 pounds as a memento of her young aunt.[15] Abbot of Zbraslav Peter of Zittau took the death of the virtuous Marie 'of dove-like character' very hard, and composed the following verses in her honour:

'Many a secret did she, pious, impart to me when still alive.
I thought that she was to stay with us, oh, for a long, pleasing while
As she was to reign over such a great realm.
Hope is thwarted; a different fate has been prepared for her ...'[16]

The accounts of the French Royal Chamber have been preserved only in fragments; the more we, therefore, welcome every small piece of information on the prince of Bohemia. At the end of March and beginning of April 1324, the accounts twice mention the royal castle at Saint-Germain-en-Laye, about half a day's ride or river journey from the capital, as Charles' place of residence. This and no other was the way of treating the other children of noble or even precisely Capetian blood too, who sometimes lived together if there were more of them. As we will hear later, this was also the case with the numerous siblings of Charles V, the second most important figure at the summit in January 1378, towards which this and the following narration have been leading only gradually so far. All the indications are that Charles did not attend the funeral of his aunt at Montargis; neither did he hence meet his father there.

In the autumn of 1325, more specifically on 26 October, the position of Charles' tutor was assumed by another cleric, Huetus by name, likewise from Viviers, who by 13 May 1325 had drawn a total of 734 pounds in eleven instal-

13/ Šusta, *Král cizinec*, p. 369 further assumed that his son was also with John and that they both then headed for Avignon, where Charles was confirmed by Pope John XXII. On this mistake, see Mezník, 'Berichte', p. 292; Charles' journey to Toulouse and Avignon with his father is, however, not ruled out by Spěváček, *Jan Lucemburský*, p. 370.
14/ On the death of the unfortunate Marie, see de Puymaigre, 'Jean l'Aveugle en France', pp. 407–408.
15/ The information was reprinted by Mezník, 'Berichte', p. 294, Note 7.
16/ *Chronicon Aulae Regiae*, p. 340.

ments from the royal treasury for his ward's household – excluding the cost of Charles' new boots. Given that no separate accounts for the sojourn of the successor to the Bohemian throne were kept from May 1325 to the beginning of March 1327, or they at least have not been preserved, the hypothesis suggests itself that some major change might have occurred in his provision during this interval. What is especially striking is the temporal relation between the last payments and the wedding of Charles IV the Fair to his third wife, Jeanne, Countess of Evreux, which took place on 5 July 1325. It seems as if the customs established by Queen Marie were still being maintained up until that time. Quite surprisingly, John of Luxembourg did not attend the wedding in Paris. He did not, however, miss Jeanne's coronation on 11 May 1326, accompanied by magnificent tournaments and banquets. On this occasion, the king of Bohemia and his retinue spent 'vast sums, which had to be paid by the inhabitants of the Kingdom of Bohemia'.[17] The otherwise well-informed chronicler Peter of Zittau made no mention whatsoever of the participation of Prince Charles. He may have considered it as obvious, and so shall we. The question arises: did he then, or any other time, write a letter to his mother? He had an opportunity to do so, because his father took to his wife Elizabeth in Prague an extremely valuable thorn from the Crown of Thorns kept at Sainte-Chapelle, which was generously given to her by the king of France. Queen Elizabeth had the thorn deposited in a precious reliquary, which was placed with her treasures on 28 October 1326 with the enormous participation of the clergy and believers.[18]

An historian seeking testimony or the minor traces left by the sojourn of the prince of Bohemia in France is sometimes pleasantly surprised; other times, his efforts are futile. Too many unknowns then lead to more or less likely conjectures. Some of these can be dispelled by further accounting documents, this time not from the Highest Royal Chamber itself but from the so-called *argenterie*, the relevant office for all areas of the private life of the royal family. In the name of this component of court administration, it is possible to recognise the Latin word *argentum* (silver), and it thus comes as no surprise that it was used to pay for jewellery, ornaments, sacral items for private chapels and miscellaneous things made by goldsmiths. In addition, its accounts list expenditures on fabrics for clothing, tapestries and other decorations, as well as payments to cloth cutters, tailors, shoemakers and other craftsmen and artisans. In the fragments of these accounts from the short period from 2 March to 1 July 1327, our Charles features in a total of 39 entries, outdone only by the members of the royal family. The sum of the expenses related to his person

17/ *Chronicon Aulae* Regiae, p. 279.
18/ It is mentioned by Abbot Peter in *Chronicon Aulae Regiae*, p. 280.

exceeded an astounding 385 pounds, which was however only a little over 2% of the total expenses of the *argenterie* for this period.[19]

The accounting expenses of the above-mentioned office of the royal court shed new light on Charles' stay. Above all, we learn from them that both tutors from 1323–1325 attended to him later as well; in addition, the chaplain Jean de Viviers assumed the role of almoner and, along with Loyset of Louveciennes participated in the upbringing of five children of the royal chapel.[20] It is a mere hint yet it indirectly implies that Charles was probably growing up in the company of other children of royal blood. The expenses for himself and his small retinue were however recorded separately, thanks to which a fairly specific picture can be drawn of the standard of living and lifestyle of the young prince, whose suite included seven persons in addition to his tutors. All are known by name, and although the records otherwise do not mention them, they belong in the annals of the French education of the next Holy Roman Emperor. The retinue of 'Lord Charles of Bohemia' included three squires (*escuiers*), namely Peter of Bouves, Thomas Prieur and a certain Stanequin. Not only Charles but also his young companions seem to have been attended to by: Colin Jacquerin, Sansonnet, Gauvel le Fourrier and Girard le Queue. They must have been busy, despite much being arranged for them by the clerks of the *argenterie*, who purchased fabrics and furs and commissioned craftsmen. All of these merchants, cloth cutters, tailors and shoemakers could be named, but little would be served by doing so.

Nevertheless, this is not all that can be discovered from the accounts. For every great feast, new clothing, footwear, quilts, bedding and doubtless also other supplies in accordance with the season were procured for Lord Charles of Bohemia. The accounting period from 2 March to 1 July 1327 included three major feasts, specifically Easter (12 April), Ascension day (21 May) and Whitsunday (31 May). Court etiquette required that a member of the royal family appear in new attire even on the occasion of such holidays or other ceremonial occasions that followed quickly after another. At Easter, clothing of identical colour as well as patterns was procured for all of the members of Charles' suite as appropriate, for the squires and servants alike. The ceremonial clothing of the prince of Bohemia was recognisable from the others for the

19/ The accounts were published by Maillard, *Comptes royaux (1314–1328)*, which on pp. 185–186 also includes the overall sums that I refer to in the text. The accounts were kept by Master of the King's Chamber Jean Billouart. On his long career, see Cazelles, *La société politique et la crise de la royauté*, pp. 58–59. Attention to the importance of these data for the Czech lands was drawn, especially in terms of jewellery, by Otavský, *Die Sankt Wenzelskrone*, p. 101.
20/ For more on the position and tasks of the almoners at the French court, see La Selle, *Le service des âmes à la cour*, pp. 153–155.

quality of the fabrics and linings, the fur collars as well as trimming, and in particular the skilful sewing and composition.[21]

King Charles IV the Fair became fond of his homonymous godson, provided for him in exemplary fashion, and among other things ensured that chaplain Jean de Viviers was teaching him to read and even slightly to write. 'From this I learned to read the hours of the glorious blessed Virgin Mary,' Charles would recall years later, 'and once understanding them a little I read them daily during my youth with great pleasure, because instructions had been given to my overseers by the king that they should encourage me in this.'[22] One would think that in Paris, the city of the Sorbonne, Charles would have received the most exquisite education. In Paris, perhaps, but it is not certain whether Charles lived there long-term. No matter where he and his large entourage were, proper care is certain to have been taken everywhere to educate him well in horsemanship, in the use of hand weapons and in court etiquette. All three squires assigned to him would have made sure that the son of a knight so famous everywhere would not lag behind in this respect either. Only after several years of training could young aristocrats participate under the supervision of their trainers in tourney jousting. The last element of the edification of a young nobleman was hunting. Archery was, however, already one of the joys of boyhood years. In the last decades of the thirteenth century, a ball game that was a precursor of tennis (*jeu de paume*), which could be played by two to eight players, became popular throughout the West. It would have been strange if the young Charles had not chased the ball, just as he undoubtedly learnt to play chess.

We already know that Charles strenuously practised reading prayer books. His reading in the French of the time soon must have been complemented by the basics of Latin, because in later life he had no opportunity to learn the universal language of mediaeval scholars. With his high intelligence and well-trained memory, it may be assumed that by listening and frequent journeys in foreign environments he himself quickly mastered also other languages the knowledge of which was practically indispensible for fulfilling sovereign duties over an extensive and linguistically diverse territory. It is with a manifest but certainly justifiable pride that he writes in his *Autobiography*: 'By divine grace therefore we know how to speak, write, and read not only Czech, but French, Italian, German, and Latin so that we are able to write, read, speak, and understand any one of these languages as well as another.'[23] It is worth noting

21/ For more on this, see Šmahel, 'Výdaje francouzské komory', pp. 65–76.
22/ *Karoli IV Vita*, p. 25.
23/ *Karoli IV Vita*, p. 69. Some further details are presented by Šmahel, 'Monseigneur Charles de Bohême', pp. 34–37.

that Charles speaks of himself in the plural and that he distinguishes between the three parts of language knowledge. Since Charles could express himself in Latin both in speech and in writing, he was from the mediaeval point of view one of the true scholars, the so-called *homines litterati*.

The royal chaplains were competent enough for elementary Latin, although they did not need to attain a doctorate or any other university degree.[24] Abbot of Fécamp Pierre Roger de Rosières (later Pope Clement VI), 'a man of eloquence and learning, endowed with an entirely honest character',[25] however, was the first to have a strong influence on the adolescent boy. The twelve-year-old Charles heard his sermon on Ash Wednesday, 17 February 1328, by which he was so pleased that he 'began to think to [himself] in contemplation, and kept wondering to [himself], "What is it about this man, that causes so much grace to flow over me?"'[26] Later, when Charles had become better acquainted with the abbot, the latter cherished him with much love and paternal affection and often instructed him on Holy Scripture.[27] It would come as no surprise if precisely he had urged the religiously-aroused youth to ask for permission from the pope for the right to have his own portable altar, where he would be able to have Mass served for himself, his wife and his servants in places that would have been otherwise unacceptable. The time coincidence is at the very least remarkable in that Pope John XXII granted this right to Charles on 14 September 1328.[28] Years later, the two men would meet again in Avignon – Charles already as Margrave of Moravia and Pierre now elevated to Cardinal. In the latter's house, a conversation took place which is recorded in the biographies of both men. 'You will yet be King of the Romans,' foresaw the cardinal, to which Charles readily replied, 'You will be pope before that'.[29] Much water would pass under the bridge before both things actually came to pass. In February 1328, a more pressing issue for the adolescent Charles was who would rule France.

On Candlemas Eve (1 February 1328), King Charles IV died at Vincennes after a short illness, at the age of not even thirty-three. He departed this world

7. Detail of the tomb of Philip VI of Valois (1293–1350) in the Abbey of Saint-Denis. A work by André Beaneuveu

24/ Jean de Viviers appears in the accounts in two places as *clericus et doctor Karoli filii regis Bohemiae* (Viard, *Les Journaux du Trésor*, p. 745, No. 4482, and p. 818, No. 4906). The expression 'doctor' rather needs to be understood in the common period meaning of *praeceptor* – 'teacher' than as a reference to a university grade (on this, see *Latinitatis Medii Aevi Lexicon Bohemorum*, II: D–H, p. 240, the entry for 'doctor'). Spěváček, *Jan Lucemburský*, pp. 340–341, expressed the conjecture that both tutors coming from Viviers were recommended or selected by the bishop there Peter de Mortemart, who represented Czech interests at the Papal Curia. Charles' study at the Sorbonne was mistakenly assumed by i.a. Kalista, *Karel IV.*, pp. 33–34.

25/ *Karoli IV Vita*, p. 28.

26/ *Ibid*.

27/ However, he hardly took him with him to the lectures at the Sorbonne as assumed by Bobková, *Velké dějiny zemí Koruny české*, IVa, p. 94.

28/ Attention was drawn to the privilege by Šusta, *Král cizinec*, p. 475, Note 1; otherwise, cf. *Regesta diplomatica nec non epistolaria Bohemiae et Moraviae*, III, Nos. 1490–1492.

29/ *Karoli IV Vita*, p. 145.

8. The so-called Bohemian Court (l'Hôtel de Bohême), the residence of John of Luxembourg. The situational layout following the plan from 1572:
1. Porte de Montmartre
2. Rue d'Orléans
3. Porte St. Honoré
4. Rue de Guernelle

without a male heir, but his wife Jeanne of Evreux was seven months pregnant. The administration of the kingdom was temporarily entrusted into the hands of a regent, Philip, the eldest son of Charles of Valois, who would be the only conceivable successor to the throne if Jeanne gave birth to another, third daughter. This is exactly what happened on 1 April, and as the February assembly of peers, barons and lawyers had excluded women from the succession, the French crown fell to the regent, who as Philip VI raised a cadet branch of the Capetian dynasty into the Valois dynasty, which would rule until 1589.

It is not known exactly how, but most likely in a weighty manner, King of Bohemia John of Luxembourg by authority of his French estates expressed himself at the February parliament in favour of his relative Philip of Valois, specifically the brother of his son Wenceslas' wife. Philip, still as Regent, reciprocated in no time at all in February 1328 by granting him and his heirs in perpetuity the house in Paris called Nesle between the gates of Saint-Honoré and Montmartre. This palace and its gardens lay close to the Louvre and were still at the end of the fifteenth century sometimes labelled as the 'Bohemian Court' (*l'hôtel de Bohême*).[30] For many years, this urban residence was the Parisian refuge of King John and undoubtedly served his son Charles as his home for the remainder of his stay in France.

John used his palace until the beginning of the summer, because on 29 May 1328 he attended Philip's coronation at Rheims as well as the subsequent spectacular celebrations in Paris. Immediately afterwards, he set out for Flanders

30/ Imprecisely on this, see Spěváček, *Jan Lucemburský*, p. 430, according to whom Regent Philip gave the Nesle palace to John already in February 1328, but for a service which he had provided to him on the birthday of Blanche, i.e. 1 April of the same year (!). From the art-historical perspective, see Benešovská, 'Les résidences du roi Jean de Bohême', pp. 120–121, who places the donation in 1327. It is the same with Bobková, *Velké dějiny zemí Koruny české*, IVa, p. 94.

on another military campaign to be true to the Latin proverb of the period that 'without the King of Bohemia, none may resolve their affairs. He elevates whoever he wishes and casts down whoever he does not.'[31]

Whereas the late Charles the Fair seems to have truly liked his Czech namesake, Philip VI followed the advice of the counsellors of his predecessor 'very little and allowed himself to become avaricious'.[32] The emperor did not disclose what he meant by this in his *Autobiography*. It could have had something to do with the reduction of the appanage for Charles and his wife Blanche. It is almost certain that they both went to Rheims again. It was the third coronation that Charles had seen with his own eyes. It was not only his personal experience but also French models that would later serve him when revising the order of coronation of the kings and queens of Bohemia.[33] Rather than with his thirty-five-year-old brother-in-law, he got on supposedly better with this brother-in-law's eldest son and heir to the throne, John called the Good (in French Jean le Bon, * 1319), with whom he was allegedly united by a bond of friendship 'firmer than state treaties'.[34] For at least some time, he was growing up at the side of Isabelle, his wife Blanche's elder sister, with whom during his last trip to France in January 1378 he would movingly recall their shared childhood years. Isabelle married Duke Peter I of Bourbon († 1356), whom she outlived by almost three decades († 1383).

King Philip probably did not please his son either, when in the spring of 1330 he sent Charles and Blanche back to Luxembourg after seven years in France. This must have been discussed with King John, who had spent the previous Christmas and the beginning of the year in Paris and Rheims. John had great plans for his son, and it was also high time that Charles was introduced to European high politics in the Luxembourg fashion. Charles had also matured for it. This was shown outwardly not only by his having his own seal[35] but also by the recognition of his succession rights which his future subjects had begun to grant to him. However unreliable it sounds, at some point in 1328 he was sought out in Paris by envoys from the town council of Görlitz

9. Detail of the tomb of John II the Good in the Abbey of Saint-Denis. A work by André Beaneuveu

31/ The adage was recorded by Peter of Zittau, see *Chronicon Aulae Regiae*, p. 306.
32/ In contrast to the miserly Philip, our Charles highlights the generosity of his uncle, Charles IV the Fair, see *Karoli IV Vita*, p. 29.
33/ Cf. Cibulka, *Český řád korunovační a jeho původ*; more recently Homolka, 'Ráno a večer', pp. 169–188; and in particular Žůrek, 'Korunovační řád Karla IV', pp. 105–142. Without knowing this study Jana Fantysová-Matějková, *Jak se tvoří mýtus. Froissartova líčení smrti Jana Lucemburského v bitvě u Kresčaku*, in: Ve znamení zemí Koruny české. Sborník k šedesátým narozeninám prof. PhDr. Lenky Bobkové, CSc., Praha 2006, pp. 545–558.
34/ See Seibt, *Karl IV.*, p. 119.
35/ It is first mentioned in a document of 19 April 1330, displayed at the Luxembourg castle in La Roche-en-Ardenne (in German Welschenfels), lying in Belgium today, see *Codex diplomaticus Moraviae*, VII, p. 860, No. 273, and Spěváček, *Karel IV.*, p. 76.

with a request, which was recorded word for word by the omniscient Peter of Zittau in his *Chronicon Aulae Regiae*: 'Know, oh lord, who art the lawful heir to the Kingdom of Bohemia, that we hereditarily belong to you; although we have long been so to say under some obligation as a dowry under the power of the Margraves of Brandenburg, we beseech you, because they all have by the will of God died out, that you deign to take us and our sons back into that tribe from which we come and unite us once more in the Kingdom of Bohemia, which you are granted by your birth and entitlements'.[36] Charles allegedly responded like a statesman: he accepted their oath of loyalty and passed Görlitz and its burghers pass under the protection of his father, King John. As is clear from this first act of statesmanship of his, France had exquisitely prepared him for his future career. What is more, it had given him the opportunity to become familiar with an advanced court culture, including its dynastic cults and rituals.[37]

FRANCE ON THE EVE OF THE HUNDRED YEARS' WAR

With his departure from France, the fourteen-year-old Charles moved from his childhood directly into his majority. Unlike modern codifications, mediaeval law had not reached a uniform definition of majority regardless of class and gender. The legal practices, which differed by class and territory, usually also failed to distinguish between one's majority as legal capacity and adulthood, characterised by manifest sexual indicators. For that matter, Charles was already married, and at the very least in the issue of his portable altar thought not merely of himself but also of his wife. The year 1330 also put Charles on his own two feet in another, less joyful way: on the feast of St Wenceslas (28 September), he lost his mother, whom he had not seen since he was three years old. Charles was then in Luxembourg and according to his *Autobiography* did not learn of her death until after his return to Bohemia, namely on 30 October 1333 when he stopped at the Zbraslav monastery, where he visited his mother's grave on this occasion. Many an historian has been perplexed by this inconsistency. Would John of Luxembourg have been so insensitive that he would not have by as much as a word informed his son of what had happened to his mother? Neither does it seem likely that at a time when correspondence commonly contained inquiries about the health of relatives Charles in Italy would not have displayed any interest whatsoever in his mother's situation. In

36/ See *Chronicon Aulae Regiae*, p. 300; cf. Butz, 'König Johann von Böhmen', pp. 274–275, and Bobková, *Velké dějiny zemí Koruny české*, IVa, pp. 108–109.
37/ Otavský, 'Die Dynastie der Luxemburger und die Pariser Kunst', pp. 64–65, expressed the opinion that the Parisian cult of St Louis could have been the inspiration for Charles' intense veneration of the memory of St Wenceslas.

10. Royal family. Miniature from the Liber de Dimna et Kalila. Several figures, mentioned by Charles IV in his autobiography, can be seen on the miniature from the second half of the 14th century. King Philip IV sits in the middle, who points to his eldest son Louis X (1289–1316), the king's brother Charles of Valois sits next to him entirely on the edge. His daughter Isabelle, wife of King of England Edward III, sits on his right in a scarlet gown with golden leopards, next to her are the two younger sons of Philip IV, namely Philip V (1291–1322) and Charles IV (1294–1328) (BnF, ms. lat. 8504, fol. 1v).

the absence of any other evidence, we must consider whatever Charles himself wrote as authoritative.[38]

The beginnings of the Hundred Years' War between England and France seemed to Charles IV to be the consequence of a great dispute between Edward II, who had ruled England since 1307, and King of France Charles IV the Fair, with whom we are already familiar: 'The king of England had married the sister of the afore-mentioned king [called Isabella], but had driven her out of England [in 1325], together with her first-born son, Edward. She came to her brother and remained in exile in France with her son. The King of France was angry at the expulsion of his sister and her son, and he asked my father-in-law Charles [of Valois], his uncle, to redress the shame which had been inflicted upon their family. The latter, when he had gathered an army, invaded Aquitaine and conquered almost all of it, except for Bordeaux and some other fortifications and castles. When Charles returned in triumph to France, he

38/ See Thomas, 'Vater und Sohn', pp. 446/447.

gave the daughter [Philippa] of his daughter [Jeanne], the Countess of Hainaut and the sister of my wife [Blanche], in marriage to the son [Edward III] of the afore-mentioned king of England, Edward [II], who was still in exile; and then he sent him, together with his escort, to England. He prevailed over his father, took him captive, deposed him, and set the crown upon his own head. That same year [1327], the father of the new king was murdered while in prison. Also in that year my father-in-law Charles died, leaving behind his first-born son, who was named Philip [erroneous: he had already died on 16 December 1325]. In addition, Charles, king of the French, died that year on the feast of the Purification of the Blessed Mary, leaving behind his wife [Jeanne of Evreux], who was pregnant [also incorrect: this occurred on 1 February 1328] and who eventually bore a daughter [Blanche]. As a result of the customs of the kingdom, the daughter was not able to succeed her father, so Philip [VI], the son of my father-in-law, was elevated to the throne of France, because he was the closest heir in the male line'.[39]

This section of Charles' *Autobiography* is remarkable for several reasons. Firstly, Charles should be complimented: to retain in his mind such an intricate web of familial relationships is admirable in and of itself when one considers that the events had happened three or more decades earlier.[40] The minor corrections provided in square brackets along with specifications are immaterial. Secondly, it is impossible to overlook the number of ties by which the future emperor was related to both of the crowned heads of the first phase of the Hundred Years' War. These relationships and alliances to both the warring parties were often at odds, as they mostly led to Count Charles of Valois, the father of his wife Blanche. On the one hand, Charles, as King of the Romans and Holy Roman Emperor, had the option of holding both powers tactically in check, but on the other he had to take clear positions even when it was not particularly pleasant to do so. We will find him in one such situation later, in January 1378 during his last visit to France. Thirdly and finally, Charles' view of the conflict which was about to ensue is captivating.

The election and coronation of Philip VI on 29 May 1328 was not unequivocally accepted even within the royal domain, and it thus took several months before the new king was secure in his position. Not until then was delicate pressure applied on King of England Edward III to take, as the lord of the County of Aquitaine, which belonged to the crown of France, the appropriate feudal oath. Edward's ambitious mother Isabella, who had been deeply

39/ *Karoli IV Vita*, pp. 25 and 27.
40/ With respect to the time of the writing of *Karoli IV Vita*. From the abundant literature, cf. Hergemöller, *Cogor adversum te*, pp. 233–253, and Nechutová, *Die lateinische Literatur*, pp. 169–171.

disappointed by the course of events and otherwise was the sister of the last three Kings of France, left the French delegation waiting a long time for a reply. When it came, it was practically hostile; Edward, as the son of a king, would never pay homage to Philip, a son of a mere count, irrespective of the fact that he himself had a greater entitlement to France than his rival. When, however, a second French delegation threatened to confiscate the county of Aquitaine, Edward in April 1329 promised to come to France – and on 6 June that same year, in the presbytery of Amiens cathedral, he really took his feudal oath into the hand of Philip VI. This was followed again by tourneys as well as magnificent banquets and celebrations, by which Philip, from the beginning of his reign, had liked to demonstrate his royal status. It is not impossible that Prince Charles and his wife Blanche also came to Amiens on this occasion, but to the great surprise of all his father John did not appear at the jousts.[41]

'People of all ages wonder,' wrote the chronicler Peter of Zittau of his king, John, 'about his taking such long journeys so frequently. He is often seen on his way, as if he were not riding a horse, but rather as if he were flying; if you saw him riding, you would rather think him to be a servant than a lord.' This is not particularly respectful, but one must remember that John travelled from war to war, so that 'there is hardly a land in which he would not be involved in a war. This holds particularly true for Germany, France, Flanders'.[42] John's court poet, Guillaume de Machaut, had a different order of priorities: it was the courage and generosity that he valued the most about his provider. A day and a half would not have been sufficient for him to recount concisely the great deeds of his king and when they occurred:

'He gave out fiefdoms, jewels and land
Silver and gold; nought did he hold
But honour, by which he abode.'[43]

Thanks to his mobility, John did not even need an intelligence service. He knew everything immediately, and hardly could his opponents recover before he entered the contest on the battlefield of war and often even of diplomacy. The year 1330 brought new tasks not only for Charles but also for his father. While Charles was familiarising himself with his duties in the county

41/ John's non-participation was already ruled out by Šusta, *Král cizinec*, p. 459, Note 4. Without knowledge of the Czech literature, John's stay in Amiens is discussed by Contamine, 'Politique, culture et sentiment', p. 349. Charles' attendance is assumed by Bobková, *Velké dějiny zemí Koruny české*, IVa, pp. 94–95.

42/ *Chronicon Aulae Regiae*, pp. 290 and 312.

43/ An extract from the poem 'Le Comfort d'Ami', ed. Ernest Hoepfner, Guillaume de Machaut, *Oeuvres*, II, Paris 1921, p. 103, verses 2930–2932.

of Luxembourg, John was raising money for a military expedition to Italy at the side of Emperor Louis the Bavarian. Matters proved to be more complicated when, after the death of the Anti-King of the Romans Frederick I of Austria († 1330) and the paralysis of his brother Albert II, also the youngest of the Habsburg brothers Otto began to toy with the idea of standing against Louis as the new pretender to the throne of the Romans. And since he found encouragement for his intention on the part of Pope John XXII, who saw in it a support in his long-running dispute with the emperor, King John could hardly miss the fact that the still young and recently widowed Otto would be an excellent match for his daughter Guta. She, however, as we already know, had previously been betrothed by John several times, most recently to Duke Edward of Bar in 1323. Nevertheless, the wedding was cancelled and even the courtship with the emperor's first-born son Louis V, Duke of Bavaria and Margrave of Brandenburg, had come to nought. This matrimonial diplomacy did however have its pitfalls, and thus in June 1330 King John hurried to the French court at Poissy, near Paris, so that through King Philip VI he could resolve his disputes with Duke Edward of Bar, which had taken a significant turn for the worse with Guta's new engagement. Ultimately, even this wedding fell through, this time because of papal obstructions. Nevertheless, this was not the end of Guta's matrimonial wanderings.

Allow us to jump forward half a year to bring her story to a close. On the feast of St Nicholas (6 December) 1331, John left Bohemia in such a hurry that he astonished even those who had no longer thought that he could surprise them with anything. When asked on his journey where he was rushing, he replied that he wanted to be in Paris for Christmas Eve. He was hard pressed, as he had stopped in Frankfurt, where he successfully obtained valuable promises on the part of Emperor Louis concerning the Luxemburg domain in northern Italy. The main aim of John's trip to Paris was to obtain similar support from the French court. Considering Philip's own power interests in the same area, this was a delicate matter, which could hardly find an ultimate resolution. On the other hand, the negotiations regarding the marriage of the sixteen-year-old Guta to Philip's eldest son and legitimate heir to the throne, John, turned out to be unexpectedly promising. The Duke of Normandy, four years her junior, would indeed be an excellent match, and since Guta, who had received a French education and achieved the appropriate elegance in Luxembourg, was also a desirable match, the marriage contract was drawn up at the royal palace of Fontainebleau already around the middle of January. John promised to pay an enormous dowry of 120,000 florins in six instalments, and moreover to aid the French king militarily should there be any conflicts in Champagne, Vermandois or around Amiens by providing relatively large, precisely defined contingents of three to four hundred cavalrymen. In the distant future, another of John's undertakings might have had far-reaching consequences, namely his promise that were he or his son to become King of the Romans or Holy Roman Emperor, they would make no claim on the basis of imperial law on the dependencies of the King of France.[44]

The wedding took place still in the summer of the same year. We are not going to decide which of the five dates offered by historians is correct. The wedding festivities were preceded by a tourney, during which the groom was knighted. King John then rushed from France to Luxembourg to make sure that no one would remind him of the first instalment of the dowry, which should have already been paid at Easter.[45] The French court never saw it. Duke John, however, reacted magnanimously and did not reproach his wife, who repaid him with four sons and three daughters. Since at least half of these would be directly involved in the events of 1378, it is useful to know that these were the future King Charles V of France (* 1338), Count Louis I of Anjou, titular King of Naples (* 1339), Duke John I of Berry (* 1340), Duke Philip II the Bold of Burgundy (* 1342), and Marie (* 1344), whose third husband was Duke Robert I of Bar († 1411), one of the noble members of the emperor's retinue during his visit to France in January 1378.[46] It should be said immediately here that this was no coincidence, as in 1354 Charles IV raised the then nine-year-old Robert to the ranks of the imperial princes, namely under circumstances quite alarming for France, whose kings had held Bar as their fief since 1301. Parts of this border county on the left bank of the River Meuse belonged to the Empire, and thus Charles IV *sui juris* promoted them to the Margravate of Pont-à-Mousson.[47]

Although we have just introduced the players of the final act of this historical travelogue onto the stage, we will return via Robert of Bar to his grandfather Edward, last seen in a dispute with King John of Luxembourg at the beginning of the 1330s. If the King of France played the role of justice of the peace, John of Luxembourg was on the contrary one of the twelve lord judges (peers) in the dispute between Philip VI and Robert of Artois (1287–1342). This count was the king's brother-in-law, which made it a matter of great delicacy, the

44/ For more on this, see Šusta, *Král cizinec*, pp. 541–543, and Spěváček, *Jan Lucemburský*, pp. 495–499.

45/ John tried to pay the dowry by selling Lucca and its county in October 1334, but the sale was cancelled. See Contamine, 'Politique, culture et sentiment', pp. 352–353, and Spěváček, *Jan Lucemburský*, p. 517.

46/ The other two daughters died before 1378: the youngest Isabella in 1362 and the oldest Jeanne in 1373. Detailed data on Guta and her offspring are provided by Veldtrup, *Zwischen Eherecht und Familienpolitik*, pp. 454–470.

47/ For more on the history of the county of Bar under Charles IV, see Thomas, 'Zwischen Regnum und Imperium'.

11. Trial of Robert of Artois (BnF, ms. fr. 18437, fol. 2r)

roots of which lay in the distant past. After Robert II of Artois fell in French colours at the Battle of Courtrai in 1302, his domains passed to his daughter Mahaut, widow of Otto IV, Count of Burgundy, by which the five-year-old Robert, son of Mahaut's prematurely deceased brother Philip († 1298), was excluded from the succession. Hardly had Robert of Artois come of age than he embarked upon a campaign to recover his grandfather's estates, but Mahaut remained firmly entrenched. As the husband of Jeanne of Valois, Robert helped his brother-in-law Philip to the throne of France, who in gratitude promoted him to a peer in 1329.

Believing that he would now obtain satisfaction, Robert of Artois raised the issue of his inheritance again. Forasmuch as his claims were considered by the court as less than conclusive, Robert decided after some hesitation to substantiate them with counterfeit documents. He was apparently incited to this by his wife Jeanne, who had obtained for this purpose a person capable of anything: Jeanne of Devion, a woman with an eventful life, who had inherited from her Jewish mother not only a considerable intellect but also an interest in occultism. The ingenuity with which she acted is remarkable. In order to increase the veracity of the falsified will, in which Robert II designated his son Philip and his male offspring as his heirs, she furnished it among other things with a confirmation of its validity with the signature and seal of King Philip IV the Fair. Had it not been for a single error in the dates, the court might well have believed the counterfeits. Jeanne of Devion was burnt as a witch and Robert of Artois was conditionally sentenced to exile and confiscation of property by Philip VI on 8 April 1331. Robert took refuge at the court of the duke of Brabant, from whence he allegedly attempted to take revenge on his brother-in-law through magical practices. In retaliation, Philip had Robert's family imprisoned and sent forces led by John of Luxembourg to Brabant. The campaign soon ended in a truce, which compelled Robert to leave for England.[48]

The main reason for mentioning this affair is the original dossier on Robert's trial with the title illumination, which in a nutshell shows the 'political society' of France under Philip VI of Valois. Highest, seated on a throne with a crown on his head and wearing the royal vestment with lilies, is Philip himself. His right hand and face are turned towards two figures clearly superior to the secular lords (peers) and ecclesiastical dignitaries on the opposite side wearing bishops' mitres. On the basis of the coats-of-arms above their heads, the two bareheaded men can be recognised as John of Luxembourg, King of Bohemia, and Philip of Evreux, King of Navarre. John of Luxembourg sits closer to the king; his prominent position is also clearly implied by the index finger of Philip's left hand. Upon close inspection, it is hard to miss that the bench with the six bishops (of Rheims, Noyon, Laon, Châlons, Beauvais and Langres) is placed noticeably higher than that of the eight secular lords opposite, who according to their coats-of-arms are the Duke of Normandy, Count of Alençon, Dukes of Burgundy and Bourbon, Count of Flanders, Duke of Brittany, Count of Étamps and Duke of Guyenne. The group of the eight figures sitting on the ground most likely depicts the king's courtiers of the higher degree, whereas below are burghers from the important, so-called 'good towns'.[49] There is hardly any illustrated textbook of French history in which this illumination would not be reproduced. The attention that it has been given here is thus justified.

From all that we have said of King John thus far, it might appear that in the 1330s he spent more time in France than in Bohemia, which he actually did. Whereas between 1331 and 1340 he spent only slightly more than two

48/ On King John's contribution to the trial of Robert of Artois, see de Puymaigre, 'Jean l'Aveugle en France', pp. 426–430; cf. also Cazelles, *La société politique et la crise de la royauté*, pp. 83 and 101. For the latest on the counterfeit documents, see Poulle, 'Les faux de Robert d'Artois', pp. 519–534.
49/ *Procès de Robert d'Artois*, Paris, Bibliothèque nationale, MS fr. 18437, fol. 2r. On the interpretation, cf. i.a. Contamine, 'Politique, culture et sentiment', p. 351.

years in Bohemia, he spent thirty-three months in total in France, where he primarily devoted himself to his hobbies. After Prague, Brno, and Arlon in Luxembourg, Paris was the city that he visited most, appearing there a total of nineteen times.[50] John did not travel to France only for tourneys and other hobbies of his: he was welcomed there also as an influential political ally and skilled warrior, always ready to sally forth at the side of the king of France. Thanks to his connections and undeniable diplomatic skills, he could also open weighty games on the European political scene joined by the Holy Roman Emperor, sometimes the king of France or the Papal Curia. It is no wonder that some scholars speak of the French-Luxembourg effort to dominate the Christian world. Another external expression of this condominium was John's marriage to Countess Beatrice, the daughter of Duke Louis I of Bourbon and his wife Mary of Avesnes, daughter of John II of Hainaut.

This marriage contract was preceded by two others, which bilaterally regulated the financial obligations between the two monarchs. To pay the dowry that he owed for Guta, who become 'Bonne' in France, John sold Philip VI his Italian estates at Lucca and in the entire county at the end of October 1334. As these were amounts of more or less questionable due dates, Philip by another contract signed in December, also in the castle of Vincennes, changed John's existing annuity of 4,000 Tours pounds (*livres tournois*) for a lifelong and hereditary annuity from the castle and estates of Mehun-sur--Yèvre near Bourges.[51] We hence learn of the annuity through which Charles IV the Fair expressed his gratitude to John for his help in obtaining the throne of France. After all, John was not to come off badly, as the same annual amount of 4,000 Tours pounds was guaranteed to him by contract with the father of the bride at the county of Clermont. It was said of the bride in court circles that she had slightly wooed John with various gifts of jewels and ribbons, because he had impressed her at tourney jousting. The groom reciprocated with jewellery of the enormous amount of 4,500 Paris pounds, which he probably never paid back.[52] In addition to the various other contractual obligations, the document of December 1334 contained a substantial provision that should the marriage produce any sons, the entire county of Luxembourg along with the estates held by John in France would fall to them. This was to the manifest disadvantage of John's sons from his first marriage, Wenceslas-Charles and the

50/ On that, see Margue, *Un itineraire européen*, passim. The stays in the individual lands were calculated by Mezník, 'Pobyty Jana Lucemburského', pp. 93–98; on the number of stays in individual places, see Hlaváček, 'Verwaltunsgeschichtliche Bemerkungen', pp. 126–127.

51/ This residence later fell to John, Count of Berry, who rebuilt it into the magnificent appearance captured in his *Très Riches Heures* (Chantilly, Musée Condé, MS 65, fol. 161v). See Autrand, *Jean de Berry*, pp. 360–364.

52/ John's debt with the goldsmith Simon of Lille was assumed by Count of Flanders Louis I of Nevers as established by Otavský, 'Die Dynastie der Luxemburger und die Pariser Kunst', p. 68.

younger John Henry (* 1322), who were to complement the nuptial agreement later.[53]

Beatrice married the longed-for hero, who however already in April 1335 was seriously wounded in a tourney held without the king's approval. Philip VI had already for a longer time sought to limit such chivalric jousting because of its expense, and therefore had all the foreign participants arrested. He did not release them until at the request of the wounded John, who remained confined to his bed until July.[54] For John, his return to Bohemia began a period of intensive, and it must be added of very successful, activity. Thanks to contracts concluded in the second half of 1335 at Trenčín and at Hungarian Visegrád, John indirectly obtained from Casimir the Great of Poland recognition of the sovereignty of the King of Bohemia over Silesia, thereby strengthening the then-forming union of the lands of the Bohemian Crown. At that time, the king was being kept in Bohemia also by his newlywed Beatrice, who had resided in Prague from the beginning of January 1336. Her companion was Charles' wife Blanche, who had already learnt some Czech and had apparently thus gained greater popularity. It was perhaps also for this reason that Beatrice soon ceased to be happy in Bohemia, and immediately after her coronation on 1 July 1337 departed with her French retinue for Luxembourg.[55] It is significant that she left her four-month-old son Wenceslas in Prague as if he had not been hers. The king provided her well with a weekly allowance from the Kutná Hora silver mines, banished the well-liked Blanche to Brno and he himself, regardless of the women and all the rest as was his nature, set out for the court of Emperor Louis the Bavarian in Frankfurt. The reason was truly serious this time, because the conflict between England and France that historians would much later call the Hundred Years' War was about to break out.

At the very beginning of this chapter, we read how the very beginnings of this clash were described by Charles IV in his *Autobiography*. French constitutional (Salic) law excluded not only daughters but also their male offspring from succession to the throne. As a grandson of Philip IV, King of England Edward III had no intention of relinquishing his claims to the French Crown and with the aid of his lawyers presented them on the grounds of several continental royal courts where he was seeking allies.[56] The war of words between England and France was to become a war of arrows and swords. The rising

---

53/ For more on that, see Šusta, *Karel IV. Otec a syn 1333–1346*, pp. 176–177; Spěváček, *Jan Lucemburský*, pp. 517–518; and Contamine, 'Politique, culture et sentiment', pp. 354–355.

54/ The account of the prohibited tourney even reached Bohemia, where it was recorded by Abbot Peter of Zittau. See *Chronicon Aulae Regiae*, p. 329.

55/ For the latest on this stage of John's politics, see Bobková, *Velké dějiny zemí Koruny české*, IVa, pp. 156–163.

56/ See Ormrod, *The Reign of Edward III*; for further literature, see *Lexikon des Mittelalters*, III, cols 1588–1590.

12. The feudal oath of King of England Edward III as Duke of Guyenne, to King of France Philip of Valois in Amiens. Chroniques de Jean Froissart (BnF, ms. fr. 2646)

expenses of the luxurious life of the royal court and of the preparations for a new crusade provoked resistance to the collection of new taxes in particular in the south of France, where the royal government traditionally struggled harder than in the north. Not even Philip VI's several-month-long journey to Toulouse, Carcassonne, Montpellier and Marseille in the first half of 1337 brought the desired results. Moreover, during a stop at Avignon, Philip had to acknowledge with heavy heart that Pope Benedict XII (1334–1342) had abandoned the already-announced crusade. With this, the king's scheme collapsed and he furthermore lost the possibility to continue to collect extraordinary taxes to finance the crusade. During his journey to the south, in an attempt to strengthen royal power, Philip announced the confiscation of the duchy of Aquitaine on 24 May 1337, namely on the grounds that Edward III had not fulfilled his liege duties. For the English court, this step was a *causus belli*, which was officially declared by Edward in October through a renunciation of his obligations to Philip of Valois, 'who calls himself the King of France'.[57]

THE HEROIC DEATH OF KING JOHN

In July 1337, the development of events came to a turning point when Edward's envoys succeeded with Louis the Bavarian. For an appropriately attractive price, the emperor promised to equip for battle two thousand cavalrymen for the English, which was no small feat. We can therefore imagine

57/ The Hundred Years' War will be covered only in connection with the main plot, and therefore it should be enough to refer to the recent standard works: Favier, *La Guerre de Cents Ans*; Contamine, *Guerre, État et société* and *La Guerre de Cent Ans*; Sumption, *The Hundred Years War*, I–II.

13. Charles IV (1316–1378), Holy Roman Emperor and King of Bohemia. A bust in the inner triforium of the Cathedral of St Vitus at Prague Castle

the disappointment of King of Bohemia John when he could not dissuade the emperor in Frankfurt from supporting Edward III. He consequently headed from there hastily for France, where already on 6 August 1337 he sealed his obligation to serve King Philip with five hundred mercenaries. Although it was supposed to be at the expense of the French side, John of Luxembourg even this time showed himself to be a loyal ally and was to remain one until his tragic end. Philip VI trusted him so much that on 30 November 1338 he appointed him Vice-Regent in Languedoc. John actually assumed his task; still in January of the following year, he lingered in the south, from whence he unexpectedly departed for Germany. For King John, the good of France was of utmost importance, sometimes even over the interests of his Kingdom of Bohemia. In order to dissuade Emperor Louis from his alliance with England, he made peace with him and on 20 March 1339 placed the forced feudal oath in his hands. By accepting his lands from the emperor as an imperial fief, he broke all of the privileges of the Czech Kingdom that had been valid up until that time. John soon also encountered the disagreement of his son Charles, at that time already Margrave of Moravia, whom he met in Lower Franconia on 20 April. Charles' resistance arose not only from his position on the legally improper oath but also from personal reasons, because the emperor had falsely claimed to his father that he already had Charles' consent. It is necessary to add that John of Luxembourg was not too worried about his obligations and considered them as purposeful moves on the political chessboard. His chivalric code of values, we are not going to conceal it, had numerous gaps, namely not only with respect to women.

We have lost sight of the successor to the Bohemian throne Charles for a long time. His father entrusted him with responsible tasks in northern Italy, in Tyrol and especially in Bohemia, while always trying to make sure that he could handle Charles. As he grew older, Charles tolerated his father's arrogant methods ever less, but he had no choice other than his own interest as well as that of the entire dynasty to bite his tongue. In the case of the military aid to France, which in the summer of 1339 had to defend itself against the invasion of an English expedition in the north, it was after all not necessary to hesitate. When in the second half of August a plea for assistance came from France, both Luxemburgs set out on the march and already in October reached France with their divisions. It did not come to a battle, but the father and son lingered in Paris until the end of the year to be on the safe side. It was especially welcomed by Margrave Charles, who had returned to his second home after a long ten years. After New Year's 1340, John of Luxembourg sought renowned eye doctors at the university of Montpellier, because he had recently been suffering difficulties with his weakening eyesight. The treatment failed and John could no longer see; nevertheless, he did not want to sacrifice his lifestyle and rhythm. Charles intended to go to the aid of the King of Spain, but his father kept him in Montpellier, from whence both went to Avignon, where they were received by Pope Benedict XII. It was also then in the house of Cardinal Pierre Roger de Rosières that the already-mentioned conversation on the future career of both men with one leading to the papal tiara and the other to the imperial crown took place. From Avignon, they returned together to Paris, but Charles only for a short time, because his father sent him to his sister, the widow of Duke of Bavaria Henry, to protect her from the injustices of Emperor Louis. It is evident from this film-like cut that the apple had not fallen far from the tree. Also young Charles was with his retinue on journeys all the time, because in that and no other way was 'great' politics done then.

Whereas Edward III had failed in France militarily, he had achieved a significant political victory at the end of the same year, 1339, in Flanders and particularly in Ghent, where he was recognised as the King of France by the towns of Flanders during his stay in January 1340. This act could not remain unanswered. At the end of May, the French armada set sail for the port of Sluis in Flanders to interdict the supply routes between England and the Continent. A month later, this fleet suffered a crushing defeat, which for several years blunted the edge of the French offensive against England. On the mainland, fighting continued, although mainly only in the form of war-cries in the camps around the besieged town of Tournai, or demonstrative shifts of knight cavalry. At the end of May, Edward III abandoned the siege and withdrew from northern France. The recourse from the stalemate, as it was to be many more times in the course of the long-term conflict, became a truce concluded on 25 September 1340.

During the truce negotiations, the French side was represented in the preeminent position by the blind King John of Luxembourg, who two weeks earlier had dictated his last will and testament in his commander's tent just in case. Most of the text of the extensive document contains a list of debts, the settlement of which he principally wanted to ensure from the yields from the Bohemian silver mines and Kutná Hora mint. As his final resting place, which is also characteristic, he did not choose St Vitus' Cathedral but the Cistercian Abbey of Clairefontaine near the town of Arlon, his main base in Luxembourg. Not even the tourney in Compiègne, organised for him and the other allied knights at great cost by King of France Philip VI, seems to have dissipated his dismal mood. The less festive was the welcome given to John in Prague, where after his stay in Luxembourg and in Wrocław, Silesia he appeared at Christmas 1340.

Although he was dependent on the eyes of the others, it did not discourage King John from continuing to look sharply behind the scenes of European politics and intervene wherever Luxembourg interests were threatened. Light to his dark days and nights was brought by the election in May 1342 of Cardinal Pierre Roger de Rosières to the papal throne, vacated by the death of Benedict XII. The new pope, who adopted the name Clement VI (1342–1352), did not want to acquiesce to the toothless policy toward the long-excommunicated Emperor Louis the Bavarian. He selected Margrave Charles of Luxembourg as a suitable ally and possible man on the imperial throne, whose competence he had had a chance to see for himself. The intermediate for that became Archbishop of Trier Baldwin, who had also facilitated Charles' father John's reception in Avignon. It was not a mere formality, because the King of Bohemia with his feudal homage to the emperor had also become anathematised and therefore had to withdraw from his obligations first and achieve a revocation of his excommunication. This happened in the Papal Palace in Avignon at the end of June 1342; however, it took more than eighteen months for the issues to move forward.[58]

A sensitive point in this game of high politics was the fear of the French court that an overhasty rise of the Luxemburgs could drive Emperor Louis the Bavarian into an alliance with England again. John's attempts to adopt the role of mediator between the pope and emperor therefore aroused an energetic counteraction on the part of his son Charles, who in contrast saw his primary goal in the isolation of Louis the Bavarian from power. This was eventually recognised also by his father, so at the end of February 1344 they both left in unison for Avignon, where they were given an unusually ceremonial reception. The first significant and in its implications truly historic result of this visit was the promotion of the Prague bishopric to an archbishopric, the establishment of a bishopric in Litomyšl and the subordination of the Bishopric of Olomouc to the newly appointed Archbishop Ernest (Arnošt) of Pardubice. The second agreement was no less momentous, although it was at first kept secret, because it was the beginning of a campaign aimed at the placement of Margrave Charles on the Roman throne after a new excommunication and the consequent deposal of the ruling Emperor Louis. As soon as this intention became known, the emperor hurried to create an anti-Luxemburg coalition. The Papal Curia had to expend a great deal of effort and issue many threats to be able to declare Louis as an incorrigible heretic on Easter in April 1346 and summon the imperial electors to the election of a new King of the Romans. With the successful election on 11 July 1346, Charles IV acquired his first royal title.[59]

14. Ernest (Arnošt) of Pardubice (1297–1364), first archibishop of Prague. A bust in the inner triforium of the Cathedral of St Vitus at Prague Castle

58/ For more on this, see Šusta, *Karel IV.*, Chapters V–VI; it has been treated from another point of view by Thomas, 'Clemens VI. und Ludwig der Bayer', pp. 75–117.
59/ Charles' election as King of the Romans is lengthily described by all the basic literature; for the latest, see Bobková, *Velké dějiny zemí Koruny české*, IVa, pp. 194–201.

15. Battle of Crécy 1346.
Chroniques de Jean Froissart
(BnF, ms. fr. 2662)

Before the two Luxemburgs could properly celebrate their triumph, an urgent request from King of France Philip VI for assistance reached them at Baldwin's court in Trier, because precisely on the day of Charles' election Edward III landed with his army in Normandy.

There is a lot to suggest that Edward planned to obtain a permanent base for further conquests on the narrowest segment of the English Channel. To be able to do so, he and his forces first had to overcome the Seine, which they managed in August at Poissy, dangerously close to Paris. Whereas the English army turned to the north, Philip VI after initial hesitation began to chase the enemy. Also the two kings of the Luxemburg family, the father John and his son Charles, now already King of the Romans Charles IV, arrived with their brigades in the vicinity of Saint-Denis sometime around the middle of August. On Saturday, 26 August 1346, the two armies faced each other between the Castle Labroye and the village of Crécy. Unlike the well-disciplined English army, the more numerous units under the French standard were not united, for which also the leadership incompetency of their commander-in-chief was to blame. The knight cavalry, which had moved forward, could not be held back, did not let the tired infantry rest and plunged impetuously into battle. The feared English bowmen repulsed the attack and thus convincingly demonstrated their superiority over the conscripted Genoese crossbowmen. During the withdrawal, confusion occurred, with some groups retreating while others lion-heartedly beginning personal combat. According to contemporary testimony, the king of Bohemia refused to leave the field of battle.[60] 'When he understood the order of the battle,' we read in the *Chronicles* by Jean Froissart, 'he said to them about him: "Where is the lord Charles my son?" His men said: "Sir we cannot tell; we think he be fighting." Then he said: "Sirs, ye are my men, my companions and friends in this journey: I require you bring me so far forward, that I may strike one stroke with my sword." They said they would do his commandment, and to the intent that they should not lose him in the press, they tied all their reins of their bridles each to other and set the king before to accomplish his desire, and so they went on their enemies. The lord Charles of Bohemia his son, who wrote himself king of Almaine and bare the arms, he came in good order to the battle; but when he saw that the matter went awry on their party, he departed, I cannot tell you which way. The king his father was so far forward that he strake a stroke with his sword, yea and more than four, and fought valiantly and so did his company; and they adventured themselves so forward, that they were there all slain; and the next day they were found in the place about the king, and all their horses tied each to other.'[61]

We should not take it all literally. According to Froissart, John of Luxembourg died as befitted a foremost and well-known representative of the waning knightly era. The newly elected King of the Romans Charles IV was at the battle and escaped only slightly wounded from it. That was the last time that he had fought in France and for France. Now, the battles to ensure his succession in the Empire awaited him.

THE CHILDHOOD YEARS OF THE FIRST DAUPHIN CHARLES OF VALOIS

How intricate the fates of the primary and secondary actors of our story can be is clearly demonstrated by the following description, in which almost the same roles are played not only by both Charleses, our Emperor and the next King of France Charles V, but also by the principality called the Dauphiné since the end of the thirteenth century according to the dolphin (*dauphin*) on the coat-of-arms of the ruling family. The principality was gradually formed on the ancient cultural territory between the Rhône Valley and the Alps with seven bishoprics and two centres, Vienne and Embrun; according to the former, it was sometimes called the 'Viennois' county instead of the Dauphiné. As we will soon hear, until 1349, the Dauphiné was a relatively independent

60/ On the English campaign and the Battle of Crécy, see de Wailly, *Crécy, 1346*; Sumption, *The Hundred Years War*, I, pp. 489–534; from the Czech literature, Urban, *Kresčak*, and briefly also Bobková, *Velké dějiny zemí Koruny české*, IVa, pp. 200–210, which contains further literature.
61/ *The Chronicles of Froissart*, pp. 103–104.

principality belonging to the Holy Roman Empire as the southwestern part of the Kingdom of Arelat.[62] Although successful alliance politics was bringing the family considerable territorial gains, it also entailed debts and conflicts with its neighbours, from 1283 especially with Savoy.

When the individual lines of our story were being spun, the Dauphiné was ruled by Quido VII, every inch a knight and a man with great ambition as well as a distant relative of Emperor Charles IV, who apparently never met him but knew that Quido's grandmother was the sister of his grandmother. It can be added that the grandmothers were Guta of Habsburg (1271–1297), the first wife of Wenceslas II, King of Bohemia, and Clementia († 1293), the wife of the titular King of Hungary, Charles Martell of the Anjou family. Before her early death, Clementia managed to bear a daughter, Beatrix, who married into the Dauphiné through Count John II, after whose death in 1318 the already-mentioned Quido VII acceded to the throne.[63] In 1333, when under strange circumstances Guy entered Luxemburg history, he was fighting quite unsuccessfully with Count of Savoy Aymon (1329–1343). Likewise both Luxemburgs, the father John and son Charles, were in armour at that time and were finishing a military campaign in northern Italy also with only unclear gains. On a journey to Parma, they stopped together in the village of Terenzo on Sunday, 15 August 1333.

Now we give the floor to Charles himself, who already – which we cannot miss – speaks of himself in the plural as a self-aware ruler by the grace of God: 'That same night, after we had fallen asleep, a vision appeared to us. An angel of the Lord stood beside us in the left side of the bed where we lay and struck us on the side, saying: "Rise up and come with us!" We responded in spirit, "Lord, I do not know where or how I may go with you." And taking us by the hair of our forehead, he lifted us with him into the air and over to where a great battle array of armed knights were standing before a fortress prepared for battle. He held us in the air above the troops and said to us, "Watch and see." And behold another angel descended from heaven bearing a fiery sword in his hand, and he struck a man in the center of the battle line, cutting off his genital organ with the sword. He seemed to be mortally wounded, and sat there on his horse in agony. Thereupon, still holding us by the hair, the angel said, "Do you know the person who has been struck by the angel and mortally wounded?" Then we said, "Lord, I do not know, neither do I know this place." He said, "Know then that this is the dauphin of Vienne, who because of the sin

62/ See Heckmann, 'Das Reichsvikariat des Dauphins im Arelat', pp. 66–69, and Weiss, 'Onkel und Neffe', pp. 111–116.
63/ For the basic information, see *Lexikon des Mittelalters*, III, cols 586–592, and *Encyclopaedia of the Middle Ages*, I, pp. 411–412.

16. Charles IV's dream in Terenzo (ÖNB, cod. ser. n. 2618, fol. 27v)

of debauchery has been struck down by God in this way; now therefore take care, and you may tell your father that he ought to avoid similar sin, or even worse shall happen to you".'[64]

The curious Charles asked the angel *inter alia* whether the poor Quido would be able to confess. While the affirmative answer slightly calmed him, the anxiety in his soul remained, and upon awakening he mentioned his dream to his father's chamberlain Thomas of Villeneuve. Although the chamberlain did not believe him, he did not bridle his tongue; hence later in Parma, Charles had to also tell his father of his night experience. Being his son, he did not dare tell him everything but apparently drew the conclusions himself from this admonition. Not until the news that Guy had actually died from an arrow shot before La Perrière fort (near Voiron) did Charles' dream gain credibility. Such an occurrence could not be kept secret; it was discussed everywhere; it was recorded by Beneš Krabice of Weitmile, Jean Porta d'Annonay as well as Aeneas Sylvius Piccolomini; neither could it have been missing in the Dream Book by Laurence of Březová.[65] This was not the end of the issue for Charles. When he was staying in Pisa more than twenty years later, he went to Teren-

64/ *Karoli IV Vita*, p. 61.

65/ For more on this, see Odložilík, 'The Terenzo Dream', pp. 163–173, which includes a reference to the sources. Most recently, the entire episode was explicated from more perspectives by Nodl, 'Svár obrazu s textem', pp. 69–95.

zo and with the consent of the Bishop of Parma had the house in which the angel had appeared to him in his dream rebuilt into a chapel consecrated to the Virgin Mary and the Holy Angels. On his journey back from the Roman coronation in spring 1355, he stopped in Terenzo again, and through Bishop of Olomouc John (Jan) Očko of Vlašim had the chapel consecrated and instituted the main vicar there and two so-called mansionary canons, whom he provided with pensions.[66]

After the death of Quido, power in the Dauphiné was assumed by his brother Humbert II (1333–1349), who quickly ended the war with Savoy and ambitiously began far-reaching internal reforms. With this, he indebted the principality even more and, when he became a widower without heirs in 1347, he saw the sale of the Dauphiné to the French Crown as his only way out. The treaty concluded in Romans on 30 March 1349 guaranteed him 200,000 florins and an annual income of 4,000 of the same. King of France Philip VI allotted this profitable estate as a so-called appanage for the crown princes and assumed the obligation for himself and his successors that the first-born prince would have the title Dauphin de Viennois and the symbols of France and the Dauphiné in a quarterly coat-of-arms. Humbert II could satisfactorily live from his income while France thus significantly increased its territory in the south. For the time being, King Philip VI did not worry about the Dauphiné belonging to the Empire, because the new Holy Roman Emperor, Charles IV, had his hands full with other problems.[67]

If we look at a map, which is useful, we realise immediately that the borders of the French monarchy were still far from resembling today's (Pic. 37). In the north, the English had captured the port of Calais in 1347, which they held as an extremely important base for two centuries. While Flanders remained a part of France, its count, under pressure from his rebellious cities, could not avoid an alliance with England. The Bretons were in a similar position; their economic and other interests drove them into the arms of the English as well. For that matter, also the inhabitants of English-controlled Gascony, which included three principalities, namely Armagnac, Albret and Foix-Béarn, remained subjects of the king of France. In the south, the border with the independent Kingdom of Navarre did not strictly follow the ridge of the Pyrenees and variously ran towards the Mediterranean Sea. France around 1350 differed the most from today's here towards the north, because not only the above-mentioned Dauphiné but also Provence, Savoy and the higher sit-

66/ The chapel or rather church no longer exists today; for details on its foundation by Charles, see Hledíková, 'Fundace českých králů', pp. 11–12.
67/ On Humbert II, cf. *Lexikon des Mittelalters*, V, cols 206–207; Autrand, *Charles V. Le Sage*, pp. 49–53.

uated Free County of Burgundy (Franche-Comté) and furthermore Lorraine with its newly formed Duchy of Bar as well as the County of Hainaut were under the jurisdiction of the Roman King and Emperor following the Treaty of Verdun of 843. It is worth noting that the officials of the French Crown tried to clarify the borders, mark them and strengthen the general awareness of their course already in the second quarter of the fourteenth century. For example, it was verified in 1387 and 1390 based on official findings that the eastern border between France and the Empire was formed by the River Meuse.[68] It is not necessary to add that France under the Valois dynasty had great troubles maintaining its ruling status not only in the west but also in the east.

For Philip VI, whose prestige had greatly decreased after the loss of the Port of Calais, the gain of the Dauphiné was one of few lasting successes. The onerous economic and social situation in his kingdom was catastrophically worsened by a plague epidemic soon afterwards. The effects of the Black Death were terrifying; for instance, 30 of 80 monks died in the Abbey of Saint-Denis alone. The only reliable cure against infection was to stay where the plague had not reached. Not even in his personal life was Philip spared from the omnipresent blight of death. After the passing of his first wife Jeanne, he married again in January 1350 to the daughter of the king of Navarre Blanche, but he left this life himself already in August of the same year. As if prescient of his near end, he entrusted the Dauphiné not to his son, who succeeded him on the throne as John II, but his eldest grandson. The next king, Charles V, thus became the first Dauphin in French history.[69]

To fulfil the conditions of the Treaty of Romans was not exactly easy. First of all, it was necessary to procure money for the gratuity. As Count Humbert II decided to devote himself to a high church career, his engagement to Jeanne, a rich and beautiful daughter of Peter I, Duke of Bourbon, and Isabelle of Valois, fell through. This was only of benefit for the eleven-year-old bride, because she was selected for Dauphin Charles, who was of the same age as she was. And although their wedding did not take place until April 1350, the promised dowry of 200,000 florins sufficiently covered the sum owed for the Dauphiné. The second indispensible step was the public assumption of the insignia, which happened in Lyon on 18 July 1349 in the presence of the

---

68/ Cf. Trapp, 'Die französischen Enquêtes von 1387 und 1390', pp. 317–332.

69/ For the basic information, see Thomas, 'Karl V.', pp. 285–320, the bibliography on p. 404. The latest summary of the literature, especially on court art from the 'century' of Charles V, has been provided by Carqué, *Stil und Erinnerung*, pp. 42–54. The fundamental work of all the further research remains the five-volume biography by Delachenal, *Histoire de Charles V*. More recent information was incorporated in her masterfully written monograph by Autrand, *Charles V. Le Sage*. Both works will be frequently referred to here.

Dauphin's father John, then still Duke of Normandy. Charles was greatly impressed by his first investiture. Besides the ring, sceptre, and standard with a depiction of St George, he also accepted the ancient sword of the Dauphiné, whose handle was supposedly of the wood of the true cross of Christ. At the end of August, Charles became seriously ill in Romans and had to postpone his arrival in Grenoble until the beginning of December. Another delay occurred, so the ceremonial enthronement of the first Dauphin did not happen until February 1350. It was followed by mutual oaths, without which nothing could happen even in France, with all of this taking place in the presence of the abdicating Humbert.

The public enthronement and wedding with Jeanne of Bourbon had to be postponed because of the demise of the Dauphin's mother Bonne, who died of a plague infection on 11 November 1349. Not even the syrup which Pope Clement VI had sent King Philip VI and his relatives had helped here. Fate did not wish Bonne to become queen and so she became almost forgotten in French history – unjustly, as has been shown more and more. Her French upraising made her perceptive even to the higher religious spheres, as is proved to this day by her beautifully illuminated Latin psalter with its Old-French calendar, in which illuminators from the famous workshop of Jean Le Noir participated.[70] After the death of her father John of Luxembourg, she took his court poet Guillaume de Machaut into her service, according to whom Bonne was 'the most perfect lady to be found in this world'. As can be assumed, the poet would tell the young Charles and his numerous siblings the heroic legends of their grandfather. In the manor (*manoir*) in Vincennes, not only Charles' brothers and sisters but also several related boys of his age were being raised with him under the loving supervision of his mother. They all shared royal blood; therefore, they all ate at one table, wore the same clothes and also had the cloth decoration of their rooms changed twice a year. At Easter, the wall coverings were green and the canopy over the beds azure; on All Saints' Day, the silk and velvet cloths were dominated by the colour red. Like it had been years before in the case of his uncle Charles of Luxembourg, even now the whole group paraded in new costumes on major feast days.[71]

Education in this royal 'preschool' had not changed much either. They all learnt to read and the basics of Latin together first through listening and repeating the psalms or prayers. Vellum for writing, writing utensils as well as books were purchased en masse. The bills that have been preserved also contain

70/ For more details on this rare monument, see M. Krieger, 'Der Psalter der Bonne de Luxembourg', pp. 69–81 and Pics 12–21; on the painting studio of Jean Le Noir, see Carqué, *Stil und Erinnerung*, pp. 263–281.

71/ On Bonne and the raising of her children, see Lehoux, *Jean de France*, pp. 6–9; Autrand, *Charles V. Le Sage*, pp. 14–17 and 26–29.

items for the rebinding of books, which proves that the children often read them or at least looked through them. Their spiritual equipment was entrusted to a so-called almoner, reading the so-called Books of Hours with them. In the case of Dauphin Charles, we know that his tutor was Silvester of Servelle, who over time was promoted to an almoner.[72] As soon as the boys were able to ride horses, training in riding and later also in weapons awaited them. However, what was no less important for the future of Dauphin Charles were his good relations with his three brothers and his cousin Louis, the duke of Bourbon. According to a contemporary chronicler, these five offspring of the royal family in their childhood and youth formed a unified group as if as one.

As the betrothed were related, it was necessary to wait for a so-called papal dispensation. The wedding of the two children took place in Tain-en-Viennois on 8 April 1350 according to the contemporary perspective almost 'in privacy' since only the bride's father represented her family. In the months to come, Charles, accompanied by his Jeanne, travelled around the Dauphiné, where his counsellors had been calming the disputes of the previous years. He returned to Paris in August for the funeral of his grandfather Philip and on 26 September he participated in the coronation of his father John the Good in Rheims, with whom he set out immediately for the Dauphiné again in November. On this journey, which lasted until February 1351, he visited Avignon and the port of Aigues-Mortes, from which St Louis had set off on his famous crusade campaign. It was the first and last time that Charles saw the Mediterranean Sea. Neither did he see his Dauphiné again; not until the visit of his uncle Emperor Charles IV in France in January 1378 was he to be reminded of this land with all the memories of his youth.

After his return to Paris and its surroundings, Dauphin Charles disappears from the public scene until the end of 1355. Whereas his spouse Jeanne of Bourbon was a companion of Queen Joan of Auvergne and Boulogne (1326–1360), whom the widowed John II married in February 1350, Charles and the other princes alternately stayed in Vincennes, in the Palace de la Cité in Paris and at the castle Vivier-en-Brie, which his father had left him as his own residence. According to the accounting documents preserved, Charles' entourage had twenty-five persons in 1353, not including squires for his protection, a jester and a gifted orphan whose study he paid. The major-domo (*maître d'hôtel*) hence had under himself four secretaries, four valets, and a 'physik', whom we could call a personal physician today, a cashier, three chaplains, two stewards, a dresser and eight servants for the table. At this time, Charles was already buying jewellery, gold products and rebuilding his residence himself

72/ The earlier theories on the educators of Charles V, published by Delachenal, *Histoire de Charles V*, I, pp. 16–18, were elaborated by La Selle, *Le service des âmes à la cour*, pp. 154 and 291.

according to his own ideas. Although the Dauphin, who had already been knighted in 1350, also acted independently in other ways, his father did not rush to recognise his adulthood.

It is befitting to mention here that the portrait of the Dauphin's father, John II the Good (1350–1364), can be encountered practically in every illustrated publication on the High and Late Middle Ages. In spite of this small tempera being among the gems of the painting collection of the Louvre, it is still tangled in mystery. It is not even certain whether it is the depiction of this king, who had to face another wave of doubts of the legitimacy of the right of succession of the Valois Family to the French throne from the beginning of his rule.[73] Here and there, the English propaganda found a positive response among local aristocrats, who did not lack self-confidence and had become used to playing an independent political role. Despite his later epithet 'the Good', King John II preferred a radical approach and did not hesitate to use even brutal force against his opponents. This is how he acted towards one of the most influential men in the kingdom only shortly after his coronation, namely the Constable Raoul de Brienne, Count of Eu and Guînes, whom he had beheaded right after he his release from English captivity. The reasons for this step have never been appropriately explained.

Even the accusation of the constable for having a love affair with Queen Bonne is considered as without credibility. Either way, King John II did not improve his position much when he appointed Charles de la Cerda, called the Spaniard (Charles D'Espagne) according to his family origin, to the vacated post of the highest official of the kingdom and its supreme military commander. The new constable quickly came into conflict with another of the king's favourites, which was King of Navarre and at the same time Count of Évreux Charles II (1331–1387). Since too many Charleses appear in this story, we will somewhat unfairly add his usual appellation 'the Bad'.[74] The nineteen-year-old king of Navarre seemed to be such a good match to John II that he married him to his nine year old daughter Jeanne in February 1352. The son-in-law learnt from his father-in-law and when his dispute with Constable Charles de la Cerda grew beyond a bearable level, he had him murdered in January 1354. Considering the latent English threat, John II had to dampen his rage

73/ The basic biographic data were compiled by Thomas, 'Johann II.', pp. 267–283. The biography by Deviosse, *Jean le Bon*, conceived for the wider public, is also useful. New questions were asked by Cazelles, 'Jean II le Bon: Quel homme? Quel roi?'. The last historian mentioned also expressed the quite substantial hypothesis that the portrait in the Louvre does not depict King Jean II but his son Charles – 'Peinture et actualité politique', pp. 53–65. For the latest source on this panel painting, cf. Frinta, 'Le portrait du Louvre de Jean le Bon', pp. 402–413, who however left the disputed identification of the man from the profile aside.

74/ The basic data are listed in *Lexikon des Mittelalters*, V, col. 981. From the literature, cf. also Plaisse, *Charles dit le Mauvais*, and Leroy, 'Autour de Charles «le Mauvais»', pp. 3–17.

17. King of Navarre Charles "the Bad" at the head of his army (BL, Ms. royal 20 C VII, fol. 140v)

and reconcile with his son-in-law. From then on, however, he was always on his guard against him.

The protracted cease-fire with England was only a preparation for war, which was hanging in the air already in 1354. After the rift with Charles of Navarre, John II realised later that he could find support in Dauphin Charles. First, he entrusted him with the administration of the county of Poitiers, and when he acquitted himself well, he appointed him as governor of the Duchy of Normandy, which John still held himself, at the end of 1354. Before the Dauphin set out for Normandy in March 1355, unsuccessful peace negotiations between delegations of both warring countries took place in Avignon on the initiative of Pope Innocent VI (1352–1362). A certain role in them was played also by King of Navarre Charles the Bad, who did not hesitate to go all the way to the very edge of the betrayal of his father-in-law. If he did not join Edward, it was only because he could not accept Edward's conditions.

Dauphin Charles arrived in Rouen at the time his father's side was losing its footing in Normandy. Preparation for war costs money, which the local aristocracy was reluctant to provide, although the brunt of the tax on every hearth lay on their serfs. Nevertheless, the young and inexperienced governor acquitted himself surprisingly well and accumulated with the help of his future chancellor and historiographer Pierre d'Orgemont, whom he then chose as his counsellor, money from the tax collectors not only for the bribes for the Norman grandees but also for covering his quite numerous retinue, which included over twenty knights with three princes from the Dauphin's family clan. The Dauphin's counsellors and officials did not waste their time and on journeys around the duchy checked the readiness for defence against an English invasion as well as the efficiency of the signal fire system. The Dauphin can be credited with yet another political success. Under not entirely clear circumstances, he partook in the settlement of a conflict between his father and Charles, the king of Navarre, in August. The threat of an English invasion after the declaration of war with France by Edward III on 1 June 1355 relegated old grievances to the background and made it possible to forget fresh disputes. An amicable agreement was concluded in Valognes on 10 September and took effect fourteen days later with its ratification by King John II before his Grand Council (*Grand Conseil*). Both Charleses, the king of Navarre and the Dauphin, became closer in these months. The difficulties of the agreement and friendly relations were, however, soon to surface.

No sooner had the Dauphin returned to Paris that autumn than the English offensive began in the south and with a slight delay also in the north. The eldest son of the king of England, also Edward, aka the Black Prince of Wales († 1376), landed in Bordeaux on 20 September 1355. In black armour as was his custom, he set forth on quick marches to Guyenne and from there to Languedoc.[75] His brigades numbering seven to eight thousand men left burning villages and sacked townships behind. Despite pleas and threats of an imminent Papal Curia, not even bishops' estates and palatial monasteries were spared. After the capture of Narbonne, the English turned around with the rich booty and appeared again in Bordeaux on 9 December. They did not encounter an effective resistance during the entire campaign, because for mutual disputes and a lack of ability or competence the leaders and allies of the king of France left the land at the mercy of the brigades of the Black Prince.[76]

75/ Cf. Barber, *Edward, Prince of Wales and Aquitaine*; further also the valuable portrait by Courtenay, 'Der Black Prince', pp. 245–264. The basic data and literature are provided in *Lexikon des Mittelalters*, III, cols 1592–1593.

76/ The literature on the entire military campaign concluded by the Battle of Poitiers is abundant. From the most recent sources, I refer to the concise synopsis in the monograph by Bériac-Lainé and Given-Wilson, *Les prisonniers de la bataille de Poitiers*, pp. 25–30.

King John II was informed of the disaster in the south in Amiens, in whose environs he was assembling an army against Edward III, who landed with his military expedition in Calais in October. The county Artois found itself in direct danger, even becoming the site of several demonstrative acts by the French units. The two kings kept calling the other to a decisive battle but always backed out of it when they received a specific offer from the enemy. Although they did not fight, even this procrastination cost enormous means, which especially John II was lacking, thus leaving him no other choice but to convene the Norman estates. In Amiens, Dauphin Charles also resided with King John. The Dauphin began to realise here the inadequacy of his powers and the inferiority of his position, because upon his return from Normandy his counsellors and officials again fell under the direct authority of the king, with him not having access even to the Grand Council. At his age, he was already becoming a man, but it was as if his father had not taken it into consideration. The Dauphin's ambitious desires were also fed by people around the king of Navarre, especially the master of intrigue and leader of the entire faction Bishop of Laon Robert Le Coq.[77]

Sometime on 22 or 23 November, the Dauphin summoned Friquet de Fricamps and Gauthier de Lor, two knights from the retinue of the king of Navarre, to himself in Amiens and asked them to accompany him to the Holy Roman Emperor, who he intended to seek out. What inspired him to that remains a mystery. Perhaps he thought that his successful uncle would advise him on how to win his father over? Hardly, since Charles IV did not like his brother-in-law John II the Good.[78] It was rather an ill-advised step, which was grist for the mill of the Navarre side, especially when the Dauphin after his return to Paris asked Charles the Bad himself for help. From Pacy-sur-Eure, where he was staying, the king of Navarre suggested to the Dauphin beginning the journey to the emperor from Mantes. As soon as the Dauphin accepted the offer, Charles the Bad set out for Mantes, from which he sent the Dauphin an entourage numbering twenty to thirty men on the morning of 7 December. It had hardly happened when a letter arrived from the Dauphin countermanding the previous agreement. The conspiracy is betrayed, Friquet with his retinue fly to Saint-Cloud, where they are awaited by men-at-arms of the king of Navarre, whereas the Dauphin on the same Monday 7 December 1355 unexpectedly receives the Norman duchy from the king. Did the Dauphin baulk at the last moment and confess to his father? It is quite likely although King John II did not pardon the conspirators including Charles of Navarre until January

77/ According to Favier, *La Guerre de Cent Ans*, p. 196, Le Coq was the actual initiator of the conspiracy.

78/ Personal motives in the Dauphin's actions were sought by Deviosse, *Jean le Bon*, p. 280.

of the next year. He undoubtedly considered his son-in-law as the architect of the affair, especially when it reached his ears that he was meeting with the Dauphin again.

An opportunity to pay him back arose at the beginning of April when the Dauphin called the leaders of the Norman aristocracy to Rouen to discuss taxes. At the ceremonial feast which the Dauphin arranged for his guests, the king burst into the banqueting hall with his commando and despite the pleas of his son arrested both Charles of Navarre and the influential John of Harcourt as well as three other noblemen. Insanely angry, he had four of them executed that same day; he spared only Charles of Navarre, but he jailed him in distant Picardy and announced a search for his followers.[79] Dauphin Charles was disconsolate. As the duke of Normandy, he had lost credit in his land and learnt again that his father wanted to make decisions without him. Before we present the further course of events, we have to recall briefly the fascinating journey of the Dauphin's uncle Charles IV to the imperial crown.

79/ For the latest source on that, see Bériac-Lainé and Given-Wilson, *Les prisonniers de la bataille de Poitiers*, pp. 30–39.

Metz 1356: The First Meeting of the Two Charleses

With the election of Charles IV on 11 July 1346, the Holy Roman Empire had two heads: the emperor until then Louis the Bavarian and the thirty-year-old king from the Luxemburg dynasty. Although Charles had gained the votes of five of the seven imperial electors, who had the right to vote according to the at-that-time unwritten imperial constitution, he had to struggle for real power. Unlike France, England and other kingdoms which already in the fourteenth century had quite strong outlines of a state in our conception, the Holy Roman Empire was a state formation of a special type.[80] In the periods ideas, which Charles IV also undoubtedly shared, the Empire was a body whose head was the king and the limbs or pillars were the princes, to whose sum the truly existing whole of the objects subordinate to their authority was both substantially and legally tied. A state formation so delimited had its territorial boundaries, the form of which varied here and there in the Late Middle Ages.

THE HOLY ROMAN EMPIRE AT THE BEGINNING OF CHARLES IV'S REIGN

The largest contiguous territory of the Empire was formed by the lands of the Bohemian Crown, which included besides the Kingdom of Bohemia and the Margraviate of Moravia also Upper and Lower Lusatia and thirteen Silesian principalities. The Duchies of Luxembourg and Brabant (see Pic. 18) were also in the realm of the Luxembourg rulers on the Bohemian throne. The rise in the power of this state formation is apparent from the fact that with the exception of the rule of Rupert (III) of Germany (1400–1410) only Kings of Bohemia held the imperial throne between 1346 and 1439. A second powerful block comprised the alliance of lands controlled by the Habsburgs, i.e. the Duchies of Austria, Styria and Carinthia, and further the County of Tyrol and Duchy of Carniola. A third large piece consisted of the lands belonging to the House of Wittelsbach, namely the duchies of Bavaria on the one hand and the Electoral

80/ For the basic information, see the entry 'Regnum' and the entries beginning with the genitive 'Reichs-' in *Lexikon des Mittelalters*, VII. A pivotal work has been written by Moraw, *Von offener Verfassung zu gestalteter Verdichtung*; further cf. K.-F. Krieger, *König, Reich und Reichsreform im Spätmittelalter* and the studies in the anthology *Regnum et Imperium*.

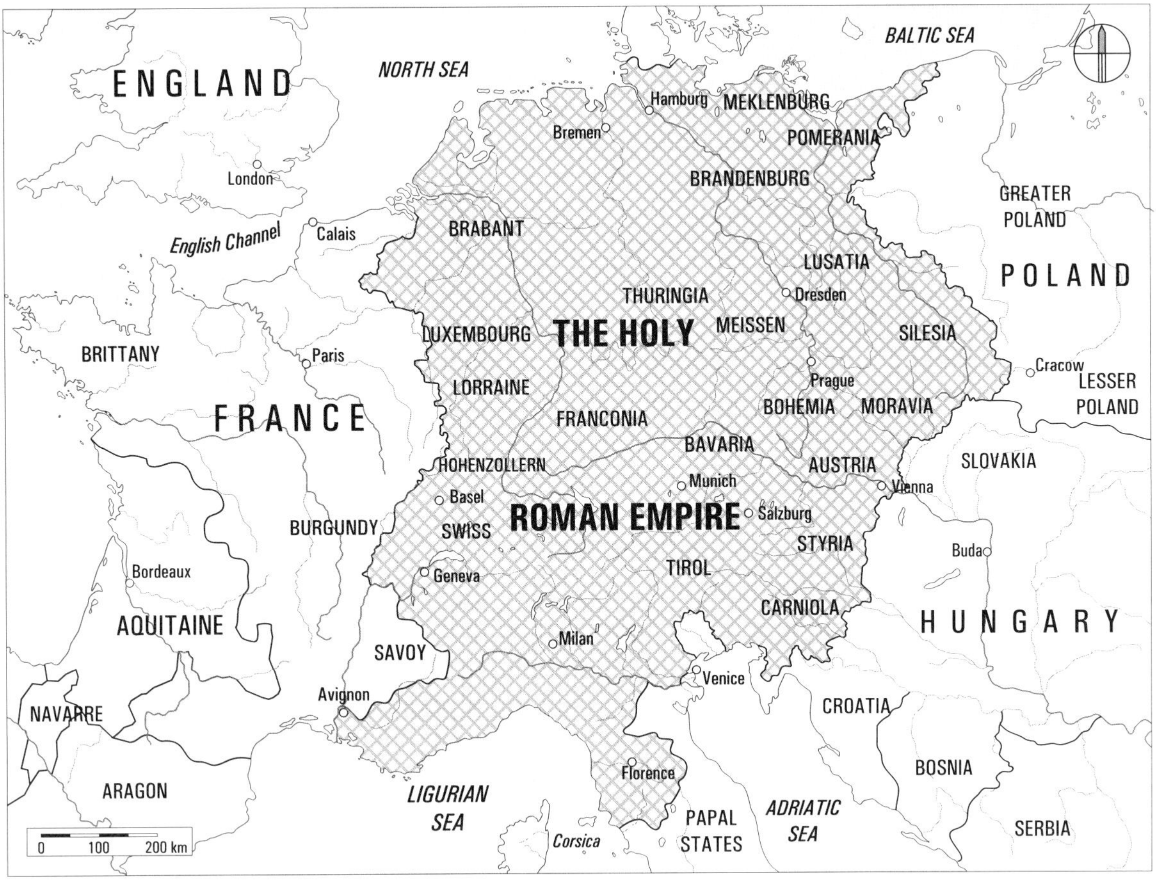

18. The Holy Roman Empire during the reign of Charles IV.

Palatine (*Kurpfalz*) on the other. The Margraviate of Meissen and Landgraviate of Thuringia were ruled by the House of Wettin; the Electorate of Saxony and the Landgraviate of Württemberg were held by dukes from the House of Ascania in the fourteenth century. When looking at the map of Central Europe during the reign of Charles IV, the overall enormous but territorially incoherent, land of the ecclesiastical electors and in the Baltic also of the Order of the Teutonic Knights strike the eye.[81]

We already know how large a land fell under the authority of the King of the Romans, but we must add that through the election and coronation he was given sovereignty only over the so-called Roman goods, which was subdivided into Roman goods in the strictest sense of the word, into imperial feudal estates and imperial ecclesiastical estates. Nevertheless, the king did not own the imperial estates, because he was merely their administrator and if possible also their augmenter, which was verbally reflected also in his title 'Augmenter of the Empire' (*zu allen Zeiten Mehrer des Reiches*). The king performed supreme power through a feudal union with the imperial princes as well as with other

81/ A general map was printed by Moraw, *Von offener Verfassung*, pp. 254–255; cf. also the map attached to the book by Spěváček, *Karel IV*.

free persons. The number of imperial princes varied; in the middle of the thirteenth century, there were around ninety of the ecclesiastical estate and only twelve secular, out of whom seven powerful so-called electors were separated out, who laid claim to the right to elect as well as depose of the Kings of the Romans from the end of the twelfth century. The first vote in this body *via facti* and later also by the constitutional law of Charles IV's decree the Golden Bull of 1356 (*aurea bulla*) fell to the king of Bohemia, with the three further secular electors being Count Palatine of the Rhine, the Duke of Saxony, and Margrave of Brandenburg. A prominent position among the three ecclesiastical electors was held by the archbishop of Trier, with the archbishops of Cologne and Mainz standing at his side.

The title of King of the Romans did not involve permanent incomes. Although he was the ruler of the largest contemporary empire, his financial chamber gained means primarily only through octroi and fees for privileges, from minting coins, from the Jewish communities, tolls and other revenues from so-called regalian rights,[82] predominantly from the imperial towns, namely Augsburg, Frankfurt, Nuremberg, Strasbourg, and Ulm. We will not attempt to define their positions precisely as no one has been able to so far. It suffices to say that imperial towns were former royal towns which had been partially exempted and continued to extricate themselves further from directly belonging in the royal goods. Hence, they had a semi-autonomous position in the process of emancipation, which never ended in complete autonomy within the territorial and temporal frame of the Holy Roman Empire. The closest to the imperial towns in terms of their size as well as their economic significance were the so-called free towns (Cologne, Speyer, Regensburg), which had shed the authority of the bishops and which were willing to recognise only the king as suzerain. Of the total number of approximately 3,000 towns on the territory of the Empire, roughly only one hundred were of one of the two types of towns with extensive internal autonomy. Only twelve to fifteen of them had more than 10,000 denizens; another twenty larger towns counted between 2,000 and 10,000 persons. Inasmuch as according to a rough estimate only ten to fifteen percent of the total population lived in towns, the incomes from them were much lower than from free land in the ownership of the princes, clergy and aristocrats. Just for a better idea, it suffices to say that the entire annual income from the imperial towns at the beginning of the fifteenth century was less than 12,000 florins, which really was not much.[83] We will not be far off the mark if we suppose that Charles IV acquired a significant part of his

82/ See the entry 'Regalien, -politik, -recht' in *Lexikon des Mittelalters*, VII, cols 556–558.
83/ For the distinction between both types of town, see Heinig, *Reichstädte, Freie Städte und Königtum*, pp. 48–54, which also contains numerical data on pp. 55 and 64.

income from his direct sovereignty in Bohemia, including the profit from the Kutná Hora (Kuttenberg) silver mines.

19. The Golden Bull of Charles IV as Holy Roman Emperor and King of Bohemia

CHARLES' COURT AND OFFICES

The decisive medium as well as instrument of the Late Mediaeval Kings of the Romans and Holy Roman Emperors was the court. As one expert says, without the court, there would not be any ruler.[84] It is not by accident that the death of the King of the Romans or Emperor also terminated all of his 'state' offices; the activity of his chancellery ended with the breaking of its seal. Charles IV, as we already know, acceded to the Roman throne as the Anti-King, so he had to build his administrative system from scratch one way or the other. Sometimes it boggles the mind how gigantic the ruler's tasks that Charles had to manage when he was thirty years old were. At the same time, we have to be aware that he – metaphorically speaking – only ruled where he dwelt. A King of the Romans who would not have been constantly on journeys would have lost his footing. There was no imperial metropolis in our sense of the word; even Prague was merely one of the residences of the Luxemburg dynasty. The court with all of its offices and especially the chancellery travelled with the king or emperor.

The inner circle of the court service included 'officials' whose task it was to care for the person of the ruler. These also to a greater or lesser extent assumed tasks of a genuinely statesmanlike, political or diplomatic nature. Having taken an oath, a courtier could be given a paid office. This needs to be understood in the sense that Charles IV did not rule through bureaucratic institutions but through his trustees. At first sight, it might seem that the most important man at the court was the Master of the Royal Household. Sometimes that was true, other times there were two, and occasionally the king did without that dignitary. In terms of influence, the Master of the Royal Household had a competition in the Chancellor, the representative of the chancellery, who was always a man with a higher religious post. On journeys, the chancellery counted twelve to fifteen scribes, clerks and other servants. The ruler would be accompanied on his journeys by the imperial court of justice led by the court justice, who also had a smaller chancellery available to him.

Along with the Arch-Chamberlain and the Marshal of the Court, the mentioned dignitaries were the leading persons in the council, which was the most important institution of the ruler's court. Whereas the role of the Lord Chamberlain is obvious, it is necessary to add the role of the Marshal of the Court that he was *inter alia* responsible for leading wars, for the guards as well

84/ See Moraw, *Von offener Verfassung*, and there his statement on p. 169, where the description of the administration of the Kings of the Romans in the Late Middle Ages begins also.

20. Charles IV, King of the Romans and Bohemian in the Codex Gelnhausen

as for ceremonial orders of the court. From the thirteenth century, the four highest court offices were traditionally given to the four lands whose rulers as electors directly participated in the election of the King of the Romans. The Office of the Arch-Steward was connected with the Rhineland-Palatinate, the Arch-Marshal's with Saxony, the Arch-Chamberlain's with Brandenburg, and finally the Arch-Cupbearer was the holder of the title of King of Bohemia. The majority of the total sum of 182 counsellors and secretaries of Emperor Charles IV known by name were from the ecclesiastical estate. Roughly three-quarters of the eighty-eight counsellors from the secular estate came from places in the domain of the Luxemburgs but not directly from Bohemia. Greater trust from Charles was enjoyed by the Přemyslids of Opava and members of the Silesian princely families. It was partially given by the developed court and land administration of the Kingdom of Bohemia and partially also by the opposition tendencies within the Bohemian aristocracy to the centralising endeavours of Charles IV.[85]

Not only did the King of the Romans have supreme court powers, but he was also responsible for their performance at the sessions of the so-called royal court, where only serious cases connected with the harshest penalties were deliberated. Although the royal court had its own smaller chancellery, the chancellery had not yet formed a permanent office in the fourteenth century, because it moved with the ruler and his court from place to place. At that time, the jurisdiction and internal rules were unsettled also in the case of the diets, which were only gradually developing from court institution into an imperial one. Only in the times when there was no ruler did the diets convene without the king; otherwise, it was essentially the King of the Romans' or Holy Roman Emperor's decision whether, when and in what composition to convoke the diet. Their resolutions however depended on the imperial princes and towns, because it was at their will in what and to what extent they would accommodate the king's demands.[86]

THE FIRST YEARS OF THE REIGN OF KING OF THE ROMANS CHARLES IV

After a look into the state mechanism of the Empire, it is possible to follow with better comprehension how Charles IV acquitted himself after his election as the King of the Romans at the ancient royal throne (*Königstuhl*) on the left bank of the Rhine on 11 July 1346. The current Holy Roman Emperor, Louis the Bavarian, secured the fidelity of the wealthy imperial towns in September

85/ For more on that, see Moraw, 'Räte und Kanzlei', pp. 285–292.
86/ In addition to the already listed literature, also cf. the synoptic entry for 'Reichstag' in *Lexikon des Mittelalters*, VII, cols 640–645.

of the same year but otherwise took no measures against Charles and did not allow himself to be upset even by Charles' coronation, which took place on 26th November in Bonn, the residential town of the Archbishop of Cologne, because the traditional coronation towns of Aix-la-Chapelle (Aachen) and Cologne had refused to open their gates to Charles. The position of the new King of the Romans was highly shaky, as is clear from the fact that he had to travel through Louis' lands to Bohemia in disguise. On the west of the Empire, Charles had steady support in his uncle Baldwin, he could even count on the Pope in Avignon Clement VI, but only at the price of hardly acceptable concessions. The new king proved his diplomatic art here, when by using postponements and excuses he avoided fulfilling his electoral promises and obligations. Charles also had to proceed with the same dexterity with respect to the rulers of the two quarrelling western powers, England and France.

War was imminent even in Central Europe, when Louis the Bavarian in an attempt to face Charles' rising influence attacked Charles' allies in Swabia and Tyrol. At the beginning of October 1347, Charles marched with a relatively strong army towards the Czech borders, where he discovered that on the tenth day of that month Louis had been felled by a stroke during a bear hunt. Charles took advantage of the situation and through a fast campaign forced the imperial and other towns not only in Franconia and Swabia but also in the Rhineland to capitulate. From that time, the powerful and wealthy Nuremberg became his important base. Charles' problems, however, did not end yet with the death of his adversary. Although the eldest son of the emperor, Louis V the Brandenburger, was under an interdict, it did not stop him from seeking a competitor to Charles IV, namely in King of England Edward III. His election on 10 January 1348 took place only through representatives, which allowed Charles to seek a path to an agreement with the assistance of his uncle Baldwin. Edward did not desire a conflict either and already abandoned his aspirations in April in return for Charles' contractual promise not to ally with Edward's enemies. Not only in this treaty but also in the final document on the mutual alliance of 24 June 1348, Charles left the back door open in the form of a clause on the defence of his own as well as imperial rights both in England and in France.[87] The treaty was concluded in Prague, which in the spring months of 1348 became the stage for Charles' history-making founding activities to the benefit of the metropolis, Kingdom of Bohemia as well as the entire commonwealth of the lands of the Bohemian Crown. By the privilege of 8 March, Charles founded the New Town of Prague, which was followed on 7 April by the founding of a university, the first east of Paris and north of the

87/ See Trautz, *Die Könige von England und das Reich 1272–1377*, pp. 344–352.

21. Seal of the university

Alps. The same date of 7 April is inscribed on another thirteen charters and bulls, in which Charles on the one hand confirmed the privileges of the Kings of Bohemia and on the other regulated the relations between the individual parts of the lands of the Bohemian Crown for several centuries.[88]

Charles' political successes were dimmed on 1 August 1348 by the death of his thirty-two-year-old wife Blanche, who left two daughters, Margaret and Catherine. Since Charles did not have an heir to the throne, it was obvious that sooner or later he would remarry. In his condolences, Pope Clement VI asked him to choose a bride again in France. However, that was out of the question not only because of the treaty with England but also because of the policy of the French court in the Dauphiné and the Free County of Burgundy Charles had not failed to notice the consolidation of the French positions as well as the demands on these imperial territories, and, although his hands were tied for the moment, he did not lose sight of the power situation there.[89] Also the courtship of the sixteen-year-old Isabella, the daughter of King of England Edward, tapered off.

Charles took them all by surprise again when in one masterful stroke he acquired a comely bride and an influential ally against the new Anti-King, who appeared on the horizon at the beginning of 1349. The opposition led by Louis V the Brandenburger did not allow itself to be deterred by the collapse of the English candidature and in the election on 30 January 1349 attempted to seat 'small' Count Günther of Schwarzburg on the imperial throne. On 7 February, homage was still being rendered to the new king by his sole valid elector, Count Palatine of the Rhine Rudolph II (1306–1353). However, in a few short days it was all to be different. On the basis of a secret agreement, Charles' marriage to the twenty-year-old daughter of Rudolph II, Anne of Bavaria, was arranged. The bilaterally advantageous wedding took place in Bacharach on the bank of the Rhine already at the beginning of March. Anti-King Günther lacked the forces to face Charles on the field of battle. At the end of May 1349, he renounced his claim to the imperial throne in return for a guarantee of the incomes from several towns of 20,000 silver marks. When the ill Günther of Schwarzburg died on 14 June of that year, the chronicler Beneš Krabice of Weitmile considered it to be a special grace of God that all of Charles archenemies had died without bloodshed before the king attacked them.[90] Charles honoured his rival by attending the funeral and in Frankfurt, formerly hostile to him, he ceremonially accepted the homage of the gathered

22. Anne of Bavaria (1329–1353), Queen of Bohemia, second wife of Charles IV. A bust in the inner triforium of the Cathedral of St Vitus at Prague Castle

88/ Further details can be found in Spěváček, *Karel IV.*, pp. 265–279.

89/ Cf. Thomas, 'Die Beziehungen Karls IV. zu Frankreich', pp. 170–172, and Weiss, 'Onkel und Neffe', pp. 116–118.

90/ *Chronicon Benessii de Weitmil*, p. 517.

23. The crown on the bust of Charlemagne, made in Prague before 1349

electors and imperial princes. The fierce three-year fight for the rule of the Empire culminated by Charles' second coronation on 25 July 1349, which already took place in the 'right place', i.e. in the cathedral of Aachen.

Before the gates of Aachen, Charles had to wait a few days until the flagellants had left the city. In Germany as well as other lands, they would interrupt everyday life and leave a mess behind themselves in their streets and minds. With their ecstatic expressions of religious rapture, the processions of the flagellants were an accompanying phenomenon of the plague pandemic, against which there was no effective defence. Death reaped both poor and rich in towns as well as countryside, and there was not anyone who could be certain before it. The epidemic missed Charles, but another calamity befell him, which tarnished his up until then good reputation. The day before his second coronation, an appalling extermination of the local Jews took place after a procession of flagellants arrived in Frankfurt. Although Charles IV made sure that the wave of pogroms was obstructed in the lands of the Bohemian Crown, the situation in Nuremberg and other imperial towns got out of hand. It seems not to have been in his power to avert the killing of the Jews. However, this notional exculpation ends where the body of his writs begins in which he gave out the property of the victims of the future pogroms to the bishops and lords whose favour he was seeking.[91] And since not even some of his steps on the political

91/ On Charles' policy concerning the Jews in a critical light, see Seibt, *Karl IV.*, pp. 196–200; otherwise, cf. especially Graus, *Pest – Geissler – Judenmorde*, pp. 227–240.

scene had anything to do with Christian morality, he at least was an example to others with his private penitence and publically expressed piety. There is no need to doubt his faith, but it clearly included simple-minded calculations concerning the redemption of sins on earth as well.

FINALLY EMPEROR

The earlier German historiography predominantly took critical positions towards Charles IV; many a time did it consider him to be an instrument in the hands of the pope and reproached him also for his purposeful personal policy. In this respect, there has been a significant turnaround in the last thirty years, which especially on Czech soil has been passing to the positions of one-sided glorification. It was not easy to rule in the Empire, which makes it all the more problematic to judge real policy in terms of morality.

After this diversion into a little historical reflection, we shall return to the unsettled year 1349. The triumph in Aachen was followed by an autumn connected not only with pogroms but also with the death of Charles' sister Guta-Bonne and his first daughter Margaret, otherwise the wife of King of Hungary Louis I the Great. The two women seem to have fallen victim to the fading plague, after which the 'world began to live and be happy' again. The revolutionary fashion of fitted doublets and long leggings also arrived in Bohemia, which not even Charles intended to resist. It is even possible that Charles himself promoted it, because already in February 1348 Pope Clement VI in an open letter asked him in a moralising way to wear 'loose and long attire' corresponding to his position. Since we already know in how refined an atmosphere Charles grew up, his transient fashion excesses are not very surprising. It was not always that way. For example, he appeared in Pisa in January 1355 in plain brown attire without any gold ornamentation, and likewise Guillaume de Machaut writes about Charles that he pays no regard to splendour as long as the attire is good and warm.[92]

Neither did Charles remain shielded from personal tribulation in the next two years. In October 1350, he became seriously ill with a nerve atrophy of the limbs, which confined him to bed for many months. He had barely recuperated when at the end of December 1351 he was deeply affected by the death of his two-year-old son Wenceslas, for whom he had already selected a bride – the twelve-year-old Anna who was the heiress of the important Świdnica (German: Schweidnitz) principality. Instead of his son, Charles IV became the next groom in line himself when he was widowed a second time on 2 February

92/ The document containing the pope's reprimand is cited by Spěváček, *Karel IV.*, p. 207; contemporary mentions of Charles' sober attire are recorded in Kybalová, *Dějiny odívání. Středověk*, pp. 166–167, which also contains more on contemporary fashion.

1353. Without an heir to the throne, a king's life makes no sense, and so the wedding took place already at the end of May of that year. Considering the age of the bride, Charles had to wait a few years for an heir to the throne. His prayers were answered in 1361, when, three years after their daughter Elizabeth, Anna bore a son Wenceslas, the next King of the Romans and Bohemia. Meanwhile, Charles had so strengthened his position in the Empire that he could consider an expensive journey for the imperial crown. In Italy, he had already for a longer period been awaited with hopes by Italian patriots who saw in him a restorer of Ancient Rome. Alongside Tribune of the Roman People Cola di Rienzo, the already famous Humanist and poet Francesco Petrarch then addressed Charles IV in the same spirit. Neither eloquent letters nor a meeting in Mantua with Petrarch in December 1354 could beguile Charles into a new Italian adventure. Charles set out for Rome in the autumn of the same year for his goal, which he reached on 5 April 1355, when he accepted the imperial crown from the hand of the legate of Pope Innocent VI. The coronation of the juvenile Anna was followed by a quick march back, which to some observers seemed more like a getaway than a triumphal passage by the ruler of the Empire already recognised by all.

Either way, Charles IV through the imperial crown raised himself as well as his dynasty and now could devote himself more to the legislative reinforcement of the positions that he had acquired. He was unsuccessful in this regard in Bohemia, because in October 1355 he was forced by the strong opposition of the aristocracy to withdraw his land legal code (the so-called *Maiestas Carolina*) before it ever took effect. The Bohemian lords did not want even Charles IV to have too much power over them, namely according to the old maxim that the king was only the first among them. What he was unable to do in Bohemia proved to be more passable in the Empire. Still before the opening of the Imperial Diet, which was convened in Nuremberg, the emperor concluded a number of component treaties which sealed his final reconciliation with Louis V the Brandenburger as well as other princes on the one hand and eased the actual discussion on the proposed imperial legal code on the other. Individual chapters were debated gradually over the Christmas holidays and, since the emperor was prepared for compromises during the discussions with the participants of the diet, the legal code, which was given the title of the *Golden Bull*, could be ceremonially declared already on 10 January 1356.

It was of great consequence to the emperor that he more precisely delimit the position of the secular electors, and consequently regulate all of the modalities of the election of the King of the Romans as precisely as possible. He managed to do both, and because the Golden Bull did not mention the papal right to approve the election, it was indisputably one of the greatest victories

24. The procession of the imperial couple accompanied by the electors. At the head, the archbishop of Trier. The Golden Bull for the Empire of Wenceslas IV, 1400 (ÖNB, cod. 338, fol. 39r)

of his foreign policy. Already the introduction of the code emphasised the exceptional position of the King of Bohemia, which was the first among the secular electors as well as the foremost before the other rulers at the imperial diets. Further privileges, including the free election of the ruler should the family die out, were received by the Kingdom of Bohemia. The Golden Bull also significantly strengthened the position of the other secular electors, who in fact obtained royal rights. Henceforth, electors could vote for themselves in royal elections and base their own succession on the right of the first-born son. At that time, this principle applied only in Bohemia, but soon, as we will hear later, it was to be applied also in France. On the other hand, the representatives of the imperial and other large towns, who had expected increased support for safe travel and trade, left Nuremberg disappointed. The Golden Bull expressly forbade town associations and also, because of the resistance of the Rhine ecclesiastical electors, left exorbitantly high customs and other fees unaltered. As was Charles' custom, he did not turn his back on the powerful. The three most important imperial towns were given special status in one of the supplemental chapters of the Golden Bull. The king was to continue to be elected in Frankfurt, crowned in Aachen and summon his first court diet in Nuremberg.[93] These modifications were to come into effect at the next imperial diet, which the emperor convoked in Metz for the Christmas holidays.

93/ On the Nuremberg phase of the Golden Bull, see Hergemöller, *Fürsten, Herren und Städte zu Nürnberg 1355/56*; further Kavka, *Vláda Karla IV.*, I, Chapter II; and Annas, *Hoftag – Gemeiner Tag – Reichstag*, II, pp. 43–55.

CHARLES' POLICY CONCERNING FRANCE

The selection of a town on the western border of the Empire was an expression of the emperor's interest in the adjacent areas and simultaneously was another measure against the territorial expansionism of the French Crown. Although his upbringing in France left permanent marks on Charles, it was eclipsed in his political aims like his filiation with the Valois dynasty. Already on his Italian journey, Charles accepted the tributes of several vassals from the Kingdom of Arles (Arelat) and confronted French usurpations not only here but also in neighbouring Provence with the renewal of feudal obligations and alliance acts. The influence of France was also quickly on the increase in the Free County of Burgundy, which was an imperial fief. We already know that the widowed John II the Good married Joan of Auvergne and Boulogne in 1350. It should be added here that she was the widow of Duke of Burgundy Philip I and mother of the minor heir of the Free County Philip II (1346–1361). In 1353, John II bound himself instead of his wife in the holding of the county as the guardian of his step-son Philip and began to seek a bride for him in Flanders. Part of the Burgundian aristocracy discountenanced the French interference, especially when John II in May 1355 began to recruit in Burgundy for an army against England. And since French influence had been spreading also into the Low Countries and Lorraine, namely in the bishoprics of Verdun and Cambrai, Emperor Charles IV decided to defend imperial interests much more emphatically than before.[94]

In this regard, Charles IV exhibited increased activity in August 1355, when he appointed Henry of Montbéliard as the imperial vicar for the Free County of Burgundy and simultaneously declared the ten-year-old Philips II of Burgundy to be of majority, which deprived the French king of his guardianship and hence his legal claim to govern the Free County of Burgundy. Both steps along with other acts of an administrative nature were components of a wider diplomatic activity which was to define for a longer period the emperor's positions towards both warring powers. To put it simply, Charles IV had neither the desire nor the means to participate militarily in a prolonged conflict. Forasmuch as he was however under pressure from the Avignon curia, which persistently incited him to renew the alliance with France, he decided to offer King John II a treaty on friendly relations with four conditions about which it could be supposed that he would not be able to accept them. Charles pre-eminently requested the return of the cities Verdun, Cambrai and Cateau-Cambrésis, although they had not yet been fully annexed to France.

94/ Charles IV's relations to France from his accession to the throne until 1356 were synoptically described by Mendl and Quicke, 'Les relations politiques', pp. 469–512; more recently cf. Thomas, 'Die Beziehungen Karls IV. zu Frankreich', pp. 165–201, and Weiss, 'Onkel und Neffe', pp. 101–110.

Secondly, the emperor insisted that the Dauphin accept the Dauphiné as an imperial fief and swear the relevant oath, in connection with which, thirdly, he requested the imperial town Vienne back. Finally, also the imperial fief in the Free County of Burgundy was to be recognised by a feudal oath. With demands that were hard to fulfil, Charles IV was leaving the door ajar to further negotiations with the English court, with whom he wanted to be on good terms. For that reason, the delegation he sent to Paris at the beginning of September 1355 also had in its baggage the proposal of a peace treaty between England and France.

To accelerate the discussions in Paris, the imperial chancellery prepared two parallel documents. Although the first, with the date of 26 August 1355, was furnished with the Golden Bull, it was to take effect only after the verification of the second document, which was to be done at the French court. King John II did not resolve to respond until the beginning of January 1356, when it was already apparent that the emperor's attempt at renewing the peace between England and France had foundered. In the letter, Charles' demands were politely declined, the reasons for which would be explained by the envoys who would soon resume deliberation. Several months passed, and not until May did the preparations begin to send a delegation. The sealed treaty which John offered the emperor was practically a verbatim renewal of the treaty on friendly relations of 1347.[95] In order to mitigate somewhat the impact of the indirectly refused demands, John II promised to present Charles IV through his first-born son with two thorns from the purported Crown of Thorns, which had been acquired by St Louis. And since in the eyes of the contemporary world it was a truly exceptional gift, John attested the authenticity of the relics with a special document.[96] Postponements of the convocation of the Imperial Diet in Metz could have been one of the reasons the French proposal became known in Prague only in the middle of July. In the meantime, sword had begun to flash yet again on the battlefields of the Hundred Years' War and so neither did the emperor rush to respond to the French offer.

Events snowballed rapidly at the end of August and beginning of September 1356, when John II marched with his army to the south to stem the incursion of the Black Prince, who with his numerous army was threatening Tours. Prince Edward turned again to Gascony but was caught close to Poitiers by the quickly approaching French army, which despite its advantage of being roughly twice as large suffered a crushing defeat near the village of

95/ A study with entirely essential importance for the correct interpretation of the individual documents has been written by Mendl, 'Vyjednání o česko-francouzský spolek 1355', pp. 111–123.
96/ The so-called certificate of authenticity with a preserved seal dated May 1364 was published by Podlaha and Šittler, *Chrámový poklad u sv. Víta v Praze*, p. 119, Note 3. Cf. on that Excursus – Book Gifts, Relics and the Small Mysteries around Them.

Maupertuis on 19 September. It was caused not only by the well-established sting of the English bowmen but also by the disorganised leadership of the battle on the part of the French leadership corps.[97] Unlike many feudal lords, King John did not flee the battlefield and along with his youngest son Philip fell into captivity. Dauphin Charles had been successfully escorted to safety by the knights. Little did it help the reputation of the successor to the throne; he was, however, too young for the ignominious defeat of the French colours to be blamed exclusively on him.

On the penultimate day of September 1356, Dauphin Charles marched into Paris as the self-proclaimed vice-regent to take up governance. His first test was the session of the estates-general, which was convened at the initiative of the Royal Council in the Great Hall of the Palace de la Cité on 17 October. Besides the clergy and the aristocracy, the diet was also attended by the representatives of the royal towns, which would be affected by the main burden of the new war taxes. At the diet, the towns gained the upper hand over the aristocracy, and the vice-regent had no choice but to accept the conditions that were presented by the leader of the Parisian merchants' guild, Étienne Marcel. A commission of eighty elected members of the assembly was established to control the finances and public affairs; the sessions of the diet were to be held twice a year. Other than this, the vice-regent was given the instruction to sack the royal officials, who were thorns in the sides of the representatives of the 'good' towns, but not only of them. It was such a serious limitation of royal powers that any help to the ruling family, no matter how little it may have been, was welcomed even if it was provided by the emperor, who had not displayed very amicable positions recently.[98] A welcome excuse for a meeting with Charles IV at the Imperial Diet convened at the borders in Metz were the so-far unfinished discussions on the mutual treaty, which was supposed to be facilitated by the handover of the treasured reliquary with two thorns from the Crown of Thorns and a precious sword worth an unbelievable 18,000 gold pieces.

THE EMPEROR'S CHRISTMAS READING IN METZ

The Dauphin set out on the journey to Metz on 5 December 1356. He took an indirect route, keeping as far south as possible to be in contact with the Papal Curia in Avignon, which on 12 December on behalf of Pope Innocent VI appealed to Charles with the request that he be of as much assistance to the

97/ On the Battle of Poitiers, see Tourneur-Aumont, *La bataille de Poitiers*; synoptically also Favier, *La Guerre de Cent Ans*, Chapter VII; and Bériac-Lainé and Given-Wilson, *Les prisonniers de la bataille de Poitiers*, p. 39ff.

98/ Reservations against Charles IV, whom France helped to the imperial crown while he in his cold calculations was never really interested in the needs of the Valois dynasty, were expressed by Delachenal, *Histoire de Charles V*, I, p. 269.

French successor as possible. This was to be supported also by the legation of Hélie de Talleyrand-Périgord, one of the most influential cardinals at the papal court. The arrival of both delegations caused an uproar in advent Metz. On 21 December, the cardinal arrived escorted by 400 cavalrymen; the very next day, Dauphin Charles came in with a numerous retinue along with his younger brother John, then Count of Poitiers, Duke of Brittany Charles de Blois, Count of Étampes Charles of Evreux, further with Guillaume de Melun, Archbishop of Sens, and last but not least with Chancellor and newly appointed Cardinal Pierre de la Forêt. Although contemporary sources mention by name also Marshal Jean Le Maingre, called Boucicaut, and the counts of Saarbrücken as well as Tancarville, the stated number of two thousand horsemen of the French delegation appears to be exaggerated, because it is difficult to imagine with the total number of participants of the Imperial Diet that the town would have had enough food and fodder for so many thousands of people and horses. Reduction is suggested even by the testimony of the local chronicle, according to which the heralds in Metz announced 3,300 knights not including the princes, dukes and other highly placed guests.[99]

It might be possible to allow for the number of several hundred mounted bowmen in doublets of the same colours. Even so, considering the dismal state of France it was a spectacular escort, which was a thorn in the side to the frugal emperor no less than the luxurious attire of the Dauphin and his suite. If the emperor accepted the invitation to visit his nephew, he certainly could not have believed his eyes, because the Dauphin brought for his temporary residence priceless cloths woven in Brussels with embroidered coats-of-arms of France as well as the Empire, the Kingdom of Bohemia as well as the Dauphiné. The second room was decorated with silk interlaced with gold, so-called *tartaire*, imported from Asia Minor (Tartary).[100] It is not certain whether the emperor actually displayed his resentment to his nephew, because an appropriate emphasis of his own majesty was also his main concern.[101] The Dauphin thus *nolens volens* became a spectator as well as actor in the emperor's triumph, which deeply impressed him as even French historiographers admit. The actual commencement of the Diet was preceded by feudal obeisance in an enormous

99/ I follow the explanation given by Delachenal, *Histoire de Charles V*, I, pp. 276–281, whose footnotes also include the citations of the sources. The enumeration of the persons in the emperor's retinue, invited and present guests has most recently been published by Annas, *Hoftag – Gemeiner Tag – Reichstag*, II, pp. 55–66.

100/ Both of these textile decorations are listed in the inventory of Charles V's treasury of 1363. See Gaborit-Chopin, *L'inventaire du trésor du dauphin futur Charles V, 1363*, p. 84, Nos. 934 and 948. The editor in the relevant notes 865 and 882 connects these items with the Dauphin's stay in Metz at the end of 1356; the work also contains some complementary data from an earlier inventory from around 1380.

101/ The emperor showed his displeasure according to the continuator of Richard Lescot's Chronicle, see Lemoine (ed.), *Chronique de Richard Lescot*, pp. 106–107.

wooden pavilion which had been hastily built along with wooden palisades in the fields by the stream Sailly (Champs à Sailly).

On Christmas Day, the Dauphin as well as all of the highly placed participants of the Diet had to get up earlier so as not to miss the matin. The Dauphin and all the other guests who had not yet had the opportunity to celebrate the Christmas holidays with Charles IV were surprised when the emperor in ceremonial robe with a crown on his head with a naked sword approached the lectern and intoned the seventh lection of the breviary, i.e. the first lesson of the third nocturn, containing a shortened text of the Gospel of Luke beginning with the words *Exiit edictum a Caesare Augusto* (L 2:1). At first glance, it is clear from the English translation in the King James version of the Bible, 'there went out a decree from Caesar Augustus', how fitting a place from the Bible he had chosen when at his first Christmas service in the Basel Cathedral in 1347 he instituted this annual tradition distinguishing his majesty. We shall see later that the Dauphin also attached primary importance to rituals and ceremonies after his accession to the French throne, so it would not be surprising if he wanted to discover much more about Charles' liturgical innovation in Metz. He could have hardly received a precise response, because even many historians have been deluded here by mistaken presumptions. And since some of them still survive in the literature, it will do no harm to mention that the active participation of the Kings of the Romans at the sunrise service had nothing to do with Charles' ordination as deacon and even less with his no less purported canonicates. Charles IV was only an acolyte, i.e. he had only achieved the lowest minor order of ordination, and he intoned Christmas pericopes even in churches that had no chapters. In Basel, Charles adapted in his own way the privilege sometimes granted by the Avignon popes to their notable Christmas guests of secular estate, purposely changed it and regardless of the permission of Clement VI boldly attached it to the Roman Imperial tradition.[102]

It was also fitting that the electors as well as the Dauphin already came to the first mass, at which the emperor accepted the Sacrament of Holy Communion from Cardinal Talleyrand, celebrating the mass. Two more masses followed, of which the so-called main one was celebrated by Archbishop of Cologne Wilhelm von Gennep. It is odd how lacunal the contemporary reports are on this important day, intended for the declaration of the imperial legal code. There are conjectures, i.a. on when and how a document of such fundamental character like the complemented version of the Golden Bull was announced. It most likely happened in the morning, perhaps before the main

102/ The lack of clarity concerning the matin on the feast of the Birth of Christ was removed by Heimpel, 'Königlicher Weihnachtsdienst', pp. 131–162, which also includes references to erroneous interpretations.

missa cantata.[103] This would also be indicated by the course of the ceremonial banquet, which was already governed by the newly complemented chapters of the Golden Bull. Likewise, the sources do not indicate with even a single word when during the day the other ceremonial acts about which we shall soon speak occurred. The following description will, therefore, proceed from the assumption that it was the afternoon banquet that best suited that purpose.

THE FIRST IMPERIAL BANQUET FOLLOWING THE GOLDEN BULL

The ceremonial banquet had exceptionally warm weather, so that most of it could be implemented outdoors. At the head of the ceremoniously decorated pavilion, as can be supposed, there stood a table with a canopy for the emperor at a place visible from all sides. According to the directives of Chapter 28 of the Golden Bull, the table was to be placed six feet higher than the other tables in the hall. Another prestigious position was allotted to a side table for Empress Anna of Schweidnitz, whose companions were the two preeminent guests of the diet, Cardinal Talleyrand and Dauphin Charles. Although it stood three feet below the emperor's, it was the same number of feet higher than the two tables for electors with precisely regulated seating arrangements. Beneath the emperor's table, a wide passage was left for the imperial dignitaries, who according to protocol were to serve the king on horseback.

And on the basis of the eyewitness it really was that way.[104] As soon as the emperor took the seat reserved for him, the Imperial Arch-Marshal, otherwise Duke of Saxony, came to his table on a graceful horse bringing oats for the emperor's horses in a silver chalice. After the Arch-Marshal handed the cup to a servant and the Vice-Marshal distributed oats to the servants of the most distinguished guests, the relatively complicated procedure followed of the initial benediction and presentation of seals by the Chancellor and present ecclesiastical electors. In the next point of the ceremonial order, the main role was played by the Arch-Chamberlain, otherwise Margrave of Brandenburg. His task was to bring on horseback a silver vessel filled with water along with a princely towel. After dismounting, he was to bring both to the emperor and serve him in washing his hands. The task of the Arch-Steward, who was Count Palatine of the Rhine, was to transport on horseback four silver trays with food. For a better idea, it is necessary to mention that two trays served as lids,

103/ Not even great experts know how to treat the time and means of promulgation. See i.a. Zeumer, *Die Goldene Bulle*, I, p. 181, or more recently Hergemöller, 'Der Abschluß der „Goldenen Bulle"', p. 201. Essentially, I follow the time sequence outlined by Heimpel, 'Königlicher Weihnachtsdienst', p. 162.

104/ The testimony can be found in the *Chronicon Benessii de Weitmil*, p. 526, on which I partially rely in the following text. Otherwise, I follow the text of the Golden Bull, in W. Fritz (ed.), *Dokumente zur Geschichte des Deutschen Reiches*, esp. pp. 622–627 (Chapters XXVII–XXVIII).

25. Emperor Charles IV and the empress at a banquet with the attendance of the electors following the regulations of the Golden Bull. The Golden Bull for the Empire of Wenceslas IV, 1400 (ÖNB, cod. 338, fol. 42v)

as proved by a depiction in the illuminated exemplar of the Golden Bill from the library of Wenceslas IV.[105] It was not easy for the riders or for the serving imperial dukes.

This entire spectacle had predominantly symbolic importance emphasising through the assigned acts and gestures the majesty of the emperor as well as the hierarchical relations in the College of Electors, subordinate to him. Since the emperor was simultaneously the King of Bohemia, the role of Czech Elector was assumed by his half-brother Wenceslas, Duke of Luxembourg, Brabant and Limburg. The Office of the Arch-Butler or Arch-Cupbearer was the highest among the secular electors, and therefore the bringing of the wine mixed with water and its being offered to the emperor was the final point in the introductory part of the protocol. Also in the case of the cup with wine, the weight of the silver was prescribed, because all of the horses and vessels, which had to be procured by the electors at their own cost, passed to the allowance of imperial counts and officials as specified in advance in Section Twenty-Seven of the Golden Bull.

After fulfilling their tasks, each of the electors stood at his table. Not until all of them had discharged their obligations could they be seated. We do not

105/ The manuscript comes from around 1400 and is deposited in the Austrian National Library in Vienna under shelf mark Cod. 338. The series of the depictions of the electors including the feast is, i.a. reproduced in the work *Kaiser Karl IV. Staatsmann und Mäzen*, Pics. 71–91 after p. 216.

26. Frescos of the so-called relic scenes, Karlštejn, Chapel of Our Lady

know what was served on the table, but most likely the menu was adjusted to the customs and tastes of most of the imperial diners. According to an eyewitness, the real revelry was triggered by the arrival of the Master of the Hounds, Margrave of Meissen, and the whipper-in, Count of Schwarzburg, who with the sound of hunting horns and barking hounds with great hullabaloo brought deer and boar to the ruler's table. Apparently at the same time, the less distinguished diners and perhaps also the crowd watching from behind the palisade were served the meat from roasted oxen.[106] In any case, it was a banquet of exceptional size, whose preparation and organisation required not only great financial means but also a large number of participants. The climax of the programme was the granting of the Dauphiné as an imperial fief to Dauphin Charles. The sources are silent on the course of this ceremony, but we can approximate it with the assistance of the records of other feudal oaths of Charles' time. During the ceremony, the emperor sat with all the signs of his dignity at his table under the canopy, with the court marshal standing beside him with his sword drawn. Before Dauphin Charles swore his feudal oath and oath of loyalty, he had to present the Dauphiné's colours. Only after this act were the colours returned to him as a sign of the legitimacy of his government.[107]

In the following days, the court chancellery was fully engaged. Foremost, it was necessary to draw papers connected with the investiture of Dauphin Charles, with the confirmation of his rights in the County of Vienne and

106/ Other dishes served can be inferred by an analogy with the banquet which Charles IV organised in Metz after his visit to France at the beginning of 1378. On that, see Excursus – Dramatic and Musical Productions during the Intermissions (Entremets) and pp. 159–160 below.
107/ For the feudal ceremony, see Kavka, *Am Hofe Karls IV.*, pp. 96–97.

27. Dauphin Charles presents relics to Emperor Charles IV. A copy of the fresco from the Chapel of Our Lady at Karlštejn in the so-called Heidelberg Codex from 1574–1575

with his appointment as the imperial vicar in that land. At the same time, the emperor ceremonially cancelled all protective rights in the Duchy of Lorraine including the rights of the King of France. And also since the Imperial Vicar Henry of Montbéliard granted the plenipotentiary of the minor Duke of Burgundy Philip II the investiture to his Free County of Burgundy, three of the four requirements that Charles IV had set as conditions for the treaty on friendly relations were *de facto* met. Nothing stood in the way of its renewal according to the proposal of John II from May of that year. Charles IV confirmed the treaty document of 28 December 1356 only with a wax seal, hence showing those privy that he did not attach primary importance to it. Even so, the act of sealing it had a celebratory nature, because it was most likely on this occasion that Dauphin Charles handed over the precious gifts from his father to the emperor.

The emperor especially treasured the two relics of the Crown of Thorns, which after his return to Prague he had mounted in the Land Cross, deposited at Karlštejn Castle. The donation act was later captured by one of the relic scenes in the local Church of the Virgin Mary. The emperor appears here in a magnificent robe with a high crown on his head, the successor to the French throne has a lower crown with lilies and a plain gown, such as was worn by

Parisian Masters of Liberal Arts. Experts allowed themselves to be confused by the words *Blanca regina* in the banner above the scene, which was linked to a faded text of the Litany, and they considered the dauphin to be the emperor's first wife Blanche. Not until spring 1924 did French professor Eugene Déprez on a visit to Karlštejn recognise Dauphin Charles according to his characteristic profile.[108] Without realising what confusion his depiction would evoke in Bohemia, the successor to the French throne left Metz on 28 December 1356. Besides the treaty on friendly relations, he was taking with him a loan of 50,000 gold pieces. Despite this, he was returning to France in uncertainty and with fear of what awaited him in the next year.[109]

108/ On the thorns donated from the Crown of Thorns and on the mentioned relic scene at Karlštejn, see Fišer, *Karlštejn*, pp. 144–145; on the various opinions on the authorship as well as dating of the relic scenes, see Homolka, 'Poznámky ke karlštejnským malbám', pp. 122–130, and Stejskal, 'Die Wandzyklen des Kaisers Karls IV.', esp. pp. 32–33, Stejskal, 'Ještě jednou o datování a atributech karlštejnských maleb', p. 344, and Royt, 'K datování a ikonografii tzv. Ostatkových scén', pp. 354–356. Myself, I tend towards the later dating to 1364–1365, because I consider it as proved that the relics are being handed over by Dauphin/King Charles the Wise, not by his father John the Good. On the portraits of the two kings, see Sherman, *The Portraits of Charles V of France*, and Cazelles, 'Peinture et actualité politique sous les premiers Valois', pp. 53–65.

109/ It arises from the receipt to which the Dauphin attached his seal that twenty thousand gold pieces from the Kingdom of Bohemia were to be paid within a year. For more on that and the conclusion of the imperial diet in Metz, see Kavka, *Vláda Karla IV.*, I, pp. 94–98.

Dauphin Charles 1357–1364: Basking in Glory and Eclipsed

Dauphin Charles was returning from the emperor with mixed emotions. He could not have achieved more. The feudal oath and other concessions were balanced by the treaty on friendly relations, which bound Charles IV and his successors on the throne of Bohemia to stand beside France against England, which was winning. The immediate loan was also not negligible, even though it could not avert the financial crisis of the kingdom. Also the consultations with his uncle had been valuable, who had recommended that he not release his cousin Charles the Bad from imprisonment. Good advice was more precious than gold, but the rapid course of events still put the successor to the throne in situations which he had to manage himself. Hardly had he returned to Paris on 14 January than he discovered the general opposition which had been evoked in Paris by the reform proposal of his Council concerning the minting of more valuable coins. In adversity, the kings of France abused their minting monopoly and attempted to improve the state finances through monetary reforms. However, since the reform of King John II of March 1356 had completely foundered, the general assembly of the estates of Languedoc at the instigation of the royal captain had decided on a flat increase in the quality of the coins for the purpose of higher tax proceeds. By this, it came to pass that different values began to be accepted in the south than in the north. In an attempt to reduce this abysmal difference, the Dauphin's Council adopted a compromise solution, which was less drastic by a half than in the south.[110] Even so, it was a hard blow for the merchants, for whom the changes in the rates unhinged negotiated deals. Deflation also impoverished the working people. To go out on the streets was the work of a moment. The appeal of Étienne Marcel was enough for it, and that was already in the air.

110/ For further details on this with the description of the appropriate minting conditions, see Cazelles, 'La stabilisation de la monnaie', pp. 298–299.

The Paris of crafts and trade was situated on the right bank, whereas the left belonged to the university and partially lawyers and other persons who were close to the court. Right-bank Paris, the 'city' as it was called, was controlled by roughly twenty families connected to the 'river', i.e. mainly to trade, whose transport artery was the Seine. It was no accident that also their guild or Hansa associated 'merchants from the water' (*marchands de l'eau*), whose symbol, a barque on the waves of the Seine, was included in the emblem of the town seal. The family clan from which Étienne Marcel came was one of the most highly esteemed and also one of the largest. Nevertheless, we would like to learn more about Étienne than what can be discovered from the sources.[111] Undoubtedly, he along with others could hardly stand the wrongs from some people of the king's circle. Aspirations for reforms of the system of government and an increase in the influence of wealthy burghers, however, were not an issue of Étienne alone, standing at the head of the merchants' guild. Struggles for town also rights took place in Bruges, Ypres, Ghent as well as in other towns in Flanders and Brabant. The sparks flashed from there to Paris also, which with the number of its populace represented an uncommonly strong base of potential popular discontent. Nonetheless, only the wealthiest 'good' burghers from merchant families spoke on behalf of the people of Paris and posed as them as necessary. Among themselves, they elected their representative (*prévôt des marchands*) and four aldermen. The influence of this autonomous corporation continued to increase and formed a counterweight to the royal provost (*prévôt de Paris*), headquartered in the Châtelet inside the ramparts. Paris, however, did not have a town hall as the permanent seat of the municipal government yet, but even that was to change in the foreseeable future.

The dauphin decided for a first meeting with Étienne Marcel on the sixth day after his return to Paris. On Thursday, 19 January 1357, the first glints of worse times appeared. The representative of the guild rejected the minting reform; work in workshops and on constructions sites was stopped at his orders and crowds of armed burghers formed on the streets. In the royal palace, they had an idea who the first victim would be. The dauphin yielded and repealed the decree on coinage. He had hardly done so when he was forced to call the council installed for him, which on Sunday, 5 February convoked another diet of the estates-general. When on 3 March Bishop Le Coq concluded the session, he had not mentioned a word about the 'Bad' Charles, who remained in

111/ On the French research, see Amalvi, 'L'érudition française face à la révolution d'Étienne Marcel', pp. 287–331. What is significant is the title given to his book by Cazelles: *Étienne Marcel, champion de l'unité française*. On the tragic fate of this mayor of Paris, see Cazalis, *1358. La Jacquerie de Paris*.

the donjon; notwithstanding that, the administration of the kingdom had been shaken to its foundations. Still on the same day, the dauphin had to dismiss twenty-two royal counsellors and all of the high officials. The administration of the kingdom came under the control of the estates, whose leaders had extorted the regular convocation of diets and austerity measures at the court. For his alacrity, the dauphin obtained a promise of a special tax of five million pounds for the mercenary pay for 30,000 armigers. Not even the estates-general forgot about the war and the king, who it was necessary to redeem from humiliating captivity. In this phase, however, the main issue was power, and that was already to a significant degree provided to the estates-general by the Great Ordinance reform of 3 March 1357. For the time being, it nevertheless concerned predominantly representatives of the aristocracy and clergy, in whose interest it was to increase the quality of the coins while keeping the taxes unchanged, namely even despite the unrelenting protests of Marcel's Paris.

Popular discontent, as it had been for the entire Middle Ages and even later, was not directed at the king but at his counsellors and officials. All of these were to blame for the disconsolate situation in the eyes of the disgruntled. And in France after the two heavy defeats at Crécy as well as Poitiers, there was something to complain about. Although King John II the Good did not have his hands tied in his English prison in Bordeaux, the English requirements conditioning his release were worse than a ball and chain would have been on his leg. The negotiations dragged on with neither side planning to yield, and the temporary fallback hence became a ceasefire, which the papal legates managed to conclude for two years. In the first half of April 1357, Edward III had King John transferred to London so that he could personally negotiate the conditions of the peace. He simultaneously sent a declaration to Paris that he would release the king only on the basis of the draft of the future peace treaty, according to which France would surrender sovereignty over a whole third of its territory. It was out of the question, especially when it was rumoured that the ransom would come to several million gold pieces. After 5 April, when the king's counsellors brought a ban from England on collecting taxes and convening the estates-general, the tension rapidly rose in Paris. And because rumours appeared at the same time that a military campaign was being prepared against the metropolis, Étienne Marcel declared a state of war. All of the gates except for three were closed even during the day and chains appeared in the streets. King John did not recognise the estates' governing council and the council did not challenge his orders. Marcel as well as Bishop Le Coq increased the pressure. The dauphin was unable to face it, introduced taxes and again convoked the estates-general in October.

The ground of Paris became unstable for the dauphin, albeit not dangerous yet. Whenever he could, he resided at the castles of his duchy of Normandy. He still had the counsellors of his father at his heels, acquiring experience from them, but he gradually sought new men, prelates as well as secular legists, with whose assistance he endeavoured to keep the courts functioning. He also had to consider his wife Jeanne, with whom he was expecting a child. In November, the dauphin became a father for the first time. Nevertheless, his daughter Jeanne had been measured out only three years of life. The dauphin had to wait for an heir; considering his age, however, he did not have to be troubled by it thus far. No lesser were the problems that Étienne Marcel had to face in Paris. Although he was not a member of the government council, he endeavoured with all his might to implement the Great Ordinance in the spirit of one of the tenets of Canon Law, which had worked its way from the university lecture halls to the urban milieu: 'What affects everyone shall also be discussed and approved by all.' In July 1357, Parisians finally attained a permanent place for the meetings of their representatives, when the aldermen led by Marcel purchased a spacious house on the right bank of the Seine for a relatively high price. Since that time, Paris has had its town hall, the Hôtel de Ville, in the same place.

The ceasefire remained only on parchment. There was fighting everywhere; the leaders of mercenary bands fought of their own accord; in Normandy, the Navarre party was reinforcing its positions. The roads were dangerous; trade floundered; beggared villagers were seeking refuge within the ramparts of the towns. The dauphin decided to manoeuvre and perhaps also on the advice of his uncle Charles IV[112] attempted to ensure the operation of the supreme court of law (*Conseil d'État*), among whose noble members and officials he sought support for his government. Even so, he had to compete for power with the supporters of his father, who wished for nothing other than an early conclusion of a peace treaty. Nonetheless, it was closer to war, which according to the estates' governing council was to be won for France by an army paid from the taxes levied. The dauphin, as has already been said, preferred a deal with Le Coq's government council, and therefore the invitations to the autumn assembly of the estates-general were coming from both sides. Despite that, the first steps of the estates, which began their deliberations on 7 November 1357, were directed against the dauphin. Two days later, Charles of Navarre was freed from prison and, what is worse, the session of the supreme court was postponed to the beginning of January and then to Candlemas (2 February).

112/ As suggested by Autrand, *Charles V. Le Sage*, p. 277, who described the dauphin's political intentions on the backdrop of the overall shift of powers.

28. Paris, Sainte Chapelle

Charles the Bad did not head for Paris but for his estates in Normandy. In Amiens, he allowed himself to be welcomed on entry to the city with royal honours. He was still king – at least in Navarre; he did not permit those around him to forget it. First of all, he demanded satisfaction and then he would see what chances he had for the French throne. He was after all a Capetian, which meant a lot in the eyes of the aristocracy represented in the estates-general, who saw its leader in him. Whereas Charles of Navarre fretted himself with humility, it was not the dauphin's destiny. Paris was eagerly anticipating its favourite in the early evening of 29 November. When he was approaching from Rheims, as if from a coronation, he was met halfway by a procession led by the Bishop of Paris, which ceremoniously accompanied him to his residence in the Abbey of Saint-Germain-des-Prés. All of this was under the direction of the estate leaders, who after the massive manifestation in tribute to the king of Navarre openly requested the restitution of his rights and properties, and hence also his return to the royal family. Charles the Bad acted accordingly. In Paris, he pardoned some criminals; in Sainte-Chapelle with the dauphin at his side, he knelt before the relics collected by his ancestor St Louis. Then both Charleses left Paris. The dauphin secretly mobilised loyal units. His cousin was not idle either and during his stays in Mantes and Rouen was strengthening the friendly ties with his allies.

We cannot deny the dauphin's courage. On Thursday, 11 January 1358, he spoke to Parisians assembled in the market, defending his steps and disputing slanders. The army, which he had amassed, was to fight the English, because the estates' government only fought with words. The disconcerted Marcel called another assembly for the next day at the Hospital of St Jacob. In a meeting full of shouting and emotions, the dauphin this time failed and left it before it ended. Not even then did he sit on his hands, he attempted to win over hesitant circles and along with his counsellors to supervise the return to the coins of low value announced in the mandates of 22 and 23 January. The reform reflected the change in the composition of the assembled estates-general, which were numerically dominated by the representatives of the 'good' towns. The very next day, an official of the dauphin's financial administration was treacherously killed on the streets. The marshal of Normandy Robert de Clermont along with other of the dauphin's warriors captured the murderer and hanged him without due process. In so doing, they violated the holy ground of the Church of Saint-Merry; the bishop of Paris pronounced them under anathema, by which he again expressed his inclination towards the estates-general, convoked on 11 February. The wording of the peace treaty which was brought from England in those days by confidants of King John II the Good satisfied no one. Charles of Navarre made himself heard again with his requests, which were considered as justified also by the speakers of the university.

The final resolution of the February assembly of the estates-general intensified oversight of the performance of royal power. The estates' council was henceforth to select 'good' officials, monitor the expenditures of the king as well as his son and be in charge of the selection of the commanders of the royal garrisons. The highest body in the country was to be the regular assemblies of the estates-general, from which the kings could gain better and healthier opinion than from their court counsellors. And since the resolution under certain circumstances also allowed the right to forcible resistance, it was actually the onset of a new regime, which was unimaginable until then.

Dauphin Charles would have everything important that happened in 1357 and 1358 later recorded in the official *Great Chronicles of France*. His chancellor Pierre d'Orgemont would capture the events as his master, who by no accident would be dubbed 'the Wise', i.e. in the period sense also of 'careful' or 'prudent', saw or wanted to see them.[113] The historian can also learn from other period sources, e.g. the chronicle records of Jean de Venette, an opponent of the aristocracy and admirer of Étienne Marcel, thus discovering the purported discussions of the actors of the drama as well as details which he cannot use. Yet, despite that, the historian would like to know more, for example who concocted the murder of the two marshals in the dauphin's abode which was carried out in the morning of 22 February. The marshal of Normandy Robert de Clermont has already flashed by in the previous lines. Jean de Conflans, marshal for the region of Champagne, was also very close to the dauphin. The same cannot be said of the lawyer of his father Renaud d'Acy, one of the wanted men of the king whom the crowd beat to death on the street. Marcel was supposedly trying to calm the stunned dauphin, before whose eyes the marshals died in a pool of blood with the words: 'Sire, do not marvel at what you have seen. So was it decided and it had to happen thus'.

As if it had not been enough that the dauphin remained in the Palace de la Cité alone against Marcel and three thousand of his armed supporters who he had brought with him. Marcel forced him to give his consent to an alliance with Paris in revolt, whose colours he was to acknowledge even on the outside. And since Marcel was a cloth merchant, he had one package of red and one of light blue fabric for hats sent for him as well as for his men. The dauphin kept a cool head even in the days to come when Marcel with alternating success sought support in the 'good' towns of the French language d'oïl, which was spoken north of the Loire.[114] Étienne Marcel was at the peak of his power; some time before, he had received a letter from the pope himself; now he was moving the members of the royal family like the figures on a chess board. Charles II the Bad had already received his invitation and returned to Paris on 26 February 1358. Both Charleses became close again; they were joined by the former tort of conspiracy behind the king's back as well as opposition to his peace treaty. Otherwise, their interests were quite divergent. The king of Navarre had not given up his greatest ambitions and for the time being he was flattered by his standing at

113/ On the period context of the phrase 'le Sage', see Guenée, *L'opinion publique à la fin du Moyen Âge*, pp. 139–158. For more on the testimonies of the contemporary chronicles, see Autrand, *Charles V. Le Sage*, pp. 274–276, more recently also Carqué, *Stil und Erinnerung*, pp. 419–422.
114/ 'Oïl' was the syllable of agreement which was typical for the northern area of France. In the south, especially in Provence, the 'd'oc' language (lenga d'oc, Occitan) was spoken, in which 'yes' was expressed by the syllable 'òc' (from the Latin 'hoc').

the head of the aristocracy, at least of those who participated in estate life. For that reason, Charles of Navarre must have felt hurt when the other Charles pronounced himself as the regent in the place of his royal father on 14 March.

The fragile balance of power in the spring of 1358 was most threatened by the brigandish military bands in the close and distant vicinity of the metropolis. It was still relatively safe in Champagne, where the dauphin resided from 17 March. At two convocations there, he acquired reliable allies, which allowed him to seize the fortresses in Montereau and in Meaux, which guarded the eastern routes to Paris. For Étienne Marcel, it was a message that the dauphin was wearing his hat again. It really was that way; the dauphin had cast aside the colours of rebellious Paris, begun to take the reins in his own hands and left the letter in which Marcel was requesting that he return to Paris, hand over both occupied fortresses and forgive the Parisians for their having transferred the royal cannons from the Louvre to their new town hall unanswered. This manifesto already reflected a new concept of the reform of public affairs consisting in three principles: according to Marcel and his lawyers, sovereign power was primarily to have its support in a certain kind of contract with the municipality. Protection and defence provided by the sovereign were to be counterbalanced by obedience and respect for him. Secondly, the king was to have his eyes and ears open to the complaints of his subjects and, thirdly and lastly, he was to take into account that burghers were not yeomen farmers. It was precisely the third point that came to the centre of attention in the second quarter of 1358.

Even in May the meetings were never-ending. In Compiègne, the delegates of the estates, who had been convened there by the dauphin, were in session from 4 May for ten days. Their main interest was a stable currency, around which everything revolved. It was better to negotiate than fight. Whereas the Parisians were arming themselves and digging defences, King of Navarre Charles began to play the role of mediator between his cousin and the metropolis. He did not object to further ceremonial greetings from Marcel's supporters, but as a precaution he found accommodation in Saint-Denis. While in Paris two traitors who had been secretly preparing the entry of the dauphin's men-at-arms were beheaded and quartered, in Saint-Leu-d'Esserent one of the most famous peasant revolts of mediaeval Europe began on 28 May 1358. Historians have not yet agreed whether the Jacquerie received its name after 'Jack Goodfellow' (*Jacques Bonhomme*), which was a pejorative nickname for the armed peasants, or was based on the short, padded surplices (*jacques*) worn by the villagers.[115] What actually happened in that hamlet on the

115/ Extensive information on the Jacquerie is provided by earlier literature. See i.a. Mollat and Wolff, *Ongles bleus, Jacques et Ciompi*; Dommanget, *La Jacquerie*, and Fourquin, *Les soulèvements populaires*.

right bank of the River Oise? No one precisely knows why a smaller mounted group of men-at-arms led by Raoul and Jean de Clermont had come there. When they harassed the villagers, they encountered armed resistance and nine of them remained lying in pools of blood.

Conceit from the victorious clash and fear of the possible consequences prompted the peasants to attacks on the nearby aristocratic fortifications and castles. The Jacquerie lasted a mere fourteen days yet in such a short period affected relatively extensive areas to the east and south of Paris. The destructive tornado of the elemental storms was leaving the dead bodies of the guilty as well as of the innocent victims in the burnt-out aristocratic residences. The first signs of a coordinated approach did not begin to manifest themselves until a few days later. In this regard, the most assertive of the peasant leaders was a certain Guillaume Cale, who did not lack a wider political insight and who also attempted to negotiate a common approach with Étienne Marcel. At the head of five to six thousand poorly armed villagers, Cale directed attacks on strategic points of the aristocracy and sent orders to all sides from his field office. Within a few days, armed divisions sallied forth from Paris, which attacked the nearby fortified residences of the aristocracy from which the metropolis could be threatened. The example of Paris was followed by other towns that had already become involved in the reform campaign of Étienne Marcel before, namely Amiens, Rouen, Orléans, Senlis and Meaux.

The aristocracy soon recovered from the series of withering attacks, quickly mobilised all of its armed forces and in a short time crushingly defeated the main rebellious hordes at Mello and in Meaux. The army of Guillaume Cale was gathering in Mello while the men-at-arms of Étienne Marcel headed for Meaux, where the dauphin had taken his young wife Jeanne of Bourbon with their daughter Jeanne as well as other noble ladies so that they would be in the safety of the royal residence; whereas he stayed in Sens, from which he was mobilising the military forces for the subjugation of Paris. The dangerous situation of the imperilled ladies was resolved out of the blue by a man who even then already had the reputation of an elegant cavalier and intellectually oriented *bon vivant*. Gaston III Phoebus, Count of Foix, was, along with his cousin Jean de Grailly, Captal de Buch, just then returning from an expedition to Prussia, where side by side with the Teutonic knights he had been gaining his spurs in battle against the 'pagans'.[116] In Châlons, they learnt about the situation in Meaux and as true knights set out to free the ladies. It almost sounds like a story from Old French epic poems (*chansons de geste*, literally 'songs of

116/ The figure of the man-of-letters, patron and *bon vivant* Gaston III of Foix has been treated in a number of works especially by Tucoo-Chala; of his recent work, see *Gaston Fébus, Grand prince médiéval*; in a concise abridgment, also Nejedlý, *La représentation*, pp. 467–488.

heroic deeds'), especially as they arrived in Meaux exactly on the morning of 9 June when the rural rebels, the so-called *jacques*, and their Parisian allies were about to attack the fortified residence and seize the Duchess of Bourbon Jeanne and her companions as hostages.

It will not be a waste of time to outline the local, relatively complex situation, because it will make it easier for us to understand the quite unclear record of the stop of Emperor Charles IV in Meaux on his return journey from France in January 1378. The city Meaux with its pontifical castle and St Stephen's Cathedral (*Cathédrale Saint-Étienne de Meaux*) lay on the right bank of the Marne, which formed a meander here with a favourable area for a market. Already in the fourteenth century, this market, called Marché de Meaux, acquired its own strong ramparts and, after the Cornillon canal was dug, it became an island fortress belonging to the royal domains. Both towns were joined by a wooden bridge, across which the rebels attempted to penetrate the island, where a palatial 'large house' (*la grande maison*) of the royal residence stood between the churches of St Martin and St Saintin, which today have already been destroyed. The aristocratic warriors managed to defeat the rebelling peasants, the people of Étienne Marcel as well as their local allies including the mayor, and slaughter them to a man. They were effectively assisted in this by the young Count Enguerrand VII of Coucy with weapon in hand, who was responsible for the safety of Emperor Charles IV and his retinue during his visit to France at the end of 1377 and beginning of 1378. And as the fighting in Meaux predominantly took place on the bridge to the island market, the fast-flowing waters of the River Marne carried away the victims and downstream announced that cruelty had been punished with cruelty.[117]

A day later, the same tragedy played out to the north of Paris in Mello, where Cale expected a clash with the Norman and other aristocracy, led by our well-known Charles II the Bad. The king of Navarre had *nolens volens* to revenge his noble supporters, whose estates and families had become victims of the peasant attacks. Charles approached Mello on 10 June with approximately one-thousand mounted men, including the recruited English mercenaries. Although the *jacques* were much more numerous and Cale had organised them into military formations, he paid dearly for his good will to negotiate. An eye for an eye, an intrigue for an intrigue. Just as the *jacques* had perfidiously murdered a certain Guillaume de Picquigny, the brother of one of the king of Navarre's liberators, during peace negotiations, so now was the leader of the

117/ My thanks for help in elucidating the local conditions in Meaux in the second half of the fourteenth century are owed to Mrs Paule Lerou and her husband Roger. The blood-stained description of the peasant cruelties and the defeat of the rebellious hordes in Meaux can be found in Jean Froissart, *The Chronicles of Froissart*, pp. 136–137.

rebels to fare. Guillaume Cale was seized and beheaded but not immediately, only after the massacre of his pitifully equipped peasants. Two weeks of bloody repression followed; then the situation was slightly calmed. The acts of violent reprisals continued even after the issuance of the general pardon of 10 August 1358. Dauphin Charles came out of the rebellion unblemished and as the successor to the throne had not stained his hands with blood of the French subjects.

THE PEACE TREATY OF BRÉTIGNY

It remains to be told what happened with the Parisian revolt of Étienne Marcel. Against expectations, Charles of Navarre did not seek the dauphin but preferred rebellious Paris. He was particular about spectacular entries, so the almost royal tributes with which Paris welcomed him on 14 June 1358 were definitely not against the grain for him. By allowing himself to be elected captain of the people by acclamation, he lost the trust of many of his noble friends and acquaintances. On the other hand, he exasperated the indecisive Parisians with his English mercenaries, whose offensiveness evoked unrest in the metropolis. Charles the Bad was a captain without an army. While he was trying to amass his forces north of Paris, the dauphin managed to mobilise a small army numbering as many as three thousand lances. Also the dauphin's wife Jeanne was active and attempted to win over the metropolis by negotiations. Charles the Bad was to become a mediator, and it was not going to be for free. Paris was to receive a general pardon, but for the sum of six hundred thousand gold pieces, which was planned as the first payment of the ransom for the king. The son did not forget his father, but the king of Navarre thwarted the plans of both when he scuppered the agreement at the last moment. His situation was also no longer rosey. In the last ten days of July, the English ranted and raved; Étienne Marcel and his ally Charles the Bad heaped error upon error. The help from Flanders, on which Marcel had been counting, did not arrive. In the end, it was members of the merchant guild who, although late, recognised the danger into which they were getting. The drama of the great revolt and rise of the 'estates-general' came to an inglorious end on 31 July 1358 and postponed the onset of constitutional monarchy in France by several centuries.[118] Étienne Marcel was killed by an aggrieved member of his family clan, the crowd had soon let off steam and woeful future things began to be expected.

In the evening of 2 August, Parisians with cries in his honour welcomed Dauphin Charles, who only a few days before had wanted to withdraw from

118/ I agree with the concept expressed by Lot and Fawtier, *Histoire des institutions françaises au Moyen Âge*, II, p. 569.

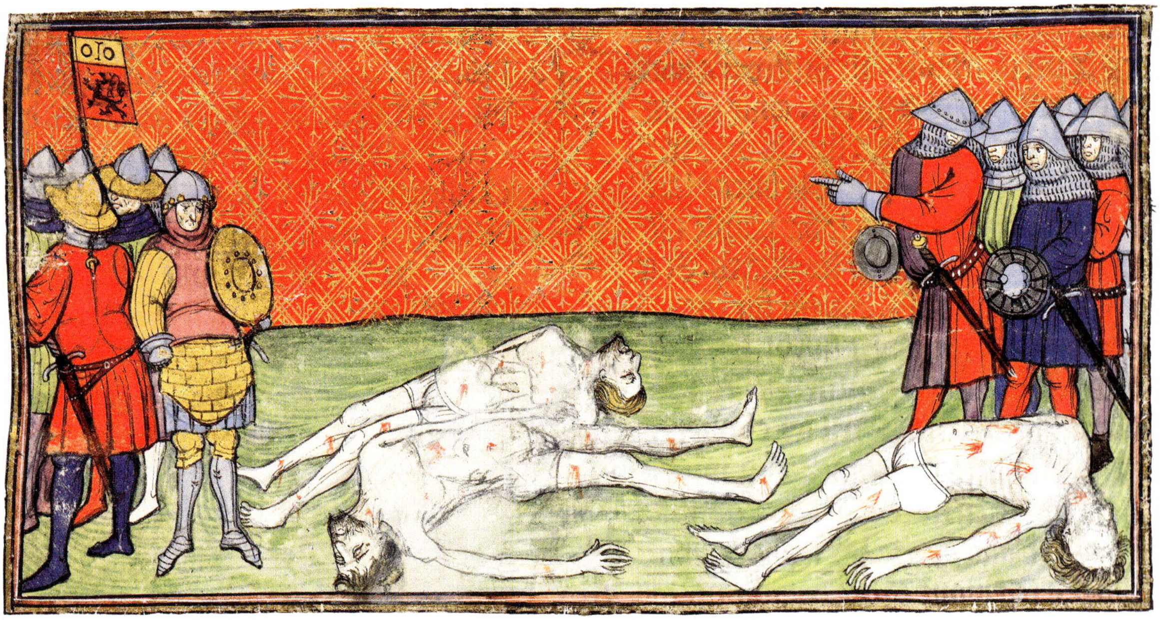

29. The death of Étienne Marcel. Chroniques de Jean Froissart (BnF, ms. fr. 2646)

the surroundings of riotous Paris to his Dauphiné. In Paris, he acted discreetly, in accord with his future epithet. He did not want the heads of his subjects; he needed their money and perhaps even their hearts.[119] Instead of frantic executions, he renewed the operation of the regularly established court. The general pardon of 10 August, however, did not apply to the actual culprits of the grand conspiracy, to the twelve men who *inter alia* wanted to make King of Navarre into King of France. Whereas Charles the Bad again sought refuge with the English, his chancellor, Bishop Robert Le Coq, paid for his political activity with his life.

The trump in the hand of King of England Edward III was his royal captive, whom along with his numerous retinue he allowed a comfortable life at a castle near London. The waiting for the ransom connected with the peace treaty had become protracted, but Edward did not have to worry that John II would escape from the well-guarded English ports. Edward had his trump not only up his sleeve but also beyond the 'sleeve' of the English Channel (in French La Manche, 'The Sleeve'), and therefore had no reason to offer special gifts to his unreliable ally of Navarre, who soon realised that secret negotiations with the enemy rather put him in danger of losing trust on the part of his noble allies from the estates-general. He began to seek a way to the dauphin with the help of Queen Blanche, the young, not even thirty-year-old widow of Philip VI, who had already extracted a thorn from his foot several times. Despite the precarious state of his finances, the king of Navarre was still a powerful man of royal blood. Even so, it took several weeks before a peace

119/ I somewhat changed the statement here of Autrand, *Charles V. Le Sage*, p. 349, according to whom the dauphin needed primarily the hearts of his subjects.

treaty was concluded in Pontoise on 21 August 1359, on whose basis the 'good people' of the city of Paris allowed Charles the Bad entry into the city again.

All of these events taking place were eclipsed by the escalating spree of thieving bands of vagrant mercenaries as well as in connection with the much more important negotiations of a peace treaty between England and France. The payments for the ransom based on the peace treaty of January 1358 were not being paid, which vexed Edward III so much that he allocated his captive John the Good a much more humble residence in Somerton. The captive king and his son Philip now had to make do with roughly half of the sixty to seventy servants, which they had had at their disposal before. Although unwillingly, John sent his librarian as well as several chaplains back to France, but he kept his physicians with him, without whom he did not take a step, further the painter Girard d'Orléans and 'king of minstrels', who moreover would repair his portable astronomical clock.[120] The more willingly did he on 24 March 1358 accede to the draft of a further treaty according to which France would lose direct access to the Atlantic through surrendering other areas, namely the coastal territories between the Somme and Calais. The conditions of the treaty were, however, unacceptable for Paris. Nevertheless, nothing was happening on the outside; negotiations were taking place only in secret and everyone was waiting for what would ensue after 24 June 1359, when the two-year ceasefire was to come to an end. The very next day, the assembly of the three estates and of the representatives of the city of Paris decided to inform Regent Charles that the conditions of the March treaty could not be accepted. The regent was of the same opinion; he only wanted to be able to declare war on England after he discussed it and consulted it with the delegates of the representative circles of the kingdom. We will see that the young successor to the throne will act as prudently and thoughtfully even later.

In the given situation, it was impossible to begin a war without allies. The regent's counsellors and diplomats had been taking steps in this direction already from the beginning of the year, because on 18 February 1359 Pope Innocent VI informed Emperor Charles IV that the regent and his brother John, Count of Poitiers, were sending a delegation to him. We know nothing of its fate, but it can be conjectured whether there was any connection between it and the truly generous gift of the relic of Christ's cross, which the regent sent in May of the same year to the imperial chancellor John (Johann) of Neumarkt. The emperor, as can be judged from his orders sent to Metz and Strasbourg, intended to send his nephew two units in support, the first of one

120/ Further details are provided by Bériac-Lainé and Given-Wilson, *Les prisonniers de la bataille de Poitiers*, pp. 142–144. Also the other imprisoned lords had to cut their staff proportionally. On the constant care of John the Good for his health, see Cazelles, *Société politique*, pp. 41–42.

hundred and the second of forty men-at-arms.[121] A similar delegation was heading for Hungary; in June, the alliance with King of Scotland David Bruce was renewed; nevertheless, the most was expected from the Danish invasion of England, which King Valdemar IV was to undertake for 600,000 florins. Everything remained unfulfilled promises; only the war, whose impact all of France was to experience heavily anew, became a reality.

The most affected by the war was John the Good himself, for whom peace was now even more important, and that at any price. The orders to his son Charles, who in his eyes continued to remain only the duke of Normandy despite his acting as the regent, were entirely unambiguous. Meanwhile Black Prince Edward undertook a military expedition in the south, whereas his brother John, Duke of Lancaster, fought in the county of Artois and in Picardy in October. The ransacked land could support neither the warriors nor their horses, and so more was being expected from the siege of Rheims in London, which happened at the beginning of December 1359. After forty days, Edward III abandoned the siege and set out with his army for Burgundy, which was one of the few lands until then spared military campaigns. The insufficiently defended duchy could not resist and concluded a peace treaty with Edward III in March, which was equivalent to a capitulation. A further advance headed for Paris, and had it not been for an ice storm which decimated a part of the English army near Chartres on 'Black Monday', 13 April 1360, Edward III would probably not have given the papal legates his consent to open negotiations.

Without having won the war, Edward III acquired everything that he dictated with the peace concluded in Brétigny on 8 May 1360. The treaty was concluded by Black Prince Edward and Regent Charles, ratified by their fathers in London on 14 June, and peace was declared with the relevant oaths in Calais on 24 October. Edward III obtained sovereignty in the surrendered areas from the Loire to the Pyrenees, further the Port of Calais with its surroundings and the counties of Guines and Ponthieu. The ransom was lowered from four to three million écus and was to be paid in six instalments within four years. After the payment of the majority of the first instalment, John II he Good was released, but in his place three of his sons went across the channel along with other dukes and aristocrats, namely as hostages for the unpaid ransom. Edward III, abiding by his device 'It is as it is', did not believe in promises of honour, because he himself did not intend to act according to his obligations. Although he was to stop asserting his claims to the French throne by November 1361, it did not happen and the war could break out again at any time.

121/ On this, see Autrand, *Charles V. Le Sage*, p. 380, and Kavka, *Vláda Karla IV.*, II, p. 144, where it is however necessary to correct the date to 25 June 1359.

30. Portrait of King John II the Good, or perhaps his son Charles V?

IN THE SHADOW OF HIS FATHER'S POLICIES

The parallel of the relations between the fathers and sons of the ruling dynasties in Bohemia and France is striking at first sight. Like John of Luxembourg, also John II the Good from the Valois dynasty constantly made it obvious to his son for whom it was befitting to rule. Undoubtedly, the Charleses had good reasons to be on alert. Personal relations usually did not play much of a role in it. For the royal children, their father was a stranger whom they seldom saw. The decisive factor was the royal blood which they shared and which was to ensure the continuity of the dynasty also in the future. *Via facti*, both Charleses in their youth had undergone a hard political school: the next emperor in the North Italian communes and the dauphin in the stormy time of his regency. The fact that they had acquitted themselves well was precisely the reason that their fathers had pushed them from the power centres to the peripheries. At the same time, a considerable, and in France sometimes the main, role was played by the individual as well as group interests of the twelve peers upon whom royal power relied.[122]

King John II the Good entered historical consciousness not through his deeds but through his appearance and his sons. His portrait in the Louvre is one of the oldest authentic depictions of European sovereigns. His four sons were in the eyes of their contemporaries the 'flowers of the lilies' symbolising the French royal family (*les fleurs-de-lis*). John's wife, the daughter of John of Luxembourg Bonne already well-known to us, alias Guta, managed to bear him ten children in 1338–1348. What is more interesting than her fertility is the fact that eight of her children survived to a greater age. Even daughters were a welcome addition in ruling families, because they expanded alliance kinship. We have already heard that John II married his eldest daughter Jeanne (1343–1373) to King of Navarre Charles II the Bad. The younger Marie (1344–1404) was the wife of Duke Robert of Bar; the youngest Isabella at age twelve received as her husband the condottiere Gian Galeazzo Visconti (1348–1372), Lord of Milan, who redeemed his low birth for the sum of 600,000 écus in cash as a contribution to the ransom for his future father-in-law.

In terms of the conservation of the dynasty, as we already know, male heirs were preferred. Whereas daughters received dowries, it was necessary to ensure so-called appanages for the sons. To the honour of King John II, it must be said that before he sent three of his sons as hostages to England in his place, he endowed them with titles and estates in due course. Like in Bohemia, also in France the permanent incomes of the king predominantly came form his direct domain. The territories where the French kings executed their power through

122/ For more on this, see Contamine, 'Essai sur la place des «XII pairs»', pp. 53–70.

their officials, the so-called *baillis* and *sénéchaux*, traditionally included Central France (Île de France), further Normandy and Champagne, around 1360 but also in other periods Picardy in the north, royal Burgundy in the south east, three *sénéchaussées* (seneschalships) in Languedoc (Toulouse, Carcassonne and Beaucaire) in the south and also a number of scattered estates which need not be listed. A sort of special component of the royal domain were the so-called appanages, with annuities and delegated rights for the male members of the wider royal family.

Before their departure to exile in London, as was already indicated, John II the Good took care of his sons, who truly did not feel like leaving France. The second-born Louis (1339–1384), who had already been Count of Anjou since 1350, received the county of Maine in addition to this appanage, with both having been raised to duchies-peerages. For another of his sons John (1340–1416), the king created a new appanage, the duchy-peerage of Berry and Auvergne, as a replacement for the county of Poitiers abdicated to the English. Finally, the third hostage Philip (1342–1404), for whom Burgundy had been sought for the future, became Duke of Touran in the autumn of 1360. Not even these just mentioned dukes were a sufficient guarantee for Edward III, and thus numerous feudal lords had to go to England with them and from the royal family the brother of John II, Duke Philip of Orléans, and their common brother-in-law Louis, Duke of Bourbon. If we name some of the members of the royal family more often than others, it is *inter alia* because we are preferentially following the actors of the great summit in January 1378.

Only after all the hostages had sworn a peace oath in Calais in the presence of both kings was John II released. Even Dauphin Charles came to greet both sovereigns. He had no reason to stay long. He still did not want to have anything to do with the peace treaty of Brétigny. In addition, as of 29 October, when his father was released, he stopped being Regent and was once again only Duke of Normandy and ruler of the Dauphiné. Of course, that was not a little, but the old-new men around the king, headed by the influential Archbishop Guillaume de Melun, along with his father made it clearer for him everyday that he had lost all of his former powers. The king began to rule again still before his arrival in Paris. Right after All Saints' Day, he appointed the president of his Chamber of Accounts (*Chambre des comptes*), two days later he established the 'grand council', of whose eight members only John II, Count of Saarbrücken, was close to the dauphin. This was followed by the nominations of the six justices of the Chamber of Petitions (*Chambre des requêtes*), six officials of the Chamber of Accounts as well as further court functionaries. Since all of these buckled down to work, the king could issue the extremely important ordinance in Compiègne on the introduction of a new currency already on 5 December, which under the name 'franc' lasted until recently. In Calais as well as at the ceremonial entrance into Paris on 13 December 1360, the second wife of the king, Joan of Boulogne, was missing, as she had died of the plague at the end of September.

31. Bonne, daughter of Charles V († 1360), head of the statue from the moment created around 1364 perhaps by John of Liège

Before John II could take up residence in the Palace de la Cité in Paris, Dauphin Charles had to leave it. The influential men of his father's grand council, in which there was no room for him, also saw to an adequate impoverishment of his external representation. For the years to come, the dauphin had to satisfy himself with a court numbering a mere one hundred and eighty people. Additionally, all of his court offices were correspondingly reduced. Nevertheless, he retained among his three first gentlemen of the chamber men who would stand by his side also in the future. Other than Adam de Melun, they were the brothers Jean and Bureau de la Rivière. Luckily, the dauphin managed to buy a residence (Hôtel) in the Saint-Pol quarter, advantageously located at the quay on the right bank of the Seine, which he gradually started to reconstruct into his magnificent residence. The sudden fall from the glory of power was accompanied also by family tragedy. On Thursday, 12 November, the dauphin buried two daughters, who had died in quick succession, at the Cistercian Abbey at Saint-Antoine-des-Champs. The younger Bonne, named after her Luxemburg-Přemyslid grandmother, was captured with a touchingly childlike expression by an excellent sculptor, perhaps Jean de Liège himself. Sentiment was rare in the royal family, which is why the testimony in the *Great Chronicles of France* on the pain which the dauphin was then experiencing deserves attention.

Dauphin and Duke of Normandy Charles spent the next three years in his father's shadow. Hence, only a few dates are enough to bring us closer to the moment when the wheel of fortune suddenly raised him. At the beginning of the 1360s, a twin calamity struck the broad regions of France. In 1360, a second wave of plague epidemics began to rage in the north, which within a year spread through central France to Aquitaine in the south. In some places, no less terrible were the effects of the robber bands of the so-called 'Great Company'. They could not be faced even by the royal army, which in April 1362 suffered an embarrassing defeat in the Battle of Brignais. King John II the Good, as if he did not have other worries, received from the hand of the new pope Urban V (1362–1370) at the end of May 1363 the leadership commission for the planned crusade expedition having as its goal, like so many times in the past, the capture of Jerusalem. Still at the end of the same year, he convened the estates-general in Amiens, after which he however entirely unexpectedly decided for a journey to London. According to some historiographers, he departed to preserve the honour of France, which had been damaged

32. Tombstone of Pope Urban V (1362–1370). Detail from the tomb in the Church of St Martial in Avignon, today's Musée du Petit Palais

by the wanton act of his son Louis of Anjou. He and his brothers were bored in England and so began to negotiate with Edward III on the conditions of their early release. King Edward in part accommodated their requests at the end of 1362 under the condition that he receive the delayed annual payment of 200,000 gold francs. That was not a little, and so the oldest of the brothers went with an armed guard to France to procure the given sum. As soon as he had disembarked in Calais, however, he used the first opportunity to escape. With the aid of his young wife, he then sought refuge in his castle Guise close to the borders of the Empire. Other historiographers judge King John's intention more soberly and conclude that he wanted to negotiate more acceptable conditions of a mutual settlement with Edward III in person. At any rate, King John II the Good left France on 2 January 1364 with a partial payment of 107,000 gold francs. He never saw his country again, because he unexpectedly died in London on 8 April 1364.

France during the Reign of Charles V the Wise

The reader may not be surprised anymore that at the beginning as well as the end of this chapter Emperor Charles IV will be reunited with his homonymous French nephew. Whereas in the first case, we shall travel back a little and fill in what we have omitted, in the second case we shall only indicate what preceded the summit of January 1378 on the French side. Whenever Dauphin Charles needed advice in a crisis situation, he sought assistance and advice from his uncle. The observation of Françoise Autrand concerns the last months of 1362, when the dauphin learnt from his brother Louis of the oppressive conditions of the treaty on the ransom as well as of the undignified position of his siblings in English captivity. As soon as it had become known that the emperor was headed from Nuremberg to the western borders of the Empire, the dauphin sent his chamberlain Count of Saarbrücken to him with a request for a meeting. Since the emperor intended to spend Christmas in Luxembourg, it was not a problem for him to accept an invitation to the nearby Mouzon, a fortress of the Archbishop of Rheims but on imperial territory. The meeting took place in the first days of January 1363, attended by the already-mentioned Count of Saarbrücken, Archbishop Jean de Craon and the dauphin's confidant Louis d'Évreux, Count of Étampes. The archbishop's mediation may suggest that this mission was instigated by King John II, but we cannot claim it with certainty. Neither do the sources indicate by as much as a word what was discussed in Mouzon. The emperor undoubtedly had an interest in a joint approach against the brigandish freebooters who threatened the safety of the routes and residences in Alsace, but it was hardly the primary reason for the meeting on the part of his nephew.[123]

THE FIRST STEPS OF THE NEW KING

Dauphin Charles did not learn of his father's death until nine days later, on 17 April 1364 at the castle Goulet near Vernon. Although he assumed government on that day, two indispensible acts had to occur according to ancient tradition before he could become the lawful King Charles, the fifth of this

123/ For the latest on the meeting of both Charleses in Mouzon, see Kavka, *Vláda Karla IV.*, I, p. 193 with the references to the literature in Note 47, and Autrand, *Charles V. Le Sage*, pp. 445–446.

name in the line of French sovereigns: the funeral of the dead sovereign and the coronation of his successor. In this interim, the successor to the throne did not have a seal yet and all of the state political affairs were conducted by the grand council along with several of the most influential men of the court offices. It had no reason to rush, because it was executing the power for the king, who until his funeral had not ceased to rule. All that the dauphin had to promise Archbishop Guillaume de Melun and the other members of his father's council, what obligations he took upon himself, can partially be identified but not entirely covered.

A month after the death of King John II, it was no longer possible to postpone the funeral rites. In the abbey at Saint-Antoine-des-Champs, the embalmers dressed the king's body in a robe interlaced with gold, placed him on a bier, put a crown with lilies upon his head and adjusted his face to express tranquil rest. On Sunday, 5 May, the funeral cortège escorted the king to the Cathedral of Notre-Dame. The next day after celebrating the Requiem Mass, the cortège again took to the streets of Paris. It was led by the three sons of the king again, the successor Charles, Louis of Anjou and Duke Philip, who were accompanied by King Peter I of Cyprus (Pierre de Lusignan). Another son of the king, Duke John of Berry, still remained in London as a hostage and thus could not attend the funeral. The denizens of the metropolis bade farewell to King John at the Hospital of Saint Lazarus, from whence his body was transferred to Saint-Denis. Only after the requiem and sealing of the tomb on the subsequent day, 7 May 1364, could Charles V assume his reign and accept the tributes of the peers and barons present. However, he could acquire the supernatural healing power which for a longer period had raised French kings above other Christian rulers only through the sacramental anointment during the coronation.

Two essential elements of the ceremonial rite in the Cathedral in Rheims were already stipulated in the coronation orders preserved from the thirteenth century. The first of them, the so-called anointment (*Sacre*), had given its name also to the actual, subsequent coronation.[124] It was precisely from the anointment with oil that the kings of France drew their miraculous power. It was not a common oil, which sufficed for the anointment of the Queen, but oil from the Holy Ampoule, which according to the legendary tradition had been brought by the Holy Spirit in the form of a dove to Bishop St Remigius (Rémy) in 496 for the christening of King of the Franks Clovis. In the fourteenth century, a similar miraculous power was also claimed by the English monarchy, which was risky considering the renewed claims of Edward III to the French throne.

124/ For more details on that, see O'Meara, *Monarchy and Consent*, Chapter 2.

It was also for this reason that learned circles at Charles V's court as well as he himself devoted extraordinary care to strengthening the legend, from which also the special position of the French sovereign as the most Christian king of them all began to be derived. It is expressive in and of itself that Charles V's renowned library had in its holdings a total of nine manuscripts treating the coronation orders not only in France but also in England and in the Empire. One of them was also the *Treatise on Anointment* (*Traité du Sacre*), which had been written by the Carmelite friar Jean (Jehan) Golein at the instigation of Charles V. Nevertheless, what was to have the greatest weight for the future was the ceremonial scroll of 1380 for the Rheims Chapter, in which Charles V practically officially confirmed his own miraculous healing power and that of all the French kings. It lay, as supposedly had been demonstrated on countless persons, in the mere touch of the royal hand healing the sick, predominantly children, beleaguered by so-called King's Evil (scrofula). It can be added with bitter irony that this miraculous touching by the hand did not work for gout or other diseases from which Charles V himself suffered.[125]

The coronation of the king and queen, which occurred with the participation of many extraordinary guests on 22 May 1364, took place in the usual, yet in the given circumstances exceptionally ceremonial peace,[126] because two days earlier Charles' commander Bertrand du Guesclin had defeated at Cocherel in Normandy the army of Charles II the Bad, which was led by the no less famous warrior and one of the victors from Maupertuis Jean de Grailly, Captal de Buch. It was one of the few victories of Bertrand du Guesclin, who despite his constant defeats became the greatest French hero of the Hundred Years' War. The court poet Eustache Deschamps even added him to cult of the Nine Worthies of the Old Testament and History (i.e. the Hebrew heroes: Joshua, David, Judas Maccabeus, the Christian heroes: Charlemagne, Arthur, and Godfrey of Bouillion, and the pagan heroes: Hector, Alexander the Great, and Julius Caesar).[127] It is noteworthy that at the end of September of the same year du Guesclin fell into English captivity after the lost Battle of Auray, which for many years decided the fate of war-beaten Brittany. In the battle, Charles of Blois, supported by King John II the Good, fell. The ducal crown in Brittany thus fell into the lap of the young John of Montfort, who had been raised in England under the tutelage of Edward III. Charles V played his cards well and,

125/ On the miraculous healing power of the French kings, see the breakthrough work by Bloch, *Les rois thaumaturges*, and there esp. pp. 136–140; the medical record of Charles V was compiled by Autrand, *Charles V. Le Sage*, pp. 472–481.

126/ On the coronation order of Jeanne de Bourbon, see O'Meara, *Monarchy and Consent*, Chapter 4.

127/ See i.a. Minois, *Du Guesclin*, pp. 195–199. The basic data and literature are provided in *Lexikon des Mittelalters*, III, cols 1440–1442.

33. Charles V hands a sword to Constable Bertrand du Guesclin. Les Grandes Chroniques de France (BL, Ms. Cotton Nero E II, fol. 220v)

when it was clear that the war was not going anywhere, he concluded a peace with John of Montfort in Guérande on 12 April 1365 and recognised him as the Duke of Brittany, who, to the displeasure of his English protector, formally paid feudal homage to Charles.

Also the further steps of the new king indicated that he did not want to rule merely under the pressure of circumstances. Not until later, however, did his new sovereign conception come forth, which lay in shifting the brunt of the battles with the brigands and centrifugal forces from the centre to the peripheral duchies. In a certain sense, Charles V thus built upon the measures of his father. Since his numerous brothers had received profitable appanages, they were to be connected with responsibilities to the French Crown. Duke John of Berry, who was still in England as a hostage, could not be counted on until his return. On the other hand, the succession crisis in the Free County of Burgundy needed to be resolved as soon as possible. In this respect, Charles V did not hesitate and within the intentions of his father raised his brother Philip to the ducal throne there on 31 May 1364. This enraged King of Navarre Charles the Bad to the greatest extreme, as he had never stopped asserting his claims in England as well as elsewhere to the succession after the immature Philip of Rouvres, who had died in 1361. Consequently, the king's brother had large worries in his princely appanage, which partially subsided only in the spring of 1365. Then, after a long negotiation, an agreement was reached between the two kings. In exchange for ceding the important city of Montpellier, Charles V obtained the nearer fortified towns of Mantes and Meulan as well as the county of Longueville. However, it soon came to light that also the king's brother Louis of Anjou claimed his right to Montpellier. This triggered prolonged disputes, which were concluded many years later by a peace in Vernon (1371).

Even greater problems arose in the north in Flanders, which appertained to the Kingdom of France but whose towns with their economic interests were dependent on good relations with England, from whence *inter alia* the wool for the local advanced cloth making was imported. The only heir of the ruling duke Louis II of Maele was originally chosen for the prematurely dead duke of Burgundy Philip of Rouvres. After the demise of her groom, immediately two royal sons competed for the hand of Margaret, as the princess was named. One was the designated Duke of Burgundy Philip of the Valois family; the second was Edmond of Langley, Earl of Cambridge since 1362 and later Duke of York. Edward III acted with his typical decisiveness and after the death of his rival John II the Good quickly negotiated the marriage for Edmund, hence they were hand in glove on 10 October 1364. It was a serious threat for France, because Margaret inherited *inter alia* also the county of Artois. French diplomacy deftly seized the only trump left to it, namely the illegitimacy of the marriage as a result of the close kinship of the betrothed pair. The war of the diplomats at the court of Avignon was to drag on for several years. In the meantime, however, Charles V could after all celebrate on 1 December 1364 the considerable success of his alliance politics, which was the wedding of his twenty-year-old sister Marie to Robert of Bar, the holder of the recently raised duchy on the border between France and the Empire of Emperor Charles IV.

IN THE GRIP OF BRIGAND TROOPS AND SMALL WARFARE

The treaty concluded in Brétigny in 1360 established a peace that lasted many years, but fighting continued in all of France. In Normandy, this everyday small war was to be blamed on the Navarrese party of Charles II the Bad, whereas everywhere else it was a form of sustenance for brigand military troops (*compagnies*). The breakdown of central power after the crushing defeat of France at Poitiers, the English conquests, the Parisian revolt as well as peasant rebellions all played into the hands of the leaders of the mercenaries, who acted similarly to the contemporary Italian *condottieri*. Their life was more important to them than anything else; they had no ideals; they did not hesitate to use any means against the defenceless and weaker. Their word could not be trusted; they maintained their position by terror, fires, murder as well as poison. The same applied also to their men. They included both knights and free-lancers without service and learned clerics as well as other life failures. They all had war as their occupation in common, and when there was no one to pay them, they had to help themselves.

It is necessary to add to this simple, too straightforward explication that ruthless behaviour of the noble as well as common warriors was to a certain extent a consequence of the conception of war in the decayed ideology of contemporary knighthood. War for these men had a predominantly individualist motivation. Each pursued adventure, joining battle at tournaments as well as on the battlefields for his own honour. For everything that he gained, he might pay with his own life. Mercenary pay from the royal treasury did not suffice; it was irregular and mostly short term. In no way could it be compared with the profit from captured booty and especially from the ransom of a wealthy prisoner. Ransom quickly became popular and gradually became higher in France from the second half of the fourteenth century. We saw in the case of King John II the Good and his sons that it was a profitable war trade even for crowned heads. On the other hand, not even the king was generally, without a special contract, obliged to cover monetary damages for his commanders. What was primarily required was obedience to one's leader as well as solidarity with him; he, on the other hand, was to cover lost horses or weapons if it was within his powers. The circle thus closes, because other than by small brigand warfare it was not possible to get their money's worth.

Unlike with professional warriors, living off of booty and ransom, the opinion prevailed in the urban milieu that it was better to kill the enemy than capture him. In an extreme form, this approach was applied by both sides in the Jacquerie, when even the aristocrats forsook their way of battle. Under the rule of Charles V, new methods and means were sought step by step to strengthen internal security and to dislodge the English gradually from the occupied territory. Among other things, the bonds of warriors in a service relationship were reinforced, and they then surrendered parts of their independence in return for the advantages provided. Instead of the ideal of the knight fighting for himself, another conception of the noble warrior gradually emerged, namely of one who was perpetually ready to stand by his king's side, particularly in case of war and other dangers. The switch to the better-paid service of the enemy was ever more considered as treason, specifically both in connection with reinforcing discipline and with the increasing emphasis on the common interests of France and of the emerging national society.[128]

128/ For more on that, see Contamine, *Guerre, État et société*, pp. 195–198.

Much of what has been suggested by the last lines remained a pious wish in the second half of the fourteenth century. Also the rulers themselves of the individual territories had a great share of the responsibility for the incessant sprees of the thieving military troops and for the devastation of the majority of the regions of the French north as well as the south. An example more revealing than others may be the career of a certain Arnaut de Cervole, originally from Périgord, whose nickname 'The Archpriest' (*l'Archiprêtre*) suggests that he once had something in common with this ecclesiastical benefice. Nonetheless, Arnaut seems not to have been a priest who had deserted his profession, because he married, received the blessing of the pope and was a guest at the table of several Avignon cardinals. His military career began in 1351 in the service of Constable Charles d'Espagne (Charles de la Cerda) and ended in May 1366, when he was murdered by one of his own cavalrymen. During the entire time, he did not win any significant battle, yet the crowned heads kept bribing him and everyone wanted to be on good terms with him. He established his reputation as an unscrupulous military entrepreneur through his violent acts, betrayals as well as frauds already in the 1350s. At the beginning of the next decade, he managed to merge various troops in the north of Burgundy into one Great Company (*Grande compagnie*), with which he set out to the south near Avignon. Pope Innocent VI at first announced a crusade against him, but then willingly paid the enormous sum of 14,500 gold florins as mercenary pay for a part of the Company for the war against the Milanese Visconti dynasty. The rest of Arnaut's men-at-arms, however, continued to ravage the villages and hamlets in Provence without restraint.[129]

It fit the dark atmosphere of the period that neither the pope nor the secular rulers were able to prevent the plunder of their lands otherwise than by mustering the military troops into neighbouring as well as distant lands. In 1362, there was a glimmer of hope that some companies would be sent to Hungary as the vanguard of a crusade, which was continuously promoted by King of Cyprus Peter of Lusignan with the help of the Papal Curia. This intention re-emerged three years later during the visit of Emperor Charles IV in Avignon. The emperor also advocated sending the bands to fight against the Turks, because they had ravaged Burgundy as well as other imperial territories in recent years. The King of Hungary was asked to cooperate in this aim, and a special delegation also headed for the Parisian court of Charles V. Should it be necessary for members of the companies to embark from Venice or other Italian ports, Charles IV bound himself according to one not very reliable testimony to contribute half of the incomes of the Kingdom of Bohemia for three

129/ The career of this warrior was described by Autrand, *Charles V. Le Sage*, pp. 494–498.

years to cover the costs. Arnaut de Cervole again showed what he was capable of. Under the pretext that he was coming in the name of the emperor, he and his troops invaded Alsace and at the beginning of July 1365 penetrated as far as Strasbourg, where Emperor Charles IV was just stopping on his return journey from Avignon. That was not all. After Arnaut collected protection money in Alsace and took what he could from the villagers, he headed for southern Germany. Since the negotiations with him were not leading to their goal, the emperor amassed regiments from the imperial towns and with the assistance of the archbishop of Trier pushed Arnaut's companies all the way back to Colmar at the end of July.[130]

Since the large cities began to defend themselves and there was nothing left to take in the rural areas, the Great Company divided into smaller troops, which then operated in both parts of Burgundy and in Champagne. When Count of Savoy Amadeo (Amadeus) VI began to organise a crusade at the beginning of 1366, Arnaut and his people saw in that a new opportunity to push into Germany. Before that could happen, 'The Archpriest' was killed. The Great Company quickly fell apart without its respected leader. Its smaller bands did not cease their ruinous activities, but they ever more collided with the renewing court system in France. The hand of justice began to fall upon individual brigand commanders and their companions as well as jackals. Minor looting stopped paying in France, so the bands started to shift gradually to Spain and elsewhere. In our summary, it is not possible to describe all of the twists and misdeeds of the Archpriest's career and hence even less possible to map the harmful activities of other robber barons, like a certain Seguin de Badefol on the English-ruled territory, who gained control of a wide area around Lyons in 1365. Even so it was evident in how onerous a situation 'sweet' France was under King John II the Good and at the beginning of the reign of Charles V the Wise. The many-headed hydra was not surrendering, but its grip had already relaxed.

THE RENEWAL OF STATE ADMINISTRATION

The new sovereign on the French throne was not a born warrior. His physical ailments as well as his spiritual disposition predestined that he take the Scales of Justice in hand rather than the sword, but it would have been impossible without a well-functioning state administration. Let us put aside the doubts of whether it is possible to speak of a state in the modern sense of the word yet. How else can we label the complex conglomerate of feudal duchies and counties, appanages, ecclesiastical estates and direct royal goods? After all,

130/ Further details can be found in Kavka, *Vláda Karla IV.*, II, pp. 24–26.

the rudiments of the modern state were hatching precisely under Charles V, namely the first in the fiscal area. All of the essential taxes of the Old Regime (*Ancien Régime*) before the French Revolution in 1789 had their roots in 1360–1370: first and foremost, the indirect taxes of five percent on sold goods (*aides*), further the tax on cultivated grapes as well as draught wine (*banalités*), the tax on salt (*gabelle*) and last but not least the hearth tax (*fouage*, i.e. the tax on every household with a hearth), which under Charles V was expanded from towns to rural residences. Unlike the permanent incomes coming from the direct royal domain, all of these new taxes were initially considered to be extraordinary, because they were collected through individual bishoprics in the entire kingdom.

It is more than surprising that the French of that time on the whole paid the ascribed taxes. According to F. Autrand, they did not do so happily; nevertheless, they were forced to comply by the common defence against the English invasions and brigand troops.[131] The collection of taxes was one thing, but the division of their profits was a different affair, in which the estates community had a primary interest. Although the role of the estates-general had significantly declined after the suppression of Étienne Marcel's uprising, the awareness of the need to control those finances of the king in which everyone contributed lingered. The king's right to give was not denied in this, but it was hindered whenever it was against the 'general good'. For the administration of extraordinary taxes, a three-member college of treasurers-general (*trésoriers généraux*) was thus established in 1360 for ransom affairs, which was joined by another college three years later, in charge of the expenditures for the defence of the country. At the assembly of the estates-general in December 1369, not only the amounts of the tax obligations but also the administration of their revenues were newly amended. Both bodies were joined in one college, the college of the so-called counsellors-general (*conseillers généraux*), which in its complete composition had twelve members: three represented the high clergy, six the military aristocracy and three were selected from the experienced burgher financiers. The real power of these supreme counsellors was indeed exceptional, and it is therefore no surprise that a number of them were members of the royal council or eminent court officials.

The anointment with oil from the Holy Ampoule gave Charles V absolute, and until his death irreplaceable legitimacy, which protected him even from possible rivals from his own family. Charles was now the king 'chosen' by God, but also simultaneously by those men of his father's former regime who had helped him to the throne. Their positions remained unshaken for many years, which was true primarily for Chancellor Jean de Dormans and Guillaume de

131/ Autrand, *Charles V. Le Sage*, Chapter XXVIII, the cited statement is on p. 676; see further Cazelles, *Société politique*, Chapter XLIV.

34. Jean de Dormans (†1373) chancellor of Charles V. A recumbent effigy (gisant) originally in the chapel of the college in Beauvais, today in the Musée du Louvre

Melun, occupant of the archiepiscopal throne in Sens. It was not by mere coincidence that their younger brothers could be found in their proximity, as such nepotism was facilitated by the high offices of both men. The careers of Jean and Guillaume de Dormans prove that even the sons of a lower royal official could achieve a high post through a legal education and their own abilities. Jean was obliged for his rapid rise to the influential cardinal Guy de Boulogne, who had procured an ecclesiastical benefice for him in Meaux and Soissons. He became Bishop of Beauvais in 1361, when he also assumed the Office of Chancellor. The cardinal's hat crowned his career in 1368, but he remained in historical awareness primarily as the founder of the famous college intended for the education of royal notaries, secretaries and officials of the Court of Justice. Guillaume de Dormans was, on the other hand, the Chancellor of the Dauphiné, which already made him close to Charles V even before his accession to the throne. Both brothers died in 1373 and until their deaths occupied exceptional positions in the royal council.[132]

According to Raymond Cazelles, Archbishop Guillaume de Melun with his energy as well as foresight helped lead France through the catastrophes and pitfalls of the 1360s to the renewal and consolidation of the administrative system. He was undoubtedly an able politician. He served two kings and managed to secure for his brother a profitable office overseeing the waters and forests of the entire kingdom. On the other hand, he need not be ascribed only merits and both kings the failures of French policy of the third quarter of the fourteenth century. Among other things, there is no reason to see in him the only author of the edict of August 1374, through which both the order of succession after the dead king was enacted and the lower limit of the successor's age at the time of succession set at thirteen years and one day. For Charles V, this act was exceptionally important, because *inter alia* it ensured the dauphin's legitimate succession and completely exempted women from it. And seeing that the king was still present as the dauphin at the ceremonial declaration of the

132/ On the career of the two brothers from Dormans, see Autrand, *Charles V. Le Sage*, pp. 702–707.

Golden Bull, it can rightly be supposed that the legislative activity of his uncle Charles IV served as a model for him.[133]

Besides his father's counsellors, whose power positions he had to respect, Charles V was surrounded by a smaller retinue of assistants and friends who had shared the good and bad with him for years. The highest position among them was held by Archbishop of Rheims Jean de Craon, whose greatest satisfaction was when he could place the royal crown on the dauphin's head. Charles V had from his childhood been closest to his cousin Louis d'Évreux, Count of Étampes, who had faithfully stood at his side for decades. They fell out shortly before the visit of the emperor, which is why we cannot find him among the participants of the summit of January 1378. On the other hand, the primary tasks at the emperor's visit were assigned to John II, Count of Saarbrücken († 1381). The origin of this man indicates that his county lay on the territory of the Empire and that he thus was a competent expert on the situation there. It was not by accident that we already encountered him at the negotiations between the dauphin and his uncle in Mouzon. Charles V renewed the court Office of High Steward for him and among others entrusted him with the presidency of the Chamber of Accounts (*Chambre des comptes*).

In the Account on the visit of Emperor Charles IV in France, we will encounter further influential men of state and court organs. Bureau de la Rivière had been along with his elder brother Jean in the dauphin's retinue from 1358. Charles V raised both knights to the aristocratic estate and entrusted them with the honorary office of the First Gentlemen of the Chamber. Out of gratitude, they stood at his side and faithfully helped him with counsel as well as sword. Both brothers immediately participated in the war against the brigand troops, with Bureau even leading an army during the reconquest.[134] Neither can we omit Pierre d'Orgemont, a layman and one of the authors of the *Great Chronicles of France*, who assumed the Office of the Chancellor in November 1373 after Guillaume de Dormans. One would assume that the king would select his chancellor himself. The reality was however different, Charles V certainly proposed his candidate, but his nomination was confirmed in his absence by a vote of the Grand Council, which consisted of a total of 130 dignitaries, beginning with members of the royal family and ending with high court officials. Pierre d'Orgemont obtained one hundred and five votes, from which it is clear that the voting was not a formal procedure.[135] In the last years of his reign, Charles V increasingly used the services of Jean Le Mercier, a member of the

133/ On the model of the Golden Bull, see Autrand, *Charles V. Le Sage*, pp. 627–629.
134/ See Cazelles, *La société politique*, pp. 546–547 and further follow the glossary, and Autrand, *Charles V. Le Sage*, pp. 699–702.
135/ On this selection of the highest officials, see Cazelles, *Société politique*, pp. 509–510.

35. Charles V in prayer. Parement de Narbonne, detail, painting on silk, around 1375

college of supreme councillors. We shall also hear of a number of other courtiers closest to the king, whether of Pierre de Chevreuse, a member of the council and Master of the Royal Household or of the royal librarian Gilles Malet.

From the end of 1375, Charles V was increasing his personal share in the government step by step. A considerable role in this was played by the prolonged illness and death of Archbishop Guillaume de Melun, the most influential man of his council, and the loss of the position of his brother Jean de Melun connected with this. If the remarks of the council and its recommendations were already relatively rare in the previous years, now they almost stop. The king predominantly ruled from his private residence, whereby the people connected with the King's Chamber (*Chambre du roi*), i.e. with regular visitors to his reception hall, gained greater importance.[136] This does not imply that the council did not meet or was not convoked during entirely exceptional cases. The visit of Emperor Charles IV was one of them, apart from fact that not even the most distant members of the council would have missed such an exceptional summit. The Account directly names some of the king's counsellors and explicitly states that the king convoked the council in his chamber when the emperor received a delegation from the University of Paris in the Louvre. On this occasion, the king also convened the council on the following day, i.e. Friday, 8 January. The Account describes in detail the course of the session, during which the king explained the principles of the French foreign policy to the emperor, and names some of the participants: 'From the people of the king's council, there were his chancellor, Archbishop of Rheims, the bishops of Laon, Paris, Beauvais and Bayeux, the abbot of Saint-Vaast and other clerics as well as laity both from the king's council and from the parliament as well as elsewhere.' Since the emperor requested time to consider it, the council heard his response on Saturday 9 January. Even more members of the council met than had the day before, but the Account does not mention their names.[137]

There do not seem to have been many more prelates sitting in the council. Those who had benefices outside of Paris and about whom the king cared would receive permanent residences in the metropolis from the king. This is the case of Nicolas Du Bosc, Bishop of Bayeux, and Jean Le Fèvre, the abbot of the monastery of Saint-Vaast in Arras. Both were, not by accident, doctors of law; the abbot, moreover, was a translator, poet and author of the memorandum *The Plaint of Bologna* (*De planctu bonorum*), in which he conducted polemics with Giovanni da Legnano on the topic of the return of the pope to Rome. It was no exception; we shall have more than one occasion to learn

136/ For more on the shift to the personal governance of Charles V and on his council after 1375, see Cazelles, *Société politique*, pp. 542–554.
137/ Delachenal (ed.), *Chronique des règnes*, II, pp. 249–251, 257 and below pp. 215–217.

about the intellectual atmosphere of Charles' court. It is also instructive to see who did not participate in the summit in January 1378 from the French side and why. It was first of all the king's younger brother Louis, Duke of Anjou. From 1364, he had been the commander-general in the south and had not associated much with the king, perhaps also because they were constantly dissatisfied with his administration in Montpellier and elsewhere. Neither can we find the famous warrior Bertrand du Guesclin in the French retinue. His influence had strongly declined, and despite his holding the Office of Constable from October 1370, everything important in the matters of war was decided by the college of supreme councillors, with whom he was at cross purposes.[138]

36. Queen Joanna of Bourbon. Parement de Narbonne, detail, painting on silk, around 1375

THE RECONQUEST OF LOST LANDS

Sunday, 3 December 1368 was especially significant for Charles V as well as for France. After three daughters, Queen Jeanne of Bourbon bore him the heir to the throne Charles, the news of which immediately spread all over the country. The royal chancellery was busy that day, because Charles V notified his 'good towns' in writing that he had addressed the just calls coming from Gascony. Not only on that territory but in all of Aquitaine, the resistance to the taxes that had been raised by Black Prince Edward to cover his enormous debts had been growing. The elderly Jean I, Count of Armagnac, former captain of John II the Good in Languedoc and faithful supporter of the royal side, had stepped to the head of the dissatisfied barons and towns. To accept the calls for defence against the tax policies of Prince Edward, who through the Peace of Brétigny had become the sovereign ruler in the surrendered territory, was already practically equal to a violation of the peace. The cold war changed into an open one when at the beginning of 1369 Duke Louis of Anjou started a mobilisation in Languedoc. At the end of April, the county of Ponthieu farther to the north was retaken and events then snowballed rapidly. In May 1369, the estates-general adopted with consent the king's decision to begin a war. King of England Edward III picked up the gauntlet that had been thrown and on 3 June renewed his claim to the French throne.

The military successes so enticed Charles V that along with his youngest brother Philip of Burgundy he started to prepare an invasion of England. Considering the situation in France, it was an imprudent, if not frankly harebrained, enterprise. A quick end to it was made by an English expedition under the leadership of John of Gaunt (Ghent), Duke of Lancaster. The younger son of King of England Edward III set out from Calais and did not end his devastating campaign along the coast until before the impregnable bulwarks of

138/ Cf. on this Minois, *Du Guesclin*, p. 357ff.

37. Military situation in France under Charles V

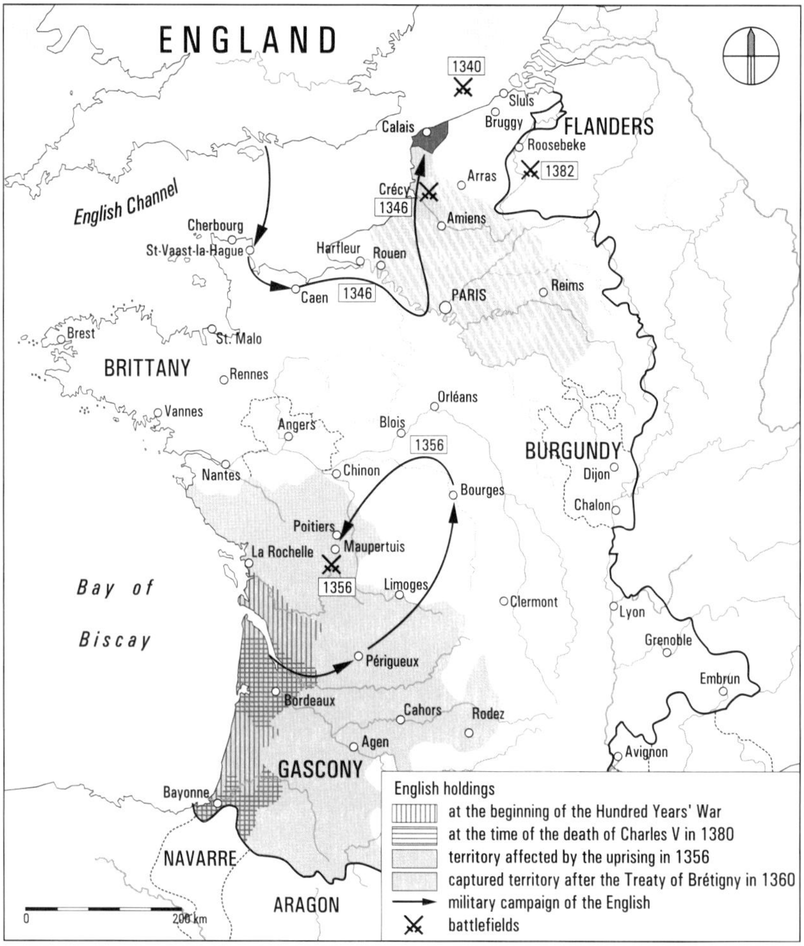

Harfleur, from which he turned back. The victorious approach of Duke Louis in the region of Guyenne was, however, so clear that Charles V no longer hesitated and on 30 November 1369 declared the confiscation of this duchy to the benefit of the French Crown.

In 1370, the war became harsher. In the first months, the French offensive fared better. The king's allies seized the lowland areas around the Garonne; Louis of Anjou did well in the south, and his younger brother Duke John of Berry with the assistance of the burghers there seized Angoulême, the residence of the Black Prince in Limousin. The seriously ill Edward requested the aid of his brothers and on 19 September won back Angoulême and mercilessly took revenge on the burghers as well as the garrison. A malignant illness, however, disqualified him from active service in which he had gained fame as one of the greatest knights of his age. In January 1371, he returned to England, which he did not leave until his death five years later.

Nevertheless, the main military event of 1370 became the summer campaign of roughly four thousand English mounted men-at-arms and bowmen led by the knight Robert Knowles, a seasoned commander from the times of the brigand troops. At the end of July, the invading army set out from Calais towards Amiens and from there past Rheims to Troyes. Knowles' people did not waste their time capturing large towns; they satisfied themselves with protection money and despite the rapid progress they were able to destroy a wide strip of rural land along the path of their march. From Burgundy, they unexpectedly turned to the west towards Paris, in front of whose gates they pitched camp on 22 September for two days. On sleepless nights, Charles V watched the flaming suburbs from his residence in Saint-Pol. As Knowles did not have enough forces to capture the metropolis, he tried to provoke the enemy into open battle. Despite the insistence of several counsellors, Charles V did not allow himself to be goaded, so there was nothing else for the English to do but turn around and continue in the destructive campaign to Brittany, where their army dissipated into several independently operating hordes.

The reaction of the period chroniclers to the actions of the king, who would hardly leave his room and yet was pushing the English step by step out of the country, is generally forbearing. Considering the physical weakness and chronic illnesses, he could no longer stand at the head of the army, and so after all even his interest in reading on the whole corresponded to the behaviour of the 'wise' sovereign.[139] Nevertheless, someone had to wield the commander's sword, as a result of which on 2 October 1370 Charles V at the assembly of the Great Council appointed as Constable of France Bertrand du Guesclin, who appears on the pages of history textbooks a little undeservedly as the only and main hero of the reconquest. The Great Council also expressed its agreement with establishing a war collection, in which chiefly only the denizens of large and smaller towns contributed. The constable's operations in Brittany did not end in an impressive victory but on the whole secured the territories that had been retaken in the last two years.

In the following year, 1371, Charles of Navarre, who had withdrawn to his Pyrenean kingdom for many years, reappeared on the French political scene. The renewal of the war forced him to defend the estates in Normandy. After landing in Cherbourg in August 1369, he endeavoured by military means as well as by negotiations to force the English captains into peace treaties. As was his custom, Charles II 'the Bad' also sought contacts with both warring kings. At the Parisian court, this effort was received with great distrust, which was nurtured especially by Duke Louis of Anjou, but later the desire for peace prevailed, and, after a numerous group of hostages was released, a stately meeting of the two kindred Charleses took place in Vernon in spring 1371. If noth-

139/ The voices of the contemporary chroniclers were accumulated by Autrand, *Charles V. Le Sage*, pp. 568–569.

ing else, France had one fewer enemy. Nonetheless, it still needed to be wary. A certain danger for example was presented by the possibility that Edward III would recruit mercenaries from the territory of the Empire. To prevent this from happening, Charles V sent Bishop of Paris Aimery de Magnac and the former governor of the Dauphiné Raoul de Vienne, Sire de Louppy, to his uncle. Both envoys were granted an audience in the armorial chamber of Prague Castle on 1 April 1372. During the audience, Bishop Aimery delivered the letter from his king and in his address appealed to the friendly ties between the Luxemburgs and the Valois dynasty. The prudent emperor probably did not commit himself to anything, but the fears of the French court were unfulfilled.[140]

Cherbourg meant a significant loss for the English, because the lost naval bases began to be recaptured in the subsequent period. Significant help in this respect was the victory of the Castilian fleet, which defeated the English galleys on the open seas before the port of La Rochelle in June 1372. King of Castile Henry II of Trastámara was induced to renew the traditional alliance with France by the aggressive policies of Prince John of Gaunt, who already saw himself as the crowned head of Castile and León. The isolation of the port was so hermetic that it forced the citizenry to surrender in September. This made the journey from Calais to Bordeaux much more difficult and longer for the English. Additionally, since Constable du Guesclin with the shadow cooperation of Duke John of Berry entered Poitiers at the beginning of August, one of the important counties lying between the Loire and the Garonne was regained for the confederation of the French Crown. The next in line now was Brittany, which was occupied in large part by du Guesclin, himself a Breton by origin, with the assistance of the aristocracy there in April and May 1373.

The English response was not long in coming. In the summer, as had become a rule in the recent years, Edward III sent another invading army to the mainland, whose leadership he this time entrusted to John of Gaunt, otherwise the duke of Lancaster (1340–1399).[141] At first it seemed that Knowles' campaign to Paris would be repeated three years later. This time, however, the opponents of the defensive tactics gained the decisive word, so the duke was forced to take a diversion and from Troyes head as quickly as possible in a southerly direction through Limousin to Bordeaux. Nevertheless, not even now did the French change their way of conducting the war. The main principle was to avoid open battle, maintain contact with the enemy, weaken him and take him by surprise. It is difficult to decide which effect was dominant here,

140/ On the stay of the French delegation in Prague, see Delachenal, *Histoire*, IV: *1368–1377*, p. 403. Documents on the stay including a brief record of the bishop's speech were issued also in Delachenal (ed.), *Chronique des règnes*, III, Appendice, pp. 147–153.

141/ What is still valuable is the biography by Armitage-Smith, *John of Gaunt*, which also contains information on his great expedition that ended badly on pp. 104–117.

whether the unpropitious personal experience of Charles V from the Battle of Poitiers or his knowledge from reading the Roman theoretician Flavius Vegetius. In any case, he had a translation of his *Epitome of Military Science (Epitoma rei militaris)* in his library. Experts also accentuate the surprisingly reliable communication between the court and the operating armies.

Even though the campaign of Duke of Lancaster John of Gaunt came to nought, his army continued to be a serious calamity for a significant part of France, which was joined by floods in the north and further epidemics of plague in the centre of the country. Since not even the following year brought a change for the better, the war fever was subsiding on both sides of the English Channel. In March 1375, Count of Flanders Louis II of Maele mediated peace discussions in Bruges, after which a year-long ceasefire was concluded on 27 June, which was subsequently prolonged to 1377. The death of King Edward III on 21 June 1377 brought a renewal of war, because the English court once again, this time in the name of the ten-year-old successor to the throne Richard II, began to assert a claim to the French Crown. Nonetheless, until the end of the reign of Charles V, military operations did not change anything about the state before the calling of the ceasefire.

THE INTELLECTUAL ENVIRONMENT OF THE COURT

The calming on the battlefield and the subsequent ceasefire allowed a intensive legislative activity at the court of Charles V. In January 1374, the great ordinance on the Royal Army was issued, followed by a series of decrees regulating the currency as well as taxes; in August, the already-mentioned edict on the succession to the French throne was declared, which was subsequently complemented by further ordinances defining the appanages, rights as well as responsibilities of the king's brothers. All of the four dukes comprised not only the most important 'flowers of the lilies' but also a special element between the king and his direct domain on the one hand and the feudal aristocracy on the other. The new hierarchical composition was reflected also in the amount of incomes. Whereas the royal incomes in the 1370s reached as much as 1,650,000 gold francs, the appanages of Dukes John of Berry and Philip of Burgundy were less than half of that. The profits of Duke Louis of Anjou from his lands in the south were apparently higher while Duke of Bourbon's lower, whereas the incomes from the county fluctuated between ten and twelve thousand francs.[142] The redistribution of profits was connected with

142/ The authoritative data for the incomes and expenditures of the royal chamber in the final decades of the reign of Charles V are listed in Rey, *Le domaine du roi et les finances extraordinaires sous Charles VI*, cf. esp. pp. 38–39. Some other comparative amounts were added by Autrand, *Charles V. Le Sage*, p. 667.

38. Duke John of Berry at a banquet. Detail from the miniature of the month of January in the Très Riches Heures du Duc de Berry. (MC, ms. 65, fol. 1r)

the decentralisation of the administration as well as the judiciary, namely with a relatively strict adherence to the Aristotelian principles of 'good' and 'just' governance, which seeped into political practice from the scholarly environment of university professors as well as court legists or notaries.

It is significant that the fully developed self-awareness of the wealthy burghers and their active role at the assembly of the estates-general in 1356–1358 found support in the academically educated counsellors and speakers. For university theologians, jurists and philosophers, the principles of autonomy were part of daily life. No less common to them also were the theoretical theorems from Aristotle's treatises on politics, economics and ethics, with which they dealt discursively from all sides in abundant commentaries. The scholars in cap and gown provided the urban delegations with not only advice but also increased prestige. We should mention by name at least one of the theoreticians, Nicole Oresme, who certainly not by accident came to the head of the prestigious College of Navarre precisely at the beginning of October 1356. His *Treatise on Money* (*Traité des monnaies*) generalised the requirements for a stable currency and with an appeal to Aristotle raised the interests of the municipality over the arbitrary behaviour of the sovereign, who becomes a contemptible tyrant if he permits counterfeit or otherwise depreciated money. Behind all of these ideological agitations, it is necessary to see a longer term penetration of Roman-law principles as well as echoes of the works of non-conformist theoreticians at the court of Emperor Louis the Bavarian.[143]

Like many radical intellectuals before him and after him, Nicole Oresme soon learnt that the slogans about the 'will of the people' and 'general consensus' could have far-reaching repercussions in a socially tense atmosphere. Therefore, it comes as no surprise that already from the end of 1357 he stood on the side of those who rejected not only the conspiring of Marcel's insurgents with Charles of Navarre but also street and other violence. This stance brought Oresme closer to the group around Regent Charles, who progressively appointed him royal secretary, chaplain and counsellor. Charles wanted to know more about the opinions and ideas that the scholars constantly brandished and so he entrusted Oresme with the translation of the weightiest of Aristotle's treatises into French. This demanding work required a longer time, as a result of which the spectacularly illuminated translations of Aristotle's *Nicomachean Ethics*, *Politics* and *Economics* were not added to the royal library until after 1372. At the same time, Simon de Hesdin translated *Facta et dicta memorabilia* (Memorable Deeds and Sayings) by Valerius Maximus, Pierre

143/ From the extensive literature, I only list those works that interpret the scholastic treatises in connection with specific political-power development: Cazelles, *La société politique*, pp. 229ff. and 302–303, and Krynen, *L'empire du roi*, pp. 422–427.

Bersuire (Petrus Berchorius) translated the *Decades* of Livy, and Denis Foullechat translated *Policraticus* by John of Salisbury. The Carmelite Jean Golein augmented the royal library with several translations at once. At the instigation of Charles V, a total of almost thirty treatises by ancient as well as mediaeval authorities were translated.[144] These manuscript books were then copied and actually read, which is evidenced by the loans from the library of Charles V. In its time, it was an entirely exceptional collection, for which Charles V reserved special areas in his residences.

Shortly after Charles V decided in 1367 to transport his books from the urban Palace de la Cité to the Louvre, extensive reconstructions began on the three highest floors of the tower in the northwest wing of the château. According to the preserved fragments of the construction receipts, the walls on the first floor intended for the library were lined with wood imported from Ireland, and the vaulting was covered with cypress wood to warm the room.[145] Although the solid bookcases as well as swivel easels for the books had been brought along with the benches from the former library, craftsmen refurbished them here. In addition, all of the windows were equipped with brass bars for protection from the falcons and other birds from the neighbouring aviary. Thirty candelabra in the niches and one silver chandelier seem to have provided the readers with enough light. A new list of the books was compiled in 1377 by the properly appointed librarian Gilles Malet, otherwise Viscount de Corbeil († 1410 or 1411). At that time, the library already had around nine hundred rare volumes including thirty-two full Bibles and roughly sixty books with tractates by Greek as well as Arab physicians. In comparison with other private libraries, what is noteworthy is not only the number of manuscripts but also the high number, roughly one-third, of secular texts of legal, natural-science as well as astrological content. Given that craftsmen were paid forty francs in gold for work more closely unspecified in the library still in November 1377, it can be supposed that it was in connection with the upcoming visit of the Holy Roman Emperor and his son. Among the readers of the loaned books, we can find the names of not only the brothers of Charles V but also of many of his counsellors and courtiers.[146]

The reform proposals of the scholarly Aristotelians sounded more convincing to those that they authorised to participate in determining things

144/ On the reception of Aristotle through translations, see Sherman, *Imaging Aristotle*, pp. 1–12, here also at length on the translations of Nicolas Oresme, on whom see also i.a. Babbitt, *Oresme's 'Livre de Politiques'*.

145/ For initial orientation, see the catalogue of the exhibition from 1968 *La Librairie de Charles V*, pp. 45–46, and the exhibits on the subsequent pages. The accounting records were printed by Delisle, *Recherches sur la librairie de Charles V*, I, pp. 367–368.

146/ See Delisle, *Recherches sur la librairie de Charles V*, pp. 120–124 (loans and book gifts), whose second volume also contains a general inventory of more than one thousand volumes. For the latest on the content orientation of the library, see B. Carqué, *Stil und Erinnerung*, pp. 419–420.

which affected them than to those who were to share their powers. After the experience that Charles V had with the diets of the estates-general, it is not surprising that he called the last of them in 1369. On the other hand, Charles V considering his intellectual background did not want to and after all could not act as an autocrat. Oresme, for example, metaphorically depicted a tyrant as a human monster with a hideously large head, which his body could not carry. We already know that Charles V at the beginning of his reign had to rely, whether willingly or not, on the influential confidants of his father and that the administrative mechanism of the French state already required a qualified administration. It was for that reason that the king's council in both its narrower and wider composition had already before held the ruler's sovereignty within acceptable boundaries, which was tacitly accepted as generally beneficial, just like the confirmation of the royal officials 'by the parliament', i.e. the supreme court of justice. Numerous members of the council and the absolute majority of judiciary and court officials boasted university titles, which were not mere decorations. An influential group was formed also by the court notaries, who had their college in the new building of the monastery of the Celestines near the royal residence in the Saint-Pol quarter.

If the opinion that practical politics should be supported by book knowledge of a good and just government really predominated in the intellectual 'club' of Charles V, then it was to the merit of the scholarly treatises by Nicole Oresme and the fictitious dialogue between a cleric and a knight presented as if it had taken place during the author's dream in a fruit orchard. Both formal means, the dream as well as the dialogue, were very popular in mediaeval literature, because they made it possible to deal with equivocal or controversial issues openly. In France at the beginning of the 1370s, these included especially the relations between secular and spiritual power on the one hand and between France, England and the Empire on the other. It is generally presumed that Évrart de Trémaugon wrote his Latin work entitled *Somnium Viridarii* (*Dream of the Orchard*) at the direct impetus of Charles V sometime in 1372–1376. The author was Doctor of Laws and Bishop of Dol, so he cannot be suspected of anticlerical positions. Although he attempted rather to smooth than to inflame the disputes, it is still apparent in many places who commissioned the work and why. The translation into French (*Le Songe du Vergier*), which was completed roughly at the time of the emperor's visit to France at the turn of 1377 and 1378, shows a number of quite serious changes, which seem to have arisen from discussions in the court circle.[147]

147/ For initial information, cf. the introductions to the editions published by Schnerb-Lièvre, *Le Songe du Vergier*, I, Paris 1982, and *Somnium Viridarii*, I, Paris 1993.

The French version of *Dream of the Orchard* became a kind of sum of contemporary French political science. In terms of the relation to the church and papacy, it is already possible to perceive the dawn of so-called Gallicanism here, which principally rejected the pope's interventions into the internal affairs of France. Thanks to their anointment with oil from the Holy Ampoule, French kings, as we know, claimed a nearly sacral status, which endowed them with exceptional privileges in the administration as well as protection of ecclesiastical property. Moreover, the newly appearing formula labelling the French king as the 'most Christian' of all European sovereigns placed him prestigiously on the level or at the side of the Holy Roman Emperor. It was understood in and of itself that the French king was *de facto* the emperor as well, because in his land he had no one above him other than God. The court legates knew how to deal even with feudal obligations in the Dauphiné or elsewhere, so that their explanation only confirmed the sovereignty of Charles V and his successors. However, we must realise that the king was in the eyes of the political theorists and practitioners of the second half of the fourteenth century a mere holder of the crown as the symbol of the sovereign kingdom of France. Even if there is no king or he is indisposed, there are other representatives of the Crown here, the regent, estates as well as council, who can fill in for him. It is precisely this duplication of the concept of Crown as transpersonal, inalienable sovereignty of the French kingdom that allowed all of the English occupations to be declared invalid and to cover legislatively the newly emerging needs of the current policy. Answers not even to these topical issues dealing with Brittany or the return of the pope to Rome were lacking in this programme dialogue.[148]

If *Le Songe du Vergier* in some chapters helped create the historical awareness of the kingdom, in others it could have served as a handbook for royal officials. Nevertheless, Charles V also thought of the future historical awareness of his reign. He was not satisfied with the Benedictines of the Abbey of Saint-Denis being responsible from time immemorial for the official *Great Chronicles of France* and entrusted their recording to his Chancellor Pierre d'Orgemont († 1389). The monks were replaced by laymen in the service of the court, mostly lawyers, who in the accounts of events did not fail to commemorate the king's masterful acts in the military and diplomatic fields. In 1375, Henri de Trévou on the king's orders made a copy of the final edition of the *Great Chronicles of France*. At the king's instigation, this volume, which went all the way back to 1350, was joined by a second, no less sumptuously decorated work, into which the copyist Raoulet d'Orleans transcribed the chancellor's records. After careful revision, both vellum volumes were bound separately in

148/ From the extensive literature, cf. i.a. Royer, *L'Église et le Royaume de France au XIVe siècle*, and Krynen, *L'empire du roi*, in particular the third part, beginning on p. 345.

1377, with fifty-two blank pages being attached to the second for a planned continuation.[149] This rare manuscript deserves our attention mainly because it also contains the original Account of the visit of Emperor Charles IV in France, including an entirely unique cycle of nineteen period illuminations. That suffices here as an introduction to the Account, with which we will soon have an opportunity to become acquainted.

Charles V did not let things take their own course when there was an opportunity to influence them. As soon as the emperor announced his visit to him in the autumn of 1377, he ordered the chancellor to have the archivists and scribes accumulate and copy into one volume all the treaties and writings of a foreign policy nature. The entire collection of 172 documents contained both the notarised copies of the Latin originals and their translations into French. The writings from the end of the twelfth century until 1374 thus amassed were sorted by content, with its being possible to find in some copies even the bulls of Charles IV from the time of his visit to France at the beginning of 1378, added later. It is highly likely that the entire collection was created shortly before as the basis for the expected negotiations with the emperor. And indeed, as we will be able to see for ourselves later, Charles V supported his conclusions at the joint session of the councils of both sovereigns with the original documents, which had been brought from the royal archives for this purpose.[150] The bases for the summit were accumulated, next came the inspections and ceremonial modifications of the palaces as well as suburban residences intended for the housing of the emperor and his retinue.

PARIS AND ITS ENVIRONS AT THE END OF THE REIGN OF CHARLES V

The venue for the heralded imperial visit was to be seven exceptionally important localities including the then still suburban Abbey of Saint-Denis and the fortress residence in Vincennes. The humiliation that he had experienced in the Palace de la Cité at end of 1357 and beginning of 1358 in the form of house arrest by the supporters of Étienne Marcel provoked Dauphin Charles still before his accession to the throne to fortify the royal residences better, increase their number and connect them to one another by routes. Also the protection of vulnerable quarters of the metropolis from the incursions of brigand bands under English mercenary pay was connected with this. Both aims led to extensive reconstruction, which for a long time endowed mediaeval Paris

149/ The research still builds on the knowledge attained during the work on the edition by Delachenal (ed.), *Chronique des règnes*, III and IV (here the Introduction, esp. pp. VIII–XII). The latest research was summarised by Guenée, 'Les Grandes Chroniques de France', pp. 189–214.
150/ The connection of the so-called 'Recueil des alliances' with the preparation of the visit of Charles IV was convincingly proved by Autrand, 'Les livres des hommes de pouvoir', pp. 99–204.

39. A dummy of the Bastille in its form from 1369–1382, which was carved from its original stone in 1790 by François Palloy

with a new urban outline as well as with monumental architecture. The area of Paris, surrounded by new ramparts and forts, among which the famous Bastille is worth noting for its modernity, roughly doubled in size as compared to the time of Philip Augustus (1165–1223), and that primarily only on the right bank of the Seine.[151] Even the Louvre was now located *intra muros* and was undergoing an entire reconstruction just like the until-then little important palace of Saint-Pol, the residence of the king and his family after 1360. The Palace de la Cité, where Charles V did not feel comfortable, was now predominantly intended for impressive purposes and for the needs of the parliament.[152]

All three royal residences were inside the walls with all of them offering the possibility of escape on the Seine, which also connected them as a thoroughfare. The construction boom was not restricted only to ramparts and royal palaces. Two bridges began to be built; in May 1365, Charles laid the foundation stone of a new church at the monastery of the Celestines; also some of the university buildings, especially the famous College of Navarre, experienced further reconstruction.[153] Unlike his Luxemburg uncle, Charles V established neither a university nor a college but all the more supported the existing colleges and in his policy also relied on university educated counsellors.[154] Likewise suburban houses were raised by one or two floors at that time. Although until recently the vedutas of Paris in the depictions of the months of June and October in the *Très Riches Heures* (*The Very Rich Hours of the Duke of Berry*) were more or less considered to be as figments of the illustrator's

151/ For more on this, see Faucherre, 'L'enceinte de Paris', pp. 78–84; on the new building of the Bastille, see Faucherre, 'La Bastille, citadelle avant l'heure?', pp. 85–90.
152/ For a synoptic view on this, see Whiteley, 'Lieux de pouvoir et résidences royales', pp. 105–111; further, see Gorochov, *Le Collège de Navarre*.
153/ See Sandron, 'Le roi et les églises', pp. 91–104.
154/ 'University policy' is discussed by Verger, 'Culture universitaire', p. 169, where further literature can be found.

40. A case with the relics and treasures from the abbey in Saint-Denis. We see two more noteworthy items on the sides of the reliquary with the head of St Denis. On the left, a large golden cross, which St Eligius his goldsmith according to legend made for King Dagobert, on the right the so-called treasury of Charlemagne before disassembly in 1794. In the lower left corner, the so-called Eagle of Abbot Suger stands coming perhaps from imperial Rome (today in the Musée du Louvre) and at the opposite end the Cup of the Ptolemies from the 1st century AD (today in the BnF, Cabinet des Médailles). An engraving from the work Histoire de l'Abbaye Royale de Saint-Denis, which Dom Michel Félibien published in 1706.

imagination, the research of the last twenty to thirty years has proved that not only those but also other period depictions of the metropolis to an almost surprising degree correspond to reality.

From today's point of view, the Abbey of Saint-Denis is an inseparable part of Paris, so we shall begin our imaginary walk in the footsteps of Charles IV right here, even though at that time it was a newly fortified town of medium size. Permission to build the ramparts was given to the population there in 1356 by the monastery's abbot, whose efforts were aided two years later by Dauphin Charles.[155] After its completion in the thirteenth century, the cathedral roughly resembled its appearance today, if we disregard the restorations which were undertaken by Violett-le-Duc in 1860. The Basilica in Saint-Denis had, as is known, a peculiar place in Charles IV's life, because it was here that he was confirmed in the church and also assumed the name Charles on that occasion. It was known about the emperor in advance that he would be interested, more than in the architecture, in the spirit of the concept of the famous Abbot Suger († 1151), in the holy relics, wonders and gems among the monastery's treasures. The most precious of those rarities can be admired to this day in the Louvre (e.g. the coronation sword and spurs, jewellery from the time of Abbot Suger etc.) or in the Cabinet of Medals and the manuscript

155/ Cf. Wyss et al. (eds), 'Atlas historique de Saint-Denis, Des origins au XVIIIe siècle'.

collection of the National Library of France.[156] The reliquaries with the relics of St Denis and two other Parisian martyrs, further one of the extremely precious nails of the Holy Rood as well as the supposed crown of St Louis had been prepared for display and dusted. Also cleaned were the areas of the tombs of King Charles IV the Fair (1322–1328), his third wife Jeanne d'Évreux, further King Philip VI of Valois (1328–1350) and his first wife Jeanne of Burgundy, with whom the emperor had grown up in his youth, and last but not least also the tomb of John II the Good (1350–1364), the father of the current sovereign. The royal necropolis in Saint-Denis was entirely destroyed by revolutionary iconoclasts in 1793. Despite that, the endeavour to preserve the marble tombs with the lying figures of almost all these people, who can be seen to this day in the Cathedral of Saint-Denis, has been successful. Another surprise for the emperor was to be the monument which was carved at the commission of Charles V *ad vivum* by sculptor André Beauneveu around 1364.[157] As far as is known, it was the first time a sovereign had been the model for his own tombstone.

The appearance of La Chapelle-Saint-Denis, which was the last stop of Emperor Charles IV before his entry of Paris, seems to have been captured quite faithfully by Jean Fouquet, who otherwise was not bothered that he had planted a green tree in the January scenery (Pic. 119 / XXXIII). This remarkable miniaturist also depicted the gate with the fortress of Saint-Denis, through which Charles IV entered the French metropolis on Monday, 4 January 1378, however not on this occasion but when illustrating the entrance of the newly crowned Charles V and his wife Jeanne of Bourbon in 1364. So as not to repeat himself, Fouquet took license and painted the gate of St Martin (Pic. 122 / XXXV). The journey along the kilometre-and-a-half-long Street of St Denis to the Castlet (Chastellet) was guarded by the Bridge of the Money Changers (Pont au Change), from which a view presented itself of the silhouette of the three round riverside towers, which were joined by a square corner tower under John II the Good, where Charles V had a large astronomical clock placed in 1370.[158] The silhouette was completed by the enormous donjon in the centre of the complex and the thin steeple on the roof of Sainte-Chapelle.

The entrance to the main gate of the Palace de la Cité, which was protected by a stalwart rampart on the street side, was framed on the extensive courtyard by bars precluding access by uninvited inquisitive persons to the stairwell of

---

156/ The basic work for learning about the original treasure is the richly illustrated work by Félibien, *Histoire de l'Abbaye Royale de Saint-Denys*, which was published in 1706. From the recent production, see the collective publication *Le Trésor de Saint-Denis*.
157/ Hilger, Hans Peter, 'André Beauneveu, Bildhauer und Maler', in *Die Parler und der schöne Stil*, I (Köln 1978), pp. 43–49.
158/ It was a novelty in its time, see Favreau, 'Jean de Berry et la ville de Poitiers', pp. 109–110.

the entrance wing of the Merchant's Gallery.[159] This public gallery, intended for the sale of rare goods, interconnected the three main parts of the complex, i.e. Sainte-Chapelle with its canon cells in the southern wing, the actual Palace with the Great Hall and the session hall of the supreme court of justice (Parliament) in the north and with private abodes for the king and his family in the western part concluded by a garden. Of the original Gothic complex, today we can only see the ground-floor Hall of the Men-at-Arms extended by the so-called Paris 'Street' and the connected Guard Room with the adjoined facilities of the original kitchens. Both impressive halls on the first floor were destroyed during reconstruction, so we know them only from later depictions. We may form an idea of the original staircase and entrance to the Great Hall, e.g. from the architectural detail on the right side of the altarpiece which until 1789 hung on the façade of the Parliament. Thanks to the iconographic evidence and building survey in recent years, it has been possible to reconstruct hypothetically in significant detail both the private and public sectors of the Palace de la Cité, in which official and other acts of the imperial visit took place from Monday to Thursday, 4–7 January 1378. It is known *inter alia* what the imperial gardens approximately looked like.[160]

Unlike most of today's tourists, Charles IV had no time left for a tour of the nearby Cathedral of Notre-Dame, which he knew well from his youth. On the other hand, he wanted to see Sainte-Chapelle and its collection of the relics of Christ's Passion, unequalled in the entire Christian world, again. At first sight, it may seem that we can see roughly the same as Emperor Charles. In the lower chapel, we can be amazed by the rich architectural décor; on both narrow spiral staircases, we can imagine how the rare guest was being pulled up by his legs and shoulders here; then in the upper chapel, your breath will be taken away by the as if ethereal space of the bluish stained-glass windows, in which the delicate columns shouldering the vaulting ribs at the height of twenty metres almost disappear. Nevertheless, appearances are deceiving, because Sainte-Chapelle is also a monument of the nineteenth century, which had to repair the damages of revolutionary vandalism. Therefore, few people know that the contemporary narrow steeple was not raised on the roof of the chapel until the World Exposition of 1855 and that not only the painted decorations but also a third of the stained-glass windows, the 'tribune' for relics,

159/ A still valuable work was published by Guérout, 'Le Palais de la Cité à Paris des origines à 1417'. Based on new research, the author added a number of details in the study 'L'hôtel du roi au Palais de la Cité à Paris sous Jean II et Charles V', cf. further Whiteley, 'Lieux de pouvoir', pp. 105–112.

160/ And that thanks to several studies by Whiteley, which are in the Bibliography. Cf. also Bennert, 'Les décors de résidences'. On the gardens, cf. i.a. Antoine, 'Jardins de plaisance'.

41. The upper chapel in Sainte-Chapelle

pavement and exterior statues come from the nineteenth century.[161] It remains to be mentioned that the original rosette with the theme of the Apocalypse, which was replaced by another with flamboyant tracery in 1485–1490 under Charles VIII, can be recognised in the already-mentioned illumination of the month of June in *The Very Rich Hours of the Duke of Berry*.

What was of primary significance for our emperor was, however, the so-called Great Case (*Grande Châsse*) for the most precious twenty-two relics of the Christian world, which St Louis acquired from Baldwin II in Constantinople after the fall of the Latin Empire in 1239–1247. For all of these relics, first precious receptacles were procured, which were then placed in a huge, three metre high case, to which only the king of France had the key. The original reliquary was rectangular without a roof, as can be conjectured from its depictions in the manuscripts of the fifteenth century. Since the miniatures capture the contents of the open cases, we can form an approximate idea of Charles' impressions. A part of the relics were saved after the Revolution,

161/ For an initial introduction, see the synoptic studies with abundant colour documentation in Dossiers d'archéologie, No. 264 (juin 2001): *La Sainte-Chapelle, l'art au temps de saint Louis.* From the essential literature, I list: Leniaud and Perrot, *La Sainte-Chapelle*, Paris 1991, further a complete catalogue of the stained glass windows: Aubert, Grodecki, Lafond and Verrier, *Les vitraux de Notre-Dame et de la Sainte-Chapelle de Paris*; on the most important statues, cf. Weber, 'Les grandes et les petites statues', pp. 81–101. *Ve znamení zemí Koruny české. Sborník k šedesátým narozeninám prof. PhD. Lenky Bobkové, CSc.*, Praha 2006.

so some have survived to our time in the treasury of the Cathedral of Notre-Dame (reliquary with the Crown of Thorns), in the Louvre (reliquary of a stone from the purported tomb of Christ) as well as in other collections (the reliquaries of Sts Lucian, Julian and Maxian).[162]

No one who walked on the pavement of the so-called Square Court at the Louvre a few decades ago could have had any idea what was found beneath his feet. Extensive archaeological excavations in 1983–1985 revealed the enormous foundations of the original square fortress from the time of Philip Augustus including the interior donjon and hall of St Louis, which were later made accessible to the visitors to the museum complex. Although the reconstruction of the fortress into a residence, which Charles V entrusted to the workshop of Raymond du Temple, concerned mainly the upper floors, archaeologists furnished proof of a new entrance from that time, which allowed direct access to the royal garden from the north side. What is much more important, however, is that the archaeological surveys confirmed the veracity of the almost fairy-tale appearance of the Louvre in the miniature of the month of October in *The Very Rich Hours of the Duke of Berry* and more or less also in a number of further depictions from the fifteenth century, e.g. on the so-called Altarpiece of the Parliament of Paris. With the assistance of these iconographic and written sources, it was then possible to reconstruct to a certain degree the impressive as well as private areas where the emperor's visit is supposed to have taken place from Thursday, 7 January, until Sunday lunch on 10 January 1378.[163]

On the same residential boat which had inspired awe for its size as well as its equipment and on which the emperor and his closest entourage had arrived at the Louvre, he went upstream on the Seine to another royal residence, called L'hôtel Saint-Pol. The word 'hôtel' in the narrow sense (part of the residence) as well as in the wider sense (the entire object) traditionally denoted a private residence. Charles V had resided here already in 1360; in the years after that, he had bought several other houses and had them renovated, so that in 1365 his entire domain here formed a complex of residences on an area of ca 190 × 300 m.[164] The advantage of the residence at Saint-Pol was not only the half-rural and thus from the perspective both then and now

162/ The reliquaries mentioned in the round brackets are deposited in the Musée National du Moyen Âge – Thermes et Hôtel de Cluny; the so-called Le Grand Camée de France can be seen at the Cabinet of Medals of the Bibliothèque nationale in Paris. For details, cf. i.a. Vidier, *Le trésor de la Sainte-Chapelle. Inventaires et documents*; Taburet-Delahaye, *L'orfèvrerie gothique*; and Durand, 'Les reliques de Constantinople', pp. 60–65.

163/ For more on that, see Fleury and Kruta, *Le Château du Louvre*, and the listed studies by Whiteley.

164/ The research arises from the study by Bournon, 'L'hôtel royal de Saint-Pol'; for the latest, cf. Whiteley, 'Lieux de pouvoir', pp. 122–124.

42. Reconstruction of the appearance of the Louvre during the reign of Charles V following the Les très riches heures du Duc de Berry. In the lower belt, the preserved (today underground) parts are marked.

'healthy' environment but also its good transport connection to another royal fortress residence in the hunting 'Wood' in Vincennes (*Bois de Vincennes*). The expensive reconstruction of the older castle continued here very rapidly, so the emperor could already at a distance feast his eyes on the creamy towers, among which the huge prism of the donjon with smaller circular towers in the corners dominated. The king ceded the emperor his bedroom on the third floor, which had a better view of the landscape than the hall one floor below: in the Account of the *Great Chronicles of France*, we learn that the emperor had himself carried around the great hall to see through the windows the surroundings of the château, where his son Wenceslas along with the brothers of Charles V were hunting fallow deer and wild rabbits. The hunting grounds can be imagined following the illuminations in the *Hours of Duke John of Berry*. The king of France was duly proud of his recently completed tower. King Wenceslas and the knights of his retinue, who had the opportunity to see also the armoury on the top floor, declared the tower 'the most beautiful and marvellous thing that

43. Donjon and "small castle" (Châtelet) of the royal residence in Vincennes. The Hours of Etienne Chevalier, miniature by Jean Fouquet, 1452 (MC, ms. 71 fol. 26)

they had ever seen'.[165] The good condition of the residential tower as well as of the entire fortress complex have simplified research in this respect.[166]

A component of the generous building activity of Charles on his hunting grounds east of Paris was also the new building of the rural residence (*manoir*) in Beauté, which was completed shortly before the emperor's visit. Charles V took to this luxuriously equipped private refuge of his, whose charms were extolled by poets, so much that he had himself brought here on 16 September 1380 shortly before his death. It hence came as no surprise that Beauté found itself in the official protocol of the final part of the emperor's visit to France, just like the Abbey of Saint-Maur-des-Fossés, selected for the renowned healing effects of the saint buried here. We will not reveal anything important in advance when we say now that the emperor recuperated during his four-day stay in Beauté, began to walk only with slight assistance and after the tour of the manor according to the testimony of the Account[167] stated, 'that he had never in his life seen a more beautiful place or a more delightful location'.[168]

165/ Delachenal (ed.), *Chroniques des règnes*, II, p. 265.

166/ From the latest period, cf. especially Chapelot, *Le Château de Vincennes*, and the treatises from the anthologies *Vincennes aux origines de l'État moderne* (1996) and *Le Château de Vincennes* (2008).

167/ Delachenal (ed.), *Chroniques des règnes*, II, pp. 266–237.

168/ The body of St Maurus the Confessor was transferred here by the Benedictines from Saint-Maur-sur-Loire in the seventh century. The Abbey of Saint-Maur-des-Fossés was destroyed in the French Revolution. Also the castle of Beauté was removed without a remnant in the eighteenth century; on its construction, cf. Chapelot, 'Le Vincennes des quatre premiers Valois', pp. 100–101.

European Dimensions of Charles IV's Reign

The newly built or expensively rebuilt royal residences of Charles V would leave a deep impression on the emperor during his visit to Paris in January 1378. There was a lot in France and its metropolis that Charles IV could admire already in his youth. The Cathedrals in Rheims, Saint-Denis as well as Notre-Dame in Paris had already been completed, the glazed walls of Sainte-Chapelle lifted the eyes and spirit, the 'Wood' in Vincennes was used for hunting, merry commotion prevailed in the Palace de la Cité, kings rested in the Louvre. Avignon surpassed Paris in various things then. The hillock above the Rhône was dominated by the enormous towers of the papal residence, whose interiors were furnished with unparalleled worldliness, but an impression on the young Charles was undoubtedly made even by the palace of his supporter Cardinal Pierre Roger de Rosières, not to mention the fortified homes of sovereigns and patricians in Italian cities. No book on Charles IV lacks his sigh after returning to Prague, so this one will be no exception: 'We found the kingdom so forsaken that there was not one castle that was free and not mortgaged together with all its royal property, so that we did not have anywhere to stay except in houses in the cities just like any other citizen. Even the castle in Prague was desolate, in ruins, and reduced from the times of King Otakar [II] so that it had crumbled almost to the ground. Here we raised up at great expense the great, new, and beautiful palace the way it appears to those who look on it today.'[169] That was only the beginning; Prague under Charles IV expanded, acquired new ramparts, within which new buildings of churches, monasteries and imposing palaces grew.

PRAGUE, HEAD OF THE LANDS OF THE BOHEMIAN CROWN

The above-mentioned complaint from Charles' *Autobiography* is ostensibly contradicted by the testimony of Abbot Peter of Zittau from the mid-1330s. According to the author of the *Chronicon Aulae Regiae*, King John at that time ordered that a great deal of construction work be done on both Prague Castle and in the Bigger Town on the house of his residence, 'and further that French

169/ *Karoli IV Vita*, pp. 68–70.

44. The house U Kamenného zvonu (At the Stone Bell) in Prague on Old Town Square, temporary residence of King John of Luxembourg and his son Charles IV

style be much applied', but not in palaces which had already begun to be built by Margrave Charles earlier.[170] John's palatial residence in Štupartská Street had long been in ruin just like his further undefined dwellings at the Castle. The chronicler Peter was a cosmopolitan man; during his journeys around France, he had seen with his own eyes the important Cistercian monasteries, many cathedrals as well as Sainte-Chapelle in Paris. He had thus definitely seen the appearance of constructions *more gallico* (*à la française*).[171] After all, King John was not the only one at that time to give commissions to French builders. During his stay in Avignon, Bishop John of Dražice acquired for his building plans a certain Master William (Vilém), who was originally to build a new bridge in

170/ *Chronicon Aulae Regiae*, p. 331; also here on p. 318, see on Charles' temporary residence in his mother's house.
171/ On the influence of French building monuments on the domestic architecture of the last Přemyslids, see most recently Kuthan, 'Pařížská Sainte-Chapelle', where *inter alia* on pp. 44–45 see on the early two-storey chapels in Plasy and in Zlatá Koruna.

Prague, reinforce the bishop's residence in the Lesser Town and *inter alia* build a monastery for the then fashionable order of Augustinians-Canons. The generous plans came to naught in Prague, but John of Dražice partially implemented them in Roudnice, where he ceremonially established the first monastery of the mentioned order in Central Europe in May 1333 and where three months later he also placed the foundation stone for a bridge across the Elbe.[172]

45. Prague Castle, north façade of the royal palace of Charles IV after the reconstruction by Dobroslava Menclová

If we take Charles IV at his word, then he could not have lived at the Castle after his arrival in Prague and must have satisfied himself with his mother's house in the Old Town for two months. It has occurred to various experts that this was the house At the White Bell on Old Town Square, whose recent reconstruction uncovered a monumental façade, with which no urban palace east of the Rhine can compete. This opinion cannot be convincingly proved, but since experts see a distant echo of period French architecture in the house At the White Bell, we can thus have at least an approximate idea of the house in which Margrave Charles and his wife Blanche temporarily lived in Prague.[173] The work on the Castle apparently proceeded quickly although the entire reconstruction of the Přemyslid palace dragged on until the end of the fourteenth century.

It is significant that another chronicler also, Francis of Prague, speaks of the royal palace that Charles built at Prague Castle in a short time 'following the model of the house of the king of France'.[174] We can form only a partial idea of its original appearance. The ground floor originally with nine pointed chamfered arcades is the most preserved; it is necessary to take into consideration that the portico gallery was not finished until around 1400. By a staircase from the northern courtyard, one entered the first floor directly, namely through a richly profiled portal, partially preserved today, which led to the largest hall

172/ More on this by Hledíková, *Biskup Jan IV. z Dražic*, pp. 144–148.
173/ The last summary of the knowledge was given by Líbal and Muk, *Staré Město pražské*, pp. 144–148; cf. also Benešovská, 'Les résidences du roi Jean de Bohême', pp. 125–127.
174/ *Chronicon Francisci Pragensis*, p. 144.

46. Cathedral of St Vitus, view from the south, the left part with the towers were not finished until 1929

with an area of roughly 30 × 16 m. On the east side, this audience hall was connected with the Romanesque chapel. On the opposite side, a narrower hallway led along a smaller room, perhaps an office, to the throne hall, to which the residential wing was connected at the western wall. Before the end of the fifteenth century, Benedikt Ried masterfully reshaped these three spaces connected by a hallway into today's Vladislav Hall and instead of the original flat ceilings impressively roofed the whole with a helical vault. The walls as well as window embrasures of the largest hall were covered by panel paintings depicting, according to the miniscule lettering found, fictitious portraits of all of Charles' predecessors on the imperial throne. The paintings were complemented by ornamented coats-of-arms, which were noticed by the delegates of King of France Charles V during their audience on 1 April 1372.[175]

175/ See Menclová, *České hrady*, II, pp. 43–46, which also contains a reconstruction of the ground plan and façades. On the portrait cycle in Charles' palace at Prague Castle, see most recently Stejskal, 'Die Wandzyklen des Kaisers Karls IV.', pp. 34–35.

Whereas with Charles' palace the French influence can only be conjectured about, in the case of the new building of the Cathedral of St Vitus it is entirely different, because the first leader of its building workshop was Matthias of Arras. The need for the new building of the cathedral which would replace the two-apse Romanesque Basilica of Sts Vitus, Wenceslas and Adalbert had appeared already in the last years of the reign of John of Luxembourg, who had in October 1341 for these and similar purposes donated to the castle chapter a tithe of all the royal incomes from all of the present and future silver mines in Bohemia. After the publication of the papal bull of 30 April 1344, which raised the bishopric of Prague to an archbishopric, it was possible to proceed quickly to the work, because both Luxemburgs, King John and Margrave Charles, had brought the above-mentioned master builder from Avignon. In autumn 1344, the clearance work east of the Romanesque basilica had progressed so much that on the feast day of the Presentation of the Blessed Virgin Mary (21 November) the first Archbishop of Prague Ernest of Pardubice could with the participation of the king and his sons lay the foundation stone for the new cathedral.

While Matthias of Arras came from the northern region of Artois, he had acquired his knowledge in the south and *inter alia* learnt at the cathedrals in Rodez, Toulouse and Narbonne.[176] Before his death in 1352, he managed to build pentagonal chapels at the apse and three chapels in the longitudinal parts of the presbytery with the adjacent galleries as well as pillars with arcades all the way to under the triforium. At the same time, he began the work on the most important chapel consecrated to St Wenceslas, whose relics had been removed already in 1348 from the tomb in the Romanesque basilica, which until that time, if not longer, continued to be used for the celebration of liturgical ceremonies. Matthias' death slowed the construction by a few years, but the delay was quickly compensated for when Charles IV in 1356 entrusted the workshop at St Vitus to Peter, son of Henry Parler, who despite his young age had managed to prove his abilities as a master in Schwäbisch Gmünd. Although the Chapel of St Wenceslas had already been structurally completed in autumn 1366 and the southern Golden Gate (*Zlatá brána*) with the entrance hall and new sacristy six years later, the cathedral could for the time fulfil its liturgical and other functions only to a very limited extent. It was true for the entire time of Charles, because the vaulting of the presbytery was not closed until July 1385. Nevertheless, the emperor could already admire with his own eyes not only the mosaics on the Golden Gate but also the new tombs

47. Matthias of Arras († 1352), the first builder of the Cathedral of St Vitus. A bust in the inner triforium of the Cathedral of St Vitus at Prague Castle

176/ See Héliot and Mencl, 'Mathieu d'Arras', pp. 103–127 and more recently Jiří Kuthan and Jan Royt, *Katedrála sv. Víta, Václava a Vojtěcha*, Praha 2011, pp. 79–175.

49. Statute of St Wenceslas in the homonymous chapel of the Cathedral of St Vitus at Prague Castle. A work of Peter or Henry Parler from 1373

48. Peter Parler (1330/3–1399), the second builder of the Cathedral of St Vitus. A bust in the inner triforium of the Cathedral of St Vitus at Prague Castle

of his ducal and royal predecessors or the gallery of the portrait busts in the triforium.[177]

While this gallery was unlike any on the European continent, the newly emerging necropolis of Czech dukes and kings could have been influenced by Charles' memories of the Abbey of Saint-Denis. French models should be

177/ The latest state of the research is captured by Benešovská, 'Gotická katedrála. Architektura', and Hlobil, 'Gotické sochařství'. French inspiration in terms of the sculptural decoration of the cathedral in Prague is allowed for also by Kuthan, 'Pařížská Sainte-Chapelle', pp. 56–60.

borne in mind – they were significantly reflected *inter alia* in Charles' intention to rebuild the Romanesque chapel of All Saints into a diminutive copy of Sainte-Chapelle in Paris. The preserved details of the chapel, which suffered heavy damage in the fire of Hradčany (the Castle District) in 1541, provide evidence of the high level of the court building workshop. With large pointed windows, Peter Parler nearly negated all of the masonry and thus fulfilled the idea of an entirely glazed wall.[178] No less superbly did he manage to deal with other commissions also, a pre-eminent place among which after the cathedral is taken by Charles Bridge.

The older, so-called Judith Bridge had been demolished by a destructive flood in 1342. For several years, Prague had to make do with a wooden provisional bridge, which however ever less suited the needs of the imperial residence. When the final decision on the construction of a new bridge was made with the laying of the foundation stone in 1357, Peter Parler shifted its line a little southwards from the Romanesque bridge, which had to remain in use for a longer period yet. The new bridge was not only two and a half metres wider but also four or five metres higher to resist floods better. For the same reason, also the massive semicircular arches lined with hewn sandstone blocks were much wider. Above the first bridge pillar, the Old Town Bridge Tower began to grow at the same time, with its vaulting in the passage way being completed by Parler after 1373. Perhaps still before his death, Charles IV could enjoy the view of the monumentally conceived eastern façade, whose second floor contains the centrepieces of the entire sculptural adornment, in its time exceptional far and wide. Under the triumphal arch on the relief of the two bridge arches here stands the patron saint of the bridge, St Vitus, with the aged emperor sitting on his right and his juvenile-appearing son on his left. A similar, publically impressive function was also fulfilled by the newly built entrance to the Louvre with statues of King Charles V and his wife Jeanne of Bourbon, just like his acquisitions for the gallery of dead kings of France in the Abbey of Saint-Denis. However, what is important is that in Prague as well as elsewhere in the Czech lands 'Parleresque' art was emerging simultaneously, so Charles IV on his visit to Paris in January 1378 could compare without blushing the transformations of both metropolises with respect to the time of his childhood.

50. Old Town Bridge Tower.
In the triumphal arch, there is the seated figure of Charles IV (left) and King Wenceslas IV,
and a standing statue of St Vitus in the centre

In this connection, a further two monumental foundations of Charles IV deserve mentioning. Although there was busy building activity also in the Older and Lesser Towns of Prague, the main actions were taking place on the construction sites of the newly founded New Town. The leading desire of

178/ From the literature, cf. Sokol, 'Parléřův kostel Všech svatých', and Homolka, 'Královská kaple Všech svatých', pp. 141–146.

51. Prague around 1400

1. Church of St Benedict
2. Strahov Gate
3. Royal Palace
4. Lesser Town Hall and church of St Nicholas
5. Monastery of St Thomas
6. Monastery of the Johanites (St John's Hospitalers)
7. Chapel of St Lawrence
8. Church of St John the Baptist Na Prádle
9. Church of the Holy Rood
10. Church of St Haštal
11. Gate at Na Františku
12. Church of St Peter
13. Church of the Holy Spirit
14. House of the Queen
15. St Valentine's Gate
16. College of poor students at St Valentine's
17. Church of St Valentine
18. Theological school at St James'
19. College of poor students at St Benedict
20. Gate of Long Avenue
21. St Benedict's Gate
22. Monastery of the Knights of the Cross before the spittal fields
23. St Clements School of the Dominicans
24. College of doctors
25. College of All Saints
26. Church of Our Lady at Na louži
27. Old Town Hall
28. Church of St Michael
29. Church of Our Lady before Týn
30. Charles College, centre of the university
31. University and college of lawyers
32. College of King Wenceslas IV
33. College of Lithuania or Queen Jadwiga (Hedvika) until 1413
34. from 1413 moved to the corner of Celetná
35. College of the Bohemian Nation
36. House belonging to the College of the Bohemian Nation
37. Gate opposite St Ambrose's
38. Charles Spa
39. Church of St Anna
40. Church of St Giles
41. Nazarene College
42. Bethlehem Chapel
43. House of Blažek, supreme burgrave
44. Church of St Gallus
45. St Gallus Gate
46. Church of the Holy Rood the Smaller
47. Theological college of the Cistercians
48. Zderaz Gate
49. Church of Our Lady of the Snow
50. Church of St Stephen
51. Church of St Stephen in the Wall
52. St Stephen Gate
53. Church of St Michael
54. Church of St Adalbert
55. House of the Magistrates
56. New Town Hall
57. Church of St Longinus
58. Church of St Wenceslas
59. Chapel of Corpus Christi
60. Church of St John
61. Church of St Jerome
62. Church of St Anthony
63. Church of the Celestynes
64. Church of St Adalbert

the founder was to connect the future right-bank buildings with the Old Town on one side and with Vyšehrad on the other. Considering the ruggedness of the already partially populated landscape, it was not an easy task, regardless of the actual interconnection of the eastern side protected by the ramparts and the moat. The foundation was definitely not preceded by an urban design, thus only with the greatest circumspection can the hypothetical scheme either imitating heavenly Jerusalem or on the other hand leading through Antique learning to the Renaissance ideal of the city be extrapolated from the geometric sketch of the ground plan.[179] Even so, there remains much that at the very least deserves attention. What is worth mentioning is not only the width of the main traffic arteries and unprecedented space of the two central squares but also the distribution of the new churches on the axis of the cross or the complementation of the network of cloisters by the convents of the orders which until that time had not had a seat in Prague. It is not necessary to list them all; it is sufficient to mention the Carmelites at the Virgin Mary of the Snows, the Benedictines with the Slavonic liturgy at Emmaus, the Servite Friars at the Church of Lady Day (also called 'Na trávníčku' /On the Grass/) or the Canons Regular of St Augustine at Karlov (Charles Quarter). In the foundation charter of the last convent mentioned, Charles IV again denoted Charlemagne as his predecessor, from whom he also derived his direct succession to the imperial throne. The wider radiation of the uniformly designed conurbation of the two towns of Prague as the residence of the Holy Roman Emperor was to arise in the first place from the octagonal Chapel of the Body of Christ on the central square, which was planned for a public exhibition of the most precious imperial relics. These were always brought before the first Friday after Easter under celebratory ceremonies from Karlštejn Castle, where they were otherwise closely guarded the entire year.

Even if Charles IV had not seen himself the fortified residence of the French kings in the 'Wood' in Vincennes in his early youth, he would still have had to establish a similar fortress near Prague. At that time, Prague Castle was one big construction site and as such could not provide appropriate security, whereas the rural royal castles lay at significant distances from the metropolis. It was precisely the proximity to Prague which co-determined the selection of the location for a new castle on a false spur over the valley of the Mořina Creek. The uncommonly large area of the castle as well as its enormous fortifications at first sight foreshadowed that its primary role was the protection of the imperial relics, the Great Bohemian Land Cross and the other sacraments deposited there. Despite its internal layout, Karlštejn, the first of many local-

179/ Cf. Lorenc, *Nové Město pražské*, pp. 41–57, which also contains ground plans and reconstructions of the city organism as a whole as well as of its individual parts.

52. Tangermünde, castle and church of St Stephen. Copper engraving by Matthäus Merian the Elder from around 1640

ities bearing the emperor's name, did not manifest building innovations. Its impressive, sacral as well as genuinely functional areas were, however, well connected operationally, so that the internal unity of its artistic decoration could be the more apparent. The group of court painters and interior decorators certainly respected the builder's instructions, but those did not limit the individual creative contribution. Of the three star artists, namely Nicholas Wurmser of Strasbourg, Master Theodoric and Master Oswald, it was the first named that was attributed with a knowledge of the galleries of the French kings on the cathedral façades, a knowledge that could be applied in the creation of an unpreserved cycle of murals of the so-called Luxemburg lineage. Nevertheless, research has not said its last word in this respect by far. Yet it is not necessary to wait for it, because many things that could at first sight connect Vincennes with Karlštejn arose from the same needs of state grandeur as well as the common taste of the both homonymous sovereigns for the accumulation and veneration of Christ's and other relics.[180]

Charles IV was however predominantly the Holy Roman Emperor and hence needed corresponding temporary residences also on the territory of the Empire. On journeys to the west, Charles regularly stopped at the imperial castle in Nuremberg. In this important imperial city which played an exceptional role in the complicated situation after his election as emperor, Charles IV sojourned at least fifty times. The city appropriately appreciated his favour and showed its gratitude by statues depicting the emperor on the frontage of the new building of the Church of Our Blessed Lady (*Frauenkirche*) and on the

180/ For a comparison of the two castles mentioned, see Dengler, 'Karlstein und Vincennes'; otherwise, cf. from the extensive literature Dvořáková, 'Karlštejn a dvorské malířství doby Karla IV.', Fišer, *Karlštejn*, and Kuthan, 'Pařížská Sainte-Chapelle', pp. 50–52 (also containing information on the French origin of the statue of the Madonna at Karlštejn, which Charles IV might have brought from France).

53. Castle Karlštejn, in which the coronation jewels and the reliquary of the Holy Roman Empire were stored

so-called Beautiful Fountain (*Schöner Brunnen*). After acquiring Brandenburg in 1373, Charles IV had the old margraviate castle of Tangermünde at the homonymous town on the confluence of the Rivers Elbe and Tanger expensively reconstructed. The emperor often stayed there at the end of his reign and even considered the castle as his main residence, *domicilium principale*, at that time. The layout of the castle was reminiscent of Karlštejn. Even here, there was a portrait gallery on the first floor with wall portraits of the emperor, electors and perhaps even other sovereigns, namely Wenceslas IV. Also the castle chapels of St John the Baptist and St John the Evangelist were given gorgeous decoration.[181]

In almost every place of the emperor's stay in the Empire as well as elsewhere (it was hundreds of localities), he has left some kind of trace, beginning with documents and ending with pious legacies to the benefit of the local ecclesiastical institutions. The map of the stays including a greater part of Continental Europe would thus figuratively be spangled with stars commemorating the great emperor to this day. Prague would have the biggest star here. Of all of the cities of Charles' empire, Prague for its size had the greatest

181/ The most recent information on this residence is in Bobková, 'Hrady Karla IV. v Laufu a Tangermünde', pp. 148–157.

chance of becoming the potential capital of the Empire and filling the role of Paris. The promising onset to this was, i.a. that some imperial dukes began to procure palaces in Prague. At least temporarily, Prague thus joined the most important European metropolises.[182]

CLERICS AND SCHOLARS ON JOURNEYS: PRAGUE – PARIS – AVIGNON

In the fourteenth century, today's France was for the denizens of the Bohemian Kingdom a quite distant land; nevertheless, the routes between Prague, Avignon and Paris were quite full of traffic. In the decades of the so-called 'Babylonian Captivity' (1309–1377), the role of the spiritual head of the Western Christian world was assumed after Rome by Avignon in southern France. This is where almost all the important decisions on what happened in ecclesiastical provinces were taken, beginning with the selection of occupants on the episcopal thrones through the collection of various fees to the granting of documents pardoning illegitimacy. While much could be arranged in writing, all of the more important applications or legal disputes before the Papal Curia required attendance in person in Avignon or sending plenipotentiary procurators. An example telling more than others can be the dispute on the provostship of Litoměřice, which was commenced by Henry (Jindřich) of Šumburk against Bishop of Prague John IV of Dražice. Henry handed the bill of complaint which he had compiled and where he had included all possible offenses of the bishop to Pope John XXII in person in Avignon. On 1 April 1318, the pope suspended the bishop of Prague, who could do nothing but clear his name before the curia. The court case dragged on for multiple years, so the bishop, who later became one of the officials of the papal court in Avignon, did not return to his diocese until 1329.[183]

The bishop's envoys travelled annually between Avignon and Prague, which expanded the circle of the clergy and their secular servants who brought a knowledge of Lyon, Strasbourg as well as other French cities through which they had passed. A small, not very numerous colony of Czech clerics in Avignon has been traced back as far as the first half of the fourteenth century. The most details have been preserved in the sources on Fridrich of Pernštejn, holder of the archiepiscopal throne in Riga, who lived at the curia permanently from 1325 until his death in 1341. We know about him that he rented a house here for himself and his household, in which he lived comfortably from his pension and from the remunerations for services at the Papal Curia. It is

182/ From the rich literature on Prague at the time of Charles IV, see Moraw, 'Zur Mittelpunktsfunktion Prags im Zeitalter Karls IV.'.

183/ See Hledíková, *Biskup Jan IV. z Dražic*, pp. 92, 97 and 98 and 138–139.

worth mentioning that five clerics of the Prague diocese died in the papal seat in 1322–1341.[184] Here and there some Czechs even bought a book in Avignon, which also had a university. In this regard, all his compatriots were surpassed by Dean of Vyšehrad William (Vilém) of Lestkov, whose library, counting 114 volumes, was purchased by Emperor Charles IV in 1370 for the newly established master's college (*Carolinum*).[185]

The regular contacts between Prague and the curia in Avignon increased even further under the reign of Charles IV. Archbishop of Prague Ernest (Arnošt) of Pardubice stayed there three times on important diplomatic missions. The first time was in spring 1343, when, i.a. he endeavoured for a confirmation of his election as the bishop of Prague. Three years later, Ernest, then already archbishop, was sent by Charles IV to Avignon in the delicate issue of the approval of his election as the Holy Roman Emperor. In a similarly pressing issue, this time the coronation in Rome, Ernest stayed at the papal court again in 1350, namely in the company of Duke of Opava Mikuláš (Nicholas). Ernest of Pardubice enjoyed great esteem at the curia, because after the death of Innocent VI in September 1362 he was being considered as a possible candidate for the vacated papal throne.

The emperor's stay in Avignon in May and the beginning of June 1365 became especially memorable. According to the period chronicles, his retinue ran between 800 and 3,000 persons, with the lower of the two sums being more than likely considering the number of the ecclesiastical and secular dignitaries known by name. It is suggested not only by the preserved bills for hay for the horses but also by the expenses for beds which had to be bought or rented from the Jews. The Czech lords participating in the expedition included Boreš of Rýzmburk, one lord of Šternberk, Beneš, John (Jan) and Peter (Petr) of Vartemberk, Půta of Častolovice and Ješek of Velhartice (German Welhartitz). Unlike Rome, Avignon could not offer the Czech aristocrats and their servants Antique scenery and Early Christian cult places, but the new papal palace and the residences of the cardinals were a wonder of the then modern architecture as well as lifestyle. Although we do not know to what extent the Czech lords after their return home attempted to adapt their residences to the higher demands, it is clear from the writings of the papal chancellor that all of Charles' courtiers to the lowest servants took with them diverse pardons from Avignon, including forgiveness of sins when leaving this world, rights to portable altars or to their own confessor. Not even the imperial jesters left empty-handed

184/ The data on the stay of this prelate in Avignon were collected by Hledíková, 'Z domácnosti Friedricha z Pernštejna', esp. pp. 394–400. The author summarised her knowledge on the Czech colony in Avignon in the study 'Češi u římské kurie'.

185/ *Chronicon Benessii de Weitmil*, p. 541. The students and professors known by name who served the two universities in Avignon were traced by Tadra, *Kulturní styky*, pp. 275–276.

having been paid one hundred gold florins at the pope's instigation so that they could marry off their daughters.[186]

France was a frequent site of the general chapters, to which monastic convents sent their representatives. At the end of May 1319, for example, the Prague inquisitor Kolda of Kolditz, who visited the papal residence in Avignon on this occasion, participated in the General Chapter of the Dominican Order in Cahors. It would again be possible to include a long list of abbots as well as other order dignitaries who became acquainted with a larger or smaller part of France on their business journeys. Only sporadically would these data include more than the dates, places and reason for the journey. All the more is it worth giving a hearing here to the travel experiences that Peter of Zittau included in his *Chronicon Aulae Regiae*. As the abbot of one of the most important Cistercian monasteries, Peter travelled to regular General Chapters in Cîteaux more frequently, but in autumn 1334 he decided to visit also Paris on this occasion, from whence he then continued to the monastery in Clairvaux, where St Bernard, who was dear to him, was buried.[187]

In the summer months, Paris was struck by plague, of whose consequences Abbot Peter still had firsthand experience. Notwithstanding that, he saw numerous things here and there in France that as he said himself delighted his soul: 'I saw the Crown of Thorns, the great relics preserved in the royal chapel there; in Paris, I saw the greatest wisdom of this word, the power of King Philip and his son John, the magnanimity of the old queen and the young lady Guta, I saw the respect of dukes and knights, the profusion of the orderly retinue, the justice of the people, the peace of the kingdom; I also visited Saint-Denis, I drank from the well lying in the tomb under the presbytery, in the love of God and St Denis, and I daubed the place of great pain I had in my thigh with the water and was immediately healed.'[188] We can hardly ask for more information, because the master of words has offered us in a nutshell his experiences not only from the visit of Guta alias Bonne, the wife of Duke of Normandy and future king John II the Good, but also from the religious tours of the holy relics and miraculous cult places in Sainte-Chapelle and in the Abbey of Saint-Denis. We shall keep these memories in mind to be able to compare them later with Charles IV's sightseeing of Paris and its environs.

If all roads for servants of the church led for most of the fourteenth century from Prague to Avignon, Paris played first fiddle for those inhabitants of

186/ Cf. Nováček, 'Císaře Karla IV. pobyt' and Bláhová, 'Příjezd Karla IV do Avignonu'.
187/ The participation of Peter of Zittau at the General Chapters in Cîteaux is evidenced in 1317, 1321, 1334, 1337 and with a question mark also in 1329. Charvátová, 'Petr Žitavský', pp. 102–103 supposes his attendance also in some other years.
188/ *Chronicon Aulae Regiae*, pp. 331–332.

the Czech lands that thought of acquiring university degrees in the liberal arts and especially in theology. The Law Faculty in Paris also had a good name, just like the instruction of medicine there; nonetheless, both of these faculties had extremely strong competition at the law school in Boulogne and in the second case at the university in Montpellier. The list of famous scholars from Bohemia and Moravia is not very extensive before 1330, after which it however becomes denser and contains almost twenty names between then and the founding of the university in Prague. The number of Czech students in Paris surprisingly remained at approximately the same level until the beginning of the Papal Schism in 1378.[189] If we were however to think that the establishment of the University of Prague in April 1348 meant the promise of a secure career for Czechs who had acquired master's and other degrees at the Sorbonne in Paris, we would be truly caught unawares. At its beginnings, the University of Prague had a vexing lack of professors who would fulfil the requirements of formal qualification. It was also true for lecturers of theology, for whom Charles IV tried to ensure the lacking titles through a requested papal bull. One of these masters, who were derisively nicknamed *bullati*, was also the Dominican John (Jan) Moravec, who following his studies at Oxford and at Paris served three years as a lecturer and instructor of clerics at the cathedral church in Prague. And since he had brought with him, i.a. commentaries on all of natural philosophy and metaphysics in the then modern form of scholarly questions, it can be reasonably supposed that after the foundation of the University of Prague he expounded also on several books prescribed for the study of the liberal arts.

Of the Bohemian and Moravian students who obtained master's degrees in Paris in the 1350s and 1360s, few left a more significant mark on the grounds of Prague tertiary education. Most of them devoted themselves to theology and after returning from abroad worked at the cathedral school or at general monastic studies. For example, Parisian Master Martin Jesconis of Veselice studied theology and at the same time worked as a professor of liberal arts in Prague in 1359–1362. His companion Master Konrád Matějův (Conradus) of Domažlice, one of the Parisian students of Vojtěch Raňkův of Ježov (Adalbertus Ranconis de Ericinio), was the administrator of the St Vitus cathedral school for ten years after his return to Prague sometime in 1361. For a long time, the liberal arts were taught only by Master Fridman of Prague, who had completed his studies in Paris at the beginning of the 1360s and who for his merits became the second dean of the already thoroughly constituted Faculty of Liberal Arts in 1368. These and other students from Paris soon brought to Prague the normative study texts of Albert the Great and especially John Buridan, whose commentaries for decades

189/ The list of these students was compiled by Černá-Šlapáková, 'Studenti z českých zemí v Paříži', pp. 70–72.

influenced the nominalistic school (of Ockham) in Prague and its offshoots in Vienna, in Cracow and elsewhere.[190]

Among the students of the University of Paris, we can find not only the already-mentioned professors of Prague but in 1372–1373 even the future archbishop of Prague John (Jan) of Jenštejn, who stayed for a short time also at the University of Montpellier. At the time of the emperor's visit to Paris, Master Matthew (Matthias) of Janov studied at the Sorbonne. Along with this influential thinker of the beginning Bohemian reformation, Charles' entrance to Paris might have been watched by two other Czech scholars, Bušek of Skopytce and Jacob (Jakub) of Prague. The most deserving of our attention in this connection is the Scholastic of the Prague Chapter Master Adalbertus Ranconis de Ericinio, who obtained a master's degree at the University of Paris on 12 June 1346. He acquitted himself well also as a professor in subsequent years, because in September 1349 and again in February 1351 he was elected Procurator of the English Nation, which also included students from the Empire and other Central European countries. In October 1352, Master Adalbertus was accepted as a member of the foremost university college which was named the Sorbonne after its founder. It brought Adalbertus a respectable income, the opportunity to study in the renowned college library, for which he compiled a preserved catalogue, and last but not least also significant prestige. Otherwise, the university would not have elected him as its chancellor on 10 October 1355. During his activity in Paris, Master Adalbertus relatively often, as was the custom, served as the examiner and promoter of his compatriots. An historian of the Middle Ages mostly contends with a lack of verified reports and so sometimes must be satisfied even with data that do not cast a good light on the great men of domestic history. The shortcomings of Adalbertus' memory include both his arrogance and his denunciatory letters on his Prague colleagues. Whereas in Paris he was constantly in debt and had to pawn even books when in dire straits, his profitable benefices at the cathedral in Prague allowed him to save a significant amount which he then in his last will allocated for a foundation for Bohemian students at Paris and at Oxford.[191] We can conclude this chapter with this commendable act to the benefit of poor philosophers and theologians of purely Bohemian provenance.

COURTIERS, DIPLOMATS AND MEN IN THE BACKGROUND

Whereas in earlier historiography attention was focused on the sovereigns, who sometimes undeservedly became the agents of all political events, more recent research has given preference to the external as well as internal lives of their courts and residences. Nevertheless, precisely in the case of the court of

190/ The latest on that can be found in Šmahel, *Die Prager Universität*, passim.
191/ Further details are listed by Kadlec, *Leben und Schriften*, pp. 2–13 and 59.

King of Bohemia and Holy Roman Emperor Charles IV we would like to know more. This is being hindered by the lack of written sources, which is particularly vexatious in comparison with the French court of Charles V and his predecessors.

At the beginnings of his reign, Charles IV had neither the time nor the requisite means for the building of an impressive court.[192] His father John had his not very numerous retinue, which substituted for a permanent court on journeys and which also assured contacts both with home and with foreign allies and partners. These worldly-wise diplomats helped Charles especially when he endeavoured for his recognition in the Empire. Since his primary interest was to maintain good relations with the papal court, he had remarkable support in his confidante, the graduated lawyer and first archbishop of Prague, Ernest (Arnošt) of Pardubice. Besides the above-mentioned complicated negotiations in Avignon, Ernest was a frequent counsellor of Charles' at the imperial diets or during meetings with European rulers. In March 1353, for instance, he accompanied Charles to a congress of Central European sovereigns in Vienna; two years later, he participated with him in the coronation journey to Italy, in 1356 he was with the emperor in Wrocław, in 1357 in Vienna, in 1358 he went to Lithuania to invite Grand Duke of Lithuania Olgerd to Wrocław to accept baptism, in 1363 he stayed with Charles in Nuremberg, which was not the first time, and again in May 1364, a few weeks before his passing, we catch him in Olomouc. Ernest was Charles' counsellor as well as assistant also on home soil (it is enough to mention here his share in the establishment of the University of Prague) and he acted on his behalf as the regent of the Kingdom of Bohemia in his absence from the country.[193]

Ernest's successor and the first Bohemian Cardinal John (Jan) Očko of Vlašim (1364–1378) acquitted himself already in his youth as a 'secretary and counsellor of the emperor'. This title had the best sound in the court titling, and its holder moreover enjoyed confidence as *familiaris* or *commensalis*, i.e. domestic companion or messmate. Most discussions really occurred during feasts, which were nevertheless attended by a much wider circle of people, sometimes also important burghers, who were however seated at one of the distant tables. Not only at the French but also at the Prague court, proximity to the sovereign was a sign of social prestige. Allow us to return to Archbishop John Očko, in whom Charles IV had absolute trust, because he appointed him regent of the kingdom during his absence in the land in 1368. It is telling that Charles never

54. John Očko of Vlašim († 1380), second archbishop of Prague and cardinal. A bust in the inner triforium of the Cathedral of St Vitus at Prague Castle

192/ On Charles' court, see especially Patze, 'Die Hofgesellschaft Kaiser Karls IV.', pp. 733–774, further Kavka, *Am Hofe Karls IV.*; on his everyday routine, see Hlaváček, 'Z každodennosti Karla IV. a jeho dvora', pp. 33–42.

193/ For the latest, see Hledíková, *Arnošt z Pardubic*, which contains further literature on pp. 328–338.

appointed Czech lords to this significant governor function with the exception of members of his own dynasty. As the Czech high nobility followed the sovereign's inclinations to centralised power with distrust and refused his proposal of a legal code, then neither Charles IV had a reason to cede to his opponents more than was necessary.[194]

Charles' close cooperation with the highest representatives of Bohemian church province was to the benefit of not only a calm domestic situation but also the royal treasury, because there was no need to pay confidants, officials or diplomats of the ecclesiastical estate, as it was after all also in France, because their livelihood was assured by the incomes from their ecclesiastical benefices. This was also the case with Bishop of Litomyšl and from 1364 Bishop of Olomouc John (Johann) of Neumarkt, who as prothonotary and court chancellor led Charles' chancellery for more than twenty years beginning in 1353. Since imperial and Bohemian matters were attended to in a single, formally undivided chancellery, John of Neumarkt had an entirely exceptional position in the exercise of the sovereign's power and in the administrative affairs of the entire enormous territory. More than seven thousand preserved documents issued at Charles IV's charge represent only a part of the writings which day after day left his chancellery.[195]

If we have at the moment an insufficient knowledge of the complex running of this office as a permanent institution in one place, it is the harder to imagine the functioning of the chancellery during the frequent and often even several-month-long journeys of Charles IV around his lands. His retinue thus always had to have several notaries and clerks aside from the trunks with official registers, which were necessary to transport from place to place. Applicants for privileges and pardons usually brought the requisite documents with them, which sped up the process. Besides the chancellor, also the members of the council and other important figures at the court had decisive influence on the positive disposal of applications submitted, because they reported to the sovereign, gave recommendation or denial positions and later as the so-called relators interpreted his decisions to the chancellery officials. It is not necessary to add that these services were not for free and that alongside the fees set in advance it was necessary to expect to pay bribes as well as provide reciprocal services.

Bishop John of Neumarkt inscribed himself permanently into the history of *Bohemica* culture as an elegant stylist, the author of model form collections and numerous translations from Latin to German and vice versa and last but

194/ A critical edition was prepared by Hergemöller, *Maiestas Carolina*. On the rejection of Charles' Code by the Bohemian aristocracy, see Mezník, 'Odvolání Majestas Carolina', pp. 53–63; on the state of the research, see Kejř, 'Die sogenannte Maiestas Carolina', pp. 79–122.

195/ Charles' chancellery awaits a comprehensive treatment. From the earlier literature, cf. esp. Moraw, 'Räte und Kanzlei', pp. 285–292, and 'Grundzüge der Kanzleigeschichte', pp. 11–42.

55. The proposal of a friendly contract between Charles IV and John I the Good. Pergamen deed with attached golden bull from 26 August 1355

not least also as a lover of beautiful books. His early Humanist interests need not be overestimated, but his correspondence and personal contacts with such important representatives of the Early Italian Renaissance as Francesco Petrarch and Cola di Rienzo at the very least testify to his cultural overview and religious orientation. Thanks to John of Neumarkt, the circle of his friends and other similar foci around the university and in some monasteries, Charles' Prague residence including the court became an important centre of European culture.[196] If in some aspects Prague lagged behind Paris, it was in the areas of political thought and politics. Charles IV did not need counsellors in this regard and it was he who conceived the main principles of his internal as well as foreign policies.

In the second half of the fourteenth century, European diplomacy was still a long way from permanent embassies and envoys named for a longer

196/ The research has recently become significantly sceptical on the Early Humanism of Charles' circle and namely also John of Neumarkt. On this, see especially Seibt, 'Gab es einen böhmischen Frühhumanismus?', pp. 1–19, Vidmanová, 'Středolatinská beletrie', pp. 140–149, and Šmahel, 'Gab es einen Frühhumanismus im luxemburgischen Böhmen?'. All the more emphasised are the almost contemporary beginnings of Humanist literature in France. I draw attention here mainly to the research school of G. Ouy and the anthologies *L'humanisme français au début de la Renaissance* (1973), *L'aube de la Renaissance* (1991) and *Préludes à la Renaissance* (1992).

period. Only the Papal Curia was a step ahead with its institution of legates plenipotentiary for certain ecclesiastical provinces and to a lesser degree also some Italian city republics, namely Venice. Most foreign policy negotiations and contacts were implemented through delegations, which were led by either members of the wider royal family or other trustworthy figures with the necessary experience, knowledge and contacts. This was especially true in the relations of Emperor Charles IV with the Papal Curia, but a certain specialisation can be observed also with diplomats, who were sent to various areas of the Empire. Although Charles was the supreme ruler here, he did not rule directly but through electors, land dukes, counts as well as other feudatories, into whose administration he would intervene only exceptionally. This can explain why the Prague chancellery could manage the entire agenda of the enormous territory and why on the other hand it was in Charles' interest to travel as much as possible and on ceremonial entry into towns to express far and wide spectacularly his presence as the supreme head of the Holy Roman Empire. With the exception of imperial cities and the so-called Bohemian fiefs, where he had his regents and officials, Charles IV exercised his rule through court diets and affiliate royal court of justice.

According to Charles' Golden Bull, a congregation or colloquium of the seven electors was to meet annually, but this regulation was never discharged, namely *inter alia* because the emperor by centralising power in his own hands indirectly limited the institutionalisation of this colloquium to the election of the sovereign. It is therefore not surprising that after the Imperial Diet in Metz all seven of the electors quite likely met only once, and that at the ceremonial baptism of Charles' first-born son Wenceslas in Nuremberg on 11 April 1361. On the other hand, another ceremonial assembly of the court diet (*solempnis curia imperialis*) mentioned in the Golden Bull, also attended by some of the electors and the highest imperial figures, convened at least ten times. In total, these ceremonial sessions were attended by around 45 dukes and almost 90 archbishops and abbots, but always in a different composition depending on the place as well as the reason for the meeting.[197]

To describe the administrative system of the Holy Roman Empire with respect to royal power is not simple. First of all, the Empire was divided into various concordant or on the other hand divergent regions. Suffice it to say that politically it comprised fourteen territories with their own administration and independent organisations. The decisive group in terms of power consisted of the imperial dukes, including even the sovereign. This group, which included the members of roughly twenty ducal dynasties and approximately

197/ See Hergemöller, 'Die „solempnis curia", pp. 451–476.

fifty imperial bishops, did not form an estate as a political corporation until the end of the fifteenth century. It arises from this that every duke represented only himself, with the entire group being characterised by a surprisingly large inequality. Special positions among the imperial dukes in the fourteenth and fifteenth centuries were held by the electors on the one hand and the three dynasties with real royal ambitions on the other. The rivalry as well as the actual positions of the Luxemburgs and Habsburgs were balanced for a long time; the Wittelsbachs had somewhat lesser power, but neither did they compromise, considering themselves as equal, and themselves never came to the seats of their rivals, always sending a deputy. It was different with most electors, especially because the Luxemburgs after acquiring Brandenburg had two votes. It was always important for Charles IV that electors be represented as much as possible at diets convoked by him. At the same time, they were independent in their decision making, because their only obligation was to meet for the election of the new king. Even an unimportant elector enjoyed higher prestige than any of the imperial dukes. All of them without a difference needed the sovereign as much as the ruler needed them, because they mutually legitimised their privileged ducal positions through the elections or formal procedures.[198]

It was different in the lands of the Bohemian Crown, where the actual base of Charles' dynasty lay. Wherever Charles IV was as the King of Bohemia the direct owner as well as lord, he was concerned with well-functioning administration. It is no wonder, because what was at issue were the incomes from the silver mines, the stamping of coins and other so-called regalian rights, further the profits from customs, tolls, the forests and agricultural lands around castles, and last but not least the regular taxes and so-called assistance in the form of financial loans from the royal towns, townlets and some large cloisters founded by the ruler. The administration of the sovereign's direct domain was already before that ensured by the court, partially hereditary offices, which under Charles IV mostly modified their competences in agreement with his centralising policy. What mainly gained in significance was the royal court of justice, applicable to the king's direct servants, vassals as well as bailiffs of royal villages and over time to most feudal affairs as well. Likewise the importance of the Master of the Royal Household rose rapidly. Under Charles IV, he was the actual first agent of the court, whose authority sometimes expanded even into the foreign policy sphere.

In the middle of the fourteenth century, a new important administrative body became the Office of the Master of the King's Chamber, who provided for the court and the ruler's needs financially on the basis of a central admin-

198/ I summarise here the crucial treatise by Moraw, 'Fürsten am spätmittelalterlichen deutschen Königshof', pp. 17–32.

istration of all the royal incomes. Nevertheless, the older court institutions retained their powers. They included the office of the royal Vice-Chamberlain and Judge of the Royal Court (in German *Hofrichter*, in Latin *iudex curiae*), who were responsible for the royal towns, then the offices of the Master of the Mint in Kutná Hora (Kuttenberg), Grand Master of the Hounds, and the hereditary offices of the Grand Marshall, High Steward and High Cupbearer (Butler), which were reserved for the lords of Lipá, of Házmburk (Hasenburg) and of Vartemberk (Wartemberg). Most of these court dignitaries had their deputies, further scribes and other employees, which was true also for the parallel offices of the court of the Queen of Bohemia.

From the end of the thirteenth century, the growing power of the high nobility demanded direct participation in the running of the country, namely through diets on the one hand and the establishment of a land court on the other, whose authority included the decision making in criminal affairs of the aristocracy and free landed estates. 'Finding the right' at a land court, which gradually grew into an estate institution, was exclusively in the competence of older lay judges or patriarchs from the old feudal families. The land court sat four times a year on so-called Ember days, and its resolutions were registered on several rows of land tablets (*tabulae terrae*), the registers of landed property and the resolutions on the criminal offenses of free landowners. The supreme land officials, i.e. the High Chamberlain, High Judge of the Land Court and High Land Scribe, did not have to live permanently in Prague, because each of them had his deputy, specifically the Vice-Chamberlain, Vice-Judge and Vice-Scribe. The specialisation of the land court crystallised the orientation of some formerly royal officials, who became officials of the land community of noblemen. This concerned namely also the High Burgrave of Prague, who was in charge of the execution of court resolutions.

So far we have spoken only of the Kingdom of Bohemia, the central component of the state formation of the lands of the Bohemian Crown, which Charles IV building on the territorial gains of his father completed in a framework of constitutional privileges from 7 April 1348.[199] In an attempt to preclude the unilateral connection of the land and fiefs belonging to the Kingdom of Bohemia with the person of the ruling sovereign, which could be in danger if he died, Charles conceived an impersonal or more precisely superpersonal union of lands of the Bohemian Crown, namely in an entirely specific, permanent territorial extent. The relations of the parts to the whole were regulated on the basis of historically incurred bonds as well as the current state. From his title as King of the Romans, Charles subjected the bishopric of

199/ For more detail on this, see Spěváček, *Karel IV.*, pp. 272–276.

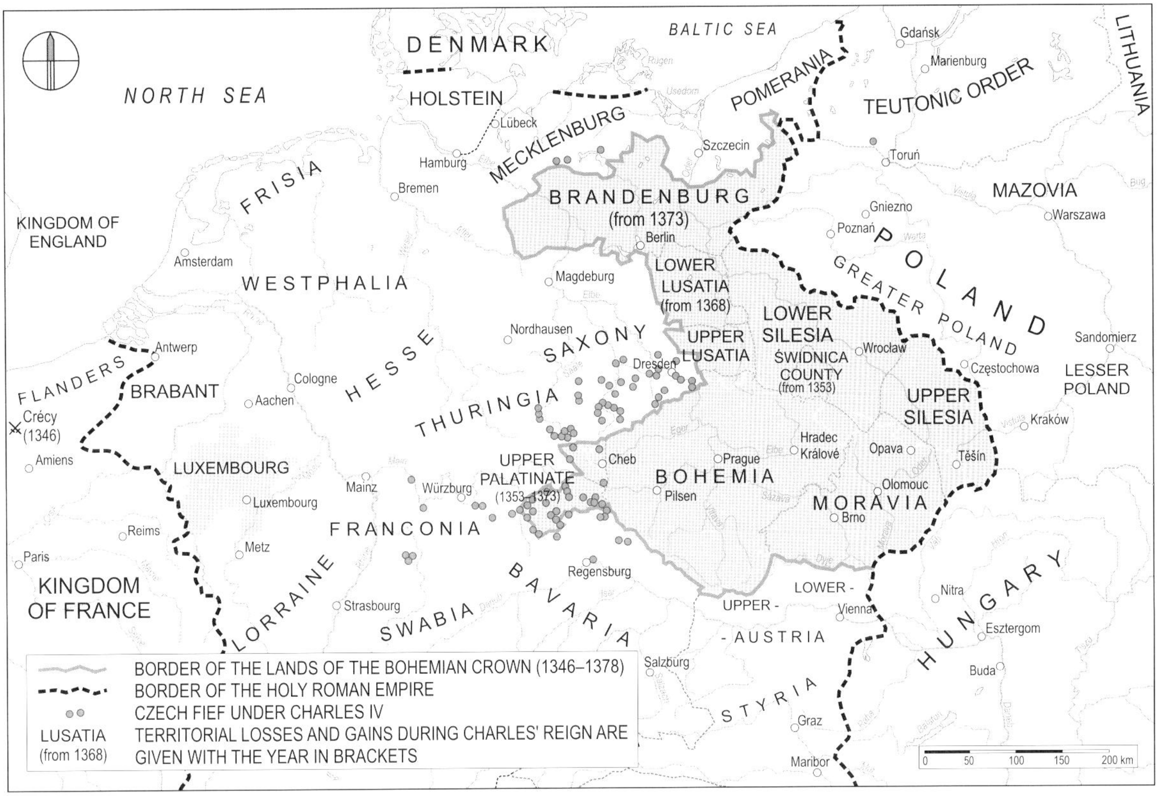

56. Map of the lands of the Crown of Bohemia

Olomouc, margraviate of Moravia and duchy of Opava as feudatories to legislation and direct rule of the Kings and Crown of the Kingdom of Bohemia. Charles IV again from the power of the King of the Romans incorporated the duchies of Silesia, the duchy of Wrocław (Breslau) with the city of Wrocław as well as the mark Lausitz of Budyšín (Bautzen) and Zhořelec (Görlitz), i.e. Lower and Upper Lusatia, into the Kingdom of Bohemia and its Crown.

In the lands that immediately fell under the sovereignty of the King of Bohemia, Charles' powers were similar to those in Bohemia. In the Wrocław district, in a part of the duchy of Głogów (Glogau), Upper and Lower Lusatia, Charles appointed his deputies, whom he mainly selected from the Bohemian aristocracy. These land commissioners (*Hauptmänner*), or reeves (*Vögte*) as they were called in both Lusatias, were among his confidants and thus often accompanied him on his journeys abroad. This was also the case with Těma the Younger of Kolditz, first a reeve in Upper Lusatia and later land governor in Wrocław, who participated in Charles' journey to France at the turn of 1378. The margraves of Moravia, the dukes of Opava and the princes of Silesia were similarly also in the closest circle of the king. All of these, as well as the dukes of Luxembourg, were direct rulers in their territories, whereas the King of Bohemia had only feudal sovereignty over them. In most of the adjacent lands, the local aristocracy or significant towns asserted themselves more or less in the local courts and diets here and there.[200] Now that we have briefly introduced the relatively complicated administrative system of Charles' enormous empire, allow us to mention at least in outline how Charles strengthened his imperial and royal majesty through court and other festivities.

IN THE PUBLIC EYE: COURT AND OTHER FESTIVITIES, RITUALS AND CEREMONIES

Practically wherever and whenever the sovereign left his privacy, his very presence added an exceptional, uncommon or directly celebratory character to even common events. This also held true for his Prague residence. We already have some idea of the spaces in which Charles IV moved at the Castle and by which noble officials he was surrounded and possibly also served. Other than these secular as well as ecclesiastical aristocrats, whom we often encounter as witnesses to the drafting of diverse political and other agreements and privileges, the court comprised more than three hundred people, from porters to royal chaplains. Service at the court brought both privileges and prestige; it is therefore not surprising that many a craftsman or supplier listed it with his name. Higher placed courtiers, like the king's physicians, Masters of the Kitchen or Commanders of the Castle Guards, owned houses in the towns of Prague. The topography of the residences of these as well as other courtiers at the time of Charles and Wenceslas IV indicated not only prosperity but also the variety of their professions. Besides the expected servants such as the valets or coachmen, it is sufficient to list the postmen, butlers, who were in charge of the table dishes, keepers of the wardrobe, shavers and barber-surgeons, fifers, heralds, trumpeters, clockmakers, armourers, lion tamers, who took care of the castle animal menagerie, and last but not least also jesters. The queen of course had her own courtiers and servants as well.[201]

The most festive of all the celebrations was the coronation. For the first of them, which took place in Prague on 2 September 1347, Charles IV with the aid of his counsellors issued a new coronation order. Its basic outline consisted of the ancient German coronation order from the tenth century, to which both traditional elements of the Old Czech ceremony and some liturgical innovations adopted from the coronation order of the French kings were added. The connection with the Přemyslid dynasty was alluded to by the ceremonies at Vyšehrad, considered to be the earliest seat of the Czech princes, which

200/ From the earlier literature, see especially Hlaváček, 'Ústřední moc a správa v českém státě za Lucemburků', pp. 37–56; an overview of the administration of the Crown lands has most recently been provided by Bobková, *Velké dějiny zemí Koruny české,* IVa, pp. 563–568.

201/ Most of the court offices and professions were captured by Tomek, *Dějepis města Prahy*, III, pp. 1–25; on the topography of the residences of the officials, see Patze, 'Die Hofgesellschaft Kaiser Karls IV.', pp. 733–773.

57. The Bohemian, so-called St Wenceslas crown, which Charles IV had made for his coronation in 1347

were attended the day before the coronation by the members of the sovereign's family, the highest ecclesiastical dignitaries, the representatives of the most important aristocratic families and five-member delegations of Prague as well as of Brno. Charles here apparently put on the bast shoes and bag of Přemysl the Ploughman, accepted the homage of the important figures present and subsequently left with them for vespers at St Vitus Cathedral. After this ceremony, which symbolically connected the pre-Christian roots of the ruling family with the protective cult of the Czech nation's patron saint, Prince Wenceslas, Charles according to the Old Czech tradition retired to the ceremoniously decorated bedroom accompanied by all those present. Only on the second day were the liturgical components of the French Coronation Order also implemented, predominantly in the associated blessing and coronation of Queen Blanche.[202]

Whereas for various reasons no other coronation of a King of Bohemia took place according to all of the requirements of Charles' order of coronation, Prague still under the emperor's reign experienced three coronations of his wives. Charles himself, always however in another place of his extensive empire, was crowned another four times in the next twenty years. Although he had himself crowned as the King of the Romans in Bonn already on 26 November

202/ The Bohemian Coronation Order was issued and interpreted by Cibulka, *Český řád korunovační a jeho původ*; the course of the coronation on 1 and 2 September was reconstructed by Spěváček, *Karel IV.*, pp. 331–338; a critical revision of the research up to now was presented by Žůrek, 'Korunovační řád Karla IV.', pp. 105–143.

1346, Charles organised another coronation in Aachen on 25 July 1347 after being generally recognised in the Empire, through which he followed the tradition of the place connected with the cult of his highly esteemed predecessor Charlemagne. His desired coronation as the Holy Roman Emperor on 5 April 1355 was preceded in January of the same year by the coronation of the King of Lombardy in the Cathedral of St Ambrose in Milan, then ten years later the coronation as King of Arelat (Burgundy) took place in Arles.

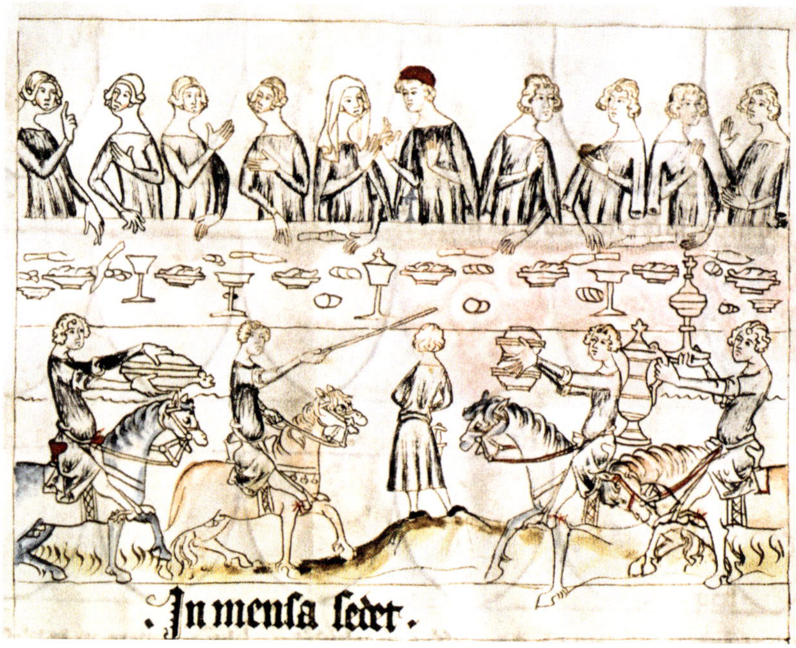

58. Feast at the court of Archbishop Baldwin in Trier (Codex Balduini Trevoriensis. Koblenz Landeshauptstadtarchiv, Bestand 1C, Nr. 1, fol. 3a)

Whereas all of these first-class representations of Charles' majesty in the period regard had their justification and their pageantry went without saying, then the coronation of the two-year-old successor Wenceslas IV did not find a positive response with his contemporaries. Already the birth and Christening of the heir to the throne were marked by exceptional festivity. Immediately after Wenceslas was born in Nuremberg in the evening hours of 26 February 1361, the bells of the churches there chimed. The joyful father had the infant weighed and for each of his sixteen pounds of the child Wenceslas' weight he donated a gold piece to the treasury of the Cathedral of the Virgin Mary in Aachen. Charles' chancellery was then busy the next days, sending letters with the news in all directions. 'We finally have a prince,' the emperor notified his subjects as well as friendly sovereigns and lords. Both the rich and poor, young and old, one like the other, simply all of Bohemia and its adjacent lands were to rejoice. Similarly, although more soberly, the empress wrote to the pope and the aldermen of the imperial towns. Charles IV connected the christening with the convocation of a celebratory court diet in Nuremberg and therefore postponed its date all the way to 11 April. The little Wenceslas was baptised immediately by three archbishops, who were assisted by six bishops and five abbots. The enumeration of the other important guests would take too much space, because it is still necessary to mention in outline the associated acts of a celebratory or otherwise exceptional nature. Charles IV *inter alia* granted an extensive amnesty to prisoners, exempted Nuremberg from paying its annual tax and had the imperial insignia and relics, which he had had brought from Bohemia for this occasion, shown from the gallery of the newly built church Frauenkirche. The christening of the small Wenceslas was followed by eight days of festivities accompanied by tournaments, banquets and theatre productions.[203]

59. Anna of Schweidnitz (1339–1362), Empress and Queen of Bohemia, third wife of Charles IV. A bust in the inner triforium of the Cathedral of St Vitus at Prague Castle

Neither was Charles' third wife and Wenceslas' mother Anna of Schweidnitz spared the sad fate of her two predecessors Blanche of Valois († 1348) and Anne of Bavaria († 1353). Her death on 11 July 1362 was borne by the emperor as another 'contrivance of a hidden enemy, which he could not avoid'. The words from Charles' letter to the bishops in which he requested requiem masses for the twenty-three-year-old Anna are the only mention of her funeral. Nevertheless, some of the rites from the mourning ritual after the death of Charles IV were undoubtedly executed also in it. It can be assumed with significant probability that also the funeral of Empress Anna stretched over several days, because her dead body always rested overnight in one of the selected Prague cathedrals, namely first at Vyšehrad, then at St Jacob in the Old Town and further at the Knights of the Cross below the Chain of the Bridge, from whence the final part of the procession led back to St Vitus Cathedral.[204]

As was his custom, Charles did not hesitate long with another marriage. The wedding to the sixteen-year-old Elizabeth of Pomerania, niece of King of Poland Casimir the Great, this time took place at Wawel Castle in Cracow. A month later, although three days before Elizabeth was crowned in Prague on 18 June 1363, the coronation of the two-year-old heir to the Bohemian throne Wenceslas IV was held in St Vitus Cathedral. Although Charles IV wanted by this entirely singular act in Czech history to prevent possible later disputes over the succession, not even his closest advisors approved of his approach. Archbishop Ernest of Pardubice considered the coronation of an immature child to be a foolish step, but he had to obey and carry out the coronation.

203/ The citations from the letters of the imperial couple along with other details on the baptism are given by Spěváček, *Václav IV.*, pp. 29–37.
204/ The similarities are provided by Šmahel, 'Spectaculum et pompa funebris', pp. 12–13.

60. King of the Romans and Bohemia Wenceslas IV. (1361–1419). A bust in the inner triforium of the Cathedral of St Vitus at Prague Castle

In the literary circle of Chancellor John of Neumarkt, a fake letter by little Wenceslas to his father was secretly passed around, in which the madness of the coronation act was expressed to the privy. A later echo of the contemporary opinion intensified by the rancorous position of the German and Catholic chroniclers towards Wenceslas IV is the anecdote in the encyclopaedia by Pavel Žídek. At his coronation, Wenceslas apparently 'cried immensely and shat all over the altar of St Maurice at the Castle on which he was standing when he was being crowned and was crying and did not calm down until a baker gave him a cake'. While the emperor achieved the agreement of the Bohemian estate community with the succession of his first-born son without greater difficulties, it took him thirteen years in the Empire before the fifteen-year-old Wenceslas was elected King of the Romans by the votes of all the electors in Frankfurt on 10 June 1376. After that, the coronation in Aachen was not long in coming. It exceptionality was obvious to all of the lofty participants, because the newly elected King of the Romans was being assisted in it by the ruling emperor and his wife.[205]

The coronations, wedding and births of descendants and other ceremonial events in the life of the royal family were occasions for fabulous feasts, tourneys and other amusements on which not even Charles IV, otherwise careful in terms of expenditures, could scrimp.[206] In the eyes of the public and even more so of the toadies and malicious foreign informers, precisely these spectacular attractions had greater weight than many state-legal affairs. Regardless of the costs, it was necessary to express that no one could match the king. Therefore, the halls of the castle palace were not sufficient for especially important banquets and it was necessary to construct provisional pavilions or tents in open areas for the numerous guests. The venue of these festivities more than once was one of the Prague squares. Especially the coronation feast which Charles IV with his spouse Blanche organised on Sunday, 2 September 1347 entered historical memory. For this purpose, a large pavilion, hung with gold-interlaced curtains and silk cloths, was built at the marketplace at St Havel. When the royal couple in ostentatious vestments sat down at the raised table, they laid aside the insignia including the crowns, which during the meal were being held above their heads by the eminent courtiers. The highest royal officials – Marshal, Chamberlain, Butler, Steward, Cupbearer and Master of the Hounds –

205/ The details are in Spěváček, *Václav IV.*, pp. 45–47 and 88–90. The quote of the anecdote has been taken from the edition by Tobolka (ed.), *M. Pavla Žídka Spravovna*, p. 178.

206/ An opportunity for celebrations was provided by Charles' numerous weddings, on which see Veldtrup, *Zwischen Eherecht und Familienpolitik*, and Kavka, *Čtyři ženy Karla IV.* Significant court festivities included also the homages and feudal oaths. The ceremonial handover of the Margraviate of Brandenburg to Charles IV was explained in detail in Bláhová, 'Pražský hrad 2. října 1373', pp. 131–139.

then one after another came in on horses decorated with trappings to the table of the royal couple and served them according to the time-honoured rituals. The generally good mood was created, i.a. by trumpeters and other musicians; the spectators were also being entertained by the tournament duels and various competitions in physical prowess. At the end of the feast, the king presented generous gifts to the significant foreign as well as domestic guests. Charles IV donated the wood from the pavilion for the royal banquet to the new cloister of the Carmelite Order that he founded the day after his coronation.[207]

The September banquet of 1347 seems to have been a prototype of many other ceremonial feasts which took place in Prague and to which the chroniclers do not pay as much attention to any more. Not even foreign observers failed to notice the munificence of the Prague celebrations. The poet Guillaume de Machaut on his last visit to the Czech metropolis was fascinated besides by the comely court damsels in the hall also by the tones of the Prague bells and the musical instrumental productions with a remarkable set of instruments. 'All the things there shone with silk / And gleamed with a golden glow'.[208] At the ceremonial feasts at Charles' court, the entertainment was to please not only the body but also the spirit. It is evidenced by *Summa recreatorum* from the third quarter of the fourteenth century, which in five treatises provides guidelines on how to increase the level of entertainment at celebratory feasts. Besides entirely factual hygienic instructions, we find here fables, entertaining stories, religious as well as secular songs and last but not least also *exempla* with the noble paragons of rulers.[209]

The menus and recipes of Charles' feasts have not been preserved. In this aspect, Czech royal cuisine seems to have lagged behind the culinary artistry of the French court. Machaut knew how to appreciate the abundance of meat and wine, unlike his younger colleague Eustache Deschamps, who did not mince his words in his remembrance of Czech food. 'Fleas, stink, pigs, mold, / The gist of the Bohemian soul, // Bread and salted fish and cold. // Leeks, and cabbage three days old, / Smoked meat, as hard and black as coal; / Fleas, stink, pigs, mold. // Twenty eating from one bowl, / A bitter drink it's beer, I'm told / Bad sleep on a straw in some filthy hole, / Fleas, stink, pigs, mold, / The gist of the Bohemian soul, / Bread and salted fish and cold'.[210] Deschamps disparages

207/ For a description of the banquet, see *Chronicon Francisci Pragensis*, p. 201, and *Chronicon Benessii de Weitmil*, pp. 514–515.
208/ Cf. Nejedlý, 'Deux poètes français', pp. 38–39; overall on court celebrations, see Kavka, *Am Hofe Karls IV.*, pp. 96–105.
209/ On this compilation, see Vidmanová, 'Summa recreatorum', pp. 170–179. According to the same author, another treatise, entitled 'Mensa philosophica', was also created at roughly the same time, cf. Vidmanová, 'Životospráva pro císařský dvůr', pp. 126–128.
210/ Eustache Deschamps, 'Rondeau', in *Selected Poems*, trans. by David Curzon and Jeffrey Fiskin, ed. by Ian S. Laurie and Deborah M. Sinnreich-Levi (New York – London, 2003), p. 195. On the poet's stay in Bohemia, see Nejedlý, 'Deux poètes français', pp. 40–42.

the dishes that he saw in pubs. The same meals were, however, served also at ceremonial feasts. At the end of his life Charles IV himself allegedly arranged a feast in three courses in the 'German way'. The very first course was rewarding, because huge chunks of beef were brought to the table, followed by boiled capons with turnips and juicy roasts with bacon. The second course was capons again, but everyone enjoyed more the roasted sucklings, prepared without any gravy and jelly. Then it was the turn of the cakes, pears, nuts and wine.[211]

Besides the celebratory feasts, also the spectacular entrances of Charles IV into the imperial and other towns remained in the memory of the participants. Charles' entries into those towns of the Kingdom of Bohemia and the Margraviate of Moravia that welcomed their sovereign for the first time undoubtedly had a celebratory character as well.[212] For that matter, it was no different in German, Swiss, Alsatian and other towns that Charles IV visited for the first time. In all these places, they welcomed the new king and later emperor according to local customs and guidelines of the court marshal. The council of the city of Zurich, e.g. asked the surrounding municipalities in writing for a report whether King of the Romans Charles was approaching yet so that he could be welcomed in time and appropriately with bells and a procession in front of the entrance gate. Part of the burghers were to meet the king on horseback; the others were to wait in the open space before the gate as was the rule here as well as elsewhere. The burghers welcomed Charles garlanded with greenery and flowers; green wreathes also adorned the wives and daughters of the local patricians, who along with the abbess and the spiritual waited for the king at the courtyard of the convent of the Capitular nuns. On this occasion, the abbess received regalian rights as proof of her renewed rights to an imperial county (*Vogtei*, headed by a reeve), which had been from time immemorial also connected with the local Capitular Church (*Großmünster*). Therefore, it was necessary to repeat the ceremony here as well.[213]

The welcome was governed also by local customs. In Strasbourg in 1365, for example, Charles IV was greeted on his arrival at the cathedral by the members of various guilds with their weapons standing along both sides of the street. If the sovereign remained somewhere for a longer period, it was necessary to entertain him. In Basel, they organised a ball for the then still young Charles in 1347, at which he purportedly 'flirted' with the local ladies. For the wives of the patricians, it was a welcome occasion to show themselves in a new dress. In Zurich on the other hand, they prepared jousting tourneys in Charles' honour. Honorary gifts were a part of the welcoming. These were usually a cup

211/ On this, see Wolfram (ed.), *Die Metzer Chronik des Jaique Dex*, p. 313.
212/ For more on the entries into Moravian towns, see Borovský and Antonín, 'Venit rex!', pp. 57–93.
213/ Peyer, 'Der Empfang des Königs im mittelalterlichen Zürich', pp. 219–233.

filled with gold or a gilded silver set of dishes if the city treasury could afford it, the king also received gold coins. Neither did the queens as well as empresses come off badly if they accompanied Charles IV on his journeys. Elizabeth of Pomerania for instance received two silver cups and two other gilded vessels in Cologne on the Rhine in 1372; four years later, precious fabrics awaited her in Aachen.[214] It went without saying that the towns would provide the retinue of the noble guest with perquisites in the form of oat, wine, meat and fish. On the already-mentioned visit to Zurich, Charles was given under ceremonial circumstances *inter alia* a herd of cattle from the surrounding alpine dairy huts. Nevertheless, not everywhere was Charles cordially seen and welcomed. When on 15 September 1353 he entered Constance with numerous ecclesiastical and secular princes, he encountered chains in the streets and burghers in arms. The reason for this provision is not known, but the burghers obeyed Charles' command and removed the chains from the streets. Then the welcome was already conducted in mutual wariness but at ease on the exterior. The Council of Constance placated Charles with the gifts of several relics from the local rich sources, for which he granted the city an advantageous privilege to the bridge toll.[215]

Charles' entry into the Eternal City on the day of his imperial coronation on Easter Monday, 5 April 1355, was entirely unique because of its singular character. Charles was riding dressed in purple coronation vestments accompanied by horsemen with plumes on their helmets and with unsheathed weapons as if prepared for battle. Before entering the bridge leading to St Angel Castle, he was welcomed by the Chancellor of the city of Rome with his syndics. After swearing mutual oaths at Collina Gate (*Porta Collina*), Charles dubbed three nephews of Cardinal of Ostia Pierre Bernard de Colombier as knights. The Roman burghers with two Senators then accompanied Charles under the canopy to St Peter's. On the way, Charles still managed to grant knighthood to numerous applicants by sword or a mere touch of the hand.[216]

The ceremoniousness of the moment for those present as well as later witnesses was increased by the attendance of other generally known and distinguished persons in the sovereign's retinue. On the entry of Charles into Lübeck on Sunday, 20 October 1375, it was possible to see with one's own eyes Empress Elizabeth of Pomerania, Margrave of Moravia Jobst, Charles'

214/ See Wilbertz, 'Elisabeth von Pommern', pp. 53–54.

215/ For details, I refer to my Excursus – 'Welcoming Processions and Ceremonial Entries'. Charles' entry into cities was last paid attention to also by Bobková, *Velké dějiny zemí Koruny české*, IVa, pp. 527–535.

216/ This event has been devoted attention thoroughly by almost all of Charles' modern biographers; its spectacular nature has been captured in detail by Kavka, *5. 4. 1355. Korunovace Karla IV. císařem Svaté říše římské*; also cf. Bobková, *Velké dějiny zemí Koruny české*, IVa, Chapter II-1, which includes further literature.

son-in-law Otto V, Duke of Bavaria and Margrave-Elector of Brandenburg, Archbishop of Cologne along with four bishops, further the Margrave of Meissen and several dukes as well as imperial counts. Before entering the castle gates, the emperor and his wife mounted parade horses. The emperor was preceded by one of the councillors with the keys to the town and the empress by Archbishop of Cologne. The procession throughout the city reached the cathedral, where it was welcomed with songs. Two houses opposite each other which were connected by a covered passage on the level of the first floor had been prepared for the imperial couple. During his ten-day stay, Charles attended a ceremonial session of the council, at which he called the aldermen of this important Hanseatic city 'lords'. Another stop was on 31 October in Wismar, where the ceremonial entry was repeated, but this time with the participation of the feudal lord Albert II, Duke of Mecklenburg.[217] Charles IV received an especially ceremonious welcome in Dortmund between 22 and 24 November 1377, because no King of the Romans or Holy Roman Emperor had visited this free imperial city since 1232.[218]

Charles IV could not be everywhere, and thus he was present somewhere at least through his depictions and statues. If we already know how common statues of Charles V were above the entrances to his residences, then it is not surprising that similar plastic portraits did not go against the grain of his uncle on the Holy Roman and Bohemian thrones. He did not live long enough to see the monumental decoration with his seated statue in larger-than-life size on the Old Town Bridge Tower. Also the so-called Beautiful Fountain in Nuremberg with the figure of the popular emperor was created only after his death. His depictions can be found not only on entrance gates, where we would most expect the emperor's portrait. Above the southern portal of St Mary's Parish Church in Mühlhausen, Thuringia, Charles IV and his wife look from the indicated balcony, namely accompanied by one courtier and one lady in waiting. Public and sacral buildings were decorated with symbols of Charles' lands more often than with demanding sculptural portraits. The murals and other paintings with the depiction of Charles IV, which we have proved in the Hanseatic League Hall of the Cologne Historic Town Hall, seem to have been more common than it would appear based on their preservation. We have already spoken of Charles' family trees and other portraits at Karlštejn and in the palace at Prague Castle.

Hopefully, the mentions of the banquets, entries into towns and other ceremonial acts of Emperor Charles IV will help us see the welcome he would

---

217/ I adopt the data which were listed by Schieche, 'Die skandinavischen Länder', p. 166.
218/ The entrance and reception of Charles IV in Dortmund were reconstructed by Weifenbach, 'Freiheit durch Privilegien', pp. 228–233.

receive in Paris in January 1378 more soberly and in a wider context. However hard his hosts would try, the emperor could not have been very surprised.

THE GREAT SUMMITS OF EMPEROR CHARLES IV

Charles' building of the Czech state and thus also his dynastic domain have already been made somewhat evident from the previous chapters, like his credit in the blossoming of Prague, the Bohemian Church province and last but not least the first transalpine university. It is not necessary to particularise here, and this holds true also for Charles' policy in the Empire, which left traces in a countless number of privileges, foundations as well as other acts. And since we are keeping Charles' visit to France at the turn of 1378 in mind, it will not be off topic to mention further of his summits with influential representatives of the Christian world, at which questions of European consequence were not uncommonly dealt with.

If we were to follow the reign of Charles IV day by day and year by year, we could not miss that he constantly had to face diverse opposition pressures. To a certain extent, it was given not only by the relatively independent components of the Empire, whose rulers had almost sovereign power on their territory but also by the undisguised ambitions of the Wittelsbachs and Habsburgs, who with their alliance and other bonds many a time overreached into the neighbouring lands. In the southern ends of the Empire, it was necessary to maintain good relations with the Hungarian Anjous, who had a significant influence also in the complicated situation in northern Italy. Charles IV first appeared in Buda still as the Margrave of Moravia during his adventurous journey through the Kingdom of Hungary to Aquileia in spring 1337. The short meeting with King Charles Robert of Anjou (1310–1342) was probably of a formal nature but set the base for the later courtship between Charles' daughter Margaret (Markéta) and the sixteen-year-old heir to the Hungarian throne Louis. Charles first met him at the funeral of his Louis' father in Visegrád and in Székesfehérvár in the second half of July 1342. At this sad event, the three great sovereigns who were to decide on the history of a great part of Europe in the third quarter of the fourteenth century met each other, because also King of Poland Casimir the Great (1333–1370) hurried to the funeral, who along with Margrave Charles thus became a witness of the coronation of Louis of Anjou, which took place on 21 July 1342.

Over time, the influence of Louis of Hungary (1342–1382) increased so much that he also attended political negotiations which might at first sight appear to have a purely imperial character. For example in March 1353, we find him in Vienna, where he came for the congress of Charles IV with Duke of Austria Albert II Habsburg and with the imperial electors. The Venetian doges

61. Prague at the end of the 15th century, woodcut from the World Chronicle by Hartmann Schedel

as well as King of Poland Casimir sent their envoys to Vienna. The questions connected with Charles' postponed journey for the imperial crown were on the agenda along with the liberalisation of the trade transit from Italy through the Austrian lands to the Kingdom of Bohemia and then especially, as was common at the meetings of crowned heads, marriage alliances. The main issue was the culmination of the marriage contracts between Charles' daughter Catherine (Kateřina) and Duke of Austria Rudolph IV of Habsburg. The wedding actually occurred in April, but greater attention was aroused by the courtship of the emperor, who had been widowed again shortly before. And again like so many times already in this account, the children of the powerful became mere objects of political bidding. The thirteen-year-old Anna of Schweidnitz, daughter of the late Duke Henry II, whom Charles had originally found for his first son Wenceslas, who had died before his second birthday († 1351), became a desirable fiancée for the thirty-seven-year-old father. Her uncle Louis of Hungary, at whose court Anne lived with her mother, was favourably inclined to the union, so soon two weddings were celebrated in Buda, because Louis, whose first wife, Charles' first-born daughter Margaret (Markéta), had died already in 1349, celebrated his wedding to Elizabeth of Bosnia at the same time. Although it might seem that we pay exorbitant attention to betrothals and weddings, it is only a small part of similar contracts which were made or implemented simultaneously within the scope of Charles' interest.[219]

Anna of Schweidnitz probably did not have to regret it. Within less than two years, on 5 April 1355, she was the first of Charles' wives to be ceremonially crowned empress in Rome and with her husband she became acquainted with a piece of the world then. In February of the following year, she again

219/ The two-volume study by Steinherz, 'Die Beziehungen Ludwigs I. von Ungarn zu Karl IV.' is still important here; see esp. p. 245ff.

visited Hungary, because Charles IV took her to Györ (Raab) for a meeting with King Louis and the envoys of the Duke of Austria Albert. The hospitality which the imperial couple received surpassed all expectations. Both were given a gorgeous golden bowl; Chancellor John of Neumarkt was rewarded with jewellery worth a thousand golden florins, and also other officials of the chancellery including the younger notaries came out of it well, each being given a reward of one hundred florins. It is not surprising that the chancellor mentioned this generosity in a letter to one of his friends.[220]

Apparently for practical reasons, both crowned sovereigns, Charles and Louis, preferred meetings half way also in the future. This was the case also with respect to Duke of Austria Rudolph IV of Habsburg, with whom they met twice in this way, first in Trnava on 15 May 1360 and second two years later in Uherské Hradiště also in May. The first meeting was called to settle the disputes created on the basis of alleged mutual slanders, on which nothing else is known. On this occasion, the emperor also agreed with the duke of Austria on the method of investiture, which until then had been postponed because of ambiguous interpretation of the questionable privileges. Rudolf endeavoured to achieve *inter alia* that the fief be granted on Austrian territory and he not have to kneel in the ceremony but sit like an elector on a horse, namely with a ducal hat on his head moreover decorated with a crown. The emperor yielded to the duke in the issue of the selection of place but himself did not sacrifice much. Seefeld, where on 21 May 1360 he granted Austrian lands as a fief to Rudolph and his brothers, did lie on Austrian land but was an imperial feudatory. The ceremony was conducted according to the customs up until then, with the duke and his lands in return receiving guarantees that it had not been done to their possible detriment.[221]

Charles IV arrived with a large suite at the meeting in Uherské Hradiště on 8 May 1363, in which besides bishops, Silesian dukes and imperial counts we can find also Margrave of Moravia John Henry and several Bohemian lords. The agenda again included mutual disagreements, which were to be muted by an extension of the truce until the arbitrator's pronouncement, which was requested to be made by King of Poland Casimir and Duke Bolek II of Schweidnitz. From Uherské Hradiště, the emperor headed to Cracow. He had a truly serious reason for it, because already on 21 May he celebrated his marriage to his fourth wife Elizabeth of Pomerania there. Charles rushed with the wedding this time, because Anne of Schweidnitz died giving birth

220/ This is interesting in relation to the gifts which the emperor and his retinue would receive in Paris in January 1378. Chancellor John of Neumarkt expressed his satisfaction in his letter from spring 1356, published by Schieche, 'Svídnický formulář Jana ze Středy', p. 150, No. 6.
221/ For more, see Kavka, *Vláda Karla IV.*, I, pp. 159–160, with additional literature.

in August of the year before. The father of sixteen-year-old Elizabeth was Duke of Pomerania Bogislaw V and her mother Elizabeth was a daughter of King of Poland Casimir III the Great, whose consent was a prerequisite of the politically motivated alliance arrangements. After the wedding banquets and tourneys in Cracow, the ceremonial coronation followed in Prague on 18 June, which we have already mentioned in connection with the antecedent coronation of the two-year-old Wenceslas IV.

Unlike the Habsburgs and Wittelsbachs, who only sent their deputies to Prague in order not to compromise themselves by receiving accommodation in the residence of the competing and in the given period more successful Luxemburg dynasty, true bearers, not only pretenders to royal crowns, appeared here and there in the capital of the Kingdom of Bohemia. Rules always have exceptions. Around Christmas 1363, we find in Prague two Dukes of Bavaria, Stephen II with his seat in Landshut and Albert I with his seat in Straubing, who moreover would be Count of Holland from 1377. Both Wittelsbachs had a serious reason for this, because by their presence they confirmed the reconciliation declaration pronounced by King of Poland Casimir and Duke Bolek II of Schweidnitz in Cracow on 12 December, namely in a dispute in which they were involved. According to this declaration, Charles IV, Margrave of Moravia John Henry, King of Hungary Louis and Duke of Austria Rudolph IV were immediately to establish friendly relations in perpetuity. The duke of Habsburg did not come to Prague, but it was possible to see at this summit his namesake, Duke of Saxony and Elector Rudolph II, two dukes of Pomerania Barnim IV and Stephen, the already-mentioned Margrave John Henry, Duke Bolek II of Schweidnitz along with other Silesian dukes; from the high clerical prelates, the archbishop of Prague and the bishops of Augsburg and Chur were not lacking. Particular attention was also enjoyed by papal nuncio Pietro Corsini, who as well as his successor on the throne of the bishops of Florence were raised by Charles IV on this occasion among the imperial ecclesiastical princes.[222]

King of Denmark Valdemar IV, who counterbalanced his unstable position with good relations to the Curia and emperor, also drew the attention of his contemporaries with his presence in Prague. Some of Valdemar's conquests were looked upon grudgingly by the northern German Hanseatic League, which not only through its economic weight but also its active policy represented a state within a state. Charles IV took this association of northern German and Baltic towns only as a union of Hanseatic merchants, but he had to acknowledge, whether willingly or not, the Hanseatic League also as a political partner. This was especially true twelve years later in the disputes on the

222/ On the Christmas summit in Prague in 1363, see also Kavka, *Vláda Karla IV.*, I, pp. 204–205.

succession after Valdemar, who died in October 1375 precisely when Charles IV was residing in Lübeck. If we wanted to trace Charles' 'northern policy', it would require several dozen pages. We would persistently encounter the names of new actors on the political scene, whose interests and roles we could not discern. All the more admiration is aroused by Charles' active policy under the conditions of an as yet little developed central administration. The emperor's constant journeys to various areas of the Empire were most likely an absolutely indispensible prerequisite for his successful reign. In this respect, Wenceslas IV did not learn very much from his father, whereas his half-brother Sigismund revived the earlier Luxemburg policy of mobile administration and thus counterbalanced the centrifugal pressures of various parts of the Empire.[223]

Unlike Louis of Anjou, who did not visit Prague even once, King of Poland Casimir III the Great (1333–1370) liked to visit Charles' residence. He first stopped in Prague on his way back from the congress of sovereigns in Visegrád in Hungary in 1335. He had a sad memory of his second visit in summer 1341, because instead of marrying Charles' widowed sister Margaret of Bohemia (Duchess of Lower Bavaria) he came to see her funeral in the Zbraslav monastery. Although the aim of his next stay in Prague at the turn of May 1356 was to gain the Bohemian feudatories in Mazovia and Płock in return for relinquishing his claims to the duchy of Świdnica-Jawor (Schweidnitz-Jauer) and to the border Silesian towns of Byczyna and Kluczbork, he also managed to fall in love very passionately with the attractive widow Christine Rokczaner here. It could have been at a ball or during a tourney at which the amazing feats of the Mazovian knight Stanislav Ciołek were admired. Christine did not refuse the king but did not want to remain in the role of a mere mistress and forced a wedding, which caused a minor international scandal, because Casimir had already been legally married for fifteen years to Adelheid, daughter of Landgrave of Hesse Henry II. The illicit wedding was to little avail to Christine – the fickle Casimir repudiated her after a while and found a replacement in the seductive Jewess Esther.[224]

As much as Casimir took a liking to Prague, Charles IV liked to travel to Cracow. We find him at Wawel Castle there again before 22 September 1364, when the congress of European sovereigns commenced there. The emperor arrived in Cracow along with King of Cyprus and Jerusalem Peter I of Lusignan, who had appeared in Prague already at the end of August. The arrival of

223/ The uncommonly complicated processes leading to an 'inspissation' of the imperial administration were traced by Moraw, *Von offener Verfassung zu gestalteter Verdichtung*, esp. in the section 'Große Krisen und große Wandlungen', starting on p. 263.
224/ All this was ascertained already by Tomek, *Dějepis města Prahy*, II, pp. 37–38. On the political agenda of the congress at length, see Szczur, 'Praski zjazd Kazimierza Wielkiego z cesarzem', pp. 81–117.

this sovereign, of whom it was known that he was organising a crusade on the authorisation of the pope, was allegedly awaited by thousands of Praguers. The aged poet Machaut, who accompanied King Peter, colourfully described the welcome in Prague and subsequent banquet in many words from which only snippets can be taken. He talked in superlatives in the praise of the emperor as well as Prague, nothing else could be expected, but the welcome itself made a significant impression on him. Charles IV generously presented his guest with gifts, according to Guillaume de Machaut even with the sword of Charlemagne, he even had himself painted with him in one of the relic scenes at Karlštejn Castle; however, he politely declined the offered leading of the crusade.[225] No less carefully did the other sovereigns whom Peter endeavoured to gain for his crusade at the congress in Cracow act.

We already know three of the crowned participants of the congress in Cracow: the host Casimir, Emperor Charles IV and King of Cyprus Peter I. Neither was a tour of the newly reconstructed Wawel Castle foregone by Louis of Anjou and Valdemar IV of Denmark, Rudolph IV of Habsburg and Louis VI of Bavaria called the Roman, Margrave of Moravia John Henry, Margrave of Brandenburg Otto V, Bogislaw V of Pomerania, Ziemowit III of Mazovia and Władysław Opolczyk (Władysław von Oppeln). To the last one, they all approved the project but conditioned it with the establishment of peace in the entire area, in which they succeeded only partially, so the crusade of Peter of Lusignan had only a very small hope of success. Although he managed to take advantage of a moment of surprise and on 10 October 1365 was able to break through the ramparts of Alexandria temporarily, the armies of the Sultan of Egypt soon forced Peter's crusaders to escape with bags full of booty. In Alexandria, the crusaders left devastation behind themselves, but Christian Europe celebrated Peter as a new hero.[226]

Several long journeys awaited Emperor Charles also in 1365. The most important led to the papal court in Avignon and from there to Arles, where the archbishop there Guillaume de la Garde placed the crown of the Kingdom of Arelat on his head on 4 June.[227] This memorable excursion has already been mentioned in another connection, and so we can move on to another journey, which Charles undertook to Buda in November of the same year. The emperor achieved his goal. Louis gave his consent to the engagement of his niece

---

225/ Guillaume de Machaut described the reception of Peter I in Prague in his composition *La Prise d'Alexandrie*. In the last edition by Palmer, *Guillaume de Machaut: La Prise d'Alexandrie*, see pp. 80–92. Cf. on that Nejedlý, 'Deux poètes français', *Fortuny kolo vrtkavé*, pp. 49–50. See Nejedlý, *Středověký mýtus*, pp. 322–323.

226/ For more on Peter's campaign, see Hroch and Hrochová, 'Karel IV. a otázka obrany Balkánu', pp. 210–211.

227/ On the political background of this coronation, see most recently Heckmann, 'Das Reichsvikariat des Dauphins im Arelat', pp. 76–78.

Elizabeth to the four-year-old King Wenceslas, although both of them had been engaged before. After all, this was not the last betrothal charade, because Wenceslas IV married Johanna of Bavaria in September 1370. In the given situation, Charles could rub his hands in satisfaction, because he *inter alia* took the French offer which the ambassador of the French court Pierre Aymon, already known to us, had presented in Buda out of play.

The death of several preeminent statesmen was significantly projected on the Central European power scene and reduced the importance as well as the pageantry of the sovereign congresses. An appreciable loss for the Austrian lands was the death of Charles' twenty-six-year-old son-in-law Rudolph IV of Habsburg in July 1365. Charles IV was even more touched by the death in December 1370 of Duke of Saxony Rudolph II, who was among his confidants

62. The Golden Gate at Prague Castle with a mosaic of the Last Judgement

63. Beneš (Benesch) Krabice of Weitmile († 1375), chronicler of the time of Charles. A bust in the inner triforium of the Cathedral of St Vitus at Prague Castle

and on whom he could rely in the body of electors. Whereas in neither case the succession evoked greater changes, the death of Casimir the Great brought a reshuffle of the ruling powers in favour of Louis of Anjou, who already on 17 November 1370, twelve days after the passing of the heirless king, succeeded to the Polish throne. Shortly before, Louis through his defensive alliance with the Wittelsbachs had made it abundantly clear to the emperor that he would have to count with him more not only in Italian but also in imperial politics. Charles IV met with Louis in person only once more, namely at the beginning of October 1372 at an unknown place on the Moravian-Hungarian borders in the presence of several dukes of Bavaria who demanded their participation in the negotiations of a truce. Weapons were then ready for battle on more sides, because Charles' relentless interest in acquiring Brandenburg aroused disconcertion at several rulers' courts.

Prague did not experience another great summit of European statesmen during the reign of Charles IV. By coincidence, several works that added a new shine to the imperial seat were completed at Prague Castle precisely at the beginning of the 1370s. Other than the sculptural, unfortunately unpreserved, decoration of the southern portal of the cathedral with the figures of the emperor and empress, the amazement of the contemporaries was aroused by the vast mosaic with scenes from the Last Judgment on the façade of the so-called Golden Gate. Since both entrances to the Castle had been newly highlighted, we yield the evaluation as well as the end of this chapter to the chronicler Beneš Krabice of Weitmile: 'In the same year [1370], our lord emperor wanted to show the splendour and fame of his Kingdom of Bohemia, because princes, fuglemen and aristocrats from all the ends of the earth were coming to it. So he had two towers of the royal castle in Prague, one on the east and one on the west, covered with lead and their surface gilded, so that these towers in clear weather gleamed and shone to a very great distance.'[228]

AN UNEXPECTED DECISION TO VISIT PARIS

If we take a look at the map of the journeys of Emperor Charles IV in the last decade of his reign, the shift of his immediate political interests to the north is apparent at first glance.[229] After returning from the second journey to Rome at the end of August and beginning of September 1369, he never crossed the Alps again, intervening in the complicated situation on the Apennine peninsula only through his diplomats. Neither did he cross the western border of his empire, gradually suppressing his own activity there. The impetus for this was

228/ *Chronicon Benessii de Weitmil*, pp. 540–541.

229/ On this, see the maps of Charles' journeys incorporated in the book by Stoob, *Kaiser Karl IV. und seine Zeit*.

inter alia the rather surprising defeat and capture of his half-brother Wenceslas by the weaker army of Duke of Jülich William II (VI) in August 1371. The emperor actively supported his brother in the dispute over the government in the duchy of Guelders but after evaluating the situation preferred negotiation to a military campaign. The outcome of his journey to Luxembourg and the Rhineland in June 1372 was the liberation of Wenceslas, however at the price of the Luxemburg dynasty's resignation of the duchy of Limburg, the county of Falkenburg and of other lands between Limburg and the River Meuse. The emperor also appointed Archbishop of Cologne Frederick as the new Chief Vicar of the Holy Roman Empire instead of his brother; on the other hand, for these large concessions he strengthened his claims to Brandenburg and increased the chances of his son Wenceslas IV of attaining the Holy Roman crown.[230]

The purchase of Brandenburg, which Charles IV acquired in December 1373 for the enormous sum of a half million florins from the Wittelsbach duke and his son-in-law Otto V, concluded his twenty-five-year contest with the six sons of Louis the Bavarian. After Louis of Anjou succeeded to the Polish throne and thus complicated the possibility of further territorial gains in northern Bavaria, Charles gained another base for his dynastic politics precisely in Brandenburg. First of all, he had it in mind as an inheritance for his son Sigismund, who had been born to Elizabeth of Pomerania in February 1368. Just like Wenceslas IV had become King of Bohemia at age two, the rank of elector passed to the five-year-old Sigismund in 1373. As the new Luxemburg residence in the north, as we already know, Charles IV selected Tangermünde, the southernmost town of Brandenburg on the River Elbe. The development of the castle complex progressed quickly, apparently also because the emperor personally supervised the construction on his frequent stays.[231] In the last three years of his life, he stayed here rather than staying in Prague, which could have been caused also by his growing health problems.

Charles had suffered the joint pain and difficulties with movement typical of gout for a longer time. His malady is likely to have been further worsened by the consequences of a spine injury from 1350 as well as a later injury to his left knee.[232] He sought assistance on all sides. At the advice of doctors, he exercised the mobility of his limbs – *inter alia* during long audiences he employed his hands with carving small sticks. For the same reason, he was interested in the healing warm springs in West Bohemia. In Vary (Carlsbad), the spa named after him which he founded in 1358 and raised to a town in 1370, he underwent

230/ Here I follow Kavka, *Vláda Karla IV.*, II, pp. 130–131 and 139–141.
231/ Synoptically on Brandenburg, see Seibt, *Karel IV.*, pp. 278–284.
232/ At large on that, see Vlček, *Čeští králové*, II-1, pp. 188–198.

medical treatment for a whole two months at the beginning of 1376. Even the Papal Curia was worried about Charles' health at that time. Where help of an earthly nature failed, it was to be achieved by intercession and miraculous healing from above. It has not been ruled out that in this regard Charles IV had already visited some pilgrimage sites purposely before, but there will be no doubt about that during his stay in France.

The election of Wenceslas IV as King of the Romans in June 1376, the beginning disputes between the sons of the dead Margrave of Moravia John Henry († 1375), the effort of the emperor's wife Elizabeth of Pomerania to provide for her sons Sigismund and John (* 1370) and most likely also his deteriorating health forced Emperor Charles to think about his political will. He published the first one on 21 December 1376; whereas the second, issued in Tangermünde on 18 October 1377, more or less only defined the borders of some territories. In essence, they specified the succession order in the royal branch of the Luxemburg dynasty, in which according to expectations the paramount position fell to King of the Romans and Bohemia Wenceslas IV. Besides the actual kingdom, Wenceslas was after Charles' death to rule in the Silesian dependencies under immediate administration, in Lower Lusatia, in the land of Budyšín (i.e. Bautzen, Upper Lusatia) and in the duchy of Świdnica-Jawor, inherited from his mother Anna. As the feudal lord, he was to reign over the margraviate of Moravia, the bishopric of Olomouc, the duchy of Opava as well as over the other Silesian principalities. Moreover, he became feudal lord in the newly created duchy of Zhořelec (Görlitz in German), which was inherited by the youngest son John, whom Charles further gave thirteen thousand talents (1 talent = 253.17g) of silver from the Kutná Hora mines. The second-born son Sigismund was as the margrave selected to be the heir in Brandenburg. In addition, the succession in the Kingdom of Bohemia was to fall to Sigismund and his sons were Wenceslas to die without male heirs. If also this second line of the royal family died out on the spear side, the branch of John of Zhořelec was to come next in line. It was also precisely stated in the will under what circumstances the Bohemian Crown would fall to the Margrave of Moravia Jobst and possibly then to his brothers John Sobieslaw and Procop.[233]

Of the three great sovereigns of Central and Eastern Europe, only Charles did not have to worry about an heir to the throne. His concern was rather how to provide adequately for his three sons. After Casimir the Great died in 1370 without leaving a male heir, the Luxemburg eastern policy failed, because his

233/ Both wills were analysed in detail by Spěváček, *Karel IV.*, pp. 457–467; for the latest on them, see Bobková, *Velké dějiny zemí Koruny české*, IVa, pp. 431–437, with more on the newly created duchy of Zhořelec.

successor, as has already been said, became King of Hungary Louis I of Anjou. All hope was not lost in this, because the aging Louis had three daughters, each of whom could bring a kingdom as a dowry. For that matter, Charles IV had already in 1365 betrothed his four-year-old son Wenceslas to the niece of the king of Hungary. When the courtship was cancelled, he arranged the betrothal of his younger son Sigismund with Louis' second daughter Marie of Hungary in 1372.[234] The attention of the sovereign courts was all the more drawn out by the oldest Catherine, who was attributed the primary inheritance rights. And since Louis still counted on having a son, he marked Catherine as the heir apparent to the Polish throne, to whom also the Polish aristocracy and towns paid homage in September 1375. Meanwhile, instead of a son, another daughter was born to him – Hedwige (known under the Polish name Jadwiga after becoming the 'king' rather than 'queen' of Poland), so *via facti* the Kingdom of Hungary had already half fallen into Mary's lap.

None of this could have been foreseen, just like the death of Catherine at the end of 1378, which opened up the Polish throne to Hedwige. It was Catherine who had appeared to the French court as the most suitable bride for the second-born son of Charles V and the next duke of Orléans Louis (* 1372). In this view, there was not only the Angevin inheritance in Hungary, but under favourable conditions the possibility of acquiring Provence for the French Crown also offered itself, albeit at the price of a dangerous engagement in the Kingdom of Naples.[235] The intention to compete for the inheritance of the childless Queen Joan of Naples had been expressed by the king of Hungary already in 1373, in which direction he also offered Charles V the betrothal of his son Louis to Catherine. The diplomatic negotiations between Paris and Buda had continued promisingly since 1374 and were to or could culminate precisely at the time when Emperor Charles was approaching France. Whereas the French delegation led by Aleaume Boistel headed towards Hungary, Louis' ambassador Chrétien de Blonnorocs reached the French court. The negotiations between Buda and Paris could not be kept secret, and hence it is no wonder that Charles IV justifiably feared a loss of his dynasty's influence not only in Italy but also in the lands thus far controlled by Louis of Anjou. During his confidential conversations with his French nephew, the emperor actually tabled this issue, so from his perspective it was a truly serious matter.[236]

234/ In this regard, two studies are weighty: Kavka, 'Zum Plan der luxemburgischen Thronfolge in Polen', pp. 257–283 and 'Karel IV. a anjouovsko-piastovské dědictví', pp. 5–63. At the same time, cf. on the same Veldtrup, *Zwischen Eherecht und Familienpolitik*, esp. pp. 402–403.

235/ For the latest on that, see Autrand, *Charles V. Le Sage*, p. 60 (the succession of the Countess of Provence Joan to the throne of Naples), 784–785 (courtship); in more detail and with better knowledge of the sources, see Kavka, 'Karel IV. a anjouovsko-piastovské dědictví', pp. 37–42.

236/ Evidence of the conversation of Charles V with the emperor on the Hungarian-French marital alliance was published by Valois, 'Le projet de mariage', the quoted passage is on p. 223.

With this, we have somewhat got ahead of events, because it is time to explain what other intentions Charles IV had on his last and for many unexpected journey to France. From the Account of the *Great Chronicles of France*, with which we will soon become acquainted in translation, we know that the emperor announced his visit of France in writing sometime already in the summer of 1377. The letter to Charles V, supposedly written in his own hand, has not been preserved but is supposed to have contained the wishes to visit the king and carry out some pilgrimages. (Pic. 64) In a later speech to the delegation of the Sorbonne, the emperor declared that he had been brought to the kingdom by three things: 'the desire to see the holy relics and perform some other pilgrimages during which he wanted to conduct some worship and then especially a great desire to see the king and speak to him'.[237] There is no reason not to believe these words since we know with what ardour Charles IV venerated and collected the relics of the saints. Also the pilgrimage to the Abbey of Saint-Maur-des-Fossés had its justification, because that saint was the patron of those ill with gout, from which the emperor in the last period of his life unbearably suffered.[238] What the emperor wanted to speak to his host about is a subject of speculation in the literature. Generally, it is judged that Charles had in mind primarily the question of succession in Hungary and Poland, i.e. in the areas of the supreme interest of Luxemburg politics.[239] A serious, not only ancillary, reason was the threat of a church schism after the return of Pope Gregory XI to Rome.[240]

Already in summer 1377, the Papal Curia also knew of Charles' intention to visit France. Nuncio Galehard, Bishop of Spoleto, was charged with entreating the emperor along with the king of France to strengthen his position in Italy energetically, but Charles IV remained constantly on guard towards Pope Gregory XI (1370–1378). They both needed the other, but each anxiously protected the power and prestigious interests of his sphere. The prolonged dispute concerning the approval of the election of Wenceslas IV to throne of the King of the Romans during the lifetime of the ruling emperor (*vivente imperatore*) was significant in this regard. The emperor resolutely refused to apply to the papal throne for authorisation of the election, and all the more sharply was this possibility refused by the electors. The pope endeavoured to save face by antedating his bull with the approval of the election to the beginning of May.

237/ Delachenal (ed.), *Chronique des règnes*, II, pp. 194 and 247–248. The contact was mediated by Duke Wenceslas, see Fantysová-Matějková, 'Cesta Karla IV.', pp. 632–633.
238/ In the literature, if I am not mistaken, it was emphasised only by Seibt, *Karel IV.*, p. 352.
239/ The literature of the past two or three decades agrees on this point. See Spěváček, *Karel IV.*, pp. 468–469; Seibt, *Karel IV.*, p. 352; Thomas, 'Frankreich, Karl IV. und das Große Schisma', pp. 156–157; Kavka, *Vláda Karla IV.*, II, p. 209; Autrand, *Charles V*, pp. 784–785.
240/ This question was emphasised by Spěváček, *Karel IV.*, pp. 467–468, and more recently also by Thomas, 'Frankreich, Karl IV. und das Große Schisma', pp. 100–104.

64. / XX. Charles V accepts a document from Emperor Charles IV (BL Ms. royal 20 C VII, fol. 194v)

The deliberations on the approval dragged on further and were not completed in Gregory XI's lifetime.[241] On the other hand, Gregory's intention to relocate to Rome suited Charles IV, because the return from the so-called Avignon Captivity promised to strengthen the interconnection of the papacy with the power sphere of the Kings of the Romans and Holy Roman Emperors. In this regard, however, the position of the French court must have been different, if not directly conflicting, namely not only for the reasons of prestige. The earlier linkages of Avignon to Paris with the exception of the Sorbonne gradually collapsed, so that Charles V failed in his application to raise the Bishopric of Paris to an archbishopric in 1377.[242] No less was the king of France irritated by the tenacity with which Gregory XI relocated to Rome in January 1377, thus if the emperor had gained any indication of understanding for Gregory's

241/ For more detail, see Klare, *Die Wahl Wenzels von Luxemburg zum römischen König*, whose monograph was taken into account by Kavka, *Vláda Karla IV.*, II, pp. 185–191.
242/ On this, see Autrand, *Charles V. Le Sage*, p. 756. Unlike Prague, Paris thus did not obtain its own archbishopric and remained dependent on Sens.

65. Elizabeth of Pomerania (perhaps 1347–1393), Empress and Queen of Bohemia, fourth wife of Charles IV. A bust in the inner triforium of the Cathedral of St Vitus at Prague Castle

approach from his nephew, he would have had to pay for it with concessions in other areas.[243]

In his final years, the emperor took his son Wenceslas IV on journeys relatively often, nevertheless the supposition that this time he had more reasons for it than just practical training in high politics will probably not be very far from the truth. Wenceslas IV arrived in France already as the elected King of the Romans, and hence his reception by Charles V the Wise represented further recognition of his legitimacy. It was also no detriment to him to become acquainted with other influential members of the wider king's family, regardless of kinship ties, which in the case of the aged emperor had a sentimental tinge. For the same reason, it is somewhat surprising that the emperor was not accompanied by his crowned wife Elizabeth of Pomerania. The last of the emperor's wives very much enjoyed travelling, participated in the coronation journey to Italy in 1368, visited Aachen twice, became familiarised with Cologne, Koblenz, Lübeck, and even went to Magdeburg and Dortmund by herself.[244] Whether the empress remained in Tangermünde in reference to the poor health of her son Henry, born in August, who also died in the following year, can only be speculated on.[245]

If they knew of Charles' journey in Rome already at the end of summer, it was to the merit of Nuncio Galehard of Spoleto, who is proved in Tangermünde as a witness on the document of 23 September 1377, in which the emperor along with Wenceslas IV promised not only never to undertake an election of the king of the Romans in their lives again but to avert it if need be and to warn the pope in time. It was a formal promise by which Charles attempted in vain to persuade the pope to a written recognition of Wenceslas' election as King of the Romans. From Wenceslas' Roman journey, Gregory XI expected a strengthening of his position in Italy, and so he *inter alia* tried to hasten it through another of his nuncios Pileus de Prato, whom Gregory sent to the court in Brussels of the emperor's half-brother, Duke Wenceslas of Luxembourg. From this it might be deduced that Rome was aware of the northern route of the emperor's journey through Brussels and not through Luxembourg and Mouzon, as was assumed in Paris. It was not the only misunderstanding in the diplomatic preparation of the summit.

243/ For further details on that, see Thomas, 'Frankreich, Karl IV. und das Große Schisma', passim.
244/ It is worth mentioning that she visited Magdeburg in 1377 and appeared on her own in Dortmund in the following year. For more on her itinerary, see Wilbertz, 'Elisabeth von Pommern', pp. 52–53.
245/ On the absence of the empress at length, see Bobková, *Velké dějiny zemí Koruny české*, IVa, p. 441, which gives other possible reasons.

LATE ARRIVAL IN FRANCE

It can be reliably proved that the emperor announced his visit to France before 12 September 1377, when King Charles V instructed that the administrator of his chamber Nicolas Martin be paid the relatively high sum of 7200 gold francs 'for the expenses of our residence connected with the arrival of our very dear and greatly beloved uncle, Holy Roman Emperor'.[246] Then, however, the mutual communication began to flag. The emperor might have originally planned to undertake the long journey in autumn, perhaps already at the end of September and in October, but had to postpone it and later moved it to the end of the year. The emperor later excused his delay 'because of certain wars which had broken out in some parts of Germany' and which he wanted to settle before his departure.[247] The mentioned reason aroused mainly perplexity, because it was not known that the emperor would have intervened directly in some ongoing military conflict. The emperor might have meant the negotiation on a peace treaty between Duke Magnus II of Brunswick and the Ascanian dukes of Saxe-Wittenberg (Albert and his uncle Wenceslas I, Prince-Elector of Saxe-Wittenberg), which was concluded in his presence in Tangermünde on 24 October. Still on 2 November, both of the last-mentioned electors entered the league for the preservation of land peace (in German *Landfried*) along with Archbishop of Magdeburg Peter, called Gelvto (in Czech *Jelito*, meaning 'black pudding').[248] Since Imperial Arch-Marshal Albert was to accompany Charles IV during his visit to France, his interest in resolving both issues before beginning the long-planned journey could have had a certain share in its postponement.[249]

Before the emperor's departure from Tangermünde shortly before 2 November, his escort already included, besides the already-mentioned, Elector Albert, Grand Master of the Court of Bohemia Petr (Peter) of Vartemberk and at Kost († 1402–1405), Master of the Imperial Chamber Thymo the Younger of Kolditz († 1383) and Chief of the Chancellery, Prothonotary Nicholas of Riesenburg († 1397).[250] On 17 November in Minden, which the emperor

246/ Delisle (ed.), *Mandements et actes divers de Charles* V, pp. 734, No. 1447.

247/ Delachenal (ed.), *Chronique des règnes*, II, p. 195.

248/ The emperor's rationale will cut no ice according to the argumentation by Kavka, *Vláda Karla IV.*, II, pp. 209–210; those mentioned in the peace treaty are listed by Böhmer, *Regesta imperii*, VIII, pp. 486–487, Nos 5819a, 5828.

249/ Only a seeming explanation of this mystery is provided by the Annals of the Imperial City of Nuremberg by Johannes Müllner. According to his later entry, Charles IV along with his son Wenceslas IV, Count Palatine of the Rhine Rupprecht and a number of other allies surrounded the rebellious town of Ulm around the feast of St Michael the Archangel (29 September), from which he then lifted the unsuccessful siege on the Thursday before Saint Gall (15 October). Cf. Müllner, *Die Annalen der Reichsstadt Nürnberg von* 1623, II: *1351–1469*, pp. 68–69. Everything would have fit together, but Müllner erroneously placed the event in 1377, although it had occurred a year earlier. See on that i.a. Spěváček, *Václav IV.*, pp. 94–85.

250/ This prothonotary with supposed Humanistic tendencies came from western Prussia, as

reached by a detour through Lüneburg, there are further known participants documented in his retinue, namely Duke of Opava Wenceslas I (1362–1381),[251] Grand Marshal of the Kingdom of Bohemia Hynek of Lipá and at Rataje and from the Bohemian lords Aleš (Holický) of Šternberk, High Chamberlain of Bohemia. Six days later in Dortmund, they were joined by Bishop of Warmia Henry Sorbom, who proved his worth as a secretary in the emperor's services.[252] Surprisingly enough, neither then nor later is it mentioned that the emperor would have been accompanied by one of his personal physicians. It is astonishing regarding his precarious health. In Paris, he however had constantly at his disposal court physicians, without whom Charles V, himself of fragile health, would not have been able to move at all.

Charles IV seems to have selected the campaign through Westphalia, which was a distant area of the Empire, deliberately so that he would for the very first time in these parts commemorate the imperial majesty of the Luxemburgs and their building on the foundational work of Charlemagne. For this reason, he turned from Herford or Bielefeld to insignificant Enger, where he had the tomb ascribed to the Saxon leader Widukind (Wittekind) restored. The placement of the coat-of-arms of Charlemagne above Widukind's head was as characteristic for the emperor's aspirations as the Czech lion at his feet. There was a deeper intent also in Charles' moving the tomb of the Dominican scholar Henry of Herford in front of the main altar of the convent church in Minden. And it would not have been Emperor Charles if he had not enriched his collections of relics by the thumb of St Felician in the cathedral there.[253] He then acquired small relics of St Reinold in Dortmund, which he reached through Paderborn and Soest on Sunday, 22 November.[254]

Almost wherever the emperor stopped he confirmed or granted privileges. It was the case not only in Dortmund, where he stayed for two days, but also in Essen, Rattingen, and Jülich, which were further stage towns. Charles IV did not treat himself to a longer, nine-day rest until Aachen, where from 29 No-

proved by Moraw, 'Grundzüge der Kanzleigeschichte Kaiser Karls IV.', p. 38. As a reward for services in the chancelleries of Charles IV as well as his son Wenceslas, he received significant benefices, i.a he was provost in Kemberg near Magdeburg, which is why he is sometimes given the title *praepositus cembergensis*. On his further career on the bishop's thrones in Constance and Olomouc, see Gatz, *Die Bischöfe des Heiligen Römischen Reiches*, pp. 515–516 (the author of the entry is Jan Bistřický).

251/ For more on him, see Prix, 'Vévoda Václav I. Opavský', pp. 54–89.

252/ Their presence is proved in the writings in Böhmer, *Regesta imperii*, VIII, p. 483, No. 5781 (Peter of Vartemberk), p. 486, No. 5819a (Elector Albert, Thymo the Younger of Kolditz), p. 487, No. 5825 (Nicholas of Riesenburg), 5829 (Wenceslas of Opava, Hynek of Lipá, Aleš of Šternberk), p. 488, No. 5834 (Henry Sorbom). On the last of the mentioned bishops, see Gatz, *Die Bischöfe des Heiligen Römischen Reiches*, pp. 184–185, with further references.

253/ These and other details are listed by Last, 'Der Besuch Karls IV. am Grabmal Widukinds', esp. pp. 307–309, 332–333 and 338.

254/ On the ceremonial reception in Dortmund, see in detail Weifenbach, 'Freiheit durch Privilegien und Schutz durch Reliquien', pp. 223–256.

66. / XXI. Charles V sends envoys to meet the emperor (BL Ms. royal 20 C VII, fol. 195r)

vember he awaited the arrival of his son Wenceslas IV, who had stayed in Luxembourg for some time before. Both monarchs met no later than 8 December, when Wenceslas IV issued several documents in Aachen. With great likelihood, his forty-person retinue included the members of the official delegation missing so far, namely Wenceslas' Master of the Court and from 1375 also Landgrave of Saxony John I of Leuchtenberg († 1407), Duke of Legnica (Liegnitz) Boleslav († 1394), Duke of Brzeg (Brieg) Henry VIII († 1399), and Master of the Royal Chamber as well as frequent companion of the emperor on journeys Lord Hašek of Zvířetice.[255] Whereas the emperor continued in a western direction through Maastricht to Brussels, Wenceslas IV with his retinue headed for Luxembourg most likely to make contact there with the messengers of the king of France, whose presence in Mouzon, as I suppose, was already known in Aachen.

255/ All of the mentioned act as witnesses in the document issued by Charles IV in Cambrai on 23 December 1377 (see Böhmer, *Regesta imperii*, VIII, p. 490, No. 5857). Data on the documents of Wenceslas IV from 8 December can be found in Spěváček, *Václav IV.*, p. 96, who erroneously believes that both Luxemburgs left Aachen for Cambrai, where they celebrated the Christmas holidays.

67. The journey of Charles IV to Paris and back

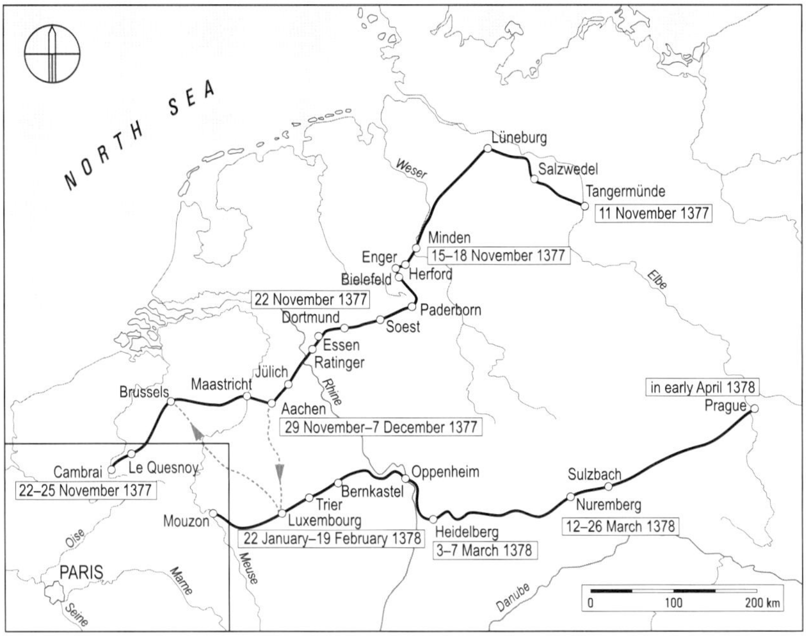

No matter how strange it may sound, the French court had no idea about the itinerary of the heralded emperor's journey or the place of his stay where he could be found. In Luxembourg, the group of mounted men which Charles V sent to acquire the necessary information found Wenceslas IV, who was awaiting the arrival of his father there incognito but with a large retinue of roughly forty horses. At least it appeared that way to the French messengers, who immediately reported it to their king. Under the presumption that the emperor was already on the way, Charles V sent the welcoming delegation through Rheims to Mouzon, the first town on French soil on the way from Luxembourg.[256] The task of welcoming the emperor was entrusted to the foremost counsellors of Charles V, Count Johann of Saarbrücken and Count Simon de Roucy et de Braine, further First Gentleman of the Chamber Bureau de la Rivière and Master of the Royal Household Pierre de Chevreuse.[257] After fourteen days, as the author of our Account tells us, Charles V called them back to Paris, because not even Wenceslas IV in Luxembourg knew yet where to catch his father.

The welcoming delegation had just returned from Mouzon when a courier appeared in Paris, who this time brought the necessary information on the approximate date of the emperor's arrival and course of his journey through Brabant, Hainaut and Cambrai. Another delay occurred, because the emperor according to this message was to arrive in Paris already seven days before

256/ These as well as the following data are taken from the Account issued by Delachenal (ed.), *Chronique des règnes*, II, p. 194 (see below for a translation).
257/ I list the careers of all the ambassadors and envoys of Charles V elsewhere.

Christmas. We will certainly not err when we connect another mandate, by which Charles V ordered to pay 7,500 francs on 12 December, with the expenses for sending a second welcoming delegation. All of the knights and pages of the delegation of three hundred horses travelled in the liveries of their lords and reached Cambrai shortly before the emperor's arrival, i.e. on 22 December 1377.[258] The above-mentioned dignitaries were joined here by Jean Le Mercier, one of the general tax collectors.

It was extremely important for Charles V that the reception in Paris surpassed all of the expectations of his 'very dear and greatly beloved uncle', as he always labelled the Holy Roman Emperor in his writings. The remembrance of the supplicant who had experienced the emperor's triumph at the magnificent feast with the imperial electors in Metz twenty years earlier was to be extinguished by the spectacular celebrations beginning with the reception through the banquets to the final gifts of exceptional value. The king of France was not the first among electors but the first among peers, among whom again special positions were held by his brothers and brothers-in-law, the 'flowers of the lilies'. Their presence at such an important state act was most desirable, and so the former acerbity and malice among the members of the royal family had to recede into the background. Only the oldest of the king's brothers, Duke Louis of Anjou, did not allow himself to be inveigled into the journey to Paris. Louis always had ambitious plans, he did not want to be satisfied with a subordinate role, and his politics in Brittany as well as in Languedoc had brought him into disputes with influential members of the king's council. The French-Hungarian courtship does not seem to have appealed to him either, as it took him out of play in the Kingdom of Naples.

Neither did Duke John of Berry have a reason to exhibit particular good favour to his brother on the royal throne, but he loved extraordinary experiences making common pastimes phenomenal and so could not be missing in Paris. In addition, in the absence of the older Louis, he was right behind the king in the titular order, with which also prestigious tasks were connected during the welcoming of the emperor. In a letter from 9 December 1377, Charles V conveyed the last instructions to John at his residence in Mehun. The duke set out forthwith on the journey to Genouilly, from whence he headed directly to Paris on 18 December. The same day, his younger brother Duke of Burgundy Philip left Dijon for the metropolis, from which it is obvious that the preparation of the emperor's visit took place with befitting lead time.[259] It was also

258/ See Delisle (ed.), *Mandements et actes divers de Charles V*, p. 771, No. 1544. On the emperor's stay in Cambrai, see Dubrulle, *Cambrai à la fin du Moyen Âge (XIIIe–XVIe siècle)*, pp. 296–297.
259/ Of the literature, precise data comes from Lehoux, *Jean de France, duc de Berri*, I, pp. 408–409.

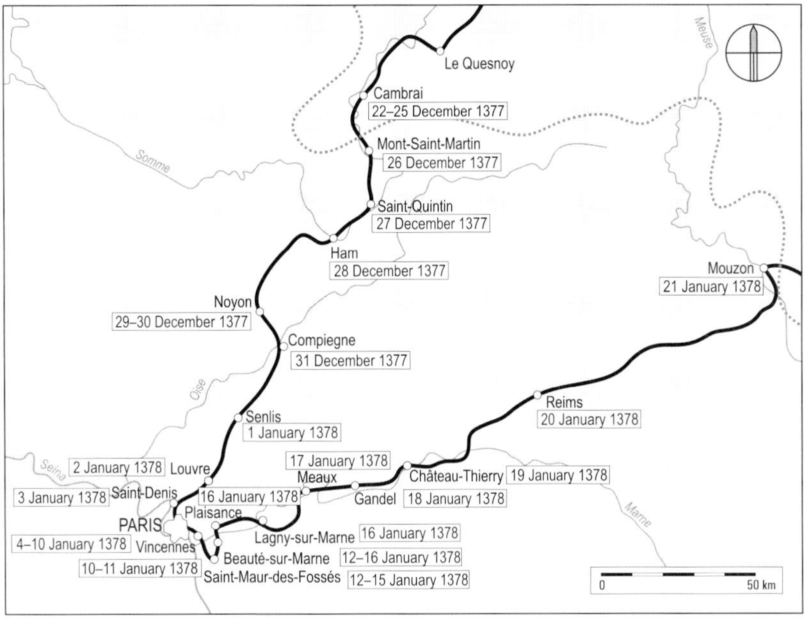

68. Places Charles IV stayed in France

true for the preparation of the royal palaces. We discover from the daily records of the Parliament in Paris that the Palace de la Cité was closed for a few days from Monday, 21 December in order to decorate its halls for the reception of the emperor and his retinue. For the entire period until 12 January 1378, the court performed only duties connected with the state visit, and on the feast of Twelfth Night and the day before the palace was entirely closed to the uninvited.[260]

As soon as Wenceslas IV had fulfilled his task in Luxembourg, he rushed to his father in Brussels. They were both received here with appropriate honours by Duke Wenceslas of Luxembourg as well as his wife. The emperor most likely caught Nuncio Pileus de Prato here, but on the other hand did not see the count of Flanders, with whom he had an agreed meeting. The count became ill on the journey from Ghent, returned and sent the castellan of Dixmude to Brussels with an apology. During his transit of Hainaut, the emperor planned to meet Duke of Bavaria Albert I, who was the regent in the county for his feeble-minded brother William III. Despite having been informed by letter, Albert left for Holland, which Charles IV most likely discovered only at Le Quesnoy Castle, where he found only the children.

Although the honorary French escort had met the emperor halfway before his entry into Cambrai, a longer conversation occurred only after the ceremonial welcome in the city and subsequent lunch. As soon as the envoys of Charles V discovered in the public audience from the emperor that he in-

260/ This is how I understand the daily records reprinted by Moranvillé, *Étude sur la vie de Jean le Mercier*, pp. 59–60.

tended to celebrate Christmas with the traditional ritual during midnight mass in Saint-Quientin, they had to, whether willingly or not, swallow a bitter pill. Nevertheless, everything turned out well, the emperor understood that he could not perform devotions on French soil with his imperial insignias, and so voluntarily agreed that he would stay in Cambrai over the Christmas holidays.[261]

With the third mandate in order with the date of 27 December 1377, Charles V ordered that five hundred gold francs be paid to Duke of Bourbon Louis II as a partial compensation for the expenses which he had with the welcoming of the Holy Roman Emperor in Compiègne. Duke Louis, otherwise the brother of the Queen of France, was accompanied by the king's cousin John of Artois, Count of Eu, Miles II de Dormans, Bishop of Beauvais, and his Parisian colleague Aimery de Magnac during the ceremonial toast on the territory of the Îlle-de-France on Thursday, 31 December 1377. In this connection, the Account mentions more than three hundred horses, with the duke's men wearing outfits in his half-white, half-blue colours. Another ceremonial welcome, given to the emperor and his son according to the carefully prepared protocol the following day before Senlis, further increased the official character of the act itself. This time, the emperor and his son were already welcomed by both of the king's brothers, i.e. Duke John of Berry and Duke of Burgundy Philip the Bold. Their retinue included the king's brother-in-law Duke John VI of Harcourt, further Adhémar Robert, Archbishop of Sens, and Cardinal Pierre Aycelin de Montaigu, Bishop of Laon. It need not be added that the mounted men of the welcoming delegation were clad in the same colours – this time in black and grey. According to the preserved accounting documents from 28 and 31 December, Charles V ordered that both of his brothers, John of Berry and Philip the Bold, be paid two thousand francs each without delay as compensation for their expenses. The final accounting for the other expenses connected with the imperial visit was to be done in January.[262]

The king's brothers and their companions returned from Senlis to Paris, whereas Duke Robert of Bar, the husband of the king's sister Marie, whose task was to welcome the emperor before his entry into the city of Louvres, travelled in the opposite direction. The flowers of the lilies, i.e. the members of the royal family, but also peers, nearly all of the highest officials, and leading ecclesiastical dignitaries of the French Crown assembled in Paris to welcome Emperor Charles IV, his son Wenceslas, and the members of their retinue

261/ On the ceremonies see Schwedler, *Deutsch-französische Herschertreffen*, pp. 71–74.

262/ See Delisle (ed.), *Mandements et actes divers de Charles V*, p. 782, No. 1571. The instruction for refunding the costs of Duke of Berry was published by Delachenal (ed.), *Chronique des règnes*, III, pp. 207–208, Appendice 27. On the overall account of the expenses of the Royal Treasury, see Excursus – The Final Account of the Expenditures of the King's Treasury.

69. Wenceslas of Luxembourg (1337–1383), Duke of Luxembourg, Brabant and Limburg. A bust in the inner triforium of the Cathedral of St Vitus at Prague Castle

there. Both the highest representatives of the Empire as well as the Kingdom of Bohemia were in themselves an ample counterweight to the French side. From the other members of the expedition, the hosts ascribed the primary position to the emperor's half-brother Wenceslas, the duke of Luxembourg, Brabant and Limburg[263], followed in hierarchical order by Elector of Saxony Albert, Duke of Brzeg (Brieg) Henry VIII, Duke of Legnica (Liegnitz) Boleslav and then Duke of Opava Wenceslas I. The imperial retinue used to have greater shine in the past, but we have to take into account the circumstances which accompanied the unexpected and not very well organised journey to France.

We have almost reached the ramparts of Paris with Emperor Charles IV, and it is time to give the floor to the official raconteur of the French court, namely a most capable man, the king's chancellor Pierre d'Orgemont. From his Account, we shall also discover further details on the emperor's journey from Cambrai to Paris. And since it is quite an enthralling testimony which would be a pity to interrupt with notes and insertions, we will allow the text to flow and will expound on everything connected to it in the excursuses and investigations in the second part of the book.

263/ Jana Fantysová-Matějková, *Wenceslas de Bohême, un prince au carrefour de l'Europe*, Paris 2013.

AN INTRODUCTORY WORD TO THE READERS

The author of the book considers it appropriate to stop the flow of the interpretation here and again remind the reader of the reason he or she is precisely now encountering the original testimony of the period source or more precisely the official protocol of the summit of the three crowned heads from 1377/78. It is not usual; normally, we do not encounter the reprint of the sources until the appendices. However, not every source is the same. This has internal coherence, every word in it is important and a historian would be embarrassed to merely paraphrase what can be offered to the reader in pure, unbiased form. It is therefore proper here, because in the relation of the Great Chronicle of France the word combines with the image. So, as a picture, it is better to see than to describe; it is in its way an experience to read the period version of exceptional historical events. Yet, a large danger of a one-sided view hides here. Since similar relation of the imperial court, if it ever existed, has not been preserved, it is all the more necessary for the historian to devote critical attention not only to the overall tendency but almost every sentence in the French protocol. It is the task of the commentary which follows the chronological line of the entire story after the epilogue. The author relies on this commentary not being an uninteresting hodgepodge of data into which only the specialists will delve.

THE ACCOUNT OF THE GREAT CHRONICLES OF FRANCE ON THE JOURNEY OF HOLY ROMAN EMPEROR CHARLES IV TO FRANCE

70. / I. Message of Emperor Charles IV (BnF, ms. fr. 2813, fol. 467ra)

HOW CHARLES, THE HOLY ROMAN EMPEROR, WROTE THE KING THAT HE HAD DECIDED TO COME TO FRANCE

In that year of one thousand, three hundred and seventy seven, Holy Roman Emperor Charles, the fourth of this name, wrote to the king a letter in his own hand and sent two delegations to him, the second quite soon after the first, that he had decided to come to France and that he had already begun the journey to visit the king and conduct some pilgrimages with devotions, which greatly obliged the king with gratitude. And since he announced neither the time of his arrival nor from which side he intended to enter the kingdom, the king sent his couriers to him to find out, who then reported to him that upon entering Germany, in the duchy of Luxembourg, they found the King of the Romans, son of said emperor, who was already residing in said Luxembourg, where he had come in disguise with a small retinue of his people numbering about 40 horses. When the king learnt about this, he reasoned that the emperor would not wait long after the arrival of his son, whom he had sent ahead. He thus hastily sent Counts of Saarbrücken and of Braine, his counsellors, and in their retinue also Lord de la Rivière, his First Gentleman of the Chamber, and Lord Pierre de Chevreuse, his Master of the Royal Household, as well as others of his servants to Rheims and from there all the way to the city of Mouzon, the gate of his kingdom, and in all directions from which the emperor was to arrive in order to meet him and welcome him with honours on his entry to the kingdom. The mentioned king's men remained in Mouzon a good fourteen days, during which time they had no news on the said emperor, although they would travel to the said place in Luxembourg to his son to be on the safe side. When he expressed that he himself knew nothing for certain, the king recalled them. Nevertheless, quite soon after their return, an imperial envoy came to the king bringing letters written in his own hand in which he apologised for his delay caused by certain wars which had broken out in some parts of Germany and which he had partially already reconciled and which he wanted to settle entirely before his departure; he further announced that he would come to the king in Paris, unless something prevented him from that, eight days before Christmas, however, that for certain reasons, namely also for a more comfortable and shorter journey, he had changed his mind and would not come through Luxembourg but through Brabant, Hainault and Cambrai. And therefore he invited his son in Luxembourg to come to him in Brabant, where in the meantime his half-brother, the duke of Brabant along with his wife and the good people of the area had welcomed him with great honours. The emperor was to be joined there by the count of Flanders, who with a retinue of 40 knights had already left Ghent for Brussels, where accommodation was prepared for him. Nevertheless, when the said count was not far away, he excused himself for an illness which had struck him. He sent the Castellan of Dixmude as well as others of his people with his apology and himself returned to his land without having seen said emperor. From Brabant the said emperor set out for Hainault, where he hoped to find Duke Albert the vice-regent there, to whom he had sent a letter but who had already left for Holland. Even though the said duke was not there at all, the said emperor went to see his children in Le Quesnoy, where he stayed one day and saw said children.

71. / II. Emperor Charles enters the cathedral in Cambrai (BnF, ms. fr. 2813, fol. 467va)

HOW KING OF FRANCE SENT AN HONOURABLE DELEGATION TO THE CITY OF CAMBRAI TO MEET THE EMPEROR, WHO WAS SUPPOSED TO ARRIVE THERE, AND HOW THEY ESCORTED HIM WITH GREAT HONOURS ALL THE WAY INSIDE THE SAID CITY, IN WHICH HE WAS JOYOUSLY RECEIVED WITH PROCESSIONS, AND ON THE WORDS THAT THE EMPEROR PRONOUNCED TO THE PEOPLE WHOM THE KING HAD SENT TO HIM.

At that time, the king sent his delegation to the emperor in Cambrai, including Lord of Coucy, the counts of Saarbrücken and of Braine, further Lord de la Rivière as well as Jehan (Jean) Le Mercier, whose retinue counted a great number of knights and squires, well dressed in the liveries of said lords, namely in the number of a good three hundred horses. On the Tuesday before Christ mas, 22 December, they were in Cambrai early in the morning and walked at least one mile towards the emperor in such an arrangement as to welcome him on behalf of the king and accompany him so augustly as was described above, telling him that the king sent his greetings to him and was entirely happy for

72. / III. Emperor Charles IV reads the seventh lesson of the Christmas service (BnF, ms. fr. 2813, fol. 467vb)

his arrival and had a great desire to see him. The emperor received them very graciously, thanked the king as well as them greatly for having arrived there there, promising to speak to them at greater length once he came to the city. When the emperor approached the city of Cambrai, the bishop as well as the burghers of the city came before him with a good two hundred horses or even more, whereas the commoners along with the municipal arbalesters, although without the usual crossbows, waited at the gate of the city, ranged on one and the other side in quite a nice arrangement. The emperor was approaching on a grey riding horse (*roncin*), in a mantle and hat of grey cloth, trimmed with marten, and at his side his son, the king of the Romans, rode with him the same distance ahead. In this way on horses, they rode almost all the way to the city, where they met the bishop with a procession of canons. There the emperor and his son dismounted and at the head of the procession went on foot to the church. When the emperor had prayed there, the emperor went to the bishop's palace, whose halls and chambers were very nicely decorated, and he covered the bishop's expenses on him in full. After lunch, the emperor commanded that they find the head of the above-mentioned king of France's men, whom he then told publically and in front of all that although he was planning to perform a pilgrimage to the monastery of St Maurice, he had principally come to visit the king, queen and their children, whom he desired to see more than any other being on earth. He said that once he had seen him and spoken to him and when he had commended his son, the king of the Romans, to him, whom he had brought for him to be entirely his, he would happily accept death whenever God called him to Him, because through this he would have fulfilled one of his greatest desires. And as said people of the king discovered that the emperor had the intention to be in Saint-Quentin at Christmas, they managed that he would spend Christmas in the city of Cambrai, which is a city and place subject to him, in which he could appear in his magnificence with the imperial insignia, whereas the king could not suffer or allow him at all to use them in any way in the Kingdom of France. And since the emperor was used to reading the seventh lection of the matins in ceremonial vestments and the insignia of his magnificence, he was warned in advance by the king's people that he could not do so in France and that it would not even be allowed. He then agreed in good will to remain in Cambrai to perform his service according to the order common in the Empire.

THE NAMES OF THE CITIES THROUGH WHICH THE EMPEROR PASSED FROM CAMBRAI ALL THE WAY TO SENLIS AS WELL AS OF THE NOBLE PEOPLE WHO CAME TO MEET HIM.

The next day, the emperor left Cambrai and for the night came to the abbey called Mont-Saint-Martin, which already lay in the kingdom, and there not only slept but even had lunch the next day, after which he went to Saint-Quentin for the night. In that place, Saint-Quentin, people and officials of the king, burghers and the populace of the city came to meet him on horseback and welcomed him with honours, telling him that he was very welcome in the royal town and gave him grand presents of meat, fish, wine, bread, hay, oats and wax. And it is appropriate to take into consideration that neither in said town nor in any other city that he visited on the way to Paris or on the return journey from there was he welcomed in any church by a procession or by the sound of bells and that no insignia of his rule or estates were used, which in all of the Kingdom of France no one else has the right to use except the king or those who represent him. In Saint-Quentin, he remained one day and having left it, he came to Ham for the night. He was constantly accompanied by the king's men, who went in advance. In Ham, the people of the town appeared before him and paid him reverence with gifts, as had been done before by the burghers of Saint-Quentin. Then, the next day after breakfast, during which he only had something to drink, he departed and went to Noyon for the night. Also here, he was met by the bishop, chapter and burghers of said city on horses in a great and beautiful procession to pay reverence and give presents to him, as was mentioned above, presenting similar speeches as were delivered by the burghers in Saint-Quentin, saying that he was welcome in the royal city. The emperor remained in the city for two days and visited the Abbey of St Eligius to see saint's body.

On Thursday, the thirty-first and last day of December, the emperor left after breakfast and arrived for the night in Compiègne, where he was met one mile before the city by the people of said city in a beautiful arrangement and good company, counting a good two hundred horses. And quite soon thereafter from the king there came to meet the emperor Duke of Bourbon, the queen's brother and with him also Count of Eu, the king's germane cousin, the bishops of Beauvais, and of Paris and more other notable lords and knights in their retinue, numbering as many as three hundred horses and more, all in the liveries of the duke, half in white and half in blue colour. The duke told the emperor that the king was sending greetings to him, that he was very grateful that he had come and that he would be extremely glad to see him and that he had sent them there to accompany him. Then when the emperor arrived in the town and was accommodated in his hostel, the duke of Bourbon asked the lords and knights from the emperor's house to come with him to eat dinner at his palace. They indeed came, and the emperor to show him even greater honour and pleasure sent his son, the king of the Romans, to him with the message that if he were able to help himself [because already in Noyon he had been struck again by gout, which inhibited him in walking], he would come to dine with him in person. The duke of Bourbon ceremonially feted the king and all the others with a great and abundant dinner, to which he assembled and convoked the ladies from the city and the environs. The next day, which was Friday, the first day of January, the emperor lunched in Compiègne, and then at vespers, as he could not ride a horse, he left by coach to the city of Senlis, before which he was awaited by the bailiff with the royal officials, in whose retinue there were also people from said city, with one hundred horses, paying homage to him and saying that he was welcome in the royal city.

HOW THE LORDS OF BERRY AND OF BURGUNDY, DUKES AND BROTHERS OF THE KING OF FRANCE, ACCOMPANIED BY NUMEROUS NOBLE KNIGHTS, BARONS AND PRELATES, CAME BEFORE THE EMPEROR TO ESCORT HIM ON HIS ENTRY INTO THE CITY OF SENLIS, AND HOW SAID KNIGHTS AND SQUIRES WERE NOBLY DRESSED IN THE SAME COLOURS.

Soon thereafter, after a short journey, approximately a mile from the city or more, the king's brothers Dukes of Berry and Burgundy, Count of Harcourt, Archbishop of Sens and Bishop of Laon came to meet the emperor having

73. / IV. Meeting of the emperor with the brothers of the French king near Senlis (BnF, ms. fr. 2813, fol. 468va)

been entrusted by the king of France. The lords were accompanied by knights and squires, dressed all in the same clothes, the knights in black and grey velvet, the squires in silk of the same colours, and there were a good five hundred horses in their procession. The duke of Berry presented the emperor with a greeting from the king, who greatly desired to see him and who had sent them to pay homage to him and escort him as much as they could. The emperor very gratefully thanked both the king and them for it. When he then dismounted to his hostel, to which he had been escorted by them, they returned to their abodes so as not to bother him any more, because he was very ill and tired. The people of the town then presented him with their gifts as was written above with other towns.

HOW THE EMPEROR ARRIVED FROM SENLIS IN LOUVRES AND HOW THE KING SENT HIM A CARRIAGE AND LITTER WITH A NOBLE TEAM, AND HOW HE ARRIVED FROM THERE TO SAINT-DENIS IN FRANCE.

The next Saturday, which was the second day of the month of January, he left Senlis after breakfast and came for the night to Louvres, where he was met by the duke of Bar, who had been sent by the king and who came to him for the first time after the departure of the king's brothers. His retinue included some counts, knights bannerets, knights and squires, and also there, although it was a non-fortified town, he was given presents just as great and honourable as in the cities mentioned above. And the next day, on Sunday, the third day of January, he left Louvres after breakfast. As the king had discovered that the emperor's gout had worsened greatly, so that he could not travel on horseback and the journey in the carriage caused him pain, he sent to him the same, Saturday night, one of his personal carriages, beautifully decorated and pulled by white horses, and the litter of his first-born son, the dauphin of Viennois, also nobly adapted and drawn by two mules and two coursers, so that he would arrive in it more comfortably. The emperor was very grateful for that and thanked the king in his absence greatly when he accepted said carriage as well as the litter from the messengers of the king. In the mentioned litter he arrived as far as the city of Saint-Denis and from Saint-Denis the abbot of the city came to him a good mile or even more, accompanied by a good hundred men on horseback, and they all gave him reverence. Soon afterwards, the archbishops of Rheims, Rouen and Sens, further the bishops of Laon, Beauvais, Noyon, Paris, Bayeux, Lisieux, Meaux, Évreux, Thérouanne, as well as Condom and the abbot of Saint-Vaast, all from the King's Council, came from the city and gave him reverence, saying that he was welcome and that the king had sent them to him to honour him and accompany him. When he then arrived in Saint-Denis, he had his litter lowered and carried by hand, because for his above-mentioned illness of gout he could not walk. He therefore had himself carried on the litter to the Church of Our Lord St Denis in front of the great altar of St Louis to be able to perform his prayer piously there. He was then carried from there in the mentioned litter all the way to his room, where the abbot acquainted him with gifts in the form of large fish, rabbits, cattle, sheep, poultry and oats, and where he offered him as much wine as his people could consume. He was also presented with very valuable gifts by the people of the city. After a longer rest, the emperor expressed a great desire to see the holy relics there. So he had himself carried in a chair to the treasury room, where he saw the relics, crowns and gems. He stayed there for very long, finding great pleasure in it as was apparent from his face according to the reports of those who were there. When he was again taken to his room, the said brothers of the king and some prelates who had stayed there until then said goodbye to him and returned to the king in Paris; he then remained in said abbey the entire day.

HOW THE EMPEROR, AFTER HE HAD SEEN THE RELICS IN SAINT-DENIS, BOTH IN THE TREASURY AND ELSEWHERE, AND HAD VISITED THE TOMBS WHICH HE WANTED TO SEE, LEFT SAINT-DENIS FOR PARIS.

The next Monday, the fourth day of the month of January, the emperor rose early in the morning, because he was to arrive in Paris that day. He had himself taken to the Church of Our Lord St Denis, before the holy bodies, and there performed his devotions. He then had himself carried around the chests and kissed the relics, the head of St Denis, the nail and the crown, and then asked to be shown the tombs of the kings, particularly King Charles and his wife Queen Jeanne, King Philip [and] Queen Jeanne of Burgundy, his wife, about whom he said that at their courts he was nurtured in his youth and that they had done very great good for him. He also wished to see the tomb of King John and after it happened, he had the abbot and the cloister assembled and ardently asked them to deign to intercede with God on behalf of those good lords and ladies who lay there. He later left the church and returned to his room, which he had left, where at the king's order the said Lord de la Rivière, his First Gentleman of the Chamber, and Colart of Tanques, First Squire of the King's Stables, stopped; they both then went into the courtyard in front of the window of the emperor's room and there presented at the king's order the gift of a beautiful destrier with a gorgeous and rich saddle with the coats-of-arms of France, and in addition a beautiful courser; and they brought the same horses for his son, the king of the Romans. The emperor thanked the king warmly and promised that he would get on the horse and ride on it to Paris, no matter how difficult it was for him due to his disease; therefore, he sent the horse ahead to La Chapelle-Saint-Denis and had himself carried there in the richly and nobly adorned litter with the gorgeous team which the queen had sent him for this purpose. When he had drunk instead of breakfast, he left on the litter, as has already been said, for Saint-Denis, and between there and La Chapelle-Saint-Denis he was met by the provost of Paris and the knight of the night watch with a large number of their mounted sergeants dressed in the same uniforms. Also here were the provost of merchants, the municipal aldermen, and burghers of Paris, all on beautiful horses and in the same half-white and half-purple clothes. And at that place there were a good eighteen hundred to two thousand mounted knights in the same robes, among whom then the provost of Paris along with the provost of the merchants, the knight of the night watch, with the aldermen and with a great number of other burghers were nobly mounted on beautiful destriers and coursers, arrayed in the plains along the path in a very beautiful orchestration.

74. / V. The representatives of the Parisian counsellors and merchants welcome Emperor Charles IV (BnF, fr. 2813, fol. 469rb)

HOW THE PROVOST OF PARIS WITH THE PROVOST OF THE MERCHANTS AND THE KNIGHT OF THE NIGHT WATCH SEPARATED FROM THE COMMONERS, WHO WERE ARRANGED IN THE FIELDS, AND APPEARED BEFORE THE EMPEROR TO GIVE HIM REVERENCE.

Then, the provost of Paris with the provost of the merchants and the knight of the night watch drew forward from the others, and when they approached the emperor, the provost of Paris delivered a speech, saying: 'Very excellent prince, we, the officers of the king in Paris, the provost of the merchants as well as the burghers of this good city, have come to give you honours and offer our services for your good pleasure, because the king, our lord, wishes it thus and so did he order us to do.' And the emperor thanked the king as well as them for that very cordially. Then, the provost of Paris with the provost of the merchants, the aldermen and with the good people left together directly for Paris, so that the procession of the royal officers and the city people counted a good four thousand horses and more. Thus accompanied, the emperor arrived at La Chapelle-Saint-Denis, at one of whose courts he had himself taken down from the queen's litter and was placed on the destrier which the king had sent to him in Saint-Denis and which was black; the king of the Romans similarly mounted on that [destrier] which the king had sent him and which was just as black. And it was intentionally that the king of France had given them horses of this coat, which was furthest from white and its opposite, because according to the customs in the Empire, the emperors were to arrive in the good towns of their empire which were in their domain on a white horse. The king did not want that to happen also in his kingdom, so he ensured that no sign of the emperor's dominion could be seen.

HOW THE KING OF FRANCE LEFT HIS PALACE
TO MEET THE EMPEROR, HIS UNCLE.

At the same time and hour, the king left his palace, mounted on a great white palfrey, richly saddled entirely in the symbols of France. He was clad in a scarlet riding jacket and a gown-like mantle richly lined with animal fur. On his head, he wore a pointed hat following old fashion, embroidered and very richly set with pearls. His escort included four dukes, namely of Berry, of Burgundy, of Bourbon, and of Bar, further the counts of Eu, of Boulogne, of Coucy, of Saarbrücken, of Tancarville, of Sancerre, of Dammartin, of Porcien, of Grandpré, of Salm, of Braine, and more other great lords, knights bannerets as well as others, countless knights, and other great aristocrats. There were also prelates present, all those written above, who came out of the gate of Saint-Denis before the emperor and were all in Roman capes as ordered and commanded by the king, mounted on beautiful horses and accompanied by their chaplains as well as other people, of whom each was in the colours of his lord. The above-mentioned lords and princes rode on commendably large horses, higher than coursers, in a rich procession of knights and squires, each of whom was in the livery of his lord. And also the king had his officials of all the estates, of a great number, dressed in uniforms according to their offices, namely: chamberlains in two types of costumes, some in velvet, the others in scarlet of two colours; masters of the royal household in clothes of two kinds of velvet – of azure blue and tawny colours, and honorary knights in vermilion velvet; squires of the king's bodyguard and his stables in blue camocas; officers of the palace guard in two kinds of camocas of blue and red stripes; the heads of the court services – breadmasters (*panetiers*), butlers and carvers at the table in a costume of two kinds of satin of white and tawny colours; and also the officials of the dauphin of Viennois, the first-born son of the king, were dressed analogously; and the masters and squires of cuisine were dressed in silk mantles called houppelandes and in otter fur coats with mother-of-pearl buttons; valets of the chamber, of whom there were fifty-two, all were all dressed in liveries with grey-white stripes on black cloth; the sergeants of the palace guard, of whom there were fifty to sixty, were dressed in blue-black uniforms; the sommeliers with stripes in brown and vermilion colour; and analogously also each of the other court offices had uniform clothing. The king needed more than half an hour to pass the courtyard of the palace for the great number of people on horseback that were there. He thus rode through the centre of the city with a great amount of people by a route directly to Saint-Denis through the gate and fortress of Saint-Denis. And the arrangement of the king's people was so well performed that there was only little press of the throng considering the number that came. All of the knights and squires, the mounted arbalesters and sergeants of the palace guard rode ahead. And before the king rode the Marshall de Blainville and the squires of his guard, who had two swords on their belts and parade helmets. He was immediately preceded by the son of the king of Navarre and the counts of Harcourt and of Tancarville, behind whom rode their officers. Then followed the four dukes mentioned above and more of the other counts, barons and above-mentioned prelates, who went arranged always two and two.

HOW THE KING OF FRANCE AND THE EMPEROR WITH HIS SON, THE KING OF THE ROMANS, MET BETWEEN CHAPELLE [SAINT-DENIS] AND THE WINDMILL, AND ON THE REVERENCE WHICH THEY GAVE EACH OTHER ON THEIR MEETING.

Behind them, then first rode the archbishops, followed by bishops, after whom came the large steeds and palfreys of the king, very richly saddled, which were led by valets in their right hands; the valets themselves rode on other horses (*roncins*), all in the same clothing, and on their belts they had the coat-of-arms of France following the common fashion. The king's *palefrenier* (groom) rode on a large courser in front of the squires of the bodyguard and carried the ceremonial coat-of-arms of the king, which was of velvet with embroidered *fleurs-de-lis*, and sewn with pearls; the groom wore it on the belts around the neck, as it was common to wear it. In front of the sergeants of the royal bodyguard, there were two royal trumpeters, who had silver French horns, decorated with embroidered pennons, and they sometimes blew a signal for the people on horseback to come forward. Thus the king rode from his palace to half way between the windmill and the Chapelle [Saint-Denis] before he and the emperor met; it happened on an extensive place so that they could approach one another when there was such a huge throng of people present. At that encounter, the emperor removed his beret and hat as did the king; nevertheless, the king did not want to come too close to the emperor so that his horse would not rub against the emperor's legs, in which he had gout, but they took each other by the hands and so greeted one another; the king in so doing told the

75. / VI. The meeting of King of France Charles V and Emperor Charles IV (BnF, ms. fr. 2813, fol. 470ra–b)

emperor that he greatly welcomed him and that he had had a great desire to see him. Then the king moved on to greet the king of the Romans and took him by the hand in the same way as he had the emperor. Then he returned before the emperor so that he would have him on his right side, even though the emperor apologised for a very long time therefore and did not want to do so; and beside him on the left side he put the King of the Romans. So the king rode in the middle, between the emperor and his son, for the whole trip and through the entire city of Paris to his palace in the orchestration and manner as follows.

ON THE NOBLE ORCHESTRATION IN WHICH THE KING, THE EMPEROR AND HIS SON ENTERED PARIS.

Primarily, it was ordained by the king that the people of the city, since there were too many of them, remain in the fields and not enter the city until the emperor, the king and all of their people had entered and passed through the city, and this was also conducted. The day before, the king had it announced that no one dare block the way leading down Grand Rue to the palace, neither by person nor cart, and that the people not move out of the places that they had assumed to be able to see the emperor, the king and the king of the Romans passing. And there were truly sergeants deployed to watch the ends of streets which lead into Grand Rue and they guarded there and kept people from crossing there. This is where thirty sergeants at arms then dismounted to take the whole length of the street and, walking before the officers of the king's

76. / VII. Parade of the royal guards (BnF, ms. fr. 2813, fol. 470rb)

bodyguard, they carried their maces in their hands and on their belts swords inlaid with silver. And the emperor had already let the king know on his way to Saint-Denis that, on his entry into Paris, he did not want any of his people at his side but that he would trust the guards and government of the king and his people who he deigned to choose for him; and he asked the king very urgently to select such that would protect him well from the press; and he also asked the king to deign to order some people to take all of his people to the palace in advance, which the king did, having them taken first and guided by the lord of Coucy, the count of Saarbrücken and the count of Braine, who had constantly been with the emperor since he had entered the kingdom. As the emperor's bodyguard, the king ordained six of his chamberlains and four officers of his guard, namely Lord de la Rivière, Lord Charles of Poitiers, Lord Guillaume des Bordes, Lord Hutin de Vermeilles, Lord Jean de Berguettes, and [a lord called] le Barrois [Jean de Barres, i.e. of Bar], and so many again did the king ordain for his bodyguard, while to the king of the Romans assigning four valets of the chamber [chamberlains] and two officers of the guard. All of these chamberlains, knights and officers of the guard also dismounted and arranged themselves in the guard with which they had been entrusted in a beautiful and good orchestration.

77. / VIII. Ceremonial entry of the sovereigns into Paris (BnF, ms. fr. 2813, fol. 470va–b)

ON THE ORCHESTRATION OF THE NOBLE BARONS, KNIGHTS, PRELATES, SQUIRES AND PEOPLE OF PARIS, WHO TRAVELLED BEHIND THE THREE PRINCES MENTIONED ABOVE.

Item, the emperor's people, who first entered the city, were followed by knights and squires of the French kingdom, of whom there were a good eight hundred knights without pages, whose number is not known; and [all] were beautifully dressed and trimmed and on very nice horses, which was a precious and marvellous thing to see. Behind them rode the Chancellor of France and the secular counsellors of the king. Then, behind them, the guards of the gates, with their commanders walking in a single line, holding their verges in their hands and wearing identical uniforms. And further the provost of the city of Paris rode on horseback, followed by more counts and barons. Next behind them was Marshall de Blainville and behind the Marshall were the squires of the king's bodyguard and his stables as is described above. Closest to the emperor, the king and the King of the Romans was a number of foot knights, all with staves in their hands; also the chamberlains and the officers written above were around the emperor, the king and the King of the Romans to prevent anyone from approaching or even pressing them. And behind the horses of the emperor, the king and the King of the Romans, the officers of the guards were arranged on foot, and they also had staves in their hands. These were then followed by the king's brothers, the Dukes of Berry and of Burgundy; and between the two of them was the Duke of Brabant, the emperor's brother and the king's uncle, followed by the Duke of Saxony, otherwise an imperial elector, the Duke of Bourbon and the Duke of Bar and the other German dukes, one called Duke Henry [of Brieg /Brzeg/], Duke Boleslav [of Liegnitz /Legnica/ in Silesia] and [Wenceslas], Duke of Troppau [Opava]. Behind said dukes, there were twenty foot knights and squires from the king's bodyguard and twenty-five arbalesters, all in full armour, with a sword in one hand and verge in the other, and they held tightly together to protect the emperor, the king, the King of the Romans as well as the above-named dukes, who rode behind them, from the multitude of people who went behind them on horseback. Then rode all of the prelates written above and behind them the royal show horses and all the rest of the multitude of horses and people. And all the way at the back rode the provost of the merchants, the knight of the night watch, mounted sergeants, and the burghers of Paris. Thus and in such an orchestration, the emperor, the king as well as the King of the Romans rode on horses, namely without being pressed or stopped. And thus, soon and shortly, they arrived very easily and without difficulties at the palace, at which many marvelled, because they had never seen such a great number of people in such good order, without disarray and press. At the gate of the palace, at the entrance to the Mercière [Gallery] and also at the entrance to the Great Hall, certain barriers had been built and the sergeants of the guard as well as other sergeants had been ordered to guard them rigorously; and they were so watched that the emperor, the king, the King of the Romans as well as the other great lords who entered there were not in greater number than forty horses, [for] it had been ordained that no one stop before said gate at the entrance or exit of the palace, but that everyone ride on horse further and everyone spread onto the adjacent streets so that there would be less crowding. And so, at about three in the afternoon, they reached the marble staircase [in the courtyard]. And since the emperor could not walk because of his mentioned disease and it was necessary to carry him in arms, the king entrusted one of his secretaries, whose name was Master Philip Ogier, who was then the administrator of his palace, with preparing a chair covered in a gold-interlaced cloth for him in the courtyard under said staircase and had him placed in it.

78. / IX. Charles V welcomes the emperor and his son Wenceslas in the Palace de la Cité in Paris (BnF, ms. fr. 2813, fol. 471va)

HOW THE KING OF FRANCE CAME TO THE EMPEROR AT THE STAIRCASE WHERE HE WAS SEATED, GREETED HIM AND KISSED HIM AND THEN KISSED THE KING OF THE ROMANS, AND ON THE SEATING ARRANGEMENT AT THE DINNER ON THE SAME DAY.

While the emperor was sitting and resting in the chair mentioned above, the king came to him and told him that he greatly welcomed him in his palace and that he had never seen any of the princes with greater pleasure, after which he kissed him; and the emperor entirely removed his hat and humbly thanked him; the king then also greeted his son, the King of the Romans, and kissed him. Afterwards, the king gave the command to his knights to lift the emperor and carry him in his chair up the stairs; the king went up on one side of the stairs and led the king of the Romans on his left, and so the king went at the side of the emperor all the way to the chamber which he had had prepared for him, i.e. to the chamber inlaid with Irish wood, which lies next to the Green Chamber and which has a view of the palace gardens on one side and of Sainte-Chapelle on the other. The king also left all of the other rooms in the rear for the emperor, whereas for his son, [the King of the] Romans, he left the lower chambers, where the queens of France normally took refuge, and ordered that they be prepared. The king himself then stayed in the upper garrets, which

King John, his father, had had built. As soon as the emperor had rested a little, the king came to his chamber to visit him; and as he was approaching him, he took off everything, even his chaperon, and said that he was coming to visit him and show him his coif which he had apparently never seen. The emperor also removed his chaperon, but they soon covered their heads again, both the king and he, and sat in two chairs, placed side by side. Subsequently, the king gave the speech which follows here: 'My great uncle, know that I have such great joy from your arrival, as great as I can have, and I beseech you, believe me, to have everything that I have as if it were yours, and that before I manage to offer it to you myself.' Thereafter the emperor took off and so did the king, and the said emperor answered with these words: 'My lord, I thank you for your honours and what you have done for me, and I offer you [what follows] and I wish you to take my word for it, please, that I and my son, whom I have brought here to you, and all the other of my children, as well as anything I have, we are all yours, and that you can consider it all as yours.' And more people were present for these speeches, who took great pleasure and joy from this great friendship and good will. And then the king left. And for the illness of the emperor, which was very serious, because he also had a fever and was very tired from the mentioned journey, the king had dinner made for him in his chamber and invited the King of the Romans and the dukes, lords and knights who had arrived with him to have dinner with him. A very large supper was served there with a great crowd of courtiers. The seating arrangement of the persons was the following: the first was the Bishop of Paris, the king and then the King of the Romans, the Duke of Berry, the Duke of Brabant, the Duke of Burgundy, the Duke of Bourbon, and the Duke of Bar; and since two of the other dukes were not knights, they ate at another table, accompanied by Master Peter, son of the King of Navarre, the Count of Eu, and more other lords. It is worth mentioning that the Great Hall of the Palace, the [Great] Chamber of the Parliament, the Hall above Water, the Green Chamber and all of the other notable chambers of the royal residence in the palace, Sainte-Chapelle and the chapel attached to the Green Chamber were in general very richly decorated and trimmed, both in the palace and in the Louvre, in Saint-Pol, in the Bois de Vincennes, as well as at the castle of Beauté-sur-Marne. The king introduced the emperor to all of these places, accommodated him and ceremonially hosted him in them. And so proceeded said Monday when the emperor arrived in Paris. After having wine and deserts served after supper, the king, the King of the Romans and the other lords each went to his room.

79. / X. Emperor Charles IV accepts the gifts of the city of Paris (BnF, ms. fr. 2813, fol. 472ra)

ON THE PRESENTS WHICH THE BURGHERS OF THE GOOD CITY OF PARIS GAVE THE EMPEROR AND HIS SON, THE KING OF THE ROMANS.

On the following Tuesday, which was the fifth day of January, at the hour when the emperor was eating lunch in his chamber, the provost of the merchants and the Parisian aldermen appeared before him to present him in the name of the city with a *nef*, weighing one hundred and ninety marks (1 mark = 253.17g) of silver, very richly gilded and chased, two large gilded and enamelled flacons, worth seventy silver marks. And they presented his son with a silver wine bottle, gilded and richly chased, weighing ninety-three marks, with two large platters of gilded silver, very richly worked, weighing thirty marks. And on that day, the king did not visit the emperor publically at all, because he was ill and had slept poorly at night; when he had eaten, he wanted to lie down to sleep for the afternoon, before the king performed his devotions and heard the *missa cantata* as was his custom. However, the emperor sent the king a very affectionate wish to deign to come so that he could speak to him in private, because he had a certain issue on which he wanted to speak to him and requested and beseeched that the Chancellor of France be present with the king. And on that day, the king ate in the [Great] Hall with a great abundance of people, with the presence of the Duke of Saxony, who had not had dinner with the king the day before, the Bishop of Braunsberg, the emperor's chancellor, and all or the majority of the princes, lords and people of the emperor's household; the King of the Romans did not eat with them, because the king allowed him to keep the emperor, his father, company. When the king had eaten and retired to his room, he went secretly with a very small number of people to the emperor, as he had requested, and brought with him his chancellor. The emperor and the king sat down in two chairs, one next to the other, and ordered that everyone leave, except the Chancellor of France, who they stopped and called back. The emperor then spoke for a long time to the king, and so they were together for a good three hours, and finally, before their leave-taking, the emperor's chancellor was called. Nothing is known on the conversations or the affairs which they discussed.

The king then went to hear the vespers of that Tuesday, which was the eve of the feast of Epiphany, in Sainte-Chapelle, and at his left guided the King of the Romans; there were two oratories, one placed on the right next to the pews, the second on the left next to the sacristy, and the king was in the one on the right while the King of the Romans in the left one. The service was conducted by the Archbishop of Rheims, and Sainte-Chapelle was so nobly decorated and the altar so richly and abundantly furnished with gems of the church and relics and so illuminated that it was a beautiful and marvellous thing to behold. And at vespers there were so many noble people that they could hardly fit into Sainte-Chapelle. At the dinner of said Tuesday, which was the eve of the feast of Epiphany, the great Hall was very nobly decorated and trimmed. Many plates [with candles] were hung there, many torches on poles were fixed in many places of the hall and numerous servants, dressed in the same liveries, held a great abundance of torches, so that in said hall it was so light at night as if it were day; and it was there that the king dined with the King of the Romans, the prelates and the princes, who follow here in the form and order in which they were seated. It is necessary to know that the first was the bishop of Paris, who sat under the large canopy at the marble table, accompanied by the Bishop of Braunsberg, the emperor's councillor, the Archbishop of Rheims, the king, King of the Romans, the Dukes of Berry, of Brabant, of Burgundy, of Saxony, of Bourbon, Duke Henry and the Duke of Bar. The other dukes and princes sat under the second canopy, which was between the marble table and the entrance to the parliament. The dinner was long, a great number of meals were served, which would take too long to record. According to the report of the heralds, there were between eight hundred and a thousand knights and a great number of other noble people at the mentioned dinner in the hall, and hence there was an immensely large throng, although everyone was served in a very organised manner and without disorder, so that the tables were quickly and well cleared and all who ate in the palace were served, just as swiftly at the lower and further tables as at the higher and closer. After dinner, the king left with the King of the Romans for the [Great] Chamber of the Parliament, and their entourage included the prelates, princes, lords and knights written above, as many as could enter there. Musicians with string instruments awaited them and played in the customary way. The entire chamber was nobly decorated with *fleurs-de-lis* and richly lit; on both sides of the throne with a canopy, there were two raised chairs also with a canopy above them with embroidered *fleurs-de-lis*. When the wine and desserts were being served, the king was served desserts by the Duke of Berry and wine by the Duke of Burgundy. Then, the king left through the back door to his chamber and sent the King of the Romans through the hall escorted by the king's brothers, the dukes mentioned above, and more other lords and knights. Thus ended the day of Tuesday, which was the fifth day of January.

HOW THE KING SHOWED THE EMPEROR THE RELICS IN SAINTE-CHAPELLE OF HIS PALACE.

The next Wednesday, the sixth day of January and the day of the Epiphany, the emperor asked the king to deign to show him the holy relics, because he wished to see them that day, be carried to and present at mass and then eat lunch with the king in the palace. Thus they rose, the king and the emperor, early in the morning, and the king ordered that the knights and squires of his court guard the gate of the palace more vigilantly than before, because the day before the sergeants of the bodyguard as well as the provost's sergeants from the Châtellet had allowed too many people to pass through it. And the gates were really so well guarded that no one came in except knights, squires or other noble people. And therefore the emperor and the king went to the chapel calmly and without a great crowd. And since the emperor wanted to ascend before the Great Reliquary no matter how to be able to see the holy relics in it, and as the staircase was so steep and narrow here that he could not be carried in his chair, he had himself pulled by the shoulders and legs up the spiral staircase, and in the same manner he was carried down, which caused a great strain, difficulties and pains to his body, which he suffered for his great desire to see the said holy relics up close. When he was up above and the king opened the Holy Reliquary, the emperor removed his hat, clasped his hands and prayed there for a long time and very devoutly as if in tears. Then he had himself lifted and moved closer [to the reliquary] to be able to kiss the holy relics. The king showed him and presented all of the objects that are in the reliquary. When all of the princes present had kissed them, the king turned the reliquary towards the chapel and had it guarded by the Bishops of Beauvais and of Paris, wearing pontificals in the form of mitres and crosiers. When the emperor was then carried down, he did not want to be seated in the oratory which the king had had prepared for him but wanted to be in the chair where according to custom the treasurer of the chapel is seated to be able to see better and longer the holy relics and to be better [positioned] opposite the front of the reliquary. They prepared the chair for him there and covered it beautifully and nobly with a gold-embroidered drapery. The king was seated in his oratory, which was at the entrance to the sacristy, and because the emperor did not have any curtains, the king had his removed as well. At the beginning of the mass, the king had holy water and also the text of the Gospels sent to the emperor, by means of the Archbishop of Rheims, before himself, no matter how strongly the emperor was refusing it. Nevertheless, the king truly wanted to do this to honour the emperor, because he had come to visit him in his kingdom and was a guest in his palace. And when it came to the offerings, the king had three pairs of oblations, of gold, frankincense and myrrh, prepared to give for himself as well as for the emperor such as is the custom. When the king asked the emperor whether he would give an offering, he apologised saying that he could not walk or genuflect or hold anything because of his gout and asked the king to deign to give the offering himself and perform it according to his habit. The king's offering took place in the following manner: three knights, his chamberlains, were holding high three beautiful, gilded and enamelled cups; in the first there was gold, in the second frankincense and in the third myrrh. And all three went before the king in line behind one another, as the offering is supposed to be properly conducted, and the king behind them; the knights genuflected, the king also genuflected before the archbishop; the first oblation, which was gold, was given to the king by the one who was holding it and the king gave the offering while kissing the archbishop's hand. The second oblation, which is frankincense, was handed by the second knight, who was holding it, to the first, and he gave it to the king, who offered it, kissing the hand of the archbishop. The third, which is myrrh, was handed by the third knight, who was holding it, to the second, by the second to the first, and the first gave it to the king, and he, kissing the hand of the said archbishop, made his offering a third time. Thus he finished his oblation, devoutly and honourably. And since it was late, there was no sermon at the said mass; for the kiss of peace, two crosses of peace had been prepared, brought by the deacon and the subdeacon, one for the emperor, the other for the king, who both kissed them simultaneously, one like the other. After the mass was completed, the king climbed up to the Holy Reliquary and had the princes and the emperor's people, who had never been there before, kiss [its relics]. And because it took a long time, the emperor retired to a sanctuary at the side of Sainte-Chapelle where the ecclesiastical and other guards are headquartered, which the king had had prepared well and honourably for the emperor's rest. When the Holy Reliquary was then closed, the king left for his chamber through the chapel. Subsequently, the king sent to the emperor in the sanctuary at Sainte-Chapelle his first-born son, the dauphin of Viennois, for whom he had sent to his residence in Saint-Pol to ask him to come to see the emperor. The dauphin was accompanied by the king's brothers, the Dukes of Berry and of Burgundy, further the Duke of Bourbon, a brother of the queen, and the Duke of Bar; and there were also a large number of other lords and knights of great estates there. When the emperor learnt that the dauphin was coming to him, he had himself lifted from his chair, removed his hat, hugged him and kissed him. The dauphin bowed before him without kneeling. Not long afterwards, the king left his chamber and went to seek the emperor for them go to eat in the Great Hall of the palace; they carried the emperor there in a chair, with the king walking at his side and having the emperor's son, the King of the Romans, at his left side. The knights carrying the dauphin on their shoulders went in advance, namely accompanied by very numerous lords and knights. The procession went without great press through the Mercière [Gallery] and the Great Hall of the palace all the way to the high canopy behind the marble table, at which the seating arrangement was as described here and as is depicted in the illumination below.

ON THE LUNCH WHICH WAS IN THE GREAT HALL OF THE PALACE, AND ON ITS ORCHESTRATION.

The Archbishop of Rheims sat first, followed by the emperor, then the king, namely in such a way that he was in the centre of the front of the hall; beside the King of France sat the King of the Romans, with the same distance between the two kings as between the king and the emperor. The emperor, king, as well as the King of the Romans each had for himself a firmament of drapery interlaced with gold and lined with velour with the symbols of France, and above these were other, very large canopies, which went along the table, along all of the pillars as well as the window jambs. The windows behind the table were richly decorated with golden cloth, as was the firmament. Three bishops sat next to the King of the Romans, far away from him, at the end of the table: the Bishop of Braunsberg, the Bishop of Paris and the Bishop of Beauvais. Under other firmaments, which were between the marble table and the en-

80. / XI. Banquet in the Great Hall of the Palace de la Cité (BnF, ms. fr. 2813, fol. 473va–b)

trance to the parliament, the Duke of Saxony sat first, followed by the Dauphin of Viennois, the king's first-born son, and next to him sat the Dukes of Berry, of Brabant, of Burgundy, the son of the King of Navarre, the Duke of Bar, Duke Henry and at the end of the table, the emperor's chancellor, who was not a bishop. The Duke of Bourbon, the Count of Eu, the Lord of Coucy and the Count of Harcourt were not seated but stood around the dauphin to keep him company and protect him from the crowd. The other dukes and princes ate under other firmaments, in a beautiful and good arrangement. Above the canopy under which the dauphin ate, there was [yet another] firmament of velour stripes and drapery interlaced with gold, which covered the wall behind the table along its whole length, with the canopy being arranged likewise. Also the Great Hall of the Palace was along its whole length decorated all around by tapestries hung high above and pictures so beautifully trimmed and so well placed that the stone statues of the kings which were all around the hall were not covered at all or prevented from being well seen. There were thus five canopies in the said hall if we count the one at the marble table, and three wine cupboards, very richly adorned and equipped with vessels. The largest and closest between the large and the second canopies, in the corner of the hall, was the most laden with golden vessels and large silver, enamelled bottles. The second, which was close to the [Great] Hall of the Chamber of Petitions (*Chambre des requêtes*), was entirely covered by as many pots, flasks and other gilded vessels as it could hold. And the third, which was well in front in the middle of the hall under one of the arches, was filled as much as possible with vessels of white silver, which served the entire hall. The large as well as the second canopies and all of the mentioned racks were surrounded all around, furnished with and defended by reliable barriers, coulisses and pillars, which were well sharpened on top, so that it was impossible to enter in any way other than through certain passages, which were guarded and defended by knights designated to do so. And according to the report which was given by the heralds, a good eight hundred knights ate in the hall, not counting the other people. The king had ordered four courses of a total of forty pairs of dishes, but because of the illness of the emperor, who had already been sitting at the table for too long, the king cancelled one course and had only three served, which was thirty pairs of dishes, with the exception of two breaks with intermissions, which took place in the following manner.

The story presented showed how Godfrey of Bouillon captured the Holy City of Jerusalem. The king had this story performed on purpose, because it seemed to him that no other more important act could be commemorated and given as an example to the most powerful men in Christendom than this, because it was precisely they who best could, were supposed and obliged to implement and undertake a similar thing serving God. For a better description and comprehension of this need, everything was performed in the following way. At the end of the hall of the palace, which was so closed that nothing was visible from outside, there was a well-made ship, resembling a sea-faring ship, equipped with a sail as well as a mast and with a forecastle and an aftercastle; the ship had all of the other tackle and equipment necessary for sailing at sea and was very nicely, expensively as well as pleasingly painted and trimmed. And inside there were people, at first sight very nicely armed, who had on their weapons, shields as well as banners the coats-of-arms of Jerusalem, which Godfrey of Bouillon himself had worn. There were around twelve of them, armed as was mentioned with the weapons of the notable captains who were at the capture of Jerusalem with Godfrey. And in the front, on the bow of the said ship, Peter the Hermit stood, looking as precisely as he could according to what the legend says about him. The ship was being moved by the people inside of it and it moved very smoothly along the left side of the palace while turning so easily that it seemed as if it were a ship floating on water. In the end, it was steered all the way to the great canopy on the opposite side, which was the right side of the hall. And then the coulisse was erected at the place from which the said ship had sailed, adjusted in the manner and into the semblance of the city of Jerusalem. There was a temple depicted well corresponding to the place, and next to it there was a high tower, such as the Saracens usually build and from which they proclaim their law. On it, there stood a man wearing very authentic Saracen clothes, proclaiming the law in Arabic in the manner of the Saracens. The tower was so high that the man above almost touched the ceiling of the hall. Below, all around the city, where walls and towers with the battlement were rendered, there were Saracens armed in their manner, with banners and pennants, who had been designated to defend the city by combat. And then this coulisse was propelled by the power of the people who were hidden inside, so that they were not visible, all the way to before the great canopy on the right side. Now, the actors of the two intermissions attacked each other. Those who were on the ship descended and in a beautiful and good orchestration conducted an attack on the city and assaulted it for a long time. What was especially well performed were the falls of those who mounted the attack on ladders and were knocked down and thrown to the ground. At the end, those from the ship ascended, conquered the city and threw out those who were dressed as Saracens, planting the banners of Godfrey and the others. And it was all better and more beautifully implemented and seen than can be described in writing. Then once the entertainment concluded, all of the objects were transported to their original places.

After lunch finished and the tablecloths were removed, the emperor and the king were served water, in which they washed together, one like the other, and the King of the Romans was the first to wash after them. Since there was a very large number of participants, the king at the emperor's request ordered that the desserts and wine be brought to their chairs at the table where they had eaten lunch, although in front of the canopy where the emperor and king were, there was no crowd at all thanks to the good guards that were at the partition. And they were brought desserts and wine, because at the entrance to the [Great Chamber of the] Parliament, the emperor would have been very pressed and bothered because of his disease. When it was done, the dauphin was brought to the table and placed two feet before the emperor as well as the king while being supported by the Duke of Bourbon. At the king's order, the emperor was served pastilles by his brother, the Duke of Berry, and the king was similarly served by the Duke of Burgundy. The emperor as well as the king supplicated one another greatly to take pastilles; then they both helped themselves at the same time, each as soon as the other, and they acted in the same way also when drinking the wine, which the Duke of Brabant served the emperor, his brother, and the Duke of Bourbon served the king. Shortly afterwards, the King of the Romans helped himself to the desserts and wine; the desserts were served to him by the Count of Eu and the wine by one of his knights. When the wine and desserts had been served, the emperor was led away from the table and placed in a chair. In order to avoid the large crowd, the king and he parted with each other and the emperor was carried out through the middle of the Great Hall, through the door to the Mercière Gallery and through the great hallway directly to his chambers. The king sent his brothers and more other lords after him to escort him and the king himself on his exit took the King of the Romans with him at his side. They entered the [Great] Chamber of the Parliament, where the king spoke and kept company for a long time with the king, dukes and princes of the empire, with the bishop and chancellor, who had come with the emperor, and with numerous other lords and knights, of whom there were as many as could fit there. Then, the king and the King of the Romans left the Chamber of the Parliament through the back way and each went to his room through the large hallway. It was already late when these things occurred. Before the last had eaten, who finished as soon as the first, it was already close to night. The king did not eat his dinner in the hall that night but quite privately in the room in front of his chamber, and the emperor as well as his son ate dinner also in their chambers. Despite this there was a large party of lords from his kingdom, who were then staying in Paris, at dinner with the king. After dinner, the king left, taking with him his brothers and a few others, and went to visit the emperor in his chamber secretly. They sat in two chairs, one next to the other, and conversed and for a long time had a good discussion. Then the king left for his room and the King of the Romans went there with him and escorted him; he had wine and pastilles with the king, after which he left, escorted by the king's brothers. Then they all parted to go to bed. And so ended Wednesday, the day of the feast of the Epiphany.

HOW THE EMPEROR AND THE KING LEFT THE PALACE AND BOARDED A BEAUTIFUL AND SPLENDID BOAT TO BE TAKEN BY WATER ALL THE WAY TO THE CHÂTEAU OF THE LOUVRE.

The next Thursday, which was the seventh day of January, the king decided to go to the Louvre and take the emperor with him. The emperor broke fast in the morning before he left, whereas the king himself did not eat lunch until he was at the Louvre. The king had the emperor carried before the palace, where a large boat was prepared, built and modified in the manner of a house, which had a hall and two rooms, all with a fireplace, and numerous places of retreat and other necessary rooms. The boat was magnificently adorned and decorated, and in the rooms there were beds with stretched canopies as well as all the other equipment that can be found in a house. When the emperor and his people had entered and seen it, they wondered greatly at it and took great pleasure in it. Thus they arrived at the Louvre, and the emperor was then carried in his chair, with the king always at his side, until they came inside the château. There the king showed the emperor the new building which he had had built and had it shown to him both from the outside and inside, in which the emperor seems to have taken great pleasure. The king accommodated him in his chambers, very luxuriously adorned and decorated, and himself stayed at the other end in the rooms which were intended for his oldest son, the Dauphin of Viennois. Then the King of the Romans was lodged below in the queen's chambers, which had been equally well adorned and decorated. Generally, in the entire château, both in the halls and in the chambers and chapels, everything was decorated and arranged so that nothing would be lacking, without even having used any decorative objects of the palace. And so that it would not be necessary to repeat it and in order to speak more briefly, all of the royal residences in which the emperor stayed, Saint-Pol, the Bois de Vincennes and the folly Beauté, were furnished in the same way. This day, the king ate lunch at the Louvre with all of the knights and squires who had wanted to come there, and all were served very nobly and generously.

HOW THE UNIVERSITY OF PARIS APPEARED BEFORE THE EMPEROR TO PAY HIM REVERENCE, AND ON THE PEOPLE OF THE COUNCIL WHO THE KING ASSEMBLED IN ORDER TO SPEAK TO THEM.

After lunch, the king assembled his Council in his chamber. At that hour at the king's order, the University of Paris appeared before the emperor. From each faculty, there were twelve [masters], with the exception of the Liberal Arts, from which there were twenty-four, and all of them were ceremonially dressed in their gowns and habits. In their usual manner, they had come to pay reverence to the emperor. The ceremonial speech was presented exquisitely and in accordance with the statutes by master of theology Jean de la Chaleur, chancellor at Notre-Dame in Paris, who praised the person of the emperor in many things, his noble acts, virtues as well as dignity, and who also greatly praised and especially brought attention to the position and honour of the King of

81. / XII. Reception of the delegation from the University of Paris (BnF, ms. fr. 2813, fol. 475rb)

France and his kingdom, praising and approving the emperor's visit to the king. In the end, he well and wisely recommended the university as is proper in such a case, to which the emperor himself responded in Latin thanking for the words which had been spoken in his honour. He further said that three things had brought him to the kingdom: the pious desire to see the holy relics, pilgrimages to some other sites where he wanted to perform devotions, and especially the great wish to see the king and speak with him.

At the same time, the king and his Council were in his chambers, where his brothers and in great number likewise prelates from his Council as well as other knights, also in a quite significant number, were present, and he asked them and requested [advice] whether it seemed a good idea to them that he would show the factual basis or have it shown as well as justice of the legitimate right which he had against his enemies from England, further the great wrongdoing which they had committed against his predecessors as well as him over a long time and also the effort by which he had tried to conclude a peace treaty good in all aspects, as well as the offers which he had made for that to the emperor, his uncle, who had expressed so much love of and trust in him, namely also by having come to his kingdom and to him, and that with two goals: first, for the emperor to learn that the enemies of the king proclaim in Germany as well as elsewhere the opposite of the truth, justifying themselves, and for the emperor, princes and his councillors who are with him thus to hear and see what the king would tell them about it and what documents as well as concluded treaties on peace and alliance he would have shown to them so that they could recognise, correctly respond and defend the truth in these issues against those who had tried, were trying and would try to speak or proclaim otherwise. The second reason which had motivated the king to this was to gain the advice and expert opinion of the emperor when he had heard and seen the effort which the king had expressed as well as the offers he had made to achieve peace, whether it would seem to the emperor that he should cease in them or whether the king should exert even greater effort. In response to these requests and questions, everyone counselled unanimously and without opposition that the king do so. He then ordered the members of his said Council and also many others to assemble the next day, and also informed the emperor for him and his son, the princes and other people of his Council who had come in his escort to be at the said place in the Louvre at the said hour and to hear what the king wanted to say and show to the emperor.

Friday, the eighth day of January, came. And that day in the morning, the king came to visit the emperor privately and brought him a gift of a beautiful jewellery box of jasper, inlaid with gold and precious stones, with one thorn from the Crown of Thorns and with one of the bones of St Martin; then he gave him also a bone of St Dennis, because the emperor greatly desired to have one and had asked the king for it. That day in the afternoon, the king came along with the emperor to the reception hall in the Louvre, and the King of the Romans was already there with those [councillors] from the emperor's side that are written here: the Bishop of Braunsberg, his chancellor and two other noted clergymen, the Dukes of Brabant and of Saxony, and the three other dukes mentioned above, the Grand Master of the Royal Household and the High Chamberlain, the lord of Kolditz, and more other lords, counts, barons and knights numbering fifty and more persons. From the king's side, the number was the same or higher, with the most important and notable among them being those whose names follow, i.e. the Dukes of Berry, of Burgundy, of Bourbon, of Bar, the Lord of Coucy, the Counts of Harcourt, of Tancarville, of Saarbrücken, of Braine, his Lordship Jacques de Bourbon, Marshall of France de Blainville, the Lord of Rayneval, Lord Philibert de l'Espinace, his Lordship Thomas de Voudenay, his Lordship Arnaud de Corbie, knights and many others. From the King's Council, there were the chancellor, the Archbishop of Rheims, the Bishops of Laon, of Paris, of Beauvais and of Bayeux, the Abbot of Saint-Vaast, and other clergymen as well as laity from both the King's Council and the Parliament as well as from elsewhere. The emperor and the king with the King of the Romans were seated in three chairs, covered in drapery interlaced with gold; the others then sat in double rows, in the manner of the chairs in the Council. The king took the floor and began to explain the events and measures written above for a very long time, for two hours and more. He took his material from the first times of the Kingdom of France and then passed to the conquest of Gascony attributable to Saint Charlemagne, who conquered it and converted it to Christianity. The land was allegedly subjected to the rule of the King of France and had always remained that way without interruption and resistance from that time and even those who had held estates there, especially the Dukes of Guyenne, also the Kings of England as well as other lords, had always entered into a direct liege bond and recognised the King of France as their legitimate lord, who owned their feudatory. If it had not been different starting with the time of the recently deceased Edward of England, there would not be any doubt today. Edward himself had acted thus inappropriately, because he had sworn homage to King Philip, the king's grandfather, which was performed in Amiens, and thus recognised Philip as his lord and the King of France. When he returned to England after that oath, he confirmed the feudal bond after quite a long time with his papers sealed with a great seal and declared it as direct, namely more strongly and thoroughly than he had done orally to King Philip, which is stated in further detail on the pages written thereon, whose originals with the seals were shown to the emperor. The emperor was also shown all of the older documents of his predecessors, the Kings of England, which had once been given to Saint Louis and which recognised the feudal bonds of Gascony, Bordeaux, Bayonne, and the islands which are opposite Normandy. It is explicitly stated in the documents how the Kings of England renounced all the lands in Normandy, in Anjou, in Maine, in Touraine, in Poitiers, and that they had no dominion there as is more plainly contained in the documents which were shown to the emperor. The king also showed him the peace treaty [from Brétigny] and proved how his father and he had paid dearly for it and how the English had kept it badly, construing it in their own way: they either neglected to return the occupied fortresses that they were to return or were holding them as security, which in contradiction of the content of the treaty they extorted, other times they continually kept military troops in the Kingdom of France, or usurped and used the rights of sovereignty, which appertain only to the King of France and which they were not to use at all; they also provided forces to the King of Navarre, at that time an enemy of the kingdom, as well as his adherents and supporters with their people, subjects as well as allies, English and Gascon alike, and allowed them transit, gave them sustenance as well as succour; all of that against the wording of the contracts concluded, sworn, terminated and made under an oath as strongly as can only occur between Christians. These contracts were shown and read also to the emperor in French and in Latin so that everyone could better comprehend them. In addition, the prince of Wales caused many outrages and damages to the land as well as the people of Gascony, which are and remain under the sovereignty and jurisdiction of the king, because no renunciation had been declared as the king showed the emperor in the document, which contains an article beginning 'It is well-known' and so on. The king also provided evidence on how the Count of Armagnac, the Lord of Lebret and more other barons as well as good towns had appealed from the prince to him and how they had come to request in person that a day and sentence in the issue of the appeal be set, and how the king had needed a long time and had had to overcome great obstacles before he could do this with the council of many notables constituted for that purpose, with the members of his Council and after hearing the opinions of several studies of law – of Bologna, of Montpellier, of Toulouse, and of Orléans – and the most distinguished clergymen of the Court of Rome, which he could not refuse; and how the king had done this through an orderly way of justice and not by the power of his arms. Then, one doctor, the king's justice in Toulouse by the name of Master Bernard Palot, and one knight, by the name of Lord Jean de Chaponval, were appointed to bring the prince the king's documents and writs of summons and, having a safe conduct from the seneschal of the said prince, to go before the prince; he, however, had them apprehended and evilly tortured against God, justice and as an offense to the king and the Kingdom of France. The king also showed the emperor how, notwithstanding the offenses thus caused, he sent to king Edward the counts, knights and clergymen to challenge him legally and request that he redress the things so evilly done by his son as well as his subjects and have them redressed; the king wished for these things to be remedied in an amicable way and not by war, but the king was not given a reasonable response or any good hope. In fact, the prince had already begun a war in Gascony against those who had appealed against him, and so did the people of the King of England in Ponthieu, when they invaded the king's land. Wherefore the king, out of necessity, and also in accordance with the Council of his kingdom, assembled for this purpose in the [Great Chamber of the] Parliament, undertook to defend his justified right against his enemies.

When the king had described the cause of the war and using the responses and sealed letters well informed the emperor and his Council, he also listed and drew his attention to the tasks he had accomplished to reach a good contract with his adversaries. Finally, he also showed the emperor the offers which he had made to this end, concluding his speech to the two ends listed above: on the one hand to demonstrate his royal right against the fabricated words of the English, which are not to be trusted, and on the other hand for the emperor to provide him with advice. He also touched on, very briefly, the graces and good fortune that the merciful God had granted him in his war, for which certainly also the emperor would be very grateful to God. The king said all of these things and many others connected with this matter, which would take too long to record, so wisely and so orderly that everyone marvelled at his good memory and excellent elocution, thereupon the emperor and everyone who had been able to listen to him said that they were happy to hear it. After that, the emperor in a short speech in German told his people who had been present and had not understood the French what the king had said, and also elucidated the content of the papers which he had heard read on it. He then gave the king such an answer as follows, i.e. that he had very carefully listened to everything that the king had very wisely presented, that he had also seen and learnt well both from the documents and otherwise the justification of his dispute and right, and that he would proclaim it everywhere and issue his own testimony on it. If the English in Germany then attempted to spread the opposite as they had done before, he himself would defend and support the king's right as he had seen it and learnt it well, because he himself had been present in Amiens when the King of England had sworn his feudal loyalty to the King of France. If he were to give advice, then he would say, considering the justified right of the king and the great injustice done by his enemies as well as the advantages which he had over them in war and the allies of the king, of whom he named the Kings of Castile, Portugal, as well as Scotland, that he had not advised nor would he advise him to offer so much in advance to his enemies. The emperor expressed the opinion that the king had already done much in this respect and that he had done so only for the love of God; he then added that he knew well the way of the English, who ask for and want to have peace when they are at a disadvantage; however, as soon as they are at an advantage, they do not maintain the peace at all, which, as he had seen himself many times, they had been doing to the Kingdom of France. Then, the king took his leave and returned to his chamber.

82. / XIII. Emperor Charles IV offers allied aid to the French king (BnF, ms. fr. 2813, fol. 476vb)

HOW THE EMPEROR HAD THE COUNCIL OF THE KING AS WELL AS THE EMPEROR'S PEOPLE GATHERED THE NEXT DAY FOR THEM TO HEAR THE OFFERS THAT THE KING WANTED TO MAKE TO THE KING IN THEIR PRESENCE.

The next Saturday, which was the ninth day of the month, the emperor announced that he had not offered the king enough in the recommendation which he had given him in his answer. He therefore had the king asked to assemble after lunch those of his Council who had been present before, and in the same way had those from his own Council who had been present informed. When they had gathered in the manner of the day before, namely in an even greater number than the last Friday, the emperor began to speak so loudly that everyone could hear him well. He declared that he wanted to apologise that he had not offered his services to the king to a greater extent in his response which he had given. He therefore wished for everyone to know and for it to be conveyed and announced to all and everywhere that he as well as his son, the King of the Romans, whom he had brought with him for this purpose, all of his other children, his allies, subjects and supporters wanted and offered the king to be all his, to support and guard his good and honour, as well as those of his kingdom, his children as well as his brother against all persons. After that, he handed him a scroll on which his allies, with whose help he could gain greater power, were declared and named. The king very gratefully thanked him for it and with that they took their leave.

HOW THE EMPEROR WENT TO VISIT THE QUEEN IN HER RESIDENCE IN SAINT-POL.

The next Sunday, which was the tenth day of January, the emperor left along with the king. When the emperor had lunched, he was carried all the way to the water on the bank at the Louvre, to the above-mentioned boat, and the emperor with the king and the King of the Romans went on it upstream under the great bridge directly to Saint-Pol, in which residence the queen and the infants of the king were waiting. When in said residence, they had reached the centre of the courtyard, the king's sons, the first-born dauphin and Lord Louis, Count of Valois, knelt before the king and then went to greet the emperor in the chair in which he was being carried. The emperor kissed them while removing his hat. Then, the king's sons were carried before the mentioned lords, and the king with the King of the Romans went in advance to the great hall and ascended the staircase with apertures, whereas the emperor was brought in his chair later. When he was upstairs, he wished to visit the queen, and the emperor, king and the King of the Romans went to see her together. There was a great throng and crowd of lords, knights, and noble people everywhere, so that it was hardly possible to pass through the entrance. Nevertheless, they came all the way to the queen's old chamber, which is next to the hall where the story of Theseus is depicted. The queen was waiting for the emperor and king there, having a very rich circlet on her head and surrounded by a noble accompaniment of grand dames, who are listed here: primarily, there was the Countess of Artois, the Duchess of Orléans, the daughter of the King of France, further the Duchess of Bourbon, the mother of the queen, the niece of the king, the daughter of his brother the Duke of Berry, the daughter of the Lord of Coucy, the Lady of Préaux and a number of other countesses and ladies, wives of feudal lords and knights bannerets and countless other ladies and girls, who would take too long to list. When the emperor saw the queen, he had himself carried all the way to her chair, removed his hat, and the queen greeted and kissed him. Then he was carried a little further in the chamber all the way to before the bed, with

83. / XIV. Emperor Charles IV on a visit at Queen of France Jeanne of Bourbon (BnF, ms. fr. 2813, fol. 477ra)

the queen staying at his side and the king in front escorting the King of the Romans, whom the queen also greeted and kissed. The emperor and the King of the Romans then kissed all of the ladies who were related and came from the French royal family. Afterwards, the emperor wished very dearly to see the queen's mother, the Duchess of Bourbon, who was standing in one of the corners of the said chamber outside of the throng; and she was brought to the emperor. When they stood next to one another, the emperor began to weep so strongly, and so did the duchess, that it was very pitiful to see. The causes of this were the memories of the emperor's first wife, who was a sister of the duchess, and also of the Duchess of Normandy, who was the emperor's sister and the king's mother, with whom the duchess had been raised as a companion. Nevertheless, they could not speak to one another at that place, and so the emperor asked for permission to visit her after lunch and speak more with her alone, and thus it happened. Afterwards, the emperor, the king as well as the King of the Romans took their leave of the queen and left. The emperor was carried to the room of the Dauphin of Viennois, the oldest of the king's sons, which was richly decorated for him, just like the whole residence, as has been said above. The king then went to eat lunch in the so-called Hall of Sens, where he led the King of the Romans and all of the emperor's people with a host of knights as practicable. While they were eating lunch, the emperor had himself prepared to sleep. After lunch, when the wine and desserts had been served, the king retired to his room and had the King of the Romans taken to the room of Lord Louis, his son, otherwise the Count of Valois. The King of the Romans then wanted to go see the lions and the king's brothers also went along with him. When the emperor awoke, the already-mentioned Duchess of Bourbon was led to him and both then talked with each other for a long time. Quite soon afterwards, the king sent the queen and his sons, the Dauphin of Viennois and the Count of Valois, to the emperor, for which the emperor was very grateful to him. The queen sat for a long time at his side and they conversed for a lengthy period. The queen gave him a gorgeous golden reliquary in the form of a great, vaulted temple, very richly inlaid with precious stones, which had a little piece of wood from the true cross inside. The dauphin then gave him two very beautiful hunting dogs on ornate leads with collars of silk embossed with golden *fleurs-de-lis*. The emperor expressed great joy with it, was extremely pleased with the gifts and thanked the queen as well as the said dauphin for them. As it was evening and the emperor was to travel with the king to the 'Wood' in Vincennes, the king came to the emperor's room to invite him to leave, because it had been agreed that they would go together. Therefore, the queen as well as the children took their leave of the emperor and left to the room next door. Then, the King of the Romans came to the queen to take his leave and she gave him a beautiful and expensive gold buckle inlaid with precious stones. Soon afterwards, they all left; the king in advance with the King of the Romans to mount their horses while the emperor sat down in the queen's litter, and so they left directly for the 'Wood'. When they arrived at the 'Wood', it was already late, and therefore a great amount of torches were carried in front of them. The king then had the emperor carried and lodged in his beautiful tower, in the room where he used to sleep, and himself was accommodated in the room which is called the Fallow Deer Room and which is in the tower. He further had the emperor's son, the King of the Romans, accommodated in the room of his oldest son, the Dauphin of Viennois. Afterwards, the king dined in the hall with his people, namely without the foreigners, who had all returned to Paris.

HOW THE EMPEROR HAD HIMSELF CARRIED AROUND IN THE ROOM WHERE HE WAS ACCOMMODATED TO SEE THE SURROUNDINGS OF THE CHÂTEAU IN THE 'WOOD' IN VINCENNES, AND ON THE BOOKS OF HOURS WHICH THE KING GAVE HIM.

The next Monday, which was the eleventh day of January, the said emperor had himself carried around in the room mentioned above to see the surroundings of the château through the windows, because he could not go there. The king then sent his son, the King of the Romans, accompanied by his mentioned brothers, to hunt fallow deer and wild rabbits in the game preserve for their entertainment. That morning the king did not see the emperor at all, because in the early morning the king had listened to mass and then had eaten lunch while the emperor wished to sleep until the king had performed his devotions according to his customs and order. However, the king came to visit the emperor after lunch, because the emperor had already slept in the meantime.

84. / XV. King of the Romans Wenceslas IV swears an oath to the French king (BnF, ms. fr. 2813, fol. 478ra)

Afterwards, they remained in a friendly conversation and entertainment for a long time, during which time the emperor asked the king to give him one of his Books of Hours, saying that he would pray to God for him [from it]. The king sent him two, one large and one small, and let him know that he could choose which he wanted or both if he liked them both. He kept them both and thanked the king for them.

HOW THE EMPEROR ORDERED HIS SON, THE KING OF THE ROMANS, TO PROMISE BY AN OATH SWORN INTO THE HAND OF THE KING OF FRANCE THAT HE WOULD LOVE HIM MORE THAN ALL THE PRINCES OF THE WORLD AND THAT HE WOULD SERVE HIM AND HIS CHILDREN, AND HOW THE KING OF THE ROMANS THEN ASCENDED ALL THE WAY TO THE TOP OF THE TOWER TO SEE ITS FLOORS.

While the king lingered with the emperor in his room, the King of the Romans returned [from hunting]. As soon as the emperor saw him, he called him, took him by the hand and had him swear an oath into the king's hand on his faith that he would love him and serve him as long as he lived before all the princes of the world, and the king's children as well. The king thanked him for that and was of good will. Afterwards, the king returned to his room and still on that day had the King of the Romans and the other princes and the knights shown the tower, its floors, armoury and equipment, so that they were all the way at the top. They all then reckoned the tower to be the most beautiful and marvellous thing that they had ever seen. The King of the Romans then received arbalests from the king. On this day, nothing more happened that would be worth recording.

HOW THE EMPEROR LEFT THE 'WOOD' IN VINCENNES AND LEFT FOR SAINT-MAUR, AND ON THE PRESENTS WHICH THE LOCAL ABBOT GAVE HIM.

On the next Tuesday, the twelfth day of January, the emperor early in the morning left the 'Wood', namely on the dauphin's litter. He had decided to wit to perform a pilgrimage to Saint-Maur-des-Fossés and did not wish to be accompanied by the king's brothers. The king then did not go either, as he had his responsibilities. On the manner in which the emperor was received in Saint-Maur, we shall tell you this:

The king sent word to the abbot and commanded that they receive him with a procession at the entrance to the monastery as a pilgrim, and they did so. The emperor then listened to the famous mass sung by the abbot, and offered one hundred francs, leaving the gifts which the abbot had given him,

85. / XVI. Emperor Charles IV during a service in the Abbey of Saint-Maur-des-Fossés (BnF, ms. fr. 2813, fol. 478rb)

namely fish, cattle, sheep, wine, bread and other things, to the convent. After the mass, the emperor went to have lunch in one of the rooms of the church, which, along with the hall next to it, the king had had beautifully decorated and tapestried for him. Since his arrival in Paris, the emperor had been hosted at the king's cost and in all of his needs served by the king's people and servants from all of his offices. When he had had lunch and slept a little, he was put in his litter and carried to Beauté-sur-Marne, where the king had been awaiting him for a long time. When the king had discovered that the emperor had been delayed and was too late, he returned from there to the 'Wood'. At said residence in Beauté, the emperor was accommodated very well. The entire residence was very luxuriously decorated and furnished in his honour and for his pleasure as has been said above, so that in the given residence his health improved remarkably. He began to walk again and saw the whole residence from top to bottom, and that only with slight assistance. He told everyone who was there with him that he had never in his life seen a more beautiful place or a more delightful location. Every day after lunch, the king arrived to visit him, and they stayed together a great deal of time. They sometimes went to the room entirely alone and there secretly spoke of their needs. The king then always left for dinner and the night at the 'Wood', where he also had lunch, and thus it was until the emperor's departure, which fell on Saturday, the sixteenth day of the month of January. On the Thursday before, the fourteenth day of the month, the king had presents given to the emperor and his people as will be written below. Since the emperor had expressed his desire several times to see the crown which the king had had made and of which he had heard told that it was very beautiful and splendid, the king sent it to him in Beauté to see it. It was brought by Gilles Malet and Hennequin, the king's goldsmith. The emperor examined it with great liking, holding it and inspecting it everywhere for a very long time, finding great pleasure in it. When he had looked at it to his content, he said that it should be deposited back in the strongbox and added that he had never seen so many noble and rich precious stones all together. On the Wednesday before, which was the thirteenth day of January, the king had a message sent to the emperor that he invite his people to Beauté for the mentioned Thursday. From Lord de la Rivière and Gilles Malet, the emperor discovered very confidentially that it was so that he could present them with gifts. No matter how much the emperor apologised, because, as he said, he did not wish the king to give him or his people anything, he sent for them on said day in order to fulfil the king's will. That Thursday after lunch, the king sent his brothers, the Dukes of Berry and of Burgundy, and with them also the Duke of Bourbon, Lord de la Rivière and other of his chamberlains and other officials to bring the jewels which were presented and given by the king to the emperor, his son and their people. The dukes gave the king's presents to the emperor in his chamber and in the emperor's presence also to his son. The gifts intended for the emperor were such as follows.

ON THE RICH PRESENTS WHICH THE KING OF FRANCE GAVE AND HAD PRESENTED TO THE EMPEROR AND HIS SON.

The Duke of Berry, presenting the things listed here to the emperor, said that the king greeted him and was greeting him and sending him such gems as they knew how to make in Paris, namely: one gold chalice of great weight, inlaid with precious stones on the foot as well as on the lid, with very fine enamel depicting the heavenly sphere with the zodiac, the signs, the planets and the fixed stars and their images. He also presented him with two large gold flasks, very nobly elaborated, whose reliefs depicted how St Jacob showed St Charlemagne the route to Spain in a revelation. Each of the mentioned flasks was shaped like a shell. The Duke of Berry told the emperor about it that the king was sending him shells, as he was himself a pilgrim. He then also presented him with a very beautiful and large gold pot, placed on a tripod decorated with

86. / XVII. The gifts of French king to Emperor Charles IV (BnF, ms. fr. 2813, fol. 478vb)

precious stones, and also a gold goblet with a pitcher, very adroitly enamelled and inlaid with precious stones.

Item, he presented the emperor with two great pots, elaborated like lions' heads. His son was then given a large goblet with a pitcher, also of gold, and two large gold vessels whose lid had decoration of ivory, sapphires and pearls; besides that, he was given a very expensive gold belt, richly decorated with stones along its entire length, of a value of a good six to eight thousand gold francs. The emperor thanked the king very much for it, and so did his son. Afterwards, the emperor went through the hallway in front of his chamber, where all of his princes, the bishop, the chancellor, the knights and other people who had come with him were, so that he could see the gifts which had been presented and consigned to them. They were great and honourable gifts, as is clearer from their list on the *rotulus*, where they are completely and individually described. In this place, however, we shall pass this over for the sake of brevity. Everyone seemed very satisfied with and excited about the gifts from the king, and they also expressed it.

HOW THE EMPEROR AFTER HIS RETURN FROM SAINT-MAUR TO BEAUTÉ THANKED THE KING FOR THE SUMPTUOUS GIFTS WHICH HE HAD SENT HIM, HIS SON AS WELL AS THEIR PEOPLE.

The next Friday, the fifteenth day of the month of January, which was the feast of St Maurice, the emperor performed a pilgrimage to [the Abbey of] Saint-Maur, where the bishop of Paris sang the Pontifical Mass in his presence. Although lunch had been prepared for him in the said abbey according to the king's command, he wanted to return to Beauté for lunch. After lunch, the king visited him and the emperor thanked him very much for the gifts which the king had dedicated to him, his son as well as his people, saying that they were too great. Afterwards, the emperor and the king retired to the cloakroom next to his room, sent everyone out and spoke together for a long time until it was very late. Then, the king left, with the emperor accompanying him to in front of his room, and left for the 'Wood' for the night.

On Saturday, the sixteenth day of January, the king ate lunch earlier than was his custom, but the emperor still sooner and then fell asleep. The king left his castle at the 'Wood' accompanied by a great number of lords, prelates and knights to escort the emperor, because he wanted to do so. He then arrived at the residence in Beauté-sur-Marne precisely when the emperor was already up, prepared for departure and ready to set out on the journey.

ON THE RINGS THAT THE KING AND THE EMPEROR EXCHANGED, AND HOW THE EMPEROR AND THE KING AMICABLY AND PLAINTIVELY TOOK THEIR LEAVE OF EACH OTHER, AND ON THOSE WHO ACCOMPANIED THE SAID EMPEROR.

When the king was in the room of the emperor, who was already awaiting him, the emperor approached him, took off his finger-one ring with a ruby and another with a diamond and gave them both to the king with honest words of great friendship. The king in return took a very expensive and large diamond which he had on his finger and gave it to the emperor in the same manner. Then in front of everyone, they mutually hugged, kissed and soon left so that they could go together out into the courtyard, where the king mounted his horse and the emperor climbed into his litter which the king had given

87. / XVIII. The mutual exchange of rings and leave-taking of both rulers (BnF, ms. fr. 2813, fol. 479rb)

him and which was pulled by three very beautiful mules. When the emperor set out, the king was at his side on the horse, and a great multitude of people waited outside in the fields before the residence all the way to the proximity of the folly in Plaisance. The king was accompanied by the already-mentioned princes, except for the Duke of Bar, who had left with the king's permission the day before, further by all of the prelates who had been with him before, and moreover by the archbishop of Ravenna, who had come here again. The Provost of Paris, the knight of the night watch, the provost of the merchants, aldermen as well as the people of the city who stood outside in the fields came to accompany the emperor and rode ahead on horseback. Near the residence in Plaisance, the emperor and the king then took their leave. The king returned sooner, and in so doing obeyed the emperor, who had told him more times and sent word to him to return. During the leave-taking, the emperor as well as the king cried so much that the people noticed it. And as it was hard for them to speak to each other, they took each other by the hands and so took their leave. The king returned to the 'Wood', whereas the Dukes of Berry, of Burgundy and of Bourbon left with the emperor. The King of the Romans returned and escorted the king for part of the journey, then took his leave of him, and so did the princes and dukes who were in the emperor's retinue. The mentioned king's brothers then went further with the emperor and led him to Lagny-sur-Marne for the night; the next day, they also went with him to Meaux. In both of the above-mentioned cities, the emperor was ceremonially received and given presents, as had happened at his arrival in all of the already-mentioned cities. On that Sunday, the seventeenth day of said month, when he was in Meaux, he departed from the bishop's palace, where he was lodged, to have dinner in Marché de Meaux. There, he along with his son, the princes and all of his people were richly, promptly and ceremonially received as well as served by the Dukes of Berry and of Burgundy although both of the king's brothers had had little time to prepare for it from when they had found out about his arrival.

HOW THE EMPEROR LEFT MEAUX AND HOW THE KING'S BROTHERS AND MANY OTHER LORDS WHO HAD ACCOMPANIED HIM TOOK THEIR LEAVE OF THE EMPEROR.

The next Monday, the emperor as well as his son, the King of the Romans, left Meaux, and the mentioned brothers of the king accompanied them a good mile on the way from the city, where they took their leave of them and returned to the king. It cannot be left out that the emperor of his own impetus and from his goodwill to the king and to his oldest son, the dauphin, had named and appointed said dauphin as his vice-regent and general vicar in the Kingdom of Arles (Arelat), and that irrevocably until the end of the dauphin's life. On that, he issued documents with a golden seal with such great and complete power as was possible, which was not usual. In a similar way, he made him vice-regent and vicar general in said Dauphiné, in its fiefs and in other domains with no exceptions through another document, furnished with a similar seal and with the same power. He further presented him with the castle Pipet sur Vienne and another house in said city, called Canaux. He also declared him to be adult and removed everything that could prevent the dauphin for his young age from receiving this favour and government. After his departure, the emperor left his chancellor in Paris for three or four days so that he would prepare and seal the letters and so that these and other things could be performed for the pleasure and to the benefit of the king as well as his children.

THE JOURNEYS WHICH THE EMPEROR UNDERTOOK DURING HIS RETURN FROM THE KINGDOM OF FRANCE.

Afterwards, the return journey began, which the emperor undertook according to the king's schedule all the way to the border of his kingdom. After his departure from the city of Meaux, he went for the night to Gandelu, where he received gifts like in other cities. From there, he went on Tuesday, the nineteenth day of January, to Château-Thierry, where the king had had a residence belonging to him provided, decorated and prepared for his arrival. Also there the emperor was very well provided for by the king's officials in the halls, rooms and in all the needs as it had been in all of the other residences of the king. From the king's side, the emperor's escort included the Lord of Coucy, the Counts of Saarbrücken and of Braine, Lord de la Rivière, and Jehan Le Mercier, all or most of whom accompanied and led him all the way to the frontier of the kingdom. His route ran from Château-Thierry to Rheims, from Rheims to Mouzon, and that without lodging between them. In every place, the emperor received presents, the same in open towns as in fortified, and was ceremonially and richly received and feted everywhere as on his arrival. It is also appropriate to mention that it was the king that had more or less paid and defrayed the entire expenditure which the emperor and his people had in the palaces in Paris, as was the case also with all the gifts that cost great expense; similarly, everything from the time the emperor entered the kingdom until he

88. / XIX. Dauphin Charles receives a deed from the imperial chancellor (BnF, ms. fr. 2813, fol. 480ra)

was outside of it, even though it was given in the name of the cities, was at the cost and expenditure of the king.

ON THE EMPEROR'S DOCUMENTS CONTAINING THE ABOVE-MENTIONED AFFAIRS, WHICH HIS CHANCELLOR GAVE TO THE DAUPHIN.

When the king returned to Paris, the emperor's chancellor brought and presented to the dauphin, who was staying at the king's, the sealed papers with the privileges which the emperor had granted him, for which the dauphin thanked the emperor and then sent to the chancellor in his dwelling a beautiful silver, thickly gilded bowl with a thousand counted golden francs, which the dauphin gave him for the effort that he had needed to exert in that.

EPILOGUE
REPERCUSSIONS AND IMPLICATIONS OF THE PARISIAN SUMMIT

In terms of political history, the meeting of the three crowned heads in January 1378 did not bring anything earth-shattering, but it was not entirely fruitless. Both sides strengthened their positions on the power chessboard by maintaining in essence the status quo. For the host country, it meant support in the ongoing war with England; for both Luxemburgs, good relations with France balanced the opposition pressures from the Rhineland electors. Not even the emperor's documents for the dauphin on the one hand or the personal contacts which the still young King Wenceslas IV acquired in Paris and elsewhere on the other were negligible. The farewell of the king of France with the emperor was thus sincere and emotional. They both knew that they would never meet again in this world, but they could not have had any idea that the coming year 1378 would bring hardly anything from which they could take joy. In their personal lives, they would undergo painful tests; also as statesmen they would face great difficulties. Some of the problems had roots in the recent past; others would emerge as a result of the Papal Schism. The shift of Pope Gregory XI to Rome would be considered more positively in the Empire than in France. It was certainly by no chance that the papal nuncio, Pileus de Prato, the man who would also direct imperial ecclesiastical policy in the next years, appeared at the emperor's farewell in Plaisance.[1] The splitting of Christian Europe could have a far-reaching impact, and it was not successfully averted until the end of the 1410s. However, our epilogue does not extend that far, because soon the uncommonly fruitful and numerous contacts between Prague and Paris were to be damped down as well.

1/ From 1367, the palatial residence in Plaisance on the edge of the 'Wood' in Vincennes had belonged to Duke of Burgundy Philip the Bold, a brother of Charles V. The evidence and further bibliography are presented by Paravicini, 'Die Residenzen der Herzöge von Burgund', p. 211.

The emperor's visit ended; life in Paris and at the court began to return to its everyday routine. The craftsmen in the palaces removed the decoration; the officials of the royal chamber began to pay the bills for the supplied goods and reimbursement for services. Especially large expenses had been incurred by the king's confidants John II of Saarbrücken, Simon de Roucy et de Braine and Bureau de la Rivière, who had gone twice to meet the emperor at the border and who then in the second half of January accompanied him on the return journey from Meaux through Gandelu and Château-Thiery to Rheims and from there to Mouzon on the border. For this reason, the king had already instructed on 12 January 1378 that the first two mentioned be paid 20 francs for every day, namely already including the reimbursements for the return journey. In a conservative estimate, it was a total of around 60 days, which would amount to 1,200 francs each. A similar sum was almost certainly paid also to Bureau de la Rivière, namely from the sum of 6,000 francs, which Charles V ordered on 15 January 1378 to be transferred from the Parisian *octroi* for military purposes to the treasury of the general receiver of *octroi* (*receveur général des aides)*. This high amount was otherwise intended to cover the money which Chancellor (*le Chancellier de France*) Orgemont had 'loaned' some members of the emperor's retinue. Not even Jean Le Mercier came off badly, having obtained 180 francs for the two trips, one to Cambrai and the other to Mouzon. Even though we do not know all of the expenses connected with Emperor Charles IV's protective and ceremonial escort, the amounts documented come to a substantial sum of 32,262 francs in gold.[2]

A special type of expenditure which was charged to the king's treasury were the fees for the preparation of five documents by the imperial chancellery. Prothonotary Nicholas of Riesenburg could be satisfied with his remuneration of a thousand francs, but his subordinates received significantly less. Including the expenses for the gold in the seals and for other taxes, the imperial chancellery was paid a total of 1,647 francs. Neither did the servants of the two Luxemburgs leave empty-handed. The valets, porters and bearers of the imperial litter shared 410 francs. The officials of the chamber were especially busy on 18 January when they dealt with the bills for the presents given to Charles IV, his son Wenceslas IV, and for the noble as well as otherwise important members of their retinue.[3] In all, these expenditures reached 21,569 francs. If we add up all of the items, we come to a sum of almost 56,000 gold francs. The numbers

2/ Details and evidence are provided in Excursus – The Final Account of the Expenditures of the King's Treasury.

3/ There is more on the gifts and their values in Excursuses – The Gifts for the Emperor and His Retinue and Book Gifts, Relics and the Small Mysteries around Them.

remain mere numbers unless we form an idea of what they actually represented. Due to the lack and unreliability of contemporary sources of a financial nature, we are limited only to an indication. The mentioned 56,000 francs formed roughly one-eighth of all the known expenditures of Charles V's royal treasury from the beginning of April 1368 to the end of July of the next year, or one-fifth of the costs of the war with England in the same period. The exceptional amount of the mentioned sum on an international scale is evidenced also by the loan of 40,000 gold pieces which Emperor Charles provided to Pope Gregory XI in March 1378.

Not all of the participants in the summit came into their own. Duke John of Berry lived up to his reputation and at every opportunity acted like a lord for whom money did not matter. It is then no wonder that he had to pay the final feast, which he organised along with his brother Philip the Bold in honour of the emperor and his retinue on 17 January 1378 in Marché de Meaux, with promissory notes.[4] He had to borrow money from his brother Philip and from the Florentine merchant Bernardo di Gino even for the purchase of the valuables that he procured for himself during his stay in Paris. Besides a white Saracen bitch, he purchased an ivory mirror along with six tablets of wood and ivory for holding a candelabra when reading novels.[5] He had just left Paris on 4 February when he received a message that his sister-in-law had passed away.

Queen Jeanne of Bourbon gave birth to her daughter Catherine precisely on 4 February but died two days later, being only forty. Ten years of life awaited the newborn daughter Catherine while her six-year-old sister Isabelle soon followed her mother to the great grief of her father. Of her eight children, Jeanne of Bourbon was outlived only by two sons: the older Charles, successor to the throne, and Louis, the future Duke of Orléans. A tragic end awaited them both. There will be more on the insanity that progressively engulfed Charles VI. Duke of Orléans Louis, an ambitious but not very successful politician, attempted to continue in the footsteps of his father as a patron of intellectuals and humanists but was murdered in November 1407 by assassins in the pay of Duke of Burgundy John the Fearless.[6] As is indicated by much, Charles V had a deep relation with his wife and lost in her not only a life partner but also a good advisor. Her body was displayed on a catafalque under a gold-interlaced canopy for an entire week. At her funeral in the abbey of

---

4/ We already know that the royal fortress of Marché de Meaux was joined with the episcopal city of Meaux by a bridge, so that the royal residence on the island was quickly reachable from the bishop's palace. After the feast, the emperor returned with his entourage to the bishop's palace for the night.
5/ For pertinent information on these expenditures, see Lehoux, *Jean de France, duc de Berri*, pp. 412–413.
6/ Newly on this, see Guenée, *Un meurtre, une société. L'assassinat du duc d'Orléans, 23 Novembre 1407.*

89. Funeral procession with the body of Queen Jeanne of Bourbon. Miniature in the manuscript of Les Grandes Chroniques de France (BL, Ms. Royal 20 C VII, fol. 200r)

Saint-Denis on 14 February only her body was laid in the grave, whereas the heart was deposited in the Chapel of the Cordeliers (Franciscans of the Strict Observance) and her entrails in the Church of the Celestines.

In no time, Charles V had a head full of worries. First, they were caused by King of Navarre Charles the Bad, who again lived up to his name. In the expensive war with Castile, he was lacking means, and therefore he pawned the port of Cherbourg to the king of England for three years in return for a company of five hundred armigers and the same number of arbalester. This treason to the French Crown could not remain unpunished. *Inter alia*, the Navarre estates and strongholds in Normandy were seized and Cherbourg attacked by an army. The English held the port, which did not come into French hands until the reign of Charles VI. A similar threat to the interests of the Crown appeared in Brittany, where the English intensified the attacks on Saint-Malo. The loss of another port was to be prevented by the court confiscation of all the fortifications and the entire domain of Duke of Montfort John IV, who had been collaborating with the English for several years. This was implemented by a judicial ruling of December 1378, but the Breton barons did not intend to lose the liberties of their duchy and formed a defensive alliance in April of the next year. The king entrusted the government of Brittany to his brother Louis, Duke of Anjou, who appointed Constable Bertrand du Guesclin, whom we already met in the Prologue, as commander of the military operations. Perhaps also because the constable himself was a Breton, who employed many compatriots in his personal guard, only smaller skirmishes occurred, which were ended by a mutual truce in November 1379. Only Duke John of Montfort refused to accept the truce and on 1 March 1380 concluded an alliance with King of England Richard II, from whom he expected military support. He did not receive it and so embraced it when after the death of Charles V he could conclude an agreement with his brothers on the basis of which he gained the duchy of Brittany back.[7]

In the absence of Louis of Anjou, serious urban disturbances occurred in Languedoc, which was under his governance. These had their causes in the dismal economic situation of the entire area, which had been the long-standing target of invasions by English armies as well as brigand military troops (*compagnies*) on the one hand and in the short-sighted tax policy of the duke's officials on the other. Louis had brought them from elsewhere, so they, like he, did not have ties to the local aristocracy and city authorities. The cup of dissatisfaction overflowed with the introduction of a tax of twelve francs for each family hearth. In 1378, Duke Louis with a harsh approach still handled the storms in some towns, but in spring and summer of the next year the social unrest in Languedoc was being worriedly watched even at the royal court, especially when the terrible raids of gangs of the so-called *tuchins* came to be known there. These castaways of predominantly peasant origin lived in forested knolls, and since they had helpers in the villages as well as the cities, it was difficult to apprehend them.[8] Nevertheless, they had nothing to do with the bloody uprising which broke out in Montpellier on 21 October 1379. A disorderly mob of municipal taxpayers murdered the duke's tax collectors, who had not heeded the royal order to lower taxes and intended to collect them again in the amount of twelve francs. In the rioting, nearly eighty people died, and, as numerous houses were being destroyed, Montpellier began to fear reprisals. These really threatened the city. The commander of the army du Guesclin along with Duke Louis moved from Brittany to Languedoc, and, had it not been for the intervention of King Charles V and Avignon Pope Clement VII, not only estates but also throats would have been at stake.

The woeful conditions and fears for the future provoked the representatives of the urban communities of Languedoc to a joint approach against the regent Louis, in whom they saw the main culprit of the long-term decline. The unheard of became reality when their delegation after three months of deliberations at the royal court achieved the recall of the duke. Through the

90. Detail of the tombstone of Queen Jeanne of Bourbon in Saint-Denis by the sculptor André Beauneveu

7/ The complicated situation in Brittany was clarified in a wider timeframe by Kerhervé, *L'État breton aux XIVe et XVe siècles*.
8/ The label *tuchin* was derived from the Old French *tuche*, meaning a grove or thicket. From the literature, see especially Charbonnier, 'Qui furent les Tuchins'?

Ordinance of 25 April 1380, Charles V concluded a truce with his rebellious subjects, significantly easing their taxes and entrusting the government there to Constable du Guesclin, whom he appointed Captain General. The renowned commander was to defend not only Languedoc but also Auvergne and Guyenne, namely both against the English and against the brigand companies. In the midst of a generally successful campaign, du Guesclin died on 13 July 1380 after a short illness. Charles V had his remains transferred to the Abbey of Saint-Denis and allotted them an honourable place in the chapel, where Queen Jeanne already rested and where he himself was soon to repose.

91. Tombstone of Constable Bertrand du Guesclin (1320–1380) in the Basilica of Saint-Denis

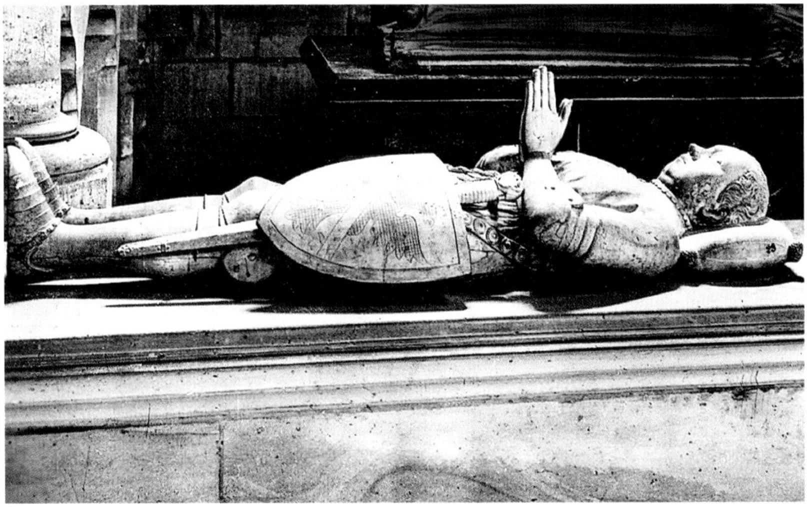

The first serious signs of Charles V's illness manifested themselves in the middle of 1379. It had been raining hard since spring; the precipitation did not cease even in the summer. Crop failures and the prospects for bad wine were joined by a plague infection in the environs of Paris. The king as well as his court removed to Montargis in the middle of July, in whose sylvan landscape he spent six months. Charles V escaped the epidemic, but on his return journey to Paris in January 1380 he was struck by such a strong attack of gout that he had to remain in bed for a year. He faced the disease of kings worse than his older uncle, the Holy Roman Emperor. Thanks to a diet and concoctions, he recuperated and after his return to Paris he resumed the affairs of the state. He continued in the negotiations with England, constantly dealt with the consequences of the church schism and in advance ensured the defence of the cities against the expected invasion of an enemy army. In June, he still travelled by horse to Rheims, and, since his health did not arouse more serious worries, none of his closest relatives and counsellors considered it necessary to stay near him in summer.

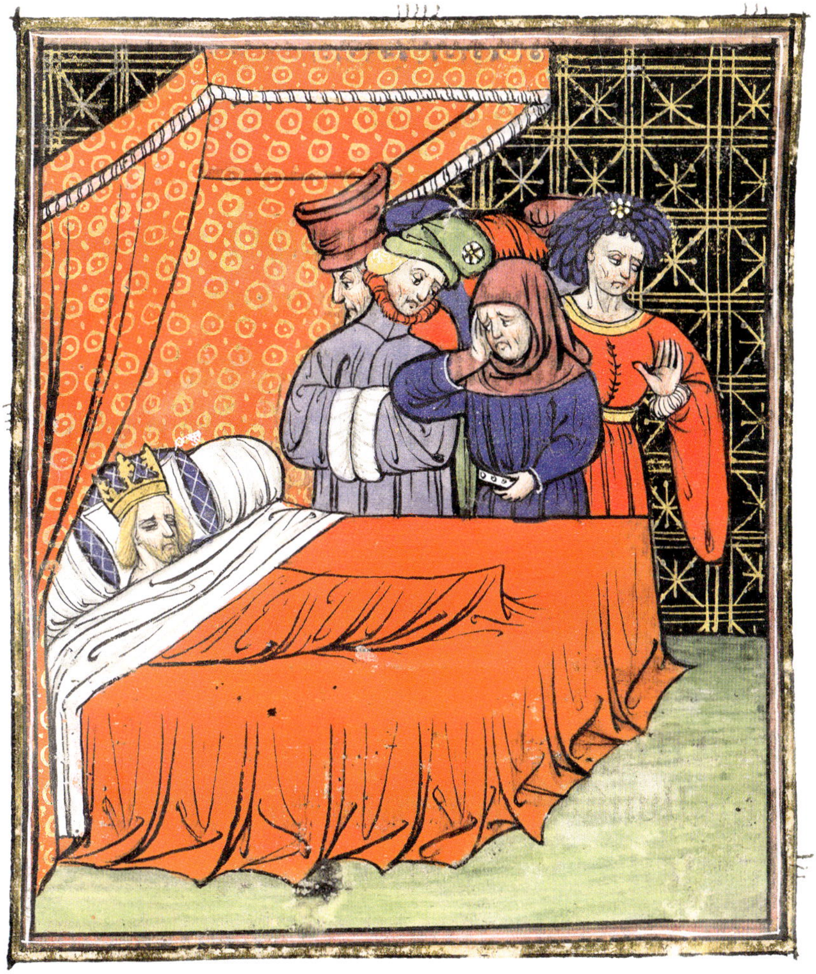

92. King of France Charles V on his death bed (BL Ms. royal 20 C VII, fol. 215r)

At the end of June, Charles V's condition deteriorated, so that on 2 August he had himself taken to his castle at Beauté, where his uncle Charles IV had drawn vitalising energy two years earlier. A serious heart attack on the night between 13 and 14 September caused a sensation in the metropolis. All sorts of people, including the bishop of Paris, Chancellor Pierre d'Orgemont and librarian Gilles Malet, rushed to Beauté. Of the barons close to the king, the Counts of Harcourt and of Saarbrücken arrived; at the last moment, even his faithful counsellor Bureau de la Rivière made an appearance. Most of them were present at the last three wills of their king. The first was of a private nature, because it concerned his financial obligations, which were to be covered from the 200,000 francs in cash deposited in the fortress tower in Vincennes. By the second act, he crowned his excise policy, and regardless of the possible consequences repealed the so-called *fouage*, the burdensome tax on the family hearth (hearth tax). Finally, in front of the notary and witnesses, Charles V published his declaration appealing for the church schism to be

93. Detail of the tombstone of Charles V in Saint-Denis by the sculptor André Beauneveu

overcome. With his gaze fixed on the crown which the abbot of Saint-Denis had brought with him, Charles V called the Wise collapsed in agony and on Sunday, 16 September 1380, yielded up the ghost.[9]

THE BEGINNING OF THE ECCLESIASTICAL SCHISM IN THE HEAD AND IN THE LIMBS

The news of the passing of Pope Gregory XI, who died in Rome on 28 March 1378, reached Paris as well as Prague unusually quickly. The emperor learnt about it immediately after his return from his long journey at the beginning of April. Even the powerful die; nothing could be changed about the thing itself. Charles IV cared much more about how and under what circumstances Wenceslas' election would be formally approbated by the new pope. Despite all of his promises, Gregory XI had not issued the approbation, although even before his death he had accepted a loan from the emperor's envoy Kuneš of Veselé (Dean of the Vyšehrad Chapter) of 40,000 gold pieces, which was to accelerate his decision. What is worse, because of the confusion after the sudden death of the pope, Kuneš did not obtain a receipt, and they could have thrown the gigantic sum out of the window. Uncertainty also reigned at the Parisian court. The energetic defender of the interests of the French Crown Cardinal Jean de la Grange had not yet arrived in Rome, six French cardinals refused to leave Avignon, and it could be foreseen that the election of the new pope would take place in a stormy atmosphere.[10]

And thus it happened. On the eve of the election by the so-called conclave, armed mobs of the Roman people assembled in front of the Vatican Palace and shouted 'Roman, Italian' extorting the election of a Roman or at least an Italian. In that late afternoon of 7 April 1378, the same demand was threateningly lodged with the cardinals by the representatives of the local administration and the leaders of the important Roman families. Of the twenty-three cardinals who were alive, only sixteen were present, of whom eleven were French, four Italian and one Spanish. Among the French, the so-called 'Limousins' dominated, who intended to vote through the fourth pope of their faction. This group from Navarre, with whose influential role in those last two decades we have already become acquainted, could not be confronted by the smaller pro-king group of the so-called 'French', and therefore during the night and the

9/ On the last moments of Charles V, see Autrand, *Charles V. Le Sage*, pp. 844–851.
10/ The outcomes of the earlier literature were summarised by Fink, 'Das große Schisma bis zum Konzil von Pisa', pp. 490–516, which includes further references. On the role of France, the fundamental source of knowledge remains the first volume of the tetralogy Valois, *La France et le grand schisme d'Occident*; the positions of Emperor Charles IV were elucidated in great detail by Steinherz, 'Das Schisma von 1378 und die Haltung Karls IV.'; more recently on the issues in this chapter, see Thomas, 'Frankreich, Karl IV. und das Große Schisma'.

next day steps were being taken to reach a compromise. And in as much as the election of a member of the College of Cardinals was out of the question in the given power distribution, fifteen electors subsequently gave their votes to Bartolomeo Prignano, Archbishop of Bari, who had run the Papal Chancellery in Avignon for years. Nevertheless, before the election of this Neapolitan native could be announced in the afternoon of 8 April, an armed impatient mob burst into the conclave and in the mistaken belief that Roman Cardinal Tebaldeschi, an aged prelate, had been elected, they placed him on the papal throne in spite of his protests. The terrified cardinals managed to escape but it was possible to convene only twelve to complete the election the next day. Through their finishing their task and attending the ceremony of ordination on 18 April, the cardinals, albeit in a limited number, legitimised the election. The dispute which broke out immediately thereafter over its validity has not yet ended and hardly ever will be.[11]

As has happened more than once in small as well as great history, power changes people and distorts their characters. The new pope, who entered history as Urban VI, certainly had already had authoritarian tendencies before, but he had not unbridled them until then. In so doing, he acted extremely incautiously. Instead of ingratiating himself with cardinals by providing them with privileges or otherwise, he rebuked them for their pompous lifestyle, urged them towards a spiritual purge in the evangelical sense and began to hector them in other ways. The cardinals were not used to it, because the popes in Avignon normally preferred collegial decision making and left religious exhortations to the mystics. Under the pretence of excessive heat, the dissatisfied cardinals departed from Rome for Anagni, where they issued a proclamation on the invalidity of the election on 2 August 1378. A week later in a second manifesto, they declared Urban to be a Schismatic, whom all of Christianity had to renounce. Urban VI sought support with Emperor Charles IV and by a bull of 26 July expressed agreement with the election of Wenceslas IV as King of the Romans. With the delegations that he was sending to the European rulers' courts, however, also covert supporters of the cardinals' opposition were leaving, spreading entirely contradictory information around Europe.

In autumn, events began to snowball. With the consent of Queen Joan of Naples, whom the new pope had already managed to antagonise, the cardinals resorted to Fondi. As soon as Urban VI discovered that of the original college only the Roman Tebaldeschi remained loyal, he appointed 29 cardinals, mostly Italians, on 17 September 1378. It was precisely on this occasion that the first Bohemian, Archbishop of Prague John (Jan) Očko of Vlašim, was adorned

11/ In my opinion, doubts remained even after the validity of the election was confirmed based on a revision of the sources by Brandmüller, 'Zur Frage nach der Gültigkeit der Wahl Urbans VI'.

94. John Očko of Vlašim, detail from the votive image of John Očko of Vlašim

with the cardinal's hat. If Urban VI attempted to gain favour with the emperor with his nomination, then he exasperated him at the same time by appointing Adolf I of Nassau as the archbishop of Mainz, against whom the Luxemburg side supported its adherent, Elector of Mainz Louis of Meissen. The opposition cardinals no longer hesitated and at a conclave of 20 September elected Cardinal Robert of Geneva as their pope. With his neutral origin, the antipope, who adopted the name Clement VII, was acceptable for the 'French' as well as the 'Italian' factions.

Most scholars think that an election of an antipope would not have occurred if the opposition cardinals had not had support at the French court. One of the two envoys whom Pope Urban VI sent with the announcement of his election and with gifts to Paris enclosed informed the king in a confidential conversation on the background of the events and gave him a letter from Pierre de Cros, Archbishop of Arles and chamberlain of the Camera Apostolica (Latin: *Camerarius Apostolicus*). The recommendation of this influential curial was apparently decisive for Charles V, who thus told Urban's delegation that he was waiting for further documents on the validity of the election. Before Urban VI could accommodate his request, two envoys of the Collage of Cardinals appeared in Paris with a declaration of the invalidity of the election. Under these circumstances, Charles V decided to act; in August, he sent twenty thousand francs to the cardinals for their expenses and requested that Queen Joan of Naples take them under her wing.

Whether the intervention of Charles V was truly demonstrated at the election of the antipope through Cardinal Jean de la Grange remains an open question, because the king's written consent with the anti-election comes from as late as 6 October 1378. And considering that the connection between Paris and the south of Italy took more than three weeks, it is questionable how much the rebelling cardinals negotiated on their own.[12] Also the emperor's envoy Dietrich Damerow arrived in Fondi when the die had already been cast. In a document of 25 September, Emperor Charles IV essentially recognised the legitimacy of Urban's election and simultaneously recommended in a different letter that Queen Joan of Naples have the college of opposition cardinals dispersed. Even before the schism came to be known, the cards had already been dealt for the next power play. The political situation at first appeared more favourable for Clement VII, who was joined by most of the curial officials with their funds, official registers, and seals. However, as soon as Urban VI took

12/ Emphasis on the letter of Charles V is placed by Autrand, *Charles V. Le Sage*, p. 833; in the literature, most remember another of Charles' letters, which is supposed to have arrived in Fondi on 18 September, i.e. two days before the election. For the latest on that, see Thomas, 'Frankreich, Karl IV. und das Große Schisma', p. 98.

hold of the castle of St Angelo in spring 1379 and hence prevented his adversary from residing in Rome, Clement VII despite the support of the queen of Naples was losing his footing in Italy and in May 1381 settled permanently in Avignon.

It arises from the sequence of events that Rome had a greater value in the eyes of the antipope than Avignon. The initial reserved position of the French Crown also took into consideration the adverse impact of the election of Clement VII, and perhaps even for this reason he was not crowned with the papal tiara until 31 October 1378. Then Charles V no longer had any other option than to announce officially which of the two popes he considered to be legitimate. He did so after consultations with prelates and theologians in an ordinance of 16 November, through which he ordered his subjects to recognise Pope Clement VII. Although his declarations of the next year are also along the same lines, the schism worried him; in discussions with his closest scholars, he was seeking a way out of the crisis in calling a council, and he defended himself against possible slander ascribing him a part in the ecclesiastical schism even in a declaration made on his death bed.[13]

The position of the lawyers and theologians of the Sorbonne in Paris was far from being unequivocal. Many of them, especially the so-far materially unsecured young masters, were tormented by the question of to which pope to address the so-called *rotuli* with supplications for vacated ecclesiastical benefices. Their uncertainty and unrest were further increased by both questions of conscience and relations to the national or territorial corporations. Although the reports coming from Italy were conflicting, it was still possible to deduce from them doubts not only on the legitimacy of the violently forced election of Urban VI but also on the approach of the opposition College of Cardinals. Shortly after the election of Antipope Clement VII augured the beginning of a religious schism, the first tractates and polemics started to appear. With the passage of time, they grew in number, so that the Vatican Library alone accumulated almost sixty manuscript works dealing with the schism. Also in this regard, the Sorbonne in Paris played first fiddle but soon its competition was to emerge also within the Empire, where universities were springing up like mushrooms after rain.

Already at the early discussions on the soil of the Sorbonne, the irreconcilability of the positions revealed itself, and therefore on 7 January 1379 the University of Paris issued a declaration of its neutrality. The king's pressure on behalf of the so-called Clementists did not stop with this and already in February evoked a critical response especially in the corporation of the English

13/ This 'spiritual' will was issued by Valois, 'Déclaration faite par Charles V à son lit de mort', esp. p. 253 there.

nation, which also associated masters and students from imperial territories. For that matter, everyone still remembered well the ceremonial *Te deum* with which the Sorbonne welcomed the election of Pope Urban. Charles V was used to debating with the scholars in person and therefore met with the representatives of the university again on 7 May to tell them what he expected of them. He put an end to all of the possible conjecture with his letter to the university of 21 May 1379 in which he ordered all of its members to recognise the legitimacy of the election of Clement VII. Since the lawyers and doctors had already done so in practice by having sent their requests for vacated benefices to Avignon, it was necessary to wait for the theologians and territorial corporations of the Faculty of Liberal Arts. Whereas two university 'nations', the French and the Norman, expressed themselves for Pope Clement the very next day, the corporations of the English and Picard 'nations' along with the Faculty of Theology requested time for further internal debates. The king's negative response had an effect on the theologians, who at their congregation on 24 May expressed themselves for Clement. Although the 'English' and the 'Picardines' remained in opposition, on 26 May the University of Paris as a whole formally recognised the legitimacy of the papacy in Avignon.[14]

This did not end the discussions in the university colleges and in the homes of the professors. The calls for neutrality, as it could be expected, were the strongest in the corporations of the two opposition 'nations', but they were also heard by prudent Clementists, who were likewise seeking a way out of the critical situation. The king's absence in the metropolis in the second half of 1379 allowed the discussion to take an entirely free course. Not even after the return of the king did the discord exceed an acceptable level. With the death of Charles V in September 1380 and the introduction of the regent government for the minor successor to the throne, however, the situation significantly changed within a few months. Even though all of the brothers of the late sovereign were to rule on behalf of the underage Charles VI, a decisive influence was seized by the eldest Louis of Anjou, who was also the first to usurp the cash and jewels of the royal treasury. Pope Clement had designated Duke Louis as the successor of Queen Joan on the throne of Naples, and hence his violent intervention in university autonomy surprised no one.[15]

Oil on the fire of the university dispute was poured by Bishop of Paris Aimery de Magnac, who on 17 May 1381 labelled all of the opponents of Clement VII as 'schismatic heretics'. The reluctant response of the university

14/ Further details with references to the literature and sources are provided by Swanson, *Universities, Academics and the Great Schism*, pp. 22–44.

15/ The time of Charles VI's reign was described by Autrand, *Charles VI. La folie du roi*; a useful synopsis of the issue was published by Leguai, 'Fondements et problèmes du pouvoir royal en France (autour de 1400)', pp. 41–58.

on 15 June, placing emphasis on removing the schism through a council, would probably not have stopped further development even if it had arrived in time. In the meantime, Clement VII instructed the bishop to remove the university titles of all Urbanists and grant these vacated benefices to his sympathisers. Furthermore, the bishop on 15 July installed John Blanchard as the university chancellor, instructing him not to allow Urban's 'schismatics' to graduate. These made use of a peculiarity of the University of Paris, i.e. the office of the second chancellor for the schools of artists in the abbey of St Geneviève on the left bank of the Seine, thanks to whose understanding they could continue obtaining bachelor's, licentiate's, and master's degrees for some time. When Clement VII on 15 April 1382 appointed new officials to St Geneviève, most of the members of the English 'nation' refused to recognise them and continued to be in opposition until November of that year. The final decision came in February 1383. Duke Louis of Anjou compelled the University of Paris to an unconditional recognition of Clement VII, whereby the supporters of Urban VI could do nothing else but seek work at general studies colleges of Roman obedience. At first it seemed that their paths would lead mainly to Prague, where we shall also head in the explication below.

THE REPERCUSSIONS OF THE SCHISM IN PRAGUE AND THE EMPEROR'S DEATH

The documents sealed with the golden bulls which Prothonotary Nicholas of Riesenburg ceremonially handed over to Dauphin Charles were, as everything indicates, the only specific outcome of the Parisian summit.[16] All of the other agreements remained on the level of promises. The emperor's concession in the issue of Arelat did to a certain extent strengthen the results of French expansive politics but it at the same time counterbalanced its neutrality in the conflict between the two warring great powers. In this point, so important for him, Charles V failed.

Only indirectly do we discover how the negotiations on marriage alliances proceeded. Charles V mentioned them in a few words in a letter which an envoy to King of Hungary and Poland Louis I carried to Buda at the end of January or the beginning of February 1378.[17] And since these negotiations are not mentioned in the Account on the Emperor's Visit, it can be presumed

16/ These documents were last published by HECKMANN, 'Das Reichsvikariat des Dauphins im Arelat 1378', pp. 86–93, Nos. 2–3.

17/ This letter was questioned by LINDNER, *Geschichte des deutschen Reiches*, p. 391; in the opinions of most researchers, his objections were conclusively refuted by VALOIS, 'Le projet de mariage', pp. 209–223 (pp. 221–223 there include a new edition of the letter of Charles V). The state of research is captured in KAVKA, *Vláda Karla IV.*, II, pp. 221–222, Note 28. Cf. further KAVKA, 'Karel IV. a anjouovsko-piastovské dědictví', pp. 39–40.

95. Charles IV, detail from the votive image of John Očko of Vlašim

that they probably happened during the confidential meeting of the crowned heads and their chancellors on 5 January 1378. The king accepted his uncle's interest in the Kingdom of Poland, referred to in the letter as a possible inheritance for the Hungarian bride of the emperor's son Sigismund, but with the awareness that it was essentially Louis' business. Therefore, there was purportedly no agreement. If it really were so, the emperor was returning to the Empire without a written confirmation of the claims laid, nevertheless with the awareness that the French court did not intend to stand in the way of his Eastern Policy. It does not alter the fact that Sigismund acquired by marriage to Marie the Lands of the Crown of St Stephen instead of Poland. So much for the additional information for those readers who are also interested in the ends of the suggested discussions.

Although the emperor unbent in Beauté, the return journey through Mouzon tired him, so that he stayed at his brother Wenceslas' in Luxembourg for an entire month. Instead of a trip to Cologne, where he was to meet the empress, Charles IV selected a journey through Trier and Bernkastel to Oppenheim and from there apparently by boat to Heidelberg. Before he arrived in Nuremburg around 12 March, he learnt about the death of Queen of France Jeanne of Bourbon. During a stay of roughly a fortnight there, he handled the urgent issues which were related to the ongoing struggle for the archbishop's throne in Mainz.[18] At the beginning of April, the emperor after a longer period appeared in Prague, where the news of the death of Pope Gregory XI reached him at the end of the month. Regardless of the mutual personal, often intense, relations, Gregory's passing brought Charles worries in two aspects at once. First of all, it dimmed the overall good prospects for a quick approbation of Wenceslas' election. With no less concern, Charles IV had to take into consideration that the confirmation of the election of Louis of Meissen to the archbishopric of Mainz would have to be discussed again with the new pope. What was at stake was the elector's vote connected with that throne, and therefore both Ludwig and the two Luxemburgs could consider the promise of a lifelong alliance which they concluded together with Rupert II, Count Palatine of the Rhine, at a congress in České Budějovice (Budweis) on 7 May as a success.

This contract could have a factual significance only if the new pope confirmed Ludwig. In the middle of June, when the delegation of the new pope arrived in Prague, it was difficult to anticipate anything, because the emperor was informed on doubts on the validity of Urban's election at the same time.

18/ During his visit, the emperor issued on 24 February 1378 for the city of Nuremburg the substantial privilege dealing with the environs to a distance of one mile (cf. Müllner, *Die Annalen der Reichsstadt Nürnberg von 1623*, II, p. 70).

They were allegedly conveyed confidentially both in writing and orally to the emperor by the two men. The first was Bertrand de Veyrac, brother-in-law of French Cardinal Guillaume d'Aigrefeuille († 1401), with the second being Václav Strnad, who authorised by Dean of Vyšehrad Kuneš of Veselé, already known to us, had joined the delegation. Only the second of them was successful, but even so a seed of doubt had been sewn. The emperor received the delegation with all of the usual honours, heard the request to send a ceremonial delegation with a view of confirming Wenceslas' election and in response to the pope assumed no obligation. Now, we understand better the rush with which on 26 July Urban VI pronounced his agreement with the election of Wenceslas IV as King of the Romans, without awaiting the arrival of the delegation.

The pope, who a few months earlier had vaunted his power to enthrone as well as dethrone emperors and kings, now had to proceed more circumspectly. His second delegation, which arrived in Prague before the middle of September, brought, along with the approbation bull and memorandum on the development of events, an urgent request for support against the cardinals' opposition. Not even this time was the bull tied to Wenceslas' taking of the oath transferred, whereby the emperor indicated to the pope that he did not intend to observe curial interventions in the imperial state of affairs meekly. On the other hand, it was clear to Charles IV that he could no longer hesitate in supporting Urban VI, because it was easy to recognise in the approach of the opposition cardinals the attempt to return to the papacy in Avignon under the guardianship of the French court. Without being able to know that the anti-election of Clement VII of 20 September had already begun the schism in the church, the emperor in a letter dated five days later explicated to the College of Cardinals why he continued to consider Urban VI, elected and ordained by him, as the pope. With a sharper position, having undoubtedly consulted it with his father, Wenceslas IV reached out to each of the cardinals individually in letters sent on the same day. As King of the Romans, he threatened to resort to harsher measures to protect the church if they continue in their opposition to the pope whom they themselves had selected. Still before he learnt about the second conclave in Fondi on 28 October, Charles IV entrusted his foremost counsellor, Bishop of Bamberg Lamprecht von Brunn, to acquire from the imperial princes their recognition of Urban VI as the legitimate pope. In the letters which he sent from Prague in diverse directions, the emperor urged the neighbouring as well as distant sovereigns, including his nephew on the French throne, to be obedient to Pope Urban. We already know that it was futile in the case of Charles V.[19]

19/ The basic outline of the events was presented already by Steinherz, 'Das Schisma von 1378', cf. esp. pp. 622–635; more recent literature was considered by Kavka, *Vláda Karla IV.*, II, pp. 235–240.

Sometime after 2 November 1378, Charles IV during a fall from a horse or from the stairs broke his left thigh's cervix. The longer stay in bed apparently evoked pneumonia, to which the sixty-three-year-old emperor succumbed three hours after sundown on Sunday 29 November. Shortly thereafter, a fire visible from far away broke out in the monastery of the Knights of the Cross with the Red Star in the Old Town, to which many people from both sides of the bridge gathered. The news of the emperor's death thus spread immediately in Prague. Still that night, the royal chancellery sent envoys with the funeral notice in all directions. The preparation of the funeral lasted almost two weeks. The funeral itself started on 11 December and concluded with requiem *missa cantata* in St Vitus' Cathedral four days later. On the memorial prepared in advance in the uncompleted cathedral, an epitaph had already been inscribed, which Cardinal and Archbishop of Prague John Očko of Vlašim included in his funerary speech:

> *In the year one thousand, three hundred and seventy-eight, on 29 November.*
> *Lo, I, Charles IV, once terror of the entire world,*
> *an emperor who never knew defeat, save by death, was laid low;*
> *in this tomb here am buried, Oh Lord, if only my soul rises to the stars,*
> *I now ask only that all pray for me,*
> *those I abandoned in death and favoured in life.*
> *And so let his soul rest in holy peace.*[20]

BOHEMIA AND FRANCE AT THE BEGINNING OF THE REIGN OF WENCESLAS IV

In the same exemplar of the *Great Chronicles of France* that preserved the Account on the Summit in Paris, we also find a brief record of the death of the Holy Roman Emperor and King of Bohemia. On his successor, Wenceslas IV, we read here that he supported Pope Urban in Rome in return for the promise of imperial coronation.[21] It truly was so, and because the links between Prague and the Roman Curia continued to increase, French politics had to take them into account.

With his father's death, the entire burden of government in the lands of the Bohemian Crown as well as in the Empire fell on the shoulders of the not even eighteen-year-old Wenceslas IV. The cards in high ecclesiastical politics were not yet definitively dealt, because after Urban VI also Clement VII expressed consent with Wenceslas' election as King of the Romans. He did so in October

20/ On the probable cause of Charles IV's death, see Vlček, *Fyzické osobnosti českých panovníků*, II-1, p. 197; for detailed information on the funeral, see Šmahel, *Zur politischen Präsentation*, pp. 1–37, where there are also references to the literature and sources.
21/ Delachenal (ed.), *Chronique des règnes*, II, p. 349.

1378, but his bull became known in Prague much later. Thanks to Charles IV, the Roman throne had unseen prestige, and therefore it was no wonder that the envoys of both popes were constantly passing each other in the doors to the Prague court. Wenceslas IV had no reason to change anything in his father's support for the pope in Rome, so he was markedly surprised when at the Imperial Diet in Frankfurt in February 1379 he again met Bishop of Paris Aimery de Magnac, who as the speaker of the delegation of King of France Charles V had come to gain sympathy for the antipope in Avignon Clement VII. Wenceslas had no other option than in declarations issued in agreement with the four electors to adopt an unequivocal position again in favour of the validity of the election of the pope in Rome.

96. King Wenceslas IV enthroned. Miniature from the Bible of Wenceslasa IV, 2nd volume, before 1395 (ÖNB, cod. 2760, fol. 74r)

Even though it happened in accord with the policy of his father, Wenceslas was thus losing the support of the French court, which he needed to strengthen his as yet little solidified position in the Empire. It might be also for this reason that he fully authorised his uncle Margrave Jobst sometime in 1379 to negotiate with King Charles V. French diplomacy did not sit on its hands either, so that at the next Imperial Diet in Frankfurt in September of the same year the issue of the possible recognition of the pope in Avignon was raised again. It was extremely unpleasant for Wenceslas IV that an influential word in the French delegation was held by his half-uncle, Duke of Luxembourg, Brabant and Limburg Wenceslas. Although he had not seen him since his stay in Paris in January 1378, Wenceslas preferred to avoid the meeting and did not appear at the opening of the diet.[22] After all, nothing serious happened; the clash of the two sides continued both behind the scenes and at the next Imperial Diet in April 1380.

Although Wenceslas IV did not cease announcing his support for the pope in Rome at imperial diets and on other occasions, there was intensive diplomatic activity between Paris and Wenceslas' court, which was located in the Rhineland in the long term, in the late spring and summer of 1380. Meanwhile, Count Palatine of the Rhine Rupert I 'the Red' had taken advantage of the ecclesiastical schism to strengthen his position, such that an effective counterbalance could be the renewed French alliance. To that end, Wenceslas on 15 June authorised his delegation for negotiation, namely Přemek (Premislaw) I, Duke of Těšín, Landgrave John I of Leuchtenberg, Kraft IV von Hohenlohe-Weikersheim and Thymo the Younger of Kolditz. The landgrave and Thymo of Kolditz knew their way around Paris and in addition had met not only King Charles V in person but also his brothers Duke John of Berry and Duke Philip the Bold of Burgundy. After the preliminary discussions in

22/ For more on that, see Spěváček, *Václav IV.*, pp. 125–129; on the delegation of powers to Margrave Jobst, see Štěpán, *Moravský markrabě Jošt*, p. 141.

Meaux on 5 May, the negotiations on behalf of the French were entrusted to Bishop Pierre de Malleaux, Minister-General of the Friars Minor (Franciscans) Angelo of Spoleto, knights Guy de Harcourt and Raimund Bernard Flaming and the king's secretary, doctor of law Jean d'Ailly. The result of these bilateral negotiations were alliance treaties of 21 and 22 July 1380, into which both sovereigns included their brothers and the king of France even his son, Dauphin Charles.[23]

After the death of Charles V, neither side rushed to an irreversible solution; the diplomats were continuously on journeys and everyone more or less waited to see who would come with what. In spring 1381, a joint Bohemian-Hungarian delegation, which as it could have been expected had failed in its defence of the election of Urban VI in front of the regents, was probing the ground in Paris. The French court monitored the simultaneously ongoing courtship between Wenceslas IV's sister Anne (1366–1394) and the heir to the English throne Richard II of Plantagenet (1367–1400) with well-founded distrust but at the end of 1381 ensured safe passage by ship for the bride to the Port of Calais and from there to England. Not even the Clementists, who had influential supporters in Bohemia in Kuneš of Veselé as well as in several other powerful prelates, slackened in their endeavour to swing Christian lands to their side.[24] The new archbishop of Prague John of Jenštejn, to whom John Očko of Vlašim vacated his throne by his resignation in October 1378, deprived the Clementists of benefices, but not even in the function of Wenceslas' Chancellor could he preclude diplomatic activities which a representative delegation of King of France Charles VI arrived in Prague to support at the end of June 1383.

97. John of Jenštejn († 1400), third archbishop of Prague. A bust in the inner triforium of the Cathedral of St Vitus at Prague Castle

More than in the ecclesiastical positions of Wenceslas IV, the regent Louis of Anjou, who had already defended his Kingdom of Naples militarily in Italy since May 1382, was interested in the direction of Luxemburg policy in Italy. In this regard, the negotiations of the French delegation in Prague and in Žebrák were surprisingly successful, because Wenceslas IV through a document of 21 August 1383 charged Margrave Jobst as the newly appointed imperial vicar in Italy with concluding an alliance contract with the king of France and his brothers. Louis of Anjou could hardly have wished for more. With Margrave Jobst, another important Luxemburg entered European politics, who finished his career in 1410 by acquiring the title of King of the Romans.[25] In December of the same year, 1383, death removed Wenceslas

23/ On the origin of the contracts, see Hlaváček, 'K diplomatice úmluv Václava IV. s Karlem V. z r. 1380'; further cf. Neumann (ed.), *Francouzská husitica*, pp. 57–59, No. 3.
24/ For details, but with an evident pro-Roman bias, see Polc, *Svatý Jan Nepomucký*, I, pp. 96–101.
25/ For the latest information, see Štěpán, *Moravský markrabě Jošt*, but for more details on the negotiation of the French delegation in Prague, see Valois, *La France et le grand schisme d'Occident*, II, pp. 280–283.

98. Oriel of the college of Charles IV, the so-called Carolinum

of Luxembourg, one of the foremost participants of the Parisian summit five years before, from the Western European political scene. According to the inheritance contract still arranged by Charles IV, the widow of this rhapsodising duke retained Brabant and Limburg, whereas Luxemburg fell to the Bohemian Crown.

The schism, as we already know, deeply affected even academic life. Soon after the accession of Wenceslas IV to the Roman and Bohemian thrones, the University of Prague was given the opportunity to adopt the leading role of the Parisian Alma Mater in the lands of obedience to Pope Urban VI in Rome. The intended transfer of theological studies from Paris to Prague, which was announced by Archbishop of Prague John of Jenštejn at the Imperial Diet in Frankfurt on the Main in September 1381, had been supported by the sovereign in advance by his having founded a new college of masters (*Carolinum*). Also the shift of Charles College to the impressive palace of John Rotlev can be put in connection with the arrival of a number of Parisian professors and students to Prague. Not until the act of 28 October 1383 and the subsequent reconstruction of the *Carolinum*, as the building began to be called, did the University of Prague acquire a truly representative seat for the ages. However, the consent of Pope Urban VI of 20 February 1384 with the establishment of a competing faculty of theology in Vienna definitively scotched Jenštejn's plans.[26]

It was not the only defeat to affect the archbishop of Prague that year. His abiding disagreements with the sovereign spilt over into an open rift in June 1384. Wenceslas IV divested Jenštejn of his office of chancellor and requested that the pope in Rome recall him from the archbishop's throne. Urban VI did not accommodate him, which only increased Wenceslas' aversion to the Roman Curia. Also Wenceslas' political orientation on France and on Duke of Anjou Louis postponed the imperial coronation to the unforeseeable. Wenceslas IV likewise from time to time maintained tentative contacts with the Avignon court of Clement VII. In July 1387, Wenceslas IV, for example, sent Archbishop of Salzburg Pilgrim II of Puchheim, who had already belonged for a long time among the covert adherents of Clement VII, to Avignon.[27] Not even the death of Urban VI, who was replaced by Boniface IX on 2 November 1389, dampened these confidential contacts, especially when immediately at the beginning of the next year Charles VI approached Wenceslas IV with a proposal of a closer alliance including recognition of the existing borders. From the

26/ From the literature, see Bartoš, 'Příspěvky k dějinám Václava IV.', II-10, pp. 11–14; further Weltsch, *Archbishop John of Jenstein*, pp. 157–159; and from a wider Central European perspective, see Rexroth, '„... damit die ganze Schule Ruf und Ruhm gewinne"', esp. pp. 520–523.
27/ According to Polc, *Svatý Jan Nepomucký*, I, pp. 199–203.

beginning of November 1388, Charles VI had already reigned independently, and therefore he had a genuine interest in good relations with the king of the Romans, with whom he had become personally acquainted as a young boy in January 1378. The negotiations that began soon hit a stumbling block, when Clement VII staked a claim to his consent with the wedding of the Aragonese princess to the Margrave of Moravia Procop. Therefore, at the end of October 1390, alliance contracts were not exchanged in Prague but in Heidelberg, where the authorised representatives of the two sovereigns drew up the relevant documents.[28] A personal meeting of the two kings was still anticipated in May of the next year, but it was scuppered for a longer time by the interruption of contacts between the Prague court and Avignon.

Almost whenever the Luxemburgs faced strong opposition in the Empire, they sought support in France. In the 1390s, several complicated political tests awaited Wenceslas IV. He failed most of them on the domestic scene in the lands of the Bohemian Crown. The conflict with the archbishop ended in 1396 with the resignation of John of Jenštejn († 1400), but it was a Pyrrhic victory, which boomeranged detrimentally for the sovereign in his intractable struggle with the Bohemian lords, who felt threatened in their estate privileges by the omnipotent group of Wenceslas' favourites of not very noble birth. When we add to that the discord inside the ruling dynasty, Wenceslas had his hands full and the less he could dedicate himself to imperial politics.[29] How important it was for rulers in the fourteenth century to rule before the eyes of the subjects has been written here many times already. Wenceslas' absence of several years from the Empire weakened his power influence and proportionally strengthened the ambitions of some of the imperial princes, namely Count Palatine of the Rhine Rupert II and his son, Rupert III.[30]

In 1397, nothing yet indicated that Rupert of Germany would become Anti-King of the Romans in three or four years. Wenceslas IV acted accordingly. During his stay in Nuremberg from the middle of September 1397, he ignored the accusations of the Imperial Diet and incensed the Rhineland electors with his unwillingness to meet with them in Frankfurt. Subsequently, Wenceslas had no alternative but to come to Frankfurt in December and listen to further complaints here from the Rhineland electors. This influential imperial city lay on the route to France, which suited the king, because he was to meet Charles VI in Rheims in March. Officially, the ending of the ecclesiastical

28/ For more on that with references to the sources, see Spěváček, *Václav IV.*, pp. 205–206.

29/ For details, I refer the readers to the three comprehensive czech works on the government of Wenceslas IV: Bartoš, *Čechy v době Husově*, esp. Chapter III; Spěváček, *Václav IV.*, Chapters IV–V; Bobková, *Velké dějiny zemí Koruny české*, IVb, Chapter Six II.

30/ For the latest on the opposition associations against Wenceslas in the Empire, see Dürschner, *Der wacklige Thron*, pp. 25–34.

schism was on the agenda, but Wenceslas IV's goal was also to strengthen his position in the Empire through a demonstration of French alliance.

The French position on the papacy in Avignon began to change after the death of Clement VII († 1394), who was succeeded by Spaniard Pedro de Luna, with his new name Benedict XIII. It might also have been because he was not a Frenchman that the counsellors of Charles VI listened more to the voices of the university theologians and lawyers calling for the unification of the church. It was not to happen through a convocation of a general council but through the abdication of both contending popes, which would have required the consensus of the great powers. The initiative was assumed by the Sorbonne in Paris, where after Oxford envoys also visited a number of Central European universities in the spring and summer of 1396. In Prague, as it appears, they were not very successful in July; King Wenceslas refused to give them an audience and supposedly sent them to preach in a church. When in November of the same year, 1396, the widowed king of England Richard II took the seven-year-old daughter of Charles VI Isabelle as his wife, both temporarily reconciled countries also found common ground in ecclesiastical politics. It did not remain merely an intention. In July of the following year, an English delegation appeared in Prague, whose task was, i.a. to win over the King of the Romans for a common approach in the question of the ecclesiastical schism. Envoys of the king of France arrived in Prague in August with the same aim, delivering a memorandum on the ecclesiastical question to Wenceslas IV. On this occasion, the poet Eustache Deschamps also came to Prague. His task was apparently to negotiate the wedding of Elizabeth (Eliška), the then eight-year-old daughter of the recently passed John of Görlitz († 1396), to Charles, a son of Duke of Orléans Louis.[31] The Parisian memorandum aroused the displeasure of Rupert II, who along with the other Rhineland electors shared interests with the Roman Curia of Boniface IX. King Wenceslas did not allow these anti-French attitudes discourage him, setting out on the journey on 24 January and after a stop in Luxembourg arriving in Mouzon on 5 March.

The King of the Romans was welcomed on French soil by the king's brother Louis of Orléans, who invited him to his residence in Ivoix (today's Carignan), where on 16 March 1398 they both signed the nuptial contract negotiated in Prague. A week later, Wenceslas IV was greeted by King of France Charles VI two miles before the gates of Rheims. The ceremonial welcome in the Cathedral of Rheims, accommodation in the Abbey of St Remigius and spectacular banquets matched the importance of the meeting.[32] Wence-

31/ See Nejedlý, 'Deux poètes français du quatorzième siècle en Bohême', pp. 39–47.

32/ A colourful description of the meeting of the two kings in Rheims was captured by the *Chronique du religieux de Saint-Denis*, II, pp. 565–571.

99. King Wenceslas IV and his second wife Sophia of Bavaria, miniature from the Bible of Wenceslas IV (ÖNB, cod. 2760, fol. 2r)

slas was accompanied by his second wife Sofia of Bavaria; his suite comprised the foremost Czech and imperial dignitaries, but the host was disappointed by the absence of some of the electors. On the French side, the king's uncles were missing. Wenceslas enjoyed the excellent wine which Duke of Burgundy Philip II the Bold had sent to Rheims as a courtesy so much that he was supposedly not able to come to the ceremonial lunch in his honour until the third day. The lunch was followed by a meeting of the two kings, during which Charles VI was apparently afflicted by a fit of mental illness from which he had already suffered for several years and which was to bring the country a deep internal crisis. After Charles VI abruptly left for Paris, the role of host was assumed by Louis of Orléans, with whom King Wenceslas signed an alliance contract on 31 March 1398, the last day of his stay in Rheims. On this occasion, Wenceslas borrowed from Louis 30,000 francs, which he never repaid.[33] Since Wenceslas IV predominantly acted in Rheims as the king of Bohemia, whose rapidly decreasing influence in the Empire was already known there, it was not possible to expect too much on the ecclesiastical question from his meeting with Charles VI. And it truly was to take another two decades before the church was successfully united again.

33/ For concise information on this, see Bartoš, *Čechy v době Husově*, pp. 154–158 and Spěváček, *Václav IV.*, pp. 285–287, who in addition provides the names of the members of the king's retinue. On the ceremonies see Schwedler, *Deutsch-französische Herschertreffen*, pp. 90–97.

100. King Wenceslas IV had the representative Castle Točník built

In the number of celebrations as well as the amount of wine drunk, the meeting of the sovereigns in Rheims approached the summit in Paris. However, the main actors had changed. Instead of the fathers, the sons met; instead of great statesmen, quandaries evoking figures with crowns on their heads.[34] The summit in Rheims concluded the century in which France and Bohemia were closer to each other than ever before or after, perhaps only with the exception of the First Republic of Czechoslovakia. Historical memory has preserved the knightly feats of King John, the education of his son Charles in France and now maybe also the summit in Paris of January 1378. Other than by the written sources, this bilaterally beneficial proximity is also witnessed by noteworthy architectural monuments, which have along with excellent works of mural as well as book painting overcome the adversity of the ages. The possible inspiration which Wenceslas IV could have gained during the tour of the magnificently illuminated manuscripts in the library of Charles V has already been mentioned. It would be no less tempting to follow whether and how France influenced the construction activities of Wenceslas IV. The grandiose

34/ On the unsuccessful reigns of not only these two sovereigns but also their English contemporary Richard II, cf. the deliberation of Graus, 'Das Scheitern von Königen: Karl VI., Richard II., Wenzel IV.', esp. pp. 10–23.

royal residences which Wenceslas had seen in Paris as well as elsewhere in his youth must have left a deep impression on him.[35] Suffice it to mention the new building of the grandiose palace at Wenceslas' castle Točník, whose hall with its size (34 × 9 m) outdid the great hall on the ground floor of the Louvre.[36] The fact that Bohemia gained more in the area of culture than France does not alter anything about it, because Bohemia paid its debt on the level of political and military alliance.

35/ On the whole issue tentatively, see Durdík and Chotěbor, 'Projevy přímého působení francouzské stavební huti v české architektuře', pp. 225–237.

36/ For the basic information, see Durdík, *Ilustrovaná encykloppedie českých hradů*, pp. 553–556; also Krakovec Castle is noteworthy for the same reason (ibid. pp. 287–289). An exceptional fate was that of the last of Wenceslas' castles; on that, see also Durdík, 'Nový hrad u Kunratic a jeho postavení ve vývoji české hradní architektury'. On book painting, see also Excursus – Pictorial Series and Illustrations below.

EXCURSUSES AND INVESTIGATIONS

The introductory story and closing epilogue on the Account of the Journey of Charles IV from the *Great Chronicles of France* (hereinafter mostly only as the Account) will be followed by a search for hidden connections, contradictions and clues preserved in the sources of a written, graphic as well as material nature. Not even then will everything have been said, but it is almost always that way in learning history.

Looking Back at the Existing Literature

Gone are the times when František Martin Pelcl (Franz Martin Pelzel), the first of the Modern historians who dealt with the journey of Charles IV to France, progressed on unexplored territory. His explanation from 1781 is surprisingly detailed and truly remarkable for its time.[1] On the other hand, *Dějiny národu českého v Čechách a v Moravě* [The History of the Czech Nation in Bohemia and Moravia] by František Palacký limited itself only to a casual comment.[2] And since it had not been otherwise in the other synoptic works, the earlier knowledge was not enriched at the end of the nineteenth century until Václav Tille, namely through his breakthrough edition of the abbreviated Account of the Journey of Emperor Charles IV to France.[3] A promising step forward in terms of art history were the two studies by Josef Cibulka,[4] who could already build upon the critical edition of the *Great Chronicles of France* from the time of John II the Good and Charles V.[5] At the impetus of Josef Šusta, the full Account was translated into Czech shortly afterwards by Jakub Pavel.[6] The handsome publication with a foreword by Šusta has remained the main buttress of Czech biographers of Charles IV until our day.[7] And since

1/ Franz Martin Pelzel, *Kaiser Karl der Vierte, König in Böhmen*, II (Prag, 1781), pp. 924–933. In this introductory part and partially even later, I shall list some of the titles in full, because the data on their place and year of publication are directly tied to the text, complement it or are otherwise important for the reader.

2/ Franz Palacky, *Geschichte von Böhmen*, II-2 (Prag, 1842), pp. 399–401.

3/ Václav Tille (ed.), 'Francouzský rukopis o cestě císaře Karla IV. do Francie v letech 1377–1378', *Věstník Královské české společnosti nauk*, třída filosoficko-historicko-jazykozpytná (Praha, 1899), Section XIV, pp. 1–16. In connection with this study, attention to another manuscript in the Parisian Bibliothèque nationale, MS fr. 5729, was drawn by Jaroslav Hrubant, 'Pařížské rukopisy o cestě Karla IV. do Francie a Paříže (1377–78)', *Časopis Musea Království českého*, 87 (1913), pp. 362–365. I will return to both manuscripts in the following excursuses.

4/ Josef Cibulka, 'Iluminátoři Velkých kronik Francie' (Bibliothèque nationale in Paris, MS fr. 2813), in *Recueil d'études, dédiées à la mémoire de N. P. Kondakov* (Prague, 1926), pp. 229–238, Cibulka, 'Iluminované popsání cesty Karla IV. do Francie v soudobém rukopise Národní knihovny v Paříži', *Památky archeologické*, 35 (1926–1927), pp. 63–69 and Tables XV–XXIV.

5/ Roland Delachenal (ed.), *Les Grandes Chroniques de France. Chronique des règnes de Jean II et de Charles V*, II: *1364–1380* (Paris, 1916); III: *Continuation et appendice* (Paris, 1920); IV: *Miniatures du manuscrit de Charles V*, (Paris, 1920).

6/ *Cesta císaře Karla IV. do Francie.* Translated from the contemporary French chronicle by Jakub Pavel. Foreword by Prof Josef Šusta (Praha, 1937).

7/ Also briefly in the main jubilee monograph by Jiří Spěváček, *Karel IV. Život a dílo (1316–1378)* (Praha, 1978), pp. 470–472. It is even truer of his later work *Václav IV. 1361–1419* (Praha, 1986), pp. 96–97.

František Kavka a short time ago rendered the political background of Charles' journey and moreover outlined Charles' visit in detail in the second volume of his large monograph, it could seem that there is no need to return to that theme, especially when another reliable portrayal of the period is available from the pen of Lenka Bobková.[8]

So far we have paid attention to Czech historiography. In France, a significant shift in terms of the provision of more information on the summit of January 1378 was not brought by the critical edition of the *Great Chronicles of France* itself but only later by the monumental five-volume monograph in which Robert Delachenal described the period of the reign of Charles V the Wise day by day.[9] With the exception of a few narrowly focused, but for that deeper probes,[10] French historiography has not felt the need to deal with this episode, which has been related to the long-term departure from narrative, predominantly political history.[11] The first robin had not yet brought spring, because in 1971 Marcel Thomas more or less limited himself to a paraphrase of the Account of the Journey of Charles IV included in the *Great Chronicles of France*.[12] However, it was not long before French historiography again began to explore in the second half of the fourteenth century interesting and beneficial topics of the newly conceived political history. From the broad spectrum of publications, I shall highlight only those upon which I relied most. Whereas Philippe Contamine provided an enormous amount of information on wartime France, Raymond Cazelles extended the knowledge on the political, power and administrative structures during the reigns of John II the Good and his son Charles V.[13] An historian also appreciates the extensive biographies of the sovereigns as well as other eminent personalities of French history in the fourteenth century, not to mention the numerous essays elucidating the contemporary conception of royal power and its ceremonial representation.[14] Nevertheless, it is not

8/ František Kavka, Karel IV. a anjouovsko-piastovské dědictví, *Sborník historický*, 36 (1989), pp. 5–63 and František Kavka, *Vláda Karla IV. za jeho císařství*, II: *(1364–1378)* (Praha, 1993), pp. 207–222. For the most recent work, see Lenka Bobková, *Velké dějiny zemí Koruny české*, IVa: *1310–1402* (Praha – Litomyšl, 2003), pp. 439–451 and 641–642.

9/ Roland Delachenal, *Histoire de Charles V*, I–V (Paris, 1909–1931); the author described the emperor's visit at length in the last volume on pp. 61–122.

10/ As an example, I provide the treatise on the Palace de la Cité, published by Jean Guérout, 'Le Palais de la Cité à Paris des origines à 1417. Essai topographique et archéologique' (Paris, 1953).

11/ The earlier French historiography dealing with our theme was captured by Heinrich Neureither, *Das Bild Kaiser Karls IV. in der zeitgenössischen französischen Geschichtsschreibung*. Inaugural-Dissertation (Heidelberg, 1965), cf. esp. Introduction and pp. 112–115.

12/ Marcel Thomas, 'La visite de l'empereur Charles IV en France d'après l'exemplaire des «Grandes Chroniques» exécuté pour le roi Charles V', in *Congrès International de bibliophiles* (Wien, 1971), pp. 85–98.

13/ Philippe Contamine, *Guerre, État et société à la fin du Moyen Âge. Etudes sur les armées des rois de France 1337–1494* (Paris – Mouton – La Haye, 1972) and Raymond Cazelles, *Société politique, noblesse et couronne sous Jean le Bon et Charles V* (Genève – Paris, 1982).

14/ It does not make sense to enumerate the books and studies listed both in connection with the commentary and in the final bibliography of the sources and secondary literature.

only about the imperial visit itself but also about its local colour, which has been provided with unexpected authenticity by the archaeological surveys in the Louvre. Also the artistic works of this peak period of the French Gothic have reached the forefront of attention at several exhibitions, and a number of treatises and collective publications brought Paris to life at the end of the reign of Charles V as well.[15] A kind of key to the latest research on our topic is represented by the enthrallingly written biography of Charles V the Wise, into which Françoise Autrand inserted the outcomes of her own extensive studies.[16]

Research not only wends from jubilee to jubilee[17] but also progresses through circuitous routes, digressions and knowledge acquired in special disciplines. At a certain point, interdisciplinary overlaps begin to yield new connections, which sooner or later result in new questions being asked. Not all of them receive an answer immediately. At the same time, it is typical that similar questions are asked by several mediaevalists. With the number of researchers constantly increasing, parallel stimuli are an ever more frequent phenomenon. Some episodes, e.g. the prestigious question of the colour and type of the horses or the theatrical performance at the ceremonial dinner of the feast of the Epiphany in January 1378, repeatedly attracted attention already in the past, but only since 1965 have studies begun to appear that again brushed up the ceremonial colourfulness of the official account of the visit of the Holy Roman Emperor. The French-Imperial relations in the Luxemburg period have been elucidated in a number of studies by Heinz Thomas, the best German expert on this issue today, who commendably issued the contemporary 'Memorandum', as I will following him refer to another written record on the imperial visit.[18] Systematic research of the illuminated manuscripts of the

15/ Cf. particularly the catalogue *Les Fastes du Gothique. Le siècle de Charles V* (Paris, 1981) and the collective work *Paris et Charles V. Arts et Architecture.* Sous la direction de Frédéric Pleybert (Paris, 2001). I will mention other monographs and catalogues later.

16/ Françoise Autrand, *Charles V. Le Sage* (Paris, 1994), there esp. pp. 779–805. The author has dealt with the emperor's visit in two studies: 'Mémoire et cérémonial: la visite de l'Empereur Charles IV à Paris en 1378 d'après les Grandes Chroniques de France et Christine de Pizan', in *Une femme de Lettres au Moyen Âge. Études autour de Christine de Pizan* (Orléans, 1995), pp. 91–103; 'Aux origines de la diplomatie européenne: la visite de l'Empereur Charles IV à Paris en 1378', *Bulletin de la Société des amis de l'Institut historique allemand*, I (1995), pp. 15–28.

17/ The large jubilee in 1978 fared poorly for our topic. It is also true for the biographies of Charles IV issued on that occasion. It is, however, necessary to take into account that their authors could not particularise. See Ferdinand Seibt, *Karl IV. Ein Kaiser in Europa 1346 bis 1378* (München, 1978). Seibt dealt in detail with the imperial vicariate in the Dauphiné, which played a significant role also during the imperial visit: 'Zum Reichsvikariat für den Dauphin', *Zeitschrift für historische Forschung*, 8 (1981), pp. 129–158. From the more recent works, cf. i.a. Heinz Stoob, *Kaiser Karl IV. und seine Zeit*, (Graz – Wien – Köln, 1990), pp. 394–397 and Jörg K. Hoensch, *Die Luxemburger* (Stuttgart, 2000), pp. 141–143.

18/ Heinz Thomas, 'Ein Zeitgenössisches Memorandum zum Staatsbesuch Kaiser Karls IV. in Paris', in *Festschrift für Hans-Walter Herrmann zum 65. Geburtstag*, ed. by W. Haubrichs et al. (Saarbrücken, 1995), pp. 99–119. On the Memorandum, see more below, otherwise cf. further important treatises by the same author: 'Die Beziehungen Karls IV. zu Frankreich von der Rhenser Wahl im Jahre 1346 bis zum Großen Metzer Hoftag', *Blätter für deutsche Landesgeschichte*, 114

Great Chronicles of France, which was meritoriously undertaken by American researcher Anna Dawson Hedeman, also contributed to a better understanding of the external ceremonies connected with the emperor's visit to France in January 1378.[19] Year after year, the interest in the relations of Charles IV to France and particularly in the rituals tied to his last visit rise, which already makes it difficult to monitor the new literature.[20] And since the repercussions of the foreign research wave also appear in Czech historiography,[21] especially in the breakthrough works by Martin Nejedlý[22] and in the proliferating studies of an art-science orientation,[23] there is no need to complain about a lack of specialised literature.

(1978), pp. 165–201; 'Frankreich', in *Kaiser Karl IV. Staatsmann und Mäzen*, ed. by Ferdinand Seibt (München, 1978), pp. 152–156 and 448–449; 'Frankreich, Karl IV. und das Große Schisma', in *'Bündnissysteme' und 'Außenpolitik' im späteren Mittelalter*, ed. by Peter Moraw, (Zeitschrift für historische Forschung, Beiheft 5; Berlin, 1988), pp. 69–104. I list the other titles in the Bibliography. For the latest, see Bernd Carqué, *Stil und Erinnerung. Französische Hofkunst im Jahrhundert Karls V. und im Zeitalter ihrer Deutung* (Göttingen, 2004), esp. pp. 447–455.

19/ Anne D. Hedeman, i.a. compared the contemporary picture reportages from Charles' visit to France in two English manuscripts: 'Les perceptions de l'image royale à travers les miniatures: l'exemple des Grandes Chroniques de France', in *Pratiques de la culture écrite en France au XVe siècle* (Louvain-La-Neuve, 1995), pp. 539–549.

20/ Two publications of a similar orientation come from Gerald Schwedler: *Herrschertreffen des Spätmittelalters. Formen – Rituale – Wirkungen* (Mittelalter-Forschungen, 21, Ostfildern, 2008); 'Deutsch-französische Herrschertreffen im 14. Jahrhundert. Dynastische und staatliche Beziehungen im Wandel', in *Regnum et Imperium. Die französisch-deutschen Beziehungen im 14. und 15. Jahrhundert. Les relations franco-allemandes au XIVe et au XVe siècle* (Pariser Historische Studien, 83, München, 2008), pp. 55–99. The same anthology also included a study by Stefan Weiss, 'Onkel und Neffe. Die Beziehungen zwischen Deutschland und Frankreich unter Kaiser Karl IV. und König Karl V. und der Ausbruch des Großen Abendländischen Schismas. Eine Studie über mittelalterliche Außenpolitik', pp. 101–164 (there esp. pp. 146–156: IX. Die Reise nach Paris). Cf. the latest work, Kintzinger, Martin, 'Zeremoniell und politische Repräsentation bei dem berühmten Treffen zwischen Karl IV. und Karl VI. von Frankreich', in *Die Goldene Bulle. Politik – Wahrnehmung – Rezeption*, I, ed. by Ulrike Hohensee et al. (Berlin, 2009), pp. 299–326.

21/ I have to mention here the thesis from the Brno seminar of Prof. Jaroslav Mezník, a part of which came out in print: Martina Lechová, 'Zpráva o návštěvě Paříže Karlem IV. roku 1378', *Sborník prací Filozofické fakulty Brněnské univerzity*, C 43 (1996), pp. 49–60; the edition of the Memorandum mentioned above is on pp. 50–56. More recently, see also Jana Fantysová-Matějková, 'Cesta Karla IV. do Francie. Příspěvek ke kritice Velkých francouzských kronik', *Český časopis historický*, 106 (2008), pp. 627–650.

22/ See selectively: Martin Nejedlý, 'Deux poètes français du quatorzième siècle en Bohême. Rencontres et confrontations', in *Prague Papers on the History of International Relations* (Prague – Wien, 1997), pp. 30–53; *Fortuny kolo vrtkavé. Láska, moc a společnost ve středověku* (Praha, 2003); *La représentation des pouvoirs et des hiérarchies dans les Chroniques de Jean Froissart* (Villeneuve d'Ascq, 2007); *Středověký mýtus o Meluzíně a rodová pověst Lucemburků* (Praha, 2007).

23/ See i.a. Karel Stejskal, 'Výstava „La Librairie de Charles V" a některé otázky českého umění XIV. století', *Umění*, 18 (1970), pp. 31–60; Karel Otavsky, *Die Sankt Wenzelskrone im Prager Domschatz und die Frage der Kunstauffassung am Hofe Kaiser Karls IV.* (Bern, 1992); Karel Otavský, 'K relikviím vlastněným císařem Karlem IV., k jejich uctívání a jejich schránkám', in *Court Chapels / Dvorské kaple* (Praha, 2003), pp. 392–398; Jaromír Homolka, 'Poznámky ke karlštejnským malbám', *Umění*, 45 (1997), pp. 122–140; Klára Benešovská, 'Les résidences du roi Jean de Bohême: leur fonction de représentation', in *King John of Luxembourg (1296–1346) and the Art of his Era* (Prague, 1998), pp. 117–131; Jiří Kuthan, 'Pařížská Sainte-Chapelle a trny z koruny Kristovy', in Jiří Kuthan, *Splendor et Gloria Regni Bohemiae* (Praha, 2008), pp. 387–426; Peter Kováč, 'Poznámky k popisu pařížské Sainte-Chapelle z roku 1378', in *Court Chapels / Dvorské kaple*, pp. 413–418; Mojmír Frinta, 'Le portrait du Louvre de Jean le Bon', *Umění*, 52 (2004), pp. 402–413. Further studies will be listed in the relevant places.

I. THE ACCOUNT OF THE GREAT CHRONICLES OF FRANCE AND ASSOCIATED WRITTEN SOURCES

At the very beginning of this excursus, a smaller surprise awaits us. Despite the journey of Charles IV and his son Wenceslas to France being one of the longest and most notable state visits of the crowned heads of the Kingdom of Bohemia in all of its history, the Czech chronicles do not mention it with even a word. Of the chroniclers of Charles' time, the only one alive then was the old Přibík Pulkava of Radenín, who soon followed the emperor from this world.[24] Whereas Emperor Charles had not managed any more to make sure that his journey home entered historical awareness, all the more interest in this regard was expressed by his French nephew Charles V. It is not entirely clear whether he entrusted the writing of the official account directly to his chancellor, Pierre d'Orgemont. According to R. Delachenal, it was apparently not the case, because the chancellor could not have written about a meeting which he himself attended that nothing was known about its deliberations.[25] On the other hand, the chancellor was bound to silence on affairs which were still of a confidential or directly secret nature. Besides, it would be difficult to find another man in the narrow circle of the confidants of the king of France who would be informed on the course of the imperial visit in such detail.[26]

Either way, the revision and copying of the gorgeously illuminated manuscript of the *Great Chronicles of France* were approaching their end, because for the relatively detailed Account, which formed roughly a fourth of the extent of the historical records on the government of Charles V, it was necessary to attach blank vellum folios to the second volume. So that there be no confusion, we are speaking of the codex created at the direct commission of Charles V, MS fr. 2813 today in the Bibliothèque Nationale in Paris (hereinafter mainly only as the 'BN'). In this manuscript, the Account begins in the left column of fol. 467r and finishes again in the left column of fol. 480r. It is followed by other historical records, including the report on the death of Emperor Charles IV. The text ends abruptly in April 1379, from which it can be deduced that King Charles V could enjoy the commissioned manuscript still before his death. To wit, other manuscripts of the *Great Chronicles of France* take the chronicle all the way to the death of Charles V, or even to the coronation of his successor, but they mainly contain only a shortened record of our Account. After the death of Charles V, both superbly illuminated volumes found their way into the no less famous collection of his brother Duke of Berry John.[27] Only later, most likely in the eighteenth century, were both parts bound together in one whole in a red Moroccan leather cover.[28]

24/ Přibík Pulkava died sometime between 18 September 1378 and 24 September 1380.

25/ See Delachenal (ed.), *Chronique des règnes*, III, Introduction, p. XVII. The disputed line is in the Account in the description of the private meeting of Charles V and the emperor on 5 January 1378.

26/ It is significant that the question of d'Orgemont's authorship or its extent is avoided by the literature. Only Heinrich Neureither, *Das Bild Kaiser Karls IV.*, p. 66, quite unequivocally expressed himself against the doubt of Delachenal.

27/ See Léopold Delisle, *Recherches sur la librairie de Charles V, roi de France, 1337–1380*, I (Paris, 1907; reprint Amsterdam, 1967), pp. 312–314, No. 90.

28/ The manuscript is on display only on exceptional occasions. From the post-war period, see the catalogues: *Les manuscrits à peintures en France du XIII*[e] *au XVI*[e] *siècle* (Paris, 1955), pp. 60–61, No. 123; *La Librairie de Charles V. Catalogue de l'exposition de la Bibliothèque nationale* (Par-

Still a few years ago, it was possible to find information which the entire text could be read only in MS fr. 2813 of the BN.[29] This assumption, however, is mistaken, as R. Delachenal already mentioned another eleven codices containing unabridged versions of the Account.[30] Nevertheless, he himself ignored them in his edition and satisfied himself with their model in MS fr. 2813 of the BN. The Old French text of the Account in this unique manuscript has twenty-eight unnumbered chapters, each of which is introduced by a graphically impressive initial and a very short summary of the content of the following episode. The incorporation of the accompanying miniatures thematically corresponded to the text, with the illuminations being eight fewer than the number of chapters.

After the death of Charles V, it became a fashion in the highest circles of the French aristocracy to own an expensive, usually also illuminated copy of the *Great Chronicles of France*.[31] Of the total number of the 107 manuscripts known so far, only fewer than twenty were created before 1375, and their owners and readers were almost exclusively found in Paris and its closest proximity.[32] Besides the main branch, derived from MS fr. 2813 of the BN, a numerous group of copies appear, *inter alia* characterised by containing an abridged version of the Account of the Emperor's Journey, which finishes in the midst of the ceremonial banquet in the Great Hall of the Palace de la Cité on 6 January 1378, namely before the description of the theatrical interludes presenting the capture of Jerusalem by Godfrey of Bouillon.[33] Whether the Account was shortened for its unsuitable length or for some other reason can only be surmised. In any case, it is interesting that this abridged version circulated even on its own, although its preserved copies do not come from before the turn of the sixteenth century.[34] What provided the stimulus for the creation of these marvellously prepared books written on soft vellum and with the title illumination is a mystery. One of the books undoubtedly served for the book edition prepared by Théodore Godefroy in 1614.[35]

The Account of the Visit of Emperor Charles to France was soon given its distinctive paraphrase in a prose work by the famous writer Christine de Pisan (1364–1430 ?), extolling the acts and 'good manners' of King Charles V.[36] The name of this exceptional writer is somewhat misleading, because her family was not from Pisa but from the North Italian city Pezzano. Christine arrived in Paris in 1368 as a four-

is, 1968), pp. 112–113, No. 195; *Les Fastes du Gothique. Le siècle de Charles V* (Paris, 1981), pp. 329–331, No. 284; and *Paris 1400. Les arts sous Charles VI* (Paris, 2004), p. 38, No. 5.

29/ The same opinion was also held by Autrand, 'Mémoire et cérémonial', p. 91.

30/ Delachenal (ed.), *Chronique des règnes*, III, pp. V–VII.

31/ One illuminated manuscript from the circle of the Master of the Berry Apocalypse is deposited in the library at Kynžvart Castle in West Bohemia. On that, see Hedeman, *The Royal Image. Illustrations of the Grandes Chroniques de France, 1274–1422*, pp. 261–262, and Pavol Černý et al., *Du bon du coeur*, pp. 124–131, No. 22.

32/ On that, see Bernard Guenée, 'Histoire d'un succès', pp. 121–129.

33/ For more on that, see Delachenal (ed.), *Chronique des règnes*, III, p. VII. Some of the manuscripts of this group bridged the omitted text with a short summary, which was published by Delachenal (ed.), *Chronique des règnes*, II, pp. 238–239, Note 3.

34/ The text in manuscript 5128 of the Parisian Bibliothèque de l'Arsenal was issued in a critical edition by Tille, 'Francouzský rukopis o cestě císaře Karla IV. do Francie', pp. 1–16. Attention to the second known exemplar in the Bibliothèque Nationale, MS fr. 5729, was drawn by François Avril, 'Jean Fouquet, illustrateur des Grandes Chroniques de France', in François Avril, Marie-Thérèse Gousset and Bernard Guenée, *Les Grandes Chroniques de France*, p. 280, Note 22.

35/ Godefroy, *Entrevues de Charles IV, Empereur, de son fils Wenceslaus, Roy de Romains, et de Charles V, Roy de France, à Paris l'an 1378* (Paris, 1614).

36/ The earlier editions and literature were registered by Edith Yenal, *Christine de Pizan: A Bibliography*, 2nd ed. (Metuchen – London, 1989), pp. 41–45, Nos. 192–206; the bibliography for 1991–2002 was issued by Angus J. Kennedy, *Christine de Pizan. A Bibliographical Guide: Supplement 2*. A standard edition was prepared by Suzanne Solente, *Le livre des fais et bonnes meurs du sage roy Charles V par Christine de Pisan*, I–II (Paris, 1936, 1940). The relevant sections are in the second volume, pp. 89–132 (reprint Genève, 1977). In the edition prepared by Eric Hicks and Thérèse Moreau, *Le Livre des Faits et Bonnes Moeurs du Roi Charles V le Sage* (Paris, 1997), the depiction of the emperor's visit in Paris can be read on pp. 250–279. On the idealisation of the figure of Charles V in this book as well as in other works by Christine de Pizan, see Cazelles, *Société politique*, pp. 49–50.

year-old girl with her father, a renowned astrologer, whom Charles V had invited to his court and whose recommendations he often followed.[37] When she was fourteen, Christine experienced the commotion around the ceremonial banquet of 6 January and might have even been a witness to another act in honour of the emperor and his son. Nevertheless, she could not have relied too much on her own memory, because she wrote her book after a significant time lapse, namely between 30 January and 30 November 1404. The impetus for it came from Duke of Burgundy Philip the Bold, who intended to honour the memory of his late brother in this way. In order to refresh her memory, the duke also gave her a complete copy of the Account of the Journey of Charles IV.[38] Christine refers to it herself and really also described the emperor's visit according to this Account, which she only abridged here and there.[39] It is questionable whether she herself added anything. Despite all my care, I found only a few details, which are not worth mentioning. A comparison with the original text of the Account would be rewarding for a number of researchers who by neglecting the model reached unfounded, mostly misleading conclusions of the independence of the author's female view.[40] Short, usually only general, mentions of the summit of the two crowned Charleses can be found also in other French chronicles, of which the *Chronique des quatre premiers Valois* and *Chronographia regum Francorum* deserve mentioning here.[41]

101. Christine de Pisan dedicates an anthology of her work to Queen Isabeau of Bavaria. Christine de Pisan, Oeuvres, around 1413 (BL, Harley 4431–1, fol. 3r)

Next come two valuable records in the form of broadside folios, which are distinguished from each other *inter alia* by their titles. The paper folio which in the Archives Départementales du Nord in Lille is labelled as B 654 No. 10.688 begins with the words 'C'est la manière comment l'empereur entra à Paris et fut le lundi IIII iour de Januier l'an LXXVII'.[42] The second, with a higher serial number (B 654

37/ Some specific examples are given by Nejedlý, *Fortuny kolo vrtkavé*, p. 306.

38/ If it really were the text of only the Account, which is not entirely certain, it would be the first evidence of its separate circulation. For more on that, see Solente (ed.), *Le livre des fais et bonnes meurs*, Introduction, pp. XXXVIII–XL, who drew the conclusion that this text has the same mistakes and omissions as the copy in the manuscript in the Vatican Library, Vat. lat. 4791.

39/ Solente (ed.), *Le livre des fais et bonnes meurs*, II, Chapter XLIX, p. 131.

40/ I do not mean here only the popular science and feminist literature, for which Christine de Pisan is directly a cult figure. See i.a. Régine Pernoud, *Christine de Pisan*, pp. 21–25; see also the following, who have, however, remained on the superficial level: Autrand, 'Mémoire et cérémonial: la visite de l'Empereur Charles IV à Paris en 1378 d'après les Grandes Chroniques de France et Christine de Pizan', and Armand Strubel, 'Le «chevauchier» de Charles V. Christine de Pizan et le spectacle de la majesté royale', pp. 385–399.

41/ Siméon Luce (ed.), *Chronique des quatre premiers Valois (1327–1393)* (Paris, 1862), pp. 264–265 (a mere mention without an informative value); Henri Moranvillé (ed.), *Chronographia regum Francorum*, II: *1328–1380* (Paris, 1893), p. 358 (which contains, e.g. a different report on the Christmas mass in Cambrai). Cf. also Étienne Baluze, *Vitae paparum avenionensium*, I, ed. Guillaume Mollat (Paris, 1914, p. 464, which only says: 'Iste idem imperator ivit Parisius peregre ubi coronavit filium Karoli V, regis Francorum, de facto in regem Arelatensem, ad decennium tantum'.

42/ The Memoir was known already to Delachenal, *Histoire de Charles V*, V, p. 97; see also *Chronique des règnes*, II, p. 238, Note 2, which contains a reference to the shelf mark of the source. Broadside folios were known also to other researchers; their importance was recognised first by Thomas, 'Frankreich', p. 449, Note 74, which reported their publication, namely in the appendix of his study 'Ein zeitgenössisches Memorandum zum Staatsbesuch Kaiser Karls IV. in Paris', pp. 116–119. The other broadside folio (referred to as B by Thomas) was simultaneously dealt with by Lechová, 'Zpráva o návštěvě Paříže Karlem IV. roku 1378', pp. 49–60.

No 10.689), contains in its title the word '*Mémoire*', which conveys its content and perhaps even the function of both documents well, which is the reason that I will hereinafter refer to them so for short. Considering the place of deposition of the broadsheets as well as their lettering, their publisher expressed the opinion that they were intended for Count of Flanders Louis de Male.[43] Both versions truly remind one of some kind of instruction on the ceremonial manner or method (hence 'la manière' in the title of one of them) during the ceremonial welcoming of foreign sovereigns and on their seating arrangement as well as on the model menu for banquets in their honour. These useful data could really be of interest to the authors of court protocols. Although the *Mémoire* describes the emperor's visit on Monday, 4 January 1378, relatively briefly, it brings some greater, some smaller changes as compared to the Account, to which we will pay heed later. However, the *Mémoire*'s main contribution is that it complements the other sources with detailed specifications of the menus of the three ceremonial banquets on Tuesday and Wednesday, 5 and 6 January, which are not known from anywhere else.[44] From these data which are different or unknown from elsewhere, it cannot however be deduced that the Account was a 'protocolic fiction' or an 'ideal' version of the official protocol while the *Mémoire* was an authentic record of what actually happened.[45]

43/ See Thomas, 'Ein zeitgenössisches Memorandum', p. 116. This speculation was rejected by Fantysová-Matějková, 'Cesta Karla IV. do Francie', pp. 640–643, according to whom the *Mémoire* was written down at the instigation of Duke Wenceslas, the half-brother of Charles IV.

44/ The differences between the Account and the Memoir are emphasised by Thomas, 'Ein zeitgenössisches Memorandum', pp. 103–111, whose deductions on the menus can already be expanded and elaborated today. At the same time, he himself did not sufficiently take into account the differences between the two broadside folios, A and B, which are so large that they were probably made from different originals. Thomas' edition offers the variant interpretations in the notes, but only from the photocopies is the formal difference of text B also apparent.

45/ Following in the footsteps of Thomas, it was thus concluded without proper justification and with a number of inaccuracies by Fantysová-Matějková, 'Cesta Karla IV. do Francie', pp. 629–631.

It will probably not be far from reality if we assume that both broadsides drew upon the written instructions for court personnel, in this case for employees of the so-called 'palace' kitchen and wine cellars. Chancellor d'Orgemont or administrator of the Palace de la Cité Philip Ogier issued more such directives. One of them, a list and description of the gifts prepared for the emperor and his retinue, is mentioned in the Account itself.[46] The unpreserved inventory of the gifts can be partially reconstructed from the mandates of Charles V ordering that refunds for this purpose be paid, further from the accounting receipts and other documents whose copies can be found in MS 26.014 of the BN and sporadically also in several other manuscripts.[47] It is not necessary to go into detail here, as the gifts and their period value will be covered in a special excursus.

The last-mentioned group of writings deviated from the so-called narrative sources and is closer in its character to official letters and documents. The collection of contracts and documents of a foreign policy nature entitled *Recueil des traités de la France* (or the *Livre des alliances*), which King Charles V had made around 1378, can be considered as a transitional link of its type. The entire collection of 172 documents contained both notarised copies of the Latin originals and their translations into French. The writings accumulated in this way from the end of the twelfth century to 1374 were sorted into several groups. The first section, called *Des Empereurs et Roys des Romains*, contains especially the documents necessary for the negotiations with Emperor Charles IV, whether concerning the Dauphiné, Lucca in Italy or Burgundy.[48] Also the contracts and documents

46/ Delachenal (ed.), *Chronique des règnes*, II, p. 270.

47/ These mandates and other documents from among the manuscripts of the National Library in Paris were issued by Delisle (ed.), *Mandements et actes divers de Charles V (1364–1380)*; for further details, see the introduction to that edition.

48/ The original exemplar, evidenced in Charles V's library in the Louvre, has probably been destroyed, but four copies have been preserved, of which three come still from the fifteenth century. For more on that, see Andrée Artonne, 'Le recueil des traités de la France composé par ordre de Charles V', pp. 55–63.

of other sections which confirmed the rights of the kings of France in Normandy, Brittany as well as elsewhere, namely with respect to both Edward III and King of Navarre Charles the Bad, could have been important for the meeting with the emperor. It is hence immensely likely that, as Françoise Autrand presumes, the entire collection was created shortly before that date as the basis for the anticipated meeting with the emperor.[49] According to the testimony of the Account, Charles V at the joint session of the counsellors in the Louvre even presented some of these documents while referring also to the expert opinion of a number of schools of law.[50] In general, it is necessary to say that the host did not want to omit anything from the constitutional standpoint, so in this respect also the chancellor of the University of Paris and its spokesperson Master Jean de la Chaleur († 1380 or 1381) during his speech to the emperor had to act not only with due reverence (*notablement*) but also with respect to the primary position of the king of France on his domestic soil (*legalment*).[51]

It remains to mention the letters and documents connected with the summit in Paris. We know the first letter, by which the emperor announced his visit to the king of France, only from the Account and from the accompanying illuminations. Similarly, not even other letters tied to the postponement of the journey have been preserved. Of the originals or at least copies, we on the other hand know the texts of six antedated letters from 5 to 7 January 1378, which Prothonotary Nicholas of Riesenburg gave the dauphin in the presence of his father after the emperor's departure from Meaux:

(1) 5 January 1378: Emperor Charles IV authorises Dauphin Charles of Vienne to issue lawfully all acts in civil affairs; orig. parchment with the golden bull, Paris, Archives nationales J 612, No. 48.[52]

(2) 6 January 1378: Emperor Charles IV in the Kingdom of Arles (Arelat) presents the dauphin with the castles Pipet and Canaux, which until that time had been in the administration of the Chapter in Vienne.[53]

(3) 6 January 1378: Emperor Charles IV revokes the authorisation for the administration of both castles by the dean and chapter in Vienne.[54]

(4) 7 January 1378: Emperor Charles IV appoints Dauphin Charles lifetime regent in Arelat except for the Dauphiné and Savoy; orig. parchment with the golden bull, Paris, Archives nationales J 612, No. 46.[55]

(5) 7 January 1378: Emperor Charles IV informs all of the populace of Arelat that he has appointed Dauphin Charles the lifelong regent and general vicar in the Dauphiné; orig. parchment with appended seal, Paris, Archives nationales Archives, J 612, No. 47.[56]

49/ Cf. Autrand, 'Les livres des hommes de pouvoir', pp. 99–204.

50/ In the first place here, besides the domestic law schools in Montpellier, Toulouse and Orléans, there appears a puzzling school in 'Bouloigne la Crasse', identified by Delachenal, *Histoire de Charles V*, V, p. 106, as the famous university in Bologna. Even so, it is surprising that the law faculty of the domestic Sorbonne was omitted. This could be explained by the Sorbonne's purely canonical orientation.

51/ On the meaning of the newly coined adjective *legalment*, see Delachenal (ed.), *Chronique des règnes*, II, p. 247, Note 2. On this, I add that the chancellor acted here also on behalf of the numerous members of the university corporation of the English nation, a significant part of which comprised the emperor's subjects from various ends of the Empire.

52/ See Johann Friedrich Böhmer (ed.), *Regesta imperii*, VIII, p. 490, No. 5858.

53/ See Böhmer (ed.), *Regesta imperii*, VIII, p. 490, Nos. 5859; cf. Claude Faure, 'Histoire de la réunion de Vienne à la France', p. 462.

54/ See Böhmer (ed.), *Regesta imperii*, VIII, p. 490, No. 5860; Faure, 'Histoire de la réunion de Vienne à la France', p. 462.

55/ See Böhmer (ed.), *Regesta imperii*, VIII, p. 490, No. 5862, ed. Marie-Luise Heckmann, 'Das Reichsvikariat des Dauphins im Arelat 1378', pp. 86–90, No. 2. The model of the document, which was, based on the copybook of the Abbey of Melk, issued by Pelzel, *Kaiser Karl der Vierte*, II, pp. 250–254, No. 244, has not been found. Heckmann, 'Das Reichsvikariat des Dauphins im Arelat 1378', p. 65, Note 6, determined that Pelzel's text corresponds to the letter inserted in the confirmation of Pope Clement VII of 6 November 1389 (edition ibid., pp. 93–97, No. 4).

56/ See Böhmer (ed.), *Regesta imperii*, VIII, p. 490, No. 5863, ed. Heckmann, 'Das Reichsvikariat des Dauphins im Arelat', pp. 90–93, No. 3.

The uniqueness of the complete copy of the Account in the manuscript MS fr. 2813 of the Bibliothèque nationale in Paris lies not only in its being an exemplar intended directly for King Charles V but also in its accompanying cycle of nineteen illuminations of relatively high artistic and informational value (Pics I–XIX). They were reliably described by Roland Delachenal in the third volume of his edition of the *Great Chronicles of France* during the reigns of John the Good and Charles V (*Les Grandes Chroniques de France. Chronique des règnes de Jean II et de Charles V*), to which he attached black-and-white reproductions of a relatively good quality.[57] Shortly thereafter, Josef Cibulka became acquainted with this edition as well as with its manuscript model. In an article intended for an anthology in honour of N. P. Kondakov, he first attempted to specify the share of painter 'A' as the designing draughtsman and partially also the painter who illuminated the Account of the Journey of Charles IV with the exception of fol. 473v. According to Cibulka, the central depiction of the feast on the mentioned folio was the work of an anonymous master 'E' (Pic. 80 / XI).[58] In another article for Czech readers, Josef Cibulka focused on a precise description of the illuminations which have an exceptional meaning for the cultural history of both sovereigns.[59] His descriptions following the originals are very valuable especially in terms of the precise determination of the colour shades.

Such an outstanding work continued to attract the attention of researchers. Within more broadly conceived or on the contrary thematically conceived studies, the cycle was dealt with by Charles Sterling among others.[60] According to the latest knowledge, also a student of the Master of the Bible of Jean de Sy contributed to MS fr. 2813, *inter alia* by painting the banquet in honour of Emperor Charles IV.[61] It was precisely this large illumination taking more than three-quarters of a manuscript page that became best known, namely thanks to the dramatic scene of the capture of Jerusalem. The miniature differs from the clear majority of the depictions through its explicit relation to the text of the Account as well as the enrichment by details of a narrative character which are not mentioned in the text.[62] The author of the Account also anticipated its creation, when before describing the seating arrangement at the Epiphany table he referred to the depiction that was to follow. He had no idea as yet that the illuminator would not capture at the table one of the three bishops on the left from the king of the Romans Wenceslas IV.[63]

57/ R. Delachenal (ed.), *Chronique des règnes*, IV: *Miniatures du manuscrit de Charles V* (Paris, 1920), with descriptions on pp. 30–40 and reproductions XXXI–XLIX. The numbering of the reproductions varies between 18 and 19, because fol. 478r contains a twin miniature. For information, I add that this parchment codex is of a size of 350 × 240 mm.

58/ Cibulka, 'Iluminátoři Velkých kronik Francie', pp. 229–238.

59/ Cibulka, 'Iluminované popsání cesty Karla IV. do Francie', pp. 63–69 and Tables XV–XXIV.

60/ Charles Sterling, *La peinture médiévale à Paris 1300–1500*, I (Paris, 1987), pp. 245–248, No. 38.

61/ According to the entry on the Grandes Chroniques de France de Charles V, in *Les Fastes du Gothique*, No. 284, p. 330.

62/ As emphasised by Hedeman, *The Royal Image*, p. 131. For more on the depiction of the scene, see below in connection with banquets.

63/ In Delachenal (ed.), *Chronique des règnes*, II, p. 236, we read: 'ci après pourtraite et ymaginée' ('as is depicted in the illumination below'). In fact, the illumination on fol. 473v begins immediately on top without any text.

In accord with the written Account, the large series of almost reportage depictions in MS fr. 2813 of the BN was to emphasise the exceptional importance of the imperial visit, and even this visual form was to make the superiority and sovereignty of the king of France on his domestic soil evident at first glance.[64] The respect and reverence which Charles V felt for his uncle were not to be affected by that. The intimacy of the relation, which found its expression in the mutual embrace (fol. 471va – Pic. 78 / IX) as well as the exchange of rings (fol. 479rb – Pic. 87 / XVIII), was of a purely private nature, and therefore the only other person present was the emperor's son Wenceslas.

The other four scenes in which the king of France appears along with both crowned Luxemburgs are already of an entirely public nature. The first of them in the order, illustrating the meeting of the three sovereigns in La Chapelle-Saint-Denis, occupies two columns (fol. 470r – Pic. 75 / VI) and already with that gains in importance. The dominance of Charles V is shown here by his grace as well as the white colour of his horse, as will be discussed in another place. The illuminator resolved the joint entry of the rulers by fronting the domestic Charles V before the emperor and King of the Romans (fol. 470va–b – Pic. 77 / VIII). At the same time, no less important is the central position of the King of France, which we encounter also in the depiction of the offer of an alliance (fol. 476vb – Pic. 82 / XIII) and the Epiphany banquet (fol. 473va–b – Pic. 80 / XI). The emperor's place is usually, but not always, at the right hand of his younger nephew. For compositional reasons, an exception here is the scene of the first meeting between La Chapelle-Saint-Denis and the windmill, which deviates from the version in the Account.[65] A special case is the illustration of the promise of love and service which was made by King of the Romans Wenceslas IV by presenting his hand at the impetus of his father (Pic. 84 / XV). Thus it is written in the Account, which however does not mention the genuflection in which Wenceslas was depicted by the illuminator. In this place, the Account is quite unreliable and kneeling before court functionaries almost unthinkable for the King of the Romans.

In spite of a certain attempt to individualise the main actors, mainly in the indication of age, which in the case of Charles V is further manifested also by highlighting his typical long and sharp nose and with the emperor by his stooped figure,[66] the main aim of the creators was a clear-cut typification of the monarchs as the representatives of European powers. Consequently, the emperor always wears the imperial crown with the small arc on his head, although he wore a beret or hat on his head according to the Account. The same also holds true in the case of the crown of Charles V, who based on the Account was also coming from Paris to meet his uncle in a pointed traditional hat richly decorated with pearls. Only in this miniature does Charles V wear – this time in accord with the verbal description in the Account – a scarlet riding jacket and a large mantle bountifully lined with fur. In all of the other scenes, Charles V is recognisable by a blue ceremonial mantle decorated with distinctive golden lilies, whereas the characteristic feature of the emperor's clothes is usually a fur-lined scarlet mantle.

Anne D. Hedeman in her fundamental and so-far unsurpassed monograph on the illustrations of the *Great Chronicles of France* registered seventy manuscripts before 1500 with eight others that she had not managed to study.[67] Hardly any manuscripts of that large collection contain a depiction related

64/ On the deliberate highlighting of the majesty of the King of France in the depictions of the Great Chronicles, see Hedeman, 'Les perceptions de l'image royale à travers les miniatures', Annexe pp. 542–544.

65/ The Account explicitly states that Charles V returned before the emperor in such a way as to have the emperor on his right side and the King of the Romans on his left. On this ceremonial politeness, see below in Excursus – Welcoming Processions and Ceremonial Entries.

66/ On the individual and typical features of the depiction of Charles V in the *Great Chronicles of France*, see Claire Richter Sherman, *The Portraits of Charles V of France (1338–1380)*, pp. 41–44.

67/ Hedeman, *The Royal Image*; cf. Appendix II there: 'Surviving Manuscripts of the Grandes Chroniques and Their Provenance', pp. 187–192.

to the visit to France undertaken by the aged emperor Charles IV and his entourage at the turn of 1378. It is so because fourteen manuscripts were created before that time as well as because even those manuscripts that provide an abridged record of the Account on the visit were left without a graphic illustration of the January summit. However, this circumstance is counterbalanced not only by a series of reportage illustrations in MS fr. 2813 of the BN but also two further cycles of nine and eight illustrations of the emperor's visit to France which accompanied a shortened text of the Account.

The sumptuously illuminated manuscript in the codex of the British Library in London (hereinafter only as the 'BL'), Royal 20 C VII, from 1400–1415 remained unnoticed for a surprisingly long time although its detailed description had been available already in the catalogue by G. F. Warner and J. P. Gilson of 1921.[68] The codex came from the royal workshop in Paris[69] and according to A. D. Hedeman was quite likely created at the order of either Louis II of Anjou, nephew of King Charles V, or even commissioned by the next king Charles VI. Hedeman preferred the second possibility, because the activity of the so-called Master of Virgil (Maître du Virgile), who participated in the ornamentation, has been evidenced up to the 1410s. The cycle of the nine illuminations on the visit of Charles IV in Paris is the work of a fourth (anonymous) painter (Pics XX–XXVIII).[70] Although the central idea of the cycle also places emphasis on the superiority of the king of France to the emperor (meaning on French soil), the main actors lost their historical authenticity. The artist was not aware of their appearance, from which it arises that not even the workshop had samples of the portraits available. The means of typification are not very imaginative. The main distinguishing feature is the shape of the crowns. In this regard, we may speak of the set visual awareness, which even in France connected the emperor with the crown with the small arc. The garments of the monarchs are dominated by shades of red. A certain superiority of the domestic sovereign can be perceived in the clarity or luminosity of the colour of his mantle. The colour blue with lilies appears only in the background of the depiction of the banquet (fol. 199r – Pic. 152 / XXVIII).

Also the last of the three mentioned manuscripts owes its origin to a royal commission, namely with high likelihood on the part of Charles VII, who entrusted its decoration to one of the greatest masters of French book painting Jean Fouquet shortly before 1460. The sumptuously decorated manuscript of the Bibliothèque nationale in Paris MS fr. 6465 has a truly imposing size of 460 × 350 mm. From our perspective, the manuscript is noteworthy already for the fact that eight of the total of fifty-one illuminations were again devoted to the visit of Emperor Charles IV (Pics XXIX–XXXVI). The manuscript did not become more widely known until later, thanks to the authority of Léopold Delisle, who in 1868 placed it among the works of the famous painter Jean Fouquet (ca 1420 – before 1480). Other scholars accepted this attribution, but some of them only to a limited degree. Nevertheless, the cycle illustrating the emperor's visit is generally considered to be the work of Fouquet without reservations. The manuscript was not missing in any significant catalogue or work on the French book painting of the fifteenth century. Considering that replicas of all of the depictions of this manuscript came out in 1967 with the expert commentaries by F. Avril, M.-T. Gousset and B. Guenée, that authoritative work can be referenced.[71] The latest state of the research was captured in the catalogue of the exhibition *Jean Fouquet. Peintre et enlumineur du XVe siècle*, which took place from

68/ George. F. Warner and Julius P. Gilson, *Catalogue of Western Manuscripts in the Old Royal and King's Collections*, II (London, 1921), pp. 372–374.

69/ This opinion was expressed by Bernard Guenée in Avril, Gousset and Guenée, *Les Grandes Chroniques*, p. 24. Seven miniatures are shown there in black-and-white reproductions (pp. 25, 42, 44–45, 52 and 55).

70/ Hedeman, 'Les perceptions de l'image royale', pp. 539–541 and 547–549 (specification of the illuminations).

71/ See Avril, Gousset and Guenée, *Les Grandes Chroniques de France*, also including detailed iconographic descriptions of all the depictions.

25 March to 22 June 2003 in the 'old' building of the Bibliothèque Nationale in Richelieu Street. The manuscript of the *Great Chronicles of France* was one of the gems of that exhibition.[72]

No matter how it might seem, considering how late Fouquet's illuminations were created, that they would lack historical authenticity, it is only partially so. In the first place, Fouquet followed the text of the Account quite closely. In accord with that, both Charleses wear hats which roughly correspond to the descriptions in the outdoor scenes. Also the colours and types of horses are in agreement with the Account. The illuminator even respected the 'gorgeous and rich saddle with the coats-of-arms of France' on the horses sent to the emperor and his son. The shift in the fashion of the gear is however pronounced, which is true for all the costumes. The trend towards naturalism with Fouquet does not exclude a certain idealisation. We encounter it especially in the conception of the landscape at the welcoming of both Luxemburgs by the representatives of the city of Paris on the plains between Saint-Denis and La Chapelle-Saint-Denis (fol. 442v – Pic. 126 / XXXII). Although the meeting took place at the beginning of January, the fresh greenery of the landscape and bright sky suggest another season. Apparently the closest to the eighty-year-removed reality is the depicted architecture. Whereas in the cases of Cambrai and Saint-Denis we do not have the possibility to confirm the veracity of the depicted buildings, certain clues are available in the case of the Parisian exteriors. Nonetheless, not even here does fiction take a backseat. According to the Account, the emperor with his escort entered Paris from the north through the gate of Saint-Denis. However, since Fouquet had depicted that gate for the entry of Charles V into Paris in 1364 (fol. 417r), so as not to repeat himself, he transferred the emperor's welcome

102. / XXXIX. Banquet in honour of the emperor in the Grand Hall of the Palace de la Cité. Les Grandes Chroniques de France, perhaps 1415 (BL, Ms. Cotton Nero E II, 2nd part, fol. 229vb)

to in front of the neighbouring gate of St Martin (fol. 444r – Pic. 122 / XXXV).[73]

Thanks to the American researcher A. D. Hedeman, it is possible to proceed not only from a parallel comparison of all three cycles [74] but also from a detailed list of the other illuminated manuscripts which accompany the Account with a single illustration available. Until now, the research has mostly focused on the manuscript of the British Library Cotton Nero E II, the second volume of which contains a relatively decent illustration of the banquet in the emperor's honour (Pic. 102 / XXXIX). The codex was noticed already by Léopold Delisle;[75] Millard Meiss ascribed most of the miniatures to a Master working for Marshall Boucicaut (Maître de Boucicaut) and his assistants,[76] which was accepted even by A. D. He-

---

72/ *Jean Fouquet. Peintre et enlumineur du XVe siècle*. Sous la direction de François Avril (Paris, 2003), cat. No. 26, pp. 219–248. In terms of our issue, the articles by François Avril, 'Jean Fouquet et ses fils' (pp. 18–28), and Erik Inglis, 'Fouquet: peintre d'histoire' (pp. 70–75, esp. 72), deserve attention in the catalogue.

73/ On this shift, see Avril, Gousset and Guenée, *Les Grandes Chroniques de France*, p. 257.

74/ Hedeman, 'Les perceptions de l'image royale à travers les miniatures', Annexe pp. 547–549.

75/ Delisle, 'Notes sur quelques manuscrits du Musée Britannique', pp. 183–238.

76/ Millard Meiss, *French Painting in the Time of Jean de*

103. / XXXVIII. Meeting of the French king with the emperor and his son. Les Grandes Chroniques de France, 1410–1420 (BL, Ms. Sloane 2433, Vol. C, fol. 149va)

deman, who added a specification of the elements and depictions.[77] The text on the visit of Charles IV begins on fol. 226va and finishes on 230rb; the sole square miniature with each side having roughly 9 cm has a gilded frame and can be found on fol. 229v with an explanatory vermilion descriptor: 'Du dinner qui fut en la grant salle du palais de l'ordonance'.

Another theme appears in the manuscript of the British Library in London MS Sloane 2433, Vol. C, fol. 149va from 1410–1420.

According to Millard Meiss, the artistic embellishment was mainly the work of a Dutch artist living in Paris in the 1510s.[78] A. D. Hedeman expressed agreement with this opinion,[79] whereas Jeffrey Hamburger found not only Dutch but also Flemish and Rhinish influences in this codex.[80] It is the only illustration of Charles' journey, namely of the chapter on the meeting of the three crowned heads in the fields between Chapelle and the wind mill. The square miniature with each side having approximately 9 cm has a gold frame, sober colours, with silver-grey shading being dominant with the exception of the crown, which shines with gold. The scene shows two groups of horsemen. The two sovereigns on white horses and in long, loosely hanging mantles without any symbols are greeting each other with their hands outstretched to shake. The king on the right is wearing a crown; one of the men on horseback in the group behind him is depicted with a typical Burgundian hat. The bearded ruler on the left – apparently the emperor – has a cap which in later depictions often marks Sigismund of Luxembourg. An identical hat is worn also by the rider behind him, who thus could be Wenceslas IV.

The subject of the meeting of the sovereigns was immensely popular with the illuminators of the *Great Chronicles of France*, because it allowed them to depict the most powerful men on the continent. It is true also of the miniature of the Municipal Library in Besançon MS 863, fol. 413vb from the beginning of the fifteenth century (Pic. 127 / XXXVII). Under No. 863, the catalogue of the Municipal Library in Besançon lists the *Chronique de Saint-Denis*, which corresponds to an earlier idea.[81] The literature has put the manuscript in the first years of the fifteenth century, namely on the basis of the women's costumes, which supposedly preceded the fashion introduced by Queen Isabeau of Bavaria after 1385. The origin of the manuscript can be traced all the way to the collection of Cardinal Granvelle. The illuminations are indisputably the work of one master; according to A. D. Hedeman, his style corresponds to the Master of the Berry Apocalypse.[82] Like with all of the earliest miniatures, the background of the meadow where the meeting took place is only indicated. In

Berry. The Boucicaut Master; the knowledge on the manuscript is on pp. 92–95; on our 'splendid' miniature, see p. 55, Pic. 429.

77/ Hedeman, *The Royal Image*, pp. 210–212.

78/ M. Meiss, *French Painting in the Time of Jean de Berry. The Limbourgs and Their Contemporaries*, p. 25, Note 62 (it also speaks on the Rhinish influences).

79/ Hedeman, *The Royal Image*, pp. 226–228, also containing the details of the depiction.

80/ Jeffrey Hamburger, 'The Casanatense and the Carmelite Missals', pp. 161–171, see p. 166 on this manuscript briefly.

81/ *Catalogue général des manuscrits des bibliothèques publiques de France. Départements*, XXXII (Paris, 1897), pp. 546–547.

82/ Hedeman, *The Royal Image*, pp. 196–197.

terms of depicting landscapes and architecture, Jean Fouquet was peerless, but also the illuminators of the title pages of both the already-mentioned separate copies of the abridged Account from the end of the fifteenth century coped with their tasks in a rather dignified manner. One of these exemplars, which is preserved in the Bibliothèque de l'Arsenal in Paris under MS 5128, was presented in the literature already by Václav Tille. There is little to add to his precise description.[83] The illumination lacks greater significance for historians; its creator did not bother to become more familiar with the text and depicted the emperor as a middle-aged man without a beard. In the landscape with trees, we can see the ruin of a windmill in the centre on a hillock, on the right on a high hill there is a distinct château or castle. Both rulers are just reaching out their hands in a mutual greeting. Dating may be determined on the basis of the fine vegetal décor (red poppies, cornflowers, acorns with leaves).

The second manuscript, MS fr. 5729 in the National Library in Paris, is not only similar to the previous one (ca 220 × 142 mm) for its incipit and explicit but also for its size. The printed catalogue places the book roughly to the fifteenth century.[84] It differs from manuscript No. 5128 in the Bibliothèque de l'Arsenal by its light and undoubtedly also earlier binding, which does not have to mean that both manuscripts would have been created in different workshops. The correspondence of the writer's scribe's execution with the introductory table of contents and initials is astonishing. The same is true for the title miniature, which has a similar conception and composition but differs in its higher quality execution. It is as if this illuminator had created a model for his assistants. It holds true for the landscape, which has more trees (five), we see a ruin instead of the windmill on the hillock in the centre, on the right on a high hill there is a distinct château or castle. Both rulers are just reaching out their hands in a mutual greeting. Charles V is arriving on a white horse; he is wearing a blue cape, with lilies and with an ermine collar, thrown over his red tunic. The head cover has the form which we encounter with Fouquet. Also the four other riders wear caps with indicated crowns. The emperor is arriving on a dark horse; of the horse of Wenceslas IV, only the front hooves are visible. Both Luxemburgs are beardless with long fair hair. The face of Charles IV appears to be somewhat older. On their heads, they have unusual caps with a rosette in the centre. They seem to be for travel, just like their dark clothes with gold orphrey. An answer to the final question of where the interest in this shortened account came from at the end of the fifteenth century has not been answered even by François Avril. However, some satisfactory explanation will certainly appear in the future.

83/ Tille (ed.), 'Francouzský rukopis o cestě císaře Karla IV. do Francie', pp. 1–2; briefly on the manuscript, see Avril, Gousset and Guenée, *Les Grandes Chroniques de France*, p. 280, Note 22.
84/ *Catalogue général des manuscrits français*, V, *Anciens petits fonds français*, Nos. 5526–6710 (Paris, 1902), p. 85. A detailed description taking into consideration the earlier manuscript, Bibliothèque de l'Arsenal MS 5128, was provided by J. Hrubant, 'Pařížské rukopisy o cestě Karla IV. do Francie a Paříže', pp. 362–365.

Understanding the sense of the ostensibly prestigious formalities in the protocol of the imperial visit presupposes a return to the relatively distant past when the theory of the sovereignty of the king of France was emerging step by step on the basis of Roman law. The legal support of the ruler's sovereignty gained in importance in the twelfth century, when the Bolognese and other canonists acknowledged the German emperors' legitimate succession of the Roman emperors and thus also their precedence over other Christian kings. This primacy derived from the Corpus of Civil Law (*Corpus juris civilis*) diverged from political reality already at the time of its creation, such that in 1202 Pope Innocent III in a decree beginning with the words *Per venerabilem* allowed for the interpretation that the kings of France should have supremacy in worldly affairs.

That did not satisfy the French legists. In an attempt to justify the independence of the king of France not only of the emperor but also of the pope, they began to proclaim that his power was of divine origin.[85] The construct of 'royal religion', as the system of sanctifying the power of the French sovereign is sometimes called, was created gradually and reached its zenith at the end of the reign of St Louis IX (1226–1270). Its fundamental element was the liturgy of the anointment preceding the actual coronation, which was ascribed such major significance that the coronation order of Charles V was still labelled as *sacre*. The sanctity connected with this word lay in the transfer of the supernatural power by means of the holy chrism, i.e. a mixture of olive oil and balsam (*crème*), which was according to a legendary tradition miraculously delivered in 496 by the dove of the Holy Spirit to Bishop of Rheims St Remigius in the Holy Ampoule for the baptism of the king. The Holy Ampoule with the chrism was deposited in the Abbey of St Remigius at Rheims, whence the local Abbot would bring it for the coronation.

Through the sacramental anointment, which the archbishop of Rheims performed with a silver spoon, the king of France acquired for himself and indirectly also for his people divine protection and inspiration, namely for life both in this world and the next world. The sanctity of the king's position was further marked by the handover of the royal insignia during a complicated, multi-stage coronation ritual. Whereas the anointment on the forehead, chest, shoulders as well as hands represented, figuratively speaking, a kind of inspiration of supernatural powers, the handover of the insignia symbolised the main attributes of the king's actual power. First of all, the king was given royal attire, because until that time he was present at the ceremony only in an undergarment. The putting on of boots and attaching of spurs was followed by the dressing in an azure coronation mantle decorated with golden fleurs-de-lis. Blue as the colour of the Virgin Mary had been considered perhaps since St Louis as a colour of the kings of France, whereas the sun symbology of the golden fleurs-de-lis was, along with the war banner (Oriflamme), which we will soon discuss in greater detail, was interpreted as a sign connected with heavenly heights.[86]

85/ For more details on that, see Jacques Krynen, *L'empire du roi*, pp. 348–351.

86/ This interpretation was explained by Anne Lombard-Jour-

104. The abbot of the monastery of St Remigius hands the holy ampule to the Archbishop of Rheims before the coronation of Charles V. The Coronation Book of Charles V. (BL, Cotton Tiberius B VIII, fol. 46r)

Whereas in dressing the king was assisted by his secular peers, the royal insignia themselves were handed over by the archbishop of Rheims under the prescribed ritual acts. First the archbishop put the ring on the king's finger, marking his dignity, Catholic faith and perhaps also the marriage which God was concluding with his people through him.[87] It was followed by the sceptre, the symbol of holy power, for the king's right hand, whereas for his left hand the so-called 'hand of justice' (*main de justice*) was intended as a symbol of his sovereign jurisdiction clear to all. Only in the next phase did the placement of the crown come. During this act, the archbishop was assisted by twelve secular and ecclesiastical peers, namely as an echo of the legendary coronation of Charlemagne. The peers then helped the king ascend to the tribune, where the ceremony culminated with the archbishop's kiss and the joint acclamation of *vivat rex* – 'long live the king'. After the offering and the kissing of the archbishop's hand, the new king received the sacrament of Holy Communion in the form of bread and wine.

While some of the contexts of this sacred ritual could be comprehensible only to a handful of the initiated, as a result of which their real role may be questioned, the reception of Communion under both species had long been reserved only for priests by the Church and therefore could on the outside quite clearly suggest the priestly character of royal power. The coronation ritual truly evoked certain similarities with the ordination of ecclesiastical persons. Besides the already mentioned Communion, it was, for example, the anointment of the king on the forehead, which otherwise appertained only to bishops. All of these singular parities or privileges were, however, related only to this particular ceremony and by no means created a special status of king – priest

DAN, *Fleur de lis et Oriflamme*; for the time around 1400, cf. an earlier treatise by Colette BEAUNE, 'Costume et pouvoir en France à la fin du Moyen Âge', pp. 141–146.

87/ This possibility was mentioned by Jacques LE GOFF, *Saint Louis*, p. 830.

105. Charles V on the tribune after the coronation among the prelates and peers. The Coronation Book of Charles V. (BL, Cotton Tiberius B VIII, fol. 40r)

(*rex – sacerdos*). Neither did the kings of France seek this position.[88]

It was somewhat different with the miraculous healing ability, albeit limited to King's Evil – scrofula, which both English and French kings began to tie to themselves in the thirteenth century. It was a gradual and still quite obscure adaptation of the ancient belief in the healing ability of kings, which from the beginning had been limited to one single disease. That disease changed over time. Whereas according to St Jerome the king could miraculously cure leprosy, for the encyclopaedist Saint Isidore of Seville († 636) this 'royal disease' (*morbus regius*) was jaundice. The miraculous healing was not regularly applied until Saint Louis, whereas in the case of his predecessors it was apparently only sporadic incidents.[89]

Not only for the Divine origin of their power but also for the obligatory defence of the church on which they swore during the coronation and which they also performed, the French rulers were 'the most Christian kings' in the eyes of their court theologians and legists. From the beginning, this titling had a predominantly political context. Saint Louis, for instance, was *princeps christianissimus* even for the papal chancellery in 1239 and again six years later. On its part, it was an expression of curial willingness, which was ruined at the end of the century when the ambitions of Pope Boniface VIII (1294–1303) to dominate the world encountered the rock-solid resistance of Philip IV the Fair (1285–1314). In the long-term conflict with Boniface's canonists, Philip's legists amassed a full arsenal of arguments, which when needed could serve also as a justification for

88/ It is explicitly related to kings from the Capetian dynasty by Le Goff, 'Aspects religieux et sacrés de la monarchie française', p. 22; it is even truer for kings from the Valois dynasty.

89/ The fundamental work on the miraculous healing abilities of the English and French kings continues to be the monograph by Bloch, *Les rois thaumaturges*. I have used the edition from 1983 with the foreword by Le Goff, who later also rectified some of Bloch's conclusions and datings in the treatise 'La genèse du miracle royal'.

the sovereignty of the king of France over the Holy Roman Emperor. The label of the most Christian, *christianissimus*, already appeared in common in connection with the king or kingdom of France.[90] The chronicler Guillaume de Nangis, a Benedictine from Saint-Denis, did not leave it at that, stretching the label *christianissimus* to the selected Capetian dynasty and making Saint Louis a new Charlemagne, a king with the image of an emperor, whom as the peacemaker (*auctor pacis*) he placed in sharp opposition to the unworthy, incompetent and treacherous holders of the imperial throne. In the eyes of this chronicler, not only Saint Louis but also his successors *de facto* assumed the role of the emperors in the Christian world. Guillaume de Nangis thus attempted to transfer the empire from Germany to France shortly before the end of the thirteenth century.[91]

Imperial ambitions mainly remained only a pious wish everywhere. Even in spite of its long-term power decline, the universal Roman Empire continued to have its ideological supporters and defenders, including men of such high renown as, e.g. the Italian poet Dante Alighieri (1265–1321)[92]. The French legists had to face them especially under Emperors Henry VII and Louis the Bavarian. When, for example, Henry VII of Luxembourg, a grandfather of 'our' Emperor Charles IV, in connection with his coronation in 1312 made it obvious in writing to the European kings and princes that the Roman Empire is by God's grace superior to all worldly hierarchies, he received an entirely blunt response from Philip IV the Fair: 'The Kingdom of France is in particular dear to Christ and the Church and as such will defend its ancient sovereignty with all its might'.[93] Not only this standpoint but also the other, both the earlier and later proclamations of the sovereignty of France echo the maxim which was expressed in 1302 by the author of the scholarly treatise entitled *Quaestio in utramque partem*: 'Everything that makes an emperor an emperor is no less true for the king of France, who is the emperor in his kingdom.'[94] The Italian lawyers but also the French legists had a lively debate on whether that could be only *de facto*, because only the emperor had unlimited sovereignty *de iure*. It was not a grey theory.

The formula making the French king emperor on his land suited both the last Capetian Charles IV in his dispute with England in 1324 and his successors from the Valois dynasty, who frequently had to assert their majesty against the centrifugal ambitions of the rulers of the border lands. In other words, the equivalence of king – emperor was valid not only in foreign affairs but also in domestic politics, because the shift of sovereign majesty from the emperor to the king entailed the court application of an offence against the dignity of the reigning sovereign (*crimen laesae maiestatis*, 'the crime of injured majesty'), the most serious of all mediaeval crimes. Here everyone, including peers and high aristocrats, had to be on guard because the kings from the Valois dynasty progressively began to derive from their majesty the privilege of changing and issuing independently not only laws but also the decrees of excise tax or currency policy.[95]

The accession of the Valois dynasty in 1328 in essence brought a substitution of the direct line of the Capetians by a branch line, in which to a certain extent the principle of the election of the king was applied again after more than one hundred years.

90/ The evidence is provided by Beaune, *Naissance de la nation France*, pp. 208–211. It is necessary to point out that the expression 'Nation France' in the quotes as well as the title of the book refers to France as a state and not the French 'nation'.

91/ Mireille Chazan, 'Guillaume de Nangis et la translation de l'Empire aux rois de France', esp. pp. 466–468 (Le roi 'très chrétien') and 476–477 (Le roi-empereur).

92/ I refer here to the classic explanation provided by Ernst H. Kantorowicz, *The King's Two Bodies*, Chapter VIII. 'Man-Centered Kingship: Dante'.

93/ This episode along with other evidence of a similar type is presented by Sophie Petit-Renaud, *«Faire loy» au Royaume de France*, pp. 23–25.

94/ 'Quaestio in utramque partem', ed. Melchior Goldast, *Monarchia S. Romani Imperii*, II, p. 98: 'omnia enim pro quae pro imperatore faciunt, valent nihilominus pro rege Franciae, qui imperator est in regno suo'.

95/ For more on that, see Petit-Renaud, *«Faire loy» au Royaume de France*, pp. 37–40.

This circumstance became more significant in connection with the hereditary claims of the young King of England Edward III, whose mother was Isabella, a sister of the last three Capetian kings. The lawyers and scholars disagreed on the question of an election of the sovereign. We shall not go into detail here; it is sufficient to draw attention to the different opinions of two famous theoreticians, John of Jandun and Marsilius of Padua. Whereas the first expressed himself for the hereditary nature of the monarchy, the author of the renowned work *Defensor pacis* preferred the election to the throne. In 1328, not even the chancellor of the Sorbonne John Buridan kept himself aloof, who somewhat hesitantly inclined towards the election of the new king in the commentary to Aristotle's *Politics*. Not even in France did they forget the election to the papal and imperial thrones during these considerations.[96]

Even an elected king of France could through his anointment with the chrism from the Holy Ampoule acquire all of the sacral and thaumaturgical attributes of his sovereignty. Nevertheless, he was obliged to the peers and other barons for his election, which under certain circumstances could lead to a separation of powers. From the introductory outline of the political development, we already know how the defeat and capture of King John II the Good at the Battle of Poitiers made way for the conveners of the estates-general. Things affecting everyone were no longer to be decided only by the king himself, after all absent, and so much the less by the mere members of his council. The idea of the reforms which had hung over Paris for several decades found its theoreticians in the university masters. Speculation on Aristotle's books on politics, morals as well as ethics was their everyday occupation. They were now given a higher mission in the services of the urban communities, which chose them as their delegates at the sessions of the estates-general. This utilisation of scholarly potential when forming active politics was not to be limited to the two-year period of the onset of constitutional monarchy, but exactly this very short stage is among the most remarkable chapters in the history of mediaeval constitutional theories.[97]

It was by no accident that Nicole Oresme, a fresh doctor of theology and head of the College of Navarre, began to deal specifically with coinage and excise tax policy in 1356–1357. Both were at the centre of attention of the strongly dissatisfied urban communities as well as their representatives at the sessions of the estates-general. On the basis of Aristotle's treatises, Oresme *inter alia* proclaimed the famous principle according to which those who were also immediately affected by the issue of coinage were to participate in the decisions on it. And since coins by natural right belonged to urban communities and individual persons, none of their changes, even less so for the worse, were to be the affairs of the sovereign alone. Under certain circumstances, the unstable currency could thus be understood as a manifestation of a tyranny, which, as Oresme warns, usually does not last long.[98]

This passing mention of those emotional years which culminated with the rural Jacquerie and the urban revolt of Étienne Marcel complements the previous explanation, in which the opinions of the theoreticians of the communal authorities were not given much opportunity to be expressed. After 1358, their voices after all lost their resonance in France, although precisely Nicole Oresme soon reached the circle of the dauphin's counsellors. This, however, did not happen until his break with the party of King of Navarre Charles the Bad and until his bitter refusal of the violence which the reform move-

96/ This is again a summary of a complicated issue. For detailed information, see i.a. Kantorowicz, *The King's Two Bodies*, pp. 313–335. For the France of our time, see synoptically Cazelles, *Société politique*, pp. 456–457, and Susan M. Babbitt, *Oresme's 'Livre de Politiques'*, pp. 34–36.

97/ Here I build on the conclusions drawn by Cazelles, *Société politique*, pp. 301–303, and Krynen, *L'empire du roi*, there esp. the chapter 'Aristote au service de la réforme', pp. 419–432.

98/ The tractate was issued by Charles Johnson (ed.), *The 'De moneta' of Nicholas Oresme*; on its interpretation, see Lucien Gillard, 'Nicole Oresme, économiste', pp. 3–39, and Krynen, 'Aristotélisme et réforme de l'État', esp. pp. 228–232.

ment had reached. No matter how unrealistic it may sound, Dauphin Charles on the one hand drowned the uprising in blood and on the other hand did not lose the sense of the intellectual basis for reinforced royal powers. In this he acted like his father, with whom he did not particularly relate. Also John II the Good had endeavoured to overcome his insufficient knowledge of Latin by reading translations, which he himself had instigated. They included novels, morality plays, the Scriptures, and also the *Book of Chess* by Jacobus de Cessolis or the *Decades* of Livy. The translator of the last mentioned work was the Dominican Pierre Bersuire, a friend of Francesco Petrarch's, who visited Paris in 1361 as an ambassador of the duke of Milan. Although Petrarch had no especially great liking for France, his meeting with King John made a surprisingly positive impression on him.[99]

In terms of books and literary education, the apple did not fall far from the tree. All of the literature uncommonly agrees that the attempts to consolidate the royal sovereign power peaked in France exactly under Charles V, namely not only in fact but also through mythology, rituals, ceremonies and last but not least also a broad propaganda campaign. However, so we can finish speaking about the career of Nicole Oresme, we will return to it with a few more sentences. As the secretary as well as chaplain of Dauphin Charles, he served in the College of Navarre until 1362, when he resigned its management to be able to devote himself to his lucrative benefices in Rouen and Paris. In 1377, he became the bishop of Lisieux, and a year later he was appointed by Charles V to the honorary function of the King's Counsellor. In his leisure time, Oresme wrote natural-science as well as other specialised treatises and simultaneously translated Aristotle's treatises on politics, ethics and the economy for the king. He interspersed the translations, which he finished sometime in 1374, with his own commentaries, which reveal his mature

106. Tyranny, oligarchy and democracy. The title page of the translation of Aristotle's Politics and Economics by Nicholas Oresme (Brusel, Bibliothèque royale de Belgique, ms. 11201–2, fol. 1v)

positions on royal power with respect to the desired common weal.

It is of primary interest that not even after twenty years had Oresme changed his opinion on the inadmissibility of a violent uprising, albeit aimed at the implementation of necessary reforms, which however did not entirely slip his mind. He continued to consider the call for reform to be legitimate just like the right of the communities to express their opinion on public affairs and if necessary to guide the ruler. Naturally, such a far-reaching right could not be given to anyone but only to the members of

99/ For more detail on that, see Cazelles, *Société politique*, pp. 39–42; on the meeting with Petrarch, see also Guenée, *Un meurtre, une société*, pp. 75–76.

107. Blessing of the banner of Oriflamme. The Coronation Book of Charles V (BL, Cotton Tiberius B VIII, fol. 73r)

the community known for their virtues and political prudence. And since Oresme explicitly denied these qualities in farmers, craftsmen as well as merchants, it is a question of whom at all he included in this 'reasonable amount' of those who could discuss generally beneficial affairs. As a philosopher and theologian, Oresme loathed the contemporary legists. According to him, they placed the king above the law and with their fabrications of the Divine origin of his majesty reinforced the abuses towards which every power inherently tends. This mild rebuke is worth noting, because we shall soon see what our philosopher meant. Under the protective wing of ancient authority, Oresme then made his supporter on the royal throne consider also opinions which diverged from his political practice and propaganda.[100]

100/ All three of Oresme's translations and commentaries were issued by Albert D. Menut; for our purposes, it is enough to mention the edition *Maistre Nicole Oresme: Le livre de politiques d'Aristote*, which was used in his treatise by Krynen, 'Aristotélisme et réforme de l'État', pp. 229–233. In further detail, although surprisingly without a consideration of Oresme's positions in 1356–1357, the commentaries were dealt with by Babbitt, *Oresme's 'Livre de Politiques'*, there esp. Chapters IV–V.

Since Edward III had not surrendered his hereditary claims to the French throne, the circle of counsellors who were preparing the coronation of Charles V purposefully placed emphasis on all of the traditional elements of the ceremonial ritual. An exceptional source of knowledge here is an illuminated original of the coronation order, which Charles V had made for himself in 1365. What was the point of this commission? Primarily, based on a detailed analysis of the text and the depictions, it seems that the manuscript faithfully, ceremony after ceremony, captured both coronation rituals as a memorial document of its type. I have not yet mentioned that the original codex preserved in the British Library under the shelf mark Cotton Tiberius B. VIII also contains the coronation order of Queen Jeanne of Bourbon. It is precisely the interconnection of the two orders that is one of the innovations to which we will pay attention.[101]

101/ See especially Carra Ferguson O'Meara, *Monarchy and Consent. The Coronation Book of Charles V of France* (2001), including also quality colour reproductions of both painting cycles. The texts of all of the coronation orders of

108. The sceptre of Charles V, before 1380

The most consequential addition was definitely the oath of the inalienability of the rights and dignities of the Crown of France (*iura et nobilitates Corone Francie*). The transpersonal conception of the Crown as an abstract expression of the sovereign's power was quite common even in France.[102] In our case, it entailed the integrity of the territories that was threatened by some of the stipulations of the peace treaty of Brétigny. Although this part of the sworn formula is considered by some scholars as a later addition, the contemporary commentaries suggest its authenticity. Even if Charles V had not done so, in his foremost counsellors' opinion it would have applied anyway that he could not give as a gift or yield when forced the slightest part of the sovereignty and the highest authority appertaining to the Crown of France, which is separate and superior to both him and the kingdom.[103] The second, undisputed innovation was the blessing of the war banner of the French kings with the legendary motif of the flaming gold (the so-called Oriflamme), which was added at the end of the coronation mass in the Cathedral in Rheims. The reverence of this banner, deposited in the Abbey of Saint-Denis, had a long and remarkable history, but it had never before been given such a paramount ceremony. It is worth noting that after the coronation of Charles V and his wife Jeanne the Oriflamme was blessed by the archbishop of Rheims and not the abbot of Saint-Denis. It is as if in this way the Oriflamme became another sign of the heavenly origin of the king's power, especially when in historical consciousness it was connected with the tradition of Charlemagne.[104]

In the case of Dauphin and later King Charles V the Wise, the cult of Charlemagne had a personal tie given by the adopted first name. During the coronation itself, Charlemagne was present through his miniature figure enthroned on top of the sceptre of the new king. As the illuminations in the Coronation Order in the manuscript of the British Library are ascribed great credibility, then it must be so also in the case of several depictions of the sceptre held by Charles V. They all depict a seated Charlemagne but in an execution significantly different from the rarely preserved original sceptre which was last an

the Frankish and French kings have been most recently made accessible in two volumes by Richard A. Jackson, *Ordines Coronationis Franciae.* The coronation orders from 1364–1365 are included in Volume II.

102/ On the exaltation of the Crown of France under John II and Charles V, see Cazelles, *Société politique*, pp. 507–508; on its transpersonal conception, see Krynen, *L'empire du roi*, pp. 125–160.

103/ On the differing opinions in the literature, see O'Meara, *Monarchy and Consent*, pp. 120–121.

104/ On the history of the banner, see Lombard-Jourdan, *Fleur de lis et oriflamme*, pp. 129–207. Attention should be paid to the tripling of the Oriflamme in the final illumination of the painting cycle on fol. 73r, which is explained by O'Meara, *Monarchy and Consent*, pp. 126–127.

embellishment of the exhibition on Parisian art under Charles VI around 1400 (Pic. 108). *Nolens volens*, I must therefore take into account the possibility that Charles V did not have this insignia made until shortly before his death.[105] The artistic accompaniment of the Coronation Order of Charles V has high informative value *inter alia* for its several depictions of the throne and especially of the enthronement itself, which became a new part of the coronation ritual in 1364 as well. Its deeper meaning seems to have laid in the emphasis on parallel with a bishop's ordination. Yet the question is whether the slight differences between the text and the depictions of the relevant parts of the coronation ritual may suggest hidden intentions.[106]

The seemingly petty innovations in the coronation order did not have merely transient importance at the given time, because they were relatively widely popularised in the treatise included by Jean Golein in his translation of the liturgical compendium by Guillaume Durand († 1296). The translation as well as the tractate were created at the commission of Charles V himself, whose deeper interest in the *sacre* is further proved by dozens of manuscripts with copies of domestic as well as foreign coronation orders in his library. In the translation of Durand's *Rationale divinorum officiorum*, the king was most likely interested in the differences in the anointment of the bishops and kings. The canonist Durand strictly adhered to the orthodox explanation of Innocent III and therefore in the case of the king's coronation regardless of the French legend of the Holy Ampoule he speaks *inter alia* only of oil and not of chrism. If what was concerned were details of such a subtle but important nature, it is not surprising that Charles V wanted to have precise edification in this aspect.

The Carmelite Jean Golein (ca 1325–1403) studied theology at the Sorbonne and as the prior

109. Charles V in his library. *Policraticus* by John of Salisbury, and Old French translation by Denis Foullechat (BnF, ms. fr. 24287, fol. 2r)

of a Parisian convent as well as the provincial of his order had close ties to the court. His short treatise must have satisfied the king. In it, the author describes the complicated ceremony step by step, here and there giving his own explanation and indicating the symbolic meaning. At the same time, he does not fail to mention everything that could emphasise the sanctity of the kingdom. In so doing, Golein fulfilled the wishes of the client, but as a theologian he tried to remain within the bounds of orthodoxy. On the one hand, he explicitly states that anointment with the chrism from the Holy Ampoule does not make a king a priest, much less a saint, but on the other hand he allows that the same anointment brings the king closer to the priestly order (*ordre prestal*). In this connection, Golein does not even hesitate to speak of the royal religion.[107]

105/ The reasons for dating it to 1380 are presented by Elisabeth Taburet-Delahaye in the catalogue *Paris 1400*, pp. 38–41.

106/ For more on that, see O'Meara, *Monarchy and Consent*, pp. 128–136.

107/ This is my translation for *religion royale*. On Golein's tractate, see Marc Bloch, *Les rois thaumaturges*, pp. 197–198, 210–211 and especially then Appendix IV on

110. Raoul of Presles dedicates his translation of Augustine's treatise The City of God to King Charles V (BnF, ms. fr. 2292, fol. 3r)

The interest of Charles V the Wise in the mystery of his majesty, in the roots of his dynasty as well as in the rules of successful governance bordered almost on obsession. It was as if Oresme's translations from Aristotle's *Politics* did not suffice him. His advocate Raoul de Presles (1316–1383) first translated for him the collection of polemics and pamphlets from the time of the conflicts between Philip V and Boniface VIII and then in 1372–1375 the famous treatise by St Augustine *De civitate Dei*.[108] The translator, who attained the lucrative function of the Master of Petitions (*Maître des requêtes*), knew well what was expected of him. In the preface to his translation, he summarised the royal chronicle in a few short sentences in the form that it acquired in the years of the reign of Charles V: 'In terms of your birth,' we read here, 'it is certain that you are the son of the king of France, who, as King of France, is the greatest, supreme and most Catholic and most powerful Christian king. In accord with that, you also come from the progeny of the Roman Emperors, who first had the eagle in their symbol. Through the anointment with oil, you are the most august Christian king, because, besides the holy chrism with which you were anointed at birth like every good Christian, you are a sanctified king par excellence, namely thanks to the Holy Ampoule, [...] about which we firmly believe that it was brought from Heaven by the dove of the Holy Spirit for the baptism of King Clovis, the first Christian king. Out of reverence for that great and magnificent mystery, all of the kings of France who have ruled since that time have been consecrated in Rheims with the liquid from this Holy Ampoule. Neither you nor anyone else can assume that this consecration could be possible without this extremely grand and sublime mystery, because precisely through it you have that great power from God to perform miracles in your lifetime and cure the ill of the terrible King's Evil, which none of the earthly rulers with the exception of you can do.'[109]

The individual elements of this saga are already known to us. It is worth noticing that in France especially in the 1370s the elements appear like mushrooms after the rain and that sometimes they emerge even in unsuspected connections. In the relatively known depiction of Charles V in meditation in the library, we are at first sight more captivated by the rotating lectern of a relatively complicated construction than by the blessing hand pointing at the king as God's vicar on earth. Along with the

pp. 478–489. I mainly refer to p. 486, where Golein speaks of the thaumaturgical healing of King's Evil and on the king's receiving Communion under both species.

108/ For more on that, see Lombard-Jourdan, 'À propos de Raoul de Presles'.

109/ At the end, I again slightly shortened the original version. I followed the citation printed by O'Meara, *Monarchy and Consent*, p. 324, Note 32. A contemporary manuscript of the translation with the introductory dedication miniature is preserved in the Bibliothèque Nationale under shelf mark MS fr. 22912.

sentences from Ecclesiasticus 14:22: 'Blessed is the man that shall continue in wisdom, and that shall meditate in his justice', to which Charles V points with his hand as if to justify his label 'the Wise', the blessing hand craftily confronts the tendency of the translated text at the beginning of whose prologue the illumination is placed,[110] namely the *Policraticus* by John of Salisbury († 1180), a very influential and widespread work defending the primacy of ecclesiastical power and its supremacy over the secular rulers. The translation was made in 1372 by the Franciscan friar Denis Foullechat, namely at the commission of Charles V, for whom at the same time Simon de Hesdin was translating Valerius Maximus and Jean de Bourgogne the fictitious travelogue of Sir John Mandeville.[111]

During all of this consolidation and development of the French royal reputation, it was not only about making it special through decoration of the sovereign and the ruling dynasty. It was not possible to forget the English hereditary claims, especially when Charles V even had a second male child. With an innate sense of assiduousness and thoroughness, which he proved *inter alia* during the accumulation of the contracts and other documents before the visit of Emperor Charles IV, he charged his lawyer Évrart de Trémaugon († 1382) with the task to process synoptically the earlier as well as the more recent opinions on the relation between ecclesiastical and secular powers. In France, it went without saying that the focus would be on the current questions related both to the war with England and to the Holy Roman Empire. Évrart, otherwise a professor at the law faculty and Master of the Chamber of the Petitions (*Maître des requêtes*), proceeded systematically, as he was accustomed. To make his compilation more comprehensible, he wrote it in the form of a scholarly dispute between a clergyman and a knight that in the presence of the king himself and the personified characters of the two 'powers' took place as if in his sleep in a fruit orchard. This gave the name to the work, *Dream of the Orchard*, which appeared in the original Latin version (*Somnium Viridarii*) in 1374–1376.[112]

111. The title depiction of the work, Le Songe du Verger (BL, Ms. Royal 19 C IV, fol. 1v)

Charles V had to wait for the French translation (*Le Songe du Vergier*) until the end of 1380.[113] Although at that time the visit of Emperor Charles was already a half-forgotten past, all the more topicality was gained by the dispute between ecclesiastical and secular powers considering the beginning schism. It is quite apparent on the introductory illumination decorating the beautiful vellum manuscript created in 1378 at the king's direct commission.[114] The scene

110/ Based on the caption in Beaune, *Les manuscrits des rois de France au Moyen Âge*, p. 18.

111/ The individual exemplars are listed in the catalogue *La Librairie de Charles V*, pp. 87–119.

112/ A critical edition was prepared for print in two volumes by Marion Schnerb-Lièvre, *Somnium Viridarii*, I–II.

113/ Also the French translation was issued by Schnerb-Lièvre, *Le Songe du Vergier*, I.

114/ The manuscript from Charles V's library ended up in London as the British Library MS Royal 19 C IV.

takes place in a marvellous garden, which in the period symbolic language began to symbolise 'sweet France'.[115] In accord with the prologue of the work, in which Évrart placed in the king's mouth the declaration 'I am God's earthly representative', Charles V in the fullness of his majesty sits on the throne as a judge between the contending ladies, who personify ecclesiastical and secular powers. In the bottom plan, we can see the dreaming author and the two protagonists of the scholastic joust, the cleric and the knight. From the orchard dotted with flowers, where game also do well, a spring issues in accordance with the idea that the source of all the sciences is in Paris and in France. The orchard is surrounded by two alleys symbolising the king's two sons. Pope Clement VII, whose Franciscan habit is worn by the ecclesiastical power, has nothing to fear in France; on the contrary, he will be in comfortable safety here.

As against the Latin version, the French translation differs in the length, number of chapters, internal organisation and partially also a shift in the doctrinal effect, because not only Nicole Oresme, at that time Bishop of Lisieux, but also other scholars from around the king had sharply criticised the original *Somnium viridarii*. Évrart de Trémaugon accepted the comments and in a revised French version deepened the conception of the sovereignty of France so comprehensibly that his *Dream of the Orchard* for a long time became an instrument of the French state propaganda of the Valois dynasty.[116] The dispute between the theologians and the legists on the nature of the anointment during the *sacre* was resolved acceptably for both sides here. The *sacre* no longer makes a king a king, and neither does anointment add anything to his power, which is already by its essence of Divine origin, but they both increase the shine, dignity as well as the honour of the majesty of the king of France in the eyes of the people.[117] *Le Songe du Vergier* in this way transformed into an apology of the king's power both inside and outside of France. Évrart de Trémaugon through his late work for many definitively excluded any kind of subordination of France to the Holy Roman Emperors on the one hand and to the popes in Avignon or Rome on the other. In 1378, the sovereignty of France had already been firmly anchored in the minds as well as on the parchment. This was the atmosphere during the visit of the emperor and the King of the Romans. All of the prestigious questions of a ceremonial nature captured in the Account of the *Great Chronicles of France* have now been given a deeper meaning.

115/ For more on that, see C. Beaune, *Naissance de la nation France*, pp. 318–322 (Le jardin de France).

116/ On that, see i.a. Jean-Pierre Royer, *L'Église et le Royaume de France au XIV*e *siècle d'après le «Songe du Vergier»*, p. 225.

117/ This shift in the conception of the power of the French king was described especially by Cazelles, *Société politique*, pp. 348–351.

In *Le livre des fais et bonnes meurs du sage roy Charles V par Christine de Pisan* (*Book of the Deeds and Good Morals of the Wise King Charles V*), Christine de Pisan placed special emphasis on the rules and relevant customs of private as well as public life, typical for the government of her favourite and revered ruler. The desired ideal is expressed by the key words 'beautiful orchestration' (*belle ordonnance*).[118] We would have expected to learn more in this regard from the chapters that she dedicated to the visit of Emperor Charles IV. Christine, however, as I have indicated elsewhere, more or less only provided an abridged paraphrase of the longer version of the Account of the *Great Chronicles of France*, although she must have also had other testimonies available. She mentions them herself in the chapter where she recapitulates the importance of the emperor's visit.[119] We shall thus begin our own search during which we shall first attempt to penetrate the relatively complicated power and administrative mechanism of France shortly before 1380.

In several places in this book, the well-worn phrase 'flowers of the lilies' (*fleurs-de-lis*) has already been mentioned. After the time of Saint Louis, the king of France had never had so many relatives as precisely under Charles V of Valois. The men, women and children of royal blood created through their mutually intertwined family relations a rather wide and internally structured community. The closest to the king, if we omit Queen Jeanne of Bourbon and the two as-yet minor sons, Charles and Louis, were his brothers (Pic. 112). The oldest, Louis, Duke of Anjou, a man of high ambitions, preferred his personal interests in Languedoc during the emperor's visit, and therefore we can leave him out of consideration.[120] On the other hand, neither of the other

112. Jean Golein presents to Charles V and Joanne de Bourbon his translation of the work by Guglielmo Durando, Rationale divinorum officiorum. It is a rare depiction of the royal family. Next to the king, there stand the sons Dauphin Charles and Duke Louis de Orleáns, at the side of the queen are the daughters Marie (1370–1377) and Isabella (1373–1377) (BnF, ms. fr. 437, fol. 1r)

118/ For an apt description of that, see Strubel, 'Le «chevauchier» de Charles V', esp. pp. 386–389.

119/ See Solente (ed.), *Le livre des fais et bonnes meurs*, II, pp. 131–132. I will present unique additions concerning the Account, e.g. the information on the reward for the imperial chancellor, continuously in the following excursuses.

120/ For an attempt to explain the reasons for his absence, see Françoise Lehoux, *Jean de France, duc de Berri, sa vie,*

113. / XXII. Duke John of Berry and Duke Philip of Burgundy on the way to the emperor (BL, Ms. royal 20 C VII, fol. 196va)

114. / XXIII. Meeting of the Duke of Bar with the emperor and his son (BL, Ms. royal 20 C VII, fol. 196vb)

brothers, the dukes John I of Berry and Philip II the Bold of Burgundy missed the unique occasion of the emperor's visit (Pic. 113 / XXII). Particularly for the duke of Berry, it was a singular opportunity to distinguish himself as the second man of France.[121] Both princes, along with their brothers-in-law, the 'good' Duke Louis II of Bourbon and Robert I, Duke of Bar, assumed the roles of the royal plenipotentiaries during the various ceremonial acts of court protocol (Pic. 114 / XXIII).[122]

All four belonged to the *fleurs-de-lis*, whereas the feudal lords of the second circle of the royal extended family (predominantly the counts) were in the court hierarchy still a level below. Of these, we will be primarily interested in the two Johns that we already know from the Account. John of Artois, Count of Eu (1321–1387), was the king's direct cousin, whereas John VI of Harcourt (1342–1388) was married to Catherine of Bourbon, a sister of Queen Jeanne.[123] The wider royal relatives also included another John, Jean (II), Viscount of Melun and Count of Tancarville (ca 1318–1382), who could not be absent from the confidential proceedings of the King's Grand Council with the two Luxemburgs.[124] The members of this council naturally were also the highest prelates of the kingdom, who in special cases even appear

son action politique (1340–1416), I, p. 408. He also seems not to have liked the French-Hungarian courtship being conducted then, which took him out of play in the Kingdom of Naples.

121/ For an explicit example of that opinion, see Lehoux, *Jean de France*, pp. 408–413; regarding Philip the Bold, the biography by Richard Vaughan, *Philip the Bold. The Formation of the Burgundian State*, does not devote much attention to the imperial visit, but we know from his accounts that he also did not take this exceptional occasion lightly.

122/ On the participation of Duke Louis II of Bourbon, see Olivier Troubat, *La Guerre de Cent Ans et le Prince Chevalier*, pp. 643–647.

123/ Both men were so significant that they were mentioned in *Lexikon des Mittelalters*, IV, col. 64 (John of Artois) and col. 1931 (John VI of Harcourt).

124/ On the influential position of this Norman feudal lord already under John II the Good, see *Lexikon des Mittelalters*, VIII, cols 454–455.

before dukes and counts in the documents.[125] Six of them were traditionally among the twelve 'peers', i.e. the archbishop of Rheims and the bishops of Beauvais, Noyon, Châlons-sur-Marne, Laon and Langres. In the election of the sovereigns and in other state ceremonies of the highest importance, the peers most likely fulfilled a role similar to that of the electors in the Empire. The peers are not mentioned in the Account of the *Great Chronicles of France*, so we do not have to speculate which of the secular dignitaries were adorned with the title of peer.[126]

The welcome given to the emperor in Saint-Denis (Pic. 115 / XXXI) which was reserved for the ecclesiastical aristocracy, was attended by not only Archbishop of Rheims Richard Picque but also three other peers, namely Miles II de Dormans, Bishop of Beauvais (1375–1387),[127] Gilles de Lorris, Bishop of Noyon (1352–1388), and Pierre Aycelin de Montaigu, Bishop of Laon (1371–1385).[128] In Saint-Denis, the emperor was awaited by still further prelates, namely Guillaume de Lestrange, Archbishop of Rouen, further his colleague from Sens Adhémar Robert (1376–1385), seven bishops, whom we will soon mention, and Jean VI Le Fèvre († 1390), who had been abbot of the important Abbey of Saint-Vaast in Arras since 1370.[129] The Account mentions the bishops in the order which undoubtedly corresponded to the protocol. Bishop of Paris Aimery de Magnac (1368–1385) appears in first place,[130] followed by Nicolas Du Bosc, also Du Boi, Bishop of Bayeux (1375–1408);[131] Nicole Oresme, already well-known to us, had been the bishop in Lisieux only since 1377 but is named before Guillaume IV de Dormans, Bishop of Meaux, and before Bernard de Caritis, Bishop of Évreux. Another of the prelates was the chancellor's son Pierre II d'Orgemont (1343–1409), Bishop in Thérouanne from 1374; the group of bishops is then concluded by Doctor of Laws Bernard Palot, holder of the episcopal throne in Condom. According to the author of the Account of the *Great Chronicles of France*, all of these bishops were members of the King's Grand Council. Whether they all attended the session on Friday, 8 January 1378, is not entirely certain, because the Account on this occasion mentions only the archbishop of Rheims, the bishops of Laon, of Paris, of Beauvais, and of Bayeux, and the abbot of Saint-Vaast.

The appropriate arrangement (*ordo Franciae*) in the sense of the political and power hierarchy had already clearly come to the surface and would have indubitably suited even Christine de Pisan. The third circle is comprised of further counts, barons and large-scale landowners (*grands terriens*), without royal blood and the highest ecclesiastical dignitaries yet with an influential position at the royal court. It is significant how differently they were addressed by the king in his letters. Most familiarly, Charles V addressed his siblings, who were his 'very dear and very beloved' (*très cher et très amé*) brother(s). The cousins and relatives on their level were also 'very dear', but only 'beloved' or 'faithful' (Old French *féal*). The rest, albeit barons and high court officials, were only 'our beloved and faithful'.[132] Of the counts (*comtes*) whose names have not been heard here yet, the ceremonial welcome of the emperor on 4 January 1378 was further attended by the member of the Council Charles de Trie, Count of Dammartin, and Marshal

125/ It is so in several documents from the period of John II the Good; see Contamine, 'Essai sur la place des «XII pairs»', pp. 61–62.

126/ Both of the king's brothers, Duke John of Berry and Duke of Burgundy Philip the Bold, were undoubtedly peers; also the dukes of Bourbon were usually titled as peers. For more on that, see Contamine, 'Essai sur la place des «XII pairs»', pp. 62 and 66. This treatise is complemented in some points by the entry 'Pairs de France' prepared by Élisabeth Lalou for *Lexikon des Mittelalters*, VI, cols 1627–1628.

127/ On his numerous posts, see Lalou, *Lexikon des Mittelalters*, III, col. 1317.

128/ See Cazelles, *Société politique*, p. 478.

129/ For his achievements in the king's services, the lawyer Jean Le Fèvre became Bishop in Chartres in 1380. For more on his career, see Cazelles, *Société politique*, p. 349.

130/ See Cazelles, *Société politique*, pp. 482–483.

131/ For more on him, see Cazelles, *Société politique*, pp. 548–549.

132/ These subtle but nevertheless telling differences in the ways of addressing were pointed out by Autrand, *Charles V. Le Sage*, pp. 655–656.

115. / XXXI. Arrival of Emperor Charles IV at the Abbey of Saint-Denis. Les Grandes Chroniques de France, illumination by Jean Fouquet (BnF, ms. fr. 6465, fol. 442r)

of France (*maréchal de France*) Louis de Sancerre (1340?–1403).[133] In this connection, the Account names also John IV, Count of Salm (1368–1381), and Counts John II of Boulogne, Jean II of Grandpré and Jean I de Châtillon of Porcien, who have not been further identified.

It would take us far into the past if we wanted to understand the differences between the Bohemian and French administrative systems. It may suffice to say briefly that in France we do not find such sharply defined powers of the so-called land and court offices. It was partially given by the much earlier formation of the administrative bodies in France than here, which sometimes disappeared, other times assumed other tasks while retaining their old label. An example here can be immediately two of the five highest offices (*grands officiers*) of a crown nature. The first was the formerly important office of the seneschal (*sénéchal* from the Latin *senescalcus*), which held ground in the duchies, counties and other territories that had fallen to France during the twelfth and thirteenth centuries. It is enough to mention here among others Normandy, Maine, Anjou, Poitou, Limousin and Languedoc.[134] In these administrative

133/ The count of Dammartin is listed as a member of the Council by Contamine, *Guerre, État et société*, p. 61, which contains also the biographical data on Louis de Sancerre on pp. 587–589.

134/ On the office of the seneschal in France and Western Europe, see the entry 'Seneschall' in *Lexikon des Mittel-*

units, seneschals exercised court and other powers for the overlords, in the second half of the fourteenth century mainly the king's brothers and brothers-in-law, who had their 'appanages' there.[135] In his own domain, the king was represented by so-called *baillis* (from the Latin *ballivus*), whom we could label according to the circumstances as governors or regents. During the emperor's visit, they were apparently not given any special tasks, and therefore we can leave them out of consideration.[136]

The second ancient office, which had an analogy elsewhere in the offices of the so-called butler (*pincerna*), has remained here but with the title complemented as *bouteiller de France* became an explicitly honorific dignity. The actual execution of the office shifted to the court high cupbearer (*maitre-échanson*) and his subordinate cupbearers. However, what we must be interested in is the fact that Charles V entrusted this honorific office to John II, Count of Saarbrücken († 1381), who was also President of the Chamber of Accounts (*Chambre des comptes*), chamberlain and member of the King's Council. He was the king's man and a friend for rainy days; he was the only counsellor remaining from 1360, led the negotiations with the English and prepared the journey of Emperor Charles IV.[137]

A relatively complicated transformation was experienced also by the third of the highest crown offices, for which the title *chambrier de France* became established. We will have problems finding an English equivalent as the meaning approaches the expressions *chambellan* and *valet de chambre*. For the second service, the apt label is 'footman', but as the office was performed mostly by pages and lower aristocrats, I have used for them the title 'valet'. For *chambellan*, I have selected the term 'chamberlain', which creates the impression of a higher-placed official. Concerning the term *chambrier*, it appears quite frequently with the adjective *grand*, thus we could say the high chamberlain, which also distinguishes this office from the Office of the First Gentlemen of the Chamber, as we will translate the French phrase of *premier chambellan*. We will not taint anything in this approach, because the Office of the High Chamberlain already under Charles V had the character of an honorific, albeit lucrative title. It was taken advantage of by Duke Louis II of Bourbon, who was thus the second highest official of the kingdom engaged in the preparation of the visit of Emperor Charles IV.[138]

The remaining two highest officials had a real, and not small, share in the executive power, which in the case of the constable, we would say the commander-in-chief of the armed forces, goes without saying in a period of an ongoing military conflict with England. We also already know his name from the Prologue as well as the Epilogue. From October 1370, it was the famous warrior Bertrand du Guesclin, who however during the emperor's visit was leading a military operation in Normandy.[139] That leaves the Office of the Chancellor (*le Chancellier de France*), whose holders stood at the peak of the state administration under the kings from the Valois dynasty. Their authority was not limited only to the chancellery, which ensured the drawing of the legal and administrative decrees and the further

alters, VII, cols 1751–1754; for France in an outline, see also Lot and Fawtier, *Histoire des institutions françaises*, II, p. 52.

135/ For the essential information, see the entry 'Apanage' in *Lexikon des Mittelalters*, I, cols 741–742; on the new statute of appanages under Charles V, see Autrand, *Charles V. Le Sage*, pp. 661–664, and also Autrand, *Jean de Berry. L'art et le pouvoir*, Chapter XV.

136/ How the duties involved in this post transformed in the Late Middle Ages was dealt with by Robert-Henri Bautier in the entry 'Bailli, bailliage', *Lexikon des Mittelalters*, I, cols 1356–1357.

137/ On the office itself, see the entry 'Bouteiller' in *Lexikon des Mittelalters*, II, cols 518–519. John II of Saarbrücken (in French Sarrebruck) received numerous goods from the king, which after his death returned to the Crown. Cazelles, *Société politique*, on p. 546 mentions that he was in charge of the preparation of the emperor's visit.

138/ Cf. the entries 'Chambellan' and 'Chambrier' in *Lexikon des Mittelalters*, II, cols 1671 and 1677. We shall learn more about the complicated system of French royal finances in the last study, Excursus – The Final Account of the Expenditures of the King's Treasury.

139/ For a recent source, see the extensive biography by G. Minois, *Du Guesclin*; the essential data and literature are listed in *Lexikon des Mittelalters*, III, cols 1440–1442.

written agenda.[140] The chancellors gradually acquired their exceptional position in all three of the bodies of assembly (*assemblées*), i.e. in the King's Council, in the Supreme Court of Justice (*parlement*) and in the Chamber of Accounts. In all of these bodies, in some of which the interests of the estate components were implemented more and in some of which less, the eminent feudal lords and prelates were in session, but they did not perform their honorary posts regularly, so the burden of the agenda lay on the royal confidants on the one hand and on the advocates, clerks and other administrative officials on the other.

When the king was absent or ill, the chancellor as the representative of the king had a position to such an extent superior that it was desirable for his appointment to be an issue of a wider consensus. It was probably for that reason that Charles V, himself a great admirer of Aristotelian principles of proper administration, for the first time in February 1372 acceded to the election of the new holder of the chancellor's office, vacated by the abdication of Jean de Dormans. The King's Grand Council, numbering two-hundred persons, elected as the successor his brother Guillaume de Dormans, who however died already on 11 July 1373. The guardian of the seal again became Jean de Dormans, this time only for a short time, because on 7 November of the same year he followed his brother into eternity. The new election took place in the Louvre on 20 November, namely with the attendance of the princes of the royal family, the prelates, the barons, the representatives of the supreme court of justice and other court offices. The election confirmed as chancellor Pierre d'Orgemont († 1389), a reliable official, diplomat and long-term member of the King's Council, who received 105 of the 130 votes.[141]

The diversion into the apparatus of the power mechanism of the French state under Charles V was hopefully not a waste of time, especially when what was concerned was the nomination of the man who was the author of the Account of the *Great Chronicles of France* and on whose shoulders lay the diplomatic, protocolary and organisational preparation of the emperor's visit at the turn of 1378.

As the direct representative of the king, Pierre d'Orgemont opened the sessions of the supreme court of justice, actively participated in the appointment of its officials, presented the king's orders (*ordonnances*) and *inter alia* supervised their proper registration. The French title of this institution (*parlement*) is quite confusing, because we would expect parliament to refer to the representative assembly of the estates. Even so, the supreme court of justice in its three chambers associated almost one-hundred members of the secular as well as ecclesiastical estates including the procurator, advocates and executors of court judgements, i.e. judicial bailiffs (*huissiers de justice*).[142] We do not have to go into further detail here, because according to the daily records of the court registers the supreme court had a few days off starting on Monday, 21 December 1378, to ensure everything necessary for the reception of the emperor and his retinue. For the entire time until 12 January 1378, the supreme court of justice hence performed only the duties connected with the state visit, and on the feast of the Epiphany and the day before the Palace de la Cité was entirely closed for the uninvited.[143] It had been necessary to vacate the so-called King's Grand Chamber (*Grand Chambre*) especially, where the four presidents and thirty members of the most influential chamber of the supreme

140/ From the earlier literature on the chancellery, see Lot and Fawtier, *Histoire des institutions françaises*, II, pp. 85–96 and Georges Tessiers, *Diplomatique royale française*; selected bibliography of the more recent literature was presented by Bautier in the entry on Chancelier, chancellerie, in *Lexikon des Mittelalters*, II, cols 1691–1696.

141/ On the office of the chancellor and his election, see Lot and Fawtier, *Histoire des institutions françaises*, II, pp. 60–65; on the first elections of the chancellors, see Cazelles, *Société politique*, pp. 509–510; on the career of Chancellor Pierre d'Orgemont, see *Lexikon des Mittelalters*, VI, cols 1452–1453.

142/ Synoptic and precise instruction was provided by Autrand in the entry 'Parlement', *Lexikon des Mittelalters*, VI, cols 1731–1733.

143/ These daily records were reprinted by Moranvillé, *Étude sur la vie de Jean le Mercier*, pp. 59–60.

116. Convocation of the parliament in the presence of Charles V. The king is seated under the baldachin on his legendary throne (lit), at his feet are the chancellor with a scroll and the constable with a sword; on the right in two rows of benches, the secular, on the left ecclesiastical members of the parliament, on the opposite side, the lay counsellors sit on benches. Bartélemy l'Anglais, Le livre des propriété des choses (BnF, ms. fr. 22532, fol. 9r)

court of justice sat. This spacious impressive room, in which the homonymous great chamber was often presided over by the king himself, was adjacent to the Great Hall and *inter alia* allowed passage to the private wing of the palace. Also the other two bodies, the Chamber of Inquiries (*Chambre des enquêtes*) and the Chamber of Petitions (*Chambre des requêtes*), had areas reserved for them in the palace, but these were not necessary to be made available.[144]

The members and officials of the supreme court of justice represented the court elite by their education, influence and often also their origin or family ties and, last but not least, also by their group self-awareness.[145] Since 1366, its four presidents had been elected by the King's Grand Council, to which most of them also belonged. After the acces-

144/ The *Chambre des enquêtes* had its own building for its forty members in the northeast wing of the Palace de la Cité; the eight Masters of Petitions (*maîtres des requêtes*) mainly met directly in the king's residence of Saint-Pol. On both, see Guérout, 'L'hôtel du roi au Palais de la Cité', pp. 270–271.

145/ For details on that based on a prosopographic analysis, see Autrand, *Naissance d'un grand corps de l'État. Les gens du Parlement de Paris (1345–1454)*.

sion of the Valois dynasty, almost all of the foremost representatives of the state and court bodies came to be members of the King's Grand Council (*conseillers*); under John II the Good, this applied also to his favourites from among the burgher financiers. Numerous provincial seneschals, regents (*baillis*) and large-scale landowners were more or less titular councillors, who mostly did not attend the sessions of the Grand Council.[146] We could already form a rough idea of the size of the King's Grand Council based on the number of 130 to 200 votes in the election of the chancellors.

The huge ransom which had to be paid for the imprisoned King John II the Good as well as for other prisoners of royal blood from the Battle of Poitiers, further also the growing war expenditures and the implementation of a far-reaching coinage reform necessitated the establishment of two new colleges in 1360. The mission of the first of them, associating the treasurers-general for the ransom (*généraux trésoriers pour la rançon*), is clear from its name. The second, twelve-member, college of the so-called counsellors-general (*conseillers généraux*) was responsible for the defence of the country, and, since it also decided on the expenditures from the war and other excise taxes, it to a certain extent also controlled the economy of the court.[147]

The majority of the treasurers-general and counsellors-general were members of the King's Grand Council or had access to it. *Via facti*, it came to be that the influence of these two colleges began to limit the king's sovereign power in the affairs of defence and finances. When these officials began to use the formulation '*De par le roy*' (in the sense of 'at the king's command') in the written dispositions for decrees of their own initiative, Charles V responded

117. Bureau de La Rivière († 1400), the first gentleman of the chamber of Charles V, one of the organisers of the imperial visit of Paris. A statue on the so-called Beautiful Pillar: of the cathedral in Amiens

to it by beginning to sign his actual orders himself.[148] This seemingly marginal procedure suggests that the so-emphasised theory of the sovereignty of the king of France had alarming cracks in practice. Beginning in 1374, Charles V step by step took the counsellors-general out of play, circumvented them or divested them of their lucrative office, as was the case with Jean de Melun, otherwise the Count of Tancarville, who lost chief supervision of the forest and water husbandry of the royal domain. Neither did the king forget his diseases, and therefore in the interest of his minor heir he created around himself a narrow council comprised of his confidants, who would, should he die, stand as custodians at the side of the queen and the regents from among the *fleurs-de-lis*.[149]

146/ An overview of the gradual transformation of the King's Council was presented by Bautier in the entry 'Conseil A. Conseil du roi', *Lexikon des Mittelalters*, III, cols 145–150; for the early period of the reign of Charles V, see Cazelles, *Société politiques*, pp. 466–467.

147/ For details on both colleges, see Cazelles, *Société politique*, pp. 478–487.

148/ For more on that, see again Cazelles, *Société politique*, pp. 490–493.

149/ Valuable observations on the King's Council under

Nearly all of the members of the King's Grand Council who appear in the documents of the second half of the 1370s were among the long-term and reliable confidants of Charles V. Almost all of them were also engaged in the preparation of the emperor's visit. We have already spoken of John II, Count of Saarbrücken; a no less significant position was held also by Bureau de la Rivière († 1400), the king's first gentleman of the chamber (*premier chambellan*), who had already been in the services of Charles V since 1358 and who had acquitted himself well as a knight banneret, diplomat as well as the captain (*capitaine*) of the fortress in Vincennes. Charles V therefore entrusted him without hesitation with the responsibility for the protection of Emperor Charles IV and his retinue and most likely placed him in charge also of other tasks arising from the ceremonial protocol.[150] Another man from this close circle was Jean Le Mercier, who had been the counsellor-general for exceptional excise taxes from 1374, and who, interestingly enough, participated at the king's behest in the protection of Beatrice of Bourbon, the widow of John of Luxembourg (of Bohemia).[151] During the emperor's visit, Jean Le Mercier had similar tasks to those of Johann of Saarbrücken and Bureau de la Rivière. Among the secular members of the King's Grand Council, the Account further mentions Count Simon de Roucy et de Braine, and Pierre de Chevreuse († 1393). Both were counsellors-general for exceptional excise taxes, Pierre moreover Master of the Royal Household.[152]

The Account names the other members of the Grand Council who met the emperor among the attendees of the plenary session of both delegations in the Louvre on 8 January 1378. Not only his position but also his proximity to the king brought First President of the Supreme Court of Justice Arnaud de Corbie here, who was to have a great career as the Chancellor of Charles VI in the following years.[153] The warrior Jacques de Bourbon appeared less in the foreground,[154] whereas the name of one of the Marshals of France Jean de Mauquenchy called Mouton de Blainville occurs relatively often in the sources.[155] Also knight Thomas de Voudenay († 1380) earned his spurs on the battlefield, whereas Philibert de l'Espinace († before 1395), otherwise one of the eight Masters of Petitions, despite his not being of very noble birth asserted himself in important deliberations.[156] Lord Jean de Rayneval, for whom the Account does not even list his first name, remains a little of an enigmatic figure.[157]

The members of the Grand Council included even Enguerrand VII of Coucy († 1397), one of the large-scale landowners, who in spite of his relatively young age acquired such military renown in Prussia as well as in Italy that Charles V entrusted him with the responsible task of ensuring the emperor's safety for his entire stay on French soil.[158] Along with him, as has already been mentioned, this task was fulfilled by Count Johann of Saarbrücken and Count Simon de Roucy et de Braine. Charles V designated as the emperor's bodyguard six of his chamberlains led by First Gentleman of the Chamber Bureau de la Rivière. At the end of the reign of Charles V, the title of

Charles V were published by Autrand, 'Un certain sens de l'État: les conseillers de Charles V', where there is also on p. 345 a mention of the king's testament of 1374.

150/ Concise biographical information was presented by Autrand in the entry 'Rivière, Bureau de la', *Lexikon des Mittelalters VII*, cols 881–882.

151/ The basis of our knowledge continues to be Moranvillé, *Étude sur la vie de Jean le Mercier*; on the fate of the widow Beatrice, see Troubat, 'Béatrix de Bourbon, reine de Bohême', esp. pp. 269–271.

152/ For brief information on both men, see Cazelles, *Société politique*, p. 548.

153/ He is listed among the confidants of Charles V by Cazelles, *Société politique*, p. 546.

154/ Contamine, *Guerre, État et société*, on p. 580 mentions him as a cousin of Jacques de Bourbon, Count de la Marche.

155/ The data on him were gathered by Contamine, *Guerre, État et société*, pp. 565–566, where also the judicial authority of the Marshals in military and war affairs is covered on pp. 199–201.

156/ For more on both of these members of the Council, see Delachenal (ed.) *Chronique des règnes*, II, p. 250, Notes 1–2; on the Burgundian knight Philibert, see also Cazelles, *Société politique*, p. 348.

157/ He is listed as Jean de Rayneval by Maurice Rey, *Les finances royales Charles VI. Les causes du déficit 1388–1413*, p. 407.

158/ On the career of Enguerrand of Coucy, see Contamine, *Guerre, État et société*, pp. 573–574.

chamberlain was held by a total of forty-five lords and knights, who alternated in the service of the king, so that not all of them stayed at the court simultaneously. During such an exceptional occasion as the visit of the emperor and his son was, everyone was on alert, and therefore the same number of six chamberlains comprised the bodyguard of Charles V and of Holy Roman Emperor Charles IV, with four others being designated for King of the Romans Wenceslas IV.

Of the sixteen chamberlains, the Account names only seven including Lord de la Rivière. Charles of Poitiers, a descendant of the dynasty of the counts of Valentinois and Diois, had already acquired the title of chamberlain in 1364. As chance would have it in the same year, also Guillaume des Bordes, an exceptional warrior and standard-bearer of the Oriflamme, became a chamberlain († 1397).[159] According to the record in the *Mémoire*, chamberlain Guillaume des Bordes led the horse of King Wenceslas by the bridle during the entry to the Palace de la Cité. From the other side, Wenceslas' horse was held by another chamberlain, Adam de Galonguet, otherwise unknown to me.[160] The three remaining chamberlains of the seven whose names we know were at the same time military captains (*capitaines*) of important castle and other garrisons. Hutin de Vermeilles was in charge of guarding the fortress in Vivier-en-Brie for an annual salary of 300 gold francs.[161] Jean de Berguettes served the king in Normandy, were he was captain of the castle in Vatteville. It is necessary to understand the chamberlain by the name le Barrois as Jean de Barres (i.e. of Bar), who also served the king for many years in arms.[162] The bodyguard of the three monarchs comprised another ten officers of the palace guard (*huissiers d'armes*), on whom we will speak later.

We have crossed almost imperceptibly the imaginary and yet still quite permeable line between the feudal lords listed by name and unnamed servants. In the records of an accounting or other nature, we here and there encounter the names of other persons engaged in the preparation and organisation of the emperor's visit, but we no longer find them on the pages of the Account or *Mémoire*.

A reconstruction of the organisational preparation of the summit of the three crowned heads in January 1378 is complicated by the onerous lack of sources. For the period of the reign of Charles V, neither the court orders (*ordonnances*) nor the accounts of the court offices have been preserved. The earlier ordinances from the period of the last Capetians were not in force forever, the later ordinances from the beginning of the reign of Charles VI are incomplete on the one hand and not always authoritative for the previous period on the other.[163] To be able to form an idea of the multitude of court personnel of higher as well as lower ranks, it is first necessary to mention that according to rough estimates the *curia regis* for 1380 numbered between 700 and 800 persons including the personal servants of the higher-ranking officials. To that, we have to add approximately 200 other servants at the independent court of the queen and her children. Not all of them stayed in the Palace de la Cité, in the Louvre or in the residence at Saint-Pol every day, because the higher-placed courtiers alternated in service. At the time of the emperor's visit, as it can easily be imagined, the demands for personnel increased so much that every helping hand was needed.

The king's court, which in France is traditionally called the *Hôtel* or *Maison du roi*, was an institution as old as the monarchy itself and included all the offices and services without which the sovereign as

159/ See Contamine, *Guerre, État et société*, pp. 567–568.
160/ On that, cf. Thomas, 'Ein Zeitgenössisches Memorandum', pp. 106–107 and 116–117.
161/ Cf. Delisle (ed.), *Mandements et actes divers*, p. 780, No. 1566.
162/ He is named among the captains of 1369 by Contamine, *Guerre, État et société*, p. 166; the data on all three of the last-named chamberlains were accumulated already by Delachenal (ed.), *Chronique des règnes*, II, p. 219, Note 1.

163/ For the earlier period, see Lalou, 'Les ordonnances de l'hôtel des derniers Capétiens directs', esp. pp. 96–101; the sources from the beginnings of Charles VI's reign were last registered by Guérout, 'L'hôtel du roi au Palais de la Cité', pp. 267–268. For the latest on the issue of research with respect to court customs and orders, see Carqué, *Stil und Erinnerung*, pp. 385–397.

the representative of the Crown as well as a private person could not do,[164] first of all the officials and servants of the so-called King's Chamber (*Chambre du roi*). We have already become acquainted with the highest of them, beginning with the Constable and ending with the Chancellor. This group also comprised both of the Marshals of France mentioned above (Louis de Sancerre and Jean de Mauquenchy called Mouton de Blainville), Admiral Jean de Vienne († 1396),[165] Grand Master of Arbalesters (*grand maitre des arbalétriers*) Hue de Châtillon († 1390)[166] and standard-bearer of the Oriflamme, from 1372 Pierre de Villiers, otherwise Grand Master of the Royal Household (*grand maitre*, or *souverain maître de l'Hôtel*), who stood at the head of the court precisely in 1377–1378.[167] This high dignity reserved for members of an important aristocratic family did not require special organisational skills, because this dignitary had several Masters of the Royal Household at hand. One of them was, as we already know, Pierre de Chevreuse; the same post was also occupied by the already-mentioned Jean Le Mercier. Shortly after the death of Charles V, there were twelve Masters of the Royal Household, but we have to bear in mind that they alternated in service after a few months, which also applied to other court officials and servants.[168] The secretary Philip Ogier († 1381), who had been raised to the aristocracy, and had already proved himself in the service of John II the Good, had an entirely distinctive position at the court. Ogier was one of the confidants of Charles V already because he oversaw of the king's great construction works. We also encounter him again as one of the men caring for Emperor Charles IV during his visit to the Palace de la Cité in January 1378.[169]

Lower positions in the King's Chamber were those of the Grand Breadmaster (*grand panetier*), Grand Cupbearer (*grand échanson*), Grand Master-Chef (*grand queux*), and almost on an equal footing with them also the knight in charge of the table carvers (*chevalier tranchant*). Unlike the other highest officials, of whom there were a total of fourteen according to a later ordinance of 1389 (however with the Chancellor and Grand Master of the Royal Household there were actually sixteen), all four were obliged to serve the king on great holidays, i.e. over Easter, Pentecost, All Saints and at Christmas.[170] With this, we have not by far exhausted all of the officials and servants of the King's Chamber. It is necessary to mention also the Masters of Petitions (*Maîtres des requêtes*), which sat at the residence of Saint-Pol. At the end of the reign of Charles V, there seemed to have been already another two officials of a similar position, i.e. the master at the head of the service of the Royal Falconers (*Fauconnerie*) and the Master of the Royal Huntsmen (*Vénerie*, i.e. fox hunting). We know the names of both of these masters, who almost certainly participated in the hunt for fallow deer and wild rabbits in the 'Wood' in Vincennes on 11 January 1378. The first was Enguerrand de Dargic; at the head of the royal huntsmen was the knight Philip de Courquilleray.[171]

A large group of higher and lower servants-in-arms (*gens d'armes*) was in charge of guarding the

164/ The entry 'Hôtel du roi' in *Lexikon des Mittelalters*, V, cols 140–141, is not sufficient; therefore, I drew information, i.a. from the standard overview by Lot and Fawtier, *Histoire des institutions françaises*, II, pp. 66–74, from the works listed in the previous note and from the book by Rey, *Les finances royales*, Chapter I (where on p. 25 he also estimated the number of people at the king's court to be between 700 and 800 persons).

165/ His biographical data were compiled by Contamine, *Guerre, État et société*, pp. 591–592; during the emperor's visit, he is likely to have served in Normandy.

166/ For more on him, see Contamine, *Guerre, État et société*, pp. 579–571. In the sources on the emperor's visit, Grand Master Hue does not appear by name.

167/ On the Office of the Grand Master of the Royal Household, see Rey, *Les finances royales*, pp. 34ff., where also Pierre de Villiers is mentioned. On his great honour (*porte-oriflamme*), see Contamine, *Guerre, État et société*, p. 672.

168/ See again Rey, *Les finances royales*, pp. 43–45.

169/ The basic data on this secretary originally from Sens were collected by Jean Chapelot, 'Le Vincennes des quatre premiers Valois: continuités et ruptures dans un grand programme architectural', pp. 70–73, where on p. 71 he expresses the opinion that Philip Ogier was one of the organisers of the emperor's visit.

170/ According to Rey, *Les finances royales*, pp. 24, 88 and 480 (see also here on the order of 1389).

171/ On both establishments of the court, *Fauconnerie* and *Vénerie*, see Rey, *Les finances royales*, pp. 132–135.

Palace de la Cité and other residences of the king. Of the above-mentioned highest military commanders, the primary role during the emperor's visit was given to Marshal Jean called Mouton de Blainville and the squires of his unit (*écuyers de son corps*).[172] The function of the knights of honour (*chevaliers d'honneur*), who were right below the masters of the royal household in the court hierarchy, remains questionable. I believe that they were high officers and commanders of the garrisons of the knightly estate who were then living at the court without having permanent duties there.[173] The external entrances to the Palace de la Cité were guarded by gatekeepers (*varlets de la porte*), who were commanded by so-called *portiers*, whereas responsibility for the internal guard was borne by the officers and sergeants of the palace guard (*huissiers* and *sergeants d'armes*).[174] The squires of the royal bodyguard (*écuyers du corps du roi*) were responsible for the armour and arms of the king himself. These were led by the First Squire (*Premier écuyer du corps*), an officer of a high rank who enjoyed the king's complete trust. At the time of the imperial visit, this post was held by Colart de Tanques († 1397), otherwise also the 'Master' of the King's Stables (*Maistre de son escuierie*), who led the squires of the said stables (*écuyers d'écurie*) and was responsible not only for the stablemen and grooms but also for the appropriate equipment of the royal chargers.[175] The subordination of both groups of squires to Colart is also implied by their common livery of blue camocas.

We should still mention two components of the chamber whose task it was to care for the king's soul and body. Charles V had been of frail health from his childhood, and therefore the medical emergency service in his residences enjoyed his constant attention.[176] Neither can we forget the valets (*valets de chambre*), who despite their ostensibly inferior label were the heads of various services.[177] In isolated cases, we can find among them a lower aristocrat or a man raised to the knighthood. This was true of the administrator of the royal library Gilles Malet, on whom we will hear more in another connection. The second group comprised court suppliers of burgher origin: goldsmiths, merchants, furriers, tailors as well as other tradesmen, for whom this title was a high honour of its sort. Jean de Viviers, with whom the relics and other gems intended as a gift for the emperor were ordered, was for example a footman.[178] It is necessary to distinguish these footmen from the many other *valets* in charge of different services.

The Royal Chapel (*Chapelle royale*), i.e. the body of clerics at Sainte-Chapelle, which from the reign of Philip V (1285–1314) had been a permanent component of the court, comes last in order although not at all in significance. It was headed by master chaplain (*maître chapelain*), whose subordinates were two chaplains, two to three clerics (*clercs de chapelle*), three to four butlers and cupbearers (*sommeliers*) and several servants (*valets*).[179] They were all certainly

172/ *Écuyers* – squires in the military sense – were professional warriors mostly of noble origin with leadership positions who had the hope of being raised to knighthood. For more on that, see Contamine, *Guerre, État et société*, pp. 13–15.

173/ Neither Delachenal (ed.), *Chronique des règnes*, II, p. 214, Note 1, knew how to deal with this rare phrase.

174/ *Huissiers* and *sergeants d'armes* are usually mentioned separately. Especially the officers of the palace guard had high positions, as arises from their hierarchical inclusion as well as the quality of their uniforms. On the military terminology, see Contamine, *Guerre, État et société*, pp. 12–16; see also *Lexikon des Mittelalters* V, col. 183 (Huissiers), 1848–1894 (Leibwache) and VII, cols 1784–1785 (Sergent).

175/ On the obligations of the listed squires and on the person of Colart de Tanques, see Delachenal (ed.), *Chronique des règnes*, II, p. 214, Note 1. In 1391, Colart served also Charles VI in this function; on that, see Contamine, *Guerre, État et société*, p. 657 (where he is written as Tenques).

176/ For more on the diseases and cures of Charles V, see Autrand, *Charles V. Le Sage*, pp. 472–481.

177/ As expressed by Delachenal (ed.), *Chronique des règnes*, II, p. 214, Note 8.

178/ On the court suppliers labelled as *valets de chambre*, see Rey, *Les finances royales*, p. 165. Jean de Viviers, for instance, appears as '*nostre orfévre et varlet de chambre*' in the mandate of Charles V from 18 January 1378 (Delisle (ed.), *Mandements et actes divers de Charles V*, p. 795, No. 1602).

179/ For more on the ecclesiastical administration at the French king's court, see Xavier de La Selle, *Le service des âmes à la cour. Confesseurs et aumôniers des rois de France du XIIIe au XVe siècle*; on the placement of the dwelling for the chaplains inside the complex of the Palace de la Cité hypothetically, see Guérout, 'L'hôtel du roi au Palais de la Cité', pp. 277–278.

on full alert during the emperor's tour of the relics in Sainte-Chapelle on 6 January 1378, at which an especially important role was entrusted to the guardian of the treasure there. Charles V augmented the treasury with many rare relics and acquired from the pope the privilege of carrying a mitre for its guardian (*trésorier*).[180] The chaplains had to economise for one to three days, because the king had their adjacent abode adjusted in advance for the repose of the ill guest. It apparently did not affect Master Chaplain Guy de Champdivers (Magister Guido de Campodiverso), who had his own house. Following the English pattern, two further spiritual services, namely the offices of the almoner (*aumônier*) and the confessor (*confesseur du roi*), became independent from this body also at the French court already at the turn of the fourteenth century. Whereas the first *officium* (*Aumônerie*) was a real office with quite numerous personnel and with a constant, albeit changeable, source of income,[181] the confessor was the king's confidant in intimate moments. At the time of the emperor's visit, the confessor of Charles V was Dominican Maurice de Coulanges († 1395), who was also support for his king in the last days of his life. With the consent of the papal throne, high episcopal or canonical benefices were reserved not only for confessors but also for almoners. In this aspect, not even Pierre de Proverville, who held the Office of the Almoner at the court of Charles V from 1371, came off badly.[182]

Before the King's Chamber (*Chambre du roi*) became independent in the fourteenth century, it was one of the six so-called *métiers*, i.e. main branches of court services.[183] Like the word *chambre* (in Latin *camera*) originally referred to the actual room in the royal palace designated for a certain office, the word *métier* (from Latin *ministerium*) meant a specific service. To maintain the traditional number of six, the chamber was replaced by the so-called *Fourrière*, which ensured the sovereign's transportation and accommodation on journeys.[184] At the beginning of the fourteenth century, the court exchequer with the strange title *Chambre aux deniers*, which sounded like a lower unit of the French currency but in this case collectively referred to incomes and expenditures, separated itself out of the original King's Chamber. Although it was an important component of the court, the master of this chamber remained on the level of the head of the accounting office in a position subordinate to the relevant Master of the Royal Household. More will be said on this court exchequer as well as on the so-called 'silver-smithy' (*Argenterie*), which provided for the needs of the royal family, in connection with the overall accounting of the emperor's visit.[185]

Five other court services were labelled according to the type of activity they involved. To be able to cover precisely the meaning of the first service, the so-called *Paneterie*, we would have to coin a new word 'breadery', because it was neither a bakery nor a mere storage room for bread. The *Paneterie* furnished not only for the royal but also for the 'common' kitchen all types of bread, tarts, desserts and other goodies, but *inter alia* provided even tablecloths. Its personnel numbering roughly twenty persons included butlers, bread-bearers or confectioners and further also assistants (*sommeliers*, *lavandières*), who were in charge of setting the table and laundering tablecloths.[186]

180/ This did not happen until 1380, two years after the emperor's visit. On that, see Jannic Durand, 'Le grand trésor gothique', pp. 83–85.

181/ Besides an almoner (*aumônier*), his assistant (*sous-aumônier*) and accountant (*clerc de l'Aumônerie*), the office also had numerous servants (*valets*). On the incomes and expenditures of the almoners, see Rey, *Les finances royales*, pp. 135–136.

182/ The biographical data on both named dignitaries were compiled by La Selle, *Le service des âmes à la cour*, pp. 271–272 (Maurice de Coulanges) and 292 (Pierre de Proverville).

183/ For more on that, see Lot and Fawtier, *Histoire des institutions françaises*, II, pp. 67–70.

184/ On this service, cf. i.a. Guérout, 'L'hôtel du roi au Palais de la Cité', pp. 274–275.

185/ For the basic information, see *Lexikon des Mittelalters*, I, cols 922–923 (Argenterie du roi), and II, cols 1675–1676 (Chambre aux deniers); for our period, see Rey, *Les finance royales*, pp. 55–62 (La Chambre aux deniers) and pp. 137–146 (L'argenterie).

186/ Briefly but concisely on that, see Lalou in the entry

Whereas we do not know the name of the master at the head of the *Paneterie* at the time of the emperor's stay, the head of the court cupbearers (*Échansonnerie*) was then Elion de Lignac and the accounting was done by the clergyman Gilot Evrart.[187] At the end of the thirteenth century, the personnel included five cupbearers, five 'bottlers' or sommeliers, who cared for the bottles (*bouteillers*), six servants taking care of the wine in barrels (*barilliers*, *porte-barils*) and one *potier*, who may have been responsible for the drinks in ceramic pots. However, this *métier* surprisingly did not procure wine, because that was dealt with by the supplier (also called *maître*) of the court cellars (*les garnisons des vins du roi*), closely connected to the court exchequer. I wonder what all was covered by the clergyman Evrart out of the enormous sum of 4712 gold francs, which he charged for the stay of Emperor Charles IV and his retinue. This sum roughly corresponded to the half-year expenditures for the purchase of wine for the entire royal court.[188]

I am going to omit the court kitchens (*Cuisine*) and stables (*Écurie*) here, to which I will pay adequate attention in the following excursuses; the next is the last so-called *metier*, which was responsible for the procurement and storage of fruit (*Fruiterie*). This relatively small unit with roughly ten experts and servants was allotted the cellar areas close to the kitchen. The expenditures of this service were also among the lowest; in the winter it was approximately 7%, which in comparison with the expenditures for the kitchen (ca 50%) was not much, because besides fruit, the *Fruiterie* provided candle wax as well as seals for the court. For a certain idea, it can be stated that in January 1417 a consignment of almost 1600 kg of wax for the court was made.[189]

It was precisely the units of the so-called *métiers* that provided for the stay of the emperor and his retinue in the Parisian residences in advance. The preparations already began in the first half of September 1377, when Master of the Court Exchequer Nicolas Martin was paid the first large amount of 7,200 gold francs for the expected expenditures.[190] The postponements of the visit certainly caused complications for the 'masters' in charge, which however had to be endured, because the anticipated summit was one of the greatest events of the French metropolis in the second half of the 1370s.

'Paneterie', *Lexikon des Mittelalters VI*, cols 1654–1655.

187/ We know of them from the king's mandates; see Delisle (ed.), *Mandements et actes divers*, p. 797, No. 1605 (premier échançon Elion de Lignac/d'Alignat), pp. 823–824, Nos 1664–1665 and p. 846, No. 719 (clerc de nostre éschançonnerie Gilot Evrart).

188/ For details on the provision of wine for the royal court, see Rey, *Les finance royales*, pp. 101–108, which also has a table of the half-year expenditures and the biographical data on Étienne Porcher, 'master' of the court cellars in 1355–1385. I calculated the amount of 4,712 gold francs from the mandates listed in the previous note.

189/ These data related to January 1417 are provided by Rey, *Les finances royales*, pp. 95–96; on the localisation of the '*métiers*' in the Palace de la Cité, see Guérout, 'L'hôtel du roi au Palais de la Cité', pp. 270–273.

190/ On this expenditure and the overall balance of the emperor's stay, see the final Excursus – The Final Account of the Expenditures of the King's Treasury.

In the Late Middle Ages, the entries of sovereigns into large towns were among the principal presentations of their majesty and unforgettable spectacles for all the other participants.[191] The Account of the *Great Chronicles of France* also paid due attention to them. Its records are uncommonly valuable for researchers, because they provide a unique opportunity to compare three different manifestations of these festivities. Whereas in Cambrai the emperor was welcomed as the sovereign ruler of the city, in Senlis and in several other French cities he was given a welcome only as a precious guest and close relative of the king of France. Finally, he entered Paris at the side not only of his son Wenceslas IV, King of the Romans and of Bohemia, but also of his host Charles V. While in places the Account may seem like a later retold directive in the form of a script of the entire visit of the emperor prepared in advance, then in the case of his welcome in Cambrai it was quite likely a record of an eyewitness. We do not know with certainty whether it was the author of the Account himself, because Chancellor Pierre d'Orgemont does not appear by name among the members of the delegation of Charles V. In any case, someone in the delegation must have been so acquainted with the domestic and imperial ceremonial customs that he could prevent the undesirable proceedings. What was especially delicate in this regard was the emperor's wish to spend the Christmas holidays on French soil in Saint-Quentin. Both sides diplomatically recognised the priority of domestic protocols, which were then thoroughly respected on both sides of the border.

The ceremonial welcome in Cambrai thus took place according to the traditions of the imperial cities. It was precisely in this border city, as has already been spoken of elsewhere, that it was necessary to respect sensitively the emperor's claims, whose recognition had been a bottleneck in the negotiations of an alliance treaty in 1355–1356. Besides that, Charles IV at the end of 1377 entered Cambrai for the first time as a sovereign, which made this event a juridic act of its type. The handover of the keys to the city, which in connection with the mutually sworn oaths of maintaining obedience on the one hand and the legitimacy of the privileges on the other was a visible fulfilment of the legal relation between the sovereign and his subjects for everyone present, is not mentioned in the Account. It cannot be entirely ruled out that it was so with a view of the long-term French interests, from time to time reinforced by accommodating the representatives of the city in their disputes with the local Chapter. Emperor Charles reacted to these tendencies completely unequivocally with his legal decrees, which he also published in Cambrai in the form of documents. It is not necessary to go into the details; suffice it to say that Enguerrand VII of Coucy, a foremost figure of the delegation of the king of France, appears as a witness in one of them.[192]

191/ The so-called 'neo-ceremonialistic school', which considers the royal rituals as a theological-juristic discourse or as a form of 'dialogue' between the king and his subjects, sometimes goes so far in its interpretations that it destroys their comprehensibility for the contemporary public. On that, cf. Joël Blanchard, *Le spectacle du rite: les entrées royales*, esp. pp. 475–479, where further literature is provided.

192/ It may be speculated that precisely he could have mediated the experiences from this phase of the emperor's journey to the chancellor.

118. / XXX. Arrival of Charles IV in Cambrai. Les Grandes Chroniques de France, illumination by Jean Fouquet (BnF, ms. fr. 6465, fol. 441r)

As was usual on the emperor's first visit of imperial cities, Charles IV pardoned outlaws with the exception of traitors and convicted murderers and under certain conditions allowed them a full-fledged return to Cambrai.[193]

At first sight, the description of the entry of Emperor Charles IV into Cambrai in the version of our Account does not differ from other known cases of his ceremonial entries into imperial and other towns. There are not many of them; we mentioned some of them already in the Prologue, and since no faithful or model order was preserved until the fifteenth century, we will focus only on the welcoming processions (Pic. 71 / II). The author of the Account does not fail to tell the reader right after the description of the arrival of the emperor on French soil that he was not welcomed in any church in the entire kingdom by a procession or the sound of bells. The arrival of the sovereign (*adventus regis*) was announced identically in France and in Germany by bells.[194] Nevertheless, it has so far eluded researchers that this honour was denied to kings from elsewhere in the first of the two countries, even though they were arriving as welcomed guests. The prohibition valid for the arrival in towns apparently did not apply to the Abbey of Saint-Maur-des-Fossés, because at the king's command Charles IV was received there by a procession upon entering the cloister, albeit only as a pilgrim (Pic. 85 / XVI). It is evident even from this small fragment that in the period perception the welcoming procession was reserved for only a limited group of people.

The 'beautiful orchestration', on which Christine de Pisan placed special emphasis, included aesthetic perceptions, but first and foremost it was related to the principles which were to mark royal dignity. It is certainly not by accident that we encounter the phrases *belle et bonne ordonnance* or *noble ordonnance* also in our Account, namely *inter alia* in the description of the emperor's entry into Paris.[195] In this connection it is also worth mentioning the abundant appearance of adverbs and adjectives of the type *noblement*, *honorable*, *joieusement*, *riche* or at least *bonne*.[196] The externally visible order, the moderate proportions and the omnipresent noble presentation of the majesty were to demonstrate the desired status of the entire state organism, in the mediaeval imagery

193/ One of Charles' documents with the date of 23 December 1377 has been registered by Böhmer (ed.), *Regesta imperii*, VIII, p. 490, No. 5857*; the content of others is shown by Hüttebräuker, 'Cambrai, Deutschland und Frankreich 1308–1378. Untersuchungen zum Kampf um die deutsche Westgrenze', pp. 131–133; on the pages before, there is also more on the ties of Emperor Charles IV to this city.

194/ For France, cf. Guenée and Lehoux, *Les entrées royales françaises de 1328 à 1515*, p. 23, Note 5. This fundamental work on this theme was complemented by, i.a. Noël Coulet, 'Les entrées solennelles en Provence au XIVe siècle. Aperçus nouveaux sur les entrées royales françaises au bas Moyen Âge', p. 64; for Germany, see Haverkamp, '„... an die große Glocke hängen". Über Öffentlichkeit im Mittelalter', p. 92.

195/ Delachenal (ed.), *Chronique des règnes*, II, pp. 217 and 219.

196/ In the edition by Delachenal (ed.), *Chronique des règnes*, II, it is enough to read the chapter titles (see e.g. pp. 197, 217, 268).

thus of the entire body, not only of the head but also of the limbs.[197] It applied also to the king's mounted procession (*chevauchier*), to which Christine devoted a separate chapter (I, 18). Not even during this, often purely practical, need could the king neglect anything in his external presentation. Already based on the great number of finely dressed barons and aristocrats, everyone was to recognise that the king himself was arriving. His place was at the centre of this noble entourage so that it would be immediately obvious who it was. Not only the clothes but also the horse made the king. The king's company (*compagnie*) included a uniformed guard in full armour, which separated him from the aristocracy. Since the king's blood relatives often arrived with him in the case of a ceremonial entry, the men-at-arms in front of him were to wear belts with symbols of the lilies, whereas the task of the groom of the royal palfreys and his subordinates was to parade augustly the mantle of ermine, hat and sword. The middle group was followed by chargers from the royal stables. So much for the general division of the royal official ride according to Christiane de Pisan, who might have also included some ceremonial innovations from the reign of Charles in her description.[198]

The procession is a projection of the secular hierarchy. The king is surrounded by his aristocracy. He is the first among equals – *primus inter pares* – but at the same time through his holy anointment and other attributes of his majesty he personifies the superpersonal France, the land as well as its community separated into estates, for which the expression 'state' would be found in the Modern Period. It arises from this that it must be clear who it is to everyone at first sight. The colour and gracefulness of the horse themselves are not sufficient. After all, the king's brothers and other relatives could not ride on nags. It was different with the gear; the king's parade horse, a *palfrey* (in French *palefroi*) had to have 'rich' gear and entirely in the symbols of France. Period illuminators leave us slightly in doubt. Was it only tiny gilded lilies on the saddle and harness, or already the horse cover so impressively depicted by Jean Fouquet a few decades later?

119. / XXXIII. Emperor Charles and his son Wenceslas change horses in La Chapelle-Saint-Denis. Les Grandes Chroniques de France, illumination by Jean Fouquet (BnF, ms. fr. 6465, fol. 443r)

The majesty did not exclude the love of the king for his people and *vice versa*. However, it was up to the king to demonstrate it. The spectacle itself which the king provided to the people through the ceremonial welcome given to the emperor must have sufficed in the January cold, because if on this occasion artificial fountains with wine or milk had been installed at selected places, the Account would not have forgotten to mention them. With great likelihood it was a novelty, which we do not encounter until two years later at the ceremonial entry of Charles VI into Paris on 11 November 1380. It was

197/ For more on that, see STRUBEL, 'Le «chevauchier» de Charles V', pp. 387–388.
198/ See SOLENTE (ed.), *Le livre des fais et bon meurs*, I, Chapter 18, the interpretation was provided by STRUBEL, 'Le «chevauchier» de Charles V', pp. 389–392.

also the first time for dramatic productions to be employed during the king's entry, but we do not know of what type.[199]

The sources on the ceremonial entries of the kings of France into Paris are surprisingly poor for the fourteenth century; nevertheless, a certain basic scheme can be derived from them. The starting point after the coronation in Rheims was the Abbey of Saint-Denis. The Parisian burghers rode out to meet the new king at La Chapelle-Saint-Denis,[200] from which they headed together towards the gate of Saint-Denis, as it had been also during the first entry of Charles V on 19 June 1364, and along the homonymous street across the Grand Bridge, otherwise also the Bridge of the Money Changers (Pont-aux-Changeurs) to the Cathedral of Notre-Dame. That is the greatest change so far as compared to the itinerary from 4 January 1378. Before the closed door was opened in front of the sovereign, he had to read the notice with the oath that he would guarantee their canonical privileges, statutes and jurisdiction to the procession of the ecclesiastical dignitaries.[201] After the relevant rites in the cathedral, the welcome culminated in the Palace de la Cité, where the new king *inter alia* accepted gifts from the burghers, prelates and secular feudal lords. This was followed by banquets, tourneys and other entertainments, lasting two to three days.

The cloth decoration of the streets and bridge had been utilised before during the welcome given to John II the Good in October 1350, when also the burghers and members of the various crafts wore uniform clothes. The official record of the *Great Chronicles of France* on the first entry of King Charles V on 28 May 1364 pays greater attention to the queen, who was welcomed independently a few hours after her husband.[202] Along with the escort of ladies-in-waiting, she headed directly for the Palace de la Cité, from which it can be deduced that the ritual with the ecclesiastical procession before the cathedral had been reserved only for kings. If already the ceremonial entry of Charles VI was captivating for its novelties, everything in this regard was surpassed by the welcome of his spouse, Queen Isabeau of Bavaria on 22 August 1389. In this connection, the report of the monk from Saint-Denis deserves attention, according to whom Charles VI asked Blanche, the widow of Philip VI († 1398), as the oldest of the ladies at the court to direct all of the ceremonies, namely, as it is explicitly stated there, 'relying on memories from the past'.[203] From this, it can at the very least be deduced that no written order had existed for the ceremonial entries of queens up until then. While we have abundant written and iconographic sources available on the ceremonial entry of Queen Isabeau, they primarily testify merely on the event itself, so that for the reconstruction of the welcome of Emperor Charles IV they can be used only marginally.[204]

199/ See Guenée and Lehoux, *Les entrées royales françaises*, pp. 12–13. Also the manifold stands or podia and other constructions and placards on the procession route were of later origin. On these so-called *establiées*, see Blanchard, 'Le spectacle du rite: les entrées royales', pp. 475–519. From the other literature, I mention selectively: Lawrence M. Bryant, 'The Medieval Entry Ceremony at Paris', esp. p. 107; the spectacular symbols of royal power, emblematism and symbolism during the entry of French kings were dealt with in two studies by Christian de Mérindol, 'Le prince et son cortège. La théâtralisation des signes du pouvoir à la fin du Moyen Âge' and 'Entrées royales et princières à la fin de l'époque médiévale' (here on p. 29 is a list of the kings' entries into town in 1328–1548).

200/ While the riding out of the burghers on horses and their welcoming the king at La Chapelle-Saint-Denis is not proved until the entry of King Charles VI on 11 November 1380, it was undoubtedly an old tradition. The reporter, who was a monk from Saint-Denis, would not have forgotten to record a novelty, like he did not forget in the case of the artificial fountains with wine, water and milk (see Guenée and Lehoux, *Les entrées royales françaises*, pp. 56–57).

201/ This ritual during the entry of John II the Good on 17 October 1350 was recorded in detail in a notary instrument which was published by Guenée and Lehoux, *Les entrées royales françaises*, pp. 48–55.

202/ Whereas the king entered Paris around noon, the queen at the so-called *hora nona*, i.e. at roughly mid-afternoon. On that, see Guenée and Lehoux, *Les entrées royales françaises*, pp. 55–56 (Note 1 here provides further period testimony).

203/ Attention to this significant testimony was drawn by Bernard Ribémont, 'L'Entrée d'Isabeau de Bavière à Paris. Une fête textuelle pour Froissart', pp. 515–516.

204/ For detailed testimony, see chronicler Jean Froissart, *Chroniques* XIV, ed. Kervyn de Lettenhove, pp. 5–25. From the period iconography, I refer especially to the manuscript

120. The arrival of Queen Isabeau of Bavaria in Paris. Chroniques de Jean Froissart, 15th century (BL, Ms. Harley 4379, fol. 3)

Also the sources on the first 'joyous' entries (*joyeuses entrées*) of the kings of France into provincial towns can be instructive. In advance, the streets and bridges were repaired, cleaned and sometimes covered with sand so that the horses' hooves would not slip. Private houses as well as public buildings were decorated with cloths, and, weather permitting, also with green sprigs and with flowers. Still before entry into the city, gifts similar to those that the emperor received on French soil awaited the king.[205] In October 1389, the people of Lyon, for instance, gave Charles VI rams, bulls and wine.[206] The day of the ceremonial entry was the day of the king's pardons. The municipal councils would submit petitions, but the king's dialogue with the subjects was preceded by mutual oaths, which were usually confirmed in writing. During the sovereign's stay, prices rose sharply, because hoteliers and innkeepers tried to take advantage of the occasion. No less did the participants remember spectacles unseen at other times. During the entry of Charles VI into already-mentioned Lyon, wooden platforms were built on the corners, from which children in clothes of the king's colours were loudly hailing the king. The canopy was carried by four beautiful, exquisitely dressed girls, who escorted the king all the way to the cathedral. Balls and theatre performances then took place in the city for four days.[207]

The welcome procession was also begun in Provence by children with bannerettes, who recited memorised greetings and praises. The king was welcomed in front of the ramparts only by men; women usually waited for him in an allotted place before the church, where the procession ended. On the other hand, children are not mentioned at the welcoming of Emperor Charles, which may be explained by both the season of the year and the overall arrangement of the procession, in which mounted men predominated. Parisian women welcomed the emperor and both kings in the streets; for noblewomen, a reception was prearranged in the residence at Saint-Pol.

Allow us to linger in Provence a little longer. The municipalities had the streets cleaned; the homeowners according to their possibilities hung cloths on the façades or somehow decorated them. The welcoming procession of the burghers was rhythmicised by the banners of the guilds. To avoid disputes, it was already prescribed in Marseille in 1320 that the first place belonged to the money changers and the last to the publicans. Also the earliest regulations on the two-coloured uniforms (the so-called *mi-parti*) come from Provence, where also canopies, the so-called heavens, were already commonly used before 1350.[208]

in the British Library MS Harley 4379, fol. 3r (reproduction in the catalogue *Das goldene Rössl*, p. 19).

205/ On a typology of these gifts, see Jean-Pierre Leguay, 'Banquets, cadeaux alimentaires et autres présents de marque dans les villes françaises à la fin du Moyen Âge', pp. 204–213.

206/ See Guenée and Lehoux, *Les entrées royales françaises*, pp. 21–22 (the appearance of the streets) and 143 (Lyon 1389).

207/ Guenée and Lehoux, *Les entrées royales françaises*, p. 143.

208/ The existing knowledge was enriched by Coulet, 'Les

After this general overview, we can proceed to the reconstruction of the emperor's ceremonial entry into Paris. In this regard, the Account provides appreciated details but sometimes somewhat confusingly or imprecisely. The first small mystery awaits us right at the beginning. According to the Account, Charles V sent one of his First Gentlemen of the Chamber along with the First Squire of the King's Stables to the Abbey of Saint-Denis in the morning of 4 January 1378 to take the emperor and his son the black horses as gifts that they were both to ride when entering Paris. On this occasion they also, as it can be conjectured, brought a team with the queen's litter. The emperor thanked for the gift of the horses and promised to observe the ceremonial regulations.[209] On the other hand, there is nothing said in the *Mémoire* on this purely special-purpose mission, yet we read in it about the ride of the four dukes to Saint-Denis and their return to Paris. It arises from the context that both of the king's brothers, their brothers-in-law and other barons, all already in festive clothes, did not meet the emperor. And since an escort of 120 mounted policemen rode in front of them, it is possible that the role of the dukes was to ensure and check the first phase of the ceremonial welcome between La Chapelle-Saint-Denis and the Abbey of Saint-Denis. It would not be right to disregard this possibility as indecorous, because we thus would cast doubt upon other, elsewhere unproved data from the *Mémoire*.[210]

The three-stage arrangement of the emperor's entry clearly stands out in the time sequence of the Account. The first stage was the business of the metropolis and its denizens. It was followed with a slight delay by the second phase, i.e. the departure of the king's ceremonial procession for La Chapelle-Saint-Denis. After the reciprocal meeting of the three monarchs, the welcome climaxed with their joint entry into Paris. The Account describes the first phase so suggestively that it need not be paraphrased. Only the numerical data and the mentions of the uniform clothes have smaller discrepancies. Whereas the Account lists 1,800 to 2,000 riders dressed in uniform, the *Mémoire* has the numbers two hundred higher. According to the *Mémoire*, Parisians had rubicund berets and half-white, half-blood-red costumes, whereas the Account mentions only a white-purple combination of the *mi-parti* uniforms. At the same time, neither source mentions the names of the main actors of the first phase, i.e. the highest royal official in the metropolis and the representative of the local government there.

It will do no harm to say a few words in advance elucidating the posts of both urban figures. The first of them, the *prévôt de Paris*, executed at the king's commission judicial and other authorities in the metropolis and its suburbs, namely on the level of provincial regents with the title of *bailli*. At the turn of 1378, the Provost of Paris was Hugues Aubriot,[211] who like his predecessors was headquartered in the fortress called the Grand Châtelet on the right bank of the Seine, which was also the place of work of both numerous auditors, investigators and notaries of the provost's court on the one hand and the roughly 160 members of the police guards on the other. A part of them armed with staves served directly in the city (*sergents à verge*); a part rode around on horses and guarded the territory of the metropolis (*sergents à cheval*).[212] A special group of police officers (*sergents du guet*) was selected for night patrols in 1367, which were led by the knight of the night watch (*chevalier du guet*). At the time of the emperor's visit, this post was held by Philip

entrées solennelles en Provence', see esp. pp. 64–67. Its pp. 75–78 also provide earlier evidence on the use of the canopy (*le dais*) than is presented by Guenée and Lehoux, *Les entrées royales françaises*, p. 19.

209/ This episode was described completely identically by Christine de Pisan, *Le livre des fais et bonnes meurs*, II, ed. Solente, pp. 96–97.

210/ On that, see the factually precise interpretation by Thomas, 'Ein zeitgenössisches Memorandum', pp. 105–106, and the editions on p. 116.

211/ I have not been able to procure a copy of the monograph dedicated to him by Eugène Déprez, *Hugo Aubriot, praepositus Parisiensis et urbanus praetor* (Paris 1902).

212/ Sufficient information can be found in *Lexikon des Mittelalters*, II, cols 1771–1772 (Châtelet de Paris) and VII, cols 199–200 (Prévôt III. Der Prévôt von Paris).

121. / XXV. Representatives of the metropolis welcome the emperor and his son (BL, Ms. royal 20 C VII, fol. 197v)

de Villiers, a son of the Grand Master of the Royal Household Pierre de Villiers. Twenty of the total number of sixty of these night-police officers served on horseback and were dressed in the same uniforms as the twelve other horsemen who comprised the escort of the provost of Paris during the welcome of the emperor.[213] The second man in Paris after the king's provost was the so-called *prévôt des marchands*, who as the leader of the merchants' guild (*confrérie des marchands de l'eau*) stood at the helm of a narrow and closed municipal government composed of four aldermen and twenty-four associate judges of the municipal court. The 'primate', as this provost could be called, was at the time of the emperor's visit Jean Cocatrix, called de Bonnes.[214]

At an opportune place between the Abbey and Chapel of Saint-Denis, likely selected in advance, the mounted policemen and burghers spread out in the fields along the path in the manner of the spreading of a battle array.[215] From the centre of this 'very beautiful orchestration', the provost along with the primate and commander of the guard came to meet the emperor. Provost Aubriot delivered a short greeting, which was captured word for word in the Account. The emperor briefly thanked for the compliments and offered services and both cavalcades jointly passed on to La Chapelle-Saint-Denis. In the meantime, those waiting were joined by further groups of royal officials and Parisian burghers, so that all together there were almost four thousand horses in the procession. The Account either greatly exaggerated here or referred to the overall number of persons who participated in the welcome and ceremonial entry. In La Chapelle-Saint-Denis, the servants first carried the emperor in a litter to some dwelling, apparently a vicarage, which has been proved there already in the thirteenth century.[216] It has not been ruled out that the emperor rested for a while there and only when the report came that King Charles V was approaching with the welcoming procession, he and his son Wenceslas mounted the gift black horses.

The second phase with the welcoming procession of the king, courtiers and the clergy began after a while. Considering the short distance between the Gate and La Chapelle-Saint-Denis (of perhaps one mile), it was necessary to time the entry so that the meeting of the three monarchs could take place

213/ These details including the name of the knight of the night watch are given by Delachenal (ed.), *Chronique des règnes*, II, p. 209, Note 2.

214/ See again *Lexikon des Mittelalters*, VII, col. 200 (Prévôt IV. Der Prévôt des marchand in Paris); the name of the primate is presented by Delachenal (ed.), *Chronique des règnes*, II, p. 209, Note 4. See also Contamine, *Guerre, État et société*, p. 88, where he appears as 'Coquatrix'. On the other hand, Cazelles, *Nouvelle histoire de Paris de la fin du règne de Philippe Auguste à la mort de Charles V, 1223–1380*, pp. 418–419, lists a certain Jean Fleury as the Primate of the Merchants in the overview of the Parisian functionaries for those years.

215/ According to the *Mémoire*, it was as if 'en manière de bataille', see Thomas, 'Ein Zeitgenössisches Memorandum', p. 116.

216/ Jan Fouquet captured only the chapel in his miniature in the manuscript of the BN Paris MS fr. 6465, fol. 443 (Pic. 119 / XXXIII); further see a facsimile of *Les Grandes Chroniques de France*, eds Avril, Gousset and Guenée, pp. 246–247, with further local data and literature references. La Chapelle-Saint-Denis echoes in the names Porte de la Chapelle, Rue de la Chapelle and Boulevard de la Chapelle.

without a longer delay near the windmill, which lay roughly halfway between the two mentioned points. Even so a slighter delay might have occurred, since the king needed more than half an hour to get out of the courtyard of the Palace de la Cité because of the great number of mounted people (Pic. 124 / XXVI). The Account first records in detail everyone who was in his procession and in what clothes. Yet this order differs from the 'arrangement of the king's people' which the Account presents at the end of the same and beginning of the next chapter. The literature has ignored these discrepancies, only Françoise Autrand listed them but did not comment on them with a general scheme of the royal escort: at the head rode trumpeters, behind them sergeants of the palace guard, mounted arbalesters, knights and squires. These were followed by the group of the king and his court, first Marshal de Blainville, the groom of the royal palfreys (*le palefrenier du roi*), two squires of the his guard, the son of the king of Navarre Peter and the counts of Harcourt and of Tancarville, King Charles V surrounded by the officers of the palace guard, four dukes, the great lords of the King's Council, all in pairs. The next group comprised the prelates, and the procession was closed by the royal steeds and palfreys.[217]

To resolve some questions, e.g. the placement of the court officials and servants, with a certain amount of likelihood, it was necessary to take into account the arrangement of the closing procession, which formed the third and crowning phase of the ceremonial entry. At the same time, it was shown that the author of the Account omitted some of the participants of the second phase, i.e. the king's departure, so the partial reconstructions brought additions and specifications for both of the subsequent phases. First, we shall proceed to a hypothetical scheme of the second phase. In the square brackets, we can find the omitted dignitaries or other participants.

217/ Autrand, *Charles V. Le Sage*, pp. 793–794. There are also two to three valuable interpretational proposals here, which I am going to use later.

THE ARRANGEMENT OF THE KING'S ESCORT DURING THE DEPARTURE FROM THE PALACE DE LA CITÉ TO LA CHAPELLE-SAINT-DENIS

I. Two royal trumpeters with French horns[218]
II. Mounted arbalesters and mounted sergeants of the palace guard
III. Knights and squires of the Kingdom of France
[IV. Chancellor of France Pierre d'Orgemont, the highest officials and secular members of the King's Council]
[V. Foot guards of the gates and their commanders][219]
VI. Marshal Jean, called Mouton de Blainville, with the squires of the bodyguard
VII. Pierre, son of the king of Navarre, otherwise Count of Mortain, Count John VI of Harcourt and Count Jean II of Tancarville
VIII. King Charles V with the officers of the palace guard
IX. Pairs of Dukes: first the king's brothers John of Berry and Philip the Bold of Burgundy, followed by their brothers-in-laws Louis II of Bourbon and Robert I of Bar
X. Pairs of Counts: John of Artois, Count of Eu – Count of Boulogne // Enguerrand VII of Coucy and John II of Saarbrücken // Louis de Sancerre and Charles de Trie, Count of Dammartin // Count of Porcien and Count of Grand-Pré // John IV of Salm and Count Simon de Roucy et de Braine[220]
XI. Other lords, knights bannerets and knights uncounted
XII. Archbishops, bishops and other prelates

218/ Autrand puts the trumpeters at the head of the procession; I abide by her solution with the addition that I could imagine further trumpeters in front of the second, i.e. king's, section.
219/ In this order, the Account presents these important functionaries and their guards when describing the ceremonial entry into Paris.
220/ I cannot guarantee the precise composition of the pairs, because the Account lists among them also the count of Tancarville, who formed a threesome along with the son of the king of Navarre and with John of Harcourt.

[XIII. Court dignitaries, officials and servants of various *métiers* in the relevant clothes and insignias][221]

XIV. The final group of richly saddled royal steeds and palfreys, which were led by uniformed valets with the coats-of-arms of France on the usual belts

As soon as the head of the welcoming procession came within the proximity of the windmill,[222] where the meeting of King Charles V with his Luxemburg guests had been agreed, it was necessary to undertake a somewhat complicated but entirely indispensible manoeuvre. We can only surmise its form. The head of the procession turned in the opposite direction and thus created an aisle for the king and four dukes. These all rode forward, whereas the back part of the procession formed the other side of the ceremonial lane.[223] Charles V rode forward to meet his uncle and removed his hat as well as lower cap. According to the Account, the emperor supposedly did so as well, but the *Mémoire* indicates that it was a fur cap, the so-called almuce.[224] The consideration that Charles V demonstrated towards his uncle by being careful for his horse not to rub the emperor's sick legs is in itself worth noting. At the same time, however, precisely this comment helps resolve the question of whether the Account appeared in advance as a script or on the contrary as an additional record of the events in their time sequence. Details of this sort were not possible to foresee in advance (Pic. 124 / XXVII).

For the same reason, it can also be supposed that, after greeting both guests, Charles V placed himself to have the emperor on his right and King of the Romans and of Bohemia Wenceslas IV on his left. The polite hesitation of the emperor proves that all of the actors were aware of the honour of the place on the right.[225] Also all of the depictions of the ceremonial tables in the emperor's honour consistently preserve this order. In the situation in front of the windmill, however, this arrangement formed a sequence in threes. Whereas according to the Account the king of France rode along the entire route until his palace between his two guests, the *Mémoire* speaks of pairs. The first was allegedly composed of both Charleses, the second of King of the Romans and Bohemia Wenceslas IV and his uncle Wenceslas, otherwise Duke of Brabant, Luxembourg and Limburg. They were purportedly followed by the king's brothers and many other princes and barons. The editor of the *Mémoire* Heinz Thomas tried to support its testimony *inter alia* by referring to the narrowness of the street leading from the gate of Saint-Denis to the Palace de la Cité.[226] That however is not very tenable; the street was called 'Grand', which certainly referred not only to its length. Besides, even the *Mémoire* speaks of threes, namely during the entry of the gate of the Palace de la Cité, when the horses of both Luxemburg guests were led from both sides by the chamberlains allotted to them. This account cannot be ignored, because it has its logic. Nonetheless, I will adhere to the Account during the reconstruction of the ceremonial entry, because otherwise it would be necessary to relinquish all of its colourful description. Besides, the arrangement by threes could better meet the demands of court protocol.

221/ The author of the Account presented this numerous group in a certain order and listed the materials and colours of their clothes but then forgot to include them in the processions of the second and third phases. I do not rule out that this group of courtiers preceded the prelates.

222/ It was located in the areas of today's Gare Saint-Lazar.

223/ The arrangement in a semicircle with such a large number of participants would apparently not have been practicable.

224/ The expression is interpreted this way by Thomas, 'Ein Zeitgenössisches Momerandum', p. 107.

225/ Nevertheless, I consider it necessary to add that Charles V did not follow the ceremonial regulations or customs very literally. It is to his honour that he mostly acted very considerately towards his dear guest and uncle, a typical example of which is the scene of their joint visit of Sainte-Chapelle, when Charles V had the canopy taken down in his oratory to avoid being superior to the emperor.

226/ For more on that, see Thomas, 'Ein Zeitgenössisches Momerandum', pp. 106–110 and the text of the *Mémoire* on pp. 116–117. My solution was rejected by Fantysová-Matějková, 'Cesta Karla IV. do Francie', pp. 637–639, who followed Thomas' solution; on the other hand, the column of threes in agreement with the Account is supposed by Schwedler, 'Deutsch-französische Herrschertreffen', p. 78.

122. / XXXV. Meeting of the crowned heads before the entry into Paris. Les Grandes Chroniques de France, illumination by Jean Fouquet (BnF, ms. fr. 6465, fol. 444r)

The assembly of the main actors of the magnificent celebration, true *pompa celebris*, was a signal for the head of the procession, behind which the mounted groups lined up according to the order set in advance. Notwithstanding that, the arrangement of so large a number of horsemen and inclusion of the rear rank of the Parisian burghers was not an easy task. It probably did not anticipate the emperor's escort being at the head of the procession. That happened at the emperor's request which he expressed immediately after his arrival at the Abbey of Saint Denis, namely along with the wish that considering his health problems he be protected against the press of the crowd. Charles V had most likely already earlier charged Lord Enguerrand VII of Coucy, further Simon, Count de Roucy et de Braine, and John II, Count of Saarbrücken with escorting the emperor's people to the palace from the windmill in advance.[227]

It arises from the time context that exactly this group could ride at the head of the procession. It was followed, also on horseback, by the knights and squires of the domestic kingdom, who thus represented their own estate. The further arrangement is difficult to explain. A certain hierarchical grading can be perceived but only in some sequences leading linearly from both sides towards the central trio of the crowned heads. If I am not mistaken, it was so for the king of France to be able to take the central position in the procession on the way to Chapelle as well as back without greater regrouping.

THE ARRANGEMENT OF THE CEREMONIAL PROCESSION DURING THE ENTRY OF EMPEROR CHARLES IV INTO PARIS ON 4 JANUARY 1378

The suite of Luxemburg officials and servants escorted by Counts Enguerrand VII of Coucy, Simon de Roucy et de Braine, and John II of Saarbrücken.

* * *

- I. Two royal trumpeters with silver French horns decorated with embroidered pennons
- II. The front cavalcade of mounted arbalesters and 50–60 members of the palace guard in blue-black cloth uniforms
- III. Knights and squires of the Kingdom of France numbering about 800 persons not including pages in the liveries of their lords, all in beautiful clothes and on very nice horses
- IV. Chancellor of France Pierre d'Orgemont, the highest officials and secular members of the King's Council, who did not have special tasks
- V. Foot guards of the gates and their commanders with verges in their hands
- VI. Royal Provost of the City of Paris Hugues Aubriot along with unnamed counts and barons
- VII. Marshal Jean, called Mouton de Blainville,

227/ Part of the emperor's retinue could stay at the Parisian residence of the emperor's brother Wenceslas, see Fantysová-Matějková, 'Rezidence Václava českého, vévody lucemburského a brabantského, jejich funkce a úloha v rodinných a „mezinárodních" vztazích', pp. 527–573.

with the squires of the bodyguard and the royal stables, who had swords on their belts and parade helmets[228]

VIII. Peter, son of the king of Navarre, otherwise Count of Mortain, Count John VI of Harcourt and Count Jean II of Tancarville

IX. The knights of honour (*chevaliers d'honneur*) in vermilion velvet and dismounted knights with staves[229]

X. King Wenceslas IV – King Charles V – Emperor Charles IV under the protection of sixteen chamberlains in velvet and scarlet clothes and ten officers of the palace guard in uniforms of blue and red camocas. We know seven of the chamberlains by name: Bureau de la Rivière, Charles of Poitiers, Guillaume des Bordes, Adam de Galonguet, Hutin de Vermeilles, Jean de Berguettes and Jean de Barres

XI. The rear guard of foot guards of the gates with verges in their hands

XII. Duke John of Berry – Duke Wenceslas of Brabant – Duke Philip of Burgundy – Duke Louis of Bourbon – Elector of Saxony Albert [230] – Duke Robert of Bar – Duke of Brieg (Brzeg) Henry VIII – Duke of Liegnitz (Legnica) Boleslav – Wenceslas I, Duke of Troppau (Opava) – Landgrave of Saxony Leuchtenberg Johann I and further lords of the imperial retinue who were not at the head of the entourage

XIII. Twenty foot knights and squires of the royal bodyguard and twenty-five arbalesters with a sword in one hand and a verge in the other

XIV. Archbishops and bishops in richly decorated copes. We know three of the archbishops by name: Richard Picque (Rheims), Guillaume of Lestrange (Rouen), Adhémar Robert (Sens). Ten bishops can be further listed, i.e. Miles II de Dormans (Beauvais), Gilles de Lorris (Noyon), Pierre Aycelin de Montaigu (Laon), Aimery de Magnac (Paris), Nicolas Du Bosc (Bayeux), Nicole Oresme (Lisieux), Guillaume de Dormans (Meaux), Bernard de Caritis (Évreux), Pierre II d'Orgemont (Thérouanne) and Bernard Palot (Condom). The abbots of the Cloisters of Saint-Vaast (Jean VI Le Fèvre), Saint-Denis and Saint-Maur-des-Fossés took the foremost place among the prelates[231]

[XV. Court dignitaries, officials and servants of various *métiers* in their relevant clothes and insignias: Masters of the Royal Household in costumes of two kinds of velvet, azure and tawny, breadmasters (butlers), cupbearers and carvers at the table – in clothes of two kinds of satin, striped white and tawny, master-chefs as well as stewards in silk mantles and in otter fur coats with mother-of-pearl buttons, and fifty-two valets of the chamber in black uniforms with grey-white stripes]

XVI. Master of the King's Stables Colart de Tanques[232] at the head of a cavalcade of richly saddled steeds and palfreys, which were led by uniformed valets with the coats-of-arms of France on the usual belts

228/ Autrand, *Charles V. Le Sage*, pp. 793–794, judged that there were two of these guards, one of whom carried the king's sword and the other his helmet. On this occasion, it would have been truly strange, since the king was not going into battle. The original text has *écharpe*, which according to the editor is necessary to understand in the given period as a belt around the neck (see Delachenal /ed./, *Chronique des règnes*, II, p. 216, Note 3). Fragments of a parade helmet (*casque de parade*) from the time of Charles VI acquired during archaeological excavations in the Louvre were reconstructed using the galvanoplastic method. On that, see Michel Fleury and Venceslas Kruta, *Le Château du Louvre*, pp. 74–76.

229/ I include here also the honorary knights – *chevaliers d'honneur*, whom I do not know where else to place, because the host and his Luxemburger guests were guarded by both chamberlains and officers of the palace guard (*huissiers d'armes*).

230/ I assume that he rode in the middle; the ordering of the other feudal lords cannot be set precisely either.

231/ They are listed in the Account when the highest prelates of France and the emperor met in Saint-Denis. It can only be conjectured whether these prelates were joined by Bishop Henry Sorbom from the emperor's escort.

232/ I only speculate here.

123. Palace de la Cité, entry to the so-called Gallery of the Merchants (Mercière). Altar of the Parisian Parliament, detail, 15th century

XVII. Provost of the Merchants Jean Cocatrix, Knight of the Night Watch Philip de Villiers, aldermen and burghers, all on horseback

XVIII. the concluding cohort of Parisian mounted policemen

Already on the day before the ceremonial procession, Charles V had a ban announced in the entire metropolis on the entrance of carts into Grand Rue, leading form the gate of Saint-Denis to the Palace de la Cité. The curious who assembled in the street were ordered to stay in place. The observation of the ban on both ends of the route was overseen by municipal policemen. The smooth passage was ensured by thirty members of the palace guard, who dismounted at the beginning of Grand Rue and proceeded with maces in their hands in front of the king and his guests. Also predetermined chamberlains dismounted and from both sides led the horses of Emperor Charles IV, King Charles V and probably even of King Wenceslas IV.[233] According to the author of the Account, the monarchs very easily, without difficulties reached the palace admirably quickly, where road blocks had been set up, which were guarded along with all the entrances by sergeants of the palace guard and bodyguard. With the exception of the king, his guests, brothers, brothers-in-law and chamberlains designated in advance, officers of the bodyguard and grooms numbering about forty persons in total, no one else was allowed entry to the Palace de la Cité. All of the horsemen in front and behind, just like the participants in the procession on foot, were ordered to continue and disperse along the adjacent streets.

In front of the marble staircase at the entrance to the gallery called Mercière, a chair covered in a gold-interlaced cloth stood which the administrator of the Palace de la Cité Philip Ogier had had prepared for the emperor. Once the emperor had settled himself in the chair, Charles V approached him and welcomed him in his palace. It was three o'clock in the afternoon; the emperor's ceremonial entry into Paris had just finished.

233/ According to the *Mémoire*, the emperor's horse was led by Charles of Poitiers along with Bureau de la Rivière while the horse of the king of France by Adam de Galonguet and Guillaume de Bordes. There is nothing mentioned of a similar measure in the case of Wenceslas IV here, from which it can be inferred that he continued on his own along with the other French and imperial feudal lords. On that, c.f. Thomas (ed.), 'Ein Zeitgenössisches Memorandum', pp. 116–117.

In the Account of the *Great Chronicles of France* on the visit of Emperor Charles IV and his son Wenceslas IV, horses appear in thirty-two places in one form or another, so they can be considered along with the crowned heads, dukes and counts as major actors of all of the events.[234] If the Account mentions horses without distinguishing between their types, sizes and colours, then it usually gives their numbers. These are sometimes reasonable, like in the case of the cavalcade of forty horses which the guards allowed into the closely guarded courtyard of the Palace de la Cité at the end of the ceremonial entry of the emperor into Paris. It was a group including, besides the three sovereigns, four dukes and four counts from the French side, also the foremost members of the emperor's suite.[235] With lesser certainty, it is possible to estimate the number of horses in the emperor's entourage. If we count an extra one or two servants for each of the twelve aristocrats and at least four attendants for serving the emperor and his son, then we reach a number of roughly forty people, to whom we however have to add the notaries and other personnel of the travelling chancellery.[236] Including coachmen, we could allow for between eighty and one hundred horsemen, which does not seem particularly exaggerated.[237] This has provided us with a kind of module for the numbers of horses listed below.

The second lowest number of a mere one hundred horses is related to the size of the entourage of the abbot of Saint-Denis, which waited for the rare visit from the Empire roughly one mile in front of the gate of the city of Saint-Denis. Since we know from elsewhere that Saint-Denis was a fortified city of medium size,[238] this number, corresponding to a tenth or even a smaller fraction of the real state, does not seem to be the figment of the common mediaeval numerical fantasy. The same holds true for the welcome procession in Senlis (to below one hundred horses) and perhaps even in the episcopal city of Cambrai and the royal Compiègne, where they managed to amass roughly two hundred riders for the prelude to the emperor's ceremonial entry.[239] Whereas in Cambrai and in Compiègne the emperor and his retinue were besides the local notables welcomed by a delegation of King Charles V numbering three hundred horsemen, before Senlis this royal cavalry had already grown to five hundred horses. A partial explanation for this disparity is offered by the Ac count itself. In Cambrai, the emperor was greeted by the delegation led by Enguerrand VII, Lord of Coucy, Count John II of Saarbrücken, Count Simon

234/ Delachenal (ed.), *Chronique des règnes*, II, cf. esp. pp. 218–222.

235/ The lower-ranking members of the escort had already been led to the Palace de la Cité at the emperor's request.

236/ According to what I was told by Ivan Hlaváček, the emperor's chancellery could have numbered six to eight people on long journeys.

237/ In the Czech edition, I listed a number of between fifty and sixty horses, which was rightfully refused by Fantysová-Matějková, 'Cesta Karla IV. do Francie', p. 635, according to whom there were more than 160 horses. This number, on the other hand, seems exaggerated to me considering the circumstances of the emperor's journey, even if it included the horses from the escort of the emperor's half-brother Wenceslas, Duke of Brabant.

238/ See, i.a. Michaël Wyss (ed.), *Atlas historique de Saint-Denis. Des origines au XVIIIe siècle*, in Documents d'archéologie française, 59, (Paris, 1996). On the welcome of the emperor, see Delachenal (ed.), *Chronique des règnes*, II, p. 205.

239/ Delachenal (ed.), *Chronique des règnes*, II, pp. 197 (Cambrai), 201 (Compiègne), 202 (Senlis).

de Roucy et de Braine, and the foremost counsellors of the king Bureau de la Rivière and Jean Le Mercier. All of these men returned to the court, whereas the finer welcoming delegation led by the queen's brother Louis II, Duke of Bourbon, the king's cousin John of Artois, otherwise Count of Eu, and two prelates, Miles II de Dormans, Bishop of Beauvais, and Bishop of Paris Aimery de Magnac, headed for Compiègne, lying on French soil.[240]

In the last case mentioned, nothing changed about the number of horses. It was different in front of Senlis, where the emperor was awaited by the king's brothers John, Duke of Berry, and Philip the Bold, Duke of Burgundy, who were accompanied by John VI, Count of Harcourt, further by Adhémar Robert, Archbishop of Sens, and Bishop of Laon Pierre Aycelin de Montaigu.[241] The welcoming cavalry had already grown to five hundred horses, probably also because it had been joined by the participants in the previous delegation. From Senlis, both of the dukes returned to Paris, and therefore the emperor during his next stop in Louvres, where he spent the night between 2 and 3 January 1378, was greeted by the king's brother-in-law Robert, Duke of Bar. That was most likely with a smaller entourage, because the grandiose welcome of the distinguished guests, which was to take place on Monday, 4 January, was already being prepared in Paris.

The protocol of the welcoming ceremony, as we already know, had several phases for this day. The emperor, who had left the Abbey of Saint-Denis immediately after breakfast, was met half way by Provost of Paris Hugues Aubriot, Knight of the Night Watch Philip de Villiers, Provost (*prévôt*) of the Merchants Jean Cocatrix along with aldermen, burghers, uniformed servants and sergeants of the palace guard on horseback numbering overall between 1,800 and 2,000 horsemen. Not even these numbers seem too exaggerated if we consider that Paris had around 100,000 inhabitants. After welcoming the emperor, both groups set out 'in a beautiful orchestration' towards the metropolis.[242]

It is worth repeating that in La Chapelle-Saint-Denis the emperor with the help of his servants alighted from the litter and mounted the black horse which King Charles V had sent him. Meanwhile the Parisian mounted entourage, led by the provost of Paris, moved to the open plain roughly halfway between the mentioned settlement and Paris, where it spread out into a formation 'in the manner of a battle array'.[243] Since the distance between La Chapelle-Saint-Denis and Paris was 2 miles (a so-called *lieue* or league, what we would call a *lieu metrique*), i.e. about eight kilometres, there was enough room in the open space for this manoeuvre. Also the numerous group of horsemen that accompanied Charles V from Paris had to spread out and regroup to be able to create the trios or pairs of riders for the actual procession, which headed for the city citadel at the gate of Saint-Denis and from there along Grand Rue to the Palace de la Cité.[244]

In one place, the Account of the *Great Chronicles of France* lists a total number of 4,000 horsemen who participated in the welcome of the emperor between Saint-Denis and Paris. Should we include the roughly 2,000 horses in the procession organised by the authorities of the metropolis in this number, roughly the same number would be left for the participants from the court suite. On this occasion, the Account mentions four dukes, eleven counts, an unspecified number of barons, prelates and other great lords; it further enumerates 800 knights and squires (without their pages), fifty-two valets of the chamber, fifty to sixty armed sergeants of the palace guards, forty-six bodyguards, twenty-five arbalesters, two royal trumpeters and an unreported number of

240/ Delachenal (ed.), *Chronique des règnes*, p. 201.
241/ Delachenal (ed.), *Chronique des règnes*, p. 203.

242/ The *Mémoire* also tells us of this arrangement, see Thomas, 'Ein Zeitgenössisches Memorandum', the cited place is on p. 116.
243/ This detail is again provided in the *Mémoire*, see Thomas, 'Ein Zeitgenössisches Memorandum', p. 116, and Lechová, 'Zpráva o návštěvě Paříže', p. 51.
244/ For more detail on that, see the reconstruction of the ceremonial entry in the previous excursus.

court officials, chamberlains, Masters of the Royal Household, honorary knights, royal and armed grooms, butlers, cupbearers, carvers of roasts at the table, master-chefs and sommeliers. It truly does not seem that the number of horses mentioned on this singular occasion could not correspond to the reality long ago. Were we to seek a lower limit, then it would at the most be a half, not a tenth of the reported amount.

Such a large number of horses required appropriate stabling. Even though most of the feudal lords and high court officials had their own palaces (*hôtels*) in Paris, the royal stables had to provide for hundreds of horses. The Master of the King's Stables (*maître de l'écurie*), who was Colart de Tanques from January 1377 until his death in August 1397,[245] was at the head of one of the six court offices headquartered in the Palace de la Cité, but the stables he cared for were in several *dépendances* called *séjours*. One lay in the direction of the gate of Montmartre in today's Rue du Jour, whose name was originally du Séjour; a second, much larger one was located in Charenton on the route to the fortress in Vincennes. In the Palace de la Cité, in the Louvre and in the residence of Saint-Pol, there seem to have been only small cowsheds for temporary stabling and for the equestrian gear.[246]

From the end of the thirteenth century, the Office of the Master of the King's Stables increased in importance, which corresponded also to increasing expenditures. High amounts are already recorded by the first preserved accounts from 1298–1301 and 1322–1325. Since there are no accounting registers available for the reign of Charles V, the expenditures from the first decade of the rule of Charles VI are more authoritative. These varied significantly but on average were between 11,000 and 13,500 gold francs, i.e. roughly a tenth of the total amount spent for the needs of the court by the so-called *denier* chamber (*Chambre aux deniers*).[247] Also the number of personnel grew proportionally to that. An approximate idea can be acquired on the basis of the accounting data from February 1389, when the Master of the King's Stables was in charge of almost 100 persons, including twelve squires (*écuyers*), three clerks (*clercs*), the first groom (*premier marechal*), the groom responsible for the king's parade horses (*palefrenier*), forty-one equerries with precisely set tasks, and nineteen mounted couriers (*chevaucheurs*).[248]

Not all horses were the same. Why not admit that a problem arises here with the contemporary specialised terms, for which not only Czech or German but also other languages do not have the apt equivalents.[249] Mediaeval France was one of the countries where a horse (*cheval*) was more than just an assistant and symbol of the social status of the owner, as is already clear from the name for the knightage (*chevalerie*, reflected in English 'chivalry'). The breeding of noble horses had its own long tradition there, and therefore it is also not surprising that we know of scholarly treatises of a veterinary nature complemented with practical advice already in the fourteenth century.[250] In this however France was not

245/ On him, see already Delachenal (ed.), *Chronique des règnes*, II, p. 208, Note 1; in more detail, see Rey, *Les finances royales*, pp. 121–132.

246/ On that, see again Rey, *Les finances royales*, pp. 118–119 and Guérout, 'L'hôtel du roi au Palais de la Cité', pp. 273–274. Both authors allow for only temporary stables in the residential palaces.

247/ For more on that, see Rey, *Les finances royales*, pp. 116 and 124–126. There is also an edition of these accounts from 1381–1387 newly available, published in 1995 by Guy-Michel Leproux, *Comptes de l'Écurie du roi Charles VI*.

248/ The rest comprised grooms. I adopted the data from Rey, *Les finances royales*, p. 117.

249/ For the German language area, see Herbert Kolb, 'Namen und Bezeichnungen der Pferde in der mittelalterlichen Literatur', pp. 151–166. For this study, I have drawn information, i.a. from the work of Brigitte Prévot and Bernard Ribémont, *Le cheval en France au Moyen Âge*, which has the mediaeval terminology for the individual types of horse among others on pp. 173–202. From another perspective, see Noëlle Cherrier, 'Les chevaux de Philippe le Hardi (1371–1404)', pp. 107–148 (containing, i.a. data on the prices of horses, suppliers, stabling etc.). Horses were of primary importance in the period military; on that, see, i.a. Contamine, *Guerre, État et société*, namely according to its index. For an informed view of the entire problem, see Nejedlý, *La Représentation des pouvoirs et des hiérarchies dans les Chroniques de Jean Froissart*, pp. 343–361.

250/ Mediaeval natural scientists (e.g. Thomas of Cantimpré, Bartholomeus Anglicus and Vincent of Beauvais)

first, because two treatises on equestrian medicine, *Liber de cura equorum* (also *Practica equorum*)[251] and Old German *Rossarzneibuch* by Master Albrant (also Albret, Hilbrant, Hildebrant), had already gained exceptional popularity in the thirteenth century. The second of these veterinary aids has been preserved in more than two hundred manuscripts and eight incunabula, with the earliest Czech translation being known from a manuscript from around 1440.[252]

It comes as no surprise that the Account of the *Great Chronicles of France*, which is so particular about court protocol and refined etiquette, distinguishes between five types of horse. The least difficulty in terms of terminology is caused by the white horses (*chevaux blancs*), pulling one of the beautifully decorated personal carriages which Charles V sent on the night between Saturday and Sunday 3 January to Louvres, after he discovered that his uncle suffered from gout and could not therefore travel on horseback.[253] If we call them 'draught horses', we will not be mistaken, especially when they appear here for the first and simultaneously the last time in our history.[254]

Also the second case can be managed since we perceive the name *coursier* (*courcier, corcier*), in English courser, as a derivative from the root of the word *cours* (course), referring to a fast horse. '*Coursiers*' appear in the Account a total of four times: Charles V sent two horses of this type with the litter of the dauphin of Viennois to Louvres; then he sent one beautiful coarser as a gift to the emperor as well as one for his son Wenceslas in Saint-Denis; a great number of burghers came to meet the rare guests mounted on beautiful coursers and finally the king's personal groom saddled a large courser for himself.[255]

With the type of horse called *destrier* in Old French as well as in English, one with a knowledge of Latin may recognise the origin of the word in the term *dextrarius*, which referred to a tourney horse or a charger that was held by a squire in his right hand (in Latin *dextera*) until the knight mounted it.[256]

The most valued horses were of Spanish breeding (*spanjol*, *kastellân*, i.e. Spanish horse and Castilian war horse),[257] but the destriers from Provence or from Burgundy were no inferior to them.[258] As one definition states, a destrier 'was a battle horse, very large, very strong, able to carry not only a horseman in full armour but also the barding with which the horse itself was covered… The courser, which could also serve war purposes, was less formidable for its size and weight but also easier to control and faster than the *destrier*.'[259] When he presented the two Luxemburgs with horses, Charles V generously

adopted mostly knowledge of Antique literature in their own encyclopaedic works. For France, cf. the cited work by Prévot and Ribémont, *Le cheval en France au Moyen Âge*, passim.

251/ For a first orientation, see Gundolf Keil, 'Liber de cura equorum', in *Die deutsche Literatur des Mittelalters. Verfasserlexikon*, 5, cols 752–756.

252/ The basic information was summarised by Rainer Rudolf, 'Meister Albrant', in *Die deutsche Literatur des Mittelalters. Verfasserlexikon*, 1, cols 157–158. For the oldest copy of the Czech translation, see the manuscript of the National Library of the CR shelf mark XI C 2, fols 289r–291v.

253/ Delachenal (ed.), *Chronique des règnes*, II, p. 204. It is however worth noting that Christine de Pisan mentions four white mules (*IIII beaulx mulez blans*) in her panegyric of Charles V. See Solente (ed.), *Le livre des fais et bonnes meurs*, II, p. 94.

254/ Draught horses were often labelled as so-called sumpters or pack animals (*sommiers*), a forerunner of the Breton Horse today; they were mainly horses of village origin, which, e.g. the poet Eustache Deschamps scornfully puts in the lowest category (on that, see Contamine, *Guerre, État et société*, p. 18, Note 50).

255/ Delachenal (ed.), *Chronique des règnes*, II, pp. 208, 209, 213 and 216.

256/ An echo of this practical habit from the age of knights can be found in the description of the procession both in the Account and in the paraphrase by Christine de Pisan: 'Aprez les prelaz et leur route venoient les grans destriers de parement du roy menez en destre…', i.e. 'after the prelates and their group followed destriers led from the right'. See Solente (ed.), *Le livre des fais et bonnes meurs*, I, p. 99.

257/ Among the sought-after horses of Spanish breeding, there were also small, easily manoeuvrable 'jennets'.

258/ For a concise description of that, mainly with consideration of the German sources, see Ortwin Gamber, in the entry 'Pferd', *Lexikon des Mittelalters VI*, cols 2029–2030. Under Charles VI, the royal stables purchased horses at the markets in Compiègne, Lendit as well as in Paris, with the expenditures for them sometimes surpassing half of the annual budget. For more on that, see Rey, *Les finances royales*, pp. 129–130.

259/ In both cases, I refer to the characteristics by Duke of Aumale, which are quoted by Delachenal (ed.), *Chronique des règnes*, II, p. 208, Notes 2 and 3.

also added to the coursers two black destriers, i.e. black (*morel*) horses.[260] We shall soon discover why.

Both Charles IV and his son Wenceslas arrived in France on horses called *roncins*, roussins or rouncies, which referred to resilient horses of German as well as other breeding (so-called *Roß*) that were intended for war as well as hunting.[261] Charles' horse was grey, which may not have played a greater role, since valets also came on rouncies to welcome the emperor.[262] King Charles V naturally rode on a parade palfrey (*palefrois*), a graceful horse which attracted attention for its build as well as its height.[263]

Not even this developed terminology sufficed the author of the protocolary Account of the *Great Chronicles of France* for covering all of the features that he considered to be important, and he therefore helped himself by using adjectives. What he says about the above-mentioned lords and princes is significant from this perspective. All of these 'rode on commendably large horses, higher than coursers'.[264] It thus went without saying that also the king's parade palfreys (*palefrois*) had to be duly high.[265]

The qualities of the horse as well as its size on their own were not enough to represent the king's majesty. No less important also was its colour, especially when what was concerned was a meeting of the two most influential sovereigns of contemporary Europe. The Account also does not conceal why Charles V presented both of his relatives with black horses: 'And it was intentionally that the king of France had given them horses of this coat, which was furthest from white and its opposite, because according to the customs in the Empire, the emperors were to arrive in the good towns of their empire which were in their domain on a white horse. The king did not want that to happen also in his kingdom, so he ensured that no sign of the emperor's dominion could be seen.' Therefore, it was also no wonder that Charles V rode to meet his uncle on that important Monday, 4 January 1378 'mounted on a great white palfrey, richly saddled entirely in the symbols of France'.[266] This memorable event was recorded also by other witnesses and following them almost unanimously by all of the biographers of both crowned Charleses.[267] It only remains to note how carefully the Account was read by its illuminators.

The basic cycle of illustrations in manuscript of the Bibliothèque Nationale in Paris MS fr. 2813 depicts horses in four of the total of nineteen illuminations.[268] The very first miniature of the mentioned four has a deviation in the colour as against the Account, because the emperor's rouncy is not grey but chestnut brown (a sorrel) (Pic. 73 / IV). The three other horses ridden to the meeting by Wenceslas IV as well as Dukes John of Berry and Philip the Bold,

260/ Delachenal (ed.), *Chronique des règnes*, II, pp. 208–210, mentioning also horses of this type, on which some Parisians came to welcome the emperor.

261/ It would probably be misleading to see this type of horse in the statue of the white horse with golden gear in the lower part of the magnificent goldsmith's work which Charles VI gave his wife Isabeau of Bavaria as a new year's present in 1405. The traditional German name for this exceptional gem is 'Das göldene Rössl', but from the French perspective it was rather a parade horse (palfrey). French researchers transcribe the German name neutrally as *cheval d'or* ('gold horse'). On the work itself, see esp. the catalogue from 1995 *Das goldene Rössl*; for the latest on the French label, see the catalogue *Paris 1400. Les arts sous Charles VI*, p. 174, No. 95.

262/ Delachenal (ed.), *Chronique des règnes*, II, p. 198, p. 216.

263/ Delachenal (ed.), *Chronique des règnes*, II, pp. 211 and 216. The term palfrey, which has been proved already back to 1190, came from the Lower-Latin *paradeverdus*, echoing the Celtic word for horse, i.e. *veredus*.

264/ See Delachenal (ed.), *Chronique des règnes*, II, p. 213: 'grans chevaux moiens, plus hauls que coursiers'. The expression *moien* in the sense of *honorable* is presented by *Le petit Robert 1. Dictionnaire alphabétique et analogique de la langue française* (Paris, 1983), p. 1240, entry 'moyen, enne'.

265/ See Delachenal (ed.), *Chronique des règnes*, II, p. 216: 'les grans chevaux et palefrois du Roy'.

266/ Cf. Delachenal (ed.), *Chronique des règnes*, II, pp. 210–211.

267/ See identically Christine de Pisan (ed. Solente, *Le livre des fais et bonnes meurs*, I, p. 98). The *Mémoire* in this regard is a compromise, it satisfied itself with a mention of the black colour of the emperor's horse: cf. Lechová, 'Zpráva o návštěvě Paříže', p. 51 and Thomas, 'Ein Zeitgenössisches Memorandum', p. 116.

268/ The research still proceeds from the information gained during the work on the edition by Delachenal (ed.), *Chronique des règnes*, III and IV (the Introduction there, esp. pp. VIII–XII). The most recent knowledge is summarised in Excursus – Pictorial Series and Illustrations.

124. / XXVI. Meeting of King Charles V and Emperor Charles IV (BL, Ms. royal 20 C VII, fol. 198va–b)

differ only in colour, not in stature. The fact that the head of the emperor's sorrel is slightly bowed cannot be ascribed symbolic meaning, because only so could the illuminator capture the heads of the other horses.[269] On the other hand, the next miniature to which we pay attention distinguishes the horses not only by size but also by colour, and we can gather only on the basis of the Account that the representatives of the city of Paris ride on the two types of chargers (i.e. destriers and coursers). At the same time, the emperor himself is crouching in the litter carried by two greyish mules (Pic. 74 / V).[270] The third miniature is of crucial significance, because it depicts the meeting of the three crowned sovereigns (Pic. 75 / VI). The host's white horse (*palefroi*) is proudly holding its head high here, whereas it is as if the emperor's black horse (probably a *destrier*) with its hung head were indicating its subordination. Wenceslas IV is sitting on a sorrel; two of the feudal lords of the Luxemburg escort are arriving from the left also on white horses. With the last miniature with the motif of horses, which depicts the entry of the three monarchs into Paris, the illuminator does not seem to have read the Account very carefully (Pic. 77 / VIII). In discrepancy with the text, the emperor rides to the left of the king of France, although Charles V had insisted that he would have his honourable uncle on his right. The illuminator evidently attempted to comply here with the common conception that the first in France is always the king, only then the emperor. At the same time, he mastered it skilfully: he slightly fronted the white horse of Charles V within the trio of the walking chargers, so that the three sovereigns follow in a proper hierarchical succession in the order of the king of France, the emperor and his son. A lesser flaw of the beauty is that the colour of the horses does not correspond to the protocol. The parade horse (palfrey) is slightly grey, the emperor's destrier this time has a dark-grey coat and Wenceslas' horse is not black but sorrel (fol. 470v).

The second, only a little later, cycle of illuminations from the very beginning of the fifteen century decorates the abridged version of the Account in manuscript of the British Library in London Royal 20 C VII.[271] The illuminator appears to have liked

269/ BN in Paris, MS fr. 2813, fol. 468va.

270/ BN in Paris, MS fr. 2813, fol. 469rb. According to Christine de Pisan, the mules were white (see Note 19 above), whereas the Account in connection with the litter speaks of two mules and two coursers (*coursiers*), which as I assume alternated. See Delachenal (ed.), *Chronique des règnes*, II, p. 204.

271/ For more on this manuscript, see Hedeman, *The Royal Image*, pp. 221–226.

125. / XXVII. Joint journey of the rulers to Paris (BL, Ms. royal 20 C VII, fol. 198vb)

126. / XXXII. Welcome of Emperor Charles IV by the representatives of the city of Paris. Les Grandes Chroniques de France, illumination by Jean Fouquet (BnF, ms. fr. 6465, fol. 442v)

horses; I counted twenty-nine of them in five of the nine miniatures of our cycle. Not even this master always adhered to the model. He depicted Charles IV as arriving in France on a white horse (Pic. 114 / XXIII), but during the meeting with the Parisian notables both he and Wenceslas sit upon the prescribed black horses (Pic. 121 / XXV), just like during the more momentous scene of the mutual greeting with Charles V (Pic. 124 / XXVI). Finally also during the ride of the monarchs in an even line, the host has his uncle and emperor in one person on the appropriate right side (Pic. 125 / XXVII). It is gratifying that in at least two cases the valets hold the emperor's black horse from the right as befit a destrier.

The third cycle was created by Jean Fouquet, a master among masters, before 1461. Paris had not changed much from the time of Charles V, and Fouquet knew how to capture it exquisitely. As against the abstract decoration of the background of the previous two manuscripts, the events take place here in realistic coulisses. Horses figure in six of the overall number of eight miniatures. Fouquet endowed them with grace, noble movement as well as sparks in their eyes. He also has to be forgiven for not having read the Account very carefully. He placed the emperor and his son on white horses not only during the entry into the city of Cambrai (Pic. 118 / XXX), which was on imperial land, but also during the meeting with the Parisian notables on the plains between Saint-Denis and La Chapelle-Saint-Denis (Pic. 126 / XXXII). In both cases, they are horses worthy of an emperor. This is evidently what a parade palfrey looked like! On the other hand, at the church in the already-mentioned La Chapelle-Saint-Denis, the emperor and Wenceslas are correctly mounting black destriers, which are however covered all over in azure-blue covers with golden lilies according to the period fashion. The white horse of Charles V struggles in identical gear, namely both when leaving Paris and when standing, at the moment the nephew

127. / XXXVII. Meeting of the French king with the Holy Roman Emperor and his son. Les Grandes Chroniques de France, beginning of the 15th century (Besançon, Bibliothèque municipale, ms. 863, fol. 413vb)

is greeting his uncle with a handshake (Pics 129 / XXXIV, 122 / XXXV). Fouquet was partial to horses, so he preferred them to mules in the scene with the litter during the arrival in Saint-Denis (Pic. 115 / XXXI).

Several other illuminated manuscripts of the *Great Chronicles of France* limited themselves to a single illustration of the emperor's visit. Popularity was enjoyed by the ceremonial banquet and the first greeting of the sovereigns in the foreground of Paris. Two of these manuscripts come from the first decades of the fifteenth century and thus are still close in time to our summit. An anonymous Dutch or Flemish master depicted not only Charles V but also his uncle on white horses in the square miniature in the manuscript of the British Library in London Sloane 2433, Vol. C, fol. 149va (Pic. 103 / XXXVIII). It seems that the white colour suited the illuminators from their artistic perspective better than the black stipulated by protocol. It is true as well of the creator of the miniature of the Municipal Library in Besançon MS 863, who also preferred a white horse in the case of Charles IV, whereas he put his French host on a no less noble horse with a fair coat (Pic. 127 / XXXVII), which with its golden shade suitably fit the lilies on the king's blue mantle.[272]

There remain to be mentioned two more, almost identical, illuminations from the turn of the sixteenth century, which form a kind of title page for the calligraphically written, abridged versions of our Account. In the landscape with trees, we can see the ruin of a windmill in the distance on a hillock, on the right on a high hill there is a distinct château or castle. Both sovereigns are just reaching out their hands in a mutual greeting. It was certainly heartfelt, but it is no less important for us that the illuminators depicted the colour of the horses correctly in agreement with the protocol. The king of France in a red tunic with white ermine around his neck has arrived from the left on a white horse in blue gear, the emperor then from the right in a purple robe on a black horse in red gear.[273]

Our equestrian study can be concluded with the finding that the illuminators of the *Great Chronicles of France* took the ceremonial prescriptions of the royal court into account, but only when it suited their artistic feeling. Our creators expressed significant arbitrariness also in the depiction of the build and other characteristic features of the parading grey, black, sorrel, chestnut as well as white horses. Then, like today, everyone liked horses, but only few understood them.

272/ On this manuscript, see i.a. Hedeman, *The Royal Image*, pp. 226–228.
273/ For more on both manuscripts, see Excursus – Pictorial Series and Illustrations.

Ceremonial occasions required proper attire. And since we are in the court milieu of France, we can anticipate that costumes will parade before our eyes like at a fashion show.[274] The verbal description of the clothes in the Account is surprisingly detailed but requires both extensive knowledge and significant imagination. The main iconographic series in manuscript MS fr. 2813 is astonishingly quite frugal and with its focus on the crowned heads also rather narrow in its scope. If we consider the somewhat later depictions in the manuscripts of the British Library and the Municipal Library in Besançon, we will find minor differences in cut but on the whole will still remain in a quandary on how to harmonise the text of the Account with the visual representation. If we employed *The Very Rich Hours of the Duke of Berry* or other illuminated manuscripts from the library of Duke John of Berry for assistance, it would soon be evident that we have the fashion of a more advanced period in front of us. For this reason, the series of illuminations by Jean Fouquet from the time around 1460 is even more out of question. If it is so, nothing else remains but to follow the Account step by step, attempt to convey well the distant past and find suitable equivalents for the period items of clothing. Neither will be easy.

The discussion will first deal with the clothes and their colours during the description of the emperor's entry into Cambrai on 22 December 1377. The emperor was arriving on a grey riding horse, dressed in a mantle and hat of grey cloth, trimmed with marten. The expression *mantel* from the Latin *mantellus* has denoted an outer garment with or without sleeves which was to protect the body from cold.[275] We learn nothing else of the clothing of both Luxemburgs. Nevertheless, many places mention the hats which the emperor and undoubtedly also his son removed when meeting the king of France and his relatives. The Account always speaks only of a hat (*chaperon*); the only exception is the meeting of the emperor and his nephew between La Chapelle-Saint-Denis and the windmill, when the emperor removed along with his hat also his beret. It arises from the context that it was a kind of cap which protected the ears and other parts of the head from the winter cold under the hat.[276] On the other hand, the contemporaneous *Mémoire* states that the emperor removed a so-called *aumuche*, otherwise also *aumusse* (in English *almuce* or *amice*, from the Latin *almucia*), which in this case most likely referred to a fur hood with a cape.[277]

The period illuminators of the *Great Chronicles of France* depicted both Luxemburgs only with crowns;

274/ I will not be far from the truth here, because according to numerous historians of clothing the phenomenon of fashion was born in the middle of the fourteenth century. For the initial orientation in that, cf. Françoise Piponnier and Perrine Mane, *Se vêtir au Moyen Âge*, p. 81. The Czech reader has the advantage of being able to rely on the excellent overview with a rich pictorial documentation by Kybalová, *Dějiny odívání. Středověk*. Mediaeval clothing has otherwise been devoted extensive literature, but it usually fails if detailed information is sought. Therefore, I shall further mention only works relevant in the given context.

275/ Cf. Kybalová, *Dějiny odívání. Středověk*, pp. 163–166.

276/ See Delachenal (ed.), *Chronique des règnes*, II, p. 217 (*barrete et chaperon*), the expression *chaperon* appears on pp. 198, 224, 225 (2x), 233, 235, 258 and 260. For beret or biretta, see also Kybalová, *Dějiny odívání. Středověk*, p. 185.

277/ See Thomas, 'Ein zeitgenössisches Memorandum', p. 116; for the interpretation, see p. 109 ibid. On the interpretation, cf. Čeněk Zíbrt and Zikmund Winter, *Dějiny kroje v zemích českých*, I, p. 421, and II, p. 221; for further information, see the entry 'almucia', *Latinitatis Medii Aevi lexicon Bohemorum*, I, p. 136.

128. Parade helmet of the royal body guards of Charles VI. Galvanoplastic replica of fragments found in archaeological research of the Louvre

the hat, or rather cap, which the emperor in Fouquet's miniatures wears on his head corresponds to the fashion of an entirely different period. On that, it is necessary to add that the expression *chaperon* referred to, rather than a hat in today's sense, a taller cap or even a hood. After all, French also has an expression for hat in our sense of the word, i.e. *chapeau* (Old French *chapel*). In the Account, if I am not mistaken, this word appears only once in connection with the bodyguards of Marshal de Blainville, who wore decorative helmets (*chapeaux de parement*) as part of their uniforms. With a significant likelihood, it was the so-called *casque* or more precisely the *chapel doré*, the parade helmet of the king's bodyguard. Fragments of one exemplar with the emblems of Charles VI, which were found during archaeological research at the Louvre in 1984, have been successfully reconstructed by the galvanoplastic method.[278]

What may be closer to the reality at the end of the 1370s is the pointed hat (*chapel à bec*) 'following old fashion, embroidered and very richly set with pearls',[279] with which Jean Fouquet covered the head of the king of France in accord with the version of the Account (Pic. 129 / XXXIV). Charles V apparently had a special liking for tradition even when the small decorative cap or rather coif (*coiffe*) was concerned. According to the expert testimony of poet Christine de Pisan, the kings of France had worn them under their hats from ancient times.[280] And as it was a singularity, Charles V showed it to his uncle when he came to visit him in his chamber in the palace.

In contradiction to all the period miniatures of the *Great Chronicles of France*, the Account does not mention crowns, which were worn – as we would quite rightly expect – on their heads, even once. Neither was it the case at the ceremonial banquets. The only exception in this respect is the mention of the richly decorated circlet or coronet worn by Queen Jeanne at the reception in Saint-Pol. In this case, the expression *cercle* certainly meant a gold coronet, because it could have also been a crown of cloth or flowers, also called a *chapel*.[281] Even if we were to allow that the monarchs were adorned with crowns anyway, these would have had to be travelling crowns, namely in the case of both Luxemburgs, or crowns for 'everyday' purposes. We find support for this opinion in the Account itself, and therefore we should mention again that the king complied with the repeated wish of the king and sent him his new crown to see. It was brought to the country residence in Beauté-sur-Marne by Gilles Malet and the king's goldsmith Hennequin du Viviers. When the emperor had examined it with great pleasure, the two entrusted courtiers placed it back in its strongbox.[282]

278/ For more on that, see Fleury and Kruta, *Le château du Louvre*, pp. 74–78, with pictorial documentation as well. I offer a somewhat different opinion here, because I cannot imagine that the king himself would have ridden with such a helmet.

279/ Delachenal (ed.), *Chronique des règnes*, II, p. 212: 'brodé et couvert de perles tres richement'.

280/ S. Solente (ed.), *Le livre des fais et bonnes meurs*, I, p. 104. It is surprisingly one of the few places where the poet added a detail as against the Account, from which she proceeded.

281/ On that, see Delachenal (ed.), *Chronique des règnes*, II, p. 259, Note 2.

282/ The interest of Charles IV in the French crown was examined in a wider context by Otavsky, *Die Sankt Wenzelskrone im Prager Domschatz*, p. 92.

129. / XXXIV. King of France Charles V rides with his retinue to meet the emperor. Les Grandes Chroniques de France, illumination by Jean Fouquet (BnF, ms. fr. 6465, fol. 443v)

This episode seems to have a wider significance, because it warns against the common idea suggested by mediaeval miniatures. The crown was almost a relic, a sacred symbol which with the exception of the coronation and especially important court and imperial ceremonies belonged more in a strongbox than on a head. The emperor for instance transported the imperial crown with other insignia to Nuremberg in 1361.[283] Also Elizabeth of Pomerania liked to be seen with the crown on her head. During the visit of Dortmund in 1378, she even carried two with her. She had one of gold with precious stones on her head during the ceremonial entry, while the second, even more costly, at the ball at the city hall. It is also necessary to take into consideration that wearing the crown on ceremonial occasions was not a privilege only of 'crowned heads'.[284]

If we have already mentioned the hat of the king of France, it is necessary to add in what clothes he was coming to meet the emperor. His travelling outfit consisted of two parts according to the Account. The undergarments were comprised of a *cote hardie d'escarlate vermeille*, i.e. a riding jacket with sleeves, which was worn outside unlike the so-called *surcot* (surcotte or surcoat) and was popularly used when horseback riding.[285] *Escarlate vermeille* only seems

283/ For a source with further valuable details with references to the literature, see Arno Mentzel-Reuters, 'Die goldene Krone. Entwicklungslinien mittelalterlicher Herrschaftssymbolik', pp. 168–173. On Empress Elizabeth, see Gisela Wilbertz, 'Elisabeth von Pommern', pp. 61–62.

284/ On that, see Otavsky, 'Die Dynastie der Luxemburger und die Pariser Kunst unter den letzten Kapetingern', p. 67.

285/ The explanation was presented by Louis-Claude Douët d'Arcq, *Comptes de l'argenterie des rois de France au XIVe siècle*, p. 365. Most of the special terminology was clarified already in the footnotes to his edition by Delache-

to be a double colour marking, because scarlet (*escarlete*) designated a special cloth of various colours of bright shades which was treated by soaking in a solution with kermes, i.e. a type of coccus (*Coccus ilicis*). Scarlet cloth was thus originally not only red but also pink, purple, blue, brown, white as well as black, and only later did the meaning shift to its most common colour, i.e. red in a dark crimson shade, which was reserved for high secular as well as ecclesiastical dignitaries.[286] Also the outer mantle (*mantel à fons de cuve fourré*) requires explanation. It is a cloak similar to a gown with a round cut, which in winter was usually lined with fur and in summer with silk or half-silk fabric, the so-called *sendal*.[287] Although the Account does not especially emphasise it, it went without saying in the court milieu that the king would be recognised at first sight not only in the throne room but primarily in the public spaces (Pic. 130 / XXIX). All the more did it hold true of the ruler of France, anointed with holy oil, in whom according to Philippe de Mézières 'royal, or it is possible to say even divine, authority is outwardly represented through appropriately honourable vestment, different from others.[288]

The court marshals were keeping in mind the overall impression of the ceremonial reception and did not therefore hesitate to give binding instructions in the king's name even to highly placed participants in the procession. In so doing, they did not forget even the prelates, who were told to wear *chappes romaines*, i.e. most likely a richly adorned

130. / XXIX. Charles V receives the envoys of the Holy Roman emperor. Les Grandes Chroniques de France, illumination by Jean Fouquet (BnF, ms. fr. 6465, fol. 440v)

sleeveless sacral vestment (a cope), for the ride on the horses.[289] It was further applied also to them that their chaplains and servants were to be in the colours of their lords. It went without saying just as well that the knights, squires and servants of the princes and other feudal lords would be similarly dressed in the relevant liveries. In Senlis, the knights in the escort of the dukes of Berry and Burgundy wore clothes of black and grey velvet; the squires had the same colours in silk. At least it says so in the Account,

nal, who relied upon Victor Gay, *Glossaire archéologique du Moyen Âge et de la Renaissance*. Besides this glossary, which only goes to the letter G, I further took into account another earlier work of a similar focus whose author is Léon de Laborde: *Glossaire française du Moyen Âge à l'usage de l'archéologue et de l'amateur des arts*.

286/ Gay, *Glossaire archéologique*, I, p. 593. The meaning of colours in mediaeval life and art is dealt with by extensive literature, see, i.a. Michel Pastoureau, 'Les couleurs médiévales: systèmes de valeurs et modes de sensibilité', pp. 35–49; from the Czech literature, see most recently Markéta Dlouhá, 'Symbolika barev ve středověku', pp. 14–38.

287/ Gay, *Glossaire archéologique*, I, p. 726. On *sendal* or *cendal*, cf. also Zíbrt and Winter, *Dějiny kroje*, I, p. 116.

288/ George W. Coopland (ed.), *Philippe de Mézières, Chancellor of Cyprus, Le Songe du vieil pèlerin*, II, p. 225.

289/ It was thought so also by the Roland Delachenal (ed.), *Chronique des règnes*, II, p. 212, Note 4. In the word *chappe*, it is possible to recognise the Latin word *cappa*, on the meaning of which see Harry Kühnel, *Bildwörterbuch der Kleidung und Rüstung*, p. 44. However, also here on p. 129 is an explanation of the outer clothing called a cape, French *chappe*, which was derived from the Roman cloak called *paenula*.

whereas it arises from the records of an accounting nature that these colours were selected for his people by Duke of Burgundy Philip II. At the same time, it is not ruled out that Philip the Bold procured the same liveries also for the escort of his brother, because he had bought one mantle of the houppelande type and two ceremonial costumes, one of wool and the other of velvet, for him in Ghent. At the same time, he made do with one pair of both clothes, whereas the duke of Berry even ordered a gold-interlaced canopy for himself for the same ceremony.[290] Particularly the high court officials took pride in their uniform costumes indicating their position.[291] The chamberlains, of whom there were at least sixteen in the procession, were in two types of costumes. The First Gentleman of the Chamber, who was Bureau de la Rivière, and also Count of Tancarville, Grand Chamberlain of France, if he was present, was dressed in velvet of an unspecified colour, the others then in a scarlet robe of two colours. This is however only a supposition, because the distinction by person is not clear from the text.

According to the court hierarchy, next came the masters of the royal household. Not even in their case is it said whether all four led by Grand Master of the Royal Household Pierre de Villiers attended the welcome. They were also dressed in velvet of two colours, namely in azure blue and tawny brown.[292] The so-called honorary knights, whose court status not even the publisher knew how to resolve very well, walked or rode in the procession in velvet costumes of a vermilion hue. The squires of the bodyguard and the royal stables followed in blue camocas (in Latin *camocatus*), i.e. precious silk cloth from India, which ranked with damask and was closest to the so-called lampas.[293] The officers of the palace guard did not differ from them in the material of their uniforms but in their execution called *mi-parti*, i.e. in blue and red stripes. The liking for glaring colours placed side by side was typical not only for mediaeval art but also for some spheres of everyday life. Dichromatism found a particular use in the court milieu, where *mi-parti* clothing was not only a social but even a heraldic sign for the servants and the squires of various lords. At the same time, various executions in terms of the colour and quality of the materials indicated the tasks, missions or authorisation of the wearers.[294] Whereas a numerous group of breadmasters, butlers and carvers at the table along with the officials of Dauphin Charles had clothing of two kinds of satin in white and tawny colours, the masters and squires of the cuisine were wearing silk mantles with wide, richly textured sleeves, the so-called houppelandes, and otter fur coats (*aumusse*) with mother-of-pearl buttons.[295]

The next part of the procession comprised numerous groups of servants, who differed from one

290/ According to the fragment of the receipt from 12 February 1378, which Duke Philip II had paid in Ghent (ed. Bernard Prost, *Inventaires mobiliers et extraits des comptes des ducs de Bourgogne de la Maison de Valois (1363–1477)*, II, pp. 15–16, No. 96).

291/ On clothing as a sign of social stratification generally, see Mérindol, 'Signes de hiérarchie sociale à la fin du moyen âge d'après le vêtement. Méthodes et recherches'; for France, see Michèle Beaulieu, 'Le costume, miroir des mentalités de la France médiévale' and from a European perspective orientationally, see Kühnel, 'Kleidung und Gesellschaft im Mittelalter', and there esp. p. XLVII–L. and the selected bibliography on pp. 317–331. In terms of *mi-parti* costumes, see Veronika Mertens, *Mi-parti als Zeichen*, pp. 15–20, but with only exceptional evidence from French sources.

292/ On the meaning of the terms *ynde* and *tenné*, see Delachenal (ed.), *Chronique des règnes*, II, p. 213, Note 4.

293/ Gay, *Glossaire archéologique*, I, p. 265.

294/ On the mediaeval liking for bright colours concisely, see Umberto Eco, *Art and Beauty in the Middle Ages*, pp. 43–51. On the *mi-parti* clothing, which is proved already in the tenth century, at length, see Mertens, *Mi-parti als Zeichen*, esp. pp. 8–22, further Kühnel, 'Kleidung und Gesellschaft im Mittelalter', pp. LIV–LV, and Kybalová, *Dějiny odívání. Středověk*, pp. 131–132.

295/ On mantles of the houppelande type, which were a sign of the highest level in France, Burgundy as well as Holland until the middle of the fifteenth century, cf. i.a. Kühnel, *Bildwörterbuch der Kleidung und Rüstung*, pp. 120–121, and Kybalová, *Dějiny odívání. Středověk*, pp. 159–161. These expensive mantles lined with precious furs were also quite common New Year's presents. On that, see Jan Hirschbiegel, *Étrennes. Untersuchungen zum höfischen Geschenkverkehr im spätmittelalterlichen Frankreich der Zeit König Karls VI. (1380–1422)*, p. 176, with further references. On the fur mantle 'aumusse, aumuce' (from the Latin *almucia*), see Zíbrt and Winter, *Dějiny kroje*, I, p. 421, II, p. 221.

another by the colours of their stripes of the drapery, hence less expensive, dresses. The valets of the chamber wore liveries with grey-white stripes on black cloth; the uniforms of the sergeants of the palace guard had blue and black stripes; the sommeliers then were characterised by brown and vermilion stripes. Costumes of the *mi-parti* type, as it seems, set the tone in the procession, because the costumes of the Parisian burghers, who rode out to meet the Luxemburg delegation, were also in a white-purple design.[296] At the same time, they were not, and this should be mentioned here, the traditional colours of Paris, which had played a role during the uprising of Étienne Marcel. The colours on the ceremonial entries of the rulers varied, e.g. during the welcome of Charles VI on 11 November 1380 the *mi-parti* clothes of the Parisian burghers were green and white. Similarly, the prescribed colours of the costumes altered in Tournai, but other cities preferred their heraldic colours.[297] In connection with the reception of the delegation of the Sorbonne, the Account further mentions that its members ceremonially appeared in their gowns and habits (*chappes et habiz*). On the other hand, not a word comes on the clothing of the numerous ladies during the emperor's visit to the residence in Saint-Pol, because this private part of the programme did not have the character of a state presentation.

It has already been said of the accompanying illuminations that one cannot expect too much from them. Nevertheless, also trifles may be valuable. We shall start with head covers. We most frequently encounter crowns in the male and female versions; high ecclesiastical dignitaries have mitres, university masters birettas. Only the large pointed hat of the man in the depiction of the entry into Paris (fol. 470v – Pic. 77 / VIII), which could mark the First Squire of the King's Stables (*premier écuyer de corps*), attracts attention for its shape. The high hats of the dukes with clasps or insignia, which sometimes decorate also the lower circular caps of other feudal lords, are much more striking. Both are a favourite object of depiction of the illuminator of the manuscript in the British Library in London Royal 20 C VII (cf. fol. 194v and 196v, Pics 64 / XX and 113 / XXII). From the head, we jump to the feet. Whereas riding boots with gilded spurs stick out from the riding mantle of the emperor (fol. 468v – Pic. 73 / IV), his envoy is shod in moccasins with a buckle at the reception by King Charles V (fol. 467r – Pic. 70 / I). We can see similar shoes with a buckle on the feet of the young lady from the suite of Queen Jeanne (fol. 477r) and surprisingly also as the outdoor shoes of the officers of the palace guard – the *huissiers d'armes* (fol. 470v – Pic. 77 / VIII). Nevertheless, the most common type of footwear are the riding boots in various colours from grey through blue all the way to red.[298]

Allow us to linger for a little longer at the last-mentioned guards. Their tight doublets with low-placed black belts are *mi-parti* but with red and purple, not red and blue, stripes. In their hands, they all hold staves, with which they were to maintain order, just like the foot knights in unicolour doublets of red velvet and gilded belts in the opposite lower corner of the miniature on fol. 470v (Pic. 77 / VIII). Their monochromatic leggings are of various shades, as is true also in the case of the five sergeants of the palace guard (*sergents d'armes du roi*) of the king, depicted on fol. 470r (Pic. 76 / VII). Their uniforms comprise vertically striped cloth doublets in black and grey, which is somewhat in disagreement with the wording of the Account, prescribing blue instead of grey. They wield maces as a weapon as well as symbol of their service in their right hands; on their chests they have silver-decorated belts with sheaths for swords.

It is now the turn of the main actors in the story. King of France Charles V is depicted in seven of

296/ In this case, also the original text mentions *mi-parties de blanc et de violet* (ed. Delachenal, *Chronique des règnes*, II, p. 209).

297/ See Guenée and Lehoux, *Les entrées royales françaises*, pp. 11–12 and 58 (here the colours in Paris in November 1380 according to the chronicler Juvénal des Ursins).

298/ In checking the colours, I relied on the expert descriptions of the individual miniatures by Cibulka, 'Iluminované popsání cesty Karla IV. do Francie', pp. 64–69.

the nine miniatures either in a dark-blue coronation mantle with golden lilies and ermine collar or at least in dark-blue vestments. It is always that way inside, which needs to be understood as both an obligation for the traditional representation[299] and as a manifestation of the majesty of the King of France on his home soil. Yet around 1380 it was not appropriate to ride a horse in a royal mantle of this type,[300] and therefore the travelling costume of Charles V comprised a vermilion mantle with an ermine collar and blue riding boots. Any other colour than vermilion was also out of question for the singular depiction of Dauphin Charles on fol. 480r (Pic. 88 / XIX), whose mantle with ermine lining is decorated with a collar of the same fur. In terms of the king's brothers, John of Berry and Duke of Burgundy Philip, who welcomed the emperor near Senlis, their travelling mantles in a combination of blue, grey and black are lined with fur. However, in the handover of the presents on fol. 478r (Pic. 86 / XVII), we can see one in a vermilion robe with a blue mantle and the other in a grey-purple robe.

Depending on the circumstances, the clothes also of Emperor Charles IV alternate in the miniatures. During the Christmas reading of the gospel, he is wearing a white alb under a bluish dalmatic (fol. 467v – Pic. 72 / III); in the scene of the oath of his son, he appears in a grey-purple vestment, probably because the vermilion mantle befitted King Wenceslas more this time (fol. 478ra – Pic. 84 / XV). In this act, the emperor's chancellor is assisting in a long lilac robe; behind him, one of the knights is standing in the same red doublet with a gilded belt as we saw with the foot knights of the French side. The emperor otherwise always had a mantle or at least a robe in vermilion (cinnabar), whereas under the mantle a robe in decent grey, purple or blue shades is sometimes visible. The mantles are sometimes lined with fur; exceptionally they are decorated with a gold clasp (fol. 473v – Pic. 80 / XI); the collars are ermine, but other times brown or grey.

The king of the Romans is in most cases marked by a mantle, or at least an under-robe, of blue. It is so on fol. 468v (Pic. 73 / IV), where his travelling costume comprises a blue doublet with a gold belt and a mantle with ermine around the neck. The long blue mantle with narrow sleeves and with a stand-up collar is sometimes without decoration (fol. 470v – Pic. 77 / VIII), other times with a gold clasp (fol. 471v – Pic. 78 / IX) or with an ornate metal belt (fol. 477r – Pic. 83 / XIV). Despite the dominant blue, however, the clothes of Wenceslas IV exhibit the widest palette of colours. Other than by the already-mentioned scene of the oath, it is evidenced also by the depiction of the procession on fol. 467v (Pic. 71 / II), in which Wenceslas is walking in a robe as well as mantle of a pink colour. He has a pink robe, but this time with a grey-purple mantle, also when receiving the presents on fol. 478r (Pic. 86 / XVII). Just for the sake of completeness, it is possible to mention that Wenceslas' undergarments do not shun even shades of green and purple grey.

In terms of the costumes implemented, the large miniature of the Epiphany banquet on fol. 473v (Pic. 80 / XI) is a real feast for the eyes. The ceremonial robe of the kings has already been mentioned, and therefore the first to follow in the order are the ecclesiastical dignitaries. The first from the left should be Archbishop of Rheims Jean de Craon, who is depicted in a white alb and in a dark-green cope, under which a piece of vermilion unidentifiable material is visible. Bishop of Warmia Henry Sorbom next to King Wenceslas wears a light-blue cope with pink lining, whereas his neighbour, most likely Bishop of Paris Aimery de Magnac, is dressed in a red cope in a vermilion shade. All three bishops have white, gold-decorated mitres; orphrey has been used also on their amices with the rectangular ends of the corners of the collars.[301] Likewise the figures of the three

299/ In this regard, the twin miniature of the coronation of Charles V and Jeanne of Bourbon in the same manuscript, BN Paris MS fr. 2813, fol. 439r, is significant.

300/ It naturally did not bother the illuminator Fouquet anymore as is apparent from Pic. 129 / XXXIV.

301/ The amice (in French *amict*, in German *Amikt*; also

court officials or servants in front of the table covered with white tablecloth decorated in grey attract attention. There can be no doubt about the function of the cutter at the table in the purple-grey tight doublet with the low-placed gilded belt on which a shorter sword is hung in a black sheath. It is worth noticing not only his leggings or puttees in the *mi-parti* style but also the square pillow with fringes serving as a leg support. His two colleagues in bright-red and bright-blue doublets resemble him, but their posture with crossed arms tells us that they stood higher in the court hierarchy. Their task was to order and supervise, which in the case of the man with the double chin is marked perhaps also by his decorations on his sleeves and left leg.

There is no reason to doubt that the master who created this splendid illumination was acquainted with contemporary court costumes, which is proved even by the then modern armour of the Harnisch type, worn by the actors presenting the capture of Jerusalem.[302] Notwithstanding that, the absence of the richly adorned as well as pleated mantles with wide sleeves, with appliqués and padding, the so-called houppelandes, is however surprising. Seeing that the illuminators of both later depictions in the manuscripts of the British Library already knew this mantle well, it is necessary to count with a certain time lag of court fashion. The houppelandes of the three courtiers serving at the table in the miniature of the manuscript Nero E II-2, fol. 229v (Pic. 102 / XXXIX) differ in the execution as well as colour. Whereas the man with the walking stick has a red mantle, the servant in the middle has a dark-blue one and his colleague on the left a light-red one. I add that counter to expectations the emperor is in a green and the king of France in a vermilion ceremonial robe. Also the mantle of the court dignitary in front of the set table in manuscript BL Ms. Royal 20 C VII, fol. 199r (Pic. 152 / XXVIII) has the characteristic form of the houppelande. In the same manuscript, also the decorated travelling mantles and the high angular hats of both dukes on fol. 196va (Pic. 113 / XXII) draw the reader's attention.

I have left women's clothing for last. We already know that according to court protocol Sunday, 10 January 1378, was reserved for the emperor's meeting with the queen and her ladies-in-waiting. The Account does not mention a word on the women's costumes, and so we have to satisfy ourselves with the miniature of the main cycle in the manuscript of the Bibliothèque nationale, ms. fr. 2813, fol. 477r (Pic. 83 / XIV). At the embrace with the emperor, the standing queen, Jeanne of Bourbon, is wearing a long fitted gown of the *cote* type in grey-purple with silver dots, with a train and oval neckline. The hairstyle, as it also is with the ladies-in-waiting, is decorated by side braids. The first of them, perhaps Princess Bonne, a daughter of Duke John of Berry, differs in her clothing from the other ladies by having a so-called *surcot* with the large armholes fashionable then on her lilac undergarment.

I am sure that if I have left out any minor point, the sharper eye of the female readers will remedy it.

superhumeral, ephod, or pallium) was a part of the liturgical vestments from the eighth century; it was usually a square piece of linen covering the neck and shoulders, which in the Late Middle Ages could be adorned with the parure or *parura* embroidered with gold, silver as well as pearls. Orientationally on that, see *Bildwörterbuch der Kleidung und Rüstung*, pp. 6 and 188.

302/ For the introductory information, see *Bildwörterbuch der Kleidung und Rüstung*, p. 101 and Table XI on p. 302.

Whoever would like to form an approximate idea of the French metropolis in 1378 would have to get off at the metro station Strasbourg – Saint-Denis and walk along Saint-Denis Boulevard towards the monumental arch of the gate built by architect François Blondel in 1672. This is where Paris began and ended at the time of the emperor's visit. The appearance of the gate at that time is sketched for us by the miniature by Jean Fouquet depicting the ceremonial entry of Charles V into Paris after his coronation in Rheims in May 1364.[303] Most of the Parisian gates were small fortresses. This was also true for the monumental gate with four turrets making it possible to see as well as fire in all directions. The illuminator also depicted the three saints under the stone baldaquins very faithfully. In the centre, we can recognise St Denis, which in accord with *The Golden Legend* (in Latin *Legenda Aurea*) holds his chopped off head in his hands; beside him, holding their heads high for the moment, stand Saints Rusticus and Eleutherius, who died the same martyr's death. When looking left, which is a view that also the emperor and his son were offered, it is possible to see a line of ramparts, whose forward defensive position was not entirely completed at the time of Charles V, the fortress gate of St Martin, further the tower with corner turrets of the former seat of the Knights Templar, which was given to the Maltese Knights, and all the way at the back the silhouette of the Bastille, the huge fortress completed in 1382 for the protection of the nearby residence in Saint-Pol.

131. Ceremonial entry of Charles V into Paris through the Saint-Denis Gate on 19 June 1364. Miniature by Jean Fouquet, Grandes Chroniques de France (BnF, ms. fr. 6465, fol. 417r)

303/ The authenticity of Fouquet's miniature is confirmed by early engravings as well as archaeological research. For more on that, see Avril, Gousset and Guenée, *Les Grandes Chroniques de France*, p. 217.

132. Palace de la Cité viewed from the east. Engraving from around 1640

Having ridden through the city gate, the emperor reached Grand Boulevard, today's Rue Saint-Denis, which in those times led to the area before the urban fortress of Grand Châtelet, seat of the royal provost. The high tower of St Jacob, so characteristic for this area today, did not yet stand. The access to the Île de la Cité, the largest of the three isles in this part of the Seine and historic base of Paris, was opened from this side by the Bridge of the Money Changers (*Pont-aux-Changeurs*). These wealthy financiers had their stalls in small huts along both sides of the carriageway, from which the river was thus not visible at all. Only with the end of the bridge did the emperor's eyes perceive the sight of the complex of the Palace de la Cité, which was already well known to him. On the left, he certainly did not fail to notice the protruding towers of the Cathedral of Notre-Dame, but is likely to have been more engaged by the quadrangular tower with its astronomical clock which Charles V had made around 1370. The old royal Palace de la Cité lay along the entire right side of Rue de la Barillerie (today's *Boulevard du Palais*) all the way to St Michael's Bridge (*Pont Saint-Michel*). According to an engraving from around 1640, two large fortified gates led from the street to the Palace. Emperor Charles IV with his escort entered the first of them, leading to the so called May Courtyard (*Cour du Mai*),[304] where a chair with a cover interlaced with gold awaited him under the main staircase.

The royal palace with an area of 4.9 ha and with a perimeter of roughly 1 km encompassed an entire third of the Île de la Cité under Charles V. Already in earlier times, it comprised three parts, i.e. Sainte-Chapelle and the canons' residences in the south, the so-called Grand Palace with public halls in the north, and finally the residences of the king and queen in the western part, to which enclosed gardens were connected. For initial orientation, we will use both a small schematic plan (Pic. 133) and a reconstruction of the layout at the beginning of the sixteenth century whose creator is the famous architect Eugène Emmanuel Viollet-le-Duc (Pic. 134).[305]

304/ The courtyard was named according to the 'maypole', i.e. the beautiful tree from the king's forests that was raised here for the May Day festival each year.

305/ I preferred this vivid illustration to the reproduction of a detailed but poorly readable map which was published

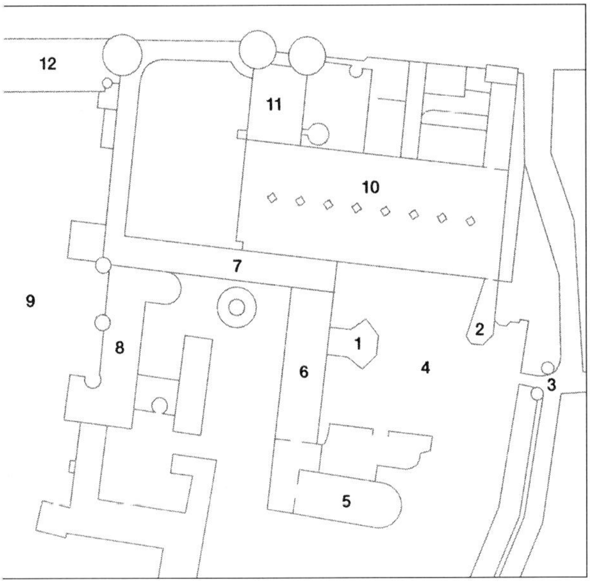

133. Schematic plan of the Palace de la Cité at the time of Charles V following Jean Guerout. 1 = monumental staircase, 2 = side entrance to the Great Hall, 3 = large gate, 4 = Cour du Mai – also the Great Court, 5 = Sainte-Chapelle, 6 = Gallery of the Merchants (Mercière), 7 = Grandes allées, 8 = Logis du Roi, 9 = Jardin du Roi, 10 = Grand salle, 11 = Grand Chamber (Grande Chambre), 12 = La Salle sur l'eau – Hall over Water, also called the Hall of St Louis.

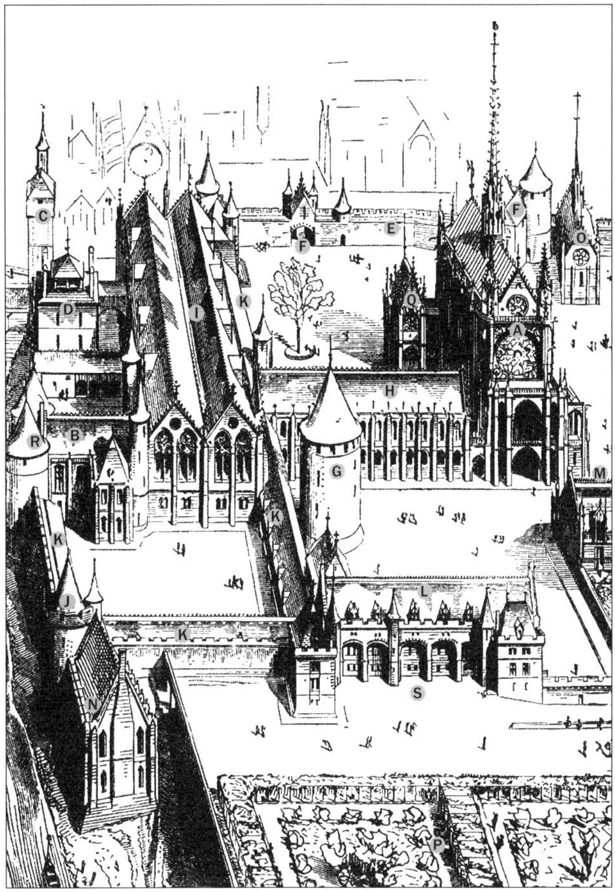

134. Palace de la Cité according to a reconstruction by Viollet-le-Duc. A – Saint-Chapelle, B – Hall of the Bodyguards, C – Tower with an astronomical clock, D – Kitchen, E – Bulwark wall, F – Wall with two gates, G – Great Tower (donjon), H – Gallery of the Merchants (Mecière), I – Great Hall of the Men-at-Arms, J – Tower called Bonbec, K – Main gallery (covered connecting walkway), L – Residential wing of the king and his family M – Accounting chamber, N – Hall of St Louis, later called the Hall on the Water, O – Grand Chamber (Grande Chambre), P – Decorative garden, Q – Royal chancellery, archive of deeds and workshop for the production of vellum sheets, R – Pair of towers, S – Courtyard of St Martin

What resembles its state today most is Saint-Chapelle (A) from 1242–1248. Also the archives of documents lying next to it along with the chancellery and the workshop for the production of parchments (Q) come from the time of Saint Louis. In the top right-hand corner, we can see another palace chapel of St Michael, which does not play any role in our story. On the right side, the dwellings of the canons and the riverside shops of the goldsmiths, which gave this bank its name so well known to all of the readers of detective novels with Inspector Maigret (*Quai des Orfèvres*), did not fit in the small drawing.

Although the royal palace was protected by the river on three sides, it was still properly fortified. The central donjon, called the Great Tower (G), from the time of Louis VI had more or less lost its primary defensive function, because the entire complex was protected in the open areas by bulwarks (E) with two gates (F) on the one hand and the towers still standing today in the continuous front line of buildings from the quadrangular tower with its astronomical clock (C) through the twin towers (R) to the tower

based on later knowledge by Guérout, 'Le Palais de la Cité', Appendix to Volume II (État vers 1360). On the Palace de la Cité, cf. also Cazelles, *Nouvelle histoire de Paris*, pp. 159–167.

135. Towers of the Palace de la Cité. Très Riches Heures du Duc de Berry. Month of May, beginning of the 15th century (MC, ms. 65, fol. 5v)

called Bonbec (J) on the other. The public sector was dominated by the two-nave building with the Great Hall on the first floor and the Hall of the Men-at-Arms (*Salle des Gens d'armes*) on the ground floor (I), which were adjoined by kitchens (D). The upper served the king, high officials and distinguished guests, the lower the armigers, members of the bodyguard and the servants. On the west side, both large halls were connected to another vaulted building, whose upper floor housed the Great Chamber (*Grande Chambre*, O) of the supreme court of justice (Parliament) and the ground floor the Hall of the Bodyguards (B). It is worth mentioning that both lower halls along with a part of the lower kitchen have been preserved to our time; during the reign of Charles V, two chambers served for administrative and control purposes, namely the Chamber of Accounts (M) and the original Hall of St Louis, later called the Hall on the Water, in which the college of the so-called counsellors-general met (N).

In his sketch, Viollet-le-Duc captured all of the main galleries, i.e. the covered joining corridors or passages (K) which connected Sainte-Chapelle, the Great Hall and the residential wing of the royal family. The most impressive of them was the Gallery of the Merchants (*Mercière*, H), where Parisian traders occasionally displayed their luxurious goods. John II the Good had the mansards on the upper floor (the so-called *galetas*, garrets) added for his adolescent son, Dauphin Charles. The gallery was entered from the May Courtyard by the so-called great stairs, which led to the two-part entry with a statue of Philip the Fair on the central column.[306] It is not certain

306/ The appearance of this staircase and the façade of the Mercière Gallery can be seen in detail on the panel altar from 1452–1454, which was originally placed in the Great Chamber of the Court of Justice and today is a part of the collections of the Museé du Louvre (Pic. 123). For more on this staircase, see Mary Whiteley, 'Deux escaliers royaux du XIVe siècle: les «grands degrez» du palais de la Cité et la «grande viz» du Louvre', pp. 137–142.

whether the emperor was brought into the Palace de la Cité this way, because another, special staircase led to the Great Hall.[307] Although experts may raise a number of objections to the reconstruction by Viollet-le-Duc, its strength is its situational clarity. His sketch provides the least support in terms of the residential wing of the king and his family (L), connected to the *Galerie Mercière* by a passage called the *Grandes Allées*. Before we look at these purely private chambers with the adjacent courtyard of St Martin (S) and ornamental garden (P), we will outline the overall appearance of the Palace de la Cité as it was captured by the illuminators of *The Very Rich Hours of the Duke of Berry*.

In the illuminations of the introductory calendar, depictions of our palace appear in the miniatures for two months. In the May scene of the ride of young aristocrats and their ladies, the silhouettes of the gables and towers with their quite characteristic shapes rise above the dense woods (Pic. 135). On the right, it is possible to recognise the round Great Tower and in the centre the somewhat raised tower with the astronomical clock; greater effort would be required to identify the protruding gables. Whereas this miniature is generally ascribed to one of the Limburg brothers,[308] the second, pertaining to the month of June, has recently been attributed to a later, anonymous master. The time shift to around 1440 somewhat removes this veduta further from the last years of the reign of Charles IV but does not reduce its authenticity considering the stagnancy of the building activity in the complex of the Palace de la Cité. The June veduta offers a panorama of the entire western part of the palace complex as if from the view of the tower of the residence of the dukes of Berry on the other side (Pic. 136).[309] All the way

136. View of the Palace de la Cité. Très Riches Heures du Duc de Berry. Month of June, beginning of the 15th century (MC, ms. 65, fol. 6r)

on the right, we can see the unmistakeable appearance of Sainte-Chapelle with its then small spire and rosette. Roughly in the centre, the Great Tower protrudes, under which the oblong residential wing is visible with four arcades and the gemel windows facing the garden. The fronted quadrangular tower with the adjoining staircase in the circular turret separates the private royal chambers from one of the galleries, behind which we recognise the rear gables of the Great Hall; the covered staircase leading to the Hall on the Water was probably not added until the fifteenth century. We already know the group of towers in the quay-side line well; a new building for us is the small house with a steam bath in the lower left-hand corner, from which the river could be accessed by stairs. Beyond the bulwark, it is possible to expect a relatively extensive garden of an area greater

307/ For more detail on the galleries and the staircases, see Guérout, 'L'hôtel du roi au Palais de la Cité', pp. 258–262.

308/ For more on that, see Raymond Cazelles and Johannes Rathofer, *Das Stundenbuch des Duc de Berry. Les très riches heures*, pp. 222–227 and 231. Further arguments were summarised by Guérout, 'L'hôtel du roi au Palais de la Cité', pp. 220–221, where specialised literature is given in the annotations.

309/ The palace was called 'Nesle' like the former Parisian residence of John the Blind of Bohemia. For the different positions of the homonymous buildings, see the map of Paris from the time of Charles V (Pic. 144).

than one hectare, whose trapezoid ground plan was formed by a framework of overgrown pavilions interconnected by aisles of bushes and by arbours. With the exception of the grape vines, the accounting and other sources do not mention any botanical terms, but a certain support is provided by the period depictions even here. Either way, the only thing Emperor Charles IV could see through the windows of his chamber in the middle of winter was the overall arrangement of the royal gardens.[310]

Given that we already know where the private part of the Palace de la Cité, which was intended only for the king and his family (the actual '*ostel*' or *Logis du Roi*), lay and approximately what it looked like, it is then necessary to add that precious testimony concerning the layout of the interior is provided precisely by our Account.[311] We should first mention again what it says: '...and so the king went at the side of the emperor all the way to the chamber which he had had prepared for him, i.e. to the chamber inlaid with Irish wood, which lies next to the Green Chamber and which has a view of the palace gardens on one side and of Sainte-Chapelle on the other. The king also left all of the other rooms in the rear for the emperor, whereas for his son, [the King of the] Romans, he left the lower chambers, where the queens of France normally took refuge, and ordered that they be prepared. The king himself then stayed in the upper garrets, which King John, his father, had had built.'[312] It arises from this testimony as well as from other sources that the so-called Green Chamber was located on the first floor, apparently next to the king's private oratory. The Green Chamber with its rich decoration of coats-of-arms and ubiquitous lilies served as a reception hall. In size, it probably had a match in the chamber inlaid with Irish wood,[313]

137. Interior of the royal Palace de la Cité. Miniature depicting the royal secretary and writer Pierre Salmon bowing before Charles VI (Pierre Salmon, Dialogues, around 1409, Paris, BnF, ms. fr. 23279, fol. 53r)

because it had windows on both sides. Two lateral, slightly higher three-storey towers were attached to the central tract. Besides bedrooms, they also housed closets with clothes. The lower floor, allotted for the queen, probably had an identical layout, including an independent oratory, which formed the lower part of the building of the chapel.

Charles V was already as Dauphin used to keeping in his treasury all kinds of valuables, including rare tapestries and room textiles. It is hence not surprising that after the emperor's departure and the death of his wife Jeanne of Bourbon he had the

310/ Further details are presented by Elisabeth Antoine, 'Jardins de plaisance', pp. 155–161, also with several contemporary depictions of artificial gardens.

311/ It was used especially by Guérout, 'Le Palais de la Cité', pp. 74–77, and 'L'hôtel du roi au Palais de la Cité', pp. 244–250.

312/ Delachenal (ed.), *Chroniques des règnes*, II, pp. 224–225.

313/ Irish wood meant quality wood of fir, larch, cypress and sometimes even of cedar. On that, see Gay, *Glossaire archéologique*, p. 165.

equipment of some rooms taken to the Louvre, where he withdrew from his permanent residence in Saint-Pol.[314] The inventory of Charles V's chattels from 1379–1380 also really contains under item No. 3584 textile embroideries with the symbols of France and the Dauphin and of the Holy Roman emperor and Bohemia placed diagonally across from one another. The editor of the inventory therefore concluded that these textiles had been procured for the emperor's visit in Paris in January 1378. However, since these embroideries are listed in the inventory of the treasure from 1363, it is clear that they had served already before in the decoration of the Dauphin's living quarters in Metz when he met the emperor in 1356. That does not rule out their further use at the turn of 1378 though, when they were joined by curtains, bedding, tapestries and square pillows.[315]

The host retired, as it is in the Account, to the upper garrets above the Mercière Gallery, in which he had experienced his deepest humiliation. We shall return for a moment to twenty years before. The day after 21 February 1358 when the ordinance was issued by the revolting estates-general essentially limiting royal power, Étienne Marcel burst into the garrets with a crowd of rebels and forced the dauphin to look out of the window at the bodies of his two murdered marshals lying under the marble stairs down in the courtyard.[316] Even though Marcel's re-

138. The Louvre. Très Riches Heures du Duc de Berry. Month of October, beginning of the 15th century (MC, ms. 65, fol. 10r)

volt and the simultaneous Jacquerie were drowned in the blood of the urban and especially the rural rebels, Charles V for his greater safety began to reconstruct the Louvre and the fortress in Vincennes even before his accession to the throne in 1364. From that time, the Palace de la Cité in the centre of Paris became even more the site, instrument as well as symbol of the sovereign power of the ruler.[317]

Until the middle of the fourteenth century, the Louvre was primarily a fortress protecting the open forefield of Paris from the west. The repeated endangerment of the metropolis after the crushing defeat of France at Poitiers in 1356 called for the accelerated construction of fronted ramparts. By its inclusion in the protected urban complex, the Louvre in part lost its original purpose, although the armoury and cells for prominent prisoners in its huge donjon contin-

314/ On that, see Jules Labarte (ed.), *Inventaire du mobilier de Charles V de Charles V, roi de France*, p. IV.

315/ Because the inventory from 1363 states explicitly: '934 – Item une chambre de broderie croisiée aux armes de France et de l'Empereur et de dalphins, sans tapisserie et sans quarreaux' (ed. Danielle Gaborit-Chopin, *L'inventaire du trésor du dauphin futur Charles V, 1363. Les débuts d'un grand collectionneur*, p. 84, which also in Note 865 elaborates the idea of J. Labart). On the other hand in the inventory from the end of the reign of Charles V, we read under item No. 3584: 'une chambre de broderie, escartelée aux armes de France et à daulphins et croisiée aux armes de l 'Empereur et de Behaigne, garnye de ciel, dossier, coultepointe et troys courtines de cendal azuré, avec six carreaulx et quinze tappis de mesmes...' (ed. Labarte, *Inventaire du mobilier de Charles V*, p. 369).

316/ On these cruel episodes, see the Great Chronicles of France, Delachenal (ed.), *Chronique des règnes*, I, pp. 149–151; for a more recent source, see Autrand, *Charles V. Le Sage*, pp. 298–301.

317/ Here I am paraphrasing the concise formulation of Jean Favier, 'Conjoncture politique et chantiers de construction dans le Paris de Jean II et de Charles V', p. 289.

139. East wing of the Louvre. Altar of the Parisian Parliament, detail, 15th century

ued to be here; Charles V began the reconstruction of the Louvre during his regency. We do not know precisely in what order the work progressed, but it is not excluded that it took place on the outside and inside of the fortress simultaneously. The protection of the new royal residence from the side of the Seine was foremost ensured by a wall connecting the old and new fortification lines. Its appearance with its round turrets and fronted quadrangular embrasures was faithfully depicted by the miniature representing the month of October in the calendar of *The Very Rich Hours of the Duke of Berry* (Pic. 138).[318] The main entry was situated opposite the river, and it therefore seems that this gate lay to the left of a small postern. The second entry, also protected by a pair of semi-circular towers, headed towards the city. The eastern façade of the Louvre is outlined for us by the somewhat later *Altarpiece of the Parliament of Paris* (Pic. 139).

Charles V did not change the basic, roughly square disposition of the Louvre of an area of 72 × 78 metres. After all, it was hardly possible, because the fortification besides the central donjon was formed by another ten enormous towers surpassing 8 metres in diameter.[319] Despite that, the construction intervention of Charles V was far-reaching. Other than adding the new buildings of two residential inner wings on the site of the original curtain (perimeter) walls, he had the entire complex raised by one floor and superstructures attached to some tow-

318/ The latest research also shifts this miniature to before the middle of the fifteenth century; on that, see Note 308 above.

319/ Besides the four corner towers, it is necessary to include also the two already-mentioned pairs of entry towers and the central towers on the opposite sides. The entire layout was clarified by archaeological research of one of the courtyards (the so-called *Cour Carrée*) of today's Louvre in 1983–1985. On that, see Fleury and Kruta, *Le Château du Louvre*, with situational sketches illustrating two phases of construction on pp. 50 and 70.

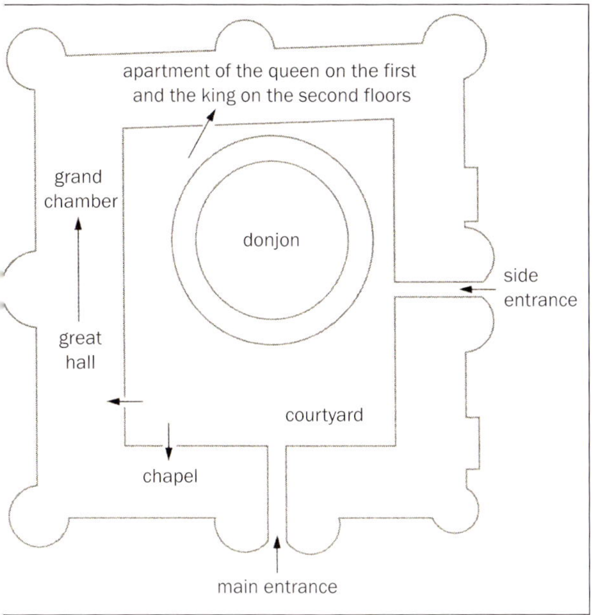

140. Scheme of the paths in the Louvre following Mary Whiteley

141. Standing statue of Charles V, originally perhaps from the façade of the Louvre

142. Standing statue Jeanne of Bourbon

ers. For vertical movement, the older narrow spindle staircases no longer sufficed, and thus roughly in the middle of the northern wing a grandiose newel spiral staircase was built (the so-called *Grande vis*). The ground plans of the ground floor and the second floor according to the reconstruction by Mary Whiteley may serve for a better idea of the new French residence in the Louvre, which became the temporary residence of Emperor Charles and his son Wenceslas from 7 to 10 January 1378 (Pic. 140).[320]

The emperor was conveyed to the Louvre on a comfortable residential boat, which apparently served for the transport of the king and his family between all of the Parisian residences easily accessible from the Seine. On the quay, the emperor again moved to the portable chair and on the way he toured the expensively rebuilt château with the host at his side; when they arrived in front of the main entrance, the emperor could not miss the statues of the royal couple, who with insignia in their hands

320/ See Whiteley, 'Le Louvre de Charles V: dispositions et fonctions d'une résidence royale', pp. 62–63, Pics 5–7. By the same author, cf. i.a. also 'Lieux de pouvoir et résidences royales', pp. 113–121.

welcomed all comers; Charles V thus had the opportunity to also introduce to his uncle his wife Jeanne of Bourbon, who because of her advanced pregnancy did not leave the residence in Saint-Pol. It had been assumed by experts in Gothic art that the statues of Charles V and his wife Jeanne which adorn the entire exposition of the mediaeval and Renaissance sculpture in the Louvre Museum were removed from the mentioned portal. This supposition is no longer accepted without reservations, and it is therefore possible that the preserved royal couple of figures used to decorate the entrance to the original Louvre (see Pic. 141, 142).[321]

The sculptural decoration and the ornamental architectural members embellished the otherwise cramped area of the courtyard, whose significant part was occupied by the enormous donjon. The emperor could have still remembered from his youth the left part of the ground floor with the portals into the chapel and the Great Hall, which remained unchanged.[322] The greater the surprise that awaited him before entrance to the main staircase, which in itself aroused admiration for its size, height as well as layout. The eighty-three steps wider than two metres were followed by a narrower spiral staircase with forty-one steps, which the king's architect Raymond du Temple completed with an observation terrace.[323] The external sculptural decoration was a joint work of the most important period artists, namely Jean de Liège, Jean de Launay, Jacques de Chartres and Jean de Saint-Romain, the last of whom created the figures of the armigers guarding the entrances to the staircase on the ground floor on both sides as well as to the suite of the queen on the first floor and the king on the second. The outer walls of the quadrangular staircase were adorned by six life-sized statues of the members of the royal family, each of which stood on a pedestal and had a stone canopy over its head. Here again, the emperor had the opportunity to see the figures of his host, his wife and moreover also of their two sons, who were most likely holding the hands of their parents.[324] Not even the king's brothers, the dukes Louis of Anjou, John of Berry and Philip II of Burgundy were missing here, accompanied by their late uncle Philip of Orléans († 1375). This gallery of the members of the royal Valois dynasty in the upper section of the staircase was protected by the figures of the Virgin Mary and St John the Baptist.[325]

There was simply enough to marvel at, and not only on the staircase. Through a richly adorned portal on the level of the second floor, one entered directly into the king's residential wing, which Charles V ceded to his uncle. It now behoves us to consult the ground plan of the second floor; the king's suite covered the entire northern wing. The largest, central room with an area of 19.5 × 11.8 metres served as the reception hall (*chambre à parer*). This was reflected also in the embellishment, ranging from the marble tiles and the large decorative fireplace through the ubiquitous tapestry and murals, with a predominance of mythological and legendary scenes complemented by heraldic ornaments, all the way to furniture of exotic 'Irish' wood. The same held generally true of also other chambers, which according to Christine de Pisan were also 'very richly adorned and embellished'.[326] On the very first day of his stay

321/ The political motivation for the monumental sculptures of Charles V was emphasised by Sherman, *The Portraits of Charles V of France*, p. 15. The original placement of the preserved statues of the married couple on the front of the Louvre was in my opinion justified convincingly by Gaborit, 'Les statues de Charles V et de Jeanne de Bourbon du Louvre. Une nouvelle hypothèse'.

322/ On the sculptural decoration of the Louvre under Charles V, see Frédéric Pleybert, 'Les sculpteurs du roi', pp. 201–204.

323/ On this builder, see Philippe Henwood, 'Raymond du Temple, maître d'oeuvre des rois Charles V et Charles VI', pp. 55–75.

324/ This opinion was expressed by Uwe Bennert, 'Les décors de résidences', p. 146.

325/ The description of the sculptural and other decoration of the Louvre was bequeathed by historiographer Henri Sauval, who in 1650–1660 could still use the written sources that were destroyed later. His records were published with a significant delay in the second volume of the *Histoire et recherches des Antiquités de la ville de Paris* (Paris 1724; reprint Paris – Genève 1974); on the staircase, see p. 23 here. The place in question was reprinted by Carqué, *Stil und Erinnerung*, pp. 437–439.

326/ Solente (ed.), *Le livre des fais et bonnes meurs*, II, p. 106.

in the Louvre, Charles IV received the large delegation of the University of Paris here, whereas his host convened his council in another hall, which we will mention later.

A kind of extension of the reception hall was a no less decorative, more or less already private chamber, where the king sometimes met with his council (*chambre de retrait*). A narrow hallway led from here to both the private oratory and the king's day room. From there, he had access to the three floors of his library in the adjacent tower, which had earlier been used by the falconers, as is reflected in its name (*Tour de la fauconerie*).[327] Everything suggests that two chambers from the other side of the reception room were reserved for the night's repose of the king. However, the king did not use them during the emperor's stay, as arises from a hint in the Account, according to which the host lodged 'at the other end', in the rooms intended for the accommodation of his older son, the dauphin of Viennois, so that the emperor could use his chambers. This suite also had a small oratory and indispensible toilet. It can be inferred from various mentions that the royal family and the numerous everyday visitors were well taken care of also in this regard.[328]

The standard of hygienic facilities provided testimony of a land and its residences in the Middle Ages no less than today. Let us not be ashamed to peek into the small rooms where even kings had to do without the help of others. Nevertheless, it will not be in the Louvre, but in the tower that formed an important component of the Parisian palace of Duke John the Fearless (*Tour Jean sans Peur*). We do not yet find a water closet even in Paris around 1380. However, instead of a quiet corner, a toilet was a small comfortable room kept at a moderate temperature by the back wall of a fireplace, with a roughly woven carpet on the floor and cloth drapes on the walls; the stone seat was covered by wood and upholstered; it was possible to wash one's hands in the small room at a prepared wash-basin, next to which stood a jug with water. Instead of toilet paper, the distinguished users of the toilet had pieces of linen or cotton cloth available, whereas the commoners had to satisfy themselves e.g. with a large leaf of mullein.

We have not yet mentioned the first floor. The northern wing, intended for the queen, had the same layout as the king's suite a floor above. It even seems that all of the royal residences had suites composed of a reception hall, a large day chamber, a bedroom, wardrobes, toilets and the indispensible oratory.[329] And since Queen Jeanne in the advanced stage of her pregnancy preferred an undisturbed stay in the residence of Saint-Pol, her chambers in the Louvre became the dwelling of King of the Romans and Bohemia Wenceslas IV for a few days. Because of the emperor's immobility, all of the state-political negotiations which were extremely important for the host took place on the second floor. The reception hall was so spacious that roughly sixty standing masters of the Sorbonne could be received in it, but it was hardly sufficient for the joint session of the King's Council and the emperor's confidants.[330] Nonetheless, the Account clearly says that the session took place in the *chambre à parer*. It is all the harder to resolve this discrepancy as on the ground floor of the Louvre there was the Great Hall (*Grande salle*), which was roughly 30 metres long and whose vaulting at the height of the second floor made it a truly grandiose area. An inspection of the ground plan of the ground floor reveals that the Great Hall neighboured upon a somewhat smaller but equally impressive chamber

327/ We will become more acquainted with the library in Excursus – Book Gifts, Relics and the Small Mysteries around Them.

328/ For more on the sanitary facilities in the Louvre, see Whiteley, 'Le Louvre de Charles V', pp. 69–70.

329/ It was precisely this circumstance that allowed a hypothetical reconstruction of the Nestle Palace, see Benešovská, 'Les résidences du roi Jean de Bohême', p. 121.

330/ According to the Account, besides the chancellor, there were twelve professors from each of the three higher faculties and twenty-four masters from the greatest, artistic faculty. The group of the emperor's people alone numbered almost fifty people or more according to the Account, but it is possible that both groups of counsellors were included in this number. I judge so based on the fact that the Account lists by name roughly forty highly placed participants.

(*Grande chambre*). And since the main palace chapel lay on the ground floor right next to the entrance, it would be strange if Charles V had forgotten to show this part of the Louvre to his guests. He had an opportunity to do so already on the first day, because the path from the main portal to the great staircase went past both the chapel and the lower halls.[331]

The emperor paid a visit to the third royal residence in Saint-Pol only for an afternoon visit of Queen Jeanne of Bourbon and her mother Isabelle, a sister of his first wife Blanche. The emperor could again appreciate the comfort of the residential boat which transported him up the Seine to the quay of the mentioned palace complex. Unlike the Palace de la Cité and the Louvre, L'hôtel Saint-Pol was entirely the building work of the ruling king, because the older palaces which were in this district had undergone a complete reconstruction. Not only the towers of the Bastille and the recently finished fortification walls but also the annexes of several monasteries in the vicinity and palaces of the feudal lords who had settled in proximity to the king were sparkling new.[332] While the residence Saint-Pol was destroyed before the middle of the sixteenth century, its appearance has been preserved in a miniature in the chronicle by Jean Chartier from around 1470 (Pic. 143) and an illumination in the *Chronicles* by Jean Froissart from approximately the same time.[333] The information accumulated by historiographer H. Sauval is no less valuable for an approximate reconstruction of this royal residence.[334]

143. Funeral procession of Charles VI on leaving the residence of Saint-Pol. Chroniques de Jean Chartier (BnF, ms. fr. 2691, fol. 1r)

The enclosed complex of the residence in Saint-Pol was entered through two gates. The main entrance from Rue de Saint-Pol was embellished by a sculptural decoration of lions and the royal coats-of-arms. The lion was not only a popular but also emblematic animal of the ruling king and thus appeared in diverse forms in other places also. The appearance of the second gate, leading to the quay, can be seen in the miniature in the already-mentioned chronicle by Jean Chartier; when the emperor was entering it with his retinue, he certainly did not miss another version of the statues of the royal couple with clear stone canopies, which along with the coloured coat-of-arms accentuated the façade of the not very high tower. In the middle of the spacious courtyard almost 80 metres in length, the emperor could observe from his chair the arrangement of the palaces mutually connected by galleries and corridors. These numerous connections facilitated internal communication on the one hand and on the other hand protected the dignified inhabitants from inclement weather as well as the prying eyes of the many officials, servants and advocates who would come here to have their

331/ For more detail on the ground floor, see Whiteley, 'Le Louvre de Charles V', p. 64.

332/ The historical circumstances connected with the beginnings of the residence in Saint-Pol were summarised by Autrand, *Charles V. Le Sage*, pp. 760–766.

333/ London, British Library, MS 4379, fol. 3r, reproduction in *Paris et Charles V*, p. 26.

334/ On both depictions, see Whiteley, 'Deux vues de l'hôtel royal de Saint-Pol', pp. 49–53; colour reproductions are available in the work *Paris et Charles V*, pp. 26–27. For the sake of completeness, I refer also to Sauval, *Histoire et recherches des Antiquités de la ville de Paris*, II, pp. 273–278. The research is based on the study by Bournon, 'L'hôtel royal de Saint-Pol à Paris'; a concise summary of the current knowledge was most recently presented by Whiteley, 'Lieux de pouvoir et résidences royales', pp. 122–124.

issues resolved. The residence of Saint-Pol was thus not only a popular refuge of the royal family but also a place of the meetings of the King's Council, Chamber of Petitions and Chamber of Accounts.

After the emperor was welcomed in the courtyard by both of king's sons, the ten-year-old Dauphin Charles and Count Louis, who was four years younger than the dauphin, it was time for his reception in the great hall of the otherwise independent palace of Jeanne of Bourbon, which was entered by the grandiose newel spiral staircase. The palace was located around the internal courtyard with a lion fountain, where the queen *inter alia* distributed alms to the poor. It went without saying also that her palace had an imposing chapel; the queen was not in the reception hall, because she was resting in a bed in the side chamber with tapestries and the murals with the then popular motifs. We know, for instance, that on one wall of the reception hall there were scenes from the Old French treatment of the Greek fable of the hero of Theseus (*Le Roman de Thèbes*) and that another room was named after Mathebrune, heroine of the chivalric romance of a knight with a swan in his coat-of-arms (*Chevalier au cygne*).[335]

As soon as the meeting with the queen and her ladies-in-waiting was over, the emperor was taken in his chair to the chambers of Dauphin Charles, which were along with the dwellings of the younger prince Louis connected by galleries to the central palace of the entire residence; Charles had had it rebuilt from the former seat of the archbishops of Sens, after whom the reception hall almost 30 metres long and not quite 12 wide on the first floor was still called. If I am not mistaken, it was precisely in it that lunch was served for King of the Romans and Bohemia Wenceslas IV and the noble members of his retinue. After a short rest in the rooms of Prince Louis, Wenceslas IV set out escorted by the king's brothers for a tour of the famous lion menagerie. Whereas in the Louvre the lions were kept in a private sector of the gardens, in the residence of Saint-Pol they were at the fore, because their cages closed one side of the great courtyard. Meanwhile the emperor received the duchess of Bourbon in the room allotted to him and after her Queen Jeanne as well, who also came with both of her sons. The reception culminated with the presentation of valuable gifts, after which the queen and her children withdrew to the neighbouring chamber, where Wenceslas IV said his farewell. And since the day was drawing to a close, Charles V came to tell his uncle gently that they still had the joint journey to the fortified residence in Vincennes ahead of them.

At first sight it might appear that it was precisely in Vincennes that Charles V struggled hardest in the unannounced competition with his uncle on the imperial throne. A comparison with Karlštejn also really has a certain justification and to a certain extent can be useful,[336] just like a look at Windsor after its reconstruction by Edward III.[337] On the other hand, it is impossible to miss significant differences. Whereas Karlštejn was built by the emperor entirely from its base with a clear, pre-determined intent, Vincennes had its own long prehistory, in which also Charles V the Wise made his mark through his construction activity. However attractive it would thus be to take Karlštejn and its overintellectualised interpretations into account, we will limit ourselves to a brief description of Vincennes when the emperor saw it again. The word 'again' must have a question mark added to it, because it is only possible to conjecture that Charles IV had seen Vincennes as a boy with his aunt Marie of Luxembourg, the second

335/ For more on the internal decoration of the residence of Saint-Pol, see Bennert, 'Les décors de résidences', pp. 138–141, also with a reproduction on p. 139 of the miniature from a later manuscript with the works of Christine of Pisan (London, British Library MS Harley 4431, fol. 3r, ca 1410), which the author considers to have quite faithfully captured the interior of the period ladies' salon.

336/ Of all the authors who have broached the parallel between the two royal fortresses, see Frank Dengler, 'Karlstein und Vincennes', pp. 75–85. While it is possible to find inaccuracies in this study, it can serve overall as a starting point for further possible comparisons.

337/ On the similarities with Windsor, see i.a. Whiteley, 'Lieux de pouvoir et résidences royales: Le château de Vincennes', p. 126, with a reference to further literature.

wife of Charles IV the Fair, who had died here on 1 February 1328. If it was so, the new Vincennes must have taken his breath away. For that matter, it is impossible to resist a strong impression when visiting it even today.

Jean Chapelot distinguished between three stages in the building development of the royal residence in Vincennes.[338] In the initial, longest and also least known period from the end of the twelfth century until 1361, Vincennes was a favourite place for temporary stays of the royal family because of its 'good air', forest hunting grounds as well as its proximity to the metropolis. While from time to time, the 'Wood' in Vincennes (*Bois de Vincennes*), as the residence was most often called from the fourteenth century, assumed greater importance, it was first under John II the Good that the idea of a multipurpose residence was born. This plan was inspired not only by sentimental memories of the time when his children were born and raised here.[339] Also the felicitous distance from the metropolis, where the deadly plague epidemics rampaged in 1348 and again in winter 1360–1361, was only one of the weights on the scales. For both reasons, the imposing residence on a square ground plan continued to suffice. After the crushing defeat at Poitiers in 1356, which so weakened France that bands of brigand raiders easily penetrated all the way to Paris, consideration of the safe protection of the sovereign and his family came to the forefront. The 'Wood' in Vincennes lying east of Paris was favourable in this respect already for its position, because danger threatened chiefly from the west and from the north at that time; in addition, in case of serious danger, the king and those near him could withdraw from the unprotected residence in Saint-Pol first to the nearby Bastille and from there to Vincennes. In this way, however, we have already advanced quite deeply into the second stage of the construction under Charles V. We will be interested only marginally in the last period after 1380, which was characterised by the completion of the building of the second royal Sainte-Chapelle.

Immediately after his return from English imprisonment in December 1360, King John II the Good undertook the first indispensable steps for the construction of a defensive system, which the residence in Vincennes severely lacked. In accordance with tradition, it was an enormous donjon surrounded by ramparts. Such an expensive construction, with estimates being around half a million gold francs,[340] required exceptional measures at the expense of other items in the royal expenditures. The decisive role in this regard fell to the royal builder already known to us, Raymond du Temple, from 1365 joined by Philip Ogier, entrusted by the heir to the throne Charles V with supreme supervision over the royal constructions.[341] Thanks to the inscription carved by Ogier into the wall of the castlet around the donjon some time before March 1372, we know that the foundation work had already begun in 1337 under Philip VI. His son continued in the interrupted construction and managed to build the first three floors in 1361–1364. The donjon with its adjoining castlet (*Châtelet*) was finished by Charles V, who subsequently complemented the entire complex of the royal residence with an enormous fortification wall with nine towers in 1373–1380. The regular ground plan with a square module and main pathways truly corresponds to the ideal conception of a royal administrative metropolis.

Emperor Charles IV thus had the opportunity in January 1378 to see the residence in Vincennes in its full glory. Already from a distance, he could

338/ See Chapelot, *Le Château de Vincennes*, p. 54. I will further rely on this extensive treatise and the other studies from the anthology in which it was published.

339/ The successor to the throne Charles V was born in the 'Wood' in Vincennes on 21 January 1338. Two more of John's sons, Louis (1339) and John (1340), also first saw the light of day there in the following years.

340/ In this regard, the discussion on the paper by Chapelot, in *Vincennes aux origines de l'État moderne*, pp. 118–120, is enlightening.

341/ His title originally was 'général maître des oeuvres', then from February 1372 'général visiteur des oeuvres du roi'. For more on his sphere of authority, see Chapelot, *Le Château de Vincennes*, pp. 69–73.

144. Map of Paris under Charles V

145. The towers of Castle Vincennes. Très Riches Heures du Duc de Berry. Month of December, beginning of the 15th century (MC, ms. 65, fol. 12r)

notice the richly profiled donjon, which with its height of 55 metres towered not only over the forest vegetation but also over the fortress towers around 40 metres high. When the sun struck the towers, their white shone from far away, as it was also in the depiction of the month of December in *The Very Rich Hours of the Duke of Berry* (Pic. 145); when the view of the entire residence opened before the emperor, he could have had the feeling that a smaller, strongly fortified city lay before him. For a better idea, it is necessary to add that the entire circumvallated complex on a ground plan of 389 × 226 m had and still has an internal area of over 8 hectares. When excavating the 7 m deep and 25–30 m wide moat in front of the fortification wall, it was necessary to remove or shift ca 350,000 m^3 of earth; nearly 260,000 hewn ashlars were used on the internal and external lining of the wall ca 18 m high and 2.6 m wide. The residence was protected on three sides by nine quadrangular towers, each of which was if needed an independent blockhouse. Only one of them has been preserved, by chance the most important one, through which Emperor Charles IV entered on the early winter evening of 10 January 1378. This so-called *La tour du Village* 25 m long rises more than 10 m above the fortification wall and ascends to a height of almost 42 m.[342]

After entering the circumvallated area, the emperor saw on his right the old royal residence, which still served for the accommodation of the queen, her children and the court servants. The oblong wing of the superstructure connected the seigniorial residence with an internal irregularly structured courtyard on the construction site of Sainte-Chapelle, which was to replace the chapel from the time of Saint Louis. Even this was characteristic for the residence that was newly being built that unlike Karlštejn it had a primarily worldly if not directly military and power role. Although other buildings (yet we do not know what they looked like and for what they served) were situated on the vast area besides the old residence, vacant areas almost strikingly predominated here; Charles V here apparently confided to his uncle his

342/ The data on the length and width provided in the literature quite vary. In the text, I proceed from the precise measurements conducted by Chapelot, *Le Château de Vincennes*, pp. 95–96 and p. 120 (which also contains the data on the extent of the construction work).

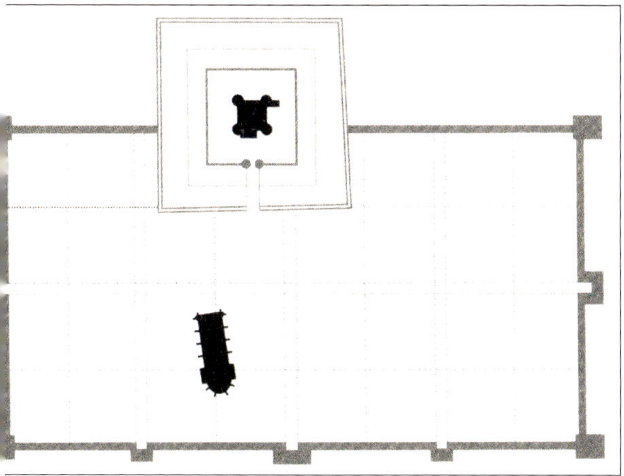

146. Regular layout of the fortress in Vincennes with a donjon, protective small castle (Châtelet) and oriented to the east, and the somewhat eccentrically situated Sainte-Chapelle

plan to transfer some offices to Vincennes and also build palaces for the highest political figures here. The project of the enclosed royal city (*Cité royale*) in the manner of the later Versailles is not a construct of historians. It was somewhat known to contemporaries, and it was highlighted by Christine de Pisan with her usual passion for the deeds of Charles V, according to whom lords, knights and others 'of his faithful' were to have here not only beautiful residences but also lifelong annuities.[343] Nevertheless, this onset of modern, centralised administration was ruined by Charles V's death.

It cannot be helped, even in the dusk of the early winter evening the most attention was attracted by the enormous and at the same time picturesque Great Tower, later called the donjon, rising above the fortification wall, and twin towers of the square 'castlet' (Pic. 146). The whole of this fortress surpassing 50 m on the side was in fact a castle in the castle complex, which is also reflected in the period sources distinguishing sometimes between the 'big castle' (*castrum magnum*) and the 'little castle' (*petit chastel*). However, all of the terminology pitfalls did not end here – the mentioned castlet (*châtelet*) was understood at that time to be a defensive system of

343/ See Solente (ed.), *Le livre des fais et bonnes meurs*, Vol. II, p. 40.

147. Reception chamber on the first floor of the defensive tower (donjon) of the fortified residence in Vincennes

the main entrance characterised at first sight by the twin towers with a gate in the middle and with a fronted barbican. During the reign of Charles V, the necessity for continuous protection of the residences from the raids of military and brigand bands led to a significant modernisation of this specific element of fortification architecture. The upper floors of the towers were connected by a terrace, from which it was possible to fight not only against an enemy outside but also if need arose inside the fortress. The external defence was ensured primarily by the barbican guarding the access to the drawbridge. The castlet had two gates, one for those on foot, the other for horses and carriages, so there were also two drawbridges across the deep moat, one smaller and one larger. Castlets were further marked by the third floor being reserved for the dwelling of the officer entrusted and by the access to all the floors being provided by a relatively wide staircase partially advanced from the back wall. Whereas the back side had an impressive décor in the large rectangular windows of the staircase with a stone balustrade, the front façade received a rich sculptural embellishment, as is proved by the five niches, three in the centre above the ogive of the gate and two in the corners on the sides. The statues did not survive the revolutionary iconoclasm, but it can be rather justifiably judged that the figures of the king and queen were not missing here. Even though it has not been possible to reconstruct the composition of the group of statues reliably, it is possible that a programme of a church portal was shifted here to a construction of a secular nature.[344]

The emperor was already entering the Great Tower by the light of many torches. Not even so could he miss the huge construction of the quadrangular donjon on a square ground plan having 16.2 m on each side with rounded corner turrets of a diameter of 6.6 m. Through a bridge from the castlet, one directly entered the reception hall (*chambre à parer*) on the first floor, (Pic. 147) from which by a wide newel spiral staircase in the left corner tower it was possible to climb up to another hall, where the king conducted discussions with his relatives and confidants (*chambre du roi*) on the second floor. This is also where a corner chapel was, to which the main access was along the hallway leading from the staircase. Also a smaller oratory was attached to the chapel. Otherwise, all the floors were connected by a narrow spiral staircase in the adjacent side wall. The toilets, whose comfort need not be questioned, were placed for the entire Great Tower in the quadrangular annex of the tower in the right back corner. The central quadrilateral halls having 9.72 m on each side were vaulted to the central column with decorative capitals. The third floor served as the king's private retreat, which was characterised by independently heated rooms in the corner towers, but even here there was a huge central fireplace like in the hall on the second floor. At least one of the corner rooms served as a bedroom, the second as a 'cabinet', where the king had his reference library, and the third was where he conducted private conversations. From the bedroom, as can be presumed, there was access to the toilet. On all three of the main floors, the eye was attracted to the expensive stone work, which was complemented by three-dimensional emblems of Charles V. Tapestries hung on the walls and coloured lilies alternated with other ornaments on the ribbing.

The host let the emperor use his bedroom on the third floor and stayed, as mentioned in the Account, himself in the 'Fallow Deer' room in the corner tower. Wenceslas IV was accommodated in the dwelling of Dauphin Charles again, which along with the chambers for the queen and her other children was located in the royal residence, because the Great Tower was only for the king. However, the emperor could not enjoy the view of the open landscape until after daybreak the following day, when he had himself carried to the windows all around the great hall on the third floor. Not even King Wenceslas, who in the meantime was with the dukes on a hunt for fallow deer and wild rabbits, missed the view from the tower. After returning from the hunt, Wenceslas with the noble lords and knights of the emperor's retinue saw not only the armoury on the fourth floor but also the superstructures on two other floors with a large observation terrace.

The emperor did not stay in Vincennes for long, because already on Tuesday, 12 January, he set out in the early morning on a pilgrimage to the Abbey of Saint-Maur-des-Fossés, from whence still on the same day, the emperor with his retinue and escort moved to the king's favourite rural residence in Beauté-sur-Marne; Charles V had had this smaller but luxurious residence of his built shortly before,

344/ On the basis of the period testimonies, it is usually inferred that there was a group of statues of the Holy Trinity, and perhaps even a statue of St Christopher, on the façade. On the 'small castle' and its appearance, see Chapelot, *Le Château de Vincennes*, pp. 81–84; on the sculptural decoration of the façade, cf. also Bennert, 'Les décors de résidences', pp. 144.

in 1373–1377.[345] The emperor, who had a temporary respite, toured the ceremonially decorated residence from top to bottom. He admitted to his guides that he had never seen a more beautiful residence in such a delightful location. Although already by the end of the eighteenth century the residence was destroyed almost without a remnant, its appearance, or rather location, was captured in ornate language by poet and servant of Charles V as well as his successor Eustache Deschamps. He considered the name of the place itself (beauté = beauty) as characteristic: 'His eldest son, the dauphin of Viennois,/ Gave this spot the name of Beauty./ And justly, for it is very delectable:/ One hears the nightingale sing there;/ The river Marne surrounds it,/ the lofty pleasant woods/ Of the noble park may be seen waving on the wind./ Meadows are near, pleasure-gardens,/ The fine lawns, beautiful and dear fountains,/ Also vineyards and arable lands,/ Turning mills, plains beautiful to view.'[346] It is no wonder that the forty-two-year-old sovereign selected precisely Beauté as the place of his departure from this world. The emperor said goodbye to his host here on Saturday, 16 January 1378, and set out through Lagny-sur-Marne to Meaux and further on the return journey to the Empire.

345/ On the dates of the construction of Beauté, see Chapelot, *Le Château de Vincennes*, p. 100; the remnants of this residence can be found on the cadastral area of the town of Nogent-sur-Marne.

346/ The translation of the poem on the château of Beauté by Eustache Deschamps has been taken from Johan Huizinga, *The Waning of the Middle Ages*, p. 294. The poet exaggerates here, because the local name Beauté is proved already from 1206 (on that, see Delachenal /ed./, *Chronique dès regnes*, p. 266, Note 1).

Emperor Charles IV's stay in Paris from Monday, 4 January, to the Saturday of the next week, 16 January 1378, left in historical memory the impression of a single celebration consisting of several parts. Nothing could compare to the entry into the city, when the public of the French metropolis most came into its own. In terms of outer pageantry, this was followed by the excellence of the receptions and banquets intended for a relatively wide circle of feudal lords, court as well as other dignitaries. They all took place in the Palace de la Cité, as it had been since the time of Saint Louis. That does not mean that lunches or dinners in the Louvre, in Vincennes or in the newly built residence of Saint-Pol would have receded into the background in the summit protocol. From the Account of the emperor's visit, it is clear that the all-day programme was adjusted to fit the banquets or was directly determined by them. Their importance, however, lay more in the political and other discussions, often only tête-à-tête, than in the representation of the sovereign's majesty. Because of his chronic pain, the emperor did not attend some of the lesser feasts; instead of lunch, he often rested or had food brought to his chamber.[347] The emperor's absence must have been especially regretted by the young duke of Bourbon Louis II, who arranged a 'great and abundant' New Year's Eve dinner in his palatial residence in Compiègne, to which he invited ladies from the city as well as the vicinity.[348]

We already know that the iconographic evidence and building surveys have made it possible to reconstruct the private as well as the public sectors of the Palace de la Cité, in which the official and other acts of the emperor's visit took place from Monday, 4 January, to Thursday, 7 January 1378, in significant detail.[349] The so-called Great Hall (*Grande salle*), the main site of all three great banquets, was approximately 75 metres long and roughly 26 metres wide.[350] After a destructive fire in 1618, the hall was ruined; *inter alia* the famous Viollet-le-Duc attempted to reconstruct its approximate form. Unlike the much later Vladislav Hall at Prague Castle, whose length is 'only' 62 and width 16 metres, the Great Hall of the Palace de la Cité in Paris was divided by a central row of eight columns into two oblong naves ending in a truss in the form of a reversed keel. Because of the central colonnade, its arrangement was consequently less transparent. The hall was quite high, approximately the height of the second storeys of

347/ According to the Account, the emperor did not for instance attend the ceremonial lunch in the so-called 'Sens' Hall of the residence in Saint-Pol; instead of lunch, he rested on a bed in Vincennes, etc.

348/ We should mention again that the Account lists among the more significant banquets of the emperor and his retinue also lunches in the episcopal palace at Cambrai, in the abbey of Le-Mont-Saint-Martin and especially in the abbey of Saint-Maur-des-Fossés, where the king had the refectory and its adjacent chamber 'beautifully' decorated and tapestried for the emperor.

349/ See especially Guérout, 'Le Palais de la Cité'. The author included a number of valuable details based on new research in his study 'L'hôtel du roi au Palais de la Cité', pp. 219–288. New knowledge has further been brought meritoriously in a number of studies by Whiteley, 'Royal and Ducal Palaces in France in the Fourteenth and Fifteenth Centuries: Interior, Ceremony and Function', pp. 47–63; 'Ceremony and Space in the Châteaux of Charles V, King of France', pp. 178–197; 'L'aménagement intérieur des résidences royales et princières en France à la fin du XIVe siècle et au début du XVe siècle', pp. 299–303, and 'Lieux de pouvoir et résidences royales', pp. 105–112.

350/ According to the plan in Guérout, 'Le Palais de la Cité', lettres h.-t.

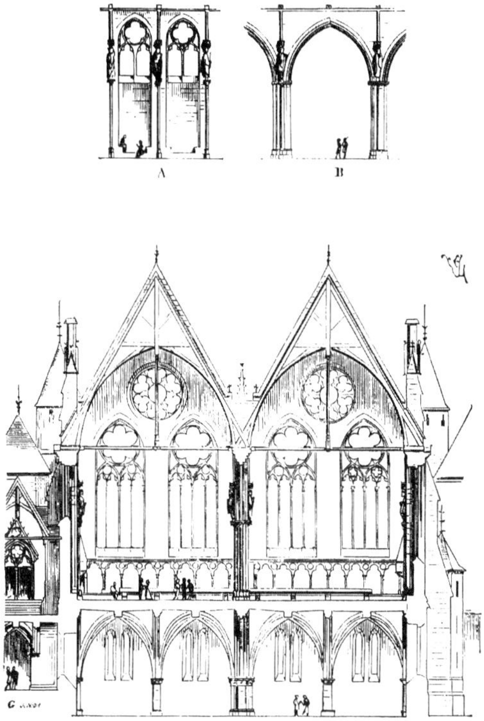

148. Hypothetical reconstruction of the upper and lower hall of the Palace de la Cité following Viollet-le-Duc

the structures around, which is evidenced, i.a. by the depiction in *The Very Rich Hours of the Duke of Berry*. Besides the windows with tracery, portals, fireplaces and other architectural members, attention was attracted by the colourful ornaments on the walls, on which the skins of exotic animals were hung. A gilded wooden stag, the emblematic animal of the ruling king and at the same time also the original symbol of French justice, hung under the arch in the central line of columns which was opposite the entrance to the adjacent Great Chamber of the Royal Court of Justice (*Grande chambre*).[351]

The entire hall was optically dominated by a gallery of the figures of the kings of France, beginning with the legendary Pharamond and finishing with Charles IV. A total of forty-eight polychromed, life-sized statues stood on the corbels of the central columns (always in pairs) and of the side pillars. If Charles IV could have gained somewhere the inspiration for the pictorial genealogy of the Luxemburg rulers, it was precisely here where he was a witness to the ceremonial assemblies as a young boy. Since that time, however, through the care of Charles V, the statues of the last kings had been added on the pillars of the southern wall.[352] Along almost the entire face of the western wall of the hall stood the famed marble table, whose length aroused the wonder of the already-famous philosopher John of Jandun († 1328).[353] The windows behind the honorary table were decorated with drapery interlaced with gold; the construction of a canopy was in front of the windows along all of the pillars and the entire length of the table. From this screen, another three smaller canopies protruded with velvet curtains above the chairs of the Holy Roman Emperor and both kings. A visual image is provided here by an illumination in ms. fr. 2813 (fol. 473v) of the Bibliothèque nationale, which also depicts the valuable tablecloth on the marble table (Pic. 80 / XI).[354] Special honours were otherwise received only by the dauphin and his noble companions, above whom a canopy with velour stripes and gold cloth vaulted as well. The second table stood between the marble table and the entrance to the Great Chamber of the Parliament, from which it arises that it was placed lengthwise. In line with it along the northern wall, there were perhaps three more tables under canopies, which are also mentioned in the Account.[355] The idea of the

351/ This symbolic connotation had already been forgotten in the sixteenth century. On that, see Guérout, 'Le Palais de la Cité', pp. 135–136, with earlier literature.

352/ For more on that, see again Guérout, 'Le Palais de la Cité', pp. 132–135, also with a list of the rulers by name according to their placement.

353/ The statement of this famous Averroist with anticurial opinions was used in his explanation by Delachenal, *Histoire de Charles V*, V, p. 95, Note 3.

354/ On the other hand, tapestries with historicising themes can be seen in the illumination of the feasts of Duke John of Berry in his *Very Rich Hours* (Pic. 155). It is also worth noting here the construction of the canopy and fireplace in the background, because the feast also takes place in January.

355/ The Account explicitly mentions a total of five canopies including the one at the head marble table. This formulation allows the explanation that the reporter counted only the large canopies along the entirety of the tables. In this case, there would have been a total of five such decorated tables for the feudal lords, as judged also by Delachenal, *Histoire*

149. Ceremonial banquet at the Burgundian court around the middle of the 15th century. The depiction of the feast illustrates one episode from the popular chanson de geste on the four sons of Aymon, known under the name of one of them, Renault de Montauban. The five-volume illustrated cycle was commissioned for Duke of Burgundy Philip the Good. The Bibliothèque de l'Arsenal owns four parts (mss. 5072–5075), one volume ended up in the Bayerische Staatsbibliothek München, Cod. Gall. n°7. This illumination has documentary significance for us in several ways. First of all, we can learn of the placement of the tables in an L, which I suppose also in the case of the feasts in the Great Hall of the Palais de la Cité. Such a placement of the sideboard likely corresponded to the custom, which cannot be said of the small balcony for the bugler who can be found also in other places in similar depictions. Also the overall operation in the hall divided by a central row of columns deserves attention. (Bibliothèque de l'Arsenal, ms. 5075, fol. 239v)

placement of the tables in the form of the letter L is based on a depiction of one of the feasts at the Burgundian court under Philip the Good. If that was so, the right half from the perspective of the honourable table was free for a dramatic production after the first intermission. For the same reason, the king of France did not sit in the middle of the marble table but 'as if at the centre of the front of the hall', i.e. in the centre axis of the hall of the space defined by the columns in the centre of the two-nave area.[356]

The proposed solution is quite likely considering the placement of the first, largest and richly decorated dresser or more precisely cupboard with shelves for wine (*dressoir à vin*), which according to

de Charles V, V, p. 96. However, it is not possible to rule out entirely the possibility that there were only five canopies in total, i.e. two large-area and three individual.

356/ This was thought by Delachenal, *Histoire de Charles V*, V, p. 95.

the Account was to stand in the corner.[357] The second cupboard with gold tableware in the form of nefs and with large silver, sometimes enamelled bottles stood close to the entrance to the Chamber of Petitions (*Chambre des requêtes*), where petitions and other pleadings to the sovereign were dealt with; finally, the third cupboard was placed all the way in the middle of the hall under one of the arches, because its tableware of white silver served all of the less dignified participants in the feast, of whom there might have been several hundred.[358] In order to prevent the king and his valued guests from being bothered, both the tables under the canopies and the cupboards with the precious tableware were separated by barriers of sharpened posts, with the pathways through them being guarded by designated knights. The diners at the tables under the canopies were served first, but the other dignified participants in the feast apparently did not have to wait long either. The author of the Account did not spare words of recognition in this regard when he said that 'everyone was served [food and drinks] in a very organised manner and without disorder, so that the tables were quickly and well cleared and all who ate in said palace [Palace de la Cité] were served, just as swiftly at the lower and further tables as at the higher and closer'.

The basic arrangement of the tables including the expensive decoration of the entire hall did not change during the entirety of the emperor's visit; according to circumstances and needs, individual canopies were only removed or added. The marble table and the richly equipped cupboard at one of the pillars is mentioned, e.g. by the chronicler Froissart when describing the feasts in the same hall in honour of Queen Consort Isabeau of Bavaria in 1389.[359] In January, it was necessary to light the hall complementarily even during lunch, namely with tallow and wax candles on pewter plates raised to the ceiling as well as with torches secured on poles. Besides that, numerous servants dressed in identical liveries with flaming torches would walk around the black-and-white tiles of the marble floor during the ceremonial dinner, 'so that … in said hall it was so light at night as if it were day'.[360] The greatest burden always lay on the staff of the kitchen, the stewards and the butlers, who had independent lodging house (*Échansonnerie*) reserved in the complex of the Palace de la Cité.[361]

It is necessary to complement the brief information on the Great Hall, because we have only mentioned its upper floor so far. In the lower hall, the Hall of the Palace Guard (*Salle des gens d'armes*), preserved to this day, which is connected to the so-called common kitchen (*la cuisine du commun*), the armigers, members of the bodyguard, the servants of the king, of the queen as well as of their children ate everyday. For the celebratory feasts in the upper hall, a special kitchen for the mouths of gourmets (*cuisine de bouche*, a.k.a. *cuisine du Palais*) was assigned, but when need arose both kitchens, connected to the Great Hall by special ramps, were engaged in food preparation. Since both kitchens along with their pantries and winecellars[362] were located in the buildings attached to the northeast wing of the Great Hall, the mentioned fences most likely were also to form a corridor for the quick transport of food to the honourable tables at the opposite end of the hall.[363]

357/ There is more on the cupboard and tableware in Excursus – Tableware.

358/ At the dinner on 5 January 1378, the Account mentions besides the great amount of other noble people eight hundred to a thousand knights; it also talks about eight hundred knights at lunch the next day, 6 January, not counting the other people. Both of these numbers might include also the participants who dined in the lower halls.

359/ *Oeuvres de Froissart*, XIV: *Chroniques*, ed. Kervyn de Lettenhove, pp. 14–15. On the ceremonial entry into Paris which preceded this feast, see Ribémont, 'L'Entrée d'Isabeau de Bavière à Paris', pp. 515–522.

360/ The function of the hung plates was explained by Delachenal, *Histoire de Charles V*, V, p. 87, Note 2, who besides that expressed the opinion that the 'torches à étendards' (battle standards) were in fact oil burners.

361/ Guérout, 'L'hôtel du roi au Palais de la Cité', p. 271.

362/ It is significant that besides the winecellars and the cold-storage rooms for meat and venison special sections of this catering complex consisted of storage rooms for bread (*Paneterie*) and fruit (*Fruiterie*), because both types of food were among the essential parts of the French diet. On that on the basis of narrative sources, see Nejedlý, *La représentation des pouvoirs et des hiérarchies*, pp. 328–334.

363/ For more detail on that, see Guérout, 'L'hôtel du roi au Palais de la Cité', pp. 270–271 and 285–288.

150. Lower hall of the palace guards (Salle des gens d'armes) in the Palace de la Cité

It was similarly considered also for the sovereigns to be able quickly and without squeezing their way through the crowd to arrive in their private rooms. Besides the official entrance to the internal residences through the Great Hall and the so-called Gallery of Prisoners (*Galerie des prisonniers*), the rulers still had at their disposal a private route through the Great Chamber of the court of justice. Both of these possibilities were also utilised during the visit of Charles IV. In order for the servants with the litter to avoid the press after the feast of the Epiphany, they carried the emperor directly to his chambers. Information in this respect is provided by the record of the Account related to the night before: the king of France headed 'through the back door to his chamber and sent the King of the Romans through the [Great Hall] escorted by his brothers, the dukes mentioned above, and more other lords and knights'. On the site of the banquets, we already know almost everything that could be determined. It only remains to mention their timing briefly. This timing could differ quite significantly with individual kings and feudal lords. It is known of Charles V that he usually ate lunch already at ten o'clock in the morning, whereas he had supper served around six p.m.[364] We can only speculate on whether it was an iron-clad habit which he forced also on his guests of Luxemburg.

The seating arrangement was of great significance for the strictly hierarchal court society, since precisely the banquets helped strengthen the order of this closed world, in which not only the sovereign's generosity but also his every word or gesture could be and often also was a component of the ceremonial codex. Whereas the marble table, as we have already heard, had its permanent position at the head of the Great Hall, the placement of the diners varied depending on the circumstances. The place of honour belonged to the host, who in the Palace de la Cité could only be the king of France. The tired and fever-weakened

364/ On the normal time of the lunch of Charles V, see Jean-Louis Flandrin, 'Les heures des repas en France avant le XIVe siècle', p. 203; the data on dinner time is presented by Mireille Vincent-Cassy, 'La gula curiale ou les débordements des banquets au début du règne de Charles VI', p. 93.

emperor was missing at the first dinner in the Great Hall on Monday 4 January, because he was eating in his room. Bishop of Paris Aimery de Magnac sat on the right of Charles V, the places on his left were then taken by King of the Romans Wenceslas, Duke John of Berry, Duke of Luxembourg and Brabant Wenceslas, Duke Philip of Burgundy, Duke Louis II of Bourbon and Robert, Duke of Bar. The other two unnamed dukes, both most likely from Charles' and Wenceslas' retinues, were not yet knights[365] and therefore ate at another table along with Peter, the younger son of King of Navarre Charles II the Bad, further with John of Artois, otherwise Count of Eu, and other lords.

The emperor was missing at the marble table also during lunch the next day when his son Wenceslas kept him company in his private refectory. The king of France dined with the feudal lords from the emperor's retinue, namely with Elector of Saxony and Duke of Brunswick-Lüneburg Albert, further Bishop of Warmia Henry Sorbom and Chancellor Nicholas of Riesenburg. The seating order of the table of honour has been preserved by the period *Mémoire* of the emperor's visit (see the upper box).[366] Bishop of Warmia Henry next to him at the edge of the table. The order on the king's left therefore did not change as compared to the night before, only Elector of Saxony and Duke of Brunswick-Lüneburg as well as Imperial Arch-Marshal Albert was added between Duke of Burgundy and Duke of Bourbon.

Bishop of Paris	Bishop of Warmia	**King of France Charles V**	**King of Bohemia Wenceslas**	Duke of Berry	Duke of Burgundy	Elector of Saxony	Duke of Bourbon	Duke of Bar

All three crowned sovereigns did not meet at the same table until the ceremonial lunch on the Epiphany. Charles V could not have chosen a more opportune moment for paying tribute to his uncle and cousin. Already the morning service in Sainte-Chapelle had the character of a political act, when Charles V with the permission of his uncle offered three beautiful cups with gold, frankincense and myrrh. According to the sharp acumen of Françoise Autrand, Charles V thus in this paraliturgy himself filled the roles of the three great Biblical kings. It is not ruled out that on his part it was a liturgical reprisal (*revanche*) for the emperor's demonstrative attempt to serve at Christmas Mass on French soil.[367] The seating arrangement at the marble table of this feast of feasts, also with three kings present, was as follows (see the lower box).

Whereas the distance between the king of France and his immediate crowned neighbours was

Archbishop of Rheims	**Holy Roman Emperor Charles IV**	**King of France Charles V**	**King of the Romans Wenceslas IV**	Bishop of Warmia	Bishop of Paris	Bishop of Beauvais

The ceremonial banquet on the eve of the Epiphany also had to do without the emperor, so that Archbishop of Rheims Richard Picque sat under the 'first canopy' on the king's right and Bishop the same on both sides, the Account mentions of the bishops that they sat far away from Wenceslas IV, all the way at the end of the table.[368] Such a less worthy place at the end of the second table under the canopy

365/ One of those who were not knights yet was most likely the seventeen-year-old Duke of Opava Wenceslas I; whether the second was Duke of Brzeg (Brieg) Henry VIII or Duke of Legnica (Liegnitz) Boleslav is impossible to determine. On the other hand, Duke of Saxony and of Lüneburg Albert is out of question, as he did not attend the dinner.

366/ See Thomas, 'Ein Zeitgenössisches Memorandum', p. 112, and Lechová, 'Zpráva o návštěvě Paříže Karlem IV. roku 1378', pp. 52–53.

367/ Autrand, 'Mémoire et cérémonial', pp. 96–97, and again in *Charles V. Le Sage*, pp. 795–796.

368/ And since we already know the names of the other

fell to the emperor's chancellor Nicholas of Riesenburg, because he was not a bishop. According to the Account, his neighbour was Henry VIII, Duke of Silesian Brzeg. On the other hand, honourable places were given to the Elector of Saxony and Duke of Brunswick-Lüneburg along with the dauphin, who sat closest to the marble table:[369]

Elector of Saxony	**Dauphin Charles**	Duke of Berry	Duke of Brabant	Duke of Burgundy	Duke of Bar	Duke of Brzeg (Brieg)	Chancellor Nicholas

The four foremost feudal lords, Duke Louis II of Bourbon, John Count of Eu, Enguerrand of Coucy and Count John VI of Harcourt were honoured to keep Dauphin Charles company and ensure his safety and therefore stood around the table. The remaining members of the emperor's retinue and the French aristocrats sat at the other tables, again ordered according to their dignity.

Apart from the House of Luxembourg, which was besides Charles IV and his son Wenceslas IV represented by the emperor's half-brother Wenceslas, Duke not only of Brabant but also of Luxembourg and Limburg, the prominent members of the Dynasty of Valois and affiliated families were also represented here at the side of the ruling king. First of all, they were the heir to the throne Dauphin Charles, both of the king's brothers, Duke John of Berry and Duke of Burgundy Philip, further Robert, Duke of Bar, husband of Charles V's sister Marie, Duke Louis II of Bourbon, brother of Queen Jeanne, Count Jean VI of Harcourt, husband of the queen's sister Catherine of Bourbon, and last but not least also the king's cousin John of Artois, Count of Eu. In essence, it was a male company, which *inter alia* can be explained by the advanced stage of Queen Jeanne of Bourbon's pregnancy.

Before we come to the actual content of the banquets, i.e. to the dishes and drinks served in the individual courses, it will do no harm to recollect the latest knowledge of a more general nature. The ideas of the Dark Middle Ages with barbaric cuisine are mostly no longer valid, but also the suppositions of the continuity of Western European cuisine from the Middle Ages almost until the present have proved to be no less misleading.[370] The opposite was closer to reality: already in the second half of the fourteenth century not only at the courts but also in burgher households, they ate exquisitely and from today's perspective also more healthily than it had been judged until recently.[371] While vegetables still remained a secondary part of the menu and we will soon learn why, fats were overall used in a moderate form, and that not only at the time of frequent fasts. It is no accident that also precisely at the turn of the fifteenth century in France, England, Italy as well as on the Pyrenees peninsula the first 'cookery books' in the full sense of the word appear.[372] In comparison with the recipes of the sixteenth to eighteenth centuries however, other flavours predominated in the Late Middle Ages. Especially in France, the majority

bishops attending, it is necessary to add that the holder of the episcopal throne in Beauvais was Miles II de Dormans († 1387).

369/ The abridged text of the Account in the manuscript of the Parisian Bibliothèque de l'Arsenal MS 5128 mentions moreover between Duke of Burgundy and Duke of Bar the son of the king of Navarre Peter. See Tille, 'Francouzsklý rukopis o cestě císaře Karla IV. do Francie', p. 14.

370/ For this conception, quite common in the North American literature, a typical book is by Constance B. Hieatt and Sharon Butler, *Pain, vin et veneison* from 1977. For a critical view of this, see, i.a. Flandrin, 'Brouets, potages et bouillons', p. 8, and Bruno Laurioux, 'De l'usage des épices dans l'alimentation médiévale', p. 15.

371/ In all of this excursus, I have used the second edition of the collective publication *Fêtes gourmandes au Moyen Âge* (1998). Further cf. i.a. the conference proceedings *Médiévales*, No. 5 (1983), *Manger et boire au Moyen Âge I–II* (1984), Lambert (ed.), *Du manuscrit à la table* (1992) and *Essen und Trinken in Mittelalter und Neuzeit* (1987).

372/ Their list was amassed by Hieatt et al., *Répertoire des manuscrits médiévaux contenant des recettes culinaires* (appendix of the anthology *Du manuscrit à la table*). The data on the editions can be commonly found also in the other cited works, see, e.g. *Fêtes gourmandes*, pp. 174–179.

of dishes were of a sour character. The already commonly imported but still rare cane sugar was used abundantly for desserts and pastilles arriving on the table at the end of feasts. Cane sugar was so liked by, e.g. the poet Eustache Deschamps that he licked it alone as a rarity.[373] With the increasing property as well as self-awareness of the upper aristocracy, the banquets became a sign of prestige and haughty exclusivity, so that social hierarchisation began to be strongly and noticeably expressed precisely in food.[374] We shall thus keep in mind that the following explanation is more or less tied only to the tastes and menu of the aristocratic class.

Since time immemorial, health has been among the highest values of human existence, and it is hence not surprising that heed was paid to the valid principles of healthy nutrition also in the Middle Ages. *Régime du corps* by Master Aldobrandino of Sienna enjoyed considerable esteem in France from the thirteenth century, which in accordance with the majority of treatises of this type proceeded from the Aristotelian hierarchy of the four fundamental elements of the universe and their characteristics, i.e. fire (hot and dry), air (hot and damp), water (cold and damp) and earth (cold and dry).[375] At the top of the imaginary ladder, there were beings from the areas of mythology or theology; the firebird Phoenix for instance had a good position here. They were followed by birds and other creatures moving in the air. The fish swimming in water were already a step below, and all the way down were the four-legged animals in constant touch with the 'cold' earth. The underground tubers and roots of vegetables took the worst place in the whole value grouping.

In an attempt to outline this relatively complicated theory, we shall notice some of its practical impact. Fruit hanging in the air enjoyed greater trust than cereals, and these were again less vulgar than vegetables. Small birds, nightingales roasted to a golden brown, siskins, goldfinches and larks,[376] placed better than river geese and ducks, additionally walking on the ground; swimming fish were more valued than eel, shellfish and oysters, moving along the bottom. Beef was considered to be the homeliest meat, which appeared 'cold and dry' like the earth. It also mainly served to obtain bouillon as a base for most soups and sauces and having been boiled, it was given to the lower servants. Veal like the meat of other young was apparently 'damper' and thus more acceptable dietetically.[377] It is a waste of words to mention pork, which was reserved exclusively for the plebeians. The French recipe books of the fourteenth century do not know fresh vegetable salads. We already have an idea of why; by their origin, they were simply 'cold' and 'damp'. Like the majority of meats, most fish were by their nature too 'cold', and hence it was necessary to increase their digestibility. This was mostly done by spices. According to Aldobrandino, the majority of them were both 'dry' and 'hot'.[378] In general, all aromatic herbs were 'hot', so the best reputation was enjoyed by the spices from southern Oriental regions, which played a preeminent role in mediaeval aristocratic cuisine.

Whereas learned dieticians provided exhortative instructions on the one hand, a no less imperative role was played by the gastronomic function of the prepared dishes on the other hand. In this respect, the *Regimen sanitatis Salernitanum* or *The Salernitan Rule of Health* by John of Milan is clear: whatever is tastier, whatever provides greater pleasure is also more beneficial to the digestive tract.[379] Although

373/ It is recalled by Nejedlý, *Fortuny kolo vrtkavé*, p. 284, also with a list of Deschamps' favourite sweets.

374/ For more on that, see Laurioux, 'Table et hiérarchie sociale à la fin du Moyen Âge', pp. 87–108.

375/ *Le Livre de maistre Aldebrandin* was first issued in book form in Lyon around 1480. A modern edition was prepared by Louis Landouzy and Roger Pépin, *Aldebrandin de Sienne*. Also cf. *Lexikon des Mittelalters*, I, col. 348.

376/ They were a favourite delicacy again of Eustache Deschamps, who would have them put on a spit and roasted to a golden brown; see Nejedlý, *Fortuny kolo vrtkavé*, p. 280.

377/ According to Carole Lambert, 'L'ordonnance', in *Du manuscrit à la table*, pp. 16–23.

378/ For more on that, see Lambert, 'L'ordonnance', in *Du manuscrit à la table*, p. 21, with a graphic expression of the health values of vegetative foods according to Aldobrandino.

379/ On this writer, see i.a. Terence Scully, 'The Opusculum de saporibus of Magninus Mediolanensis', pp. 178–207.

not even this recommendation was valid without exceptions, the authors of mediaeval cookery books and chefs at the courts of the feudal lords had to bear in mind the common or individual tastes of their distinguished providers. Despite a certain cosmopolitanism of Western and South European mediaeval cuisine, which was sometimes expressed in the identical names of a number of dishes,[380] there were marked differences between distant regions, especially in terms of the perception of sweetness and sourness. The dishes intended for the tables of the French aristocracy of the fourteenth and fifteenth centuries were mainly without fat or acid, which is true for most sauces that today would in taste be reminiscent of Asian, e.g. Vietnamese, cuisine. In Italy, the meals were already slightly sweetened, which was even truer of Catalonia and England.

The most famous French 'cookery book' of the entire fourteenth century, the so-called *Le Viandier*, lists one or more sour ingredients in 63 % of its recipes.[381] And since in the religious-ethical code a sour taste was closer to asceticism than indulgence in sweets, the Parisians knew how to justify even their preference for dry wines from a higher perspective. It was not true for everyone and everywhere in France; nevertheless, not only in the time of Villon but already under Charles V, 'Paris led the dance'. The mentioned recipe book is also enlightening and authoritative for our topic in terms of spices, which were the most distinctive social attribute of the aristocratic table. In nearby countries, in Spain and Sicily, cane sugar was cultivated along with saffron of poor quality. The rest of the spices listed in the recipe book, i.e. ginger, cinnamon, cloves, cardamom, nutmeg, and 'long' as well as spherical pepper, were expensively imported from the Orient. Of all of these ingredients, particularly ginger and cardamom were preferred.[382]

It is no longer necessary to beat about the bush. Master Guillaume Tirel, called Taillevent, to whom the mentioned cookery book used to be ascribed,[383] was the Grand Master-Chef (*grand queux*) at the court of Charles V and thus the man who prepared the menus of the ceremonial banquets in honour of Holy Roman Emperor and his son Wenceslas. What is noteworthy about the entire issue is *inter alia* that *Le Viandier*, unlike later cookery books, does not present model menus of ceremonial or funeral banquets at all. Moreover, the recipes in Taillevent's edition are laconic, again unlike later handbooks, which are sometimes difficult to understand for their loquaciousness.[384] The Grand Master-Chef at Charles V's court eliminated twelve types of vege-

380/ The menus of the banquets in honour of the Luxemburg delegation, which we will deal with below, often mention, e.g. the word 'broet', which corresponds to the English 'brewet', Catalonian 'brouvet' or Italian 'brodetti'. Other identical terms are presented in Lambert, 'L'ordonnance', in *Du manuscrit à la table*, p. 11.

381/ This famous collection of recipes is available in two editions: *Le Viandier de Guillaume Tirel dit Taillevent*, Jérôme Pichon and Georges Vicaire (ed.), Paris 1892, ed. revised and enlarged by Sylvie Martinet, Genève 1967, and *The Viandier of Taillevent. An Edition of all Extant Manuscripts*, Scully (ed.), Ottawa 1988 (I will refer to this edition). On the question of authorship, see Note 382 below.

382/ For more detail on that, see Laurioux, 'De l'usage des épices', esp. pp. 18–19.

383/ In the post-war period, Taillevent's authorship was doubted, because *Le Viandier*, ascribed to him, was found in a manuscript from the beginning of the fourteenth century. On that, cf. Paul Aebischer, 'Un manuscrit valaisan du Viandier attribué à Taillevent', pp. 73–100; from the more recent literature, see, i.a. Margarete Zimmermann, 'Kochkunst im spätmittelalterlichen Frankreich', pp. 103–115. This question had not yet been unambiguously answered; Taillevent, as it appears, edited one of the texts and added his own instructions to it. For more on that, see Laurioux, *Le règne de Taillevent. Livres et pratiques culinaires à la fin du Moyen Âge*, pp. 103–110, and Laurioux, *Les livres de cuisine médiévaux*, pp. 25 and 39.

384/ It is the case of a burgher author of the recipe book entitled 'Le ménagier de Paris' (The Good Wife's Guide), which he wrote for the edification of his young wife, or of the famous Master Chiquart, master chef of Duke of Savoy Amadeus VIII, who began to work at the order of his master. Both handbooks are available in reliable editions: *Le Ménagier de Paris. Traité de morale et d'économie domestique composé vers 1393 par un bourgeois parisien*, Jérôme Pichon (ed.), Paris 1846, reprint Genève – Paris 1982. From the recent past, see the edition *Le Ménagier de Paris*, ed. by Georgina E. Brereton and Janet M. Ferrier, Oxford 1981, and its homonymous French translation by Karin Ueltschi (Paris, 1994). The second collection was issued by Scully, *Du fait de cuisine par Maistre Chiquart, 1420*, in *Vallesia*, 40, 1985, pp. 103–231. Otherwise for the recipe books and kitchen handbooks concisely, see Laurioux, *Les livres de cuisine médiévaux* in the editorial series *Typologie des sources du Moyen Âge occidental*, 77.

tables from his recipe book including leek, cabbage, turnip and pea, because they seemed too 'common' to him. He preferred fish, poultry and feathered game to meat from the butcher's shops, by which he to a certain extent fulfilled the mediaeval principles of a healthy diet.[385] He left a noticeable leeway to the users of his recipe book when preparing dishes, he did not stipulate to them for instance the preparation of meat by roasting or grilling, or the preparation times of the individual dishes. For that matter, fireplaces, ingles and ovens in the Late Middle Ages varied so much that instructions in this regard did not make any sense. *Mutatis mutandis*, the same may be said about period scales, and therefore Taillevent did not list the amount of ingredients either. Progress could not be stopped, however; the book publication of his *Le Viandier* of 1486 already complemented these data for numerous sauces.[386]

Before we get to the food itself, it is necessary to mention that the banquet was commenced by trumpeters with their fanfares, whereas heralds announced the names and titles of the valued guests arriving. Unlike the heralds, the trumpeters were not mentioned by the author of the Account, but one of them is captured in the depiction of the Epiphany feast in one of the illuminated manuscripts of the *Great Chronicles of France* in the British Library,[387] namely at the moment when the servants are bringing the emperor the items for washing his hands (Pic. 102 / XXXIX). Not even this propriety of every better feast was devoted greater attention in the Account.[388] What was commonplace at the French court can surprise us even today for its sophistication. The water for washing for example was prepared in sever-

151. Setting of the table for the ceremonial banquet (detail Fig. 153 / XXXVI)

al ways, with it being important that it smell nice.[389] Textile serviettes were still available for wiping the mouth and hands, sometimes forming a component of the place setting. Washing was indispensible after every course as well as after the feast ended, because meat and other parts of the dishes were eaten with the hands. Forks, unlike spoons of all types, were still a great rarity in the fourteenth century.[390] The question remains of whether the guests may have brought their own knives and cups for drinking (so-called *gobelets*) to the table. On the tables covered with tablecloths, which were sometimes changed after individual courses, bowls for eating as well as drinking (*hanaps*), receptacles with water for washing (*aquamaniles*), bowls for hand washing (*bassins*), salt cellars (*salières*), and particularly vessels (*nefs*, *vaisselles*) for fruits or other titbits which were prestigious valuables had been prepared for the guests. The other dishes and utensils were brought as needed after the commencement of the feast. It was especially true for the wooden or metal trays for cutting bread and meat (*tailloirs*, *tranchoirs*), jugs for water (*aiguières*) and table fountains for wine (*fontaines*).[391]

385/ For more on the French aristocratic diet according to Taillevent, see Scully (ed.), *The Viandier of Taillevent*, pp. 311–33.
386/ Cf. i.a. Françoise Sabban, 'Le savoir-cuire ou l'art des potages dans le Ménagier de Paris et le Viandier de Taillevent', pp. 161–172.
387/ It is the manuscript in London, British Library Nero E II, Vol. 2, fol. 229v.
388/ The Account mentions a final hand washing after the tablecloths were removed from the table.
389/ The recipes stipulated boiling the water with sprigs of sage (two for 1 litre), or camomile and marjoram (1 stalk of each). It was also recommended that water be boiled with stalks of rosemary and with the peel of bitter oranges, which were imported to Paris from the area of the Ligurian Sea. Sweet oranges were not available in Europe until the seventeenth century. On that, see *Fêtes gourmandes*, pp. 54–55.
390/ See Stéphane Vandenberghe, *Les premières fourchettes*, p. 45.
391/ I devote attention to the cutlery, plates, utensils and other aids in the following excursus.

152. / XXVIII. Ceremonial feast in the Great Hall of the Palace de la Cité (BL, Ms. royal 20 C VII, fol. 199r)

The written sources are welcomingly complemented here by period as well as later miniatures.

Nevertheless, we must not forget two essential preludes of every important feast. The first, concerning everyone, was the prayer before the food, which in the case of our three feasts was recited by the archbishops or bishops present. Although banquets were highly secular affairs, they distantly reminded of the Lord's Supper through the bread and wine available everywhere. At the court in Burgundy, the serving of the bread wrapped in napkins seemed to imitate the liturgical acts at mass.[392] The second task on the other hand took place in seclusion, because it was testing of the wholesomeness of the food served. At banquets with a great number of participants and servants, there was always an increased danger of poisoning attempts. Those who had their eyes opened included, besides the designated tasters, particularly the administrator of the Palace de la Cité (*maître d'hôtel*), the Grand Breadmaster (*grand panetier*), who seems to be captured for us in one of the miniatures (Pic. 152 / XXVIII), First Cupbearer (*premier échanson*) and master carver (*écuyer tranchant*), who were usually confidants of their lord, experts on his tastes and favourite morsels. We can see one richly dressed carver at work at the table of Duke John of Berry. The coordination of servants at the table is clearly illustrated in the depiction of the feast of the knights of the Order of the Star founded by John II the Good. At the courts of French feudal lords, and all the more at the king's residences, there were moreover poison detectors (so-called *proba* /testers/) available, which were mainly precious stones, shark teeth or extremely expensive pieces of the horn of unicorns and narwhals (sea unicorns). All of these aids, as it was believed, had the ability to indicate poisons by changing colour or otherwise and protect from them.[393] It was not without reason. Large banquets offered poisoners great opportunities, and although the tales were sometimes more terrible than the truth, a number of period affairs prompted wariness.[394]

It went without saying that mediaeval ceremonial banquets were characterised not only by the abundance of food but also by their various types and preparations. Whereas the courses in England more or less repeated in their composition, at French banquets the individual courses, so-called *mets* or *assiettes*, had different and relatively stable functions already in the second half of the fourteenth century. The so-called *service à la francaise*, i.e. dining in the French style, lay in the serving of the entire range of dishes for every course. This was also true for aperitifs in today's sense of the word.[395] They were mostly not listed in the menus, which is our case as well, and it is therefore fitting to add that it was mainly Southern French wine (*grenache*) or spiced wine (*hypocras*),

392/ According to Lambert, 'L'«assiette de table» – Le «premier mets»', pp. 48–49; it was a habit common at other courts.

393/ So far the most is known on poison detectors at the court of the popes in Avignon. It is to the merit of Robert Lentsch, 'La proba. L'épreuve des poisons à la cour des papes d'Avignon', pp. 155–162.

394/ On that, see Franck Collard, 'Le banquet fatal: la table et le poison dans l'Occident médiéval', especially pp. 337–339 there, and a more recent book by the same author entitled *Le crime de poison au Moyen Âge*.

395/ For more detail on that, see Lambert, '«L'assiette de table» – Le «premier mets»', pp. 43–78.

into which toasted bread was sometimes dipped; the food and desserts were served also with a sweet wine (*garnache*), malvaz and muscat (*muscadel*) imported from Greece, and wine from Cyprus, which enjoyed great popularity.[396]

Already with the first course, butcher's delicacies, hard and soft sausages and pâtés were thus brought to the table. They were followed by so-called *potages*,[397] i.e. various sauces and mashed dishes with fish as well as other meats and later also roasts, poultry and feathered game. After such a heavy beginning, it was time for the first intermission (*entremets*), which usually attracted attention not only with desserts and wine but also with musical or other productions.[398] Whereas during the intermezzo, it was the cupbearers (*échansons*) who were the busiest, the carvers with their knives (*écuyers tranchants*) could show their mastery during the second course, because the breadmasters (*panetiers*), who were otherwise in charge of the bread and salt, were bringing to the table roasts in all possible ways with one platter below and another on top (Pic. 153 / XXXVI). Besides the various preparations of beef and mutton, these were roasted poultry, roasted fish in two to three colours or roasted birds with sauce *à la dodine*.[399] This composition could but did not have to repeat with the third and possibly even the fourth or further courses.[400] At the end, it was time for a course sometimes called *desserte*, which did not exclude meat delicacies but mostly included compotes, medlars, sophisticated preparations of pears or apples, nuts, dried fruits, etc. Yet not even

153. / XXXVI. Banquet in honour of the emperor and his son in the Grand Hall of the Palace de la Cité. Les Grandes Chroniques de France, illumination by Jean Fouquet (BnF, ms. fr. 6465, fol. 444v)

this was the end. As soon as the tables were cleared and the hands washed – it need not be added that this took place after every course – the *issue* (or *yssue*) followed. It was literally the 'conclusion' of the banquet, during which spiced wine and fine wafers were always served. The so-called *boutes-hors* were already served in another room and, like in the later aristocratic and burgher salons, the society amused themselves over wine, ginger and other pastilles and sipped liqueurs for good digestion.[401] To list all of the variations would be quite difficult, because each name was linked with secret ingredients, which not even experts often know how to resolve. For that matter, we will have enough difficulties with the menus of the three feasts in honour of the Luxemburg delegation.

396/ For original orientation, see LAMBERT, '«L'assiette de table» – Le «premier mets»', p. 53; otherwise cf. Roger DION, *Histoire de la vigne et du vin en France des origines au XIXe siècle*, Marcel LACHIVER, *Vins, vignes et vignerons. Histoire du vignoble français*, and concisely also NEJEDLÝ, *La représentation des pouvoirs et des hiérarchies*, pp. 331–333.

397/ The expression *potages* in the French culinary dictionary had several meanings. For more on that, see FLANDRIN, 'Brouets, potages et bouillons', p. 6.

398/ See LAMBERT, 'L'entremets', pp. 103–122.

399/ This very popular preparation lay in the fact that the fat created when roasting was used in the preparation of a spicy sauce made from the roasting juices, raw liver from the bird, carrots, onions, wine and cream. On that, see i.a. *Fêtes gourmandes*, Glossaire, p. 182.

400/ See again LAMBERT, 'Le «tiers mets»', pp. 123–138.

401/ For details on the individual courses, see LAMBERT, in *Fêtes gourmandes*, pp. 57–157.

Not only the ceremonial banquets in honour of Emperor Charles IV but also most of the numerous gifts received by him as well as his entourage are more or less connected with tableware, and it may therefore be useful to deal with these artefacts in more detail. Considering the ambiguous terminology and variety of forms, this can only be a partial contribution to the existing, similarly focused studies.[402]

Noble guests were coming to the ceremonially laid table, where their home or travel cutlery, which was still chiefly comprised of a spoon and a knife, had been prepared for them.[403] Spoons were commonly wooden; the inventories of legacies no less often mention silver tablespoons and teaspoons. Knives were of various qualities; the most valuable ones could be even a welcome gift, like both pairs of knives for Charles IV and one pair of knives for Wenceslas IV for sixteen francs each from the workshop of the royal cutler Pierre Willequin, which were given to his Luxemburg guests by Charles V.[404] Period illustrations of the banquets capture knives on the set tables; they, however, do not show forks, which were no longer a rarity at the French court in the second half of the fourteenth century but were apparently not yet used at banquets with numerous guests.[405] At least some guests also brought with them their own goblets and cups, which are known to have been among travel essentials. A rare proof here is the chased and painted leather cup case from the fifteenth century in the Musée Cluny (Cl. 21362). At least some of the precious chalices and cups that Charles V gave to the emperor, his son and the members of their entourage in large amounts seem to have been in travel cases, although they are not mentioned in the accounting documents.[406] Personal cutlery as well as cups were also required by some ordained regulations, namely for hygienic reasons.[407]

402/ French researchers have two earlier handbooks available to them, namely LABORDE, *Glossaire français du Moyen Âge, à l'usage de l'archéologue et de l'amateur des arts*, and an unfinished work whose author was GAY, *Glossaire archéologique*. I advantageously used also other works: Ronald W. LIGHTBOWN, *Secular Goldsmiths' Work in Medieval France: A History*; Max HASSE, 'Neues Hausgerät, neue Häuser, neue Kleider', pp. 7–83; Miloš DRDA and Rudolf KRAJÍC, *Tzv. Husův hrneček – originál nebo dokonalý padělek?*, pp. 505–601; Dana STEHLÍKOVÁ, *Encyklopedie českého zlatnictví, stříbrnictví a klenotnictví*. The problems with ambiguous nomenclature were pointed out by Johann Michael FRITZ, *Goldschmiedekunst der Gotik in Mitteleuropa*, p. 62, but the focus of this synoptic work with many reproductions lies later, in the fifteenth century. For the specification of the technical terms, I would like to thank PhDr. D. Stehlíková, CSc.

403/ The question of whether the attendees of banquets brought their own knives also in the Late Middle Ages remains unanswered even for an author so knowledgeable in this matter as LAMBERT, '«L'assiette de table» – Le «premier mets»', p. 46.

404/ We know of them from the king's order for payment published by DELISLE (ed.), *Mandements et actes divers*, pp. 797–798, No. 1606.

405/ For initial orientation, see VANDENBERGHE, 'Les premières fourchettes', p. 45. From the second half of the fourteenth century, silver forks begin to appear also in German inventories. On that, cf. HASSE, 'Neues Hausgerät', p. 66 (Gabel).

406/ It seems to have been completely different at the meeting of Charles VI and Wenceslas IV in Rheims in March 1398, when the King of France gave his guest and his entourage all of the gold and silver dishes from the banquet rooms. On this gesture based on the testimony of the chronicler Jean Froissart, see NEJEDLÝ, *La représentation des pouvoirs et des hiérarchies*, pp. 325–326.

407/ In the case of goblets and chalices, a role was played again by the fear of poisoned drinks as well as of epidemics. Mediaeval leather covers for travelling cups, as PhDr. Dana Stehlíková, CSc. brought to my attention, can be proved also in the collections of the National Museum, Museum of Decorative Arts in Prague and Moravian Gallery in Brno.

154. Silver goblet with the inscribed band Dieu soit loué de tout (May God be praised above all). Height 11 cm, diameter 8.5 cm

We will first pay attention to the term *gobelet*, which is used for these given chalices and goblets. The word *gobelet* from the Old French *gobel* commonly refers to a vessel for drinking, usually without a stem and bigger in height than in width, similar to a chalice in English.[408] It is apparent from the accounting documents for the gifts for the Luxemburg delegation that the *gobelets* could differ in size, material and decoration. Most of the preserved cups from the second half of the fourteenth century and beginning of the fifteenth century have a height of 100 to 150 mm, as proved also by some exemplars on display in the Musée du Louvre (Richelieu Wing). The silver chalices have two gold rims (OA 9423), a central one with lettering (OA 9424 – Pic. 154), or satisfy themselves only with the upper rim (C. 7345–7346). The museum also has a chalice of amethyst in a combination with pink jasper, which deviates from our set (OA 2042).[409] Two silver chalices from the collections of that museum are only 110 mm high and 96 mm wide, they widen higher and have their upper edges emphasised by a curve (C. 7345–7346).[410] A simple cylindrical chalice of silver, 114 mm high and 86 mm wide, from before 1355 can be seen also in the Musée Cluny (Cl. 1953).[411] One *gobelet* stands on the table of the Epiphany feast in honour of Charles IV in a miniature in the codex of the British Library in London Nero E II, fol. 229va (Pic. 102 / XXXIX); two typical chalices are available to the diners at the ceremonial table in the manuscript of the Bibliothèque Nationale ms. fr. 2813, fol. 473v (Pic. 80 / XI). The accounting documents in the form of the royal mandates of Charles V prove not only the generosity of the giver but also the variety of the vessels labelled in this way. For further enlightenment, it is enough to mention the number of the relevant mandate in the given edition.[412]

1593 *un grant gobelet, esmaillez et garniz de perrerie*, a large chalice for Charles IV from Jacques d'Orgeval for 2,000 fr (along with a gold jug). Considering its high price, I suppose that it is the vessel labelled as *une coppe d'or de grant pois*, which is mentioned in the first place in the list of presents given to Charles IV and his retinue at the residence in Beauté on Thursday, 14 January. Also this cup was decorated with precious stones and was entirely covered with very fine enamel depicting the heavenly sphere with the zodiac, the signs, the planets, the fixed stars and perhaps even their images (*et leurs ymages*).[413]

408/ On this artefact, see Gay, *Glossaire archéologique*, pp. 781–783, and more recently Lightbown, *Secular Goldsmiths' Work in Medieval France*, p. 22. The equivalent in German is in my opinion the expression *Becher*. This is corroborated also by the explanation in Hasse, 'Neues Hausgerät', pp. 61–62, where there is *inter alia* a mention of the collection of five silver hexagonal chalices of Bohemian provenance from 1310–1335 (the so-called *Häufelbecher*) in the Germanisches Nationalmuseum in Nuremberg (Inv. No. HG 11 628).

409/ The *gobelet* is registered in the catalogue *Les Fastes du Gothique. Le siècle de Charles V*, pp. 216–217, No. 176.

410/ Both were also displayed at the exhibition *Les Fastes du Gothique*, pp. 258–259, No. 207 A–B. I have additionally mentioned two further typical *gobelets* in the catalogue *Paris 1400. Les arts sous Charles VI*, pp. 185–187, Nos. 102 and 105.

411/ See *Les Fastes du Gothique*, p. 257, No. 206I, and more recently Taburet-Delahaye, *L'orfèvrerie gothique (XIIIe – début XVe siècle) au Musée de Cluny*, p. 246, No. 129.

412/ See Delisle (ed.), *Mandements et actes divers*, pp. 789–799. I deal with units of coins and weights as well as the prices of silver and gold in one of the following excursuses.

413/ So we read in the Account of the *Great Chronicles of France* on the emperor's visit to France, published by Delachenal (ed.), *Chronique des règnes*, II, p. 268, Note 3, who on the other hand concluded that this object did not

1601 *un gobelet et une ayguiere d'or, pesans vii mars vi onces*, a cup with a gold jug weighing 7 marks and 6 ounces for Wenceslas IV for 700 fr from Jean de Viviers.[414]
1607 *un gobelet d'or*, weighing 3 marks and 15 sterlings (*esterlins*), one mark for 88 fr, bought for 272 fr for Duke Henry from the goldsmith Robert de Val.
1592 *un gobellet (d'or) et une ayguiere d'or* (ewer for the king), weighing 6 marks and 15 sterlings, 80 fr per mark; bought for Thymo of Kolditz from the money changer Henriet Orlant for 497.5 fr.
1608 *un grant hennap, un pot, deux flacons, un grant gobelet et un autre pot d'argent dorez*, all weighing 53 marks, 4 ounces and 10 sterlings, at 12 fr for 1 mark; purchased for prothonotary Nicholas and one knight for 642 fr and 12 sous from the money changer Simon de Dammartin.
1591 *quatre gobelés d'argent dorez*, weighing 13 marks, 6 ounces and 5 sterlings; 10 fr per mark; bought from Franchequin de Target for four *officiers* for 137 and 13 Parisian sous.
1591 *trois gobelés d'argent dorez*, weighing 13 marks, 2 ounces and 12 sterlings; 10 fr per mark; bought from Franchequin de Target for the valets of the chamber for 133 fr, 4 sous and 6 deniers Parisian.
1591 *un grand gobelet et un pot d'argent dorez*, weighing 12 marks, 11 ounces and 15 sterlings; 12 fr per mark; purchased from Franchequin de Target for one knight for 153 fr.
1592 *un gobelet et une ayguiere d'argent dorez*, weighing 7 marks, 2 ounces and 10 sterlings, 1 mark for 10 fr; purchased for one knight from Henriet Orlant for 73 fr, 2 sous and 6 Tours deniers (*deniers tournois*).
1592 *une ayguiere d'argent dorez avec un gobelet*, weighing 2 marks, 2 ounces and 5 sterlings, 1 mark for 10 fr; purchased for one squire from Henriet Orlant for 22 fr, 16 sous and 3 Tours deniers.
1596 *un gobelet d'argent dorez*, weighing 4 marks and 8 sterlings, 1 mark for 10 fr; bought for one squire from the money changer Jean de Mareuil for 44 fr and 8 sous.
1605 *un grant hennap, un grand gobelet et deux pos d'argent dorez*, weighing 32 marks and 2 ounces, 12 fr per mark; bought for two knights for 387 fr from Pierre Fatinant.
1605 *trois gobeles et une aiguiere d'argent dorez*, weighing 16 marks, 5 ounces and 10 sterlings, 10 fr per mark; purchased for three *officiers* for 166 fr and 14 Parisian sous from Pierre Fatinant.
1607 *un grant gobelet d'argent dorez*, weighing 9 marks and 2 ounces, 1 mark for 10 fr; bought for 1 knight from Germany for 92 fr and 8 Parisian sous from the goldsmith Robert de Val.
1608 *onze gobellés, neuf ayguieres et deux quartes d'argent dorez*, weighing 64 marks, 4 ounces and 1 sterling, 1 mark for 10 fr; purchased for numerous clerks, notaries and officials (*clers et officiers*) for 643 fr and 13 Tours sous from Simon de Dammartin.

For drinking at banquets as well as on journeys, they further used vessels called *pot*. It is typical for the unclear terminology that *pot* is used in reference to a jug with a handle and hinged lid from the fourteenth century from the Abbey of Maubuisson (Versailles, Musée Lambinet, Inv. No. 1141), 340 mm high, with a maximum width of 170 mm. The material combines coconut, gilded copper and silver with black enamel.[415] However, these were mostly vessels of a hemispherical shape, similar to today's tea cups or mugs, which differ from the shallow bowls called *hanap* by their depth. *Inter alia* they were among the gifts of the city of Paris for Emperor Charles and his son Wenceslas (Pic. 79 / X).[416] In the German and Central European context, this vessel seems to have a counterpart in the type with several labels (*Kopf, Schauer, Napf*, etc.), which quite varied in its material as well as shape, on a stem and without, with a lid in the form of a conical chalice of the same size upside down and placed on top (the so-called *Doppelkopf*) etc.[417] It is apparent from the following documents that vessels of silver or gold were intended for the gifts:

1593 *un pot d'or, esmaillez et garni de perrerie*, a gold ewer decorated with enamel and precious stones from Jacques d'Orgeval for Charles IV for 2,000 fr (along with a large chalice).[418]
1591 *une fontaine, hennap et pot d'argent dorez*, a table fountain, chalice and gilded silver ewer, all weighing

appear in the accounts. Only the label can be called into question here, because the descriptions otherwise agree on the whole.

414/ These seem to be the gifts for Wenceslas IV which are listed by Delachenal (ed.), *Chronique des règnes*, II, p. 269: 'un grant gobelet d'or et aiguiere de mesmes'.

415/ See *Les Fastes du Gothique*, pp. 226–227, No. 180.

416/ For more on that, see Lightbown, *Secular Goldsmiths' Work in Medieval France*, pp. 25–27. Hasse, 'Neues Hausgerät', pp. 73–75, uses for a similar type of vessels for drinking the phrase *Kopf, Napf* and other equivalents. He by mistake, however, also classifies the French term *hanap* here, on which there is a discussion below.

417/ This type was devoted attention by Drda and Krajíc, *Tzv. Husův hrneček*, here esp. pp. 518–537.

418/ It could be one of two precious chalices which the Account mentions in the handover of presents on 13 January 1378.

67 marks, 2 ounces and 5 sterlings (*esterlins*), 13 fr per mark; bought for 874 fr and 12 Parisian sous from the Parisian merchant Franchequin de Target for the duke of Saxony.
1591 *pour une autre petite fontaine, hennap et pot d'argent dorez*, all weighing 41 marks and 5 ounces, 1 mark for 13 fr for Henry of Brzeg; purchased from the Parisian merchant Franchequin de Target.
1605 *pour une grant fontaine, pot et hennap d'argent dorez*, all weighing 60 marks, at 14 fr per mark; bought for Duke Henry for 840 fr from Pierre Fatinant.
1599 *une fontaine, hennap et pot d'argent doré*, weighing 64 marks, 3 ounces and 15 sterlings, 1 mark for 12 fr; purchased for Thymo of Kolditz from the goldsmith Jean Pochart for 773 fr and 10 sous.
1607 *une fontaine, hennap et pot d'argent dorez*, weighing 61 marks and 3 ounces, 1 mark for 12 fr, for Duke de Strapo for 616 fr and 8 Parisian sous from the goldsmith Robert de Val.
1592 *une fontaine, hennap et pot d'argent dorez*, weighing 34 marks, 1 mark for 12 fr; bought for John of Leuchtenberg from Henriet Orlant for 408 fr.
1608 *un grant hennap, un pot, deux flacons, un grant gobelet et un autre pot d'argent dorez*, all weighing 53 marks, 4 ounces and 10 sterlings, at 12 fr per mark; purchased for prothonotary Nicholas and one knight for 642 fr, 12 sous from the money changer Simon de Dammartin.
1591 *un grand gobelet et un pot d'argent dorez*, weighing 12 marks, 11 ounces and 15 sterlings; 12 fr per mark; bought from Franchequin de Target for one knight for 153 fr.
1596 *deux hennaps et un pot d'argent dorez*, weighing 26 marks, 7 ounces and 1 sterling and an obole (*obule* is a coin worth a half of a denier or 1/24th of a sol), 1 mark for 12 fr; purchased for two knights from money changer Jean de Mareuil for 442 fr and10 sous.
1605 *un grant hennap, un grand gobelet et deux pos d'argent dorez*, weighing 32 marks and 2 ounces, 12 fr per mark; bought for two knights for 387 fr from Pierre Fatinant.
1609 *deux grans hennaps et deux pos d'argent dorez*, weighing 26 marks, 2 ounces, 7 sterlings and an obole, 1 mark for 12 fr; purchased for two squires for 315 fr and 9 Parisian sous from the goldsmith Thomas Pochart.

A smaller cup was the so-called quarter (*quarte*), which appears in the list of presents only once:

1608 *onze gobellés, neuf ayguieres et deux quartes d'argent dorez*, weighing 64 marks, 4 ounces and 1 sterling, 1 mark for 10 fr; bought for numerous clerks, notaries and officials for 643 fr and 13 Tours sous from Simon de Dammartin.

It is worth noting that in the collection of gifts for the Luxemburg delegation both jugs and table fountains were numerously represented on the one hand and shallow bowls called *hanaps*, which we most frequently find in depictions of period banquets, on the other. We shall first devote attention to the jugs for water or wine, the so-called *aiguières*.[419] As the origin of the word from the Latin *aquaria* indicated, they were originally vessels for water. According to period depictions, these high jugs had a handle and spout.[420] The jug from which a servant is pouring water at the edge of the table of the duke of Berry seems to correspond best to our accounting entries (Pic. 155). European collections contain many jugs; often only the most precious ones, made of crystal, are on display.[421] They could be gilded over the entire area or only partially. The generosity of the French host is proved by the total of fourteen jugs given:

1601 *un gobelet et une ayguiere d'or, pesans vii mars vi onces*, a goblet with a gold jug weighing 7 marks and 6 ounces for Wenceslas IV for 700 fr from Jean de Viviers.[422]
1592 *pour un hennap et une ayguiere d'argent dorez*, weighing 10 marks and 4 ounces, 1 mark for 10 fr; bought for one knight from Henriet Orlant for 105 fr.
1592 *un gobelet et une ayguiere d'argent dorez*, weighing 7 marks, 2 ounces and 10 sterlings, 1 mark for 10 fr; purchased for one knight from Henriet Orlant for 73 fr, 2 sous and 6 Tours deniers.
1592 *une ayguiere d'argent dorez avec un gobelet*, weighing 2 marks, 2 ounces and 5 sterlings, 1 mark for 10 fr; bought for one squire from Henriet Orlant for 22 fr, 16 sous and 3 Tours deniers.

419/ Cf. Gay, *Glossaire archéologique*, pp. 13–15. The only equivalent is the German expression *Kanne*, which also labels a vessel with a spout for pouring drinks when serving at the table. For more on that, see Hasse, 'Neues Hausgerät', pp. 70–71.
420/ We find an excellent exemplar decorated with enamel in the catalogue *L'art au temps des rois maudits. Philippe le Bel et ses fils 1285–1328*, p. 180, Pic. 1.
421/ A beautiful exemplar donated to the Prague cathedral by Charles IV before 1354 today is a component of Charles IV's treasure (see *Die Parler und die schöne Stil 1350–1400*, III, p. 179, Kaiser Karl IV., Pic. 106).
422/ These are undoubtedly the gifts for Wenceslas IV mentioned in the Account, Delachenal (ed.), *Chronique des règnes*, II, p. 269: 'un grant gobelet d'or et aiguiere de mesmes'.

155. New Year's feast of Duke John of Berry. Très Riches Heures du Duc de Berry. Month of January, beginning of the 15th century. The feast takes place according to the assignment of the scenes in the calendar also in January, but roughly 25 years later. However, we are interested in the actual feast and its provision. On the lavishly supplied sideboard on the left, we can see in addition to the two common jugs, bowls and cups also the small bottles for wine typical for the period, so-called fontains. A smaller mystery, at least for me, are the two tall gold or golden vessels in the background, which have an elongated conical shape with a cap. A tablecloth cannot be lacking on the wooden tables of which we can see only the legs. The large gold boat is on the left side of the host as prescribed by several court protocols. In front of each guest, there are small bowls shaped like so-called hanaps and écuelles. The platters with food are manifestly larger, serve just roasted chickens or other birds, which also the small dogs eat which are allowed to roam freely on the table. Even the duke's favourite hunting dog, served by the servant order to do so, gets a tasty bite. A welcome enhancement is a servant with a jug who is pouring water into the gémellion of one of the guests. He is busy trying to hold the chalice in his other hand. The carvers are trying; one cuts the meat on the platter (tranchoir), the other is preparing to fillet the roasted birds or hares. Their spectacular costumes and small swords on their belts indicates that they are noble servants. If that was the case, the clothes shawls on their shoulders could be interpreted as large towels or napkins on which the guests could wipe their hands. We should not miss even the figure of the hofmeister (master of the household) in the background who calls the waiting guests to the food with the words "aproche, aproche". (MC, ms. 65, fol. 1r)

1605 *trois gobeles et une arguiere d'argent dorez*, weighing 16 marks, 5 ounces and 10 sterlings, 10 fr per mark; purchased for three officers for 166 fr and 14 Parisian sous from Pierre Fatinant.
1608 *onze gobellés, neuf ayguieres et deux quartes d'argent dorez*, weighing 64 marks, 3 ounces and 1 sterling, 1 mark for 10 fr; bought for numerous clerks, notaries and officials for 643 fr, 13 Tours sous from Simon de Dammartin.

156. A silver, partially gilded bowl for drinking – a hanap from the 14th century

The most frequent gift was a shallow bowl for drinking, the so-called *hanap*, which could however be used also as a vessel for soup, sauce or for a portion of meat. The explanation of this object is slightly problematic. The word *hennap/hanap* comes from the Latin word *hanappus*, meaning a gold vessel, a chalice.[423] The question is to what extent this precious object resembled the so-called Royal Gold Cup from around 1380 (British Museum 92, 5-1-1), which was made for the duke of Berry.[424] It is worth noting that it is a small bowl on a round foot, not a goblet or chalice. On the other hand, the vast majority of vessels for drinking labelled in the French collections as *hanap* have the form of low round bowls, e.g. the *hanap* from the treasure found in Gaillon and displayed in the Musée Cluny (Cl. 1951) is 50 mm high with a diameter of 185 mm (Pic. 156). This silver bowl is partially gilded and has an enamel medallion in the centre surrounded by six embossed leaves.[425] In the newly arranged collection of art objects in the Louvre, we find in the Richelieu Wing immediately two groups of bowls labelled in this way from around 1350. It is a set of four simple silver bowls labelled as *hanap* of Toulouse provenance from a treasure found in Ariège (OA 11783–11786). The Toulouse hallmark can also be found on the independently displayed silver bowl (OA 11777) decorated with bubbles (*à décor boulonné*). The second set, coming from Parisian workshops, contains *inter alia* two simple, undecorated silver bowls (OA 11895, 11379). However, the other two bowls already have more expensive decoration. The first of them is partially gilded with traces of translucent enamel (OA 643); the second has an enamelled scene of a rabbit being chased by a dog in the centre (OA 11380). From our bowls and chalices for drinking (Pic. 157), it is necessary to distinguish

157. A person drinking from a bowl called a hanap. A depiction from the Hours in the Bibliothèque municipale, Rouen

423/ At least according to *Latinitatis Medii Aevi Lexikon*, II, p. 950. For more on this table utensil, see Laborde, *Glossaire français*, pp. 337–339, and Lightbown, *Secular Goldsmiths' Work in Medieval France*, pp. 20–22. It is likely that this term was used also when referring to a shallow bowl on a stem that could have had a lid as well, also serving for drinking. It has its analogue in the German term *Schalle*; for more on that, see Hasse, 'Neues Hausgerät', pp. 15 and 79–80.
424/ The catalogue *Europäische Kunst um 1400*, p. 421, No. 498 (Pic. 27) labels it as a ciborium.
425/ *Musée national du Moyen Âge Thermes de Cluny. Guide des collections*, pp. 96–97, No. 109 (also with a reproduction); this and another *hanap* were described by Taburet-Delahaye, *L'orfèvrerie gothique*, pp. 242–245, Nos. 127–128. For beautiful exemplars of *hanaps* on a stem as well as in the form of shallow bowls most recently, see the catalogue *Paris 1400. Les arts sous Charles VI*, pp. 184–6, Nos. 100–101 and 104.

so-called *gémellions*, which served for hand washing. The etymology of the name (*gémaux*, now *jumeaux*, i.e. twins) reveals that water was poured from bowl to bowl. *Gémellions* were richly decorated and could be used for liturgical as well as secular purposes.[426] From the iconographic documents, I mention the depiction of the banquet for both crowned heads in the manuscript of the British Library Nero E II, fol. 229va (Pic. 102 / XXXIX), where a large chalice with a lid, whose foot however resembles rather a calix, stands before Emperor Charles. Gold or gilded bowls and plates can be seen also on the ostentatious table of the duke of Berry (Pic. 155).[427] Here, they are serving food on platters (*écuelles*), which had flattened edges so that it could be used like a lid for food also from the other side.[428] The catalogue of the exhibition *Les Fastes du Gothique* shows four of these platters (*écuelles*) from a treasure found in Maldegem near Eecloo in Belgium, which have a diameter of ca 240 mm and a height of about 40 mm.[429] That the difference is remarkable is proved by an object in the same catalogue under No. 206 H, which is shown there as a *hanap ou écuelle*. Unlike the bowls mentioned before, it has a smaller diameter (182 mm, height 45 mm). This object belongs to the group of relatively varied Gothic utensils from the treasure of Rouen-Gaillon, whose individual pieces are deposited in the Victoria and Albert Museum, in the Musée des Thermes et de l'hôtel de Cluny and in the Hermitage today. The same perplexity with labelling occurs also with the bowl denoted as 206 D, which has a diameter of 230 mm and a height of 45 mm; the collection also clearly shows the diversity of décor:

206 A) *Hanap ou écuelle* (Victoria and Albert Museum 109-1865), Paris, first third of the fourteenth century, 183 mm, 45 mm.
206 B) *Hanap* (Victoria and Albert Museum 106-1865), Montpellier, before 1355, 184 mm, 40 mm.
206 C) *Hanap* (Victoria and Albert Museum 107-1865), France, around 1350, 210 mm, 54 mm.
206 D) *Hanap ou écuelle* (Victoria and Albert Museum 108-1865), Paris, last quarter of the fourteenth century, 230 mm, 45 mm.
206 G) *Hanap* (Cluny, Cl. 1951), France, first half of the fourteenth century, 183 mm, 55 mm.
206 H) *Hanap ou écuelle* (Cluny, Cl. 1952), Paris, first half of the fourteenth century, 182 mm, 45 mm.
206 J) *Hanap* (Louvre, OA 396), France, first half of the fourteenth century, 195 mm, 44 mm.
206 K) *Hanap* (Hermitage, unlabelled) France, first half of the fourteenth century, only a diameter of 200 mm.
206 L) *Hanap* (Hermitage, unlabelled) France, first half of the fourteenth century, only a diameter of 200 mm.
206 M) *Hanap* (Hermitage, unlabelled), Montpellier, before 1355, a diameter of 205 mm.
206 N) *Hanap* (Hermitage, unlabelled), France, first half of the fourteenth century, a diameter of 200 mm.
208 *Hanap* (private collection), Paris, second half of the fourteenth century, 158 mm, 42 mm.

Only now is it time for the given dishes of this name, which again prove their great diversity:

1595 *un grant hennap d'or à couvercle et sus un hault trepie*, a large pokale with a lid on a high tripod for Charles IV for 2,360 fr (which the host Charles V originally intended to keep for himself), purchased from the money changer Jean Brulart. It is undoubtedly the gorgeous dish decorated with precious stones mentioned by the Account of the *Great Chronicles of France*.[430]
1591 *une fontaine, hennap et pot d'argent dorez*, a table fountain, chalice and gilded silver jug, all weighing 67 marks, 2 ounces and 5 sterlings (*esterlins*) at 13 fr per mark; purchased for 874 fr and 12 Parisian sous from the Parisian merchant Franchequin de Target for the duke of Saxony.
1591 *pour une autre petite fontaine, hennap et pot d'argent dorez*, all weighing 41 marks and 5 ounces, 1 mark for 13 fr for Henry of Brzeg, bought from the Parisian merchant Franchequin de Target for the duke of Saxony.

426/ A gorgeous sample is presented in *Musée national du Moyen Âge Thermes de Cluny. Guide des collections*, p. 90, No. 100 (Cl. 954).
427/ *The Very Rich Hours of the Duke of Berry*, miniature of the month of January, beginning of the fifteenth century.
428/ This is precisely how the function of the flattened edges was described with the similar bowls in Germany called *Schüssel* and *Salser* by Hasse, 'Neues Hausgerät', p. 81. For the French milieu, see Lightbown, *Secular Goldsmiths' Work in Medieval France*, p. 17.
429/ *Les Fastes du Gothique*, pp. 245–246, No. 198. It is not insignificant that the catalogue lists them as 'différentes par leur formes des hanaps ou coups du trésor de Gaillon'.

430/ See Delachenal (ed.), *Chronique des règnes*, II, p. 269, Note 4. It is worth noting the so-called *Deckelpokal* from before 1376 in the Rijksmuseum in Amsterdam, which had a decorative lid and was on a tripod. See Johann Michael Fritz, in *Die Parler und der schöne Stil 1350–1400*, I, p. 113, on it briefly, also with a reproduction.

1605 *pour une grant fontaine, pot et hennap d'argent dorez*, all weighing 60 marks, at 14 fr per mark; purchased for Duke Henry for 840 fr from Pierre Fatinant.
1607 *une fontaine, hennap et pot d'argent dorez*, weighing 61 marks and 3 ounces, 1 mark for 12 fr; purchased for Duke de Strapo for 616 fr and 8 sous Parisian from the goldsmith Robert de Val.
1599 *une fontaine, hennap et pot d'argent doré*, weighing 64 marks, 3 ounces and 15 sterlings, 1 mark for 12 fr; purchased for Thymo of Kolditz from the goldsmith Jean Pochart for 773 fr, 10 sous.
1592 *une fontaine, hennap et pot d'argent dorez*, weighing 34 marks, 1 mark for 12 fr; bought for John of Leuchtenberg from Henriet Orlant for 408 fr.
1591 *un grant hennap d'argent doré*, weighing 8 marks, 5 ounces and 5 sterlings, at 12 fr per mark; purchased for prothonotary Nicholas for 103 fr and 14 sous from Franchequin de Target.[431]
1608 *un grant hennap, un pot, deux flacons, un grant gobelet et un autre pot d'argent dorez*, all weighing 53 marks, 4 ounces and 10 sterlings, at 12 fr per mark; bought for prothonotary Nicholas and one knight for 642 fr, 12 sous from the money changer Simon de Dammartin.
1592 *un hennap et une ayguiere d'argent dorez*, weighing 10 marks and 4 ounces, 1 mark for 10 fr; purchased for one knight from Henriet Orlant for 105 fr.
1596 *deux hennaps et un pot d'argent dorez*, weighing 26 marks 7 ounces and 1 sterling and an obole, 1 mark for 12 fr; bought for two knights from the money changer Jean de Mareuil for 442 fr and 10 sous.
1605 *un grant hennap, un grand gobelet et deux pos d'argent dorez*, weighing 32 marks and 2 ounces, 12 fr per mark; bought for two knights for 387 fr from Pierre Fatinant.
1609 *deux grans hennaps et deux pos d'argent dorez*, weighing 26 marks, 2 ounces, 7 sterlings and an obole, 1 mark for 12 fr; purchased for two squires for 315 fr and 9 Parisian sous from the goldsmith Thomas Pochart.

Problems also arise with another of the gifts, the so-called *fontaine*, i.e. usually a metal table fountain for wine with one or more taps which was brought to the table at the end of ceremonial banquets.[432] Bottles (*flacons*) with corks or screw closings of various shapes had the same function. Also the *flacons* had various shapes; frequently they were flattened round vessels standing upright, with a shorter or longer neck, which used to be also a part of travelling sets of silverware (Pic. 158).[433] It would have been odd if this precious table utensil had not appeared at the Parisian banquets in the emperor's honour, because Charles V gave several, apparently smaller fountains to his guests:

158. Two silver, gilded bottles (flacons) with screw tops from around 1400

431/ It is apparently this vessel that was meant by Spěváček, *Karel IV. Život a dílo*, p. 472, according to whom Nicholas of Riesenburg received for his work a 'splendid thickly gilded silver jug in which a thousand gold francs were deposited' (reference is not given).

432/ A gorgeous table fountain from the fourteenth century is deposited in the Cleveland Museum of Arts. For a colour photograph with an explanation of the use of the fountains, see *Fêtes gourmandes*, pp. 106–109; cf. further Stehlíková, *Encyklopedie českého zlatnictví, stříbrnictví a klenotnictví*, p. 474. One of the gifts of the city of Paris in the miniature in the manuscript in Paris, Bibliothèque nationale, ms. fr. 2813, fol. 472ra, was interpreted as a type of vessel called *fontaine* by Delachenal (ed.), *Chronique des règnes*, caption to Pic. XL.

433/ Two travel flasks (flacons) were purchased in the already more often mentioned collection of table dishes for prothonotary Nicholas and one knight (Delisle (ed.) *Mandements*, No. 1608). For enlightenment on flacons, see Gay, *Glossaire archéologique*, pp. 716–717, and more recently Lightbown, *Secular Goldsmiths' Work in Medieval France*, pp. 28–30. Two exquisite gilded silver flasks – flacons from the holdings of All Souls College, Oxford, are shown in the exhibition catalogue *Paris 1400. Les arts sous Charles VI*, pp. 187–188, No. 106.

1591 *une fontaine, hennap et pot d'argent dorez*, a table fountain, chalice and gilded silver jug, all weighing 67 marks, 2 ounces and 5 sterlings (*esterlins*) at 13 fr per mark; purchased for 874 fr and 12 Parisian sous from Parisian merchant Franchequin de Target for the duke of Saxony.
1591 *une autre petite fontaine, hennap et pot d'argent dorez*, all weighing 41 marks and 5 ounces, 1 mark per 13 fr for Henry of Brzeg; bought from the Parisian merchant Franchequin de Target for 541 fr and 2 Parisian sous.
1605 *une grant fontaine, pot et hennap d'argent dorez*, all weighing 60 marks, at 14 fr per mark; purchased for Duke Henry for 840 fr from Pierre Fatinant.
1607 *une fontaine, hennap et pot d'argent dorez*, weighing 61 marks and 3 ounces, 1 mark for 12 fr, for Duke of Opava for 616 fr and 8 Parisian sous; purchased from the goldsmith Robert de Val.
1599 *une fontaine, hennap et pot d'argent doré*, weighing 64 marks, 3 ounces and 15 sterlings, 1 mark for 12 fr; bought for Thymo of Kolditz from the goldsmith Jean Pochart for 773 fr and 10 sous.
1592 *une fontaine, hennap et pot d'argent dorez*, weighing 34 marks, 1 mark for 12 fr; purchased for John of Leuchtenberg from Henriet Orlant for 408 fr.

The most valuable tableware was gold, gilded or silver table nefs (*navette*, *nef*), which appear as one of the prestigious signs in many mediaeval depictions. Their function varied. Some of them served as salt cellars,[434] but those can be commonly found on tables alone also;[435] others contained plates, precious stones for indicating poison, or exotic spices, confetti and titbits. Their place on the tables was close to the host, because they were one of the signs of his position. Since tablecloths inhibited their movement, the tablecloths could be removed at the end of the banquet to allow them to be pulled or pushed back by hand or crooked staff. I know whereof I speak, since as a guest at All Souls College, Oxford, I had the opportunity to manipulate large nefs full of fruit in the described way at the end of the dinners. Well, there is nothing like experience. This also led some later goldsmiths to equip table nefs with wheels.[436]

Based on the inventory of the moveable valuables of Charles V from the first half of 1379, we know that for the king's table it was possible to use six gold nefs, of which at least three stood out for their size as well as decoration. Coincidentally, they are captured also in the depiction in MS fr. 2813 of the Biblitothèque nationale, fols 473va–b (Pic. 80 / XI). The flagship, figuratively, was a two-master with four enamel escutcheons with royal lilies, which were supported by six golden lions. Another large nef, entirely flat, was given to the king by the city of Paris. It weighed an incredible 120 marks of gold.[437] For comparison, we can mention that on 5 January 1378 Emperor Charles also received from the representatives of the metropolis one richly decorated nef weighing even 190 marks, but only of gilded silver (Pic. 79 / X).[438]

A total of three names label the identical shape of low round vessels which may be of roughly the same size, diameter and height. The *hanap*, which often had a decorated bottom as well as edges, has

434/ Sometimes the nef in the miniature of the month of January from the *Very Rich Hours of the Duke of Berry* is labelled as the *salière du Pavillon*. On table nefs, their shapes and use, see, i.a. Laborde, *Glossaire français*, pp. 403–405, and Lightbown, *Secular Goldsmiths' Work in Medieval France*, pp. 29–31.

435/ Undoubtedly a salt cellar alongside three gold nefs appears also in the depiction of the Epiphany feast in the manuscript containing our Account, i.e. Paris, Bibliothèque nationale, ms. fr. 2813, fol. 473v. Nothing is visible in the nefs; on the other hand, some flat tarts or stacked plates are visible in the one gold nef in the depiction of a feast of Duke John of Berry (Pic. 155).

436/ For more on this tableware, see Günther Schiedlausky, 'Tafelschiffe', pp. 30–39; one nef with the wheels from 1450–1475 was published by Birgit Franke, 'Pracht und Zeremoniell. Burgundische Tafelkunst in franko-flämischen Bildteppichen des 15. Jahrhunderts', p. 44, Pic. 18.

437/ See Labarte (ed.), *Inventaire du mobilier de Charles V*, pp. 64–65, No. 334–339.

438/ Cf. Delachenal (ed.), *Chronique des règnes*, II, p. 227, Note 2, with information on this precious utensil owned by Charles V. The representatives of Paris presented the emperor with two large gilded and enamel-decorated flasks (flacons) at a cost of 70 silver marks. Not even Wenceslas IV left empty-handed, the city gave him both a gilded silver vessel (*fontaine*) weighing 93 marks of silver and another two large vessels of gilded silver. The written testimony is in this exceptional case complemented by a miniature in the manuscript of Paris, Bibliothèque nationale, ms. fr. 2813, fol. 472r, which captures a nef with two towers on the keels, a table fountain with spouts on the sides as well as spouts in the embossed heads of two lions and two vessels with a handle and lid (Pic. 79 / X).

already attracted our attention. The copper *gémellions* of the Romanesque period, which were used later too, were sometimes adorned with gold as well as Limoges enamel and often (or always?) bore the coats-of-arms of their owners, as I noticed with the exemplars displayed in the Musée du Louvre. *Gémellions* served for hand washing and thus approached the vessel called a *bassin*, which resembled our smaller and lower metal sink (basin).[439] This dish for hand washing was commonly a part of the festive table, just like the *aquamanile*. The second of these vessels was of diverse shapes and is also well known from the Czech lands and so will not be discussed separately.[440] From the table utensils, the silver, copper or wooden platters for cutting bread and meat (*tranchoirs*), which we commonly see in period illustrations, remain to be mentioned. In accordance with the sources illuminating the journey of Emperor Charles IV to France, they were mainly metal dishes. In conclusion, it is necessary to add that it was possible to encounter simple as well as expensively decorated works of ceramics also on the tables of the feudal lords, not to mention the glass goblets and turned bowls of rare wood. That however is already a question for other scholars.

439/ In the German-speaking area, it is a vessel labelled as *Handbecken* or only *Becken*. For more on that, see Hasse, 'Neues Hausgerät', pp. 63–64.

440/ For initial information, see i.a. *Lexikon des Mittelalters*, I, cols 825–826; further see Peter Bloch, *Aquamaniles, objets sacrés et profanes du Moyen Âge*.

The menus of the feasts in the Great Hall of the Palace de la Cité in Paris on 5 and 6 January 1378, which have been preserved in two versions of the *Mémoire* on the visit of Emperor Charles IV in France, are important not only for their historic circumstances but also in and of themselves as the only evidence of Taillevent's culinary art. The menus were most likely consulted in advance with the chef or another servant of the emperor's retinue. The last word of course was that of King Charles V himself, who had originally set four courses of forty pairs of dishes for the ceremonial lunch on the feast of Epiphany, but considering the emperor's health he cancelled one course, so that only thirty pairs of dishes were served.[441] No more is mentioned in the Account on the menu; we only find out that 'a great number of meals were served, which would take too long to record'.[442]

Both manuscript versions deposited in the Archives du Nord in Lille under shelf marks B 654/ 10 688 [B] and 10 689 [A] were already known to the publisher of the *Great Chronicles of France* Roland Delachenal, to whom however some of the gastronomical terms seemed so incomprehensible that he resigned on a reconstruction of the menu.[443] This difficulty did not scare the student of Professor Jaroslav Mezník Martina Lechová, who published an edition of version [B] and translated it into Czech.[444] She did so with women's intuition, having gathered information from mediaeval cookery books, whereas the publisher of the second version [A] Heinz Thomas limited himself to an illustrative explanation of two dishes.[445] Neither edition is entirely reliable in terms of the part containing menus. By presenting my own solution in places, I do not attempt a partial critical edition but, as I hope, a materially more correct model for translation. However, not even this will help the readers much in terms of what was actually eaten at the banquets. In the notes, I have therefore attached a supplementary explanation or directly rough recipes if I could discover them. On the other hand, in the notes to the Old French version I have listed some significant differences of manuscript [A] and the different interpretations of the editors.

I have selected the menus written in the columns of version B, which in my opinion corresponds better to the original itemisation of the four courses prepared. From the form of the written record, it seems that the scribe had at his disposal the original menu, which served for the orientation of the kitchen and serving staff. The third course seems to have been omitted at the king's command only at the last moment. Not even then did any of these courses contain ten 'pairs of dishes', so the testimony of the Account in this regard remains a bit of an enigma. Whereas the Account calls the courses *assiettes*, i.e. in Old French the same as services at the table, the *Mémoire* uses the expression *mets* from the Latin *missum*, i.e. whatever has been sent to the table. In connection

441/ Delachenal (ed.), *Chronique des règnes*, II, p. 238.
442/ Delachenal (ed.), *Chronique des règnes*, II, pp. 230–231.
443/ Delachenal, *Histoire de Charles V*, V, p. 97; see Delachenal (ed.), *Chronique des règnes*, II, p. 238, Note 2, which also contains a reference to the shelf mark of the source.
444/ Lechová, 'Zpráva o návštěvě Paříže Karlem IV. roku 1378', pp. 49–60.
445/ Thomas, 'Ein Zeitgenössisches Memorandum', pp. 111–112 (commentary) and pp. 115–119 (editions).

159. A ragù with small birds (gravé de menus oiseaux), which following the recipe in the manuscript Paris, BnF, lat. 7131, fol. 100r, was prepared by Yves Pinard, chef of the restaurant Le Grand Louvre. According to the recommendation of the successor of the medieval chef, you pluck, disembowel and tie the sparrows, quails, thrushes or other birds. Them you bake them to a golden brown in an earthen skillet in salted lard. The, you cool them in wine and water, add pepper and ginger, cover the pan and keep it on low heat for twenty-five to thirty minutes. Some juice from the birds is necessary to pour over them. For preparation, you need four quails or other birds, 4 slices salted lard about 3mm thick, 15 cl white wine, 4 gr ground black pepper, 20 gr powdered ginger and 15 cl water. (After: Jean-Louis Flandrin – Carole Lambert, *Fêtes gourmandes au Moyen Age*, Paris 1998, p. 71.)

160. Wheat porridge for game of all types (fromentée) following the recipe in the manuscript Paris, Bibliothèque naionale, Lat. 6707, fol. 185r. The resulting appearance of the dish of the chef Yves Pinard. If you want to cook following the original recipe, you first rinse the husked wheat and cook it for approximately 90 minutes in salted water while mixing constantly with a wooden spoon. Then, remove from the fire and let it absorb the remaining water while cooling. Then, bring milk to a boil, add the wheat, mix and again bring it to a boil. Once the porridge has cooled a bit, add well beaten eggs. Serve warm. For cooking, you need 350 gr husked wheat, 1.5 litres water, 0.5 litres milk, 4 eggs and a pinch of salt.

with the second term, *dentremets – l'entremets* then marked an intermission between courses during which, as we already know, delicacies and drinks were served, namely accompanied by musical or other productions. Thirdly, we encounter the term *dischue* (*– yssue*) once here, apparently in the sense of *dessert*, i.e. the last food served.

So as not to remain only with names, frequently half secret, as it has been in France before as well as nowadays, we shall look at what two dishes prepared for the Epiphany table in honour of Emperor Charles IV may have looked like. The seasoned stew with small birds (*gravé de menus oiseaux*) was prepared according to the period recipes by Yves Pinard, chef of the restaurant of Le Grand Louvre (Pic. 159). A less demanding part of the menu which everyone can try was *fromentée* or the gruel of frumenty to be served with game of all types (Pic. 160).

[Dîner offert par Charles V
le 5 janvier 1378]

PREMIER MES

Un broet d'Alemaigne / un cyvé de lievres / petis patés[a)] / et grosse char

SECONT MES

Rost de plusiers manieres / un broet gaudé / un amandé blanc / pastéz norois / et tourtes lombardes

D'ENTREMES

Une queue de sangler

TIERS MES

Un rosé et un tieullé[b)] / oisons et chapons / de haute grace à la dodine / fromenteée et venoison

D'ENTREMES

Poulles doreez / verdes et jaunes[c)] / et pommes d'orenges

Menu for the Lunch Served by Charles V
on 5 January 1378

FIRST COURSE

Soup in the German style with almonds[I] / hare with black sauce[II], / small pâtés / beef[III]

SECOND COURSE

Roasted meat in several styles / yellow sauce / fresh[IV] almond milk / Karelian pastries[V] and Lombard cakes

INTERMISSION

Boar tail

THIRD COURSE

Pink soup[VI] and tieulle soup[VII] / goslings and fat capons with mushrooms and poultry sauce / gruel of frumenty with eggs[VIII] and game

INTERMISSION

Hens roasted to a golden brown[IX] / green and yellow [sauces] / meatballs[X]

I/ All French and English recipes for this soup contain almonds, and therefore it could be a confusion between *amande* (almond) and *Alemaigne*. On that, see Scully (ed.), *The Viandier of Taillevent*, pp. 69–70, No. 22; further *Fêtes gourmandes au Moyen Âge*, Glossaire, p. 180. The recipes for this soup in four ways (with beef, with rabbits, with chicken, and with eggs) are presented by Flandrin, 'Brouets, potages et bouillons', p. 14.

II/ 'Civé de lievres': the dark colour was given by the browned bread, see Scully (ed.), *The Viandier*, pp. 78–81, No. 28–29, also here on four types of toast.

III/ See *Fêtes gourmandes*, Glossaire, 182: 'char = viande: le boeuf, le mouton et parfois le porc'; it is therefore the meat of large animals, mostly beef, mutton, entirely exceptionally also pork; for more details, see Scully (ed.), *The Viandier*, chair, char according to the index; for more details, see ibid., pp. 37–39, No. 4.

IV/ Here in the sense of 'fresh' rather than 'white'; see analogically *poisson blanc* in: *Fêtes gourmandes*, Glossaire, p. 184.

V/ 'Norwegian' usually marks something Scandinavian. I used the term 'Karelian pastries', because they were fried small pancakes filled with meat, cheeses and fruit; for more on that, see Scully (ed.), *The Viandier*, pp. 262–263, No. 208, and *Fêtes gourmandes*, Glossaire, p. 184.

VI/ See *Fêtes gourmandes*, Glossaire, p. 184 = 'brouet de couleur rose', i.e. a soup of pink colour.

VII/ Not even the authors of the glossary knew how to deal with the dish 'tuille, tuillé' much. No matter how odd it may sound, it is either a soup the colour of roofing tiles or looking as if it were covered with tiles (*Fêtes gourmandes*, Glossaire, p. 186; also cf. Scully (ed.), *The Viandier*, pp. 260–261, No. 206).

VIII/ See *Fêtes gourmandes*, Glossaire, p. 184: 'fromentée = bouillie de froment liée aux oeufs', i.e. gruel of frumenty with eggs, with also the ingredients, recipe and photograph on pp. 130–131 (see Pic. 160). The connection of this gruel with venison was typical for the third course of period feasts. For more detail on that, see Scully (ed.), *The Viandier*, pp. 116–117, No. 63. Fromenté was also eaten with sea fish; see Nejedlý, *Fortuny kolo vrtkavé*, p. 283.

IX/ i.e. repeatedly coated with egg yolk during roasting.

X/ See *Fêtes gourmandes*, Glossaire, p. 185: 'pommes d'orenge = petites boulettes de viande'.

[Souper offert par Charles V le 5 janvier 1378]

PREMIER MES POUR LE SOUPER

Venoison de sangler à / la courte souppe / un broet blanc lie d'oes / un potate en manière de sayme / de connins et oisons de rivière / et un broet foule sur chapons

SECONT MES

Rost de plusiers manieres / pastes de connins et de / chapons de haute graisse / un tieullé et / un broet bare de blanc et de vert

TIERS MES

Creppes verdes et jaunes / tartes cucreez et autre / menu ouvrage de four / un broet fin vert et un / broet camelin de petis / oiseles et ni ot point / d'entremes

D'ISCHUE[d)]

Nois et poires / cucreez / et pomes verdes / item mestier / de menestrel

Menu for the Dinner Served by Charles V on 5 January 1378

FIRST COURSE OF THE DINNER

Weak bouillon from boar meat / white soup with eggs / stew with rabbits[XI] river gosling / sauce a bowl of bread crust

SECOND COURSE

Roasted meat in more ways / pastries stuffed with the meat of rabbits and fat capons / small shaped pastries / sea bass with white and green sauce

THIRD COURSE

Green and yellow crêpes / sweet cakes with small pastries[XII] / fine green sauce[XIII] / goslings in spiced sauce,[XIV] the so-called salsa and there was no *intermission*

CONCLUSION

Nuts, sweetened pears and green apples titbits and pastilles[XV] to the sound of music as well as singing

XI/ Lechová thinks that it was an a la 'Seine' method. In reality, the word 'saymé' meant the same as 'gravé', i.e. a broth of small birds (quails, swallows, etc.) prepared on grease, in which these small birds were served after a proper preparation. See the recipe and photograph in: *Fêtes gourmandes*, pp. 70–71 and here Pic. 159.

XII/ According to the *Fêtes gourmandes*, pp. 140–141, 'menus ouvrages' – they were small pastries often bought on the streets of large towns, e.g. wafers, rolled wafers, etc.

XIII/ It is so called 'sauce cameline', for ingredients, recipe and photograph, see *Fêtes gourmandes*, pp. 94–95, *Glossaire*, p. 181, and Scully (ed.), *The Viandier*, p. 44.

XIV/ An idea can be gained from the period recipe of the so-called 'gravé de menus oiseaux', see *Fêtes gourmandes*, pp. 70–71.

XV/ See *Fêtes gourmandes*, pp. 140–141, with a detailed description of the so-called 'le mestier' at large banquets.

[Diner offert par Charles V
le 6 janvier 1378]

PREMIER MES

Porée[e)] blance et pois coulez / oyes salées / et grosse char de plusiers manieres / un civé d'oistres / un broet jorge de char / une soringue d'anguiles / et une salmine sur chapons

SECOND MES

Rost de plusiers manieres / char de bre<s>mes rosties[f)] / eschinées[g)] de saumon / un tieule / un broet fulle / Et furent servi de poisson / de mer et drave[h)] douche a grant / plente et de plusiers manieres

[THIERS MES]

Un broet asure sur le poisson / un broet jaune sur chapons / anguilles renversees[i)] à la vouée[j)] / figues farsie connins[k)] de fuelle d'or / Et un broet de trois couleurs / blanc, ynde et vermeil / et pastez lorrois

THIERS MES

Conins farsis et dorez / et haricocs[l)] / let lardee / un rose / un broet de verde couleur / tartes cucrees / bourrees à la chaude sausse / un amande blanc / chapons pelerins à la dodine / tourtes parmeniens / une espinbegue / une gellee / espaules de mouton farcies / et motes de char

a) Thomas reads 'pois passéz'; b) Lechová reads 'ticulle' everywhere; c) Lechová reads 'Jannos'; d) Thomas reads 'dischnee'; e) Lechová reads 'porce', but it is understood to be 'poiree'; f) *Mémoire* A has: 'rost de pluseurs manieres de char et bremes rosties'; g) Thomas reads 'eschiveez'; h) Thomas reads 'eschiveez'; i) Lechová reads 'routeez', Thomas also incorrectly 'acucreez'; j) This is what Thomas has, whereas Lechová has, probably erroneously, 'bonne'; it might have been 'voeu', i.e. as wished; k) Thomas reads 'farchies couuers'; l) Lechová has 'us hitons'; Thomas has 'haricous'.

Epiphany Menu for the Banquet in Honour
of Emperor Charles IV

FIRST COURSE

Leek soup[XVI] and pea mash / salted geese / beef and mutton in various styles / ragout of oysters[XVII] / eel and capons with ragout of feathered game

SECOND COURSE

Various types of roasts / roasted bream[XVIII] / back of salmon / small shaped pastries / sauce and sea fish were served / .... in various ways

[CANCELLED THIRD COURSE]

Fish with a sour sauce / capon with a yellow sauce / eels 'inside out'[XIX] as wished / stuffed figs / rabbits roasted to a golden brown / sauce of three colours: white, blue and red / and fried scones stuffed with meat[XX]

THIRD COURSE

Stuffed rabbits roasted to a golden brown and ragout / milk crust / pink sauce / sweet cakes with blancmange / almond milk / Baked lean capons with sauce à la dodine[XXI] / Parma pancakes[XXII] / spiced sweets fish jelly[XXIII] / stuffed mutton shoulder and meat olives[XXIV]

XVI/ See *Fêtes gourmandes*, Glossaire, p. 184: 'Potage généralement à base de blanc poireaux'. Here also with the recipe and photograph on pp. 68–69.
XVII/ For more details on that, see Scully (ed.), *The Viandier*, pp. 145–146, No. 79; ingredients, recipe and photograph also in the publication *Fêtes gourmandes*, pp. 76–77.
XVIII/ See Scully (ed.), *The Viandier*, pp. 176–177, No. 105, and *Fêtes gourmandes*, pp. 123–124 ('la brème rôtie').
XIX/ See *Fêtes gourmandes*, Glossaire, p. 185 = 'Il faut fendre anguille sur le dos, de chaque côté de l'arête, enlever cette dernière ainsi que la tête et la queue, retourner la chair vers l'exterieur, la ficeler et la faire cuire'.
XX/ For the difference between 'pastéz' 'norrois' and 'lorrois', see *The Viandier*, pp. 262–264, Nos 208–209.
XXI/ See *Fêtes gourmandes*, pp. 125 and 182 = 'volaille rôtie dont on récupère la graisse de rotissage pour confectionner la sauce'.
XXII/ On 'tourtes parmeniens', on that in detail cf. Scully (ed.), *The Viandier*, pp. 250–251, No. 197.
XXIII/ For more on that, see again *Fêtes gourmandes*, pp. 125 and 134.
XXIV/ Enlightenment on 'espaules de mouton farcies et mots' is given by Scully (ed.), *The Viandier*, pp. 266–267, No. 212.

XII. DRAMATIC AND MUSICAL PRODUCTIONS DURING THE INTERMISSIONS (ENTREMETS)

Besides the menus of the three ceremonial banquets, the *Mémoire* provides valuable information on the musical productions. 'It is necessary to know,' it is said here, 'that with every course which was served to the king menestrels [musicians or minstrels] playing smaller horns and further menestrels playing string instruments appeared before the king'.[446] A little later but undoubtedly faithful idea is provided here by the illustration by Jean Fouquet to this record of the *Great Chronicles of France* in ms. fr. 6465 of the Bibliothèque nationale in Paris from around 1460 (Pic. 153 / XXXVI). Behind the set table, we can see only the left half of the table of honour. On the left, three trumpeters are blowing fanfares announcing the first course, namely apparently at the command of one of the four masters of the royal household (*maîtres d'hôtel*), who issued his orders *inter alia* by the blows of a decorative staff. It seems likely that everything on this exceptional occasion was orchestrated by the Grand Master of the Royal Household himself, who was Pierre de Villiers.[447] The Account mentions the masters of the royal household on another occasion, just like the cupbearers (*échansons*), meat carvers (*varlets tranchants*) and breadmasters (*panetiers*), two of whom we can also see with large platters full of food in Fouquet's miniature.[448]

All of these masters and servants of the royal kitchen were participants at the emperor's entry to Paris, so we also know their uniforms. The masters of the royal household had velvet costumes in combined azure blue and tawny colours, whereas breadmasters, cupbearers and carvers, subordinated to them, wore satin clothes with stripes in white and tawny colours.[449] However, none of this corresponds to the preserved illustrations. The grand master of the royal household with folded arms in the miniature in the manuscript of the Bibliothèque Nationale ms. fr. 2813, fol. 473v, has a dark-red uniform of the same cut as one observing breadmaster and the carver with his utensils, i.e. with a platter for cutting meat and a large knife (Pic. 80 / XI). Both are distinguished by colour; one has a bluish outer garment, the other greyish. In his depiction, Jean Fouquet captured the fashion of around 1460, which prescribed a uniform dark-red colour for long as well as short doublets.

446/ Lechová, *Cesta Karla IV. do Francie*, p. 54 had in her translation literally 'high instruments', by which she meant stringed instruments with high tones. A part of the sentence is unclear; the editor understands that the musicians played *plancta* (songs of lamentation) on horns, which seems to be inappropriate for this occasion, in addition to the fact that *plancta* were considered to be songs. On their use in period France, see *Lexikon des Mittelalters*, VI, cols 2199–2200.

447/ The Account does not mention Pierre de Villiers in connection with the emperor's visit, but Master Philip Ogier appears in it as the 'concierge' of the Palace de la Cité, who at the king's command prepared a chair covered in a gold-interlaced cloth for the emperor.

448/ Avril, Gousset and Guenée, *Les Grandes Chroniques de France*, pp. 264–265, also with a reproduction. The announcement of a new course with musical instruments is quite apparent in the depiction of the feast of the knights of the Order of the Star in 'our' manuscript of the *Great Chronicles of France* in the Bibliothèque nationale, MS fr. 2813, fol. 394r. While the butlers are bringing full platters from the right, a trumpeter stands on the left along with a bagpiper. A reproduction can be found in the publication *Paris et Charles V*, p. 57. Bagpipes were among the popular instruments at wedding or other ceremonial feasts, on that, see Catherine Homo-Lechner, 'De l'usage de la cornemuse dans les banquets: quelques exemples du XIVe au XVIe siècle', in *Fêtes gourmandes*, pp. 111–119; the author published a more concise explanation under the title, 'La cornemuse, un instrument «de bouche»', in *Fêtes gourmandes*, p. 109.

449/ On that, see Excursus – Nothing but Horses: Their Numbers, Types and Colours.

161. The feast of the knight of the Order of the Star founded by John II the Good. Les Grandes Chroniques de France, around 1380. This miniature is valuable both for being the work of the same artist as the depiction of the banquet of the Epiphany in the same manuscript and the relatively rich tableware. The lower social status of the stewards and carvers, who have no sword at their belts, corresponds to the lesser importance of the feast. The feast in in full swing, although the musical production of the two musicians could indicate rather some entremet. One steward is bringing food in plate-like, reciprocally closing bowls (écuelles), his colleague is already kneeling offering it to the diners, also the carver is kneeling ever ready to assist. The first knight on the left is cutting bread himself, a knife is also prepared before the knight on the right. One cup in the form of a chalice, a jug for water or wine, one small cup and two bowls are available on the table with a white tablecloth. They are taking pieces of the dish, perhaps a cutlet, from both of the stewards. We should mention the sideboard (*dressoir*) in the backgrouns with prepared jugs and other tableware. (BnF, ms. fr. 2813, fol. 394r)

Since the servants at the court of Duke John of Berry had costumes of a different cut and in the colours of their lord, their period depiction in the *Very Rich Hours of the Duke of Berry* is not conclusive for us either (Pic. 155).

The depiction of the feast of the Order of the Star in our fundamental manuscript in the BnF ms. fr. 2813, fol. 394r, has a somewhat greater documentary value. In it, the staff at the table have costumes of the same cut but in different colours, which is true also for the leggings (Pic. 161). All the more valuable here is the depiction of two musicians, one trumpeter and one bagpipe player. It is apparent from this detail that musical productions could and also did involve various instruments. All of the musicians that we have seen so far in period miniatures stood at the table and blew or played for the host or his guests as if 'in their ears'. With the size of the Great Hall of the Palace de la Cité, which was 935 m^2, we might have rather expected some kind of platform for an entire musical group. That this idea has a certain justification is proved by immediately several miniatures from the illuminated set of five manuscripts with the *chansons de geste* connected with the name Renault of Montauban. In the set created in Bruges for Duke of Burgundy Philip the Good after 1462, we can find a number of depictions of ceremonial feasts. Considering the specific Burgundian fashion typical for the 'autumn of the Middle Ages', we are not interested in the clothes of the attending servants this time, but in the arrangement of the tables, placement of the cupboards and of the already-mentioned platforms for the musicians. Although the depicted solutions show significant variability, they convincingly prove both the continuing popularity of canopies and the additional function of cupboards displaying precious dishes for show. The place reserved for musicians is on the raised platforms, as it is also in the miniature on fol. 239v in manuscript No. 5075 of the Bibliothèque de l'Arsenal in Paris (Pic. 149).[450]

The testimony of the *Mémoire*, to which we return after a small diversion, complements in a welcome way the Account, which only says that there was a musical production after the dinner on the eve of the Epiphany, namely in the Great Chamber of the court of justice (*Grande chambre*), where 'musicians with string instruments [awaited] and played in the common way'.[451] The court did not have to look long for an outstanding musical composer, the foremost representative of the new musical style (*Ars nova*). It had had him for a long time in Guillaume de Machaut, whose musical expression in historical consciousness recedes somewhat into the background behind his poetic word.[452] This famous composer had died shortly before this († 1377), otherwise he certainly would not have been missing at the banquet in honour of the son of his belov-

162. Guillaume de Machaut composing one of his ballads. Guillaume de Machaut, Oeuvres (BnF, ms. fr. 1584, fol. 242r)

ed King John of Luxembourg. Machaut's student Eustache Deschamps is likely not to have forgone this feast of all feasts. Even if he had been present, however, he would hardly have been invited to perform any of his compositions. Most of the German participants of the emperor's retinue would not have understood them. Instrumental music better suited the Epiphany banquet. Not until this occasion were desserts with wine served, during which the ceremonial cupbearers were both of the brothers of the king of France. The duke of Berry served desserts to the king (we know that these were sweet pears, green apples and nuts); the duke of Burgundy, on the other hand, poured wine for him. In this way, we complement the explanation for *boutes-hors*, which we have already encountered above in passing.

A much more complicated ceremonial was implemented at the end of the Epiphany luncheon. In contradiction to tradition and protocol, a quite significant change was made at the very beginning. When the tablecloths were removed from the table after lunch finished and all three monarchs washed their hands one after another, beginning with the emperor and ending with his son, the serving of wine and desserts was to follow in the adjacent Great Hall of the Parliament, i.e. the supreme court of justice. It lay on the left side of the marble table, so that

450/ For initial information on this collection, see *Catalogue général des manuscrits des bibliothèques publiques de France. Paris, Bibliothèque de l'Arsenal*, V (Paris 1889), pp. 38–40, shelf marks 5072–5075. Volume V is deposited in the Bayerische Staatsbibliothek in Munich, Cod. gall. 7.

451/ See Delachenal (ed.), *Chronique des règnes*, II, p. 231, Note 1, with an explanation of the meaning of 'les ménestrels de bas instruments', i.e. players on the harp, viola, etc. It is thus not any tawdry, loud music, as judged on the basis of earlier literature still by Václav Černý, *Staročeská milostná lyrika*, pp. 222–223.

452/ A large entry is dedicated to him in the *Guide de la Musique du Moyen Âge*, pp. 488–510; the latest literature is listed by Miren Lacassagne, 'Actualité de Guillaume de Machaut', pp. 129–138, and Nejedlý, 'V Praze jsou tři města, mnoho výstavných kostelů a lidé zbožní…', pp. 36–48.

the diners would have easy and thanks to the guards at the partition also safe access to it; nevertheless, in front of its portal there was still significant bustle when individual courses were being served. The emperor noticed this and considering his infirmity asked the king that they remain in place. The host as always happily accommodated him and ordered that desserts and wine be brought to their marble table under the canopy. The nine-year-old Dauphin Charles, cared for by his uncle, Duke of Bourbon, was also placed on the table. 'At the king's order, the emperor was served pastilles by the Duke of Berry, and the king was similarly served by the Duke of Burgundy. The emperor as well as the king supplicated one another greatly to take pastilles; then they both helped themselves at the same time, each as soon as the other, and they acted in the same way also when drinking the wine, which the Duke of Brabant served the emperor, his brother, and the Duke of Bourbon served [Charles V, his brother-in-law].' King of the Romans Wenceslas did not have much appetite for the desserts offered to him by Count of Eu, or for the wine poured for him by one of his knights.[453]

However, what brought the Epiphany feast historical fame were neither gourmet orgies nor musical productions but the theatrical performances during the intermissions.[454] The host had the historical drama on the capture of Jerusalem by Duke of Lower Lorraine Godfrey of Bouillon presented on purpose to remind the most important sovereigns of Western Christianity through the exemplary act of the unfulfilled task of freeing the Holy Land. One of the leaders of the First Crusade soon after his death in 1100 became an idealised hero of many chronicles as well as epic songs and *chansons de geste*, which remained popular for the entire Middle Ages.[455] We will hardly be wrong, especially as we can rely here on the previous literature, if we notice in the background a politically updated echo of the relentless efforts of Philippe de Mézières (around 1327–1405). This former servant of the Viscontis of Milan and chancellor of King of Cyprus Peter I founded the Order of the Passion of Jesus Christ (*Militia Passionis Jhesu Christi*) after visiting the Holy Sepulchre and endeavoured by all means to revive the idea of a crusade. For Charles V, whose advisor he became in 1373, he began to compose *Le Songe du vieil Pèlerin* [The Old Pilgrim's Dream], in which he critically reflected on the present on the background of a fictitious travelogue. This is also the reason that this man with a spiritual bent, who bore in mind even his own entry to Heavenly Jerusalem, kept presenting one reform proposal after another to his provider, whose sons he raised.[456] It is not without interest for us that the work in question even mentions the feast in the emperor's honour.[457] After this diversion, we thus return to the actual theatrical production in two acts, which filled both intermissions – *entremets*.[458]

Here a direct quote tells more than a mere paraphrase: 'At the end of the hall of the palace, which was so closed that nothing was visible from outside,

453/ All again following the Account (in the edition of Delachenal, *Chronique des règnes*, II, pp. 242–243); the only thing that I explain here is the change of the protocol.

454/ The echoes of this staging in the verses of Chaucer's *Franklin's Tale* were attempted to be proved by Laura Hibbard Loomis, 'Secular Dramatics in the Royal Palace, Paris 1378, 1389, and Chaucer's "Tregetours"', pp. 242–255.

455/ For an initial orientation, see *Lexikon des Mittelalters*, IV, cols 1598–1600.

456/ Sufficient data including references to the editions and literature are brought by *Lexikon des Mittelalters*, VI, cols 592–593 (Mézières, Philippe de). In connection with our topic, cf. Loomis, 'Secular Dramatics in the Royal Palace', 247–249; from the more recent literature, see, i.a. Autrand, *Charles V. Le Sage*, pp. 695–698.

457/ Cf. Coopland (ed.), *Philippe de Mézières, Le Songe du vieil pèlerin*, II, p. 318. This place was already drawn attention to by Dora M. Bell, *Étude sur Le Songe du vieil pèlerin de Philippe de Mézières*, pp. 158.
On the not very flattering image of the Czech lands and especially Wenceslas IV in this literary work, see Nejedlý, "'V Praze jsou tři města, mnoho výstavných kostelů a lidé zbožní...' Obraz českých zemí a jejich panovníků ve francouzsky psané literatuře 14. století", pp. 51–52.

458/ On the additional meaning of the word *entremets* as political and propagandistic performances between courses at French feasts, see Nejedlý, *Meluzínský mýtus a rodová pověst Lucemburků*, pp. 729–730, according to whom there is a direct line between the scene in honour of the emperor and the theatrical court productions of the next century. The author also speaks of an apparent inspiration of this production in the work of Philippe de Mézières.

163. Epitaph of Philippe de Mézières, who is kneeling before the seated Virgin Mary with Baby Jesus on her lap. Originally in the Parisian monastery of the Celestines, today in Anvers, Musés Mayer van den Bergh

there was a well-made ship, resembling a sea-faring ship, equipped with a sail as well as a mast and with a forecastle and an aftercastle; the ship had all of the other tackle and equipment necessary for sailing at sea and was very nicely, expensively as well as pleasingly painted and trimmed. And inside there were people, at first sight very nicely armed, who had on their weapons, shields as well as banners the coats-of-arms of Jerusalem, which Godfrey of Bouillon himself had worn. There were around twelve of them, armed as was mentioned with the weapons of the notable captains who were at the capture of Jerusalem with the said Godfrey. And in the front, on the bow of the said ship, Peter the Hermit stood, looking as precisely as he could according to what the legend says about him.'[459]

In our imagination, we can further follow the voyage of the ship, which was being moved by the people inside of it along the left side of the hall all the way to the large canopy opposite with the marble table. According to the testimony of the Account, the model of the ship was moving so dexterously and smoothly as if it were floating on the sea. We pause here, because the first intermission has ended and it will be up to the workers to erect during the second course the coulisse with the silhouette of Jerusalem at the place from which the ship sailed. The mentioned Peter the Hermit who has been spoken of was none other that a zealous preacher whose share in calling the First Crusade further increased the later legendary mist around him.[460] His imaginary portrait was captured by another reporter of ours, namely the illustrator of the manuscript of the Bibliothèque Nationale in Paris already well-known to us, ms. fr. 2183 (Pic. 80 / XI). Let us now have a look at the likeness of the ship in his version, which is just setting out on its sail along the Great Hall. The ocean waves on which it bobs up and down are to intensify the illusion of an ancient expedition. The banner of Count of Auvergne, one of the leaders of the First Crusade who participated in the capture of Jerusalem, is flapping on the main mast. The banner with the symbols of this kingdom flies above the imitation of the Palace de la Cité on the stern, whereas the symbols of Flanders are apparent on the bow. The fourth banner is that of England and is placed on the smaller mast in the centre of the ship.[461] The crew is not visible; the two men with folded arms are the knights prepared to serve the sovereigns at the table of honour, although they both keep turning their eyes to the acts which have captured their attention.

The second course had finished; the stewards had removed the dishes; the cupbearers had already brought the drinks from the cupboards; the second

459/ See Delachenal (ed.), *Chronique des règnes*, II, pp. 239–242. As far as the mentioned arrangement at the end of the hall is concerned, it is possible that it was a kind of hung curtain, as was concluded by Franke, 'Pracht und Zeremoniell', p. 38.

460/ Again cf. *Lexikon des Mittelalters*, VI, cols 1937–1938.

461/ The coats-of-arms were determined by Delachenal (ed.), *Chronique des règnes*, IV, pp. 35–36.

act of the spectacle could begin. The attendees of the feast were offered a view of the coulisse with a temple and minaret, from which the Muslim muezzins were proclaiming passages from the Koran in Arabic. The minaret reached almost the height of the ceiling of the Great Hall. 'Below, all around said city, where walls and towers with the battlement were rendered,' as we again discover from the Account of the *Great Chronicles of France*, 'there were Saracens armed in their manner, with banners and pennants, who had been designated to defend the city by combat.' To the wonder of all those present, this entire huge coulisse was put into motion and by the power of the people hidden inside was moved along the entire hall until it was close to the ship which had been meanwhile waiting in calm for the culmination of the production in the right corner of the Great Hall from the perspective of the host and other diners at the marble table. These all now saw up close the scene of the famous capture of Jerusalem, which could begin.

The Account describes the entire dramatic production as if in one sequence. However, the capture of Jerusalem did not take place in one act but in two, i.e. during the first and second intermissions. In a very careful reading and with a knowledge of the protocol customs, one cannot fail to notice that the Old French version of the Account says 'Et lors se mistrent les deux entremés l'un contre l'autre', i.e. 'Now, the actors of the two intermissions attacked each other'.[462] In fact the ship already remained in the same place at the end of the first intermission. During the second intermission, the coulisse with the model of Jerusalem was moved towards it from the other side and the battle could then begin in front of the eyes of the monarchs and prelates sitting at the marble table.

Now, only after the moving of the coulisse with the walls of Jerusalem did the crusaders disembark from the ship 'and in a beautiful and good orchestration conducted an attack on said city and assaulted it for a long time. What was especially well performed were the falls of those who mounted the attack on ladders and were knocked down and thrown to the ground. At the end, those from the ship ascended, conquered the city and threw out those who were dressed as Saracens, planting the banners of Godfrey and the others. And it was all better and more beautifully implemented and seen than can be described in writing.' The scene of the capture of Jerusalem also offered the illuminator an excellent chance to prove his mastery. He had men-at-arms with the coats-of-arms of all four banners ascend two ladders. The count of Auvergne has managed to climb the highest; Godfrey of Bouillon on the second ladder is almost as successful. One of the knocked-down Saracens, whose fall actually could have entertained the spectators of the show, is lying in the right-hand corner of the scene. The entertainment has been concluded; the coulisses have been transported to their original places and the banquet can continue with the third course and the already-mentioned serving of the desserts and rare wine. The greatest Parisian celebration in the emperor's honour has finished with his being carried out 'through the middle of the Great Hall, through the door to the Mercière Gallery and through the great hallway directly to his chambers'.

Postscript to the pompous festivity. An inseparable part of the ceremonial feasts were not only the theatrical and musical productions but also acrobatic bits, riddles and anecdotes. Although we do not know the jokes and stories that were heard at the Epiphany banquet,[463] we do know what echo this feast of feasts had at the French-German border in Metz. Besides other anecdotes of Emperor Charles, the local patrician Jaique Dex (ca 1371–1455) preserved in his chronicle an informative anecdote which begins with a remark on the admirable number of courses and roasts at the Parisian banquet already well known to us. Everything that

462/ Cf. Delachenal (ed.), *Chronique des règnes*, II, p. 242.

463/ Two jesters standing in the background were captured in a miniature by Jean Fouquet (see Pic. 153 / XXXVI). Otherwise, their appearances or other common productions are not mentioned in our sources.

had not been eaten was apparently thrown away. It seems not to have mattered as arises from further narration. The emperor reciprocated the king of France with a feast of three courses *selong la coustume d'Allemaigne*, i.e. in the German way. The very first course was worth mentioning, because huge pieces of beef, further cooked capons with turnip and juicy roasts with bacon were brought to the table. Capons followed again as the second course, but everyone enjoyed the roasted suckling pigs more, prepared without any sauce or jelly. Subsequently, desserts, pears, nuts and wine were brought. Nothing was thrown away, because the leftovers of meat as well as wine were distributed to the poor to the greater glory of God. While the emperor allegedly admitted that the French feast had cost more money, the 'German' one was more substantial.[464] As they say, there is no accounting for taste. There would be nothing to add to this anecdote if they did not say of our emperor, a notorious cheapskate, precisely in France that there was nothing to cook in his kitchen.[465]

464/ See Georg Wolfram (ed.), *Die Metzer Chronik des Jaique Dex*, p. 313. For more on this chronicler, see Neureither, *Das Bild Kaiser Karls IV. In der zeitgenössischen französischen Geschichtsschreibung*, pp. 74–76; the anecdote in the text was recorded already by Thomas, 'Ein Zeitgenössisches Memorandum', p. 113. It would be however incorrect to think that they did not care about good cuisine and standard of banqueting in German-speaking lands. On that, see, i.a. Trude Ehlert, *Das Kochbuch des Mittelalters*, pp. 9–24 (here also with information on German recipes from the fourteenth century) and an article by the same author with the poignant title 'Les manuscrits culinaires médiévaux témoignent-ils d'un modèle alimentaire allemand?', pp. 121–136.

465/ It is told so by the advisor of King Charles V, Philippe de Mézières, who as the chancellor of King of Cyprus Peter of Lusignan visited Prague in 1364 and met the emperor in person. See Coopland (ed.), *Philippe de Méziéres, Chancellor of Cyprus, Le Songe du vieil pèlerin*, II, pp. 238–239.

Not only the gifts themselves but also everything connected with their presentation is among the attendant phenomena of human existence, or, as is popular to say today, anthropological constants. In comparison with the extensive literature which deals with the presents as a widespread form of behaviour as well as conduct, their sense, ethnological, economic or even sociobiological functions, historical research had quite ignored this topic. Ivan Hlaváček rightfully pointed out this gap in mediaeval-oriented studies in 1992,[466] but soon afterwards in connection with the intensive research on residences and the court milieu works on this topic appeared after all.[467] For our theme, the book by Jan Hirschbiegel on New Year's and other presents at the court of Charles VI is exceptionally stimulating and beneficial taking us, as Latin scholars say, *in medias res*, to the core of the issue.[468]

Knowledge of Latin is not a waste here, because if we disregard the *naturalia* already known to us which awaited the emperor on his entry to the cities, the first expensive gift about which we will soon speak belonged to a special group of New Year's tokens for which Old French had the expression *estreine*. Not only through the etymology from the Latin word *strena* (New Year's bonus) but also through tradition does this custom point to Antiquity. New Year's gifts were inveighed against to no avail by St Augustine, who wanted to replace them with alms; the pagan vices connected with Christmas 'Feast of Fools' were repeatedly and therefore unsuccessfully forbidden by local as well as ecumenical councils. Sporadic evidence can be found from the time of Charlemagne, but it does not appear to a greater degree until the fourteenth century, namely during the reign of Charles VI.[469] Not even his father, Charles V the Wise, omitted *étrennes*, as proved by his mandates, in which the recipients of expensive New Year's tokens include besides the Dauphin also the arch-sommelier and the favourite carver of roasts at the table.[470]

It is not excluded that Charles IV had learned about this New Year's custom during the years spent at the French court, when he probably not only received gifts but also gave them himself to his servants. Considering that the first meeting of Emperor Charles and his homonymous nephew, then still Dauphin Charles, occurred in Metz in 1356 at Christmas time, also the famous two thorns from the purported Crown of Thorns could have been

466/ Hlaváček, 'Überlegungen zum Geschenkwesen im Mittelalter', pp. 12–15, but valuable studies can be found already earlier, cf., e.g. Alain Guéry, 'Le roi dépensier: le don, la contrainte et l'origine du système financier de la monarchie française d'Ancien Régime'; Jürgen Hannig, 'Ars donandi. Zur Ökonomie des Schenkens im früheren Mittelalter'; Ludwig Holzfurtner, 'Schenker und Schenkergruppen. Sozialgeschichtliche Studien an Hand hochmittelalterlicher bayerischer Traditionsbücher'.

467/ The important book by Charles de Miramon, *Les «donnés» au Moyen Âge*, deals e.g. with the gifts of the subjects to ecclesiastical institutions.

468/ Hirschbiegel, *Étrennes*, here, i.a. on pp. 9–21 an informed introduction to the problem.

469/ Hirschbiegel, *Étrennes*, esp. pp. 37–46 and 80–81 (evidence from the time of Charles V). The enormous increase in the number of *étrennes* during the reign of Charles VI may partially be misleading as a result of the exceptional amount of accounting and other documents preserved.

470/ Delisle (ed.), *Mandements et actes divers*, p. 797, No. 1605. The king also received New Year's gifts, for which he sometimes gave a monetary compensation, as happened in the case of his librarian Gilles Malet (ibid. p. 784, No. 1578).

meant as a New Year's gift. Relics and reliquaries are no exception among *étrennes*; no less necessary is it however to bear in mind that King John the Good then sent the emperor as a gift also a gorgeous sword inlaid with precious stones and pearls of a value of 18,000 gold pieces.[471] We can proceed a step further in our speculations. In the copy of the inventory of the dauphin's treasure whose original was written in 1363, we can find under item No. 585 'a bell that was given to the lord [the Dauphin] by the emperor'. Should we inquire when this could have happened, then it was more likely in Metz than during the second mutual encounter in Mouzon seven years later.[472] On the other hand, the crystal reliquary with the blood of St Wenceslas decorated with gold was carefully preserved by Dauphin Charles as an inheritance from his mother, the emperor's sister Bonne.[473]

After this digression, which would have been a pity to avoid, we return to New Year, 1378, when Dukes of Berry and of Burgundy along with Count of Harcourt, with Archbishop of Sens and with Bishop of Laon welcomed the emperor in the name of the king before the ramparts of the city of Senlis. The only of these feudal lords of whom it can be assumed with certain reservations that he prepared a New Year's *étrenne* for this occasion was Duke of Burgundy Philip the Bold, however not for the emperor but for King of the Romans Wenceslas IV.[474] It was a truly magnificent gift of a sword whose golden pommel as well as hilt were inlaid with pearls. Just for the mark of gold needed for the decoration, Duke Philip paid the Parisian goldsmith Jean de Saint--Laurent 53 francs and 10 Tours sous. The sheath prepared from Alexandrian velvet cost him another 5 francs.[475] It would nevertheless have been daring to remember only the emperor's son on this occasion and moreover embarrass his brother John, who had not prepared any New Year's gift for this occasion, as far as is known. And therefore we have to take into consideration the possibility that the sword was a personal gift which Duke Philip gave his cousin Wenceslas IV on another occasion, e.g. at the final dinner in Meaux on 17 January 1378. In any case, the sword along with other expenditures during the emperor's visit so burdened the ducal treasury that his relatives this time had to be satisfied with more modest New Year's gifts.

One of a sovereign's main virtues was generosity, which as we already know was praised by the poet Machaut with John of Luxembourg. Ovid's encouragement of gifts which win the favour of the gods as well as men was handed down for the entire Middle Ages.[476] It held and still holds true for both. Generosity and gifts together formed the shine (*splendor*) of royal or imperial might (*imperii vel regni*); they augmented the prestige of the monarchs as well as their fame. In period opinion, kings and emperors were lords as far as they were givers. Considering the primordial basis of the word (*donataire* – donee / *donateur* – donor), a paraphrase of the statement in the then popular *Dream of the Orchard* can be

471/ On the gift of the sword with vaguely indicated sources, see Emil Werunsky, *Geschichte Kaiser Karls IV.*, III, p. 169; his entry was adopted by Jean Deviosse, *Jean Le Bon*, p. 396; on the contrary, it is presented with critical caution by Kavka, *Vláda Karla IV.*, I, p. 104, Note 28. On the gift relics and reliquaries on the occasion of New Year's, see Hirschbiegel, *Étrennes*, pp. 169–170.

472/ Gaborit-Chopin (ed.), *L'inventaire du trésor du dauphin futur Charles V, 1363*, p. 68: 'Item la sonnette que bailla l'Empereur à Monseigneur'. In Note 588, the editor connects the gift of the bell to the meeting in Metz but does not rule out Mouzon either.

473/ Gaborit-Chopin (ed.), *L'inventaire du trésor du dauphin*, p. 71, No. 665: 'Item un reliquiaire long où il a de saint Vincelot'. In Note 631, the editor presents supplementary data from a later inventory from around 1380. See ibidem in the introduction on p. 9 on further objects inherited from his mother.

474/ This gift is included among *étrennes* by Hirschbiegel, *Étrennes*, p. 95, Note 117, who confused King Wenceslas with the emperor. Besides the reasons I present in the text, it is necessary to bear in mind that the sword is not listed as an *étrenne* in the accounting document. In addition, the duke did not issue the order to pay until 15 February, whereas New Year's gifts were already procured in advance in December.

475/ Prost (ed.), *Inventaires mobiliers et extraits des comptes des ducs de Bourgogne*, II, p. 16, No. 97, and p. 20, No. 117.

476/ Publius Ovidius Naso, *Ars amatoria* 3, 653: 'Munera, crede mihi, capiunt hominesque deosque'. In the Middle Ages, this recommendation or saying circulated in many paraphrases and variants.

ambiguous, but in the case of the emperor's visit we are in no doubt.[477] Charles IV did not take any gifts to France, and it was on the contrary he and his retinue who were constantly given presents. Let us remember how our Account ends: 'In every place, the emperor received presents, the same in open towns as in fortified, and was honourably and richly received and feted everywhere like on his arrival. It is also appropriate to mention that it was the king that had more or less paid and defrayed the entire expenditure which the emperor and his people had in the palaces in Paris, as was the case also with all the gifts that cost great expense; similarly, everything from the time the emperor entered the kingdom until he was outside of it, even though it was given in the name of the cities, was at the cost and expenditure of the king.' In the chapter on the accounting for the expenditures of the emperor's visit, it will come out that it really was so. Now, however, we are interested more in the diversity and character of the gifts than in their monetary value.

The gifts in kind with which Charles IV and his retinue were honoured by cities as well as monasteries lying on the route of their journey comprised meat, fish, wine, bread, hay, oats and wax. With the exception of wax, they were foodstuffs and feed for everyday use. We can imagine that the guests consumed most of these gifts there or that they took some of them with them on the journey. If they were given large fish, rabbits, cattle, sheep and poultry in the abbey of Saint-Denis, then probably only in the form of prepared meals. Only in one case could it be considered that the animals were alive, namely in the abbey of Saint-Maur-des-Fossés, because the emperor left all of the gifts that he had received from the abbot there for the convent. It was different in the case of the two destriers (war horses) with rich saddles as well as with another two no less valuable coursers which Charles V sent to Saint-Denis as a gift for both Luxemburgs. Although the King of France resolved with this gift the delicate prestigious question of the colour and type of horse on which the guests would ride into Paris, horses were always a valuable item and were easy to take back on the return journey. It was similar with the rare hunting dogs which Dauphin Charles gave to the emperor in Saint-Pol even with ornate silk collars embossed with golden *fleurs-de-lis*.[478] There were probably greater problems with gifts that could not be carried in the luggage. As wagons carrying registries and provisions travelled with the party anyway, then it was not too much trouble to procure or rent another wagon with a driver. The emperor certainly did not worry himself about the question of how to transport the gifts.

It is not excluded, or it could even be so, that the gifts from the cities also included precious items. R. Delachenal, for instance, drew attention to the receipt of 6 March 1378, according to which the people of the town of Ham were paid 120 Paris pounds 'for a certain gift which they had given the emperor when he went through this town on his journey to the king'.[479] As far as is known, the metropolis did not request any compensation for its gifts for the emperor and his son, and it apparently would not have received it anyway. The labels of the precious items will not cause any problems for us because we have already encountered them all (*nef*, *flacons*, *fontaine*, *pots*) in the descriptions of the table utensils of the ceremonial banquets. Besides that, significant support is provided here by the relevant miniature of manuscript BN MS fr. 2813, fol. 472r, which is *inter alia* enlightening with its depiction of two *pots*, i.e. rounded jugs with a handle and lid (Pic. 79 / X). We can say beforehand that precisely the table utensils, both luxurious and practical, will comprise the ma-

477/ On the interpretation of the statement from *Le Songe du Vergier*, see Guéry, *Le roi dépensier*, pp. 1243–1244.

478/ The Account mentions two dogs, so-called *brachez*, whereas the king's mandate of 18 January speaks of four dogs of a Spanish race (*Espaignoz*). Not even Delachenal (ed.), *Chronique des règnes*, II, p. 262, Note 2, with further references to the literature and sources, knew how to handle these contradictory data.

479/ Delachenal (ed.), *Chronique des règnes*, II, p. 276, Note 2.

jority of the gifts for the emperor, his son as well as their numerous escort.

Just like his predecessors from the Valois family, Charles V grew up in the luxurious milieu of the court and exhibited an appreciation for expensive objects as well as sumptuous representation even in the difficult years of his reign. It was so in the only apparent contrast to his simple style in private, where he with his university gown did not differ from his favourite scholars and men of letters. The prestige 'of the French Crown' required its own even from Charles the Wise. In terms of his relation to jewellery and other precious objects, a comparison of the two inventories of his collection from the beginning and end of his reign speaks for itself. Whereas the treasure contained a little over 900 diverse pieces in 1363, the list of chattels in all four residences (the Louvre, Vincennes, Saint-Germain-en-Laye and Melun) included already almost 3,900 items in 1379–1380.[480] Also his successor Charles VI purchased jewellery on a large scale. In one, otherwise however exceptional, case, fourteen percent of the annual income was spent on it.[481] At the same time, the treasury was used by the kings chiefly as a savings office for periods of financial straits. Shortly after the death of Charles V, between May 1381 and 1382, 140 pounds of gold table utensils and 800 pounds of silver table utensils were supplied to the mint to be remade into coins. Besides that, in June 1381 Charles VI 'loaned' the duke of Anjou 50,000 francs in the form of jewellery from the treasure of his father. None of these 143 precious objects appeared any more in the later inventories. The vast majority of the other valuables from the collection of Charles V disappeared after the death of his son on 21 October 1422, when the last pieces were sold to cover the funeral costs.[482]

It would be a mistake to think that Charles V simply decreed that gifts for the emperor and his men be selected from his treasury. Everything was procured especially for this purpose, as will soon be apparent. This was undoubtedly true also for the gifts from the city of Paris. The gilded boat (*nef*) for the emperor weighed 190 silver marks and the two large gilded and enamel-decorated bottles (*flacons*) which came with it weighed a total of 70 marks. At the normal price of jeweller-treated silver of 10 francs per mark,[483] the price of only the precious metal without gilding would have been 2,600 francs. The question is whether these valuables could have been purchased merely by weight. Evidence for this surprising possibility is provided by the accounting items of the type: *pour un gobelet d'argent doré, pesant IIII mars VIII esterlin, à X frans le marc, que nous avons donné à un escuier de nostre dit oncle, XL frans, VIII s. p.*[484] In translation, this place reads: 'for one gilded silver chalice weighting 4 marks and 8 sterlings, at a price of 10 francs per mark, which we gave to one squire of our said uncle, 40 francs and 8 Parisian sous'. The conversion is simple; the result corresponds, because at the same price of a mark of silver one sterling of silver equalled one sous also in other cases.[485] Not only that but almost in all of the cases the prices of jewellery as well as other precious gifts correspond to the price for the given weight of the precious metal. We can thus also count the monetary value of the three gifts of the city of Paris for Wenceslas IV. The gilded silver fountain and two gold as well as oth-

480/ See Labarte, *Inventaire du mobilier de Charles V*. The inventory includes jewellery, reliquaries, cameos as well as precious manuscripts from Vincennes. More recently, see the catalogues *La Librairie de Charles V*, p. 35, No. 89a, and *Les Fastes du Gothique*, pp. 337–338, No. 29; further cf. Henwood, 'Vincennes, écrin de pierre de l'orfèvrerie royale', pp. 321–327, and in addition also Avril, 'Les livres de Charles V au château de Vincennes', pp. 338–340.

481/ Cf. Rey, *Les finances royales*, p. 321. For more detail on the purchases of jewellery and the gifts for the king, see Henwood, 'Vincennes, écrin de pierre de l'orfèvrerie royale', pp. 322–326.

482/ Cf. Henwood, 'Vincennes, écrin de pierre de l'orfèvrerie royale', pp. 323 and 327.

483/ In the mandates of Charles V related to the emperor's visit, the price of silver fluctuated between twelve and fourteen francs per mark.

484/ See Delisle (ed.), *Mandements et actes divers*, p. 793, No. 1596. The accounting records usually show only the weight of the valuables as proved by Leguay, 'Banquets, cadeaux alimentaires et autres présents', p. 206.

485/ I recalculated all of the items and with a few exceptions I always achieved the same results. I only add that at the same price of 1 mark for 10 francs, the price for 1 ounce was 20 sous (= 1 franc and 4 sous).

erwise richly decorated jugs (*pots*) that came with it hence cost 1,230 francs altogether.

Since the price per mark in the case of silver fluctuated in the range of 10 to 14 francs, we can justifiably assume that precisely this difference reflected either the standard of goldsmith treatment or the value of the gilding, pearls or also precious stones used. It is significant that the higher price per mark of silver can be found with the gifts intended directly for the emperor, his son and the important dignitaries of the retinue.[486] Not only this fact but particularly the period prices of silver and gold for minting validate the original supposition. The official price of silver for minting was set by the ordinance of 15 February 1376 at 105 Tours sous per mark, which corresponds to 6 francs and 9 sous. The market prices fluctuated between 107 and 116 sous. The higher prices were paid precisely in 1377–1378, from which it arises that one mark of silver for minting cost 7 francs and 4 sous then. From 63 francs and 2 sous to 63 francs and 10 sous were paid for 1 mark of gold for minting.[487] Now it is clear: the valuable objects were paid for by weight, but the price of 1 mark of precious metals expressed not only the value of the enamel, precious stones or possibly gilding but also of the goldsmith's work. In comparison with silver for minting, the price of jeweller-treated precious metals was roughly 1.5 to 2 times higher per mark; in the case of gold, only the lower of the two numbers can be confirmed.

It is worth noting that this knowledge applies generally both for valuables bought directly from the producers, i.e. goldsmiths, and from money changers and merchants.[488] It arises from this that the method of determining the price at the jewellery market was similar if we ignore pawning and sales from acute need. However, jewellery and other valuables were most often furnished to the royal court by goldsmiths. At the end of the fourteenth century, there were apparently almost six hundred in Paris alone, so there was definitely no want of suppliers.[489] Priority was given to goldsmiths with the title of valet (*valet de chambre*), namely Jean de Viviers (*Mandements* 1601, 1602)[490] or Hennequin du Viviers, who along with the administrator of the royal library Gilles Malet brought the royal crown for the emperor to see.[491] However, other goldsmiths also received orders, especially Jacques d'Orgeval (*Mandements* 1593), Jean Pochart (*Mandements* 1599), Nicolas Giffart (*Mandements* 1604), Robert de Val (*Mandements* 1607), and Thomas Pochart (*Mandements* 1609). Also the cutler Pierre Willequin was a direct producer (*Mandements* 1606). Yet the court also purchased the same items from money changers, who had apparently acquired them through forfeited pawns. Those listed by name include Henriet Orlant (*Mandements* 1592), Jean Brulart (*Mandements* 1595), Jean de Mareuil (*Mandements* 1596), Simon de Dammartin (*Mandements* 1608), and Thomassin de Nuga (*Mandements* 1610). Finally, the court was also supplied by Parisian merchant Franchequin de Target (*Mandements* 1591) and Pierre Fatinant (*Mandements* 1605), who had a competition in the Venetian Huguelin of Laza (*Mandements* 1583).

The most numerous group of objects given comprised table utensils, which may surprise with the purely male group of the donees, but, as it will soon be shown, a significant part of these vessels could be used at the table as well as on journeys. It was particularly true of the chalices – *gobelets*, of which we know what they looked like, so their utility as well as compactness is beyond any doubt. A welcome but otherwise rare proof here is the chased and painted leather cup case from the fifteenth century, which is

486/ Cf. Delisle (ed.), *Mandements et actes divers*, pp. 789–790, No. 1591, and pp. 796–797, No. 1605.

487/ For more detail on that, see Cazelles, *Société politique*, p. 559.

488/ I investigated the data of the relevant mandates also from this perspective to verify to what degree the prices of similar valuables purchased from direct producers on the one hand and the merchants or money changers on the other differed.

489/ This number is presented by Hirschbiegel, *Étrennes*, p. 74, with references here in Note 11 to the special literature.

490/ The number in round brackets corresponds to the number of the mandate in the most frequently cited edition, Delisle, *Mandements et actes divers*.

491/ See Delachenal (ed.), *Chronique des règnes*, II, p. 267.

displayed in the Musée Cluny (Cl. 21362). From the overall number of thirty-two *gobelets* given, five were large; the predominant material was gilded silver; gold was indicated exceptionally. An entirely unique gift was the large gold chalice decorated with enamel and precious stones for Charles IV, for which along with another gold vessel (*pot*) Jacques d'Orgeval charged 2,000 gold francs (*Mandements* 1593). Considering its exceptionally high price, I suppose that rather than a common *gobelet* it is the vessel labelled as a large gold cup of great weight (*une couppe d'or de grant pois*), which is mentioned in first place in the list of presents given to Charles IV and his retinue at the residence in Beauté on Thursday, 14 January. Also this cup was decorated with precious stones and fine enamel depicting the heavenly sphere with the zodiac, the signs, the planets, the fixed stars and perhaps even their images (*et leurs ymages*).[492]

Even other of the table utensils given found application on journeys, be they the seventeen chalices on a stem with a lid or without it (*pots*) or the ewers for water or wine (*aiguières*), numbering fifteen pieces, or the larger or smaller shallow bowls (*hennaps*) of identical number. This set was complemented by six flat containers (*fontaines*), two flasks (*flacons*) and two smaller chalices called quarters (*quartes*). The price of these items fluctuated according to size, the precious metal selected and possibly also further decoration. We cannot forget the large pokale, called *hennap* here, with a lid and on a high tripod, which Charles V purchased for his uncle from the money changer Jean Brulart. It indubitably is the fantastic dish decorated with precious stones which was mentioned by the Account and whose analogue could be the chalice deposited in the Rijksmuseum in Amsterdam.[493] According to the Account, the emperor received from his host *inter alia* two large vessels (*pots*) shaped like lions heads, but the financial order speaks of only one gold *pot* decorated with enamel and precious stones (*Mandements* 1593). It seems to have been a confusion with the above-mentioned valuable gold cup (*un grant gobelet*) in the same item. In the somewhat ambiguous terminology, a confusion could have easily happened. On the other hand, the accounting documents for the two most expensive flasks (*flacons*) intended for the emperor have not been preserved, but according to the Account they must have been exquisite exemplars of sublime workmanship with a relief depiction of Charlemagne, who is being shown the way to Santiago de Compostela by St James. Both flasks had the shape of mussel shells, the traditional symbol of pilgrims, which the host chose for his uncle as a souvenir of the trip to the Abbey of Saint-Maur-des-Fossés. Three pairs of knives, two for the emperor and one for his son, which were supplied by the royal cutler Pierre Willequin for the price of 49 francs (*Mandements* 1606), were a relatively singular gift in its time.[494]

And since we have already become acquainted with tableware in detail in one of the previous excursuses and since their overall price will come out in the final balance, we will focus on the gifts which deviate from the others for their character or rarity. They include the jewellery mentioned in the Account and the jewels which we know of from the preserved documents of an accounting nature. Only from the king's mandates do we know of two gifts for Bishop of Warmia Henry Sorbom. The first was a gold ring with a light pink spinel from money changer Jean de Mareuil for 100 francs (*Mandements* 1596); the second was a gold cross inlaid with precious stones, which was supplied by the court goldsmith Jean de Viviers for 110 francs (*Mandements* 1601). A gold pendant, also inlaid with precious stones, which was given to the emperor by Queen Jeanne, probably as a gift for his wife Elizabeth, was much rarer. We are aware of it also only from the king's mandate, which says that the goldsmith Nicolas Giffart was to

492/ See Note 413 in Excursus – Tableware.

493/ On this so-called *Deckelpokal* with a decorative lid and on a tripod, see Fritz in *Die Parler und der schöne Stil 1350–1400*, I, pp. 112–113 (here also a depiction).

494/ The knives were not mentioned among the New Year's gifts by Hirschbiegel, *Étrennes*, p. 149. The exception could be explained by Charles V's having purchased knives also for himself and Dauphin Charles on this occasion.

be paid 1,200 francs in gold for this object (*Mandements* 1604).

We will linger for a moment at the last mentioned gift, which according to the wording of the source are 'pictures' (*uns tableaux d'or garni de perrerie*). These golden *tableaux*, mostly with a depiction or a figure of Christ, the Virgin Mary and other saints, were among the quite common New Year's gifts. Their financial value frequently surpassed several times the presented sum of 1,200 francs, so we have to count with the fact that these pictures were intended for hanging on the wall.[495] In the catalogue of the exhibition *Les Fastes du Gothique*, *tableau* are a label for enamel tablets in miniature imitations of picture frames, which were worn hung around the neck circa 1380. The designs of these miniatures with the depictions of saints vary; they could be square as well as circular, with their size adjusted to be worn around the neck.[496] And as also paintings of a smaller format which bear the label 'tabular painting' have been preserved in the Treasury of St Vitus,[497] I leave the question of the shape and function of the queen's gift for further research.

The most expensive of all of the gifts, not only jewellery, was a gold belt richly decorated with precious stones along its entire length, which according to the rough estimate of the author of the Account could have had a value of 6,000 to 8,000 gold francs. In fact it was purchased less expensively, because the Venetian merchant Huguelin of Laza asked four thousand francs for it (*Mandements* 1583). In at

164. A clasp with a reliquary. Gilded silver, enamels, precious stones and pearls, around 1350, height and width: 185 mm

least two miniatures (Pics 13 / IV and 83 / XIV), Wenceslas' mantle is fastened by a wide gold belt, from which nothing can be deduced. Only a distant vague idea can be formed according to the preserved, for that matter very precious, relicts.[498] How abysmal the difference in the price of one and the same object could be is proved by the belt of gilded silver bought as a gift for one of the knights of the emperor's entourage for 50 fr and 12 Parisian sous from the goldsmith Robert de Val (*Mandements* 1607).

A buckle or clasp (*fermail*) for fastening clothes was a very common component of clothing of the higher as well as lower classes and in an ornate implementation suited well as a gift or token.[499] The beautiful and expensive clasp inlaid with precious stones which Queen Jeanne gave Wenceslas IV on

495/ For more on the New Year's gifts and their specific forms, see Hirschbiegel, *Étrennes*, pp. 165–169.

496/ See *Les Fastes du Gothique*, pp. 265–268 and artefacts under No. 214: *Noli me tangere* (Bruxelles musées royaux 122-3352), Paris (?) 1380–1390, 122 × 108 mm; No. 216: *Saint Jean Baptiste préchant* (Louvre, MR 2674), Paris 1380–1400, 67 × 53 mm; No. 217: *Saint Jean l'Evangeliste* (Louvre MR 2651), Paris 1380–1400, round shape, height: 82 mm, width: 72mm; No. 218: *Médaillon-réliquaire* (Cluny 676), Paris 1370–1380, round shape, diameter: 64 mm. In this series of tableaux, one differs in size and that is No. 215: Sainte Catherine d'Alexandrie (Victoria and Albert Museum M 350-1912), Paris around 1380, 650 × 500 mm.

497/ See Antonín Podlaha and Eduard Šittler, *Chrámový poklad u sv. Víta v Praze*, pp. 28–31, Nos. 20–21.

498/ The fragments of the belt from the so-called *trésor de Colmar* from the first third of the fourteenth century (Musée de Cluny, Inv. No. 20674) were displayed at the exhibition in Paris in 1961; see the catalogue *Les Fastes du Gothique*, pp. 242–243, No. 197A. It is a narrow silk belt on which small metal roses and heads have been applied.

499/ Cf. Laborde, *Glossaire français*, p. 312ff. These clasps and buckles were quite common among New Year's gifts; on that, see Hirschbiegel, *Étrennes*, p. 158.

taking leave of the residence of Saint-Pol had been purchased for 1,250 francs from money changer Thomassin de Nuga (*Mandements* 1610). The Parisian merchant Pierre Fatinant charged substantially less for a similar clasp for the duke of Saxony, but even so it was the high amount of 700 francs (*Mandements* 1605). In the case of jewellery of this type, we may rely also on other sources than period miniatures like in the case of Wenceslas IV's belt buckle (Pic. 83 / XIV). The guide to the collections of the Musée National du Moyen Âge – Thermes de Cluny from 1993 for instance lists a clasp in the form of a reliquary (*fermail-reliquiaire*), which according to the author belonged to a highly placed person in the Empire, perhaps Charles IV himself. The description would roughly correspond, because Wenceslas IV would hardly have worn the small relics of the saints on his clothes.[500]

The interests of the young King of the Romans Wenceslas IV were respected by the hosts. When hunting for fallow deer and wild rabbits in the woods around the château in Vincennes, he was undoubtedly loaned hunting weapons by the king's brothers. We are likely not to be far from the truth when we express the hypothesis that Wenceslas was very interested especially in crossbows, because shortly thereafter Charles V gave him some arbalests (*arbalestes*) from his armoury. The dauphin also could have ingratiated himself to Wenceslas rather than to his father with the gift of the already-mentioned dogs (*brachets*, *bracets*). And since Jean Brulart supplied four, not only two, silver-inlaid collars for 60 francs (*Mandements* 1595), it seems that there were four of these 'Spaniards' (*Espaignoz*), namely the other two for Wenceslas IV. This would partially resolve the discord between the Account and the wording of the mandate of Charles V from 18 January 1378, because, according to the Account, the silk collars had gold forging with chasing in the form of *fleurs-de-lis*. Apparently an even more precious collar adorns the noble white dog which is being fed by its servant (*valet du chien*) in the lower right-hand corner of the depiction of the January ceremonial table of Duke John of Berry (Pic. 155).[501]

Also the last three jewellery items presented had great value. On leave-taking in Beauté-sur-Marne, as the Account mentions, the emperor removed two rings from his fingers, one with a ruby and the other with a diamond, and gave them both to his host. It is the first and last time that the Account of the *Great Chronicles of France* has mentioned some gift or other honour for the host. Not even this time did Charles V the Wise remain a debtor to his uncle – he removed from his finger a ring with a large, very expensive diamond and gave it to him with 'nice' words of mutual friendship. Even the litter in which Charles IV set out on his journey was a gift from his host, who thus fulfilled to the last moment what he had resolved to do: to demonstrate the splendour of his majesty to the emperor and his dear uncle.[502]

500/ Pierre-Yves Le Pogam, 'Orfèvrerie et émaillerie', in *Musée national du Moyen Âge Thermes de Cluny. Guide des collections*, p. 98, No. 111. The Bohemian origin is accompanied by a question mark, but Charles IV is explicitly mentioned here as an example of a sovereign who had a collector's passion for this type of objects. Another example can be found on p. 95 under No. 106 (*Trésor de Colmar: Fermail ajouré*, second half of the fourteenth century). A number of valuable buckles from a somewhat later time are presented by the catalogue *L'art au temps des rois maudits. Philippe le Bel et ses fils 1285–1328*, pp. 239–243, Nos. 156–157. Both clasps from Colmar were displayed at the exhibition *Les Fastes du Gothique*, pp. 242–243, No. 197B–C. A special case is the *Fermail orné d'une fleur de lis* from the treasure of Saint-Denis, which was repaired in 1365–1367 by the goldsmith of Charles V, Jean de Picquigny (see *Les Fastes du Gothique*, pp. 238–139, No. 192. Three pearls originally decorated the clasp from the first half of the fourteenth century (Musée de Cluny, Inv. 15146, *Les Fastes du Gothique*, p. 245, No. 197 bis).

501/ For more on these white dogs from the menagerie of Duke John of Berry, see Hirschbiegel, *Étrennes*, p. 54, Note 81.

502/ See Delachenal (ed.), *Chronique des règnes*, II, pp. 271–272.

Even great men have moments of weakness. Not even Emperor Charles IV could help yielding to them during his stay at the château in Vincennes on his last visit to France at the beginning of 1378. We should mention again that on Monday, 11 January, the emperor, beleaguered by illnesses, as we read in the Account of the *Great Chronicles of France*, had himself carried around the hall on the third floor to be able to observe the surroundings of the château at least in this way.[503] His host, Charles V, did not see the emperor that morning, because the king listened to mass in the morning. 'However, the king came to visit the emperor after lunch, because the emperor had already slept in the meantime. Afterwards, they remained in friendly conversation and entertainment for a long time, during which time the emperor asked the king to give him one of his Books of Hours, saying that he would pray from it to God for him. The king sent him two, one large and one small, and let him know that he could choose which he wanted or both if he liked them both. He kept them both and thanked the king for them.'[504] This small episode of an anecdotal nature did not have to be the only occasion, as I will try to prove, on which the emperor or his son had a book in hand during the visit to Paris.

The cognomina of the kings are sometimes misleading. In the case of Charles V, the nickname *le Sage* (wise, respectable, prudent) has more semantic fields, but at the very least we should concede him intellectual enlightenment.[505] Although already some of his anointed predecessors liked beautiful books at hand, Charles V raised his personal interest to a state interest by founding an institutional royal library. Immediately after the books had been transported from the king's Palace de la Cité to the Louvre in 1367, reconstructions began on the three highest floors of the tower in the northwest wing of the château, which have already been mentioned above.[506] Although the solid bookcases as well as swivel easels[507] for the books had been brought along with the benches from the former library, craftsmen refurbished them here. In addition, all of the windows were equipped with brass bars for protection from the falcons and other birds from the neighbouring aviary. Thirty candelabra in the niches and one silver chandelier provided the readers with enough light. A new list of the books was compiled in 1377 by the properly appointed librarian Gilles Malet, otherwise Viscount de Corbeill († 1410 or 1411).[508] At that time, the library already had around nine hundred rare volumes deposited on the three floors of the

503/ An even better view was offered from the terrace two floors higher, but it may have been harder to access with the litter.

504/ See Delachenal (ed.), *Chronique des règnes*, II, p. 264.

505/ For more on the character traits of this 'wise' ruler, see Autrand, *Charles V. Le Sage*, pp. 464–490.

506/ For initial enlightenment, see the catalogue *La Librairie de Charles V*, pp. 45–46 and the subsequent exhibits. The accounting documents were printed by Delisle, *Recherches sur la librairie de Charles V*, I, pp. 367–368.

507/ These swivel easels are shown for us in the period miniatures depicting, i.a. Charles V in his library. See especially the French translation of the *Policraticus* by John of Salisbury in MS fr. 24287 of the Bibliothèque Nationale in Paris, fol. 2r. On this miniature and other period depictions, see Sherman, 'Representations of Charles V of France (1338–1380) as a Wise Ruler', pp. 83–96.

508/ This noteworthy man has left behind numerous works, i.a. the so-called *Osculatorium*, otherwise also the *Pacificale*; for more on this, see the catalogue *Europäische Kunst um 1400*, pp. 396–397, No. 465.

165. The towers of Castle Vincennes. Très Riches Heures du Duc de Berry. Month of December, beginning of the 15th century (MC, Ms. 65, fol. 12r)

tower.[509] Given that the craftsmen were paid forty francs in gold for work more closely unspecified in the library still in November 1377, it can be supposed that it was in connection with the upcoming visit of the Holy Roman Emperor and his son.[510]

The official Account does not mention the visit to the tower with the library, but both of the Luxemburgs stayed in its proximity for three days. Charles V ceded his chambers on the second floor to his uncle, whereas Wenceslas IV was accommodated a floor below in the rooms of the queen, who was staying in the residence of Saint-Pol at the time of the visit. On the basis of a detailed reconstruction of the palace of Charles V in the Louvre, it can be proved that the king's suite was on the left side immediately adjacent to the corner tower with the library. The rooms of Queen Jeanne of Bourbon were identically situated one floor below with the same view of the gardens, undoubtedly providing Wenceslas IV with easy access to his father.[511]

The librarian Gilles Malet was after all in the immediate proximity of the rare guests. It was he who along with the court goldsmith Hennequin to Beauté brought the newly prepared crown of the king for the emperor to see and who fulfilled the role of mediator when presents were being given to the emperor's entourage. It was undoubtedly also he who was put in charge of the task of selecting the two above-mentioned Books of Hours for the emperor, but with great likelihood they were not manuscripts from Charles' main library in the Louvre, whose catalogue does not list among the missing items any Books of Hours which could be connected with the emperor's visit. We will add that the host was in this respect almost surprisingly generous, because he loaned or gave a whole range of rare manuscripts to his relatives, friends as well as servants.[512]

This bibliophile on the French throne had smaller reference collections of books also at his other residences, particularly in Vincennes, where fifty-six manuscripts were recorded between January and May 1380, a few months before his death on 16 September of the same year. The goldsmith Hennequin du Viviers and librarian Gilles Malet participated in the list with their knowledge.[513] Unlike the wide

509/ The inventory from 1380–1411, which includes both the inventory by Gilles Malet from 1373 and its copy in the form of a *rotulus* made and complemented by Jean Blanchet in 1380, was issued by Delisle, *Recherches sur la librairie de Charles V*, II, pp. 21–165.

510/ See Delisle (ed.), *Mandements et actes divers*, p. 760, No. 1509.

511/ The issue has been dealt in more detail in Excursus – Where the Emperor Stayed in Paris. The plan of the hypothetical reconstruction of the ground floor and second floor of the Louvre in the period of Charles V the Wise was published by Whiteley, 'L'aménagement intérieur des résidences royales et princières', pp. 299–303, Pic. 26.

512/ Delisle, *Recherches sur la librairie*, I, Chapter X, pp. 120–124 ('Prêts et dons de livres faits par Charles V').

513/ The books along with the jewellery and other valuables

thematic scope of the library in the Louvre, the collection in Vincennes comprised manuscripts mainly of a liturgical character, with more than half of them being intended for the spiritual needs of the educated laity. Therefore, it is no accident that the inventory lists sixteen Books of Hours, seven psalters and five prayer books. Despite a number of these manuscripts being small in size so that they could be held easily in the hands even in intimate moments, the vast majority were expensively illuminated volumes. And since it arises from the list that the manuscripts, including Books of Hours, were placed not only in the oratory but also here and there in other rooms of the residence in Vincennes,[514] the emperor had a strong desire to take one to Prague. We already know how it ended; the circle has closed.

Emperor Charles IV did not enjoy the rare Books of Hours for much longer. Their traces have not yet been found in domestic or foreign manuscript collections,[515] but they most likely remained in the family library if it already existed then. If not, Wenceslas IV had credit for establishing it. I will probably not be far from the truth that Wenceslas acquired the model for his library in Paris, which became one of the few bright sides of his reign on the Bohemian throne. This possibility could not have escaped earlier research: especially the exhibition in Paris on the library of Charles V must have inspired questions of this type. Besides by Karel Stejskal,[516] they were asked by Josef Krása, namely in relatively sharply formulated outlines.[517] According to this expert, the court library of Wenceslas IV was undoubtedly established primarily from the impetus of the royal library of Charles V the Wise.[518] Unlike the last-mentioned library, we do not have a single written report on the establishment and development of Wenceslas' collection. According to Krása, the library at first probably did not have a solid position, travelled with the king to his favourite residences, until later after 1412, it found its last refuge at Nový Hrad (New Castle, in German *Wenzelsburg*) near Kunratice in today's greater Prague.[519] According to the chronicler Vavřinec of Březová (Laurentius de Brzezowa in Latin or Laurentius von Brösau in German), the books were placed in a vaulted room, from which they were taken away in several wagons in January 1421 after the capitulation of Sigismund's garrison. The rest were then stolen by 'avaricious commoners'.[520]

Whereas two rare books disappeared from the royal library in the Louvre, one was quite likely added to it thanks to the emperor's visit. It was a collection of documents called *Recueil des traités de la France* or *Livre des alliances*. Considering that this collection of

of the chattels in Vincennes were listed by the three-member commission composed of Bureau de la Rivière, Gilles Malet and the goldsmith Hennequin du Viviers. This uncommonly valuable inventory was published with erroneous dating by Labarte, *Inventaire du mobilier de Charles V.*

514/ I take most of the information from a study whose author was an expert more qualified than the others, the Chief-Conservator of the Department of Manuscripts of the Bibliothèque Nationale in Paris, Avril, 'Les livres de Charles V au château de Vincennes', pp. 329–340.

515/ The most important evidence of this type in the National Library of the Czech Republic in Prague was drawn attention to by Stejskal, 'Über die Illuminatoren der französischen Stundenbücher in der Prager Nationalbibliothek', pp. 715–724. These Books of Hours however do not come from before the fifteenth century, like other manuscripts of this type in our libraries. An exception is the Latin Book of Hours of French origin from the time around the middle of the fourteenth century in the Library of the National Museum of the Czech Republic in Prague, shelf mark XIII F 32. On their simple illumination, see Pavel Brodský, *Katalog iluminovaných rukopisů Knihovny Národního muzea v Praze*, p. 188, No. 163. It has been possible to determine roughly a fifth of the manuscripts from the collection of Charles V in Vincennes, which is an unusually high number. On that, see Avril, 'Les livres de Charles V au château de Vincennes', pp. 336–337.

516/ Stejskal, 'Výstava „La Librairie de Charles V" a některé otázky českého umění XIV. století', p. 31.

517/ Josef Krása, 'Dvě kresby z Louvru a česká knižní malba kolem roku 1400'. It is a study originally printed in French as 'Deux Dessins du Louvre et la peinture de manuscrits en Bohême vers 1400' in the journal Scriptorium XXIII, 1969, pp. 163–176, and most likely already taking the exhibition in Paris into account.

518/ Krása, *The Travels of Sir John Mandeville: A Manuscript in the British Library*, Add. 24189, p. 286.

519/ See Krása, *Rukopisy Václava IV.*, pp. 15–19, with information also on the fates of the library after Wenceslas' death.

520/ 'Laurentiii de Brezova', 'Historia hussitica', ed. Jaroslav Goll, p. 466.

Latin documents and their translations into French also includes a section devoted to the Holy Roman Emperors and Kings of the Romans, André Artonne expressed the opinion that it was documentation created in 1378 or 1379 for the purpose of planned diplomatic activities.[521] Françoise Autrand, the author of the large biography on Charles V, then quite convincingly connected the origin of this collection with the preparation of the emperor's visit and the diplomatic summit in the first ten days of January 1378. While the original exemplar evidenced in the inventory of the library still in 1411 has not survived to this day, what it looked like has been preserved by three copies from the fifteenth century.[522]

At the end, there is a small mystery which was left to further research by F. M. Pelzel, a historian who had a surprisingly detailed knowledge of Charles' visit to France.[523] His main, and it must be added also reliable, source was the shortened Account of the *Great Chronicles of France*, which had been issued by Théodore Godefroy in 1614.[524] When enumerating the valuable gifts received by Charles and his entourage, Pelzel also mentioned books. And since as the administrator of the library of the Counts of Nostitz[525] he had in front of his eyes a gorgeous illuminated codex of a translation of Livy into French by Pierre Bersuire, he expressed the opinion that Emperor Charles had brought it as a gift for his crowned nephew. However, it is not known when this precious manuscript was given, sold or otherwise taken, so we look for it in vain in the catalogue of 1910.[526] For this reason, Pelzel's detailed description becomes important for the possible identification of the codex:

'It is Livy translated into French by Peter Bercheur [sic] around 1361 at the request of King of France John [II the Good]. The book is magnificent and truly royal... It is entirely written on marvellous parchment and is comprised of 508 folios of a large format. It is bound in black velvet with a red spine of the same, completely smooth material, with the binding being covered with gilded brass buttons. There are golden lilies on the edge. The folios on which one Decade or one book of the same begins are illuminated with paintings of the most beautiful and most vivid colours with rich and heavy gilding. The initial letters of every chapter as well as after every full stop in the entire book are also gilded, just like the drollery on the margins shines with gold. The book is so sumptuous that it could not have been prepared for anyone else but for King John, from whose impetus the translation happened.'[527]

It is possible to suppose almost with certainty that it was one of the period copies of this work, which is one of the masterpieces of French translation of the second half of the fourteenth century. The Dominican Pierre Bersuire (Berchorius, † 1362) worked on the translation in the turbulent years 1354–1359, when the malcontents led by Étienne Marcel met in his cloister of St Eligius near the Palace de la Cité.[528] Although his Old French translation of the *Decades* by Livy has been preserved in roughly sixty manuscripts and several early printed books, the original exemplar devoted to King John II the Good has not been preserved. To believe that the

521/ Artonne, 'Le recueil des traités de la France composé par ordre de Charles V', pp. 55–63.

522/ Autrand, 'Les livres des hommes de pouivoir: de la pratique à la culture écrite. I. Pratique diplomatique et culture politique au temps de Charles V', here esp. pp. 199–204.

523/ Pelzel, *Kaiser Karl der Vierte*, II, pp. 931–932.

524/ The text was made accessible in a German translation in 1828 by Johann Ritter von Rittersberg: 'Kaiser Karl des IV. und seines Sohnes König Wenzel Reise nach Paris in den Jahren 1377 und 1378' [Nach der von Theodor Godefroy im J. 1614 zu Paris herausgegebenen 'Entrevue...'], *Monatschrift der Gesellschaft des vaterländischen Museums in Böhmen*, 2-1 (1828), pp. 201–204, 313–339.

525/ Pelzel became the Master of the Royal Household in the family of Count Anton Nostitz in 1769; see Hanuš, *František Martin Pelcel, český historik a buditel*, p. 4ff.

526/ See J. V. Šimák, *Rukopisy majorátní knihovny hrabat z Nostitz a Rhienecka v Praze.*

527/ Pelzel, *Kaiser Karl der Vierte*, II, pp. 931–932. In Note 1, we then read: 'A Prince de très Souveraine Excellence Iehann, Roy de France par grace divine, frère Pierre Berceure son petit serviteur, prieur à présent de Cloy de Paris toute humble révérence et subjection. C'est tout certain trés Souverain Seigneur que tous Excellens princes etc.'

528/ The basic information is presented by Albert Gier in the entry 'Bersuire, Pierre' in *Lexikon des Mittelalters*, I, cols 2020–2021, also with the earlier literature.

166. Pierre Bersuire gives his translation of Titus Livius to the king. Miniature from around 1410. Tite-Live, Histoire romaine (Bibliothèque de l'Arsenal, ms. 3693, fol. 9r)

rarest of all of the manuscripts with this work found its way precisely into the Nostitz Library would be rash already for the reason that Pelzel's description is quite vague as far as the age of the work is concerned, because we also know of copies from the second half of the fifteenth century that look valuable.[529] So far the earliest of the manuscripts of this provenance is a copy approximately from around 1370 made for the library of Charles V in the Louvre. This gem of book painting is listed in all of the inventories of the royal library in the Louvre until 1424, when it came into the ownership of the Duke of Bedford. This manuscript decorated the library of the Dukes of Burgundy for some time before it subsequently came into the library of Sainte-Geneviève under the shelf mark 777.[530] There was apparently great interest in the French version of the *Decades* by Livy among the educated feudal lords; Duke John of Berry alone had five of them in his library.[531] In October 1393, Duke Louis of Orléans, son of Charles VI, spent 500 gold francs for the preparation of two volumes.[532]

This is not the end to the small puzzles, but at least one will be possible to dispose of *ad acta*. In one of his articles, Konrad Burdach with reference to the above-mentioned assumption of Pelzel's mistook the translation of Livy for an illuminated manuscript by Valerius Maximus,[533] which later also misled Josef Krása.[534] It is necessary to add that this work could have been lacking in the library of Charles V also. The translation of the first four books of Valerius Maximus' Facta et dicta memorabilia (Memorable Deeds and Sayings) into French as *Faits et dits mémorables* was finished in honour of Charles V by Simon de Hesdin in 1375 and is today one of the greatest book treasures of the Bibliothèque Nationale.[535] As is evident, the mysteries are usually created by the historians themselves. It is also true for the very noteworthy Ottonian Gospel Book from around 985 which Charles V in 1379 had furnished with a gold upper tablet on the front cover and then donated it to Sainte-Chapelle.[536] Since the manuscript had been created at the order of Bishop of Trier Egbert, François Avril expressed the conjecture that our emperor had given this rare work to Charles V on his

529/ One of these illuminated manuscripts in two volumes was displayed in 1955 at an exhibition in the Bibliothèque Nationale in Paris. See the description in the catalogue *Les manuscrits à peintures en France du XIIIe au XVIe siècle*, p. 125, No. 256 (Paris, Bibliothèque nationale, ms. fr. 20071–20072).

530/ For further information, see Delisle, *Recherches sur la librairie*, I, pp. 183–284, No. 80, additionally the catalogues *Les manuscrits à peintures en France du XIIIe au XVIe siècle*, p. 58, No. 118, and *La Librairie de Charles V*, pp. 107–109, No. 189.

531/ See again Delisle, *Recherches sur la librairie*, II, pp. 310*–312*, No. 233–236 bis.

532/ It was mediated again by Gilles Malet; see the receipt published by Delisle, *Recherches sur la librairie*, I, pp. 362–364, No. IV/1–3.

533/ Konrad Burdach, 'Zur Kenntniss altdeutscher Handschriften', p. 337.

534/ Krása, *Rukopisy Václava IV.*, p. 9.

535/ The richly illuminated manuscript has the shelf mark Paris, Bibliothèque nationale, MS fr. 9749. For more on that, see Delisle, *Recherches sur la librairie*, I, p. 254, further the catalogues *Les manuscrits à peintures en France du XIIIe au XVIe siècle*, p. 60, No. 122, and *La Librairie de Charles V*, p. 109, No. 190.

536/ The manuscript is now deposited in the Bibliothèque Nationale under MS lat. 8851.

visit to Paris in January 1378.[537] Karel Stejskal soon imaginatively added the explanatory idea that the emperor could have acquired the Gospel Book along with other treasures of which he took possession after the death of his great-uncle Baldwin, Archbishop of Trier, in 1354.[538] Nothing like that can be reliably proved, not to mention that the rare Gospel Book had already been a part of the treasure of the kings of France in the thirteenth century.[539]

A unique mystery is another supposed gift for the emperor which was allegedly the mitre of St Eligius. In this regard, the Account of the *Great Chronicles of France* is surprisingly quiet, although it otherwise quite pedantically enumerates even the presents of relics. The preserved mitre, which has been deposited in the National Museum in Prague (Inv. No. HA 60701) since 1876 along with its reliquary, corresponds with its size as well as shape to similar artefacts and depictions of the High Middle Ages. The authenticity of similar relics is usually disputable; in our case, it is enough to add that in the Western Church the mitre, otherwise also *infula*, did not become the insignia of bishops and abbots until the middle of the eleventh century.[540] We can

537/ It is thus in the catalogue *La Librairie de Charles V*, pp. 40–41, No. 99.

538/ See Stejskal, 'Výstava „La librairie de Charles V"', pp. 54–55. The fact that Charles IV attended the funeral of Archbishop of Trier Baldwin can be a certain support here (see Spěváček, *Karel IV.*, p. 237). The Gospel Book however does not appear among the Trier monuments and remains which Charles IV mentions in his letter to the Prague Chapter from 17 February 1354 (the letter was published by Podlaha and Šittler, *Chrámový poklad u sv. Víta v Praze*, pp. 31–32, Note 2).

539/ It is MS lat. 8851 of the Bibliothèque nationale, which the literature does not connect with Emperor Charles IV. On that, see Marie-Pierre Laffitte, 'Les manuscrits du trésor: La Sainte-Chapelle au Moyen Âge', p. 56, and Taburet-Delahaye, 'L'orfévrerie à la Sainte-Chapelle sous saint Louis', pp. 72–73.

540/ In the Byzantine area, the mitre was the insignia of the patriarchs of Constantinople and bishops of the Eastern Rite already in the centuries before. For initial enlightenment, see *Lexikon für Theologie und Kirche*, VII, p. 490, further Kühnel, *Bildwörterbuch der Kleidung und Rüstung*, pp. 172–173, and the entry 'Pontifikalien' in *Lexikon des Mittelalters*, VII, cols 96–97. In the narrow sense of the word, *infula* labelled the two strips of cloth hanging on the back of the actual headcover.

167. Mitre of St Eligius

be much more surprised by the result of a special analysis of the fabric itself, which suggests that the material is quite likely to come from the end of the sixteenth or from the beginning of the seventeenth century,[541] because no objections have so far been raised to the authenticity of the reliquary in which the mitre of St Eligius is deposited. The case of gilded silver follows the shape of the bishop's mitre with apertures of rock crystal (Pic. 167). The framework has an elliptical base below with a two-line memorial inscription in Gothic minuscule, which after expanding the abbreviations reads as follows: *Anno domini M.CCC.LXXVIII. infula Sancti Eligii aportata est per serenissimum principem et dominum Carolum Quartum, Romanorum imperatorem semper Augustum / et Bohemie regem, donata ei a domino Carolo rege Francie, que nobis aurifabris Pragensibus per ipsum dominum nostrum imperatorem data et donata ex gracia speciali.*[542]

541/ See Stehlíková, Mádl and Heude-Levoir, 'Le reliquiaire de la mitre de Saint Éloi à Prague', pp. 81–89. Odile Valansot participated in the technological analysis.

542/ A brief description with the data on the earlier literature was presented by the catalogue [of an unimplemented exhibition] *České umění gotické 1350–1420*, p. 340, No. 432.

The inscription is entirely unambiguous: Emperor Charles IV acquired the *infula* of St Eligius as a gift from King Charles V of France in 1378 and after his return to Bohemia gave it to the Prague goldsmiths by a special grace. Since St Eligius (ca 590–660) was famous as a court goldsmith and coinmaster of the French kings before his ordination as Bishop of Noyon, he became the patron saint of numerous metalworking crafts.[543] And here the Account after all gives us guidance, because Emperor Charles IV remained in Noyon for two days, during which he also visited the Abbey of St Eligius and bowed to his relics. On this occasion, Charles certainly did not find it difficult to ask the abbot or the local bishop Gilles de Lorris, with whom he met again in Saint-Denis, for some relic for Prague. For that matter, this could have been also mediated through the host Charles V, who is mentioned in the inscription as the donor. After all, the Palace de la Cité was located in proximity of the Dominican cloister of St Eligius, which undoubtedly also owned the relics of its patron.

Whatever the case was, it then went without saying that Emperor Charles IV after his return to Prague donated the precious relic precisely to the guild brotherhood of the Old Town goldsmiths. Although it was an exceptional expression of favour, we find the first mention of this reliquary only in the *Annales Boemorum* [Chronicle of the Bohemians] by Václav Hájek of Libočany (Wenceslai Hagek a Liboczan).[544] It is also perplexing that the statutes of the goldsmith's guild entirely left out its patron and that the Chapel of St Eligius, otherwise called 'zlatnická' (the Goldsmith's Chapel) on the site of the Klementinum now is first proved only in the fifteenth century.[545] At the last moment, I add one more monument which is allegedly connected with the journey of Charles IV to France. The Bibliothèque de la Ville in Paris has in its collections the manuscript MS Res. 104 with the legend and prayer of St Eligius, which might have been ordered as a gift for the king of France after the return of the emperor and his son to Prague. It was judged so by Ulrike Jenni based on the similarity of the book ornamentation with the manuscripts of Prague provenance.[546] The uncertainties for one memorial are too numerous, and thus it is better to wait for the results of a general analysis.

The host was quite familiar with the emperor's collecting of holy relics.[547] The emperor had been famous for it already at an early age, because otherwise John II the Good would not have, as an expression of special favour, given him two thorns which he had had removed by the archbishop of Rheims from the 'Holy Crown', deposited in Sainte-Chapelle. The relic was given to the emperor by Dauphin Charles in Metz in 1356, namely along with a document proving the authenticity of both thorns deposited in the crystal protective reliquary furnished with a gold frame.[548] It was most likely on this occasion that the dauphin gave his uncle the no less precious relic from the wood from Christ's cross, which as one of the three pieces of wood of the Lord was deposit-

The mitre has been displayed at a number of other exhibitions and today is a part of the permanent exhibition of the National Museum at Lobkowicz Palace (see *Památky národní minulosti*, pp. 75–76, No. 218). The latest state of research has been captured by Stehlíková, Mádl and Heude-Levoir, 'Le reliquiaire de la mitre de Saint Éloi à Prague', pp. 77–81.

543/ The basic information on the saint is provided by Joseph-Claude Poulin in the entry 'Eligius' in *Lexikon des Mittelalters*, III, cols 1829–1830, also with references to the sources and literature.

544/ Václav Hájek z Libočan, *Kronika česká*, Praha 1541, mechanical reprint from 1819–1823, p. 349.

545/ On that, see Ferdinand Menčík, 'Pořádek bratrstva zlatnického v Praze a jeho stanovy z r. 1324', pp. 260–261.

546/ Ulrike Jenni and Maria Theisen, *Mitteleuropäische Schulen*, III, Textband, p. 121, Cat. 25, Fig. 38.

547/ For more on this mania of Charles IV, see Franz Machilek, 'Privatfrömmigkeit und Staatsfrömmigkeit', pp. 87–101; more recently Beate Weifenbach, 'Freiheit durch Privilegien und Schutz durch Reliquien', pp. 245–254, also with further literature.

548/ The so-called certificate of authenticity was issued by Podlaha and Šittler, *Chrámový poklad u sv. Víta v Praze*, p. 119, Note 3; the appearance of the protection aspect was described by František Fišer, *Karlštejn*, p. 144. It was already the second relic of this provenance. On the thorn from the Crown of Thorns from Sainte-Chapelle in the treasure of the monastery in Zlatá Koruna, see Jiří Kuthan, 'Pařížská Sainte-Chapelle a trny z koruny Kristovy', p. 45, which contains a recapitalisation of the question in this study.

168. / XXIV. The emperor with his son and retinue kneeling before the reliquary of St Denis (BL, Ms. royal 20 C VII, fol. 197r)

ed in the Great Land Cross. It is indicated by the depiction of the first of the so-called Relic Scenes in Karlštejn's Chapel of the Virgin Mary, in which Dauphin Charles with a clear gesture of the right hand puts a small cross furnished with a point in the emperor's hand (Pic. 27).[549] Whereas the dauphin's appearance in this fresco is undisputed, doubts are raised by the attempt to find the dauphin's physiognomy in the depiction of one of the young kings on the southern wall of the Chapel of the Holy Rood (KA 3779).[550]

Emperor Charles IV was also a great admirer of his illustrious namesake Charlemagne, whose relics he sought in every possible way. *Inter alia*, he managed to acquire Charlemagne's tooth or teeth. I suppose that there must have been at least two, because he otherwise would not have given one of them to Charles V, who handed this relic along with the accompanying letter from the emperor of 18 January 1367 over to the treasury of Sainte-Chapelle. What is surprising is that the tooth does not appear in the inventory which Charles V had made in February 1377 or in any other list of this type. However, it does not seem to be a fabrication, because the original of the emperor's donation letter has been preserved; its deposition in the archives in Sainte-Chapelle is mentioned in the inventory from 1622.[551]

The search for Charlemagne's teeth would probably be futile, but they have taken us back to January 1378 again. The host must have heard with what internal zeal his uncle had himself carried around the reliquaries in the Abbey of Saint-Denis, during which the precious guest was allowed to kiss some of the relics, particularly the head of St Denis and the nail from Christ's cross (Pic. 40).[552] On Wednes-

---

549/ For more detail on that, see Fišer, *Karlštejn*, pp. 144 and 248–249. The supposition that the donor is giving the emperor also a relic of the cross was questioned already earlier by Zdeněk Bouše and Josef Myslivec, 'Sakrální prostory na Karlštejně', p. 280ff. On the artistic side of these scenes, see especially Homolka, 'Poznámky ke karlštejnským malbám', pp. 127–129, who on the basis of the restoration of the Relic Scenes in 1994–1995 supported the opinion of A. Matějček that their painter belonged to the circle of Parisian court artists. It is a significant conclusion which will have to be taken into consideration also in connection with the meeting of the dauphin and the emperor in Metz. According to Homolka, the portrait of Dauphin Charles is so faithful that the painter could have worked at Karlštejn following a portrait imported from France (on that, see Note 24 on p. 138). On the latest information on this issue, see Otavský, 'K relikviím vlastněným císařem Karlem IV.', pp. 394–395.

550/ This idea was presented by Jiří Fajt, 'Magister Theodoricus', p. 311; see ibidem p. 494 with a depiction of the young monarch (shelf mark KA 3779).

551/ The emperor's letter in the Archives Nationales, shelf mark L 620, No. 7, was drawn attention to by Alexandre Vidier, *Le Trésor de la Sainte-Chapelle*, p. 339, No. 73, also with an edition of the inventory from February 1377 on pp. 63–68.

552/ The famous cabinet with the most precious relics of the treasure of the abbey (Armoire du trésor de Saint-Denis) was captured by an engraving in the work by Dom Michel Félibien, *Histoire de l'Abbaye Royale de Saint-Denys en France*, Plate IV. The monumental cross, probably with a nail, is quite evident in the depiction. Its earlier appearance was captured by a plate painting of the Mass of St Gilles from around 1500 (National Gallery, London). The valuables were put in the Cabinet of Antiquities (*Le Cabinet des médailles et des antiques de la Bibliothèque nationale de Paris*) of the Bibliothèque nationale and the Museum in the Louvre during the French Revolution. Despite several thefts and sales, some of the valuables are preserved in both collections.

169. The interior of the relic case (Grande Chasse) from Sainte Chapelle in a depiction from the end of the 15th century. The central position is taken by the crown of thorns in a case like a chalice. The rare remnants of Christ's cross are placed in a large two-armed cross, a stone from Christ's tomb is places in a so-called Victoria Cross, and a smaller equilateral cross, which the French kings carried into battle. The other valuable relics include Moses' staff and milk of the Virgin Mary

day, 6 January, Charles V fulfilled the emperor's wish and escorted him to Sainte-Chapelle. The emperor wanted at all costs to see with his own eyes the Great Reliquary in the upper chapel and therefore had himself pulled by his shoulders and legs up the spiral staircase. The king himself opened the reliquary and showed him all of the objects deposited in it (Pic. 169). When the emperor had inspected and kissed them, so did all the other princes present. The king then had said reliquary turned towards the chapel so that the emperor could observe it from below during the mass from the chair in which the treasurer of the said chapel usually sat.[553]

It might have been on this occasion, but it could have been earlier, that the emperor mentioned to his nephew his wish to acquire a relic of St Denis. The host again accommodated him generously. According to the Account of the *Great Chronicles of France*, he came to visit the emperor privately on 8 January 1378 and brought him a gift of a bone of St Denis along with a 'beautiful jewellery box of jasper, inlaid with gold and precious stones', in which there was a thorn from the Crown of Thorns and one of the bones of St Martin.[554] It was also up to the king to choose gifts on behalf of his wife which would equally please the emperor and his son. Queen Jeanne could thus on Sunday 10 January, give the emperor 'a gorgeous golden reliquary in the form of a great, vaulted temple, very richly inlaid with precious stones, which had a little piece of wood from the true cross inside'.

Charles V the Wise was a pious man; his daily routine included morning mass; he had a Book of Hours or other religious educational reading always on hand. Although there can be no doubt of his deep religious feeling, the overdone fetishism connected with the cult of the holy relics seems to have been alien to his nature. He expressed due respect to the crown relics in Sainte-Chapelle and elsewhere, but he did not pathologically cling to them. Charles V also gave splinters or chips from the 'true' Cross of Christ to other people, namely his brother John, Duke of Berry, or the Grand Master of the Order of Teutonic Knights. He himself made these splinters

553/ This famous cabinet for relics (*Grande Châsse*) has been rendered several times. The earliest depiction can be found in Manuscript 67 of the Morgan Library & Museum (formerly The Pierpont Morgan Library), fol. 1 (end of the fifteenth century); the interior is captured also in engravings from the eighteenth century). See Durand, 'Les reliques de Constantinople', pp. 60–65, and Taburet-Delahaye, 'L'orfèvrerie à la Sainte-Chapelle sous saint Louis', pp. 66-73. For the latest on the emperor's visit to Sainte-Chapelle, see Kováč, 'Poznámky k popisu pařížské Sainte-Chapelle z roku 1378', pp. 413–418, including i.a. the idea that the *Grande Châsse* was placed on a revolving pedestal.

554/ Delachenal (ed.), *Chronique des règnes*, p. 249.

170. Reliquary of the Holy Crown of Thorns from Sainte-Chappelle, today in the cathedral museum of Notre-Dame

and chips. It was also no different with the thorns of the Crown of Thorns which Saint Louis had acquired in 1238–1239 from the deposed ruler of the Latin Empire Baldwin II (Pic. 170).[555] He also gave one of the thorns to Queen Joan of Sicily.[556]

What mattered were not only the relics but also their cases, which had to correspond to their importance. For Charles V, two such reliquaries were supplied and perhaps even made by his court goldsmith and valet Jean de Viviers, namely for 116 francs in gold. According to the mandate of 18 January 1378, they were two gold reliquaries decorated with crystals and four large pearls. One was intended for the deposition of a piece of wood from the true cross and the other for the placement of other relics.[557] In the inventories of the Metropolitan Chapter in Prague, these relics cannot be reliably identified,[558] and it is no different with the later inventories of the Karlštejn relics.[559]

The *devotionalia*, some of which were intended for the queen, were less valuable.[560] Through his brother John, Duke of Berry, Charles V moreover gave his uncle two very nobly prepared large gold flasks, whose reliefs depicted Saint James showing Saint Charlemagne the way to Spain. Both flasks had the form of shells, which had a symbolic character, as the Duke of Berry explained to the emperor. The king sent him shells, because he had come to France also as a pilgrim.[561]

555/ On that in detail, see Le Goff, *Saint Louis*, pp. 140–146. Cf. also Durand, 'Les reliques de Constantinople', pp. 60–64.

556/ On that, see Vidier, *Le Trésor de la Sainte-Chapelle*, p. 340, No. 76.

557/ See Delisle (ed.), *Mandements et actes divers*, p. 795, No. 1602: 'pour deux reliquiaires d'or garniz de cristaulz et de quatre grosses perles, c'est assavoir l'un pour mettre une piece du fust de la vraye croix, et l'autre pour mettre autres reliques'.

558/ Although they mention the tooth of St Martin which Charles IV obtained from an unnamed French king, it already appears in the inventory from 1355 (see Podlaha and Šittler, *Chrámový poklad u sv. Víta*, p. 48, Note 1). It is also disputable when two fragments of rush stalk from the Crown of Thorns from Saint-Denis became parts of the golden relic cross (Inv. No. 25, or also 97). On that, see again Podlaha and Šittler, *Chrámový poklad u sv. Víta*, pp. 119–120 and 168–169 (with a description). Possibly see also the catalogue *České umění gotické 1350–1420*, pp. 337–338, No. 427.

559/ Besides other obvious counterfeits, however, the inventory of the Karlštejn relics from 1598 also contains 'the head of St Denis, bishop and martyr' (see Fišer, *Karlštejn*, p. 318).

560/ On that, see Excursus – The Gifts for the Emperor and His Retinue.

561/ Machilek, 'Privatfrömmigkeit und Staatsfrömmigkeit', p. 94.

The period Account of the *Great Chronicles of France*, with which we are already familiar, did not forget to mention in two places that the emperor and his people had been hosted at the expense of Charles V throughout their stay in France, even when the gifts were in the name of the towns.[562] In accordance with the period suprapersonal conception of the Crown of France and its prestige, it is not surprising that all of these expenditures were considered as a part of the propaganda, namely with no consideration of the overall indigence of the king's finances. The total proved expenditures for the visit of Charles IV in the amount of 55,888 francs, 6 sous and 3 deniers significantly surpass the 51,000 francs which was reached by Raymond Cazelles by an estimate based on the same sources.[563] This amount, which does not include all the expenses of a crown nature by far, is truly enormous if we compare it with the account of incomes and expenditures from the time immediately following.[564]

Considering the changing currency rate, it is necessary to add that on the basis of the ordinance of John II the Good from 5 December 1360 the new coin became the 'franc', which after conversion was equal to the earlier currency, i.e. one Tours pound (*livre tournois*). However, only through a further ordinance of 22 April 1365, this time already with the signature of Charles V, did the new means of payment acquire a steady rate for a longer period. Externally both gold coins differed in that the king on horseback with an unsheathed sword (*franc à cheval*) was replaced by a standing sovereign in a Gothic architectural frame (*franc à pied*). The two differed only insignificantly in terms of weight (3.89 g : 3.83 g); the other differences need not be discussed here (Pic. 171).[565] A smaller coin was one sou, which was one-twentieth of a franc. In the accounting data, we further encounter the Tours denier (*denier tournois*), which had the value of one-twelfth of a sou.[566] For the sake of thoroughness, it is useful to add that the écu became the main currency through the coin reform of Charles VI of 1385, with it still being converted to francs.[567]

It is no wonder that such large expenditures had to be properly registered by the officials of the royal chamber. While special registers including lists of the gifts[568] or official books have not been preserved, they are partially substituted for by the royal

562/ It is significant that the Account ends by drawing attention to all the possible expenses that Charles V covered for the emperor and his retinue.

563/ Cazelles, *Société politique, noblesse et couronne sous Jean le Bon et Charles V*, p. 556. The difference can be explained by including the amounts which Cazelles did not take into consideration.

564/ For more on that, see Rey, *Les finances royales*, cf. esp. pp. 62–63 with a tabular overview of the incomes and expenses of the court in 1380–1381. Cazelles, *Société politique*, p. 540, states that the king's treasury (*le trésor du roi*) at the time of Charles V's death had more than 200,000 francs available.

565/ For more information, see, i.a Jean Belaubre, *Histoire numismatique et monétaire de la France médiévale*, pp. 93–98 (depictions of the coins on pp. 245–246, Nos. 551–557) and Jean Duplessy, *Les monnaies françaises royales*, I, pp. 156–160.

566/ On the coin under Charles V, see Cazelles, 'La stabilisation de la monnaie par la création du franc', pp. 293–312, more concisely Cazelles, *Société politique*, pp. 558–560, and Autrand, *Charles V. Le Sage*, p. 426.

567/ Rey, *Le domaine du roi et les finances extraordinaires sous Charles VI 1388–1413*, p. 39.

568/ A special list of the gifts in the form of a *rotulus* (*en un rolle*) is mentioned in the Account; on that, see Delachenal (ed.), *Chronique des règnes*, II, p. 270, Note 1.

171. A gold franc of Charles V (Franc à pied). The inscription on the obverse KAROLUS DI GR / FRANCORV REX (Charles King of France by the grace of God), centre the standing king in ringmail with lilies on his chest, holding a sword and so-called hand of justice. The inscription on the reverse states that it is Christ who conquers, reigns and rules.

mandates, which are available in a surprisingly high number of thirty-two documents.[569] Ideally speaking, any of the expenditures for the emperor's journey could appear in several types of documents at the same time: First in the written order for payment, the so-called mandate (*mandement*), further in the receipt (*quittance*) and subsequently in the accounting (*compte*). From an administrative perspective, it was an interconnected system of offices with different functions and powers. The central financial institution of the French monarchy was the Chamber of Accounts (*Chambre des comptes*), whose main task was to control the accounts of all the people who accepted money or dispensed with it in the public interest. This relatively small office had its seat in the Louvre and in 1360 was composed of nine 'masters' and of twelve lower specialised accountants. The Chamber of Accounts *inter alia* confirmed, ratified, examined and registered the receipts as well as gifts of the separate courts of the king, queen and children of the royal family (*Enfants de France*).[570]

Later, each of the courts had its own accounting office, called a *denier* chamber (*Chambre aux deniers*) according to the small coin.[571] Not only this chamber but also another six court offices (*métiers*) were led from the beginning of the fourteenth century by the Grand Master of the Household (*grand maître de l'Hôtel*), whose position was symbolised by a staff in his hand. The Chamber of the Deniers at the king's court supervised daily expenditures, checked them and at the end of each half-year period submitted them to the Chamber of Accounts (*Chambre des comptes*).[572] The staff of this chamber comprised the 'master' (*maitre*), who – as we already know – reported to the Grand Master of the Household, further the controller of the accounts (*controleur*), two 'bottlers' (*sommeliers*) and numerous assistants (*valets*). Most of these officials accompanied the king on journeys to all of his Parisian as well as rural residences, and therefore the Chamber of the Deniers always had a carriage available with a three-horse team to transport cash as well as a registers.

In 1315, the so-called *Argenterie* (literally 'silver-smithy') formally separated from the Chamber of the Deniers; it is difficult to find an English equivalent for this office since it otherwise appeared only at the Burgundian court. The term silver-smithy does not suffice here, because besides jewellery this office also procured furniture, tapestries, textile decoration of the rooms, clothing, linen, hats and shoes for the king and his family. In addition, it ensured

569/ They were published in 1874 by Delisle (ed.), *Mandements et actes divers de Charles V (1364–1380)*, who in the Preface on p. III warns of the huge amount of documents from other collections that he could not take into account. The research so far on the journey of Charles IV to France has utilised these sources only marginally. Since the vast majority of the mandates have the date of 18 January 1378, I will refer to them in the notes and in the text mainly only with the sequential numbers.

570/ For the beginnings of this institution, see Élisabeth Lalou, 'La Chambre des comptes de Paris'; otherwise, cf. the concise entry 'Chambre des comptes' in *Lexikon des Mittelalters*, II, cols 1673–1675, where also the special literature is listed.

571/ For the period of Charles VI, but considering the development in the previous period, see Rey, *Les finances royales*, pp. 55–62.

572/ The first such receipts were preserved only from the beginning of the reign of Charles VI; nevertheless, they are a valuable source of learning for the earlier period, because they mention, i.a. people known from the mandates of his father. In the component edition arranged by Douët d'Arcq, *Comptes de l'Hôtel des rois de France aux XIVe et XVe siècles*, we e.g. encounter entries for the mantles of the court staff, namely for three main accountants (*maistres des comptes*), ten accountants (*clercs des comptes*), thirteen secretaries and twenty-three notaries (p. 29).

everything connected with travelling, celebrations, purveyance of gifts, devotional articles, etc. It is thus from our perspective an especially significant office. It was led by the *argentier*, who often administered even the highest offices of the financial administration. It sometimes eased the transfer of money, acquired by the *argenterie* both from the Chamber of Extraordinary Taxes (*Chambre des aides*) and directly from the Royal Treasury (*Trésor royal*), which under Charles V administered only the regular incomes of the king's domain.[573] Considering the sharply rising expenditures of the *Argenterie*, the post of its master was temporarily cancelled at the beginning of the 1360s and his authorities were transferred to higher financial bodies, where they remained until 1379.[574]

Whereas most of the expenditures for the household of the young Charles IV and later for his nephew Dauphin Charles went through the *Argenterie*, which always closed out its accounts on 30 June and 31 December, all the amounts for gifts and other expenses connected with the summit in January 1378 were billed through the financial administration of extraordinary taxes, which at the order of Charles V paid Nicolas Martin, master of the treasury, two advances totalling 14,400 francs, whose accounting has not been preserved. The other amounts were paid directly to the persons for whom they were intended, be they the king's brother or the suppliers from among Parisian merchants, goldsmiths and money changers. The collections of the king's mandates issued from 12 September 1377 to 15 May 1378[575] belong to the category of letters closed by the formula '*De par le roy*' and verified by one of the notaries of the *Chambre des généraux*. Without these countersigns, these royal mandates had no validity, unlike others for which the so-called visa was not necessary, or those which the King's Council (*Conseil*) did not have to submit to the monarch.[576]

Most of the mandates in relation to the emperor and his delegation were signed by the notary Louis Blanchet, from Sens by origin, who had been in the king's service at least since 5 December 1373. Several mandates bear the signature of Jean Tabari, of whom we know came from Lesterps in the Limousin Region. Having studied canon law and medicine at the university in Orléans, he entered the services of King Charles V in 1362 as a notary public and secretary.[577] On that, it is necessary to add that the proceeds from the octroi (*aides*) did not flow directly to the king, with the exception of the sums intended specifically for the king's coffers (*coffres*). The orders to pay amounts from the octroi in the name of the king had to be verified on the back by one of the so-called receivers-general (*receveurs général des Aides*), or *conseilleurs généraux*, sometimes shortened to *les généraux*. These high officials had the right to refuse payment if it did not correspond to the pre-determined purposes. In such a case, however, they had to write their negative stance on the back of the king's mandate.[578] The general receiver of the taxes, who in our cases was usually assigned certain sums by the king to disburse, was François Chanteprime, who had held this post already in 1373.[579]

It was almost certainly agreed in advance in the King's Council that all of the expenditures for the emperor's visit to France would be assumed by

573/ I refer also for these offices to *Lexikon des Mittelalters*, I, cols 234–235 (Aides, Cour des), cols 922–923 (Argenterie du roi), and VIII, cols 975–978 (Trésor royal). The preserved receipts from the fourteenth century which were issued by Douët d'Arcq, *Comptes de l'argenterie des rois de France au XIVe siècle*, are not related to the last years of the reign of Charles V.

574/ I refer here to Rey, *Les finances royales*, pp. 137–141.

575/ It is however necessary to take into account that in France until the sixteenth century the beginning of the year was counted from White Saturday, which in 1378 fell on 17 April (on that, see Bláhová, *Historická chronologie*, pp. 336–337). Therefore, all of the documents from January and February of 1378 show the previous year.

576/ For more on that, see Cazelles, *Société politique*, p. 491.

577/ These data are presented by Cazelles, *Société politique*, p. 492. The widow of Jean Blanchet is mentioned in 1392 (Rey, *Les finances royales*, p. 196, Note 4).

578/ On the authority of the so-called *conseilleurs généraux*, see Cazelles, *Société politique*, p. 485ff.

579/ Cazelles, *Société politique*, speaks of him in more places (cf. esp. p. 542); he is relatively frequently mentioned also by Rey, *Le domaine du roi* and Rey, *Les finances royales* (see the indexes).

the state treasury. It is also significant that the official Account of the *Great Chronicles of France* draws attention to this generosity in several places. The following place, which we can read in its conclusion, is especially revealing: 'It is also appropriate to mention that it was the king that had more or less paid for and defrayed the entire expenditure which the emperor and his people had in the palaces in Paris, as was the case also with all the gifts that cost great expense; similarly, everything from the time the emperor entered the kingdom until he was outside of it, even though it was given in the name of the cities, was at the cost and expenditure of the king.' The emperor must have been informed on it in advance or he took it for granted. He also settled the expenses for himself and his entourage himself with the bishop in Cambrai, which did not escape the author of our Account either. The first mandate in order related to the expenditures connected with the visit of the Holy Roman Emperor is the order of Charles V from 12 September 1377 for the payment of 7,200 gold francs into the hand of Nicolas Martin, Master of the Chamber of the Deniers.[580] The majority of the expenses of the court went through this chamber, and it is therefore not surprising that an advance was to be acquired beforehand for the accommodation, entertainment as well as the safety of the precious guest and his entourage. Three months later, on 12 December 1377, a further advance followed, also in the amount of 7,200 francs.[581] The specification of the expenditures has not been preserved, but a part of them undoubtedly covered the expenses of the diplomatic delegations which preceded the actual visit.

The third mandate, which bore the date 27 December 1377, ordered the payment of 500 gold francs to Duke Louis II of Bourbon as a partial defrayment of the costs which he had had with the welcome of the Holy Roman Emperor in Compiègne.[582] Duke Louis, otherwise the brother of Queen Consort of France Jeanne of Bourbon, was accompanied at the ceremonial welcome on the Île-de-France on Thursday 31 December 1377 by the king's cousin Count of Eu, Miles II de Dormans, Bishop of Beauvais and his Parisian colleague Aimery de Magnac. The Account in this connection mentions more than three hundred horses, with the duke's men wearing *mi-parti* costumes, half in white and half in blue. Another ceremonial welcome, which according to a carefully prepared protocol took place the following day before Senlis, further enhancing the official character of the act itself. This time the emperor and his son were welcomed by both of the king's brothers, i.e. Duke John of Berry and Duke of Burgundy Philip the Bold. Their entourage, as we have already heard, included the king's brother-in-law Duke John VI of Harcourt, further Adhémar Robert, Archbishop of Sens, and Cardinal Pierre Aycelin, Bishop of Laon. It need not be added that the riders of the welcoming delegation wore clothes in the same colours, this time black and grey. According to the preserved accounting records, monetary compensation was given to both dukes, namely in the identical amount of 2,000 francs in gold.[583]

It is however not ruled out that the king defrayed the costs also of other relatives or bishops, or that he settled with them in another way. Especially high expenses were incurred by the king's confidants Johann of Saarbrücken, Simon de Roucy et de Braine and

580/ See Delisle (ed.), *Mandements et actes divers de Charles* V, p. 734, No. 1447. After the death of his provider Charles V the Wise, Nicolas Martin was replaced at the head of this office by Guillaume Perdrier (see Rey, *Les finances royales*, p. 57, Note 4).

581/ See Delisle (ed.), *Mandements et actes divers*, p. 771, No. 1544.

582/ See Delisle (ed.), *Mandements et actes divers*, p. 780, No. 1567. Even the receipt has been preserved whose text was partially quoted by Troubat, *La Guerre de Cent Ans et le Prince chevalier*, pp. 645–646, Note 5.

583/ The mandate of 28 December 1377 with the order to pay this amount to Duke John of Berry was published by Delachenal (ed.), *Chronique des règnes*, III, pp. 207–208, No. XXVII; for the second mandate of 31 December, see Delisle (ed.), *Mandements et actes divers*, p. 782, No. 1571. Also the receipt of Duke Philip of Burgundy has been preserved; its shelf mark is listed by Lehoux, *Jean de France*, I, p. 412, Note 6. Note 7 here lists also some expenditures of Duke John of Berry for the banquet he arranged in the emperor's honour in Meaux on 18 January. The duke then indebted himself to both his brother Philip and the merchant of Florence in Paris Bernardo di Cino.

Bureau de la Rivière, all of whom went to meet the emperor at the border twice and then on the return journey escorted him to the border city of Mouzon in the second half of January 1378. For this reason, the king ordered on 12 January 1378 that the first two mentioned be paid 20 francs a day, namely including compensation for the return journey. A conservative estimate would be about sixty days overall, which would make it 1,200 francs for each.[584] It will probably not be wrong to assume that First Gentleman of the Chamber Bureau de la Rivière received a similar compensation, namely from the sum of 6,000 gold pieces which Charles V had ordered on 15 January 1378 to transfer from the Parisian taxes for war purposes to the treasury of the receiver-general of taxes, who was, as we already know, François Chanteprime. In the first place, this high amount was intended to cover the money which the First Gentleman of the Chamber had 'loaned' some people of the emperor's retinue.[585] Not even Jean Le Mercier came off badly, having received 180 francs for both trips, the first to Cambrai and the second to Mouzon.[586] I have already hinted that we do not know all of the expenditures connected with the protective and ceremonial escort of Emperor Charles IV on his last journey to Paris;[587] even so, the documented amounts roughly reach the considerable sum of 32,262 francs in gold.[588]

A special kind of expenditure which was debited to the king's coffers were the fees for the preparation of five documents by the emperor's chancellery.[589] It is enough to add here that these documents were a quite unimpressive outcome of the political negotiations of the two foremost sovereigns of Christian Europe. The first of these Letters of Majesty with the date of 5 January 1378 solemnly declared by the authority of the emperor the legal majority of the ten-year-old heir to the French throne Charles (VI). Through the documents of the next day, Charles IV granted the dauphin two residences from the property of the Kingdom of Arles (Arelat). Finally, on 7 January, the emperor appointed the dauphin the imperial vice-regent and general vicar in the County of Vienne (the so-called Dauphiné) and entrusted him in another privilege with the same authorities in the Kingdom of Arles. On such an exceptional occasion, the chancellery most likely did not charge the usual rates[590] but relied on much more generous remunerations on the part of the dauphin's father. Whether it was so or not, Charles V did not scrimp in this regard. Besides another gift, Prothonotary Nicholas of Riesenburg received as a fee 1,000

584/ Two mandates with an identical text were published by Delisle (ed.), *Mandements et actes divers*, pp. 783–785, No. 1579–1580; A third identical mandate may be assumed for Bureau de la Rivière. We know of the first journey that after fourteen days the king called the welcoming delegation back to Paris. All three of those named were then with the emperor from around 20 December 1377 until the end of January of the following year. I have added a few days for the return journey.

585/ See Delisle (ed.), *Mandements et actes divers*, p. 786, No. 1584.

586/ See Moranvillé, *Étude sur la vie de Jean le Mercier*, pp. 60–61 and 315–316 (here the payment order from 4 February 1378 is under No. XLVIII and the receipt from 8 February under No. XLIX).

587/ A special case here are the ten francs which Charles V gave to the church in Saint-Maur-des-Fossés on the occasion of the visit of the Holy Roman Emperor. The *Mandements* further mentions 100 francs 'que nous avons baillies à notre amé et feal soubz aumosnier pour faire certaines asumosnes secrètes que nous lui avons commandé estre faictes pour nous' Delisle (ed.), *Mandements et actes divers*, pp. 788–789, No. 1589). The Account of the *Great Chronicles* says that the emperor in the Abbey of Saint-Maur 'offered one hundred francs, leaving the gifts which the abbot had given him, namely fish, cattle, sheep, wine, bread and other things, to the convent' (Delachenal /ed./, *Chronique des règnes*, pp. 265–266).

588/ Cf. the overall expenditures in the Appendix. In the total sum, I also included the 20 francs for the messenger called Hennequin Saete, who Charles V sent to his uncle before 23 February 1378. The reason is that this amount is, i.a. listed in a mandate of the mentioned date (see Delisle /ed./, *Mandements et actes divers*, p. 813, No. 1644).

589/ On that, see Excursus – The Account of the Great Chronicles of France and Associated Written Sources.

590/ Some data for the chancellery of Charles IV are presented by Lindner, 'Beiträge zur Diplomatik der Luxemburgischen Periode', p. 187ff. Further comparative data were collected by Hlaváček, *Das Urkunden- und Kanzleiwesen des böhmischen und römischen Königs Wenzel*, pp. 268–289. Considering the weight of these privileges, the overall sum does not seem exorbitant. It would however be necessary to look at the taxes of the French royal chancellery; on them, see Octave Morel, *La grande chancellerie royale et l'expédition des lettres royaux*, pp. 464–466, and more recently Tessier, *Diplomatique royale française*, p. 184ff.

francs in gold,[591] his notaries and clerks were given 50 francs each, which was a total of 450 francs. It is necessary to add 108 francs for the gold on the seal and other fees or expenses for the seals in the amount of 89 francs. For the preparation of the five privileges, the French court thus paid 1,647 francs in total.[592]

The same mandate of 18 January 1378, which ordered François Chanteprime to cover the charges for the seal, provided for the payment of the servants of Emperor Charles IV and his son Wenceslas. The three doormen (*huissiers de la chambre*) and two valets (*valets de chambre*) who served or were assigned directly to the emperor received 270 francs in total. Another 80 francs were given to the valets of King of the Romans Wenceslas IV. Finally, the three bearers of the emperor's litter received 60 francs together.[593] Precisely in the last mentioned case, doubts arise whether they were always staff from the retinue of the two Luxemburgs. According to the Account of the *Great Chronicles of France*, Charles V made the litter of his son available to his uncle immediately after discovering his movement problems at the beginning of January.[594] Charles V then gave the emperor the litter including three beautiful mules at their leave-taking in Beauté-sur-Marne on 16 January. One of the miniatures illustrating the emperor's visit to France step by step in MS fr. 2813 of the Bibliothèque Nationale in Paris (fol. 469rb) clearly shows how the litter was hitched on the gear of the two mules (Pic. 74 / V).[595] Whereas the litter had been attended to by servants of the French court until that time, in Beauté-sur-Marne they were replaced by men from the emperor's retinue.

If all of the expenditures listed so far reached the accounting amount of 34,319 francs in gold, then that is not by far the overall sum which the French Royal Chamber had to expend on the emperor's visit. Nearly the same amount was reached by the expenditures for the marvellous gifts for the emperor himself, his son, accompanying feudal lords as well as lower ranking figures of the escort. Also in this regard do the mandates issued by Charles V provide surprisingly detailed data on the prices of the valuable objects, their suppliers or directly their producers. In several cases, welcome additional information may be found in the Account of the *Great Chronicles of France*.[596] We will consider them only marginally, because we have paid attention to the collection of precious gifts from the artistic-historical perspective already before. However, it is necessary to add that not even our relatively detailed accounting can include all of the expenditures of the French Royal Chamber. As has already been mentioned above, R. Delachenal drew attention to the receipt of 6 March 1378, according to which the people of the town of Ham were paid 120 Paris pounds 'for a certain gift which they had given the emperor when he went through this town on his journey to the king'.[597] Hence it is not excluded that this chamber settled also other amounts of this type *post facto*.

Even in the gifts, a hierarchy appeared, which everyone took as a matter of course, although it was not without envy. The members of the protocol staff

591/ It is explicitly stated in the Account that the dauphin sent the First Gentleman of the Chamber 'un bel hanap d'argent tres bien doré, pesant XX mars, et dedenz avoit mil frans d'or comptez' (Delachenal /ed./, *Chronique des règnes*, II, p. 277). Since a common *hennap* looked like a shallow bowl of a diameter of 18–20 cm, it is difficult to imagine that so many gold coins would have fit in this vessel. However, it was probably a larger version on a stem.

592/ All of these data are listed specifically but without further details in the two mandates from 18 January 1378 (see Delisle /ed./, *Mandements et actes divers*, pp. 787–788, Nos. 1587 and 1588).

593/ See Delisle (ed.), *Mandements et actes divers*, p. 788, No. 1588.

594/ Delachenal (ed.), *Chronique des règnes*, II, pp. 204–205.

595/ Not even the third alternating mule, which was just resting, is missing in the depiction. The reproduction was printed by Delachenal (ed.), *Chronique des règnes*, IV: *Miniatures du manuscrit de Charles V*, p. 32 and Repr. XXXV.

596/ It is worth mentioning especially the objects that we do not encounter in the mandates, because they were gifts from the royal collections, *inter alia* two manuscripts of the Books of Hours (Heures) which Charles V gave the emperor on 11 January 1378 (Delachenal /ed./, *Chronique des règnes*, p. 264) and the arbalests that he gave Wenceslas IV (ibid., p. 265).

597/ Delachenal (ed.), *Chronique des règnes*, p. 276, Note 2.

acted as was expected from them. I will further attempt to determine the sums of costs of the objects which were given to individual people.[598] First, how else, comes Emperor Charles IV himself. One of the largest gifts, the so-called *nef*, which was one of the fashionable table utensils of silver, cannot be found in the mandates, because it was a gift of the city of Paris.[599] The gilded *nef* weighed 190 marks of silver, whereas the two large gilded and enamelled bottles or vessels that belonged to it weighed 70 marks. At the common price for jeweller-treated silver of 10 francs per mark,[600] the price of the precious metal alone without gilding would have been 2,600 francs. We already know that valuable objects were paid for by weight but that the price of jeweller-treated precious metal was roughly one and a half to two times higher per mark.[601]

To avoid enumerating several dozen valuables, I will mention only the overall sums, while some other data can be inferred from the total accounting in a separate appendix. The gifts of the highest value of 5,986 francs (hereinafter mainly only as fr) were not received by the emperor but by his son Wenceslas, which was apparently by virtue of having born in mind the future significance of the heir to the Roman and Bohemian thrones. Neither can it be forgotten that some gifts could have looked more expensive irrespective of their actual price, so the relation between the accounting value and the prestigious position of the donee was made irrelevant. It might be necessary to consider from this perspective the nominal values of the gifts for Dukes Albert and Henry VIII, which we would have expected in the opposite relation.[602] It is somewhat surprising that Duke Wenceslas was given less than some highly placed members of the emperor's retinue, although the gift in the form of a clasp cost the huge amount of 900 francs.[603] The sums for gifts intended for specific persons have been summarised in the following table:

Wenceslas IV, *King of the Romans*	5,986 fr
Charles IV, *Holy Roman Emperor*	5,528 fr
Henry VIII, *Duke of Brzeg (Brieg)*	1,653 fr and 2 sous
Albert, *Elector of Saxony and Duke of Brunswick-Lüneburg*	1,547 fr and 12 sous
Petr (Peter) of Vartemberk, *Grand Master of the Court of Bohemia*	1,058 fr and 2 sous
Thymo of Kolditz, *Master of the Imperial Chamber*	1,045 fr and 10 sous
Wenceslas, *Duke of Luxembourg and Brabant*	900 fr
Nicholas of Riesenburg, *prothonotary*	746 fr and 10 sous[604]
Wenceslas I, *Duke of Opava*	616 fr and 8 sous
John I of Leuchtenberg, *Landgrave of Saxony*	408 fr
Henry Sorbom, *Bishop of Warmia*	210 fr
Total	19,952 fr and 4 sous

The important members of the emperor's delegation known by name whom the mandates do not list explicitly further included Duke of Legnica (Liegnitz) Boleslav, Aleš (Holický) of Šternberk, Grand Marshal of the Kingdom of Bohemia Hy-

598/ The synoptic balance sheet does not include all of the gifts for the emperor, his son and the other feudal lords. Some would be difficult to quantify precisely (e.g. horses, litter and books); others were covered by Paris or the king's relatives. An example here can be the sword which Duke Philip the Bold gave King Wenceslas IV (on that, see Excursus – The Gifts for the Emperor and His Retinue).

599/ Delachenal (ed.), *Chronique des règnes*, pp. 227–228.

600/ In the mandates, the price of silver fluctuates between 12 and 14 francs per mark.

601/ For more on that, see Excursus – The Gifts for the Emperor and His Retinue.

602/ According to Professor František Kavka, who pointed this discrepancy out to me, Duke Henry VIII could have deserved this attention as a relative of the wife of Wenceslas IV Johanna of Bavaria, whose mother Margaret was the daughter of Duke of Brzeg Ludwig I. However, this conjecture is contradicted by the orders at the ceremonial entry and banquets in the Palace de la Cité.

603/ The omission of this gift was brought to my attention by Fantysová-Matějková, 'Cesta Karla IV. do Francie', p. 648, Note 74. As a result of this, also the overall expenditures below have been increased correspondingly.

604/ The price includes a gift for an unnamed knight. However, the total value of the gifts for the prothonotary was undoubtedly between 600 and 700 francs.

nek of Lipá and at Rataje, and Master of the Royal Chamber Hašek of Zvířetice. The king of France, or more precisely his entrusted confidants, provided gifts also for them in the range of roughly fifty to two hundred and twenty-five francs. For eight unnamed knights, the mandates mention fifteen gifts in the total amount of 1,394 fr and 6 den; it is thus possible that each of them was allotted two objects roughly at the same price of approximately 163 francs. At the same time, it is not excluded that the more influential, albeit also unnamed, courtiers from the emperor's entourage received gifts of a much higher value. Another group were four squires, for whom seven gifts were provided for a total sum of 379 fr, 3 sous and 3 den. Around 95 francs would have thus fallen to each on average. In fact, however, two of them received a bowl and a cup in the overall value of 315 fr and 9 sous, so proportionally less was left for the other two. Finally, the Luxemburg officials (at least seven are mentioned), three of the emperor's valets and 'officers' (with no number given) were remunerated with cups and chalices (21 pieces), jugs (10 pieces) and two so-called quarters. The gifts for this last group also had a non-negligible value of 1,081 fr, 8 sous and 6 den, but the average value of each was only 33 francs.

We have come to the conclusion of our accounting balance, which will be only in numbers as is proper:

Expenditures for accommodation, food and entourage	32,262 fr
Fees and remunerations for the Imperial Chancellery of Charles IV	1,647 fr
Cash remunerations to the servants of Charles IV	410 fr
Gifts for Charles IV	5,528 fr
Gifts for Wenceslas IV	5,966 fr
Gifts for members of the entourage listed by name	8,212 fr
Gifts for unnamed members of the entourage	2,763 fr, 6 sous and 3 den
Total	**56,788 fr, 6 sous and 3 den**

The numbers remain mere numbers if an idea cannot be formed of their informative value. A summary breakdown of the expenditures of the royal treasury of Charles V from the beginning of April 1368 to the end of June of the following year will serve for comparison. Of the total sum of 405,619 francs, 248,630 fr (61 %) went for the war with England, 70,000 fr for Duke of Burgundy's wedding, 51,339 fr for other diplomatic-alliance activities, 14,000 fr for the reconstruction of the donjon in Vincennes; the expenses connected with the birthday and baptism of Dauphin Charles were 10,000 fr, the purchases of valuables required 7,000 fr, and the rest comprised relatively small amounts for alms and for the support of court artists.[605] Only now can we assume with considerable certainty that the expenditures on the last visit of Emperor Charles IV in Paris at the turn of 1378 reached an exceptional amount even by French standards.

605/ I proceed here from the calculation published by Rey, *Les finances royales*, pp. 446–447.

Appendix

ACCOUNTING FOR THE EXPENDITURES OF THE FRENCH CROWN ON THE JOURNEY OF EMPEROR CHARLES IV IN 1377/1378

Expenditures for Accommodation, Food and Entourage

1447	advance for the expenses of the court	7,200 fr
1544	second advance for the same purposes	7,200 fr
1567	travel expenses of Duke Louis of Bourbon	500 fr
1571	travel expenses of Duke Philip the Bold of Burgundy	2,000 fr
	* travel expenses of Duke John of Berry	2,000 fr
1579	travel expenses of Count Johann of Saarbrücken	ca 1,200 fr
1580	travel expenses of Count Simon de Roucy et de Braine	ca 1,200 fr
1584	expenses of First Gentleman of the Chamber Bureau de la Rivière	6,000 fr
1644	messenger to the emperor in February 1378	20 fr
1664	expenses for wine and service (*Échansonnerie*)	3,950 fr
1665	expenses for the extended stay of the chancellor and his notaries	122 fr
1719	expenses, additional payment	640 fr
	** travel expenses of Jean Le Mercier	180 fr
Total		**32,262 fr**

Fees and Remunerations for the Imperial Chancellery of Charles IV

1587	for Prothonotary Nicholas of Riesenburg for five documents	1,000 fr
1587	remuneration for the notaries	250 fr
1587	gold for the seals	108 fr
1588	fees for the seals	89 fr
1588	remuneration for the four notaries	200 fr
Total		**1,647 fr**

Cash Remunerations to the Servants of Charles IV

1588	three porters and two valets of Emperor Charles IV	270 fr
1588	chamberlains of King Wenceslas IV	80 fr
1588	three bearers of the emperor's litter	60 fr
Total		**410 fr**

Gifts for Charles IV

1593	a chalice and a cup	2,000 fr
1595	a bowl on a tripod with a lid	ca 2,000 fr
1595	four dog collars (from the dauphin)	60 fr
1602	two reliquaries	116 fr
1604	a platter from the queen	1,200 fr
1606	two pairs of knives	32 fr
	** gift of the town of Ham	120 fr
Total		**5,528 fr**

Gifts for Wenceslas IV

1583	a gold belt decorated with precious stones	4,000 fr
1601	a cup with an ewer	700 fr
1606	one pair of knives	16 fr
1610	a gold clasp from the queen	1,250 fr
Total		**5,966 fr**

Gifts for Members of the Entourage Listed by Name

1591	a fountain, a small bowl and a cup for Elector of Saxony and Duke of Brunswick-Lüneburg Albert	874 fr and 12 sous
1605	a large gold buckle for the same duke	700 fr
1605	a clasp for Duke of Luxembourg and Brabant Wenceslas	900 fr
1591	a small fountain, a small bowl and a cup for Duke of Brzeg (Brieg) Henry	541 fr and 2 sous
1605	a fountain, a cup and a small bowl for the same duke	840 fr
1607	a cup for Duke Henry	272 fr
1607	a fountain, a small bowl and a cup for Duke of Opava Wenceslas	616 fr and 8 sous
1592	a small bowl for Grand Master of the Court of Bohemia Petr (Peter) of Vartemberk	358 fr
1609	an ewer, a cup and a small bowl for the same	700 fr and 2 sous
1592	a cup for Thymo of Kolditz	ca 272 fr
1599	a fountain, a small bowl and a cup for the same	773 fr and 10 sous
1592	a fountain, a small bowl and a cup for John of Leuchtenberg	408 fr
1596	a ring with a spinel for Bishop Henry Sorbom	100 fr
1601	a cross for the same bishop	110 fr
1591	a bowl for Prothonotary Nicholas of Riesenburg	103 fr and 14 sous
1608	a bowl, two cups, two flasks, two chalices for the same prothonotary	642 fr and 12 sous
Total		**8,212 fr**

Gifts for Unnamed Members of the Entourage

1591	a chalice and a cup for one knight	153 fr
1591	four cups for four officials	137 fr and 13 sous
1591	three cups for three of the emperor's valets	133 fr, 4 sous and 6 den
1592	a small bowl and an ewer for one knight	105 fr
1592	a cup and an ewer for one knight	73 fr, 2 sous and 6 den
1592	a cup and an ewer for one squire	22 fr, 16 sous and 3 den
1596	two small bowls and one cup for two knights	442 fr and 10 sous
1596	a cup for one squire	40 fr and 8 sous
1605	a bowl, chalice and two cups for two knights	387 fr
1605	three chalices and a jug for three officials	166 fr and 14 sous
1607	a chalice for one knight	92 fr and 8 sous
1607	a belt of one knight from Germany	50 fr and 12 sous
1608	eleven chalices, nine jugs, two quarters****	643 fr and 9 sous
1609	two bowls and two cups for two squires	315 fr and 9 sous
Total		**2,763 fr, 6 sous and 3 den**
Total		**56,788 fr, 6 sous and 3 den**

* The mandate with the order to pay this sum ed. by Delachenal, *Chronique des règnes*, III, pp. 207–208, No. XXVII.

** The mandate with the order to pay this sum ed. by Moranvillé, *Étude sur la vie de Jean le Mercier*, p. 315.

*** See Delachenal (ed.), *Chronique des règnes*, p. 276, Note 2.

**** All of these items were purchased for the officials and officers of the emperor's entourage.

LIST OF ABBREVIATIONS

BnF	Bibliothèque nationale de France, Paris
BL	The British Library, London
ÖNB	Österreichische Nationalbibliothek, Wien
MC	Musée Condé, Chantilly

Family Tree of the Valois Dynasty

(up to 1422)

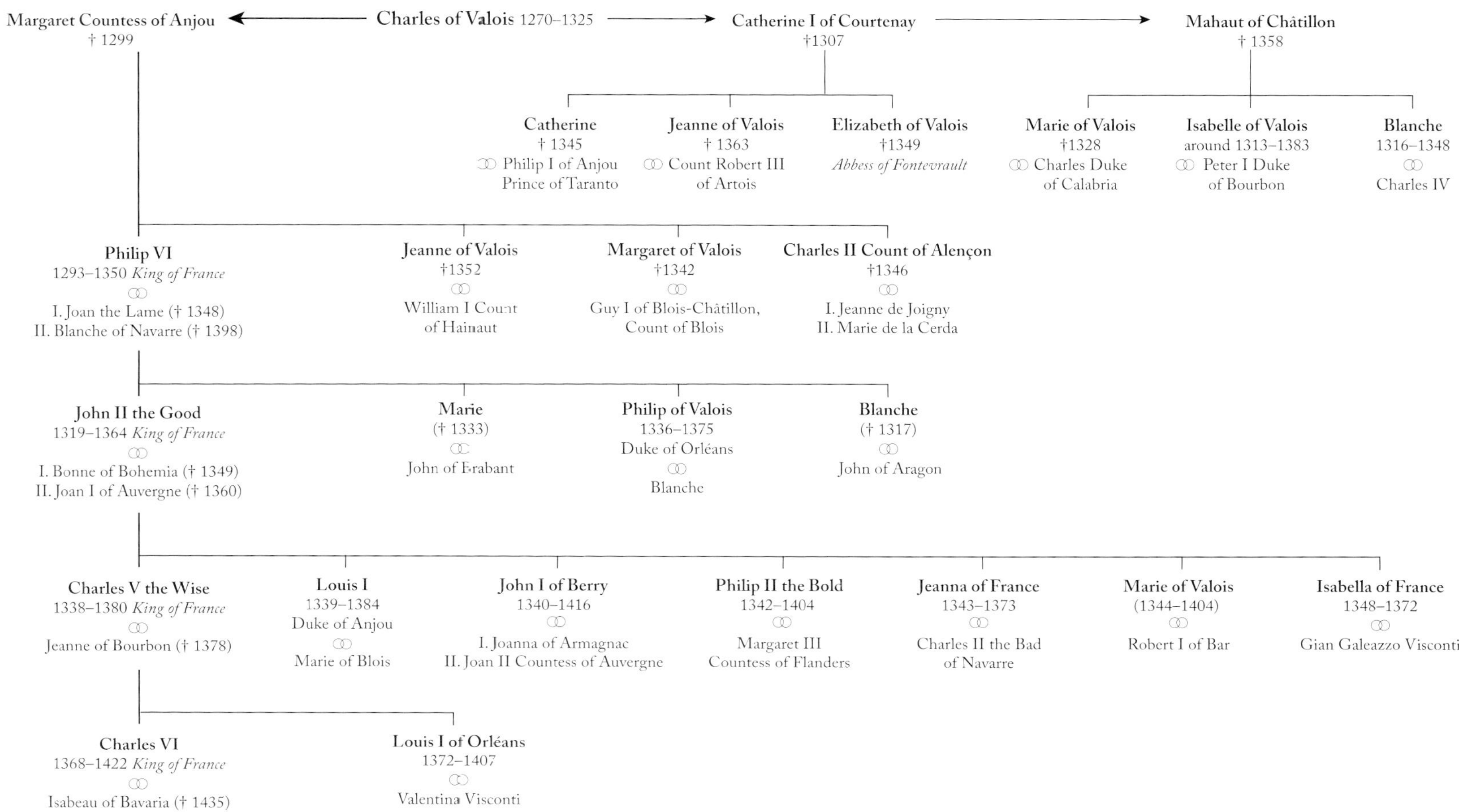

Luxemburg Dynasty

(Czech branch)

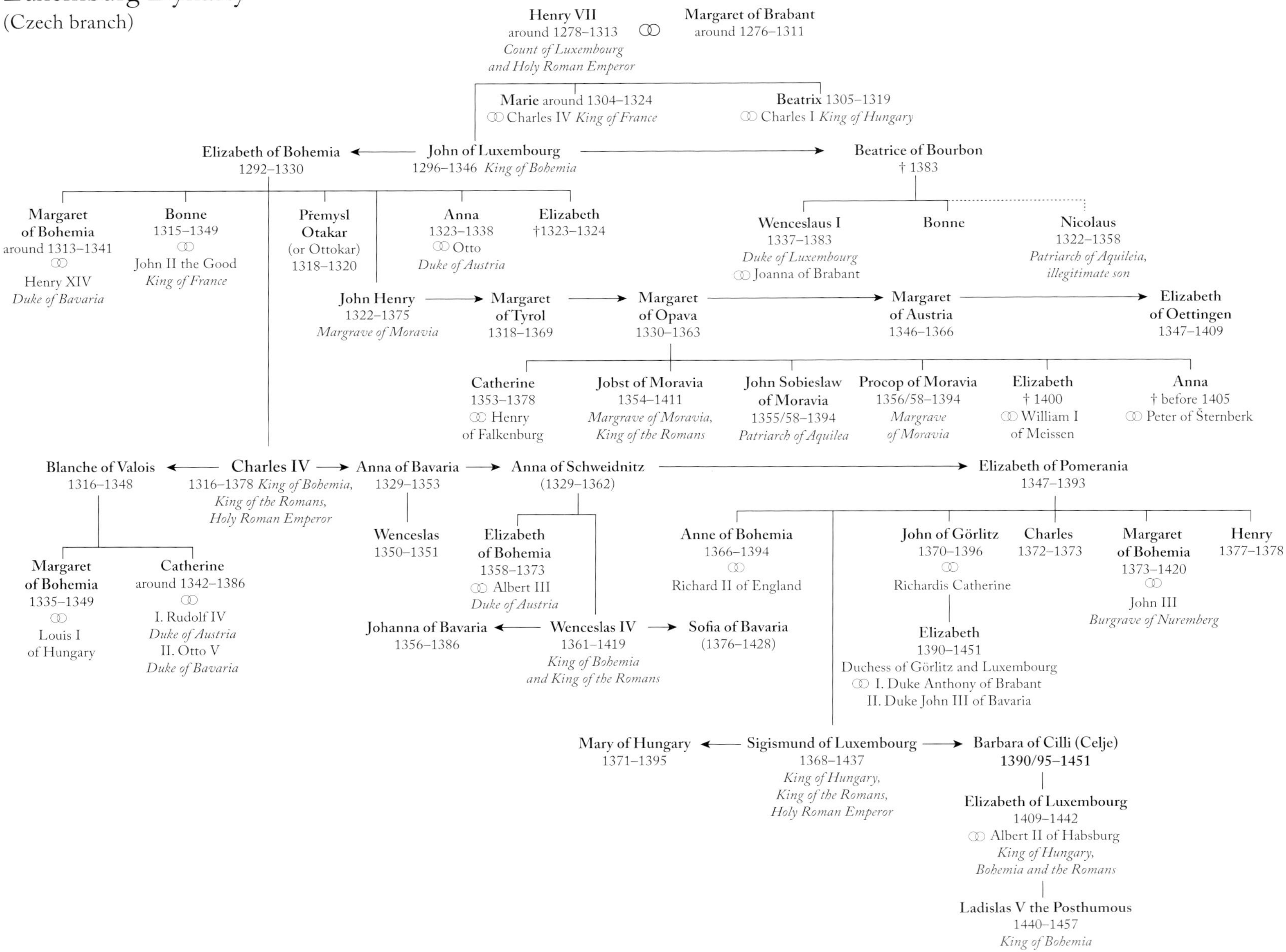

Bibliography of sources and secondary literature

ILLUMINATED AND OTHER MANUSCRIPTS

BESANCON, BIBLIOTHÈQUE MUNICIPALE
- MS 863 (*Les Grandes Chroniques de France*)

BRUXELLES, BIBLIOTHÈQUE ROYALE
- MS 11201-2 (Nicole Oresme, *Politiques et Économiques*)

CHANTILLY, MUSÉE CONDÉ
- MS 65 (*Les Très Riches Heures du duc de Berry*)
- MS 71 (*Heures d'Étienne Chevalier*)

KOBLENZ, LANDESHAUPTARCHIV
- *Codex Balduini Trevirensis*, Bestand 1C, Nr. 1

LILLE, ARCHIVES DÉPARTEMENTALES DU NORD
- sign. B 654 N° 10.688–10.689 (*Mémoire*)

LONDON, BRITISH LIBRARY
- MS Cotton Nero E II (*Les Grandes Chroniques de France*)
- MS Cotton Tiberius B VIII (*The Coronation Book of Charles V of France*)
- MS Harley 4379 (Jean Froissart, *Chroniques*)
- MS Harley 4431-1 (Christine de Pisan, *Oeuvres*)
- MS Royal 19 C (*Le Songe du Vergier*)
- MS Royal 20 C VII (*Les Grandes Chroniques de France*)
- MS Sloane 2433 (*Les Grandes Chroniques de France*)

LUCCA, ARCHIVO DI STATO
- MS 107 (Giovanni Sercambi, *Le croniche lucchesi*)

NEW YORK, THE METROPOLITAN MUSEUM OF ART
- The Cloisters Collection, Inv. Nr. 69.86 (*Psautier de Bonne de Luxembourg*)

NEW YORK, THE PIERPONT MORGAN LIBRARY
- MS 67 (*La Grande Chasse*)

PARIS, BIBLIOTHÈQUE DE L'ARSENAL
- MS 3693 (Tite-Live, *Histoire romaine*)
- MS 5075 (Renaut de Montauban)
- MS 5128 (*Les Grandes Chroniques de France*)

PARIS, BIBLIOTHÈQUE HISTORIQUE DE LA VILLE DE PARIS
- MS Res. 104 (*Vita et Officium sancti Eligii*)

PARIS, BIBLIOTHÈQUE NATIONALE DE FRANCE
- MS fr. 437 (Guillaume Durand, *Rationale divinorum officiorum*, trans. into French by Jean Golein)
- MS fr. 1584 (Guillaume de Machaut, *Oeuvres*)
- MS fr. 2292 (Saint Augustin, *La Cité de Dieu*, trad. fr. de Raoul de Presles)
- MS fr. 2646 (Jean Froissart, *Chroniques*)
- MS fr. 2662 (Jean Froissart, *Chroniques*)
- MS fr. 2813 (*Les Grandes Chroniques de France*)
- MS fr. 5729 (*Les Grandes Chroniques de France*)
- MS fr. 6465 (*Les Grandes Chroniques de France*)
- MS fr. 18437 (*Procès de Robert d'Artois*)
- MS fr. 22532 (Bartélémy l'Anglais, *Le livre des propriétés des choses*)
- MS fr. 23279 (Pierre Salmon, *Dialogues*)
- MS fr. 24287 (Jean de Salisbury, *Le Policratique*, trad. fr. de Denis Foullechat)
- MS fr. 26921 (Jean Chartier, *Chroniques*)
- MS lat. 6707 (*Le Ménagier de Paris*)
- MS lat. 7131 (*Le Viandier*)
- MS lat. 8504 (*Liber de Dimna et Kalila*)

WIEN, ÖSTERREICHISCHE NATIONALBIBLIOTHEK
- cod. 338 (*Die Goldene Bulle*)
- cod. ser. nova 2618 (*Vita Caroli*)

SECONDARY LITERATURE, EDITIONS AND CATALOGUES

AEBISCHER, Paul, 'Un manuscrit valaisan du Viandier attribué à Taillevent', *Vallesia*, 8 (1953), pp. 73–100.

ALEXANDER, Arnaud, 'Les hôtels princiers', in *Paris et Charles V. Arts et Architecture* (Paris, 2001), pp. 132–137.

AMALVI, Christian, 'L'érudition française face à la révolution d'Étienne Marcel: une histoire mythologique? (1814–1914)', *Bibliothèque de l'École des chartes*, 142 (1984), pp. 287–331.

ANNAS, Gabrielle, *Hoftag – Gemeiner Tag – Reichstag. Studien zur strukturellen Entwicklung deutscher Reichsversammlungen des späten Mittelalters (1349–1471)*, I–II (Göttingen, 2004).

ANTOINE, Elisabeth, 'Jardins de plaisance', in *Paris et Charles V. Arts et Architecture* (Paris, 2001), pp. 151–165.

ARMITAGE-SMITH, Sydney, *John of Gaunt*, 2nd ed. (New York, 1964).

ARTONNE, André, 'Le recueil des traités de la France composé par ordre de Charles V', in *Recueil de travaux offerts à M. Clovis Brunel*, I (Paris, 1955), pp. 55–63.

AUBERT, Marcel, GRODECKI, Louis, LAFOND, Jean and VERRIER, Jean, *Les vitraux de Notre-Dame et de la Sainte-Chapelle de Paris* (Paris, 1959).

AUTRAND, Françoise, 'Aux origines de la diplomatie européenne: la visite de l'Empereur Charles IV à Paris en 1378', *Bulletin de la Société des amis de l'Institut historique allemand*, I (1995), pp. 15–28.

AUTRAND, Françoise, *Charles V. Le Sage* (Paris, 1994).

AUTRAND, Françoise, *Charles VI. La folie du roi* (Paris, 1986).

AUTRAND, Françoise, *Jean de Berry. L'art et le pouvoir* (Paris, 2000).

AUTRAND, Françoise, 'La Cour des fleurs de lys', in *Paris et Charles V. Arts et Architecture* (Paris, 2001), pp. 36–39.

AUTRAND, Françoise, 'La succession à la Couronne de France et les ordonnances de 1374', in *Représentation, pouvoir et royauté à la fin du Moyen âge*, ed. Joël BLANCHARD (Paris, 1995), pp. 25–35.

AUTRAND, Françoise, 'Les livres des hommes de pouvoir: de la pratique à la culture écrite. I. Pratique diplomatique et culture politique au temps de Charles V', in *Pratiques de la culture écrite en France au XVe siècle* (Louvain-La-Neuve, 1995), pp. 193–204.

AUTRAND, Françoise, 'Mémoire et cérémonial: la visite de l'Empereur Charles IV à Paris en 1378 d'après les Grandes Chroniques de France et Christine de Pizan', in *Une femme de Lettres au Moyen Âge. Études autour de Christine de Pizan* (Orléans, 1995), pp. 91–103.

AUTRAND, Françoise, *Naissance d'un grand corps de l'État. Les gens du Parlement de Paris (1345–1454)* (Paris, 1981).

AUTRAND, Françoise, 'Un certain sens de l'État: Les conseillers de Charles V', in *Vincennes aux origines de l'État moderne* (Paris, 1996), pp. 343–353.

AVRIL, François, 'Les livres de Charles V au château de Vincennes', in *Vincennes aux origines de l'État moderne* (Paris, 1996), pp. 329–340.

AVRIL, François, GOUSSET, Marie-Thérèse and GUENÉE, Bernard (eds), *Les Grandes Chroniques de France. Reproduction intégrale en fac-similé des miniatures de Fouquet. Manuscrit français 6465 de la Bibliothèque nationale de Paris* (Paris, 1987).

AVRIL, François and REYNAUD, Nicole, *Les manuscrits à peintures en France 1440–1520* (Paris, 1993).

BABBITT, Susan M., *Oresme's 'Livre de Politiques' and the France of Charles V* (Philadelphia, 1985).

Balduin von Luxemburg, Erzbischof von Trier – Kurfürst des Reiches 1285–1354, eds. Johannes MÖTSCH and Franz-Joseph HEYEN (Mainz, 1985).

BARBER, Richard, *Edward, Prince of Wales and Aquitaine: A Biography of the Black Prince* (Woodbridge, 1978).

BARON, Françoise, 'Saint-Denis, «cimetiere aus rois» et musée de sculpture funéraire', in *Saint-Denis, la basilique et le trésor*, Dossiers d'archéologie, No. 261 (mars 2001), pp. 68–81.

BARTOŠ, F. M., *Čechy v době Husově 1378–1415*

[Bohemia at the Time of Hus, 1378–1415] (České dějiny, II-6; Praha, 1947).

Bartoš, F. M., 'Příspěvky k dějinám Václava IV., II-10. Z počátků theologické a lékařské fakulty University Karlovy' [Papers on the History of Wenceslas IV, II-10. From the Beginnings of the Faculties of Theology and Medicine of Charles University], *Věstník České akademie věd a umění*, 53 (1944), pp. 9–19.

Beaulieu, Michèle, 'Le costume, miroir des mentalités de la France médiévale (1350–1500)', in *Le vêtement. Histoire, archéologie et symbolique vestimentaires au Moyen Âge* (Cahiers du Léopard d'Or, 1; Paris, 1989), pp. 255–286.

Beaune, Colette, 'Costume et pouvoir en France à la fin du Moyen Âge: Les devises royales vers 1400', *Revue des sciences humaines*, 183 (1981), pp. 125–146.

Beaune, Colette, 'L'invention de l'histoire', in *Paris et Charles V. Arts et Architecture* (Paris, 2001), pp. 40–45.

Beaune, Colette, *Les manuscrits des rois de France au Moyen Âge. Le Miroir du Pouvoir* (Paris, 1997).

Beaune, Colette, *Naissance de la nation France* (Paris, 1985).

Begert, Alexander, *Böhmen, die böhmische Kur und das Reich vom Hochmittelalter bis zum Ende des Alten Reiches* (Historische Studien 475; Husum, 2003).

Belaubre, Jean, *Histoire numismatique et monétaire de la France médiévale (de la période carolingienne à Charles VIII)* (Paris, 1986).

Bell, Dora M., *Étude sur le Songe du vieil pèlerin de Philippe de Mézières (1327–1405), d'après le manuscrit français Bibl. nat. 22542* (Genève, 1955).

Benešovská, Klára, 'Gotická katedrála. Architektura' [The Gothic Cathedral. Architecture], in *Katedrála sv. Víta v Praze* (Praha, 1994), pp. 25–65.

Benešovská, Klára, 'Les résidences du roi Jean de Bohême: leur fonction de représentation', in *King John of Luxembourg (1296–1346) and the Art of his Era* (Prague, 1998), pp. 117–131.

Bennert, Uwe, 'Les décors des résidences', in *Paris et Charles V. Arts et Architecture* (Paris, 2001), pp. 138–150.

Bériac-Lainé, François and Given-Wilson, Chris, *Les prisonniers de la bataille de Poitiers* (Paris, 2002).

Bildwörterbuch der Kleidung und Rüstung. Vom Alten Orient bis zum ausgehenden Mittelalter, ed. Harry Kühnel (Stuttgart, 1992).

Bláhová, Marie, *Historická chronologie* [Historical Chronology] (Praha, 2001).

Bláhová, Marie, 'Pražský hrad 2. října 1373. Ceremoniál předávání braniborského markrabství českému králi v soudobých českých zprávách' [Prague Castle on 2 October 1373: The Ceremonial Handover of the Brandenburg Margraviate to the King of Bohemia in Contemporary Czech Reports], in *Verba in imaginibus*, eds Martin Nodl et al. (Praha, 2004), pp. 131–139.

Bláhová, Marie, 'Příjezd Karla IV. do Avignonu v květnu 1365 v podání soudobé historiografie' [The Arrival of Charles IV in Avignon in May 1365 as Told by Contemporary Historiography], in *Ve znamení koruny české. Sborník k 60. narozeninám prof. Lenky Bobkové*, eds Jana Konvičná and Jan Zdichynec (Praha, 2006), pp. 559–577.

Blanchard, Joël, 'Le spectacle du rite: les entrées royales', *Revue historique*, 127 (2003), pp. 475–519.

Bloch, Marc, *Les rois thaumaturges. Études sur le caractère surnaturel attribué à la puissance royale particulièrement en France et en Angleterre.* Nouvelle édition. Préface de Jacques Le Goff (Paris, 1983).

Bloch, Peter, *Aquamaniles, objets sacrés et profanes du Moyen Âge* (Milan, 1982).

Bobková, Lenka, 'Hrady Karla IV. v Laufu a Tangermünde. Panovnická reprezentace vepsaná do kamene' [The Castles of Charles IV in Lauf and Tangermünde. Sovereign Magnificence Etched into Stone], in *Verba in imaginibus*, eds Martin Nodl et al. (Praha, 2004), pp. 141–157.

Bobková, Lenka, *Velké dějiny zemí Koruny české* [The Comprehensive History of the Lands of the Bohemian Crown], IVa–b: *1310–1402*, I–II (Praha, 2003).

Böhmer, Johann Friedrich (ed.), *Regesta imperii*, VIII: *Die Regesten des Kaiserreichs unter Kaiser Karl IV. 1346–1378* (Innsbruck, 1877; reprint Hildesheim, 1968).

Bojcov, Michail A., 'Qualitäten des Raumes in zeremoniellen Situationen: Das Heilige Römische Reich, 14.–15. Jahrhundert', in *Zeremoniell und Raum*, ed. Werner Paravicini (Sigmaringen, 1997), pp. 129–153.

Borovský, Tomáš and Antonín, Robert, 'Venit rex! Panovnické vjezdy do středověkého Brna', in *Brno v minulosti a dnes*, 18 (2005), pp. 57–93.

Boureau, Alain, 'Un obstacle à la sacralité royale en Occident. Le principe hiérarchique', in *La royauté sacrée dans le monde chrétien* (Paris, 1992), pp. 29–37.

Bournon, Fernand, 'L'hôtel royal de Saint-Pol à Paris', *Mémoires de la Société de l'histoire de Paris et de l'Île de France*, 6 (1879), pp. 54–179.

Bossuat, Robert, *Manuel bibliographique de la littérature française du Moyen Âge. Troisième supplément (1960–1980)* (Paris, 1986).

Bouše, Zdeněk and Myslivec, Josef, 'Sakrální prostory na Karlštejně. Příspěvek k problematice jejich programu' [Sacral Spaces at Karlštejn. A Paper on the Issues of Their Programme], *Umění*, 19 (1971), pp. 280–295.

Brandmüller, Walter, 'Zur Frage nach der Gültigkeit der Wahl Urbans VI. Quellen und Quellenkritik', *Annuarium Historiae Conciliorum*, 6 (1974), pp. 78–120.

Brodský, Pavel, *Katalog iluminovaných rukopisů Knihovny Národního muzea v Praze* [Catalogue of the Illuminated Manuscripts of the Library of the National Museum, Prague] (Studie o rukopisech, Monographia, V, Praha, 2000).

Bryant, Lawrence M., 'The Medieval Entry Ceremony at Paris', in *Coronations. Medieval and Early Modern Monarchic Ritual*, ed. János M. Bak (Berkeley – Los Angeles – Oxford, 1990), pp. 88–118.

Burdach, Konrad, 'Zur Kenntniss altdeutscher Handschriften und zur Geschichte altdeutscher Literatur und Kunst. III. Böhmens Kanzlei unter den Luxemburgern und die deutsche Cultur', *Centralblatt für Bibliothekswesen*, 8 (1891), pp. 145–176.

Butz, Reinhardt, 'König Johann von Böhmen und die Städte in der Oberlausitz', in *Johann der Blinde, Graf von Luxemburg, König von Böhmen 1296–1346*, ed. Michel Pauly (Luxemburg, 1997), pp. 121–134.

Byrne, Donal, 'Rex imago Dei: Charles V of France and the Livre des propriétés des choses', *Journal of Medieval History*, 7, 1981, pp. 97–113.

Cadden, Joan, 'Charles V, Nicole Oresme, and Christine de Pizan: Unities and Uses of Knowledge in Fourteenth-Century France', in *Texts and Contexts in Ancient and Medieval Science* (Leiden – New York – Köln, 1997), pp. 208–244.

Carqué, Bernd, *Stil und Erinnerung. Französische Hofkunst im Jahrhundert Karls V. und im Zeitalter ihrer Deutung* (Veröffentlichungen des Max-Planck-Instituts für Geschichte, 192; Göttingen 2004).

Catalogue général des manuscrits des bibliothèques publiques de France. Départements, XXXII (Paris, 1897).

Catalogue général des manuscrits français, V: *Anciens petits fonds français*, Nos. 5526–6170 (Paris, 1902).

Cazalis, Anne-Marie, *1358. La Jacquerie de Paris. Le destin tragique du «Maire» Étienne Marcel* (Paris, 1977).

Cazelles, Raymond, *Étienne Marcel, champion de l'unité française* (Paris, 1984).

Cazelles, Raymond, 'Jean II le Bon: Quel homme? Quel roi?', *Revue historique*, 98 (1974), pp. 5–26.

Cazelles, Raymond, *La société politique et la crise de la royauté sous Philippe de Valois* (Paris, 1958).

Cazelles, Raymond, 'La stabilisation de la monnaie par la création du franc. Blocage d'une société', *Traditio*, 32 (1976), pp. 293–312.

Cazelles, Raymond, *Nouvelle histoire de Paris de la fin du règne de Philippe Auguste à la mort de Charles V, 1223–1380* (Paris, 1972).

Cazelles, Raymond, 'Peinture et actualité politique sous les premiers Valois. Jean le Bon ou Charles, dauphin', *Gazette des beaux-arts*, 92 (1978), pp. 53–65.

CAZELLES, Raymond, *Société politique, noblesse et couronne sous Jean le Bon et Charles V* (Genève – Paris, 1982).

CAZELLES, Raymond and RATHOFER, Johannes, *Das Stundenbuch des Duc de Berry. Les très riches heures* (Wiesbaden, 1996).

ČERNÁ-ŠLAPÁKOVÁ, Marie L., 'Studenti z českých zemí v Paříži' [The Students from the Czech Lands in Paris], *Strahovská knihovna*, 5–6 (1970–1971), pp. 67–88.

ČERNÝ, Pavol et al., *Du bon du coeur. Poklady francouzského středověkého umění v českých a moravských sbírkách* [Du bon du coeur. Treasures of French Mediaeval Art in Czech and Moravian Collections] (Olomouc, 2006).

ČERNÝ, Václav, *Staročeská milostná lyrika a další studie ze starší české literatury* [Old Czech Love Lyrics and Other Studies of Earlier Czech Literature] (Praha, 1999).

České umění gotické 1350–1420 [Czech Gothic Art] (Praha, 1970).

Cesta císaře Karla IV. do Francie [The Journey of Charles IV to France], translated from the contemporary French chronicle by Jakub PAVEL, foreword by Prof Josef ŠUSTA (Praha, 1937).

CHAPELOT, Jean, *Le Château de Vincennes* (Paris, 1995).

CHAPELOT, Jean, 'Le Vincennes des quatre premiers Valois: continuités et ruptures dans un grand programme architectural', in *Vincennes aux origines de l'État moderne* (Paris, 1996), pp. 53–114.

CHARBONNIER, Pierre, 'Qui furent les Tuchins?', in *Violence et contestation au Moyen Âge* (Paris, 1990), pp. 235–247.

CHARVÁTOVÁ, Kateřina, 'Petr Žitavský, opat zbraslavského kláštera (1316–1339)' [Peter of Zittau, Abbot of the Zbraslav Monastery (1316–1339)], *Sborník Společnosti přátel starožitností českých*, 2 (1991), pp. 89–107.

CHAZAN, Mireille, 'Guillaume de Nangis et la translation de l'Empire aux rois de France', in *Saint-Denis et la Royauté. Études offertes à Bernard Guenée* (Paris, 1999), pp. 463–480.

CHERRIER, Noëlle, 'Les chevaux de Philippe le Hardi (1371–1404)', *Annales de Bourgogne*, 67 (1995), pp. 107–190.

Chronicon Aulae Regiae, ed. Josef EMLER, in *Fontes rerum Bohemicarum*, IV (Praha, 1884), pp. 3–337.

Chronicon Benessii de Weitmil, ed. Josef EMLER, in *Fontes rerum Bohemicarum*, IV (Praha, 1884), pp. 457–547.

Chronicon Francisci Pragensis, ed. Jana ZACHOVÁ (Fontes rerum Bohemicarum, Series nova I; Praha, 1997).

Chronique du religieux de Saint Denys contenant le règne de Charles VI de 1380 à 1422, I–II, first published in Latin and translated by M. L. BELLAGUET 1842, introduction by Bernard GUENÉE (Paris, 1994).

CIBULKA, Josef, *Český řád korunovační a jeho původ* [The Bohemian Coronation Order and Its Origin] (Praha 1934).

CIBULKA, Josef, 'Iluminátoři Velkých kronik Francie' [Illuminators of the Great Chronicles of France] (Bibliothèque nationale in Paris, MS fr. 2813), in *Recueil d'études, dédiées à la mémoire de N. P. Kondakov* (Prague, 1926), pp. 229–238.

CIBULKA, Josef, 'Iluminované popsání cesty Karla IV. do Francie v soudobém rukopise Národní knihovny v Paříži' [An Illuminated Description of the Journey of Charles IV to France in a Contemporary Manuscript of the National Library of France], *Památky archeologické*, 35 (1926–1927), pp. 63–69.

Codex diplomaticus Moraviae, VII (Brünn, 1858).

COLLARD, Franck, 'Le banquet fatal: la table et le poison dans l'Occident médiéval', in *La sociabilité à table. Commensalité et convivialité à travers les âges* (Rouen 1992), pp. 335–342.

COLLARD, Franck, *Le crime de poison au Moyen Âge* (Paris, 2003).

CONTAMINE, Philippe, 'Essai sur la place des «XII pairs» dans l'ordo de la royauté française à la fin du Moyen Âge', in *Hiérarchies et Services au Moyen Âge* (Aix-en-Provence, 2001), pp. 53–70.

CONTAMINE, Philippe, *Guerre, État et société à la fin du Moyen Âge. Etudes sur les armées des rois de France 1337–1494* (Paris – Mouton – La Haye, 1972).

CONTAMINE, Philippe, *La Guerre de Cent ans* (Paris, 2002).

CONTAMINE, Philippe, 'La royauté française à la fin du Moyen Âge. Modèles, pratiques et circonstances', in *Europa im späten Mittelalter. Politik – Gesellschaft – Kultur*, ed. R. C. SCHWINGES, C. HESSE, P. MORAW (Historische Zeitschrift, Beihefte, NF 40; München, 2006), pp. 35–49.

CONTAMINE, Philippe, 'Politique, culture et sentiment dans l'Occident de la fin du Moyen Âge: Jean l'Aveugle et la royauté française', in *Johann der Blinde, Graf von Luxemburg, König von Böhmen 1296–1346*, ed. Michel PAULY (Luxemburg, 1997), pp. 343–361.

COOPLAND, George W. (ed.), *Philippe de Mézières, Chancellor of Cyprus, Le Songe du vieil pèlerin*, I–II (Cambridge, 1969).

COULET, Noël, 'Les entrées solennelles en Provence au XIVe siècle. Aperçus nouveaux sur les entrées royales françaises au bas Moyen Âge', *Ethnologie française*, No. 7 (1977), pp. 63–82.

Court Chapels of the High and Late Middle Ages and Their Artistic Decoration / Dvorské kaple vrcholného a pozdního středověku a jejich umělecká výzdoba, ed. Jiří FAJT (Praha, 2003).

COURTENAY, Lynn T., 'Der Black Prince: Visuelle Metaphorik unter der Regierung Richards II.', in *Herrscher, Helden, Heilige*, eds Ulrich MÜLLER and Werner WUNDERLICH (St. Gallen, 1996), pp. 245–264.

Das Goldene Rössl. Ein Meisterwerk der Pariser Hofkunst um 1400 (München, 1995).

DELACHENAL, Roland (ed.), *Les Grandes Chroniques de France. Chronique des règnes de Jean II et de Charles V*; II: *1364–1380* (Paris, 1916); III: *Continuation et appendice* (Paris, 1920); IV: *Miniatures du manuscrit de Charles V* (Paris, 1920).

DELACHENAL, Roland, *Histoire de Charles V*, I–V (Paris, 1909–1931).

DELISLE, Léopold (ed.), *Mandements et actes divers de Charles V (1364–1380) recueillis dans les collections de la Bibliothèque nationale* (Paris, 1874).

DELISLE, Léopold, 'Notes sur quelques manuscrits du Musée Britannique', *Mémoires de la Société de l'histoire de Paris et de l'Île-de-France*, 4 (1878), pp. 183–238.

DELISLE, Léopold, *Recherches sur la librairie de Charles V, roi de France, 1337–1380*, I–III (Paris, 1907; reprint Amsterdam, 1967).

DENGLER, Frank, 'Karlstein und Vincennes – zwei spätmittelalterliche Burgen als Herrschaftssymbole im Vergleich', in *Die Burg, ein kulturgeschichtliches Phänomen* (Stuttgart, 1994), pp. 75–85.

DÉPREZ, Eugène, *Hugo Aubriot, praepositus Parisiensis et urbanus praetor* (Paris, 1902).

DESCHAMPS, Eustache, *Selected Poems*, trans. by David CURZON and Jeffrey FISKIN, ed. by Ian S. LAURIE and Deborah M. SINNREICH-LEVI (New York – London, 2003).

DESPORTES, Françoise, *Le pain au Moyen Âge* (Paris, 1987)

DEVIOSSE, Jean, *Jean le Bon* (Paris, 1985).

DHÉNIN, Michel, 'Le franc et la politique monétaire', in *Paris et Charles V. Arts et Architecture* (Paris, 2001), pp. 46–47.

Die deutsche Literatur des Mittelalters. Verfasserlexikon, I (Berlin – New York, 1978); V (Berlin – New York, 1985).

Die französischen Könige des Mittelalters. Von Odo bis Karl VIII. 888–1498, ed. Joachim EHLERS, Heribert MÜLLER and Bernd SCHNEIDMÜLLER (München, 1996).

Die goldene Bulle vom 10. Januar und 25. Dezember 1356, (lateinisch und frühneuhochdeutsch), ed. Wolfgang D. FRITZ (Monumenta Germaniae Historica. Constitutiones et acta publica imperatorum et regum, Dokumente zur Geschichte des Deutschen Reiches und seiner Verfassung, 1331–1335, 11; Weimar, 1978), pp. 535–633.

Die Parler und der schöne Stil 1350–1400. Europäische Kunst unter den Luxemburgern. Ein Handbuch zur Ausstellung des Schnütgen-Museums in der Kunsthalle Köln, I–IV, ed. Anton LEGNER (Köln, 1978–1980).

DINZELBACHER, Peter, 'Der Traum Kaiser Karls IV.', in *Träume im Mittelalter. Ikonologische Studien*, ed.

Agostino Paravici-Bagliani and Giorgio Stabile (Stuttgart – Zürich, 1989), pp. 161–171.

Dion, Roger, *Histoire de la vigne et du vin en France des origines au XIXe siècle* (Paris, 1959).

Dlouhá, Markéta, 'Symbolika barev ve středověku' [The Symbolism of Colours in the Middle Ages], *Kuděj*, 3 (2001), pp. 14–38.

Dommanget, Maurice, *La Jacquerie* (Paris, 1971).

Dotzauer, Winfried, 'Die Ankunft des Herrschers. Der fürstliche „Einzug" in die Stadt (bis zum Ende des Alten Reiches', *Archiv für Kulturgeschichte*, 55 (1973), pp. 71–146 and 245–288.

Douët d'Arcq, Louis-Claude, *Comptes de l'argenterie des rois de France au XIVe siècle* (Paris, 1851).

Douët d'Arcq, Louis-Claude, *Comptes de l'Hôtel des rois de France aux XIVe et XVe siècles* (Paris, 1865).

Drda, Miloš and Krajíc, Rudolf, 'Tzv. Husův hrneček – originál, nebo dokonalý padělek?' [The So-Called Cup of Hus – the Original or a Perfect Counterfeit?], *Husitský Tábor*, Supplementum 1 (Tábor, 2000), pp. 505–601.

Du manuscrit à la table. Essais sur la cuisine au Moyen Âge et répertoire des manuscrits médiévaux contenant des recettes culinaires, ed. Carole Lambert (Montréal – Paris, 1992).

Dubrulle, Henry, *Cambrai à la fin du Moyen Âge (XIIIe–XVIe siècle)* (Lille, 1903).

Duplessy, Jean, *Les monnaies françaises royales de Hugues Capet à Louis XVI (987–1793)*, I (Paris – Maastricht, 1988).

Durand, Jannic, 'Le grand trésor gothique', in *La Sainte-Chapelle, l'art au temps de saint Louis*, Dossiers d'archéologie, No. 264 (juin 2001), pp. 80–86.

Durand, Jannic, 'Les reliques de Constantinople', in *La Sainte-Chapelle, l'art au temps de saint Louis*, Dossiers d'archéologie, No. 264 (juin 2001), pp. 60–65.

Durdík, Tomáš, *Ilustrovaná encyklopedie českých hradů* [Illustrated Encyclopaedia of Czech Castles] (Praha, 2000).

Durdík, Tomáš, 'Nový hrad u Kunratic a jeho postavení ve vývoji české hradní architektury' [The New Castle at Kunratice and Its Position in the Development of Czech Castle Architecture], *Archaeologia Pragensia*, 5 (1984), pp. 173–190.

Durdík, Tomáš and Chotěbor, Petr, 'Projevy přímého působení francouzské stavební huti v české architektuře feudálních sídel 14. stol.' [Manifestations of the Direct Impact of French Building Works in Czech Architecture of Feudal Residences of the 14th Century], *Archeologia historica*, 18 (1993), pp. 225–237.

Dürschner, Kerstin, *Der wacklige Thron. Politische Opposition im Reich von 1378 bis 1438* (Frankfurt am Main, 2003).

Dvořáková, Vlasta, 'Karlštejn a dvorské malířství doby Karla IV.' [Karlštejn and Court Painting at the Time of Charles IV], in *Dějiny českého výtvarného umění*, I-1 (Praha, 1984), pp. 311–327.

Eco, Umberto, *Art and Beauty in the Middle Ages* (New Haven, 2002).

Ehlert, Trude, *Das Kochbuch des Mittelalters. Rezepte aus alter Zeit* (Zürich – München, 1990).

Ehlert, Trude, 'Les manuscrits culinaires médiévaux témoignent-ils d'un modèle alimentaire allemand?', in *Histoire et identités alimentaires en Europe*, under the guidance of Martin Bruegel and Bruno Laurioux (Paris, 2002), pp. 121–136 and 246–254.

Encyclopedia of the Middle Ages, I–II, ed. Andre Vauchez in conjunction with Barrie Dobson and Michael Lapidge (Paris – Cambridge – Rome, 2000).

Erlande-Brandenburg, Alain, 'Les grands travaux', in *Paris et Charles V. Arts et Architecture* (Paris, 2001), pp. 68–75.

Essen und Trinken in Mittelalter und Neuzeit, eds Irmgard Bitsch et al. (Sigmaringen, 1987).

Europäische Kunst um 1400 (Wien 1962).

Fajt, Jiří, 'Magister Theodoricus, dvorní malíř císaře Karla IV.' [Master Theodoricus, Court Painter to Emperor Charles IV], in *Magister Theodoricus, dvorní malíř císaře Karla IV.*, ed. Jiří Fajt (Praha, 1997), pp. 281–340.

Fajt, Jiří and Royt, Jan, 'Umělecká výzdoba velké věže hradu Karlštejna' [The Artistic Decoration of the Great Tower of Karlštejn Castle], in *Magister Theodoricus, dvorní malíř císaře Karla IV.*, ed. Jiří Fajt (Praha, 1997), pp. 155–254.

FANTYSOVÁ-MATĚJKOVÁ, Jana, 'Cesta Karla IV. do Francie. Příspěvek ke kritice Velkých francouzských kronik' [The Journey of Charles IV to France. A Paper on the Criticism of the Great Chronicles of France], *Český časopis historický*, 106 (2008), pp. 627–650.

FANTYSOVÁ-MATĚJKOVÁ, Jana, Jak se tvoří mýtus. Froissartova líčení smrti Jana Lucemburského v bitvě u Kresčaku, in: *Ve znamení zemí Koruny české. Sborník k šedesátým narozeninám prof. PhD. Lenky Bobkové*, CSc., Praha 2006, pp. 545–558.

FANTYSOVÁ-MATĚJKOVÁ, Jana, 'Rezidence Václava českého, vévody lucemburského a brabantského, jejich funkce a úloha v rodinných a „mezinárodních" vztazích' [The Residences of Wenceslas of Bohemia, Duke of Luxembourg and Brabant, Their Function and Role in Family and 'International' Relations], in *Korunní země v dějinách českého státu*, III: *Rezidence a správní sídla v zemích České koruny ve 14.–17. století*, eds Lenka BOBKOVÁ and Jana KONVIČNÁ (Praha, 2007), pp. 527–573.

FANTYSOVÁ-MATĚJKOVÁ, Jana, *Wenceslas de Bohême, un prince au carrefour de l'Europe*, Paris 2013.

FAUCHERRE, Nicolas, 'La Bastille, citadelle avant l'heure?', in *Paris et Charles V. Arts et Architecture* (Paris, 2001), pp. 85–90.

FAUCHERRE, Nicolas, 'L'enceinte de Paris', in *Paris et Charles V. Arts et Architecture* (Paris, 2001), pp. 78–84.

FAURE, Claude, 'Histoire de la réunion de Vienne à la France (1328–1454)', *Bulletin de l'Académie Delphinale*, Ser. IV, XIX (1905), pp. 327–501.

FAVIER, Jean, 'Conjoncture politique et chantiers de construction dans le Paris de Jean II et de Charles V', in *Vincennes aux origines de l'État moderne* (Paris, 1996), pp. 289–295.

FAVIER, Jean, *La Guerre de Cent Ans* (Paris, 1980, reprint 2001).

FAVREAU, Robert, 'Jean de Berry et la ville de Poitiers', in *Fürstliche Residenzen im spätmittelalterlichen Europa*, eds Hans PATZE and Werner PARAVICINI (Vorträge und Forschungen, 36; Sigmaringen, 1991), pp. 103–135.

FÉLIBIEN, Dom Michel, *Histoire de l'Abbaye Royale de Saint-Denys en France* (Paris, 1706).

Fêtes gourmandes au Moyen Âge, texts by Jean-Louis FLANDRIN and Carole LAMBERT, 2nd ed. (Paris, 1998).

FINK, Karl August, 'Das große Schisma bis zum Konzil von Pisa', in *Handbuch der Kirchengeschichte*, ed. Hubert JEDIN, III-2 (Freiburg – Basel – Wien, 1968), pp. 490–516.

FIŠER, František, *Karlštejn. Vzájemné vztahy tří karlštejnských kaplí* [The Mutual Relations of the Three Chapels at Karlštejn] (Kostelní Vydří, 1996).

FLANDRIN, Jean-Louis, 'Brouets, potages et bouillons', in *Médiévales*, No. 5 (Novembre 1983), pp. 5–14.

FLANDRIN, Jean-Louis, 'Les heures des repas en France avant le XIXe siècle', in *Le temps de manger. Alimentation, emploi du temps et rythmes sociaux* (Paris, 1993), pp. 197–226.

FLEURY, Michel and KRUTA, Venceslas, *Le Château du Louvre* (Paris, 2000).

FOURQUIN, Guy, *Les soulèvements populaires au Moyen Âge* (Paris, 1972).

FRANKE, Birgit, 'Pracht und Zeremoniell. Burgundische Tafelkunst in franko-flämischen Bildteppichen des 15. Jahrhunderts', in *Die öffentliche Tafel. Tafelzeremoniell in Europa 1300–1900*, eds Hans OTTOMEYER and Michaela VÖLKEL (Wolfratshausen, 2003), pp. 38–47.

FRINTA, Mojmír, 'Le portrait du Louvre de Jean le Bon', *Umění*, 52 (2004), pp. 402–413.

FRITZ, Johann Michael, *Goldschmiedekunst der Gotik in Mitteleuropa* (München, 1982).

FRITZ, Wolfgang, D. (ed.), *Dokumente zur Geschichte des Deutschen Reiches und seiner Verfassung 1354–1356. Texte* (MGH – Constitutiones et acta publica 11; Hannover, 1997).

FROISSART, Jean, *Chroniques (1307–1400)*, I–IV, ed. Kervyn de LETTENHOVE (Bruxelles, 1867–1876).

GABORIT, Jean-René, 'Les statues de Charles V et de Jeanne de Bourbon du Louvre. Une nouvelle hypothèse', *Revue de Louvre*, 31 (1981), pp. 237–245.

GABORIT-CHOPIN, Danielle (ed.), *L'inventaire du trésor du dauphin futur Charles V, 1363. Les débuts d'un grand collectionneur* (Nogent-le-Roi, 1996).

GABORIT-CHOPIN, Danielle, 'Les arts précieux à Paris (ivoires et orfèvrerie) au temps de Jean de Luxembourg', in *King John of Luxembourg (1296–1346) and the Art of his Era* (Praha, 1998), pp. 53–61.

GATZ, Erwin (ed.), *Die Bischöfe des Heiligen Römischen Reiches 1198 bis 1448. Ein biographisches Lexikon* (Berlin, 2001).

GAUME, Luce and PÉNICAUT, Emmanuel, *Le château de Vincennes – Une histoire militaire*, (Paris, 2008).

GAY, Victor, *Glossaire archéologique du Moyen Âge et de la Renaissance*, I: *A–Guy* (Paris, 1883; reprint Paris 1929, 1967).

GILLARD, Lucien, 'Nicole Oresme, économiste', *Revue historique*, 279 (1988), pp. 3–39.

GODEFROY, Théodore, *Entrevues de Charles IV, empereur, de son fils Wenceslaus, roy des Romains, et de Charles V, roy de France, à Paris, l'an 1378* (Paris, 1614).

GOLDAST (VON HEIMENSFELD), Melchior, *Monarchia S. Romani Imperii: sive Tractatus de iurisdictione imperiali*, I–III, 3rd ed. (Francofurti – Lipsiae 1730, II).

GOROCHOV, Nathalie, *Le Collège de Navarre de sa fondation (1305) au début du XVe siècle (1418)* (Paris, 1997).

GRAUS, František, 'Das Scheitern von Königen: Karl VI., Richard II., Wenzel IV.', in *Das spätmittelalterliche Königtum im europäischen Vergleich*, ed. Reinhard SCHNEIDER (Vorträge und Forschungen, 32; Stuttgart, 1987), pp. 17–39.

GRAUS, František, *Pest – Geissler – Judenmorde. Das 14. Jahrhundert als Krisenzeit* (Göttingen, 1988).

GRIERSON, Philip, *The Coins of Medieval Europe* (London, 1991).

GUENÉE, Bernard, 'Histoire d'un succès', in AVRIL, François, GOUSSET, Marie-Thérèse and GUENÉE, Bernard (eds), *Les Grandes Chroniques de France. Reproduction intégrale en fac-similé des miniatures de Fouquet. Manuscrit français 6465 de la Bibliothèque nationale de Paris* (Paris, 1987), pp. 121–129.

GUENÉE, Bernard, 'Les Grandes Chroniques de France. Le roman aux roys (1274–1518)', in *Les lieux de mémoire*, II-1: La Nation (Paris, 1986), pp. 189–214.

GUENÉE, Bernard, *L'opinion publique à la fin du Moyen Âge d'après la «Chronique de Charles VI» du Religieux de Saint-Denis* (Paris, 2002).

GUENÉE, Bernard, *Un meurtre, une société. L'assassinat du duc d'Orléans, 23 Novembre 1407* (Paris, 1992).

GUENÉE, Bernard and LEHOUX, Françoise, *Les entrées royales françaises de 1328 à 1515* (Paris, 1968).

GUÉROUT, Jean, 'Le Palais de la Cité à Paris des origines à 1417. Essai topographique et archéologique', in *Fédération des Sociétés historiques et archéologiques de Paris et de l'Île-de-France: Mémoires*, I (1949), pp. 58–212; II (1950), pp. 21–204, and III (1951), pp. 7–101; reprint in one volume with identical numbering (Paris, 1953).

GUÉROUT, Jean, 'L'hôtel du roi au Palais de la Cité à Paris sous Jean II et Charles V', in *Vincennes aux origines de l'État moderne* (Paris, 1996), pp. 219–288.

GUÉRY, Alain, 'Le roi dépensier: le don, la contrainte et l'origine du système financier de la monarchie française d'Ancien Régime', *Annales: Économies, sociétés, civilisations*, 39 (1984), pp. 1241–1269.

Guide de la Musique du Moyen Âge, ed. Françoise FERRAND (Paris, 1999).

GUILLEMAIN, Bernard, *La cour pontificale d'Avignon (1309–1376). Études d'une société* (Paris, 1962).

HÁJEK Z LIBOČAN, Václav, *Kronika česká* [Chronicle of Bohemia] (Praha, 1541; mechanical reprint from 1819–1823), p. 349.

HAMBURGER, Jeffrey, 'The Casanatense and the Carmelite Missals: Continental Sources for English Manuscript Illumination of the Early 15th Century', in *Masters and Miniatures. Proceedings of the Congress on Medieval Manuscript Illumination in the Northern Netherlands*, eds Koert VAN DER HORST and Johann-Christian KLAMT (Doornspijk, 1991), pp. 161–171.

Hannig, Jürgen, 'Ars donandi. Zur Ökonomie des Schenkens im früheren Mittelalter', in Richard van Dülmen (ed.), *Armut, Liebe, Ehre. Studien zur historischen Kulturforschung* (Frankfurt, 1988), pp. 11–37.

Handbuch der Kirchengeschichte III. Die mittelalterliche Kirche. 2. Vom kirchlichen Hochmittelalter bis zum Vorabend der Reformation (Freiburg – Basel – Wien, 1968).

Hanuš, Josef, *František Martin Pelcel, český historik a buditel* [Franz Martin Pelzel, Bohemian historian and Revivalist] (Praha, 1914).

Hasse, Max, 'Neues Hausgerät, neue Häuser, neue Kleider – eine Betrachtung der städtischen Kultur im 13. und 14. Jahrhundert sowie ein Katalog der metallenen Hausgeräte', *Zeitschrift für Archäologie des Mittelalters*, 7 (1979), pp. 7–83.

Haverkamp, Alfred, '„… an die große Glocke hängen". Über Öffentlichkeit im Mittelalter', *Jahrbuch des Historischen Kollegs 1995* (München, 1996), pp. 71–112.

Heckmann, Marie-Luise, 'Das Reichsvikariat des Dauphins im Arelat 1378. Vier Diplome zur Westpolitik Kaiser Karls IV.', in *Manipulus Florum. Festschrift für Peter Johanek zum 60. Geburtstag*, eds Ellen Widder, Mark Mersiowsky and Maria-Theresia Leuker (Münster, 2000), pp. 63–97.

Heckmann, Marie-Luise, *Stellvertreter, Mit- und Ersatzherrscher. Regenten, Generalstatthalter, Kurfürsten und Reichsvikare in Regnum und Imperium vom 13. bis zum frühen 15. Jahrhundert*, I–II (Studia Luxemburgensia, 9–10; Warendorf, 2002).

Hedeman, Anne D., 'Les perceptions de l'image royale à travers les miniatures: l'exemple des Grandes Chroniques de France', in *Pratiques de la culture écrite en France au XVe siècle* (Louvain-La-Neuve, 1995), pp. 539–549.

Hedeman, Anne D., *The Royal Image: Illustrations of the Grandes Chroniques de France, 1274–1422* (Berkeley – Los Angeles – Oxford, 1991).

Heimpel, Hermann, 'Königlicher Weihnachtsdienst im späteren Mittelalter', *Deutsches Archiv für Erforschung des Mittelalters*, 39 (1983), pp. 131–206.

Heinig, Paul-Joachim, *Reichsstädte, Freie Städte und Königtum 1389–1450: Ein Beitrag zur deutschen Verfassungsgeschichte* (Beiträge zur Sozial- und Verfassungsgeschichte des Alten Reiches, 3, Wiesbaden, 1983).

Héliot, Pierre and Mencl, Václav, 'Mathieu d'Arras et les sources méridionales et nordiques de son oeuvre à la cathédrale de Prague', *Cahiers de Fanjeaux*, 9 (1974), pp. 103–27.

Henwood, Philippe, 'Raymond du Temple, maître d'oeuvre des rois Charles V et Charles VI', *Bulletin de la société d'histoire de Paris et de l'Île de France*, 105 (1979), pp. 55–75.

Henwood, Philippe, 'Vincennes, écrin de pierre de l'orfèvrerie royale: les joyaux et la vaisselle du roi sous le règne de Charles VI (1389–1422)', in *Vincennes aux origines de l'État moderne* (Paris, 1996), pp. 321–327.

Hergemöller, Bernd-Ulrich, *Cogor adversum te. Drei Studien zum literarisch-theologischen Profil Karls. IV. und seiner Kanzlei* (Warendorf, 1999).

Hergemöller, Bernd-Ulrich, 'Der Abschluß der „Goldenen Bulle" zu Metz 1356/57', in *Festschrift Heinz Stoob zum 70. Geburtstag* (Studia Luxemburgensia, 3; Warendorf 1989), pp. 123–232.

Hergemöller, Bernd-Ulrich, 'Die „solempnis curia" als Element der Herrschaftsausübung in der Spätphase Karls IV. (1360 bis 1376)', in *Deutscher Königshof, Hoftag und Reichstag im späteren Mittelalter*, ed. Peter Moraw (Vorträge und Forschungen, 48; Stuttgart, 2002), pp. 451–476.

Hergemöller, Bernd-Ulrich, *Fürsten, Herren und Städte zu Nürnberg 1355/56. Die Entstehung der „Goldenen Bulle" Karls IV.*, (Köln – Wien, 1983).

Hergemöller, Bernd-Ulrich (ed.), *Maiestas Carolina. Der Kodifikationsentwurf Karls IV. für das Königreich Böhmen von 1355* (München, 1995).

Hieatt, Constance B. and Sharon Butler, *Pain, vin et veneison. Un livre de cuisine médiévale* (Montréal, 1977).

Hilger, Hans Peter, 'André Beauneveu, Bildhauer und Maler', in *Die Parler und der schöne Stil*, I (Köln 1978), pp. 43–49.

Hirschbiegel, Jan, *Étrennes. Untersuchungen zum höfischen Geschenkverkehr im spätmittelalterlichen Frankreich der Zeit König Karls VI. (1380–1422)* (München, 2003).

Hlaváček, Ivan, *Das Urkunden- und Kanzleiwesen des böhmischen und römischen Königs Wenzel (IV.), 1376–1419. Ein Beitrag zur spätmittelalterlichen Diplomatik* (Stuttgart, 1970).

Hlaváček, Ivan, 'Johann der Blinde, König von Böhmen und Graf von Luxemburg', in *Balduin von Luxemburg, Erzbischof von Trier – Kurfürst des Reiches 1285–1354*, ed. Franz-Josef Heyen (Mainz, 1985), pp. 151–173.

Hlaváček, Ivan, 'K diplomatice úmluv Václava IV. s Karlem V. z r. 1380' [On the The Diplomacy of the Agreements beween Wenceslas IV and Charles V in 1380], *Zápisky katedry čs. dějin a archivního studia*, 3 (1958), No. 3–4, pp. 55–61.

Hlaváček, Ivan, 'Politische Integration der Böhmischen Krone unter den Luxemburgern', in *Fragen der politischen Integration im mittelalterlichen Europa* (Ostfildern, 2005), pp. 325–374.

Hlaváček, Ivan, 'Überlegungen zum Geschenkwesen im Mittelalter', *Mitteilungen der Residenzen-Kommission der Akademie der Wissenschaften zu Göttingen*, 2/2 (1992), pp. 12–15.

Hlaváček, Ivan, 'Ústřední moc a správa v českém státě za Lucemburků, zejména za Karla IV. a Václava IV., a její fungování' [Central Power and Administration in the Bohemian State under the Luxemburgs, Especially Charles IV and Wenceslas IV, and How It Functioned], in *Jenštejn 1977* (Brandýs nad Labem and Stará Boleslav, 1977), pp. 37–56.

Hlaváček, Ivan, 'Verwaltungsgeschichtliche Bemerkungen zum Itinerar Johanns von Luxemburg', in *Johann der Blinde, Graf von Luxemburg, König von Böhmen 1296–1346*, ed. Michel Pauly (Luxemburg, 1997), pp. 121–134.

Hledíková, Zdeňka, *Arnošt z Pardubic. Arcibiskup, zakladatel, rádce* [Ernest of Pardubice. Archbishop, Founder, Counsellor] (Praha, 2008).

Hledíková, Zdeňka, *Biskup Jan IV. z Dražic (1301–1343)* (Praha, 1991).

Hledíková, Zdeňka, 'Češi u římské kurie za prvních tří avignonských papežů' [Czechs at the Roman Curia under the First Three Avignon Popes], *Český časopis historický*, 102 (2004), pp. 249–272.

Hledíková, Zdeňka, 'Fundace českých králů ve 14. století' [Foundations by Kings of Bohemia in the 14th Century], *Sborník historický*, 28 (1981), pp. 5–55.

Hledíková, Zdeňka, 'Z domácnosti Friedricha z Pernštejna' [On the Household of Friedrich of Pernštejn], in *Pocta Janu Janákovi*, ed. Bronislav Chocholáč and Jiří Malíř (Brno, 2002), pp. 391–403.

Hlobil, Ivo, 'Gotické sochařství' [Gothic Sculpture], in *Katedrála sv. Víta v Praze* (Praha, 1994), pp. 66–95.

Hoensch, Jörg K., *Die Luxemburger* (Stuttgart, 2000).

Hohenberger, Nicole, 'Carolus 4 kompt binnen Dortmunde. Der Besuch Kaiser Karls IV. am 22. November 1377 in Dortmund', in *Himmel, Hölle, Fegefeuer. Jenseitsvorstellungen und Sozialgeschichte im spätmittelalterlichen Dortmund* (Dortmund, 1996), pp. 44–51.

Holzfurtner, Ludwig, 'Schenker und Schenkergruppen. Sozialgeschichtliche Studien an Hand hochmittelalterlicher bayerischer Traditionsbücher', *Zeitschrift für bayerische Landesgeschichte*, 54 (1991), pp. 299–324.

Homo-Lechner, Catherine, 'De l'usage de la cornemuse dans les banquets: quelques exemples du XIVe au XVIe siècle', in *Fêtes gourmandes*, pp. 111–119.

Homo-Lechner, Catherine, 'La cornemuse, un instrument «de bouche»', in *Fêtes gourmandes*, p. 109.

Homolka, Jaromír, 'Královská kaple Všech svatých na Pražském hradě' [The Royal Chapel of All Saints at Prague Castle], in *Pro arte. Sborník k poctě Ivo Hlobila*, ed. Dalibor Prix (Praha, 2002), pp. 141–146.

Homolka, Jaromír, 'Poznámky ke karlštejnským malbám' [Notes on Karlštejn Painting], *Umění*, 45 (1997), pp. 122–140.

HOMOLKA, Jaromír, 'Ráno a večer. Počátek korunovačního ceremoniálu podle řádu Karla IV.' [Morning and Evening. The Beginning of the Coronation Ceremony according to the Order of Charles IV], in *Verba in imaginibus*, eds Martin NODL et al. (Praha, 2004), pp. 169–188.

HROCH, Miroslav and HROCHOVÁ, Věra, 'Karel IV. a otázka obrany Balkánu proti Osmanům v polovině 14. století' [Charles IV and the Question of the Defence of the Balkans against the Ottomans in the Middle of the 14th Century], in *Karolus Quartus*, ed. Václav VANĚČEK (Praha, 1984), pp. 205–214.

HRUBANT, Jaroslav, 'Pařížské rukopisy o cestě Karla IV. do Francie a Paříže (1377–78)' [The Parisian Manuscripts on the Journey of Charles IV to France and Paris (1377–78)], *Časopis Musea Království českého*, 87 (1913), pp. 362–365.

HUIZINGA, Johan, *The Waning of the Middle Ages: A Study of the Forms of Life, Thought, and Art in France and the Netherlands in the XIVth and XVth centuries* (New York, 1989).

HÜTTEBRÄUKER, Lotte, 'Cambrai, Deutschland und Frankreich 1308–1378. Untersuchungen zum Kampf um die deutsche Westgrenze', *Zeitschrift der Savigny-Stiftung für Rechtsgeschichte: Germanistische Abteilung*, 59 (1939), pp. 88–135.

JACKSON, Richard A., *Ordines Coronationis Franciae: Texts and Ordines for the Coronation of Frankish and French Kings and Queens in the Middle Ages*, I–II (Philadelphia, 1995–2000).

JARRY, Eugène, *La vie politique de Louis de France, duc d'Orléans 1372–1407* (Paris, 1976).

Jean Fouquet. Peintre et enlumineur du XVe siècle, under the guidance of François AVRIL (Paris, 2003).

JENNI, Ulrike and THEISEN, Maria, *Mitteleuropäische Schulen*, III: *(ca 1350–1400) Böhmen – Mähren – Schlesien – Ungarn*, in cooperation with Karel STEJSKAL. Textband + Tafel- und Registerband (Die illuminierten Handschriften und Inkunabeln der Österreichischen Nationalbibliothek, 12; Wien, 2004).

JOHNSON, Charles (ed.), *The 'De moneta' of Nicholas Oresme and English Mint Documents* (London, 1956).

JOMARON, Jacqueline de, *Le théâtre en France*, 1: *Du Moyen Âge à 1789* (Paris, 1988).

JOUBERT, Fabienne, 'Les arts de la couleur', in *Paris et Charles V. Arts et Architecture* (Paris, 2001), pp. 168–185.

KADLEC, Jaroslav, *Leben und Schriften des Prager Magisters Adalbert Rankonis de Ericinio* (Münster, 1971).

Kaiser Karl IV. Staatsmann und Mäzen, ed. Ferdinand SEIBT (München, 1978).

KALISTA, Zdeněk, *Karel IV. Jeho duchovní tvář* [Charles IV. His Spiritual Face] (Praha, 1971).

KANTOROWICZ, Ernst H., *The King's Two Bodies. A Study in Mediaeval Political Theology* (Princeton, 1997).

Karoli IV Imperatoris Romanorum Vita Ab Eo Ipso Conscripta et Hystoria Nova De sancto Wenceslas Martyre, trans. by Paul W. KNOLL and Frank SCHAER, ed. by Balász NAGY and Frank SCHAER with an Introduction by Ferdinand SEIBT (Budapest, 2001).

KAVKA, František, *5. 4. 1355. Korunovace Karla IV. císařem Svaté říše římské* [5 April 1355: The Coronation of Charles IV as Holy Roman Emperor] (Praha, 2002).

KAVKA, František, *Am Hofe Karls IV.* (Leipzig, 1989).

KAVKA, František, *Čtyři ženy Karla IV. Královské sňatky* [The Four Wives of Charles IV: Royal Marriages] (Praha – Litomyšl, 2002).

KAVKA, František, 'Karel IV. a anjouovsko-piastovské dědictví' [Charles IV and the Angevin-Piast Heritage], *Sborník historický*, 36 (1989), pp. 5–63.

KAVKA, František, *Vláda Karla IV. za jeho císařství* [The Reign of Charles IV When He Was an Emperor], I–II: (1355–1378) (Praha, 1993).

KAVKA, František, 'Zum Plan der luxemburgischen Thronfolge in Polen (1368–1382). Strittige Forschungsfragen', *Zeitschrift für historische Forschung*, 13 (1986), pp. 257–283.

KEIL, Gundolf, 'Liber de cura equorum', in *Die deut-*

sche Literatur des Mittelalters. Verfasserlexikon, 5, cols 752–756.

Kejř, Jiří, 'Die sogenannte Maiestas Carolina. Forschungsergebnisse und Streitfragen', in *Festschrift Heinz Stoob zum 70. Geburtstag* (Studia luxemburgensia, 3, Warendorf, 1989), pp. 79–122.

Kennedy, Angus J., *Christine de Pizan. A Bibliographical Guide: Supplement 2* (Camden House, 2003).

Kerhervé, Jean, *L'État breton aux XIVe et XVe siècles. Les ducs, l'argent et les hommes*, I–II (Paris, 1987).

Kintzinger, Martin, 'Der weiße Reiter. Formen internationaler Politik im Spätmittelalter', *Frühmittelalterliche Studien*, 37 (2003), pp. 315–353.

Kintzinger Martin, Inszenierungen der Kaiserherrschaft bei Karl V. Überlegungen zum Verhältnis von imperialer Tradition und universalen Herausforderungen, *Francia* 38, 2011, s. 207–227

Kintzinger, Martin, 'Politische Westbeziehungen des Reiches im Spätmittelalter. Westliche Kultur und Westpolitik unter den Luxemburgern', in *Deutschland und der Westen Europas im Mittelalter*, ed. Joachim Ehlers (Vorträge und Forschungen, 56; Stuttgart 2002)

Kintzinger, Martin, 'Zeremoniell und politische Repräsentation bei dem berühmten Treffen zwischen Karl IV. und Karl VI. von Frankreich', in *Die Goldene Bulle. Politik – Wahrnehmung – Rezeption*, I, eds Ulrike Hohensee et al. (Berlin, 2009), pp. 299–326.

Klapper, Joseph, *Johann von Neumarkt, Bischof und Hofkanzler. Religiöse Frührenaissance in Böhmen zur Zeit Kaiser Karls IV.* (Leipzig, 1984).

Klare, Wilhelm, *Die Wahl Wenzels von Luxemburg zum römischen König 1376* (Münster, 1990).

Kolb, Herbert, 'Namen und Bezeichnungen der Pferde in der mittelalterlichen Literatur', *Beiträge zur Namenforschung*, 9 (1974), pp. 151–166.

Kováč, Peter, 'Poznámky k popisu pařížské Sainte-Chapelle z roku 1378' [Notes on the Description of Sainte-Chapelle in Paris from 1378], in *Court Chapels / Dvorské kaple* (Praha, 2003), pp. 413–418.

Krása, Josef, 'Dvě kresby z Louvru a česká knižní malba kolem roku 1400' [Two Drawings from the Louvre and Bohemian Illumination around 1400], in Idem, *České iluminované rukopisy 13./16. století* (Praha, 1990), pp. 253–267.

Krása, Josef, *Rukopisy Václava IV.* [The Manuscripts of Wenceslas IV] (Praha, 1971).

Krása, Josef, *The Travels of Sir John Mandeville: A Manuscript in the British Library*, trans. Peter Kussi (New York, 1983).

Krieger, Karl-Friedrich, *König, Reich und Reichsreform im Spätmittelalter* (Enzyklopädie der deutschen Geschichte, 14, München, 1992).

Krieger, Michaela, 'Der Psalter der Bonne de Luxembourg', in *King John of Luxembourg (1296–1346) and the Art of his Era* (Praha, 1998), pp. 69–81.

Krynen, Jacques, 'Aristotélisme et réforme de l'État, en France, au XIVe siècle', in *Das Publikum politischer Theorie im 14. Jahrhundert*, ed. Jürgen Miethke (München, 1992), pp. 225–236.

Krynen, Jacques, *L'empire du roi. Idées et croyances politiques en France XIIIe–XVe siècle* (Paris, 1993).

Krynen, Jacques, '"Rex Christianissimus". A medieval theme at the roots of French absolutism', *History and Anthropology*, 4 (1989), pp. 79–96.

Kubínová, Kateřina, 'Římská korunovace Karla IV.' [The Roman Coronation of Charles IV], in *Lesk královského majestátu ve středověku*, eds Lenka Bobková and Mlada Holá (Praha – Litomyšl, 2005), pp. 47–60.

Kühnel, Harry, 'Kleidung und Gesellschaft im Mittelalter', in *Bildwörterbuch der Kleidung und Rüstung* (Stuttgart, 1992), pp. XXVI–LXIX.

Kuthan, Jiří, 'Pařížská Sainte-Chapelle a trny z koruny Kristovy' [Sainte-Chapelle in Paris and the Thorns from the Crown of Thorns], in Idem, *Splendor et Gloria Regni Bohemiae* (Praha, 2008), pp. 387–426.

Kybalová, Ludmila, *Dějiny odívání. Středověk* [History of Clothing. The Middle Ages] (Praha, 2001).

L'art au temps des rois maudits. Philippe le Bel et ses fils 1285–1328 (Paris, 1998).

L'aube de la Renaissance: pour le dixième anniversaire de la disparition de Franco Simone, eds Dario CECCHETTI et al. (Genève, 1991).

L'humanisme français au début de la Renaissance, Colloque international de Tours (XIVe stage) (Paris, 1973).

La France et les arts en 1400. Les Princes des fleurs de lis (Paris, 2004).

La Librairie de Charles V. Catalogue de l'exposition de la Bibliothèque nationale (Paris, 1968).

LA SELLE, Xavier de, *Le service des âmes à la cour. Confesseurs et aumôniers des rois de France du XIIIe au XVe siècle* (Paris, 1995).

LABARTE, Jules (ed.), *Inventaire du mobilier de Charles V, roi de France* (Paris, 1879).

LABORDE, Léon de, *Glossaire français du Moyen Âge, à l'usage de l'archéologue et de l'amateur des arts. Précédé de l'Inventaire des bijoux de Louis, duc d'Anjou, dressé vers 1360* (Paris, 1872; reprint Genève, 1975).

LACASSAGNE, Miren, 'Actualité de Guillaume de Machaut', *Le Moyen Âge*, 109 (2003), pp. 129–138.

LAFFITTE, Marie-Pierre, 'Les manuscrits du trésor: La Sainte-Chapelle au Moyen Âge', in *La Sainte-Chapelle, l'art au temps de saint Louis*, Dossiers d'archéologie, No. 264 (juin 2001), pp. 52–59.

LAFORTUNE-MARTEL, Agathe, 'De l'entremets culinaire aux pièces montées d'un menu de propagande', in *Du manuscrit à la table* (Montréal – Paris, 1992), pp. 121–129.

LACHIVER, Marcel, *Vins, vignes et vignerons. Histoire du vignoble français* (Paris 1988).

LALOU, Élisabeth, 'La Chambre des comptes de Paris: sa mise en place et son fonctionnement (fin XIIIe – XIVe siècle)', in *La France des principautés. Les Chambres des comptes XIVe et XVe siècle* (Paris, 1996), pp. 3–16.

LALOU, Élisabeth, 'Le théâtre et les spectacles publics en France au Moyen Âge: État des recherches', in *Théâtre et spectacles hier et aujourd'hui. Moyen Âge et Renaissance* (Paris, 1991), pp. 9–33.

LALOU, Élisabeth, 'Les ordonnances de l'hôtel des derniers Capétiens directs', in *Höfe und Hofordnungen 1200–1600*, eds Holger KRUSE and Werner PARAVICINI (Sigmaringen, 1999), pp. 91–101.

LAMBERT, Carole (ed.), *Du manuscrit à la table* (Montréal – Paris, 1992).

LAMBERT, Carole, '«L'assiette de table» – Le «premier mets»', in *Fêtes gourmandes*, pp. 43–78.

LAMBERT, Carole, 'Le «tiers mets»', in *Fêtes gourmandes*, pp. 123–138.

LAMBERT, Carole, 'L'entremets', in *Fêtes gourmandes*, pp. 103–122.

LAMBERT, Carole, 'L'ordonnance', in *Du manuscrit à la table*, pp. 9–24.

LANDOUZY, Louis and PÉPIN, Roger, *Aldebrandin de Sienne. Texte français du XIIIe siècle* (Paris, 1911; reprint Genève, 1978).

LAST, Martin, 'Der Besuch Karls IV. am Grabmal Widukinds in Enger', in *Kaiser Karl IV. 1316–1378. Forschungen über Kaiser und Reich*, Blätter für deutsche Landesgeschichte, 114 (1978), pp. 307–341.

Latinitatis Medii Aevi lexicon Bohemorum, I–II (Praha, 1987–1993).

'Laurentii de Brezova Historia hussitica', ed. Jaroslav GOLL, in *Fontes rerum Bohemicarum*, V (Praha, 1893), pp. 327–534.

LAURIOUX, Bruno, 'De l'usage des épices dans l'alimentation médiévale', *Médiévales*, No. 5 (Novembre 1983), pp. 15–31.

LAURIOUX, Bruno, *Le règne de Taillevent. Livres et pratiques culinaires à la fin du Moyen Âge* (Paris, 1997).

LAURIOUX, Bruno, *Les livres de cuisine médiévaux* (Typologie des sources du Moyen Âge occidental, 77; Turnhout, 1997).

LAURIOUX, Bruno, *Manger au Moyen Âge* (Paris, 2002).

LECHOVÁ, Martina, *Cesta Karla IV. do Francie na rozhraní let 1377 a 1378* [The Journey of Charles IV to France at the End of 1377 and Beginning of 1378], Faculty of Arts, Masaryk University, Brno, 1994 (diploma thesis).

LECHOVÁ, Martina, 'Zpráva o návštěvě Paříže Karlem IV. roku 1378 (edice starofrancouzského pramene)' [A Report on the Visit of Charles IV to Paris in 1378 (an edition of the Old French source)], *Sborník prací Filozofické fakulty brněnské univerzity*, C 43 (1996), pp. 49–60.

LE GOFF, Jacques, 'Aspects religieux et sacrés de la monarchie française du Xe au XIIIe siècle', in *La royauté sacrée dans le monde chrétien* (Paris, 1992), pp. 19–28.

LE GOFF, Jacques, 'La genèse du miracle royal', in *Marc Bloch aujourd'hui. Histoire comparée et sciences sociales* (Paris, 1990), pp. 147–156.

LE GOFF, Jacques, *Saint Louis* (Paris, 1996).

Le Château de Vincennes – Une histoire militaire (Paris, 2008).

LEGUAI, André, 'Fondements et problèmes du pouvoir royal en France (autour de 1400)', in *Das spätmittelalterliche Königtum im europäischen Vergleich*, ed. Reinhard SCHNEIDER (Vorträge und Forschungen, 32; Sigmaringen, 1987), pp. 41–58.

LEGUAY, Jean-Pierre, 'Banquets, cadeaux alimentaires et autres présents aux visiteurs de marque dans les villes françaises à la fin du Moyen Âge', in *Jeux, sports et divertissements au Moyen Âge et à l'âge classique* (Paris, 1993), pp. 193–213.

LEHOUX, Françoise, *Jean de France, duc de Berri, sa vie, son action politique (1340–1416)*, I: *De la naissance de Jean de France à la mort de Charles V* (Paris, 1966).

LEISTENSCHNEIDER, Eva, *Die französische Königsgrablege Saint-Denis. Strategien monarchischer Repräsentation 1223 bis 1461* (Weimar, 2008).

Le Ménagier de Paris, eds Georgina E. BRERETON and Janet M. FERRIER (Oxford, 1981), trans. into modern French by Karin UELTSCHI (Paris, 1994).

Le Ménagier de Paris. Traité de morale et d'économie domestique composé vers 1393 par un bourgeois parisien, Jérôme PICHON (ed.) (Paris, 1846; reprint Genève – Paris, 1982).

Le Mesnagier de Paris, eds Georgina E. BRERETON and J. M. FERRIER, trans. into modern French by Karin UELTSCHI (Paris, 1994).

LEMOINE, Jean (ed.), *Chronique de Richard Lescot, religieux de Saint-Denis (1328–1344) suivie de la continuation de cette chronique (1344–1364)* (Paris, 1896).

LENIAUD, Jean-Michel and PERROT, Françoise, *La Sainte-Chapelle* (Paris, 1991).

LENTSCH, Robert, 'La proba. L'épreuve des poisons à la cour des papes d'Avignon', in *Les Prélats, l'Église et la société (XIe–XVe siècles). Hommage à Bernard Guillemain* (Bordeaux, 1994), pp. 155–162.

Le petit Robert 1. Dictionnaire alphabétique et analogique de la langue française (Paris, 1983).

LEPROUX, Guy-Michel (ed.), *Comptes de l'Écurie du roi Charles VI*, I: *Le Registre KK 34 des Archives Nationales (1381–1387)* (Recueil des historiens de la France. Documents financiers et administratifs, IX-1; Paris, 1995).

LEROY, Béatrice, 'Autour de Charles «le Mauvais», groupes et personnalités', *Revue historique*, 273 (1985), pp. 3–17.

Les entrées gloire et déclin d'un cérémonial. Colloque des 10 et 11 mai 1996, Château de Pau (Biaritz, 1997).

Les Fastes du Gothique. Le siècle de Charles V (Paris, 1981).

Les manuscrits à peintures en France du XIIIe au XVIe siècle (Paris, 1955).

Lexikon des Mittelalters, I–IX + Registerband (München – Zürich – Stuttgart – Weimar, 1980–1999).

Lexikon für Theologie und Kirche, I–XI, 3rd, fully revised edition (Freiburg im Breisgau, 1993–2001).

LÍBAL, Dobroslav and MUK, Jan, *Staré Město pražské, architektonický a urbanistický vývoj* [The Old Town of Prague, Architectural and City Planning Development] (Praha, 1996).

LÍBAL, Dobroslav, 'Umění gotické. Architektura' [Gothic Art: Architecture], in *Praha středověká* (Praha, 1983), pp. 167–356.

LIGHTBOWN, Ronald W., *Secular Goldsmiths' Work in Medieval France: A History* (London, 1978).

LINDNER, Theodor, 'Beiträge zur Diplomatik der Luxemburgischen Periode', *Archivalische Zeitschrift*, 9 (1884), pp. 168–192.

LINDNER, Theodor, *Geschichte des deutschen Reiches unter König Wenzel*, I (Braunschweig, 1875).

LOMBARD-JOURDAN, Anne, 'À propos de Raoul de Presles', *Bibliothèque de l'École des chartes*, 139 (1981), pp. 191–207.

Lombard-Jourdan, Anne, *Fleur de lis et Oriflamme. Signes célestes du royaume de France* (Paris, 1991).

Loomis, Laura Hibbard, 'Secular Dramatics in the Royal Palace (Paris, 1378, 1389, and Chaucer's "Tregetours"', *Speculum*, 33 (1958), pp. 242–55.

Lorenc, Vilém, *Nové Město pražské* [The New Town of Prague] (Praha, 1973).

Lot, Ferdinand and Fawtier, Robert, *Histoire des institutions françaises au Moyen Âge*, II: *Institutions royales* (Paris, 1958).

Luce, Siméon (ed.), *Chronique des quatre premiers Valois (1327–1393)* (Paris, 1862).

Lützelschwab, Ralf, 'Prag – das neue Paris? Der französische Einfluß auf die Reliquienpolitik Karls IV', in *Wallfahrten in der europäischen Kultur / Pilgrimage in European Culture*, eds Daniel Doležal and Hartmut Kühne (Frankfurt am Main, 2006), pp. 201–219.

Machaut, Guillaume de, *La Prise d'Alexandrie (The Taking of Alexandria)*, ed. and trans. by R. Barton Palmer (New York, 2002).

Machaut, Guillaume de, *Oeuvres*, II, ed. Ernest Hoepfner (Paris, 1921).

Machilek, Franz, 'Privatfrömmigkeit und Staatsfrömmigkeit', in *Kaiser Karl IV. Staatsmann und Mäzen*, ed. Ferdinand Seibt (München, 1978), pp. 87–101.

Maillard, François (ed.), *Comptes royaux (1314–1328)*, II (Paris, 1961).

Manger et boire au Moyen Âge, I–II, ed. Denis Menjot (Paris, 1984).

Margue, Michel, 'Jean de Luxembourg, prince idéal et chevalier parfait: aux origines d'un mythe', *Mediaevalia historica Bohemica*, 5 (1998), pp. 11–26.

Margue, Michel, *Un itineraire européen. Jean l'Aveugle, comte de Luxembourg et roi de Bohême, 1296–1346* (Bruxelles, 1996).

Meiss, Millard, *French Painting in the Time of Jean de Berry. The Late Fourteenth Century and the Patronage of the Duke* (London, 1967).

Meiss, Millard, *French Painting in the Time of Jean de Berry. The Boucicaut Master* (London, 1968).

Meiss, Millard, *French Painting in the Time of Jean de Berry. The Limbourgs and their Contemporaries*, Text Volume (London, 1974).

Menclová, Dobroslava, *České hrady* [Bohemian Castles], II (Praha, 1972).

Menčík, Ferdinand, 'Pořádek bratrstva zlatnického v Praze a jeho stanovy z r. 1324' [The Order of the Goldsmith Guild in Prague and Its Statutes from 1324], *Věstník Královské české společnosti nauk* (1891), pp. 257–279.

Mendl, Bedřich, 'Vyjednávání o česko-francouzský spolek 1355' [Treaty on the Czech-French Alliance 1355], in *Českou minulostí. Práce V. Novotnému k 60. narozeninám* (Praha, 1929), pp. 111–123.

Mendl, Bedřich and Quicke, Fritz, 'Les relations politiques entre l'empereur et le roi de France de 1355 à 1356', *Revue belge de philologie et d'histoire*, 8 (1929), pp. 469–512.

Mentzel-Reuters, Arno, 'Die goldene Krone. Entwicklungslinien mittelalterlicher Herrschaftssymbolik', *Deutsches Archiv für Erforschung des Mittelalters*, 60 (2004), pp. 135–182.

Menut, Albert D. (ed.), *Maistre Nicole Oresme: Le livre de politiques d'Aristote* (Transactions of the American Philosophical Society, 60–66; Philadelphia, 1970).

Mérindol, Christian de, 'Couleur, étoffe et politique à la fin du Moyen Âge. Les couleurs du roi et les couleurs d'une cour ducale', in *Actes du 112e Congrès national des Sociétés savantes. Section d'histoire médiévale et de philologie* (Paris, 1987), pp. 221–249.

Mérindol, Christian de, 'Entrées royales et princières à la fin de l'époque médiévale: jeu de taxinomie, d'emblématique et de symbolique', in *Les entrées gloire et déclin d'un cérémonial. Colloque des 10 et 11 mai 1996 Château de Pau* (Biaritz, 1997), pp. 27–47.

Mérindol, Christian de, 'Le prince et son cortège. La théâtralisation des signes du pouvoir à la fin du Moyen Âge', in *Les princes et pouvoir au Moyen Âge. Congrès de la Société des historiens médiévistes de l'enseignement supérieur* (Paris, 1993), pp. 303–323.

Mérindol, Christian de, 'Signes de hiérarchie sociale à la fin du moyen âge d'après le vêtement. Méthodes et recherches', in *Le vêtement. Histoire, archéologie et symbolique vestimentaires au Moyen Âge* (Cahiers du Léopard d'Or, 1; Paris, 1989), pp. 181–223.

Mérindol, Christian de, 'Théâtre et politique à la fin du Moyen Âge: les entrées royales et autre cérémonies, mises au point et nouvaux aperçus', in *Théâtre et spectacles hier et aujourd'hui. Moyen Âge et Renaissance* (Paris, 1991), pp. 199–212.

Mertens, Veronika, *Mi-parti als Zeichen. Zur Bedeutung von geteiltem Kleid und geteilter Gestalt in der Ständetracht in literarischen und bildnerischen Quellen sowie im Fastnachtsbrauch vom Mittelalter bis zur Gegenwart* (Kulturgeschichtliche Forschungen, 1; Remscheid, 1983).

Meyer, Rudolf J., *Königs- und Kaiserbegräbnisse im Spätmittelalter* (Köln – Weimar – Wien, 2000).

Mezník, Jaroslav, 'Berichte der französischen königlichen Rechnungen über den Aufenthalt des jungen Karl IV. in Frankreich', *Mediaevalia Bohemica*, 1 (1969), pp. 291–295.

Mezník, Jaroslav, 'Odvolání Majestas Carolina' [On the Revocation of Maiestas Carolina], in *In memoriam Josefa Macka (1922–1991)*, eds Miroslav Polívka and František Šmahel (Praha, 1996), pp. 53–63.

Mezník, Jaroslav, 'Pobyty Jana Lucemburského' [The Stays of John of Luxembourg], *Časopis Matice moravské*, 116 (1997), pp. 93 98.

Minois, Georges, *Du Guesclin* (Paris, 1993).

Miramon, Charles de, *Les «donnés» au Moyen Âge. Une forme de vie religieuse laïque (v. 1180–v. 1500)* (Paris, 1999).

Mollat, Michel and Wolff, Philippe, *Ongles bleus, Jacques et Ciompi. Les révolutions populaires en Europe aux XIVe et XVe siècles* (Paris, 1970).

Mollat, Guillaume (ed.), *Vitae paparum avenionensium par Étienne Baluze*, I (Paris, 1914).

Moranvillé, Henri (ed.), *Chronographia regum Francorum*, II: *1328–1380* (Paris, 1893).

Moranvillé, Henri, *Étude sur la vie de Jean le Mercier* (Paris, 1888).

Moraw, Peter, 'Fürsten am spätmittelalterlichen deutschen Königshof', in *Principes. Dynastien und Höfe im späten Mittelalter*, eds Cordula Nolte et al. (Residenzforschung, 14; Stuttgart, 2002), pp. 17–32.

Moraw, Peter, 'Grundzüge der Kanzleigeschichte Kaiser Karls IV. (1346–1378)', *Zeitschrift für historische Forschung*, 12 (1985), pp. 11–42.

Moraw, Peter, 'Räte und Kanzlei', in *Kaiser Karl IV. Staatsmann und Mäzen*, ed. Ferdinand Seibt (München, 1978), pp. 285–292.

Moraw, Peter, *Von offener Verfassung zu gestalteter Verdichtung. Das Reich im späten Mittelalter 1250 bis 1490* (Frankfurt am Main and Berlin, 1989).

Moraw, Peter, 'Zur Mittelpunktsfunktion Prags im Zeitalter Karls IV.', in *Europa slavica, Europa orientalis. Festschrift für Herbert Ludat zum 70. Geburtstag*, eds Klaus-Detlev Grothusen and Klaus Zernack (Berlin, 1980), pp. 445–489.

Morel, Octave, *La grande chancellerie royale et l'expédition des lettres royaux de l'avènement de Philippe de Valois à la fin du XIV siècle (1328–1400)* (Paris, 1900).

Müllner, Johannes, *Die Annalen der Reichsstadt Nürnberg von 1623*, II: *1351–1469*, ed. Gerhard Hirschmann (Nürnberg, 1984).

Musée national du Moyen Âge Thermes de Cluny. Guide des collections (Paris, 1993).

Naegle, Gisela, '«Bonnes villes» et «güte stete». Quelques remarques sur le problème des «villes notables» en France et en Allemagne à la fin du Moyen Âge', *Francia*, 35 (2008).

Naegle, Gisela, 'Im Dienst von König und Königreich? Französische „officiers" im Spätmittelalter', in *Europa im späten Mittelalter. Politik – Gesellschaft – Kultur*, eds R. C. Schwinges et al. (Historische Zeitschrift, Beihefte, NF 40; München 2006), pp. 313–338.

Nechutová, Jana, *Die lateinische Literatur des Mittelalters in Böhmen* (Köln – Weimar – Wien, 2007).

Nejedlý, Martin, 'Deux poètes français du quatorzième siècle en Bohême. Rencontres et confrontations', in *Prague Papers on the History of International Relations* (Prague, 1997), pp. 30–53.

NEJEDLÝ, Martin, *Fortuny kolo vrtkavé. Láska, moc a společnost ve středověku* [Fortune's Fickle Wheel. Love, Power and Society in the Middle Ages] (Praha, 2003).

NEJEDLÝ, Martin, *La représentation des pouvoirs et des hiérarchies dans les Chroniques de Jean Froissart* (Lille, 1995).

NEJEDLÝ, Martin, *Meluzínský mýtus a rodová pověst Lucemburků* [The Myth of Melusine and the Dynastic Legend of the Luxemburgs], *Český časopis historický* 98 (2000), pp. 693–736.

NEJEDLÝ, Martin, *Středověký mýtus o Meluzíně a rodová pověst Lucemburků* [The Mediaeval Myth of Melusine and the Dynastic Legend of the Luxemburgs] (Praha, 2007).

NEJEDLÝ, Martin: '„V Praze jsou tři města, mnoho výstavných kostelů a lidé zbožní..." Obraz českých zemí a jejich panovníků ve francouzsky psané literatuře 14. století', in *Evropa a Čechy na konci středověku. Sborník příspěvků věnovaných Františku Šmahelovi*, eds Eva DOLEŽALOVÁ, Robert NOVOTNÝ and Pavel SOUKUP (Praha, 2004), pp. 35–37.

NEUMANN, AUGUSTIN (ed.), *Francouzská husitica. Řada první. Akta a listiny z let 1383–1435* [French Hussitica. Series One. Acts and Deeds from 1383–1435] (Olomouc, 1923).

NEUREITHER, Heinrich, *Das Bild Kaiser Karls IV. in der zeitgenössischen französischen Geschichtsschreibung*, Inaugural-Dissertation (Heidelberg, 1965).

NODL, Martin, 'Svár obrazu s textem. Sen Karla IV. o smilstvu' [The Feud of Picture and Text. The Dream of Charles IV on Lechery], in *Verba in imaginibus*, eds Martin NODL et al. (Praha, 2004), pp. 69–95.

NOVÁČEK, Vojtěch Jaromír, 'Císaře Karla IV. pobyt při dvoře papežském v Avinioně r. 1365' [The Stay of Emperor Charles IV at the Papal Court in Avignon in 1365], *Časopis Musea Království Českého*, 64 (1890), pp. 151–179.

ODLOŽILÍK, Otakar, 'The Terenzo Dream of Charles IV. Critical examination of the available sources', in *Orbis medievalis. Festgabe für Anton Blaschka zum 75. Geburtstag* (Weimar, 1971), pp. 163–173.

Oeuvres de Froissart, XIV: *Chroniques*, ed. Kervyn de LETTENHOVE, (reprint Osnabrück, 1967).

O'MEARA, Carra Ferguson, *Monarchy and Consent. The Coronation Book of Charles V of France* (London – Turnhout, 2001).

ORMROD, William M., *The Reign of Edward III: Crown and Political Society in England 1327–1377* (New Haven – London, 1990).

OTAVSKÝ, Karel, 'Die Dynastie der Luxemburger und die Pariser Kunst unter den letzten Kapetingern', in *King John of Luxembourg (1296–1346) and the Art of his Era* (Praha, 1998), pp. 62–68.

OTAVSKY, Karel, *Die Sankt Wenzelskrone im Prager Domschatz und die Frage der Kunstauffassung am Hofe Kaiser Karls IV.* (Bern, 1992).

OTAVSKÝ, Karel, 'K relikviím vlastněným císařem Karlem IV., k jejich uctívání a jejich schránkám' [On the Relics Owned by Emperor Charles IV, on Their Veneration and Cases], in *Court Chapels / Dvorské kaple* (Praha, 2003), pp. 392–398.

PALACKY, Franz, *Geschichte von Böhmen*, II-2 (Prag, 1842).

Památky národní minulosti. Katalog historické expozice Národního muzea v Praze v Lobkovickém paláci [Monuments of the National Past. Catalogue of the Historical Exposition of the National Museum in Prague at Lobkowicz Palace] (Praha, 1989).

PARAVICINI, Werner, *Die Preussenreisen des europäischen Adels*, I (Sigmaringen, 1989).

PARAVICINI, Werner, 'Europäische Hofordnungen als Gattung und Quelle', in *Höfe und Hofordnungen 1200–1600*, eds Holger KRUSE and Werner PARAVICINI (Sigmaringen, 1999), pp. 13–20.

PARAVICINI, Werner, 'Zeremoniell und Raum', in *Zeremoniell und Raum*, ed. Werner PARAVICINI (Sigmaringen, 1997), pp. 11–36.

PARAVICINI-EBEL, Anke, 'Die Vita Karls IV., ein „Ego-Dokument"?', *Deutsches Archiv für Erforschung des Mittelalters*, 63 (2007), pp. 101–109.

Paris 1400. Les arts sous Charles VI (Paris, 2004).

Paris et Charles V. Arts et Architecture, under the guidance of Frédéric PLEYBERT (Paris, 2001).

PASTOUREAU, Michel, 'Les couleurs médiévales: systèmes de valeurs et modes de sensibilité', in *Figures et couleurs. Études sur la symbolique et la sensibilité médiévales* (Paris, 1986), pp. 35–49.

PATZE, Hans, 'Die Hofgesellschaft Kaiser Karls IV. und König Wenzels in Prag', *Blätter für deutsche Landesgeschichte*, 114 (1978), pp. 733–773.

PELZEL, Franz Martin, *Kaiser Karl der Vierte, König in Böhmen*, II: [1355–1378] (Prag, 1781).

PERNOUD, Régine, *Christine de Pisan* (Paris, 1982).

PETIT-RENAUD, Sophie, *«Faire loy» au Royaume de France de Philippe VI à Charles V (1328–1380)* (Paris, 2001).

PEYER, Hans Conrad, 'Der Empfang des Königs im mittelalterlichen Zürich', in *Archivalia et Historica. Festschrift Anton Largiadèr* (Zürich, 1958), pp. 219–233.

PICHON, Jérôme and VICAIRE Georges (ed.), *Le Viandier de Guillaume Tirel dit Taillevent*, ed., revised and expanded by Sylvie MARTINET (Genève, 1967).

PISAN, Christine de, *Le Livre des Faits et Bonnes Moeurs du roi Charles V le Sage*, eds Eric HICKS and Thérèse MOREAU (Paris, 1997).

PIPONNIER, Françoise and Perrine MANE, *Se vêtir au Moyen Âge* (Paris, 1965).

PLAISSE, André, *Charles dit le Mauvais, comte d'Évreux, roi de Navarre, capitaine de Paris* (Évreux, 1972).

PLEYBERT, Frédéric, 'Art, pouvoir et politique', in *Paris et Charles V. Arts et Architecture* (Paris, 2001), pp. 49–58.

PLEYBERT, Frédéric, 'Les sculpteurs du roi', in *Paris et Charles V. Arts et Architecture* (Paris, 2001), pp. 186–213.

PODLAHA, Antonín and ŠITTLER, Eduard, *Chrámový poklad u sv. Víta v Praze. Jeho dějiny a popis* [The Cathedral Treasure at St Vitus' in Prague. Its History and Description] (Praha, 1903).

POLC, Jaroslav V., *Svatý Jan Nepomucký*, I, Život [Saint John of Nepomuk, I, His Life] (Řím, 1972).

POULLE, Emmanuel, 'Les faux de Robert d'Artois et l'histoire de l'écriture', in *Mélanges Jacques Stiennon* (1982), pp. 519–534.

Préludes à la Renaissance. Aspects de la vie intellectuelle en France au XVe siècle, eds Carla BOZZOLO and Ezio ORNATO (Paris, 1992).

PRÉVOT, Brigitte and RIBÉMONT, Bernard, *Le cheval en France au Moyen Âge. Sa place dans le monde médiéval, sa médecine: l'example d'un traité vétérinaire du XIVe siècle, la Cirurgie des chevaux* (Orléans, 1994).

PRIX, Dalibor, 'Vévoda Václav I. Opavský. Příspěvek k dějinám Opavského vévodství počátkem poslední čtvrtiny 14. století' [Duke Wenceslas I of Opava. A Paper on the History of the Opava Duchy at the Beginning of the Last Quarter of the 14th Century], *Acta historica et museologica Universitatis Silesianae Opaviensis*, 3 (1997), pp. 54–89.

PROST, Bernard (ed.), *Inventaires mobiliers et extraits des comptes des ducs de Bourgogne de la Maison de Valois (1363–1477)*, I: *Philippe le Hardi 1363–1377* (Paris, 1902); II: *Philippe le Hardi 1378–1390* (Paris, 1913).

PUYMAIGRE, Théodore de, 'Jean l'Aveugle en France', *Revue de Questions Historiques*, 52 (1892), pp. 391–452.

QUILLET, Jeannine, *Charles V, le roi lettré. Essai sur la pensée politique d'un règne* (Paris, 1984).

RAYNAUD, Christiane, 'Le langage de la violence dans les enluminures des Grandes chroniques de France dites de Charles V', *Journal of Medieval History*, 17 (1991), pp. 149–170.

Regesta diplomatica nec non epistolaria Bohemiae et Moraviae, III, ed. Josef EMLER (Praha, 1890).

Répertoire des manuscrits médiévaux contenant des recettes culinaires, eds Constance B. HIEATT et al., in *Du manuscrit à la table*, II (Montréal – Paris, 1992).

REXROTH, Frank: '„...damit die ganze Schule Ruf und Ruhm gewinne". Vom umstrittenen Transfer des Pariser Universitätsmodells nach Deutschland', in *Deutschland und der Westen Europas im*

Mittelalter, ed. Joachim EHLERS (Vorträge und Forschungen, 56; Stuttgart, 2002), pp. 507–532.

REY, Maurice, *Le domaine du roi et les finances extraordinaires sous Charles VI 1388–1413* (Paris, 1965).

REY, Maurice, *Les finances royales sous Charles VI. Les causes du déficit 1388–1413* (Paris, 1965).

RIBÉMONT, Bernard, 'L'Entrée d'Isabeau de Bavière à Paris. Une fête textuelle pour Froissart', in *Feste und Feiern im Mittelalter* (Sigmaringen, 1991), pp. 515–522.

RIGAUDIÈRE, Albert, *Penser et construire l'État dans la France du Moyen Âge (XIIIe–XVe siècle)* (Paris, 2003).

RITTER VON RITTERSBERG, Johann, 'Kaiser Karl des IV. und seines Sohnes König Wenzel Reise nach Paris in den Jahren 1377 und 1378' [Nach der von Theodor Godefroy im J. 1614 zu Paris herausgegebenen „Entrevue…"], *Monatschrift der Gesellschaft des vaterländischen Museums in Böhmen*, 2-1 (1828), 201–204 and 313–339.

ROYER, Jean-Pierre, *L'Église et le Royaume de France au XIVe siècle d'après le «Songe du Vergier» et la jurisprudence du Parlement* (Paris, 1969).

ROYT, Jan, 'K datování a ikonografii tzv. Ostatkových scén v kapli Panny Marie na Karlštejně' [On the Dating and Iconography of the So-Called Relic Scenes in the Chapel of the Virgin Mary at Karlštejn], in *Court Chapels / Dvorské kaple* (Praha, 2003), pp. 354–356.

SABBAN, Françoise, 'Le savoir-cuire ou l'art des potages dans le Ménagier de Paris et le Viandier de Taillevent', in *Manger et boire au Moyen Âge*, II (Paris, 1984), pp. 161–172.

SALY, Antoinette, 'Les oiseaux dans l'alimentation médiévale d'après le Viandier de Taillevent et le Ménagier de Paris', in *Manger et boire au Moyen Âge*, II (Paris, 1984), pp. 173–179.

SANDRON, Dany, 'Le roi et les églises', in *Paris et Charles V. Arts et Architecture* (Paris, 2001), pp. 91–104.

SAUVAL, Henri, *Histoire et recherches des Antiquités de la ville de Paris*, II (Paris, 1724; reprint Paris – Genève, 1974).

SCHIEDLAUSKY, Günther, 'Tafelschiffe', *Kunst und Antiquitäten*, 12 (1991), pp. 30–39.

SCHIECHE, Emil, 'Die skandinavischen Länder', in *Kaiser Karl IV. Staatsmann und Mäzen*, ed. Ferdinand SEIBT (München, 1978), pp. 164–167.

SCHIECHE, Emil, 'Svídnický formulář Jana ze Středy' [The Świdnica Form of John of Neumarkt], *Časopis archivní školy*, 5 (1927), pp. 110–159.

SCHLOTHEUBER, Eva, 'Die Autobiographie Karls IV. und die mittelalterlichen Vorstellungen vom Menschen am Scheideweg', *Historische Zeitschrift*, 281 (2005), pp. 561–591.

SCHNEIDER, Reinhard, 'Karolus, qui et Wenceslaus', in *Festschrift für Helmut Beumann zum 65. Geburtstag*, eds Kurt-Ulrich JÄSCHKE and Reinhard WENSKUS (Sigmaringen, 1977), pp. 365–387.

SCHNERB-LIÈVRE, Marion (ed.), *Le Songe du Vergier*, I (Paris, 1982).

SCHNERB-LIÈVRE, Marion (ed.), *Somnium Viridarii*, I–II (Paris, 1993, 1995).

SCHWARZ, Michael V. (ed.), *Die Gräber der Luxemburger. Image und Memoria eines Kaiserhauses* (Luxembourg, 1997).

SCHWEDLER, Gerald, 'Deutsch-französische Herrschertreffen im 14. Jahrhundert. Dynastische und staatliche Beziehungen im Wandel', in *Regnum et Imperium. Die französisch-deutschen Beziehungen im 14. und 15. Jahrhundert. Les relations franco-allemandes au XIVe et au XVe siècle* (Pariser Historische Studien, 83; München, 2008), pp. 55–99.

SCHWEDLER, Gerald, 'Die Schwertmesse Karls IV. von Luxemburg', in *Die Welt der Rituale. Von der Antike bis heute* (Darmstadt, 2006), pp. 247–252.

SCHWEDLER, Gerald, *Herrschertreffen des Spätmittelalters. Formen – Rituale – Wirkungen*, (Mittelalter-Forschungen, 21; Ostfildern, 2008).

SCULLY, Terence, 'Du fait de cuisine par Maistre Chiquart', *1420*, in *Vallesia*, 40 (1985), pp. 103–231.

SCULLY, Terence, 'The Opusculum de saporibus of Magninus Mediolanensis', *Medium Aevum*, 54 (1985), pp. 178–207.

SCULLY, Terence (ed.), *The Viandier of Taillevent. An Edition of all Extant Manuscripts* (Ottawa, 1988).

SEIBT, Ferdinand, 'Gab es einen böhmischen Frühhumanismus?', in *Studien zum Humanismus in den böhmischen Ländern*, eds Hans-Bernd HARDER and Hans ROTHE (Köln – Wien, 1986), pp. 1–19.

SEIBT, Ferdinand, *Karl IV. Ein Kaiser in Europa 1346 bis 1378* (München, 1978).

SEIBT, Ferdinand, 'Zum Reichsvikariat für den Dauphin', *Zeitschrift für historische Forschung*, 8 (1981), pp. 129–158.

SHERMAN, Claire Richter, *Imaging Aristotle. Verbal and Visual Representation in Fourteenth-Century France* (Berkely – Los Angeles – London, 1995).

SHERMAN, Claire Richter, 'Representations of Charles V of France (1338–1380) as a Wise Ruler', *Medievalia et humanistica*, New Series 2 (1971), pp. 83–96.

SHERMAN, Claire Richter, *The Portraits of Charles V of France (1338–1380)* (New York, 1969).

ŠIMÁK, J. V., *Rukopisy majorátní knihovny hrabat z Nostitz a Rhienecka v Praze* [The Manuscripts of the Majorat (*fideicommis*) Library of the Counts of Nostitz-Rieneck in Prague] (Praha, 1910).

ŠMAHEL, František, *Die Prager Universität im Mittelalter. Gesammelte Aufsätze / The Charles University in the Middle Ages. Selected Studies* (Leiden – Boston, 2007).

ŠMAHEL, František, 'Gab es einen Frühhumanismus im luxemburgischen Böhmen?', in *Kunst als Herrschaftsinstrument: Böhmen und das Heilige Römische Reich unter den Luxemburgern im europäischen Kontext*, eds Jiří FAJT and Andrea LANGER (Berlin, 2009), pp. 22–26.

ŠMAHEL, František, 'Monseigneur Charles de Bohême. Dětství a dospívání Karla IV. ve Francii' [Monseigneur Charles de Bohême: The Childhood and Adolescence of Charles IV in France], *Dějiny a současnost*, 27-1 (2005), pp. 34–37.

ŠMAHEL, František, 'Spectaculum et pompa funebris: Das Leichenzeremoniell bei der Bestattung Kaiser Karls IV.', in *Zur politischen Präsentation und Allegorie im 14. u. 15. Jahrhundert* (München, 1994), pp. 1–37.

ŠMAHEL, František, 'Výdaje francouzské komory na zaopatření českého prince Karla v roce 1327' [Expenses of the French Chamber for the Provision for Prince of Bohemia Charles in 1327], in *Regnum Bohemiae et Sacrum Romanum imperium. Sborník k poctě Jiřího Kuthana*, eds Jan ROYT et al. (Praha, 2005), pp. 65–76.

SOKOL, Jan, 'Parléřův kostel Všech svatých na Pražském hradě' [Parler's Church of All Saints at Prague Castle], *Umění*, 17 (1969), pp. 574–582.

SOLENTE, S[usanne] (ed.), *Le livre des fais et bonnes meurs du sage roy Charles V par Christine de Pisan*, I–II (Paris, 1936, 1940).

SPĚVÁČEK, Jiří, *Jan Lucemburský a jeho doba 1296–1346* [John of Luxembourg and His Time, 1296–1346] (Praha, 1994).

SPĚVÁČEK, Jiří, *Karel IV. Život a dílo (1316–1378)* [Charles IV. His Life and Work (1316–1378)] (Praha, 1979).

SPĚVÁČEK, Jiří, *Václav IV. 1361–1419* [Wenceslas IV. 1361–1419] (Praha, 1986).

Staročeský slovník [Old Czech Dictionary], *na – obíjěti se* (Praha, 1977); *obilé – ožžený* (Praha, 1984); *paběnický – pravý* (Praha, 1996).

STEHLÍKOVÁ, Dana, MÁDL, Martin and HEUDE-LEVOIR, Marie-Flore, 'Le reliquiaire de la mitre de Saint Éloi à Prague. Étude pluridisciplinaire', *CIETA – Bulletin*, 76 (1999), pp. 76–89.

STEHLÍKOVÁ, Dana, *Encyklopedie českého zlatnictví, stříbrnictví a klenotnictví* [Encyclopaedia of Czech Goldsmithery, Silversmithery and Jewellery] (Praha, 2003).

STEINHERZ, Samuel, 'Das Schisma von 1378 und die Haltung Karls IV.', *Mitteilungen des Instituts für österreichische Geschichtsforschung*, 21 (1900), pp. 599–639.

STEINHERZ, Samuel, 'Die Beziehungen Ludwigs I. von Ungarn zu Karl IV.', *Mitteilungen des Institut für österreichische Geschichtsforschung*, 8–9 (1887–1888), pp. 217–257, 529–637.

STEJSKAL, Karel, 'Die Wandzyklen des Kaisers Karls IV. Bemerkungen zu Neudatierungen und Rekonstruktionen der im Auftrag Karls IV. gemalten Wandzyklen', *Umění*, 46 (1998), pp. 19–41.

STEJSKAL, Karel, 'Ještě jednou o datování a atribucích karlštejnských maleb' [One More Time on the Dating and Attributions of the Paintings at Karlštejn], in *Court Chapels / Dvorské kaple* (Praha, 2003), pp. 343–350.

Stejskal, Karel, 'Über die Illuminatoren der französischen Stundenbücher in der Prager Nationalbibliothek', *Wiener Jahrbuch für Kunstgeschichte*, 46–47 (1993–1994), pp. 715–724.

Stejskal, Karel, 'Výstava „La Librairie de Charles V" a některé otázky českého umění XIV. století' [The Exhibition 'La Librairie de Charles V' and Some Issues of Bohemian Art in the 14th Century], *Umění*, 18 (1970), pp. 31–60.

Štěpán, Václav, *Moravský markrabě Jošt (1354–1411)* [Margrave of Moravia Jobst (1354–1411)] (Brno, 2002).

Sterling, Charles, *La peinture médiévale à Paris 1300–1500*, I (Paris, 1987).

Stoob, Heinz, *Kaiser Karl IV. und seine Zeit* (Graz – Wien – Köln, 1990).

Strubel, Armand, 'Le «chevauchier» de Charles V. Christine de Pizan et le spectacle de la majesté royale', in *Penser le pouvoir au Moyen Âge (VIIIe–XVe siècle)*, texts collected by Dominique Boutet and Jacques Verger (Paris, 2000), pp. 385–399.

Suckale, Robert, 'Die Porträts Kaiser Karls IV. als Bedeutungsträger', in *Das Porträt vor der Erfindung des Porträts*, eds Martin Büchsel and Peter Schmidt (Mainz, 2003), pp. 191–204.

Sumption, Jonathan, *The Hundred Years War*, I: *Trial by Battle* (London 1990); II: *Trial by Fire* (London, 1999).

Šusta, Josef, *Král cizinec* [King Foreigner] (České dějiny, II-2; Praha, 1939).

Šusta, Josef, *Karel IV. Otec a syn 1333–1346* [Charles IV. Father and Son 1333–1346] (České dějiny II-3; Praha, 1946).

Šusta, Josef, *Karel IV. Za císařskou korunou 1346–1355* [Charles IV. In Pursuit of the Imperial Crown 1346–1355] (České dějiny II-4; Praha, 1948).

Swanson, Robert Norman, *Universities, Academics and the Great Schism* (Cambridge, 1979).

Szczur, Stanisław, 'Praski zjazd Kazimierza Wielkiego z cesarzem w 1356 roku', in *Polska i jej sąsiedzi w późnym średniowieczu* (Kraków, 2000), pp. 81–117.

Taburet-Delahaye, Elisabeth, 'L'orfèvrerie à la Sainte-Chapelle sous saint Louis', in *La Sainte-Chapelle*, Dossiers d'archéologie, No. 264 (juin 2001), pp. 66–73.

Taburet-Delahaye, Elisabeth, *L'orfèvrerie gothique (XIIIe – début XVe siècle) au Musée de Cluny* (Paris, 1989).

Taburet-Delahaye, Elisabeth et al., *Paris 1400. Les arts sous Charles VI*, exhibition catalogue, Musée du Louvre (Paris, 2004), pp. 38–41.

Paris 1400. Les arts sous Charles VI (Paris, 2004).

Tadra, Ferdinand, *Kulturní styky Čech s cizinou až do válek husitských* [The Cultural Contacts of Bohemia with the Abroad until the Hussite Wars] (Praha, 1897).

Tessier, Georges, *Diplomatique royale française* (Paris, 1962).

The Chronicles of Froissart, trans. by John Bourchier, Lord Berners, ed. and reduced in one volume by G. C. Macaulay (London 1924, reprint of 1895 1st ed.).

Thomas, Heinz, 'Clemens VI. und Ludwig der Bayer', in *Kaiser Ludwig der Bayer. Konflikte, Weichenstellungen und Wahrnehmung seiner Herrschaft*, eds Hermann Nehlsen et al. (Paderborn – München – Wien – Zürich, 2002), pp. 75–117.

Thomas, Heinz, 'Die Beziehungen Karls IV. zu Frankreich von der Rhenser Wahl im Jahre 1346 bis zum Großen Metzer Hoftag', *Blätter für deutsche Landesgeschichte*, 114 (1978), pp. 165–201.

Thomas, Heinz, 'Ein Zeitgenössisches Memorandum zum Staatsbesuch Kaiser Karls IV. in Paris', in *Zwischen Saar und Mosel. Festschrift für Hans-Walter Herrmann zum 65. Geburtstag*, eds Wolfgang Haubrichs et al. (Saarbrücken, 1995), pp. 99–119.

Thomas, Heinz, 'Frankreich', in *Kaiser Karl IV. Staatsmann und Mäzen*, ed. Ferdinand Seibt (München, 1978), pp. 152–156 and 448–449.

THOMAS, Heinz, 'Frankreich, Karl IV. und das Große Schisma', in *Bündnissysteme' und 'Außenpolitik' im späteren Mittelalter*, ed. Peter MORAW (*Zeitschrift für historische Forschung*, Beiheft 5; Berlin, 1988), pp. 69–104.

THOMAS, Heinz, 'Johann II. 1350–1364', in *Die französischen Könige des Mittelalters. Von Odo bis Karl VIII. 888–1498* (München, 1996), pp. 267–283.

THOMAS, Heinz, 'Karl V. (1364–1380)', in *Die französischen Könige des Mittelalters. Von Odo bis Karl VIII. 888–1498* (München, 1996), pp. 285–320.

THOMAS, Heinz, 'Vater und Sohn. König Johann und Karl IV.', in *Johann der Blinde, Graf von Luxemburg, König von Böhmen 1296–1346*, ed. Michel PAULY (Luxemburg, 1997), pp. 445–482.

THOMAS, Heinz, *Zwischen Regnum und Imperium. Die Fürstentümer Bar und Lothringen zur Zeit Kaiser Karls IV.* (Bonn, 1973).

THOMAS, Marcel, 'La visite de l'empereur Charles IV en France d'après l'exemplaire des «Grandes Chroniques» exécuté pour le roi Charles V', in *Congrès International de bibliophiles* (Wien, 1971), pp. 85–98.

TILLE, VÁCLAV (ed.), 'Francouzský rukopis o cestě císaře Karla IV. do Francie v letech 1377–1378' [The French Manuscript on the Journey of Emperor Charles IV to France in 1377–1378], *Věstník Královské české společnosti nauk,* třída filosoficko-historicko-jazykozpytná (Praha, 1899), Section XIV, pp. 1–16.

TOMEK, Václav Vladivoj, *Dějepis města Prahy* [History of the City of Prague], II, 2nd ed. (Praha, 1892); III, 2nd ed. (Praha, 1893); V, 2nd ed. (Praha, 1905).

TOURNEUR-AUMONT, J. M., *La bataille de Poitiers (1356) et la construction de la France* (Paris – Tours – Poitiers, 1940).

TRAPP, Thomas, 'Die französischen Enquêtes von 1387 und 1390. Ein Beitrag zur Linearität mittelalterlicher „Staatsgrenzen"', in *Grenzen Erkennen – Begrenzungen überwinden. Festschrift für Reinhard Schneider* (Sigmaringen, 1999), pp. 317–332.

TRAUTZ, Fritz, *Die Könige von England und das Reich 1272–1377* (Heidelberg, 1961).

TROUBAT, Olivier, 'Béatrix de Bourbon, reine de Bohême', *Revue de l'Est*, 5 (1989), pp. 259–279.

TROUBAT, Olivier, *La Guerre de Cent Ans et le Prince Chevalier, le «Bon Duc» Louis II de Bourbon, 1337–1410*, I: *Règnes de Jean le Bon et Charles V* (Montluçon, 2001).

TUCOO-CHALA, Pierre, *Gaston Fébus, prince des Pyrénées (1331–1391)* (Paris, 1993).

TUCOO-CHALA, Pierre, *Gaston Fébus, Grand prince Médiéval 1331-1391* (Paris, 1996).

URBAN, Jan, *Kresčak 26. srpna 1346* [Crécy, 26 August 1346] (Praha – Litomyšl, 2000).

VALOIS, Noël, 'Déclaration faite par Charles V à son lit de mort', *Annuaire-Bulletin de la Société de l'histoire de France*, 24 (1887), pp. 251–255.

VALOIS, Noël, *La France et le grand schisme d'Occident*, I–II (Paris, 1896, 1901; reprint Hildesheim, 1967).

VALOIS, Noël, 'Le projet de mariage entre Louis de France et Catherine de Hongrie et le voyage de l'empereur Charles IV à Paris', *Annuaire-Bulletin de la Société de l'histoire de France*, 30/II (1893), pp. 209–223.

VANDENBERGHE, Stéphane. 'Les premières fourchettes', in *Fêtes gourmandes*, p. 45.

VAUGHAN, Richard, *Philip the Bold. The Formation of the Burgundian State* (London, 1962; 2nd ed. London, 1979).

VELDTRUP, Dieter, 'Ehen aus Staatsräson. Die Familien- und Heiratspolitik Johanns von Böhmen', in *Johann der Blinde, Graf von Luxemburg, König von Böhmen 1296–1346*, ed. Michel PAULY (Luxemburg, 1997), pp. 483–542.

VELDTRUP, Dieter, *Zwischen Eherecht und Familienpolitik. Studien zu den dynastischen Heiratsprojekten Karls IV.* (Studien zu den Luxemburgern und ihrer Zeit, 2; Warendorf, 1988).

VERGER, Jacques, 'Culture universitaire, culture de cour à Paris au XIVe siècle', in *Erziehung und Bildung bei Hofe*, eds Werner PARAVICINI and Jörg WETTLAUFER (Residenzforschung 13; Stuttgart, 2002), pp. 167–176.

VIARD, Jules (ed.), *Les Journaux du Trésor de Charles IV le Bel* (Paris, 1917).

VIDIER, Alexandre, *Le trésor de la Sainte-Chapelle. Inventaires et documents* (Paris, 1911).

VIDMANOVÁ, Anežka, 'Summa recreatorum', in *Deutsche Literatur des Mittelalters in Böhmen und über Böhmen*, eds Dominique FLIEGER and Václav BOK (Wien, 2001), pp. 169–179.

VIDMANOVÁ, Anežka, 'Středolatinská beletrie, Jan ze Středy a olomoucký protohumanismus' [Mediaeval Latin Fiction, John of Neumarkt and Olomouc Protohumanism], in *Laborintus. Latinská literatura středověkých Čech* (Praha, 1994), pp. 140–149.

VIDMANOVÁ, Anežka, 'Životospráva pro císařský dvůr i městský dům' [The Regimen at the Imperial Court and Urban House], *Listy filologické*, 121 (1998), pp. 126–128.

Vincennes aux origines de l'État moderne (Paris, 1996).

VINCENT-CASSY, Mireille, 'La gula curiale ou les débordements des banquets au début du règne de Charles VI', in *La sociabilité à table. Commensalité et convivialité à travers les âges* (Rouen, 1992), pp. 91–102.

VLČEK, Emanuel, *Fyzické osobnosti českých panovníků*, II: *Čeští králové*, 1: Atlas kosterních pozůstatků českých králů přemyslovské a lucemburské dynastie s podrobným komentářem a historickými poznámkami [The Figures of the Bohemian Sovereigns, II: Kings of Bohemia, 1: An Atlas of the Skeletal Remains of the Kings of Bohemia of the Přemyslid and Luxemburg Dynasties with a Detailed Commentary and Historical Notes] (Praha, 2000).

WAILLY, Henri de, *Crécy, 1346: Anatomy of a Battle* (New York, 1987).

WARNER, George F. and GILSON, Julius P., *Catalogue of Western Manuscripts in the Old Royal and King's Collections*, II (London, 1921).

WEBER, Annette, 'Les grandes et les petites statues d'apôtres de la Sainte-Chapelle de Paris: hypothèses de datation et d'interprétation', *Bulletin monumental*, 155 (1997), pp. 81–101.

WEIFENBACH, Beate, 'Freiheit durch Privilegien und Schutz durch Reliquien. Überlegungen zur spätmittelalterlichen Inszenierung reichsstädtischer Freiheit anlässlich des Besuchs Kaiser Karls IV. in Dortmund', *Blätter für deutsche Landesgeschichte*, 137 (2001), pp. 223–256.

WEISS, Stefan, 'Onkel und Neffe. Die Beziehungen zwischen Deutschland und Frankreich unter Kaiser Karl IV. und König Karl V. und der Ausbruch des Großen Abendländischen Schismas. Eine Studie über mittelalterliche Außenpolitik', in *Regnum et Imperium. Die französisch-deutschen Beziehungen im 14. und 15. Jahrhundert. Les relations franco-allemandes au XIVe et au XVe siècle* (Pariser Historische Studien 83; München 2008), pp. 101–164.

WELTSCH, Ruben E., *Archbishop John of Jenstein 1348–1400. Papalism, Humanism and Reform in Pre-Hussite Prague* (The Hague – Paris, 1968).

WERUNSKY, Emil, *Geschichte Kaiser Karls IV. und seiner Zeit*, III.: *(1355–1368)* (Insbruck, 1892).

WHITELEY, Mary, 'Ceremony and Space in the Châteaux of Charles V, King of France', in *Zeremoniell und Raum*, ed. Werner PARAVICINI (Sigmaringen, 1997), pp. 187–198.

WHITELEY, Mary, 'Deux escaliers royaux du XIVe siècle: les «grands degrez» du palais de la Cité et la «grande viz» du Louvre', *Bulletin monumental*, 147 (1989), pp. 137–142.

WHITELEY, Mary, 'Deux vues de l'hôtel royal de Saint-Pol', *Revue de l'Art*, 105 (2000), pp. 49–53.

WHITELEY, Mary, 'L'aménagement intérieur des résidences royales et princières en France à la fin du XIVe siècle et au début du XVe siècle', in *Vincennes aux origines de l'État moderne* (Paris, 1996), pp. 299–303.

WHITELEY, Mary, 'Le Louvre de Charles V: dispositions et fonctions d'une résidence royale', *Revue de l'art*, 97 (1992), pp. 60–71.

WHITELEY, Mary, 'Lieux de pouvoir et résidences royales. Le palais de la Cité / Le château du Louvre / L'hôtel Saint-Paul / Le château de Vincennes', in *Paris et Charles V. Arts et Architecture* (Paris, 2001), pp. 105–131.

WHITELEY, Mary, 'Public and Private Space in Royal

and Princely Châteaux in Late Medieval France', in *Palais royaux et princiers au Moyen Âge*, under the guidance of Annie Renoux (Le Mans, 1996), pp. 71–75.

Whiteley, Mary, 'Royal and Ducal Palaces in France in the Fourteenth and Fifteenth Centuries: Interior, Ceremony and Function', in *Architecture et vie sociale: L'organisation intérieure des grandes demeures à la fin du Moyen Âge et à la Renaissance* (Paris, 1994), pp. 49–50.

Wilbertz, Gisela, 'Elisabeth von Pommern – eine Kaiserin im späten Mittelalter', *Bohemia*, 28 (1987), pp. 45–68.

Wolfram, Georg (ed.), *Die Metzer Chronik des Jaique Dex (Jacques d'Esch) über die Kaiser und Könige aus dem Luxemburger Hause (1307–1435)* (Quellen zur Lothringischen Geschichte, 4; Metz, 1906).

Wyss, Michaël et al. (eds), 'Atlas historique de Saint-Denis. Des origines au XVIIIe siècle', in *Documents d'archéologie française*, 59 (Paris, 1996).

Yenal, Edith, *Christine de Pizan: A Bibliography*, 2nd ed. (Metuchen – London, 1989).

Zeumer, Karl, *Die Goldene Bulle Kaiser Karls IV.*, I–II (Wiemar, 1908).

Zíbrt, Čeněk and Winter, Zikmund, *Dějiny kroje v zemích českých* [The History of Clothing in the Czech Lands], I–II (Praha, 1892–1893).

Zimmermann, Margarete, 'Kochkunst im spätmittelalterlichen Frankreich: «Le Ménagier de Paris»', in *Essen und Trinken in Mittelalter und Neuzeit*, eds Irmgard Bitsch et al. (Sigmaringen, 1990), pp. 103–115.

Tobolka, Václav (ed.), *M. Pavla Žídka Spravovna* [Master Pavel Žídek's Encyclopaedia] (Praha, 1908).

Žůrek, Václav, 'Korunovační řád Karla IV. jako ritualizovaný panovnický program' [The Coronation Order of Charles IV as a Ritualised Sovereign Programme], *Časopis Národního muzea. Řada historická / Series historia*, 176, 3–4 (2007), pp. 105–143.

List of figures

Riches Heures du Duc de Berry. (RMN-Grand Palais, domaine de Chantilly, ms. 65, fol. 1r, photo: René-Gabriel Ojéda)

39. A dummy of the Bastille in its form from 1369–1382, which was carved from its original stone in 1790 by François Palloy (after: *Paris 1400. Les arts sous Charles VI.* Paris 2004, p. 87, fig. 35)
40. A case with the relics and treasures from the abbey in Saint-Denis. An engraving from the work Histoire de l'Abbaye Royale de Saint-Denis, which Dom Michel Félibien published in 1706 (after: *Saint-Denis, la basilique et le trésor*, Dossiers d'archéologie, No. 261 /mars 2001/, p. 82).
41. The upper chapel in Sainte-Chapelle (Pixmac)
42. Reconstruction of the appearance of the Louvre during the reign of Charles V following the Les très riches heures du Duc de Berry (after: Michel Fleury – Venceslas Kruta, *Le Château du Louvre. Guide et monografie*, Dijon 2000, p. 68)
43. Donjon and "small castle" (Châtelet) of the royal residence in Vincennes. The Hours of Etienne Chevalier, miniature by Jean Fouquet, 1452 (RMN-Grand Palais, domaine de Chantilly, ms. 71, fol. 26, photo: René-Gabriel Ojéda)
44. The house U Kamenného zvonu (At the Stone Bell) in Prague on Old Town Square, temporary residence of King John of Luxembourg and his son Charles IV (photo Robert Novotný)
45. Prague Castle, north façade of the royal palace of Charles IV after the reconstruction by Dobroslava Menclová (Dobroslava Menclová, *České hrady* II, Praha 1972, p. 44, Fig. 44)
46. Cathedral of St Vitus, view from the south, the left part with the towers were not finished until 1929 (Prague Castle Administration, photo: Jan Gloc)
47. Mathias of Arras († 1352), the first builder of the Cathedral of St Vitus. A bust in the inner triforium of the Cathedral of St Vitus at Prague Castle (Prague Castle Administration, photo: Jan Gloc)
48. Peter Parler (1330/3–1399), the second builder of the Cathedral of St Vitus. A bust in the inner triforium of the Cathedral of St Vitus at Prague Castle (Prague Castle Administration, photo: Jan Gloc)
49. Statute of St Wenceslas in the homonymous chapel of the Cathedral of St Vitus at Prague Castle. A work of Peter or Heinrich Parler from 1373 (Prague Castle Administration, photo: Jan Gloc)
50. Old Town Bridge Tower (photo: Hans Peter Schaefer, http://www.reserv-a-rt.de)
51. Prague around 1400 (after: Vilém Lorenc, *Nové Město pražské*, Praha 1973)
52. Tangermünde, castle and church of St Stephen. Copper engraving by Matthäus Merian the Elder from around 1640
53. Castle Karlštejn (Prague, National Archives, ČDKM, sign. I B 1/9)
54. John Očko of Vlašim († 1380). A bust in the inner triforium of the Cathedral of St Vitus at Prague Castle (Prague Castle Administration, photo: Jan Gloc)
55. The proposal of a friendly contract between Charles IV and John I the Good (Prague, National Archives, Archive of the Crown of Bohemia 483)
56. Map of the lands of the Crown of Bohemia
57. The Bohemian, so-called St Wenceslas crown (Bohemian coronation jewels – Prague Castle Administration, photo: Jan Gloc)
58. Feast at the court of Archbishop Baldwin in Trier (Codex Balduini Trevoriensis. Koblenz Landeshauptarchiv, Bestand 1C, Nr. 1, fol. 3a)
59. Anna of Schweidnitz (1339–1362). A bust in the inner triforium of the Cathedral of St Vitus at Prague Castle (Prague Castle Administration, photo: Jan Gloc)
60. King of the Romans and Bohemia Wenceslas IV. (1361–1419). A bust in the inner triforium of the Cathedral of St Vitus at Prague Castle (Prague Castle Administration, photo: Jan Gloc)
61. Prague at the end of the 15th century, woodcut from the World Chronicle by Hartmann Schedel (Goetzfried Antique Maps, www.vintage-maps.com)

87. / XVIII. The mutual exchange of rings and leave-taking of both rulers (Paris, Bibliothèque nationale de France, ms. fr. 2813, fol. 479rb), size: 72 × 67 mm
88. / XIX. Dauphin Charles receives a deed from the imperial chancellor (Paris, Bibliothèque nationale de France, ms. fr. 2813, fol. 480ra), size: 72 × 67 mm
89. Funeral procession with the body of Queen Jeanne of Bourbon. Miniature in the manuscript of Les Grandes Chroniques de France (The British Library Board, Ms. Royal 20 C VII, fol. 200r)
90. Detail of the tombstone of Queen Jeanne of Bourbon in Saint-Denis by the sculptor André Beauneveu (after: *Paris et Charles V. Arts et Architecture*, dir. Frédéric Pleybert, Paris 2001, p. 196)
91. Tombstone of Constable Bertrand du Guesclin (1320–1380) in the Basilica of Saint-Denis (archive of the author)
92. King of France Charles V on his death bed (The British Library Board, Ms. royal 20 C VII, fol. 215r)
93. Detail of the tombstone of Charles V in Saint-Denis by the sculptor André Beauneveu (after: *Paris et Charles V. Arts et Architecture*, dir. Frédéric Pleybert, Paris 2001)
94. Votive image of John Očko of Vlašim, detail (National Gallery in Prague, inv. No. O 84)
95. Charles IV, detail from the votive image of John Očko of Vlašim (National Gallery in Prague, inv. No. O 84)
96. King Wenceslas IV enthroned. Miniature from the Bible of Wenceslasa IV, 2nd volume, before 1395 (Wien, Österreichische Nationalbibliothek, cod. 2760, fol. 74r)
97. John of Jenštejn († 1400). A bust in the inner triforium of the Cathedral of St Vitus at Prague Castle (Prague Castle Administration, photo: Jan Gloc)
98. Oriel of the college of Charles IV, the so-called Karolinum (Charles University in Prague)
99. King Wenceslas IV and his second wife Sophia of Bavaria, miniature from the Bible of Wenceslas IV (Wien, Österreichische Nationalbibliothek, cod. 2760, fol. 2r)
100. King Wenceslas IV had the representative Castle Točník built (Czech News Agency, photo: Jan Kouba)
101. Christine de Pisan dedicates an anthology of her work to Queen Isabeau of Bavaria. Christine de Pisan, Oeuvres, around 1413 (The British Library Board, Harley 4431–1, fol. 3r)
102. / XXXIX. Banquet in honour of the emperor in the Grand Hall of the Palace de la Cité. Les Grandes Chroniques de France, perhaps 1415 (The British Library Board, Ms. Cotton Nero E II, 2nd part, fol. 229vb), size: 87 × 87 mm
103. / XXXVIII. Meeting of the French king with the emperor and his son. Les Grandes Chroniques de France, 1410–1420 (The British Library Board, Ms. Sloane 2433, Vol. C, fol. 149va), size: 88 × 88 mm
104. The abbot of the monastery of St Remigius hands the holy ampule to the Archbishop of Rheims before the coronation of Charles V. The Coronation Book of Charles V. (The British Library Board, Cotton Tiberius B VIII, fol. 46r)
105. Charles V on the tribune after the coronation among the prelates and peers. The Coronation Book of Charles V. (The British Library Board, Cotton Tiberius B VIII, fol. 40r)
106. Tyranny, oligarchy and democracy. The title page of the translation of Aristotle's Politics and Economics by Nicholas Oresme. (Brusel, Bibliothèque royale de Belgique, ms. 11201–2, fol. 1v)
107. Blessing of the banner of Oriflamme. The Coronation Book of Charles V. (The British Library Board, Cotton Tiberius B VIII, fol. 73r)
108. The sceptre of Charles V, before 1380 (RMN--Grand Palais, musée du Louvre, photo: Jean-Gilles Berizzi)
109. Charles V in his library. *Policraticus* by John of Salisbury, and Old French translation by Den-

169. The interior of the relic case (Grande Chasse) from Sainte Chapelle in a depiction from the end of the 15th century (after: Jean-Michel Leniaud and Françoise Perrot, *La Sainte-Chapelle*, Paris 1991, p. 61)
170. Reliquary of the Holy Crown of Thorns from Sainte-Chappelle, today in the cathedral museum of Notre-Dame (after: Jean-Michel Leniaud and Françoise Perrot, *La Sainte-Chapelle*, Paris 1991, p. 60)
171. A gold franc of Charles V (Franc à pied), after: *Paris 1400. Les arts sous Charles VI.* Paris 2004, p. 44.

Page 421: Mask of a Green Man from the oriel window of the Carolinum (archive of the author, photo: Petr Chotěbor)

List of miniatures

PARIS, BIBLIOTHÈQUE NATIONALE DE FRANCE, MS. FR. 2813

I. / 70. Message of Emperor Charles IV (fol. 467ra), size: 78 × 68 mm

II. / 71. Emperor Charles enters the cathedral in Cambrai (fol. 467va), size: 67 × 69 mm

III. / 72. Emperor Charles IV reads the seventh lesson of the Christmas service (fol. 467vb), size: 67 × 68 mm

IV. / 73. Meeting of the emperor with the brothers of the French king near Senlis (fol. 468va), size: 74 × 069 mm

V. / 74. The representatives of the Parisian counsellors and merchants welcome Emperor Charles IV (fr. 2813, fol. 469rb), size: 73 × 105 mm

VI. / 75. The meeting of King of France Charles V and Emperor Charles IV (fol. 470ra–b), size: 75 × 150 mm

VII. / 76. Parade of the royal guards (fol. 470rb), size: 66 × 68 mm

VIII. / 77. Ceremonial entry of the sovereigns into Paris (fol. 470va–b), size: 159 × 147 mm

IX. / 78. Charles V welcomes the emperor and his son Wenceslas in the Palace de la Cité in Paris (fol. 471va), size: 67 × 71 mm

X. / 79. Emperor Charles IV accepts the gifts of the city of Paris (fol. 472ra), size: 76 × 77 mm

XI. / 80. Banquet in the Great Hall of the Palace de la Cité (fol. 473va–b), size: 192 × 197 mm

XII. / 81. Reception of the delegation from the University of Paris (fol. 475rb), size: 77 × 70 mm

XIII. / 82. Emperor Charles IV offers allied aid to the French king (fol. 476vb), size: 86 × 67 mm

XIV. / 83. Emperor Charles IV on a visit at Queen of France Jeanne of Bourbon (fol. 477ra), size: 80 × 67 mm

XV. / 84. King of the Romans Wenceslas IV swears an oath to the French king (fol. 478ra), size: 75 × 75 mm

XVI. / 85. Emperor Charles IV during a service in the Abbey of Saint-Maur-des-Fossés (fol. 478rb), size: 75 × 75 mm

XVII. /86. The gifts of French king to Emperor Charles IV (fol. 478vb), size: 82 × 65 mm

XVIII./87.The mutual exchange of rings and leave-taking of both rulers (fol. 479rb), size: 72 × 67 mm

XIX. / 88. Dauphin Charles receives a deed from the imperial chancellor (fol. 480ra), size: 72 × 67 mm

LONDON, THE BRITISH LIBRARY BOARD, MS. ROYAL 20 C VII

XX. / 64. Charles V accepts a document from Emperor Charles IV (fol. 194v) , size 78 × 78 mm

XXI. / 66. Charles V sends envoys to meet the emperor (fol. 195r), size: 78 × 78 mm

XXII. / 113. Duke John of Berry and Duke Philip of Burgundy on the way to the emperor (fol. 196va), size: 78 × 78 mm

XXIII. / 114. Meeting of the Duke of Bar with the emperor and his son (fol. 196vb), size: 78 × 78 mm

XXIV. / 168. The emperor with his son and retinue kneeling before the reliquary of St Denis (fol. 197r), size: 78 × 78 mm

XXV. / 121. Representatives of the metropolis welcome the emperor and his son (fol. 197v), size: 78 × 78 mm

XXVI. / 124. Meeting of King Charles V and Emperor Charles IV (fol. 198va–b), size: 78 × 78 mm

XXVII. / 125. Joint journey of the rulers to Paris (fol. 198vb), size: 120 × 78 mm

XXVIII. / 152. Ceremonial feast in the Great Hall of the Palace de la Cité (fol. 199r), size: 78 × 78 mm

PARIS, BIBLIOTHÈQUE NATIONALE DE FRANCE, MS. FR. 6465

XXIX. / 130. Charles V receives the envoys of the Holy Roman emperor. Les Grandes Chroniques de France, illumination by Jean Fouquet (fol. 440v), size: 108 × 142 mm

XXX. / 118. Arrival of Charles IV in Cambrai. Les Grandes Chroniques de France, illumination by Jean Fouquet (fol. 441r), size: 106 × 130 mm

XXXI. / 115. Arrival of Emperor Charles IV at the Abbey of Saint-Denis. Les Grandes Chroniques de France, illumination by Jean Fouquet (fol. 442r), size: 230 mm × 165 m (along the edges only 122 mm)

XXXII. / 126. Welcome of Emperor Charles IV by the representatives of the city of Paris. Les Grandes Chroniques de France, illumination by Jean Fouquet (fol. 442v), size: 108 × 140 mm

XXXIII. / 119. Emperor Charles and his son Wenceslas change horses in La Chapelle-Saint-Denis. Les Grandes Chroniques de France, illumination by Jean Fouquet (fol. 443r), size: 115 × 145 mm

XXXIV. / 129. King of France Charles V rides with his retinue to meet the emperor. Les Grandes Chroniques de France, illumination by Jean Fouquet (fol. 443v), size: 115 × 124 mm

XXXV. / 122. Meeting of the crowned heads before the entry into Paris. Les Grandes Chroniques de France, illumination by Jean Fouquet (fol. 444r), size: 112 × 130 mm

XXXVI. / 153. Banquet in honour of the emperor and his son in the Grand Hall of the Palace de la Cité. Les Grandes Chroniques de France, illumination by Jean Fouquet (fol. 444v), size: 112 × 142 mm

BESANÇON, BIBLIOTHÈQUE MUNICIPALE, MS. 863

XXXVII. / 127. Meeting of the French king with the Holy Roman Emperor and his son. Les Grandes Chroniques de France, beginning of the 15th century (fol. 413vb), size: 92 × 86 mm

LONDON, THE BRITISH LIBRARY BOARD, MS. SLOANE 2433

XXXVIII. / 103. Meeting of the French king with the emperor and his son. Les Grandes Chroniques de France, 1410–1420 (Vol. C, fol. 149va), size: 88 × 88 mm

LONDON, THE BRITSH LIBRARY BOARD, MS. COTTON NERO E II

XXXIX. / 102. Banquet in honour of the emperor in the Grand Hall of the Palace de la Cité. Les Grandes Chroniques de France, perhaps 1415 (2nd part, fol. 229vb), size: 87 × 87 mm

Index

Q

R

S

W

Y

Z

THE PARISIAN SUMMIT, 1377–78
EMPEROR CHARLES IV AND KING CHARLES V OF FRANCE

FRANTIŠEK ŠMAHEL

Translated by Sean Mark Miller and Kateřina Millerová
from the Czech original *Cesta Karla IV. do Francie, 1377–1378*
published by Argo Press in Prague 2006
Graphic design by Zdeněk Ziegler

Published by Charles University in Prague
Karolinum Press
Ovocný trh 3–5, 116 36 Prague 1
Prague 2014
Editor vice-rector Jan Royt
Edited by Kamila Veselá
Proof-read by Peter Kirk Jensen
Maps by Jaroslav Synek
Typeset by DTP Karolinum Press
Printed by PBtisk, Příbram
First English edition

ISBN 978-80-246-2522-5